The Word and the Book

Studies in Biblical Language and Literature

D1081626

by

ROBERT GORDIS

KTAV PUBLISHING HOUSE, INC.

New York

1976

Library of Congress Cataloging in Publication Data

Gordis, Robert
  The word and the book.

  Reprinted from various journals and Festschriften,
1930-1974.
  English and Hebrew.
  Includes bibliographical references and indexes.
  1. Bible. O.T.—Language, style—Addresses, essays,
lectures. 2. Bible. O.T.—Criticism, interpretation, etc.—
Addresses, essays, lectures. 3. Bible. O.T. Ecclesiastes—
Criticism, interpretation, etc.—Addresses, essays, lectures.
I. Title.
BS1192.G67   221.6   75-46617
ISBN 0-87068-456-6

MANUFACTURED IN THE UNITED STATES OF AMERICA

CONTENTS

EXEGETICAL NOTES

INDICES

HEBREW SECTION

FOREWORD

More than four decades have elapsed since the inception of my career in scholarship. There have been occasional forays into such fields as rabbinics, medieval Hebrew literature, and American-Jewish history and I have had an ongoing concern with the character and content of religion and its relevance to the condition of modern man. Nevertheless, my principal field of study and research has been the Hebrew Bible. The major products of this activity are embodied in about a dozen books and monographs. In addition to these larger works, several scores of papers have appeared in various scholarly journals in the United States, Great Britain and Israel.

A few years ago, some friends, including colleagues and students, urged that these scattered papers, some of which were out of print, be collected and thus made accessible to a wider public. In deference to this request, a collection of biblical studies was published by Indiana University Press in 1971 under the title *Poets, Prophets and Sages—Essays in Biblical Interpretation.*

As was indicated in the preface to that volume, the studies there included were concerned basically with the content and meaning of the Bible and some of its major components, rather than with philological or exegetical themes. My friends remained gently insistent that these more technical studies, too, be assembled in book form. In the interim, several papers of more general scope, notably on Jonah and Ruth, have been published. The present volume serves as "a city of refuge" for these more recent studies.

The first two papers span virtually the entire period of my scholarly activity. The first, "On the Methodology of Biblical Exegesis," seeks to indicate fundamental principles in exegetical method which are all too often ignored in biblical research today. The second, "The Origins of the Masorah in the Light of the Qumran Scrolls and Rabbinic literature," represents an expansion of a Hebrew paper originally delivered at the Second World Congress of Jewish Studies in Jerusalem in 1957. It appeared in English for the first time as the Prolegomenon to the new reprint-edition of my book, *The Biblical Text in the Making—A Study of the Kethib-Qere* (KTAV Publishing House, New York, 1971). It reopens the question of the origins of photo-masoretic activity which I date in the two centuries preceding the destruction of the Second Temple. This conclusion, advanced in the 1937 edition of the book, is supported, I am convinced, not only by relevant data drawn from rabbinic literature, some newly advanced here, but also, and dramatically, by the biblical scrolls and fragments emanating from Qumran and Wadi Muraba'at. Some Qumran texts, notably Isaiah B, contain what is basically our Masoretic Text, or readings substantially similar to it. Other texts represent popular, unofficial manuscripts containing textual variants differing in quality, some superior and others inferior to the *textus receptus*. The conclusion that emerges from these conflicting data is that while the official religious leadership, centered in Jerusalem, strove to establish a basic text as the norm, vulgar manuscripts containing variant readings continued to circulate among the people. These "unofficial" manuscripts were to be found in Palestine even in the hands of scholars. Their presence would be more prevalent as one moved away from Jerusalem, either physically or ideologically. Hence they were more likely to be found in Diaspora communities like Alexandria, as well as among sectarians like the Samaritans and the Qumranites. They often underly Septuagint renderings.

Basing myself on a variety of considerations, I conclude that an official, archetypal text was established during the Second Commonwealth era, in the period between the accession of Simon the Maccabee (142 B.C.E.) and the destruction of the Temple (70 C.E.). It is worth pointing out that though this early date for the emergence of a Masoretic text was originally challenged, a growing number of scholars has recognized the bearing of the Dead Sea Scrolls on the question and has arrived at similar conclusions.

The next four papers deal with Ruth, the Prophetic books, Psalms and Job. They complete the first section.

The study of language as a key to human psychology, affecting semantics, morphology, syntax and rhetoric, has always been a source of deep interest to me. Under the rubric, "Studies in Biblical Semantics and Rhetoric," seven papers deal with varied aspects of this fascinating field.

The third section, "Qoheleth Studies," consists of two groups of papers dealing with novel and sensational theories propounded by scholars on Qoheleth. The first group examines and refutes the contention that our present Hebrew text of *Qoheleth* is a translation from a lost Aramaic original. The scholarly literature which developed on this question is cited and the salient arguments against the theory are summarized in my book,

Koheleth—The Man and His World (3rd augmented edition, New York, 1965), chapter VIII and Supplementary Note A. The *coup de grace* for the translation-theory of Qoheleth was supplied by the discovery of Hebrew fragments of the book in Qumran. Most scholars today have been convinced of the authenticity of the Hebrew text of Qoheleth by the considerations we have advanced. But the theory still has some advocates, which gives the discussion more than historical interest.

Shortly after the discussion on the Aramaic original theory of Qoheleth subsided, another sensational hypothesis was advanced—that Qoheleth was written by a Phoenician, because of alleged affinities of the book with Ugaritic. Included in this volume are two papers demonstrating the untenability of this theory.

I believe that these Qoheleth studies serve to highlight important issues both of method and substance for biblical research in general and for Qoheleth study in particular.

The fourth section, "Contributions to the Biblical Lexicon," presents several papers elucidating hitherto unknown or unrecognized meanings of roots and vocables in the biblical vocabulary.

The fifth section, "Exegetical Notes," contains a series of studies of difficult biblical passages, for which new interpretations are advanced. Their justification lies in the contribution they make to a better understanding of the biblical writers.

The concluding section contains several papers written in Hebrew. I am well aware that many biblical scholars and students are not fluent in modern Hebrew, which is becoming an increasingly important language for scholarship. Translating these Hebrew papers would necessarily have meant reworking them, and the publication of this book would have been greatly delayed. These essays are printed in the back of the volume, which is, of course, the front of the book for Hebrew!

A brief indication of the contents of this section may be in order. The paper on "The Prophecy of Jonah ben Amittai of Gat Hahepher" discusses the various categories of Hebrew prophecy as a background for the role of the eighth century prophet Jonah ben Amittai, who was a contemporary of King Jeroboum II. It is suggested that two fragments of his oracles have survived in the Book of Kings (II Kings 14:25 f.), and that his words are ironically cited and rebutted by Amos of Tekoa.

The paper "Some Rhetorical Usages in Scripture" calls attention to such important rhetorical figures as *talḥin, hysteron proteron* and *hendiadys,* and indicates several scores of passages which are illumined by the recognition of these usages. The paper "Biblical Language in the Light of Rabbinic Hebrew" is a supplement to the English paper "Some Relationships of Biblical and Rabbinic Hebrew." It offers a substantial number of additional instances where the later stages of the Hebrew language shed light on biblical usage. The short note " 'My Mother—My Sister' and the Etymology of the Name 'Ahab' " utilizes Akkadian royal epistolary style to explain a problematic verse in Job (17:14). It also proposes an etymology for the Hebrew name "Ahab" for which no satisfactory derivation has been proposed.

The reader who will be interested in noting the original dates of publication of the various papers in this volume will find instances where later scholars have adopted views presented earlier in these pages. That the Rabbis (Abot 6:6) felt it necessary to declare, "He who cites a statement in the name of its originator brings redemption to the world," testifies that the practice was often honored more in the breach than in the observance. Frequently the scholar must remain content with the knowledge that his insight has been absorbed in the body of anonymous knowledge.

It is a pleasure to express my thanks to the editors of the following journals for permission to utilize material which originally appeared in their columns: *American Journal of Semitic Languages* and *Journal of Near Eastern Studies* (Chicago), *Biblica* (Rome), *Jewish Quarterly Review* (Philadelphia), *Journal of Biblical Literature* (New Haven), *Journal of the American Oriental Society* (New Haven), *Journal of Semitic Studies* (Manchester), *Leshonenu* (Jerusalem), *Vetus Testamentum* (Leiden). My gratitude is also extended to Dr. Louis Finkelstein the Chancellor (now Emeritus) of the Jewish Theological Seminary, under whose auspices the *Louis Ginzberg Jubilee Volumes* were issued, the officers of the *Hevrah Leheqer Hamiqra* in Israel which published the *Anniversary Volumes* in honor of· N. H. Tur-Sinai and Moshe Seidel, and the publishers and editors of the *Jacob M. Myers Festschrift* entitled *A Lamp Unto My Path* (Philadelphia 1974).

My warmest thanks go to Mr. Bernard Scharfstein of KTAV Publishing House, whose regard for the author and enthusiasm for this project made this book a reality. I am very grateful to my student, Steven Saltzman, who undertook the arduous task of preparing the indices. He has thus greatly enhanced the usefulness of the work.

The astronomical rise in printing costs has compelled the publication of this book by photo-offset. This has precluded updating the papers or eliminating material in areas where my views have changed. Generally, however, I believe the conclusions reached in these studies are valid today.

Moreover, I trust that some interest will inhere in the disclosure of the processes of research involved. In view of the independent provenance of each paper, a slight degree of repetition and some variations in transliteration and the mode of citation, were unavoidable. These aspects should, however, not be unduly disturbing to the reader. The original pagination of each paper has been kept to facilitate finding references.

I venture the hope that these studies will prove stimulating and valuable to scholars, students and readers of the Bible at various levels. May they be inspired to a deeper interest in the Book of Books, of which the ancients justly remarked, "Turn it over and over, for everything is in it."

These papers span all the years of my marriage. Their existence is only the slightest indication of the understanding, forbearance and love my dear wife has lavished upon me. Without Fannie's encouragement and inspiration, a scholarly career would have been impossible for me, in view of a busy career of communal activity and service. On Tu Bishvat, "The New Year of the Trees," which is our wedding anniversary on the Hebrew calendar, I pray that these fruits of the harvest will not be entirely unworthy of her planting.

February 7, 1975   ROBERT GORDIS

ACKNOWLEDGMENTS AND SOURCES

The papers in this volume originally appeared in the following journals and *Festschriften;* to the editors of which our grateful acknowledgment is made for permission to reprint.

AMERICAN JOURNAL OF SEMITIC LANGUAGES
A Note on Joshua 22:34 (Vol. 48, 1931, pp. 287-88)
A Rhetorical Use of Interrogative Sentence in Biblical Hebrew (Vol. 49, 1933, pp. 212-217)
A Note on Genesis 24:21 (Vol. 52, 1935, pp. 191-2)
Some Effects of Primitive Thought on Language (Vol. 55, 1938, pp. 270-84)

BIBLICA
Qoheleth and Qumran—A Study in Style (Vol. 41, 1960, pp. 395-410)

HAHEVRAH LEHEQER HAMIQRA
Biblical Hebrew in the Light of Rabbinic Hebrew (Sefer Tur-Sinai, 1961, pp. 149-67)
Some Rhetorical Usages in Biblical Hebrew (Sefer Seidel, 1962, pp. 253-264)

JEWISH QUARTERLY REVIEW
Studies in Hebrew Roots of Contrasted Meanings (Vol. 27, 1936, pp. 33-58)
The Original Language of Qohelet (Vol. 37, 1946, pp. 76-84)
The Translation-Theory of Qohelet Re-Examined (Vol. 39, 1949, pp. 103-116)
Psalm 9 - 10—A Textual-Exegetical Study (Vol. 48, 1957, pp. 104-122)
On the Methodology of Biblical Philology (Vol. 61, pp. 93-118)

JOURNAL OF THEOLOGICAL STUDIES (OXFORD)
A Note on Lamentations 2:13 (Vol. 34, 1933, pp. 162-163)
Critical Notes on the Blessing of Moses (Vol. 34, 1933, pp. 390-392)
A Note on *Tobh* (Vol. 35, 1934, pp. 186-188)
The Branch to The Nose—A Note on Ezekiel 8:17 (Vol. 37, 1936, pp. 283-287)
Notes on the Blessing of Moses (Vol. 37, 1936, pp.
The Biblical Root ŠDY-ŠD (Vol. 41, 1940, pp. 35-43)

JOURNAL OF AMERICAN ORIENTAL SOCIETY
The Asseverative Kaph in Hebrew and Ugaritic (Vol. 63, 1943, pp. 176-178)

JOURNAL OF BIBLICAL LITERATURE

Note on General Conditional Sentences in Hebrew (Vol. 49, 1930, pp. 200-203)

Midrash and the Prophets (Vol. 49, 1930, pp. 417-422)

Some Hitherto Unrecognized Meanings of the Verb ŠUB (Vol. 52, 1933, pp. 153-162)

Ecclesiastes 1:17—Text and Interpretation (Vol. 56, 1937, pp. 323-330)

A Note on I Samuel 13:21 (Vol. 61, 1942, pp. 209-211)

A Note on *Yad* (Vol. 62, 1943, pp. 341-344)

The Text and Meaning of Deuteronomy 33:27 (Vol. 67, 1948, pp. 69-72)

Additional Note on Deuteronomy 33:27 (Vol. 68, 1949, pp. 407-408)

Qohelet—Hebrew or Aramaic (Vol. 71, 1952, pp. 93-109)

Was Qohelet a Phoenician (Vol. 74, 1955, pp. 103-114)

The Root *degel* in the Song of Songs (Vol. 88, 1969, pp. 203-204)

The Conclusions of the Book of Lamentations (5:22) (Vol. 93, 1974, pp. 289-293)

JOURNAL OF NEAR-EASTERN STUDIES

"Na 'alam and Other Observations on the Ain Feshka Scrolls" (Vol. 9, 1950, pp. 44-47)

"Corporate Personality in Job" (Vol. 4, 1945, pp. 54-55)

JEWISH THEOLOGICAL SEMINARY

"Studies in the Relationship of Biblical and Rabbinic Hebrew," L. Ginzberg Jubilee Volumes, 1946, pp. 173-200

LESHONENU

Job 17:14 and the Name "Ahab." (Vol. 35, 1971, pp. 71-72)

TARBIS

"The Origins of the Masorah in the Light of Rabbinic Literature and the Dead Sea Scrolls" (Vol. 27, 1958, pp. 444-469)

VETUS TESTAMENTUM

"The Text and Meaning of Hosea 14:3" (Vol. 5, 1955, 88-90)

Job 40:29 (Vol. 14, 1964, pp. 492-494)

A LIGHT TO MY PATH—OLD TESTAMENT STUDIES IN HONOR OF JACOB M. MYERS,

Ed. Howard N. Bream, Ralph D. Heim and Carey A. Moore, 1974, pp. 241-263

"Love, Marriage and Business in The Book of Ruth—A Chapter in Hebrew Customary Law"

BRIT IVRIT OLAMIT

"Nebhu'at Yonah ben Amittai Miggat Hahepher" in *Hagut Ivrit Ba'amerika,* Vol. 7, 1971, pp. 112-120.

ON METHODOLOGY IN BIBLICAL EXEGESIS

SIXTY YEARS AGO THE LATE MAX L. MARGOLIS published his classical paper, "The Scope and Methodology of Biblical Philology" which graced the opening issue of the New Series of the *Jewish Quarterly Review*.[1] In this study, the incomparable master of scientific method demonstrated the proper procedure with regard to Biblical exegesis and textual criticism by a study of one verse in Job, 3:2. Unfortunately his brilliant paper cannot be described as epoch-making. Rather, it has been a voice crying in the wilderness. In the six decades that have elapsed since its publication, Biblical scholarship has gone on its way, all too often oblivious of the canons of sound methodology. Some of the simplest concepts that sound platitudinous when spelled out, continue to be ignored, both in Bible editions and commentaries.

The utilization of the ancient versions offers one of the most obvious instances. One frequently encounters "LXX reads" as though the Hebrew *Vorlage* of the Septuagint were before us. Little attention is paid to the method and purposes of the translator, his theological background, the Halachic considerations that entered into his work and the major problem of the degree of his understanding of the Biblical text. Evidence symptomatic of the widespread ignoring of sound methodology is the fact that the standard works dealing with the method and approach of the ancient versions, by Frankel[2] and Luzzatto,[3] are both over a century old. Margolis' brilliant and succinct paper on the correct method of

[1] Cf. *JQR* (NS), vol. 1, no. 1, (1910-11) pp. 5-41.
[2] Zechariah Frankel, *Vorstudien zu der Septuaginta*, (Leipzig, 1841), *idem, über den Einfluss der palästinischen Exegese auf die alexandrinische Hermeneutik*, (Leipzig, 1851), and several later works.
[3] S. D. Luzzatto, *Oheb Ger*, (Vienna, 1830).

7

establishing Semitic equivalents for the vocabulary of the Greek Versions is sixty years old.[4].

The tremendous impact of archaeology is of course the single most significant new factor in twentieth-century Biblical scholarship. Perhaps we ought to be grateful that scholars are human and are therefore susceptible to fashions which follow in the wake of important discoveries, each of which in turn is hailed as providing the key to the total understanding of the Bible. That each discovery has enriched our comprehension of Biblical literature and history goes without saying. It is the "imperialist" claims advanced for each that violate the canons of scientific method. The most familiar instance is of course the Pan-Babylonian school, which rose and fell at the turn of the century.[5] Less influential has been the Pan-Egyptian emphasis.[6] Then came the Edomite phase, which attributed much of the basic traditions of Genesis and virtually all of Wisdom literature to the Edomites.[7] This procedure was virtually incapable of refutation, since not a line of their literature has come down to us and virtually nothing is known of Edomite religion and culture.

Today it is Pan-Ugariticism which holds the field. The uncertainties of interpretation with regard to the extra-biblical texts being adduced are all too often ignored. Little or no attention is paid to the problem of the channels of communication, which are assumed to have existed between 15th century Syria and its Hebrew psalmists and Wisdom

[4] Cf. his paper, "Complete Induction for the Identification of the Vocabulary of the Greek Versions of the O.T." in *JAOS*, vol. 31, 1910, (pp. 301-10).

[5] Friedrich Delitzsch's *Bibel und Babel*, (Leipzig, 1902), is the most sensational product of this school. A. Jeremias, *Das alte Testament im Lichte des alten Orients*, (Leipzig, 1902), is a more scholarly presentation of the same viewpoint, which informs much of the work of Hugo Winckler.

[6] Cf. e.g., P. Humbert, *Recherches sur la Littérature sapientiale d'Israel*, (Neuchâtel, 1929), a work containing much valuable material.

[7] This view is presented in R. N. Pfeiffer's indispensable *Introduction to the O.T.*, (New York, 1941), pp. 159-67.

2

sages nearly a millennium later, living in another geographical religious and cultural milieu. In some quarters the Bible becomes little more than a poorly transmitted corpus of Ugaritic literature, which for two millennia has been misunderstood at hundreds of points by those unfamiliar with the "original" language.[8] The fallacy of "reductionism" is too often rampant in Biblical scholarship.

One of the outstanding gains derived from contemporary archaeology has been the rehabilitation of the credibility of the Biblical narrative, which has had important consequences for the evaluation of the Higher Criticism. Increasingly it is being recognized that tradition is itself a historical datum that must be reckoned with.[9] Unfortunately this conclusion has not penetrated fully into the field of the lower criticism. The Masoretes are frequently conceived of as the would-be creators of a uniform artificial text, which never existed before.[10] This has had important consequences in at least three directions: (1) The Tiberian system of vocalization has been assumed to be a construction of the medieval Masoretes, of relatively little value for reconstructing the authentic morphology and phonetics of Biblical Hebrew; (2) The transmission of the Biblical text has been regarded as faulty in the extreme, so that emendations, transpositions and

[8] The copious publications of M. H. Dahood, particularly his *Commentary on Psalms I, II*, in the *Anchor Bible* series, are the most consistent examples of this approach, but by no means the only ones. His work, nevertheless, contains highly stimulating observations and many valuable insights.

[9] This has been one of the contributions of the so-called "Scandinavian school," which prefers to describe itself as "traditio-historical." See I. Engnell, *A Critical Scrutiny*, (Nashville, 1969), for a trenchant presentation of this approach.

[10] Cf. P. Kahle, *Der masoretische Text des A.T. nach der Überlieferung der babylonischen Juden*, (Leipzig, 1912); *Masoreten des Ostens*, (Leipzig, 1913); *Masoreten des Westens*, (Stuttgart, 1927-1950); *The Cairo Geniza*, (London, 1947). His view of the Masoretes as seeking to *create* a non-existent *textus receptus*, a goal they never fully achieved, rather than the *conservers* of a transmitted text, dominated the field and is only now beginning to yield ground to a more balanced view.

deletions can be proposed with complete assurance. Recently a highly regarded scholar in treating one chapter of 15 verses in the Prophets proposed over 40 changes in the text. One chapter in Biblical Wisdom literature consisting of twenty-five verses was left with three authentic verses after the "proper" deletions and excisions were made. (3) The assumption continues to be made that the Masoretes themselves corrected the text in many hundreds of passages, and the *Qere* readings and *Sebhir* notations are offered as proof of this activity.

With regard to the trustworthiness of the traditional vocalic system and the morphological structure it embodies, one fundamental fact has been lost sight of and its implications ignored. When the Masoretes in the sixth to eighth centuries created the various systems of vocalic notation, both supra-linear and sub-linear, the theory of the triliterality of Hebrew roots was not yet formulated. Thus the tenth century Hebrew grammarians, Menahem ben Saruk (910-70) and Dunash ben Labrat (920-990) still operated with the biliteral theory. Not until Judah Hayyug (c. 1000) and Abul-Walid ibn Janah (985-1040) was the triliteral character of Hebrew recognized and demonstrated. *That the vocalic system which the Masoretes transmitted could receive an adequate explanation only on the basis of a triliteral theory, the existence of which they could not have suspected, is decisive evidence of the reliability of the tradition of which they were the custodians, and not the creators.*

With regard to the second assumption concerning the alleged incidence of errors in the text, a widespread and long overdue disenchantment with wholesale and arbitrary emendations has fortunately set in. In fact, the human penchant of Biblical scholars to oscillate from one extreme to the other has set in so that the legitimacy of emendations is being totally denied in some quarters.

Finally, the idea that the Masoretes "corrected" the text rests upon the failure to recognize that the sole function of the

Masoretes was to conserve the Biblical text that reached them as meticulously as possible. They would have regarded any claim to "improve" upon it as the height of impiety. To be sure, the codices that came into their hands and were chosen to serve as models because of their antiquity and general reliability, nevertheless contained errors that had previously entered the text during the centuries separating the composition of the Biblical books and the earliest "official" manuscripts—a fact that the defenders of "the new conservatism" in textual criticism seek to ignore. Once the Masoretes began their labors, however, the unconscious and ubiquitous introduction of variations in text, orthography and vocalization came to a virtual halt. The Masoretes conceived of their task to serve as guardians of the text, setting up a fence around the Torah.[11]

This evaluation of the role of the Masoretes was set forth in a study of the *Kethib-Qere*, entitled *The Biblical Text in the Making*, to which the present writer devoted a study published in 1937, many of the principal conclusions of which have since been silently adopted by scholars. In this study it was indicated that the origin of the *Kethib-Qere* apparatus is to be sought in several categories, in all of which one word is written (*Kethib*) and another is to be publicly read (*Qere*). These include the Divine Name, which was to be replaced in

[11] The statement of Rabbi Akiba מסורת סייג לתורה, "Masoret is a fence to the Torah," (*M. Abot* 3:13), has been subjected to a variety of interpretations. In view of R. Akiba's preoccupation with the niceties of *plene* and *defectiva* spelling, and the use of particles like *akh*, *gam*, and *raq* in the Biblical text, as well as the appearance of Aquila's painfully precise Greek version of the Bible, produced under the guidance of Rabbis Akiba, Eliezer and Joshua (*J. Megillah* i, 71c., *B. Meg.* 3a), the statement may well refer to the Masorah, the pre-history of which may be traced to periods much earlier than the 6th or 7th centuries C.E. For evidence of proto-Masoretic activity before the destruction of the Temple, for which the Qumran Bible texts offer indirect evidence, see Gordis, *The Biblical Text in the Making* (= BTM), Philadelphia, 1937, pp. 29-66, and "*Qadmutah šel Hamasoret ľor Hamegillot Hagenuzot*" in *Tarbiz*, vol. 27, (5738 = 1958), pp. 449-69.

the reading by *Adonai* or *Elohim*,[12] and the substitution of
words felt to be obscene by less objectionable equivalents.[13]
The same system of marginal notation was utilized for another
purpose—to help fix the pronunciation before the invention
of the vocalic system, particularly at such critical points as
the reading of plural suffixes written *defectiva*,[14] the older
masculine suffix [15] and other possible errors in reading.[16]

Once this device of marginal readings of the manuscripts
became established, it was utilized for another purpose. In
addition to the archetypal codex adopted as basic, there was
a small number of additional manuscripts that were regarded
as standard because of their antiquity and general reliability,
which contained variants adjudged worthy of preservation.
This was strongly felt by the "proto-Masoretes", to whom each
letter of Scripture was sacred. They, therefore, proceeded to
record these "respectable" variants on the margin, side by
side with the original *Kethib-Qere* notations. As a result, these
variants were subsumed under the same rubric. In all these
cases, the *Qere* is not a correction of the *Kethib*, but a variant
reading drawn from a highly regarded codex. The *Kethib-Qere*

---

[12] This *Qere perpetuum* is registered in a Tannaitic statement in the
Talmud, *B. Peshaim* 50a: אמר הקב״ה לא כשם שאני נכתב אני נקרא נכתב
אני ביו״ד ה״א ונקרא אני אלף דלת
"Said the Holy One, blessed be He, 'not as I am (i.e., my name is)
written am I read: I am written *Yodh He* (i.e., the Tetragrammaton),
but I am read *Aleph Daledh* (Adonai).' " This *Qere* is, however, far
older even than the Talmudic passage. It was universally observed in
the third century B.C.E., as the Septuagint translation of the Pentateuch attests in its reading Κύριος for the Divine name. Cf. BMT, pp.
29 f.

[13] As e.g., *Deut.* 28:27, ובעפלים Kethib; וּבַטְחוֹרִים Qere. This
category is also registered in a Tannaitic statement *B. Meg.* 25a:
תנו רבנן כל המקראות הכתובים בתורה לגעאי קורין אותן לשבח
"Passages written with unclean expressions are changed to more
seemly readings." Cf. *op. cit.*, pp. 30 f., 86.

[14] As e.g., *Gen.* 33:4, צוארו Kethib; צַוָּארָיו Qere. Cf. *op. cit.*, pp. 86 ff.

[15] As e.g., *Num.* 10:36, ובנחה Kethib; וּבְנֻחֹה Qere. Cf. *op. cit.*, pp.
92 ff.

[16] Cf. *op. cit.*, pp. 94-97, Lists 5-8.

6

variants may register orthographic differences, archaic and later forms, phonetic variants, instances of metathesis, divergences in the morphology of nouns and verbs, and other categories.

Obviously, only one of the variants, either the *Kethib* or the *Qere* could have been "original" with the author, but the Masoretes were not improving or restoring the text. They were utilizing the *Kethib-Qere* apparatus to preserve the readings that had reached them. A striking case in point, but by no means the only instance, is afforded by *Ruth* 4:4. In this verse the obvious error יִגְאָל for תִּגְאָל is left "uncorrected" by the Masorah, while the satisfactory or at least the possible reading ואדע is marked as a *Kethib*, with a *Qere* וְאֵדְעָה, on the margin.

It is decisive for evaluating the *Qere* as a textual variation of the *Kethib* that a detailed study of all Masoretic *Kethib-Qere* instances shows that in 11.38%, the *Kethib* and the *Qere* are equally satisfactory, in 12.34% the *Kethib* is superior to the *Qere*, and only in 18.57% of the total is the *Qere* preferable to the *Kethib*.[17] Nevertheless, Bible editions and commentaries often continue to speak of the *Qere* as "correcting" the *Kethib*.

Another Masoretic category, that of the *Sebhirin*, registers attractive readings, *against the introduction of which the Masoretes sought to guard scribes*.[18] Yet *Sebhirin* tend to be cited as Masoretic authority for changes in the text.[19]

To recognize that the role of the Masoretes was to conserve the text, it goes without saying, is not to maintain that the Masoretic Text at every point is the original and authentic text. Even after the inception of Masoretic activity, non-Masoretic codices continued in circulation among the people,

[17] These are classified in Lists 9-85, *op. cit.*, pp. 97-166. The results are presented *ibid.*; p. 82.

[18] On the Sebhirin, see J. Reach, *Die Sebirin der Masoreten* (Breslau 1895), and the critique in *op. cit.*, pp. 26 ff. The treatment in C. D. Ginsburg, *Introduction to the Massoretico-Critical Text of the O.T.* (reprint edition, New York, 1966) pp. 188-96, is not fully adequate.

[19] Cf. e.g., Kittel, *Biblia Hebraica* on Job 9:24c.

to which the Talmud as well as the Dead Sea Scrolls bear testimony.[20] Many of the divergences in the *Ancient Versions* go back to these vulgar non-official manuscripts. Nonetheless, a proper evaluation of the value of the Masoretic tradition, both in transmitting the structure of the Hebrew language and in preserving the Biblical text, is long overdue.

We may turn to another area of Biblical research—the utilization of comparative Semitic material for Biblical exegesis. As was pointed out twenty years ago, the comparative method, properly viewed, has two aspects which may be described as: (a) horizontal (or spatial), that is to say, the use of cognate material from other Semitic languages, and (b) vertical (or temporal), the utilization of material from later stages of the Hebrew language itself—mishnic, talmudic and medieval.[21] The one *caveat* that must be observed is the need to establish clearly that these later usages are authentic and original and not merely reminiscences of Biblical passages.

From the standpoint of method, the vertical approach, which utilizes material coming out of the *Wortschatz* of later Hebrew, has one major advantage over the horizontal, which adduces parallels from cognate languages. In the former instance, we possess the element of continuity with an unbroken tradition embodied in a continuing society, so that there is no problem of establishing the lines of communication and contact. In the latter instance, the proponent must establish how the influence of other periods and alien peoples came to bear upon Biblical Hebrew in Palestine. If, for example, Psalm 29 is "a Ugaritic psalm in a Hebrew transformation," as one scholar has alleged, it remains necessary to demonstrate how a pagan Syrian hymn of the 15th century B.C.E. or earlier, which, incidentally, is not extant, reached a Hebrew

[20] Cf. L. Blau, *Masoretische Untersuchungen* (Strasburg, 1891); V. Aptowitzer, *Das Schriftwort in der rabbinischen Literatur* (Vienna, 1906-15) for the pertinent rabbinic data and our paper cited in n. 11 above.

[21] In *Louis Ginzberg Jubilee Volumes* English Volume (New York, 1945), pp. 173 f.

poet hundreds of years later in a radically different milieu.

On the other hand, if it is argued that the newly proposed meaning or usage, which is, incidentally, often based on unclear or uncertain interpretations of the non-Hebrew source, is indigenously Hebrew, one needs to explain how the continuous tradition of a living people totally forgot and misunderstood it. When the additional assumption is made that this process has taken place, not in a few isolated cases but frequently, we must face the problem of a major discontinuity in the understanding of Hebrew by the Jewish community, for which there is no shred of evidence, and little plausibility, since Hebrew never ceased being written and read by Jews.

In his valuable, indeed indispensable work, *Comparative Philology and the Text of the Old Testament*, (Oxford, 1968), James Barr calls attention to another drawback inherent in the widespread practice of adducing Semitic parallels for Hebrew vocables—it means adding an unconscionably large number of homonyms in Hebrew which would make comprehension difficult and which, it must also be assumed, were forgotten by Hebrew readers and writers for centuries. Thus, for the Hebrew root עיר, no less than nine additional homonyms in addition to "city" have been suggested by various scholars.[22]

In at least one of these instances we wish to propose a new approach to the text that reveals an old meaning. In *Hos.* 11:9, the Masoretic Text reads:

לֹא אֶעֱשֶׂה חֲרוֹן אַפִּי   לֹא אָשׁוּב לְשַׁחֵת אֶפְרָיִם
כִּי אֵל אָנֹכִי וְלֹא אִישׁ   בְּקִרְבְּךָ קָדוֹשׁ וְלֹא אָבוֹא בְּעִיר

This has been generally rendered, "For I am God and not man, holy in your midst and I will not enter into anger." This meaning for עִיר is allegedly supported by a reference to *Jer.* 15:8, עִיר וּבֶהָלוֹת, which is rendered "excitement and terror." It will be granted that the two meanings for עִיר

[22] Cf. Barr, *op. cit.*, 125-6.

suggested are neither identical nor convincing. We propose vocalizing the final stich as וְלֹא אָבֶא בַעֵר, "and I am not willing to destroy," from the root, אבה, "be willing, desire." For the aberrant orthography with *tertiae Aleph* instead of the more common *tertiae* (*He*) *Yod*, אבה, cf., *Pr.* 1:10, אַל תֹּבֵא, "do not agree, be unwilling."

Fortunately, in this instance, we are able to document every element in the proposed revocalization. The verb אבה frequently governs a complementary infinitive without *Lamed* (cf Deut. 2:30; 10:10; 25:7; I Sam. 15:9; Isa. 28:12; 30:9; 42:4; Job 39:9). The Lord is the subject of (לֹא) אבה in Deut. 10:10; 23:6; II Kings 24:4; II Chron. 21:7.A passage exactly parallel in usage to our proposed reading —and directly opposite in meaning—occurs in Deut. 29:19: לֹא־יֹאבֶה ה' סְלֹחַ לוֹ. The *Piel* of בער signifying total destruction at the hand of God occurs in Num. 24:22; Isa. 4:4; 6:13.

Moreover, there are instances where the recognition of a new meaning does not require the assumption of a new homonym. *Pr.* 3:35 offers an example:

כָּבוֹד חֲכָמִים יִנְחָלוּ   וּכְסִילִים מֵרִים קָלוֹן

The singular participle מֵרִים (from רום) with a plural subject, כְּסִילִים, is manifestly impossible. It has therefore been emended מוֹרִשִׁים.[23] Actually, the vocable in question is to be recognized as the plural participle (ē form) of the root מור, like מֵת or נֵד (*Isa.* 17:11). The root מור generally means "change, exchange" in Hebrew, and is used in the *Hiphil* (and *Hophal*) almost exclusively. The relationship of exchange or barter to purchase and acquiring of property is, of course, a truism in cultural history, so that תְּמוּרָה in *Job* 20:18 means "wealth acquired by exchange" and "purchase" in *Ruth* 4:7. The Arabic مار (*mediae ya*) means "to procure (food)," and the

---

[23] So Steuernagel, Kittel, Oesterley, *et al.*

Aramaic מר "to buy or import (food)." The passage in *Proverbs* is therefore to be rendered: "The wise inherit honor, but fools acquire shame".

The same root (ā form) occurs also in another, difficult passage in *Isa.* 38:17, הִנֵּה לְשָׁלוֹם מַר לִי מָר, where the various efforts at interpretation and emendation may be studied in the Commentaries. When the last word of stich a is recognized as the perfect of the verb מוּר (pausal form), the verse receives a clear and unforced meaning with a striking paronomasia:

"Behold my bitterness He has changed to peace,
You have saved my soul from the pit of decay."

The ē form of the *mediae Vav* verb, which we have invoked for the exegesis of *Pr.* 3:35, occurs in another passage, where the failure to recognize it has also led to a misunderstanding of the text. The passage is *Pr.* 20:27:

נֵר ה׳ נִשְׁמַת אָדָם   חֹפֵשׂ כָּל־חַדְרֵי־בָטֶן

It is familiar in the rendering:

"The spirit of man is the lamp of God
Searching all the innermost parts of the belly."

The total absence of any relationship between the two stichs has led to emending נֵר to נֹצֵר.[24] This change has the virtue of supplying a verb in parallelism to חֹפֵשׂ,[25] except that the theme of "guarding" and "searching out" are still poles apart. Actually, no change is required if נֵר is construed as the participle of the verb נוּר, a metaplastic form of the root נהר II, "shine." While this latter root is used only figuratively in the two passages in which it occurs (*Isa.* 60:5; *Ps.* 34:6), the concrete meaning, "shine, give light," obviously underlies it, in accordance with a principle discussed below in this paper. Moreover, the root נור has its cognates in Arab نار;

[24] Cf. Kittel, *BH ad loc.* and the commentaries.
[25] Rashi intuitively grasped the need for a verb and rendered freely: הנשמה שבקרבו מעידה עליו בדין.

11

Akk, nuru, "shine." [26] While the derived noun נֵר "lamp," is common in Hebrew, the verb seems to occur only here in the meaning, "shine upon, cast a beam into," hence, "penetrate." Our verse is then to be rendered:

> "The Lord penetrates to the soul of man,
> Searching out the innermost parts of the belly."

Since the root-meanings of מֵרִים and נֵר as well as the stative (ē forms) of the participle of *mediae Vav* verbs, are uncommon, it is not astonishing that both vocables were wrongly interpreted in the light of their more frequent meanings, as "lift up" and "lamp" respectively. It should also be added that morphological form is not completely wedded to syntactic function. While it is true that stative verbs are generally intransitive, this is by no means always the case. In addition to the two new instances we have adduced here, we may note such stative forms as חָפֵץ (Hos. 6:4), אָהֵב (Ps. 99:4), שָׁאֵלְךָ (Jud. 4:20), all of which govern a direct object. With time, the stative forms of the participle Qal (*qātel*) tended to be assimilated to the dominant active form (*qōtēl*), אוֹהֵב and שׁוֹאֵל, חָפֵץ being the only common instance of resistance to this tendency. It is, therefore, entirely comprehensible that both forms of the participle of the root מור have been preserved, מֵר (Pr. 3:35) and מָר (Isa, 38:17).

In spite of considerations such as those we have advanced above in favor of the "vertical" approach, scholars continue largely to by-pass it and to prefer the "horizontal" method. The reasons for this tendency are not insignificant. In part, the ignoring of post-Biblical Hebrew language and literature often springs from unfamiliarity with rabbinic sources. Candor requires that another motive also be recognized. The "horizontal" approach, ostensibly strictly scientific, is, in some degree, a secularized version of a deeply ingrained

[26] Cf. Köhler-Baumgartner, Lexicon, *s.v.*, p. 604 b.

theological prejudice. In the past, the traditional Christian view, which regarded the Hebrew Scriptures as the inferior prelude to a higher revelation, saw in rabbinic Judaism a degenerate and petrified version of Hebrew religion that had lost all vitality and meaning with the advent of Christianity. While this view of Judaism is not as frequently explicated today as in the past, it still continues to operate, often on the sub-conscious level, frequently being transposed from the theological to the philological key. Post-Biblical Hebrew is often regarded as an artificial, scholastic dialect of little value for Biblical Hebrew. As a result, a basic resource for an understanding of the Bible is minimized, when it is not left totally unused. This situation prevails even more strongly with regard to medieval Hebrew, which is still more recondite and unfamiliar to most Biblical scholars.

Perhaps the most common, and the most justifiable, use of comparative Semitic material for the elucidation of Hebrew has lain in the use of "Aramaisms." One still encounters the simplistic argument that the existence of an alleged "Aramaism" is evidence of a late date for the document. Recently a more balanced and sophisticated analysis of "Aramaisms" has been emerging. Thus Barr divides "Aramaisms" into four categories: (a) a term for a word more frequent in Aramaic but less common in Hebrew; (b) an appeal to Aramaic for a usage not hitherto recognized in Hebrew, though well-known in Aramaic; (c) an Aramaic term based upon contact with Aramaic speakers, particularly in northern Israel; (d) "Aramaisms" due to an erroneous translation into Hebrew from an alleged but non-existent Aramaic original.[27]

The last-named category, which was advanced vigorously by some scholars a decade and more ago with regard to *Ecclesiastes*, has no real existence. While it afforded some scholars a vehicle for ingenuity, the arguments were effectively

---

[27] Cf. *op. cit.*, pp. 121 ff.

refuted in this Journal and elsewhere,[28] and received their death-blow with the discovery of fragments of the Hebrew text of *Koheleth* in Qumran.

No more convincing is the theory of a non-Hebrew original for *Job*, which has been suggested with more or less assurance by such diverse figures as Abraham ibn Ezra, Thomas Carlyle, (Arabic) N. H. Tur-Sinai, (Aramaic) and R. H. Pfeiffer, (Edomite). Here an important methodological principle is at stake. The principal argument of the proponents of the "translation hypothesis" is that the present Hebrew text is difficult and hence must be a translation from a no longer extant Arabic, Aramaic or Edomite text. Actually, the logical conclusion is directly to the contrary. A translator, faced by a difficult original, may misread it, because he lacks an adequate knowledge of the vocabulary and misconstrues the grammar. He may tacitly emend the text, read irrelevant matters into it and generally fail to penetrate its meaning. But ultimately he decides upon some view of the passage, which he then expresses in his idiom. If he commands his own language at all, his translation will be clear and intelligible, indeed far more so than the original, even though it be incorrect. For all the difficulties and possible alternatives posed by the original will have been solved, ignored or obscured in the process of translation.

One has only to compare a difficult verse in the Hebrew of *Hosea*, *Ezekiel* or *Job* with any competent English version to see how the manifold difficulties of the Hebrew "disappear" in the smooth English renderings. *Other things being equal, it may therefore be maintained that a difficult text may be presumed to be the original rather than a translation.*

One instance, chosen almost at random, will suffice to demonstrate this conclusion. A well-known crux, virtually every phrase of which is unclear, is to be found in *Hosea* 11:7:

[28] For a summary discussion of the subject and a bibliography of the literature, see Gordis, *Koheleth—The Man and His World*, 3rd ed., (New York, 1968), pp. 59-62; 324 f.; 413 f.

וְעַמִּי תְלוּאִים לִמְשׁוּבָתִי וְאֶל־עַל יִקְרָאֻהוּ יַחַד לֹא יְרוֹמֵם

The Jewish Publication Society Version renders it as follows:

"And My people are in suspense about returning to Me;
And though they call them upwards,
None at all will lift himself up."

The Revised Standard Version reads:

"My people are bent on turning away from Me
So they are appointed to the yoke,
and none shall remove it."

The two translations are poles apart from one another, testifying to the massive difficulties of the text. What is noteworthy is that both are smooth readings, intelligible and clear, free from all the obscurities and grammatical anomalies of the original Hebrew text.

With the exception of Barr's last category, his classification of Aramaisms is basically identical with ours, which is perhaps more historically oriented than his. They are to be subsumed under four distinct categories: (1) examples of the North-West Semitic vocabulary and usage indigenous to both Aramaic and Hebrew, which became frequent in Aramaic but remaining rare (or poetic) in Hebrew. Such forms are generally early and cannot be invoked for a late date and are not really "Aramaisms" at all; (2) Hebrew borrowings from nearby Aramaic during the pre-Exilic period, especially during the heyday of the Syrian Kingdom; (3) later Hebrew borrowings during the Babylonian Exile and the early post-Exilic period, when Aramaic became the *lingua franca* of the Near East; (4) idioms and morphological forms introduced into Hebrew and patterned after Aramaic usage, with which the Hebrew writer or speaker was familiar, because Aramaic had become the vernacular of the Jewish community. In view of the ambiguities and uncertainties with regard to many specific "Aramaisms", it should be clear that it is methodologically unsound to postulate a late date

15

for a literary composition solely on the basis of one or two
instances. Only when there is a heavy concentration of "Aramaisms", as in Psalm 139, and preferably other data pointing
in the same direction, is it legitimate to assign the document to
an exilic or post-exilic date.[29]

We have thus far emphasized pitfalls and errors in methodology that are to be avoided in Biblical research. We should
like to call attention to two positive and constructive principles that are intimately related: *the importance of semantic
change* and *the ubiquity of psychological association as a basic
component of the human mentality*. Association is constantly at
work enlarging and modifying the meaning of words, often
beyond the dictates of formal logic or coherence.

Thus it remains true, Barr's doubts to the contrary notwithstanding, that the original sense of words is generally
concrete and that the abstract meaning is secondary.[30] One
has only to recall words like רוח "breath, wind," then "spirit",
חטא "miss the mark" then "sin", עוה "twist" then "pervert".

A less familiar instance of this principle may be added.
The common Hebrew root בטח "trust" has its Arabic cognate in بطح which has the meanings: I "throw to the
ground", VII "be thrown to the ground, lie down, lie extended." This original concrete meaning was noted by the Karaite grammarian, David ben Abraham Alfasi and the medieval lexicographer Solomon ibn Parhon, who interpreted בטח
as "lie down" in Jer. 12:5; Ps. 22:10; Job 40:2.[31] We believe
that it is highly appropriate to Job 11:18a; 12:6; 40:23.[32]

Failure to recognize this principle of semantic change from

[29] Cf. Gordis, *The Book of God and Man—A Study of Job* (Chicago,
1963), pp. 162, 344.

[30] Cf. Barr, *op. cit.*, p. 276, who cites Eitan's view, which we endorse.
Barr may have been led to doubt the principle because he does not find
the particular application to *Ex.* 17:13 to be convincing, in which
respect he is right.

[31] Cf. J. L. Skoss in *Jewish Studies in Memory of G. A. Kohut* (New
York, 1935), pp. 549-53.

[32] Cf. our translation in *BGM*, *ad loc.* and our *Commentary on Job*
now in preparation.

16

the concrete to the abstract leads at times to radically unsound procedures in exegesis and textual criticism. A case in point is afforded by Ecc. 11:10:

וְהָסֵר כַּעַס מִלִּבֶּךָ וְהַעֲבֵר רָעָה מִבְּשָׂרֶךָ כִּי־הַיַּלְדוּת וְהַשַּׁחֲרוּת הָבֶל

The closing stich has been rendered by commentators "for childhood and youth are vanity." It has then been deleted as a pious gloss intended to counter the hedonistic counsel of stichs a and b, "Remove vexation from your body and sorrow from your flesh." Actually, *hebhel* here, as in other instances, has its primary concrete meaning of "breath, vapor", being used at times to emphasize brevity and at other times, insubstantiality. Here, as the context makes clear (see 12:1 ff.) the sage is declaring that "childhood and youth are only a breath," that is to say, "they pass all too quickly."

Doubts have been expressed with regard to the rare words חֶלְכָּה חֵלְכָּאִים (Ps. 10:8, 10 *Kethib*.[33] We find this view thoroughly unjustified, in view of the existence of the Arabic حلك; "be black", which then passes over in Hebrew into the sense "unfortunate." The same semantic development occurs in קדר "be black", hence "be miserable, mournful" (Ps. 35:14, 38:7, 42:10, 43:2; Job 5:11, 30:28; Mal. 3:14), and in חֲשֻׁכִים (Pr. 22:29) "dark", hence "obscure, lowly".

As psychoanalysis and the study of symbolism have made clear, the range of association is virtually limitless. It is so far-reaching that frequently we can only register the fact of semantic change, without being able to reconstruct the psychological process by which it was arrived at. Thus, we can speculate with little assurance concerning the connection between "branch of a tree" and "thought, opinion", yet the facts are clear. The Hebrew nouns סָעִיף and סְעַפָּה mean "branch" in Isa. 17:6, 27:10; Ez. 31:6, 8 and

[33] BDB is doubtful about the text, which Köhler-Baumgartner calls it "unexplained." Barr, *op. cit.*, pp. 228 f. shares this doubt.

"idea, opinion" in I Ki. 18:21; (סְעִפָּה‎); Job 4-13, 20:2
(שְׂעִיפִּים‎). The same root with infixed *Reš* offers סַרְעַפָּה‎
"branch" (Ez. 31:5) and שַׂרְעַפִּים‎, "opinion, idea" (Ps. 94:19,
139:23).

Obviously, when the various steps in the semantic process
can be reconstructed and the evidence appears in the same
language or in closely related ones, the proposed view is
more likely to carry assent. Nevertheless the human spirit
is one everywhere and similar psychological processes trans-
cend ethnic and cultural boundaries. As Engnell has forcefully
reminded us, "Comparing Israelite material with relatively
far-distant lands and cultures—India and Iran for instance—
actually can be more fruitful than comparing it with closer
regions, such as Arabia." [34]

To cite one instance from the area of language, the now
obsolescent English slang term "bean" for "head" has its
analogue in the legitimate French word *tête*, derived from the
Latin *testa*, "bean". In the case of idioms in particular, the
process of association is often rendered more difficult to
retrace because of truncation, so that only the end result and
not the steps involved remains clear to us.

I should like to offer as an illustration an interpretation of
a famous crux which may be regarded as an extreme example.
In Job 12:6, the poet is describing the prosperity of the
wicked:

יִשְׁלָיוּ אֹהָלִים לְשֹׁדְדִים   וּבַטֻּחוֹת לְמַרְגִּיזֵי אֵל
לַאֲשֶׁר הֵבִיא אֱלוֹהַּ בְּיָדוֹ

The enigmatic third stich has been subjected to a plethora of
interpretations and emendations. It has been explained as:
(a) the idolator, "who makes his God with his hand" (Rashi);
(b) The idolator "who brings his god in his hand;" (c) "who
holds God in his power" (Driver-Gray); (d) "who sees his God
in his strength"; (e) "who makes might his God", (Butten-
wieser, Moffat), "God's terror-spreaders, whom God brings

[34] Cf. Ivan Engnell, *A Critical Scrutiny* (Nashville, 1969), p. 8.

up for him" (Tur-Sinai). The stich has been emended to
לאשר הניף באלוה ידו (Siegfried) לאשר הביא באלוה ידו (Beer),
כאשר הביא אלוה בידם (Duhm); לאמר הכו אלוה בידי (Ehrlich).

The totally unconvincing character of these interpretations
and emendations has, predictably enough, served to suggest
deleting the clause, or the verse, or the entire section as a gloss,
leaving unexplained how and why these inexplicable words
were interpolated into the text.

It so happens, however, that in Elizabethan English we
find a well-attested idiom "to bear someone in hand", in the
meaning of "to deceive, delude." We may cite the following
examples from Shakespeare:

> "To bear a gentlemen in hand
> and then stand upon security"
> (King Henry IV, Part Two, I, 2, l.34)

> "How you were borne in hand
> how crossed . . . ."
> (Macbeth, III, 1, l. 181)

> "That so his sickness, age and impotence
> was falsely borne in hand"
> (Hamlet, II, 1, ll.66 f)

Not only is the English idiom identical with the Hebrew
phrase in question, but its meaning, "to deceive" is highly
appropriate to the context. As Kissane has correctly pointed
out, "The context is the guide to the interpretation and
disregard of the context leads to chaos.[35] The passage therefore may be rendered without recourse to emendation, as
follows:

> "The tents of robbers are at peace,
> The dwellings of those who provoke God,
> of those who have deceived Him." [36]

---

[35] Cf. E. J. Kissane, *The Book of Isaiah II* (Dublin, 1943), p. lxviii.
[36] The change of number from plural to singular (between stichs a
and b and stich c) is, of course, common in Biblical style, especially
since the relative אשר tends to be treated as a singular pronoun.

Tobit 1:13 reads: καὶ ἔδωκεν [μοι s] ὁ ὕψιστος χάριν καὶ μορφὴν ἐνώπιον Ενεμεσσαρου.

Perles suggested that the noun μορφή means "form" on the basis of the Arabic *šakl* [37]. This meaning Perles attached also to the phrase טוֹבַת שֵׂכֶל וִיפַת תּוֹאַר in I Sam. 25:3 though he did not consider it appropriate in the *Tobit* passage. The entire suggestion Barr views with considerable skepticism.[38] However, the passage in *Tobit* is obviously reminiscent of the Biblical idiom occurring in Pr. 3:4 וּמְצָא חֵן וְשֵׂכֶל טוֹב. The same meaning occurs again in Ps. 111:10 שֵׂכֶל טוֹב לְכָל עֹשֵׂיהֶם. The noun obviously means "favor" in both verses:

We believe that this significance occurs also in Gen. 3:6. וַתֵּרֶא הָאִשָּׁה כִּי טוֹב הָעֵץ לְמַאֲכָל וְכִי תַאֲוָה הוּא לָעֵינַיִם וְנֶחְמָד הָעֵץ לְהַשְׂכִּיל Here the usual rendering of the last clause, "desirable for giving wisdom" was induced by the fact that it is the Tree of Knowledge which is being spoken of. However, several strong considerations militate against this interpretation of לְהַשְׂכִּיל:

(a) The parallelism with וְכִי תַאֲוָה הוּא לָעֵינַיִם (b) the juxtaposition with נֶחְמָד "desirable, attractive", and (c) the fact that the capacity of the tree to give knowledge would not become evident to Eve by looking upon it (וַתֵּרֶא הָאִשָּׁה). The verse is therefore better rendered: "The woman saw that the tree was good for food, desirable for the eyes and attractive in form." Here too, as is too often the case, the intuitive feeling for the text of the earlier interpreters has unjustifiably been neglected. Targum Onkelos and the Jerusalem Targum both render להשכיל as לאסתכלא, "to look upon."

The technical term מַשְׂכִּיל, which occurs as a superscription in several Psalms has always been a crux. That it cannot mean "a didactic Psalm" has been generally recognized, in

[37] Cf. *JQR*, (NS) vol. XVII (1926-7), p. 233.
[38] *Op. cit.*, pp. 244-5. On the other hand, the phrase is correctly rendered "grace and favor" by D. C. Simpson in R. H. Charles, *Apocrypha and Pseudepigrapha of the O.T.* (Oxford, 1913) vol. I, p. 204.

view of the totally varied subject-matter of the Psalms
bearing this heading, including its use in the superscription
of the Royal Wedding Song in Ps. 45, and its occurrence in
Ps. 47:8.[39] We believe that the term means literally "attractive
song", and that this generic term possessed a specific
technical sense that we can no longer discover. We may compare
the modern use of *belles lettres* to refer to one specific
genre of literature. The fact that the specific sense of *Maskil*
eludes us today, as well as the variety of subject matter,
would suggest that the term referred to the melodic or instrumental
aspect of the Psalm, rather than to its content.
On the basis of the Arabic cognate, *šakl*, which means "form",
we may predicate two related semantic processes: a) from
the literal to the figurative and b) polarization, so that the
basic meaning "form, appearance" is generally used in a
positive sense, "beautiful form, attractiveness", with or
without the qualifying adjective טוב.

This meaning, "favor, attractiveness," is also more appropriate
in *Pr.* 19:11, where שכל is parallel to תפארת:

שֵׂכֶל אָדָם הֶאֱרִיךְ אַפּוֹ   וְתִפְאַרְתּוֹ עֲבוֹר עַל־פָּשַׁע

Here there is no relationship between the subjects in the two
stichs according to the usual translation, "a man's discretion,"
and his "glory." On the other hand, the passage receives an
unforced meaning in the rendering:

> It is attractive for a man to be slow to anger,
> And a glory for him to overlook a transgression.[40]

Finally, it may be added that *Josh.* 1:7 לְמַעַן תַּשְׂכִּיל בְּכֹל
אֲשֶׁר תֵּלֵךְ is translated by the Targum בדיל דתכשט, the
root of the common Hebrew and Aramaic noun, תכשיט,
"ornament, decoration." [41]

---

[39] Cf. *Psalms* 32, 42, 44, 45, 52, 53, 54, 55, 74, 78, 88, 89, 142.

[40] Reading with all commentators, the infinitive הַאֲרִיךְ (parallel to
עֲבוֹר) for the perfect הֶאֱרִיךְ.

[41] The phrase in *II Chr.* 30:22 כָּל־הַלְוִיִּם הַמַּשְׂכִּילִים שֵׂכֶל־טוֹב לה' is
unclear. The passage may refer to the Levites' teaching of the Law or

Insight into the semantic process should dispel any doubts with regard to the meaning of נִכַּר אוֹתוֹ אֱלֹהִים בְּיָדִי (*I Sam.* 23:7). The rendering by LXX, πέπρακεν, "sell," is not to be dismissed as a "lucky guess" of the translators who related it to מכר.[42] The Ugaritic *nkr*, "sell," and the usage in *Hos.* 3:2, וָאֶכְּרֶהָ, may be adduced here. In *Hosea* the *Qal* of the root means, "buy, purchase." In *Samuel* the *Piel* used causatively means, "sell," hence, "betray," a figurative use frequent with the verb מכר (*Deut.* 32:30; *Isa.* 50:1; *Ps.* 44:13, a.e.). We may note the Aramaic *Peʿal*, זְבַן, "buy," and the causative *Paʿel,,* זַבֵּן "sell." [43]

The principle of association is also a basic clue to literary structure. A writer may be led to bring together disparate matters which have in common only an external similarity of language. An excellent example is afforded by *Ecc.*, Chap. 7. Here commentators for centuries attempted to find a common theme running through the passage. What we have here is a collection of seven traditional Wisdom apothegms, with characteristic comments by Koheleth, which he assembled because they all begin with the word *tōbh*. In this instance, the arrangement seems to have emanated from the author.[44]

In other instances it is a principle employed by editors, particularly in putting together prophetic oracles, which were generally brief. *Isa.*, Chap. 19 contains five oracles, each introduced by the phrase, *bayōm hahū'* (vv. 6, 18, 19, 23, 24). Similarly, *vᵉhayah bayōm hahū'* introduces three oracles in *Isa.* 7:18, 21 and 23. Recognizing the independent character of each unit makes it unnecessary to try to find one theme

to "their good skill in the service of the Lord" (JPSV, RSV). It seems more likely that it refers to the Levites' chanting of hymns (cf. v. 21 וְהַכֹּהֲנִים בִּכְלֵי־עֹז לה').

[42] So Barr, *op. cit.*, p. 267.

[43] On the meaning of the verb and its importance for the critical questions of Hos. 1-3, cf. Gordis, "Hosea's Marriage and Message" in *HUCA* (vol. XXV) 1954, pp. 25 f., n. 26.

[44] Cf. *KMW ad loc.*

and date for the entire section; each oracle requires individual analysis.

Even greater difficulties have been encountered by interpreters attempting to find a common background and theme to Mi. 4:8-5:5. Here we have another collection of brief oracles, the nexus being the opening words אתה and עתה, which do not differ radically in pronounciation: ואתה (4:8); עתה (4:9); ועתה (4:11); עתה (4:14); ואתה (5:1). This method of editorial organization on the basis of similarity of rubric is very common in Rabbinic literature.[45]

The sovereign role played by psychological association in language and literature is far from exhausted by the instances adduced above. Thus association is the basis for most of the rhetorical figures, such as paronomasia, *talḥin*,[46] metaphor and simile. It is the basic mechanism underlying chiasmus, which is the key to many difficult passages in Biblical literature, the value of which have not yet been fully explored.[47]

In this paper, we have dealt with some widespread errors in method, both specific and general. In the final analysis, however, truly creative research, as distinct from routine research, cannot really be taught; like art and religion it must be caught.[48] Where the creative spark exists, the חלק אלוה ממעל, it wells up independently in the spirit of the scholar and makes him brother to the artist.

But whether the scholar is engaged in a creative enterprise of the first magnitude or in a routine project of modest scope,

---

[45] *M.Eduyoth*, Chaps 6-9, where otherwise unrelated matters are associated by the rubric העיד; *Yadayim*, Chap. 4, where בו ביום is the formula and *Pesahim*, Chap. 4, where מקום שנהגו serves similarly.

[46] On this subtle and richly rewarding figure of speech, see our study in *Sepher Seidel* (Jerusalem, 5722 = 1962) pp. 255-62.

[47] This is the key to the meaning and structure of Bildad's first speech (Job 8:9-22), as will be demonstrated in our forthcoming *Commentary on Job*.

[48] This is our own reformulation of the approach to research in the natural sciences expounded by Michael Polanyi in his brilliant and suggestive work, *Science, Faith and Society*, (Chicago, 1964).

he must seek to avoid one basic pitfall all too common among literary and historical scholars—their inability or unwillingness to recognize the limits inherent in the nature of humanistic studies. In the natural sciences, the verification of a theory is achieved by reproducibility of the results, agreement between determinations made by different and independent methods and the fulfillment of predictions. Yet even here, philosophers of science have pointed out all three criteria may be present and yet the statement they seem to confirm may prove to be false.[49] Generally speaking, however, where these criteria are clearly present, a high degree of certainty may be secured. Even in the social sciences, some degree of objectivity and the complete examination of all pertinent data are possible through the judicious use of statistical data, though obviously far less so than in the natural sciences. In the historical and literary disciplines, virtually none of these resources or procedures is available. We cannot reproduce the past under test conditions nor study theories within the life-situation to which they allegedly apply. It therefore follows that the terms "demonstrate" and "prove" in these areas necessarily have a far more restricted and tentative character than in the natural sciences, and should be used sparingly, if at all. At best, they can only establish a more or less plausible reconstruction of the past to explain the available phenomena, which are virtually always incomplete, and therefore always liable to misinterpretation.

There is a tendency among some natural scientists, particularly those who have never reflected seriously upon the limitations of their own discipline, to look down upon humanistic scholars. This attitude is unjustified. The phenomena with which historical and literary scholars deal involve human beings and are therefore far more complex than those of inanimate nature or of sub-human forms of life, which constitute the subject matter of astronomy, geology or biology. Yet even natural scientists, when they enter complex

[49] Cf. Polanyi, *op. cit.*, p. 30.

fields, such as nuclear physics or genetics, find their theories and conclusions becoming increasingly tentative and subject to controversy. In far greater degree, it behooves students and scholars in humanistics to develop a deep sense of humility coupled with a healthy dose of agnosticism with regard to theories, particularly those they propose themselves. That this goal is not easy to attain needs no demonstration!

The brilliant Biblical exegete, Arnold B. Ehrlich, in rebutting some of the vagaries of the Higher Criticism with regard to *Deuteronomy*, did not hesitate to incorporate a joke in his Commentary[50]. Perhaps I may be forgiven for yielding to an equally unscholarly impulse. For years, my students have been taught that an important canon of scholarly method is to be found in the phrase which characterized a popular American radio comedian some years ago: "Vas you dere, Charley ?" In similar vein, Israel Friedlander, who served years ago as Professor of Bible at the Jewish Theological Seminary, was accustomed to tell his students, "When you read a statement in a scholarly treatment containing the adverb 'undoubtedly', you may be sure there is a great deal of doubt."

In part, the dogmatism with which the views are advanced within the field of Biblical research and the violence with which differing views are often attacked, derive from a sense of inferiority among humanistic scholars vis-à-vis the natural scientists and the desire to pretend to the kind of certainty the latter seem to enjoy—though this, too, is an illusion.

In even greater degree, Biblical scholars need to recognize that Biblical exegesis is not a science but an art, which rests upon a foundation of science. The practice of medicine offers a perfect analogy. It is an art that calls upon the intuitive gifts of the practitioner, as well as such personal qualities as insight and sympathy, attributes resting upon a constellation of sciences which include anatomy, physiology, pharmacology and others. Similarly, Biblical exegesis is an art that requires

[50] Cf. his *Randglossen*, (Berlin, 1909), vol. II, p. 299.

such personal qualities as insight, empathy with the material being analyzed, constructive imagination and esthetic appreciation. These must rest upon a knowledge of Hebrew and other Semitic languages and literatures, including phonetics, morphology, syntax, and style-patterns, archaeology, ancient history, higher and textual criticism and other disciplines.

Literature is the foremost expression of the human spirit and language is its medium. Both reflect the limitless variety of man's emotions and thoughts, his impulses and desires, his fears and hopes, his memories and aspirations. The student of language, which is the key to literature, is therefore basically dedicated to the exploration of the most fascinating and elusive phenomenon in the world—human nature. It is the path of wisdom for the scholar to recognize the limitations inherent in his quest. If he approaches his task in a spirit of humility, he is more likely to be vouchsafed a few glimpses of new truth and beauty—and this is reward enough.

26

STUDIES IN BIBLICAL LITERATURE

THE ORIGIN OF THE MASORETIC TEXT IN THE LIGHT OF RABBINIC LITERATURE AND THE QUMRAN SCROLLS

I.

The distinguished Biblical scholar, Professor Max L. Margolis, was accustomed to say that any scientific question could always be reopened. The discovery of new sources, an improved investigation of data previously known, an original and novel approach to the subject—any or all of these factors might bring about a new approach to theories and conclusions that had previously been widely accepted.

More than a century has elapsed since Paul de Lagarde adopted the theory of Rosenmüller that a single manuscript was the source of the Masoretic text of the Hebrew Bible.[1] An investigation of the Biblical manuscripts collated by Kennicott and de Rossi made it clear that they all had a common origin.[2] The slight variations in *defectiva* and *plene* orthography and other similar details were to be explained as scribal errors due to anonymous copyists. On the other hand, an independent study of these manuscripts revealed that many characteristics of the accepted text, such as the large and small letters (majuscules and miniscules), the inverted *nun*, and the *Kethibh-Qere* variants were to be found in virtually all the manuscripts. From this, Lagarde concluded that all the Biblical manuscripts that reached us were copies of a single authoritative archetype or *Mustercodex*.

29

When was this official, universally accepted, text adopted? Lagarde answered with great assurance that the archetype had been chosen in the period of Rabbi Akiba, approximately 130 C.E. Rabbi Akiba, who was the creator of the very precise method of Biblical hermeneutics that derived legal and religio-ethical interpretations from such apparently unimportant words as גם,אך, and רק,[3] recognized the necessity for an official text. Hence, he and members of his school chose one manuscript as an archetype and established it for all Jewry.[4]

For several decades, Lagarde's theory was accepted as fundamental in Biblical scholarship. However, in the twentieth century it was challenged, not only in regard to the period when the archetype was alleged to have been chosen, but in regard to the basic thesis itself. The manuscripts upon which Lagarde and his colleagues had based their view arose, by and large, in the twelfth century and later. The first complete manuscript of the Hebrew Bible was written in the tenth century. The oldest manuscript of the Latter Prophets was dated 895. The new collation of Biblical manuscripts and early prints by C. D. Ginsburg, in spite of weaknesses in method, brought to light a large number of new variations, most of which, to be sure, were unimportant.[5] When the Biblical manuscripts of the Cairo Genizah were studied by Paul Kahle, they revealed many variations in vocalization and in the use of *matres lectionis*.[6] In addition, the Biblical quotations in the Talmud and the Midrash contain a large number of texts that vary from the Masoretic.[7] On the basis of this evidence, Kahle and his school concluded that there never had been an archetype, and that variations in the Biblical text were widespread in Jewish circles until the Middle Ages. One scholar went so far as to argue that there was no accepted text of the Bible until the second edition of the Rabbinic Bible by Jacob ben Ḥayyim (1521–1525).[8]

To be sure, Lagarde's theory was not totally discarded; it survived in modified form. According to the dominant view today, the process of creating an "accepted text" of the Bible was begun in the second century C.E. by Rabbi Akiba, as a consequence of his extremely exact method of interpreting letters and words in the Torah. However, according to this view his efforts did not succeed at once. Many variations in text, with regard to both orthography and vocalization, continued to fill manuscripts in the succeeding centuries until the Middle Ages.[9] Two new factors then entered the picture—the activity of Arab and Syrian scribes, who labored to preserve the text of their respective scriptures against changes and errors, and the rise of the Karaite sect, which gave primacy to the Biblical text. These events, served as a stimulus to the work of the Masoretes, particularly the families of Ben Asher and Ben Naphtali (which flourished from the second half of the eighth to the middle of the tenth centuries C.E.). It was the all-powerful influence of Maimonides in the twelfth century that succeeded in giving to the version of Ben Asher its authority as the official text of Rabbinic Judaism.[10]

Not all scholars believed that the variations remained numerous for so long a period as the centuries between Rabbi Akiba and the medieval Masoretes. Some admitted that the consonantal text (vocalization does not enter into consideration here) remained more or less fixed beginning with the second century.[11] What has been common to virtually all scholars concerned with the origins of the Masoretic text is the view that it is the result of the labors of Rabbi Akiba and his school. Hence, the beginnings of the *textus receptus* could not antedate the second century, and the conclusion of the process is to be attributed to the Middle Ages, when the *Kethibh-Qere* readings were fixed.[12]

II.

During my graduate studies under Professor Max L. Margolis, I became interested in the Masorah and undertook to study the *Kethibh-Qere*, the results of which were set forth in the volume, *The Biblical Text in the Making—A Study of the Kethibh-Qere*, which was first published in 1937. As a result of my research, I came to the conclusion that the accepted view regarding the genesis and history of the Masorah, as summarized above, is basically unacceptable, since it is unable to explain the available

31

data and the content of our extant sources. Through a careful investigation of all instances of the *Kethibh-Qere* in the Masoretic text, it became clear to me that the accepted view that the *Qere* is a correction of the *Kethibh* by the Masoretes is totally without foundation. Not only is it contradicted by much specific data, but it runs counter to the entire spirit of Masoretic activity and to its purpose, which was the preservation of the text as it reached them and not its correction or improvement.[13] That these anonymous guardians of the text, who counted the letters of Scripture, determined the middle letter and the middle verse of the Torah, established the middle letter of the Bible as a whole, compiled extensive lists of rare and unique Biblical forms, listed the number of occurrences of thousands of Biblical words and usages—all in order to help protect it from tampering and prevent scribes from introducing changes into the accepted text—would themselves engage in wholesale changes in the accepted readings is a rank impossibility.

This evaluation of the spirit and function of Masoretic activity, in general, is supported by one fundamental fact, the implications of which have not yet been fully realized: the grammatical structure of Biblical Hebrew as reflected in the Masoretic system of vocalization. All three systems of Hebrew vocalization were created before the year 900 C.E. At that time, no grammarian had as yet proposed the tri-literal theory for Hebrew morphology. On the contrary, the view that Hebrew roots were bi-literal (and perhaps originated in a single letter) prevailed until the end of the tenth century and beyond (cf. the *piyyutim,* Menaḥem ben Saruk, *c.* 910–*c.* 970; Dunash ben Labrat, *c.* 920–*c.* 990; and Rashi, 1040–1105). The bi-literal theory was first challenged by Judah Hayyug (*circa* 1000) and Jonah Abu al-Walid ibn Janah (*c.* 985–*c.* 1040). *Nevertheless, the Masoretic vocalization of Hebrew is in harmony with the tri-literal theory,* which alone is able to explain all the phenomena it contains—*conclusive evidence that the Masoretes did not invent the vocalic system but preserved an ancient reliable tradition regarding the pronunciation of the Biblical text.* To be sure, in the course of the centuries changes did take place with regard to pronunciation of the consonants and, particularly, the vowels. Nevertheless, it is clear that the Masoretes created the traditional vocalization in order to preserve the structure of a living language, and not to change the pronunciation by some newly invented system of their own.

Another line of evidence indicating that the role of the Masoretes was to conserve the text and not to make innovations upon it, has recently come to light. Basing himself on the fact that medieval *piyyutim* use the suffix *ākh* for the masculine second person singular, Kahle concluded that the Masoretes had "invented" the form *khā* perhaps because of Arabic influence. Now the Qumran Biblical manuscripts contain hundreds of instances where this suffix is written *khah,* thus attesting to the antiquity of the Masoretic vocalization. This is the form the official guardians of the text preserved in spite of the fact that it differed from the usage current in their own time.

These general considerations militating against the view that the *Qere* readings, which number 1350, represent "corrections of the *Kethibh*," are supported by an impressive array of specific data discussed in detail in the body of the book.[14] It may be useful to present them here in summary fashion and supplement them by additional evidence.

1. There are a large number of passages in which the *Kethibh,* in one instance, serves as the *Qere* in another, and *vice versa.* For example, in Genesis 39:20 the *Kethibh* is אסורי, the *Qere* אֲסִירֵי. In Judges 16:21, 25 the *Kethibh* is האסורים, the Qere הָאֲסוּרִים.

2. In almost every category of *Kethibh-Qere* listed by the Masorah there are instances in the Biblical text where the *Kethibh* occurs without the *Qere.* Thus, in Genesis 24:33 the *Kethibh* is וייׂשם, the *Qere* וַיּוּשַׂם. In Genesis 50:26 the reading is וַיִּישֶׂם with no correction in the *Qere.*

3. There are instances in which a word occurs several

33

times in a given passage, some examples of which are marked by a *Qere* and others are not. Thus, in Judges 9:8 and 9:12 a *Kethibh-Qere* occurs. In 9:9 the same form occurs without a variant.

4. At times, there is a *Qere* with regard to a *Kethibh* which offers no difficulty at all while, in the same verse, an obvious difficulty is "uncorrected" by the *Qere*. Compare Proverbs 15:14, *Kethibh* וּפְנֵי, *Qere* וּפִי, as against Numbers 33:8 מִפְּנֵי הַחִירֹת without a *Kethibh-Qere*. Note particularly in Ruth 4:4 *Kethibh* וָאֹדַע, *Qere* וְאֵדְעָה · while the impossible reading יגאל is not at all "corrected" by the Masorah.

5. At times, the *Qere* creates a *hapax legomenon,* where the *Kethibh* is the normal form, as in the first *Kethibh-Qere* in the Bible, Genesis 8:17 *Kethibh* הוצא, *Qere* היצא.

6. On the basis of an analysis and statistical summary of all instances of the *Kethibh-Qere* it becomes clear that the *Qere* is superior to the *Kethibh* in only 18% of the cases, while the *Kethibh* is superior to the *Qere* in 12%. In the remaining 62% of the instances they are of equal value. It is inconceivable that the Masoretes, who approached the text with such extraordinary reverence and meticulous care, would dare to tamper with the text in over 1300 passages, and to propose a change where the *Kethibh* is superior, or at least not inferior to the *Qere* in 74% of all instances.

7. Conclusive evidence of the attitude of the Masoretes to a difficult passage is to be found in the phenomenon of the *Sebirin*. In these cases the Masoretes warn the copyists to avoid changing the accepted text in favor of a reading which apparently seems preferable. They, therefore, note the attractive reading on the margin, accompanied by the term *sebirin*, which means "it is thought [proposed] to read so and so, but you, the scribe, must not vary from the accepted text." Thus, Psalm 144:2 הָרוֹדֵד עַמִּים תַּחְתָּי has a *sebir* עַמִּים, against which the Masorah warns the scribe. The full force of this argument has not been appreciated

because the term *sebir* has often not been entirely understood.[15]

It is, therefore, clear that the *Qere* did not serve as a correction of the *Kethibh.* Detailed research into its origin, character, and function revealed that the phenomenon of its use is not uniform, and that there were several stages in its development.

The first stage in the *Kethibh-Qere,* as its name "written-read" indicate, is to be sought in cases in which one word is written in the text and the public reader is asked to pronounce another in its stead. The oldest *Kethibh-Qere* is in the Tetragrammaton, which was recognized in the Talmud as a *Qere perpetuum*: "Not as I am written am I read. I am written *Yod He* and I am read *Aleph Daled* (i.e., *Adonai*)" (*B. Pesaḥim,* 50a).

The antiquity of this *Kethibh-Qere* is attested by the fact that it was already evident in the Septuagint version of the Torah in the middle of the 3rd cent.[16] In the Qumran Scrolls, the Tetragrammaton is frequently interchanged with *Adonai,* undoubtedly because the former was pronounced like the latter. The tendency to avoid the pronunciation of the Divine Name is reflected in several aspects of the Biblical text itself, notably the rarity (or absence) of the Name in later books, like Job, Ecclesiastes, and Esther, in the Elohistic version of Psalms and, possibly, in certain other elements of Biblical style that deserve investigation.[17] The reason for this attitude toward the Name, which apparently derived out of extraordinary reverence, is not clear, but the fact itself is beyond dispute.[18]

Not infrequently the Masoretic text contains usages which depart from conventional standards of "clean speech," especially for public reading. Such is the verb שגל, "cohabit" (Deut. 28:27 and elsewhere) and the nouns עפל, "tumor" (I Sam. 5:6 and elsewhere), חרא, "feces" (II Kings, 6:25 and elsewhere), שין, "urine" (II Kings 11:27). In all these instances the *Kethibh-Qere* apparatus was entirely appropriate, since one word was written, but another was to be read in its place. This category was also recognized by the Tannaim:

35

תנו רבנן כל המקראות הכתובים בתורה לגנאי קורין אותן לשבח.
"All passages written in the Torah in unseemly language are to be
read with a euphemism" (*B. Megillah,* 28a). This category of the
Kethibh-Qere, like the one preceding, is very ancient. The changes
of שכב· for שגל and טהור for עפל presuppose a period when the
Hebrew language, with all its nuances and idioms, was still well-
known by the broad masses of the people. Hence, their origin must
lie in a period preceding the penetration of Aramaic into the
Jewish community and its replacement of Hebrew as the spoken
language of the masses.

The substitution for the Tetragrammaton, which occurs 6823
times in the Bible, and the euphemistic changes, which number
16, created the technical term, *Kethibh-Qere,* in its original meaning, which was later to be utilized in extended forms for other
purposes.

The next level in the development of the *Kethibh-Qere*
attempts to deal with the problem of reading the Hebrew text
in the absence of vowels. A very common category is the masculine
third person singular suffix in plural nouns as, for example, ועמדו
(Exod. 27:11), where the only possible reading is ועמדיו, or in the
case of pronouns, as for example עלו (I Sam. 2:10), where the
reading is עליו. A similar problem arises with rare nouns which
end with a consonantal *vav* as, for example, השלו (Numbers
11:32), which is to be read השליו. Similarly, the old ending
for the masculine third person singular suffix as, for example,
אהלה (Gen. 9:21), could lead to errors in the reading, since it
might be read as a feminine suffix. The absence of *matres lectiones*
was also felt in the rare orthography of certain words as, for
example, לו, which is written at times as לא, and the nouns צבײם
(Gen. 14:2), and גײם (Gen. 25:23), which are to be read with
a *holem* and not a *hireq* or a *sere* in the first syllable.

There was also a practice of ancient scribes, known to us also
from the Lachish letters, of writing down only one of the vowel
letters אהוי״, instead of two, as in חיהוה, which can be found
in the Biblical texts והמבי את (II Sam. 5:2) and מחטו (Gen.

36

20:1). This absence of vowel letters naturally added to the difficulties in the reading.

In all these instances (*BTM* lists 2–8), the number of which reaches 259, it was necessary to teach the reader the correct pronunciation. To be sure, many scribes did not hesitate to change the text of the manuscript before them and wrote עָלָיו instead of עָלוֹ and אֵהֵלוֹ instead of אָהֳלֹה. But the official guardians of the text, whose fundamental function was the protection of the received version against all changes, could not make peace with such an approach. They were compelled to find means for easing the problems of reading without changing the accepted text. After hundreds of years, during which countless efforts were made to solve this problem, the Masoretes created the various systems of vocalization, following the example of Arab and Syrian grammarians. In the early period with which we are concerned, that preceded the invention of the vocalic system by many years, the guardians of the text utilized an instrument already available to them, the *Kethibh-Qere* apparatus. When they found a word written *defectiva* in the text, which was liable to mislead the reader, they wrote the *plene* spelling in the margin, e.g.,– עמדו כ׳, עמודיו ק׳ and did not modify the consonantal text at all.[19]

In sum, all the early stages of the development of the Kethibh-Qere were intended to present a reading mode differing from the written form which is the only one in existence. These two earliest categories, the change in the reading of the Tetragrammaton and the euphemisms, arose in a very early period. The function of these categories was to protect the reader against blasphemy and obscenity. The later categories sought to protect him against ignorance and lack of understanding. These too arose in an early period long before the rise of the vocalic system. The *terminus ante quem* will be delimited even further as we clarify the origin of the third stage of the *Kethibh-Qere* in which this apparatus made a fundamental contribution to the establishment of the Biblical text and its preservation.

Already in a very early period, the guardians of the text recognized that valuable, or at least significant, textual variants were to be found in the manuscripts circulating among the people. These proto-Masoretes did not want these variants to be lost. On the other hand, they could not surrender their basic objective—the preservation of the text against a flood of variants.

Not easily, nor in one leap, were the guardians of the text able to discover appropriate means for achieving this ambivalent function. Our sources provide the evidence of the slow progress that the Masoretes made in technique and sophistication in carrying out their objective. Modern scholars were mistaken in having treated these sources with undue skepticism. Indeed, their reliability is underscored precisely by the fact that they testify to phenomena which contradict the basic goal of the Masoretes—the preservation of the text against the most minute change. These early sources testify to changes introduced into the consonantal text of Scripture, a procedure which the later Masoretes would never have postulated.

An additional argument in favor of the reliability of these reports is the fact that they are attributed to Ezra and the early Sopherim, that is to say to the early Second Commonwealth period, before the destruction of the Temple, and obviously long before the Tannaim. From the Rabbinic sources which attribute these changes in the text of Scripture to these Sopherim, it is clear that Ezra, or his successors, were concerned not only with establishing the Oral Law for their contemporaries, but with fixing the text of the written Torah as well. An important historical kernel is to be found in the definition in the Talmud, "The earliest scholars were called Sopherim because they counted [שהיו סופרים] all the letters in the Torah" (B. Kiddushin 30a).

This function, that of establishing the Biblical text, is an even more central aspect of Sopheric activity, if we accept the approach proposed by Professor Ephraim E. Urbach, who makes a sharp distinction between the Sopherim and the Ḥakhamim. According to his view, the Sopherim were teachers of the Bible and guardians of its text, and were financially supported through these labors since they belonged to the lower economic classes of the people. On the other hand, he suggests, the Ḥakhamim were the interpreters of the Oral Law, who came from the upper strata of society and engaged in their work without compensation.[20]

Whether we identify the Sopherim with the Ḥakhamim who came after them, as is the general view, or we distinguish between them, as does Urbach, it is clear that very soon these anonymous teachers of the people recognized the vital need for a fixed text of Scripture that could serve as a protection against the flood of changes and errors which were multiplying in the manuscripts to be found among the masses. To be sure, they themselves found certain doubtful passages in the Scriptures and, in order to call attention to them, they fell back upon the technique of placing dots on doubtful letters and words, a practice familiar to Hellenistic scribes in Alexandria. Our old sources attribute these dots to Ezra himself.[21] This procedure had the advantage that it avoided erasing, and thus losing, the doubtful readings which are preserved, so to speak, on a tentative basis. Additional proof of the antiquity of the use of dots is their frequent occurrence in the Qumran Scrolls to mark words which the scribe wished to omit.

On the other hand, Rabbinic sources testify to a number of places in Scripture in which *tiqqunei Sopherim,* "corrections of the Scribes," were introduced into the text מפני הכבוד, "to preserve the honor of God." The various lists of *tiqqunei Sopherim* that have reached us differ in their number—7, 11, 13, 15 or 18.[22] It is reasonable to assume that these rubrics do not exhaust all instances of *tiqqunei Sopherim* and that there were other examples that were forgotten and were incorporated into the Biblical text, without leaving a trace in the sources.[23]

To be sure, some scholars have completely denied the real existence of *tiqqunei Sopherim,* arguing that the scribes never changed the text before them and that the alleged readings in our sources were intended for homiletic purposes only.[24] In his illuminating discussion of the subject, Professor Saul Lieberman demonstrates that the Rabbinic sources themselves were already divided on this question. Some, the *Mekhilta* and the *Sifre*, attributed the present reading in our texts to the original authors and, therefore, described the *tiqqunei Sopherim* by the phrase כינה הכתוב namely: "the Bible itself changed the customary idiom [in favor of the euphemism]." On the other hand, some of the Rabbinic sources, *Tanḥuma, Genesis Rabba, Shemot Rabba,* attribute the changes directly to the scribes, whence the name, "corrections of the Scribes."[25]

Whoever approaches the question without prejudice must conclude that only the latter view is acceptable. It is inconceivable that in the later period, when the spiritual leaders of the people fought as vigorously as possible against the danger of changes in the text, however slight, that the Rabbis would invent a tradition that there had ever been a time when scribes had taken it upon themselves to change the text of the Scriptures. On the other hand, this desire to stand guard over the received text explains the rise of the tendencious view that the changes reported by tradition had no real existence, but that the Biblical writers themselves had chosen to modify their style "because of God's glory."[26] There is, therefore, no basis for doubting the truth of the reports concerning *tiqqunei Sopherim* in the early period.

There is also a tradition concerning עיטורי סופרים "the separation of words by the Scribes."[27] According to this report, the scribes removed the *vav* conjunctive in five passages in the Bible. The reading with the *vav* in all these instances became widespread in manuscripts because it gives a somewhat smoother reading, as Rabbi Nathan points out in *He'Arukh.*[28] For this reason, the scribes guarding the text protected the "original" and more difficult reading (*difficilior lectio*) by calling attention to the omission of the *vav*. This tradition concerning the existence of a reading in "vulgar" manuscripts with the *vav* conjunctive is supported by the fact that it coincides with the reading of the Samaritan Pentateuch.[29] Another ancient tradition testifies to still another means employed to indicate some doubt regarding the text—the inverted *nun*—which calls attention to the uncertainty in regard to the correct position or authenticity of certain passages (Num. 10:35–36; Ps. 107:27–32; 40).[30] Through devices such as these, the scribes succeeded in avoiding tampering with the Biblical text and at the same time called attention to doubtful readings (through the dotted words) or changed texts (*tiqqunei Sopherim; itturei Sopherim*).

Nevertheless, these procedures did not fully solve the problem of textual variations that were to be found in different manuscripts, many of which seemed worthy of attention and which were often of value equal to the original. Here, the guardians of the text had recourse to a device which is familiar in virtually all literatures, and which has left many marks in the Biblical text, even though it is not specifically mentioned in our extant sources. This was the method of conflation, i.e., the combination of two variant readings into a single text.[31] Thus, for example, the Masoretic text of Exodus 6:4 reads as follows:

אֶת אֶרֶץ כְּנָעַן אֵת אֶרֶץ מְגֻרֵיהֶם אֲשֶׁר גָּרוּ בָהּ

This verse represents a conflation of two variants:

א. את ארץ כנען את ארץ מגוריהם

ב. את ארץ כנען אשר גרו בה

Conflation took place even when it created an ungrammatical form, as for example Joshua 2:7:

וְהַשַּׁעַר סָגָרוּ אַחֲרֵי כַּאֲשֶׁר יָצְאוּ הָרֹדְפִים

This verse preserves two distinct readings which occurred in different manuscripts:

א. וְהַשַּׁעַר סָגָרוּ אַחֲרֵי אֲשֶׁר יָצְאוּ הָרֹדְפִים

ב. וְהַשַּׁעַר סָגָרוּ כַּאֲשֶׁר יָצְאוּ הָרֹדְפִים

Similarly, in I Kings 10:21 the ungrammatical reading in the Masoretic text: אֵין כֶּסֶף לֹא נֶחְשָׁב בִּימֵי שְׁלֹמֹה לִמְאוּמָה represents a conflation of:

אין כסף נחשב בימי שלמה למאומה

כסף לא נחשב בימי שלמה למאומה

We called attention to this phenomenon over thirty years ago, citing a substantial number of Biblical passages containing

41

instances of conflation. We now amplify this list with 28 additional examples.[32] This technique had one important advantage; it made possible the preservation of variant readings on the theory that "both these and the others are the words of the Living God.". On the other hand, it also suffered from major defects: it created long and redundant readings radically different from the sinewy style of the Biblical writers. What is even worse, frequently, as in the instances adduced above, conflation produces a text that violates the canons of grammar and usage (e.g., ‏(אין... לא, אחרי... כאשר‎) Finally, among the various manuscripts there undoubtedly were variants which it was impossible to combine into a consistent text, however faulty in character. It is because of these drawbacks that this technique was not more widely adopted and is not explicitly mentioned in our sources. Nonetheless, its existence cannot be doubted and it is by no means limited to the instances already cited.

Conflation differs from dittography in one fundamental respect. In the former there is *no exact repetition* of the word, as is the case in dittography (as, for instance, Gen. 25:30 ‏האדם‎ ‏האדם הזה‎ which may arise from a scribal or an oral error. In conflation the subject matter is repeated *in similar words* that add no new meaning to the passage, but are not identical. It is no accident that a relatively large number of instances of conflation are met with in the Book of Samuel. This is due to the fact that many versions of this book circulated among the people, as is clear from the large number of significant variants to be found in the Septuagint which have now been confirmed by manuscript fragments from Qumran Cave 4.[33] Finally, the ancient Bible scribes became convinced that all the various procedures and techniques indicated above were unable to stem the tide of change and error which continued to increase with each copy.

An illuminating parallel to the process by which a fixed text was established may be found in the history of the text of the Koran.[34] *Ab ovo,* the Koran differs from the Hebrew Bible, being essentially a collection of utterances by a single individual, and not a collection of different books representing a wide spectrum of literary styles and historical backgrounds. A short time after Muhammad's death the traditions cited in his name increased tremendously and various religious centers adopted different manuscripts of the Koran which contradicted one another. According to Islamic tradition, the first effort to create a uniform text of the Koran was made as early as the year 12 of the Hegira by the Caliph Abu Bekr, but greater credibility attaches to the detailed reports concerning the activity of the Caliph Othman (c. 576–656 C.E.), whose reign was from 644–656 C.E. Because of his justified doubts concerning the multiplicity of extant readings and his desire to minimize the controversies that stemmed from them, Othman charged Zaid ibn Tabit and a group of scholars with him, to gather the traditions attributed to Muhammad among the people and to accept only the material confirmed by two witnesses (cf. קיימו שנים). These scholars were also empowered to establish the uniform text in the Qoreish dialect, to prepare exact copies of their archetype, and to send them to all religious centers. Finally, they were ordered to destroy all texts of remaining traditions still to be found among the people. Since this official text was in accordance with the version of Medina, the city of Muhammad and his earlier followers, it is a reasonable assumption that it was the best text available, though there was no lack of other manuscripts, some of them surely containing significant readings. These steps did not exhaust the process of the creating of an official text. The officially adopted Othman manuscript lacked the dots which distinguish various consonants in Arabic and, it goes without saying, any system of vocalization and punctuation. There therefore arose various schools of scribes and interpreters. This period of "freedom of choice" continued until the year 322 A.H. when seven systems of readings were officially recognized.

There still was no uniform text for all Muslims. The most important step, the time and creator of which are veiled in obscurity, was the choice of one manuscript as the fundamental authority. Basing himself upon this codex, al-Dani (died 444 A.H.)

43

compiled his notations for scribes in which he lists every unusual orthography in the version, and warns the copyists to preserve these rare forms with great care. This basic manuscript has remained the foundation for the version of the Koran used throughout the Islamic world. By its reproduction through lithography in modern times identical copies are to be found in all mosques.

In dealing with this problem of the multiplicity of readings, the Arab scribes had been preceded by their Hebrew counterparts in the period of the Second Temple. The guardians of the Biblical text found one ancient, meticulously written manuscript and made it the foundation for their work. They established it as the archetype from which all official copies were to be made and by which all manuscripts in private hands could henceforth be corrected. Because the selection of this standard codex had taken place in the dim past, the *process* is not recorded in our sources, but the *product* of the process is, we believe, referred to explicitly in Rabbinic literature. Similarly, we have no information regarding the time, the place, and the circumstances surrounding the introduction of such phenomena as "the dotted words," the *tiqqunei Sopherim,* the *'itturei Sopherim,* and the inverted *nun,* though their presence in the Masoretic text is evident.[35] The Mishnah, the Tosefta, and the Palestinian Talmud, as well as other Rabbinic sources, speak of ספר העזרה, "the Scroll of the Temple precincts," or ספר עזרא "the Scroll of Ezra" and inform us that it was utilized as a standard by which other codices were corrected.[36] If the latter variant be the original reading, it would suggest that the tradition regarded this codex as very ancient and attributed it to Ezra, who is credited with several other early features of Biblical text, as well as the introduction of the square Aramaic script in place of the older Hebrew or Phoenician alphabet.[37] If, on the other hand, the former reading, *Sepher ha 'Azarah* be accepted, as seems to be more likely, we have an explicit reference to a highly esteemed and presumably ancient scroll being kept in the Temple to serve as a standard for correcting other manuscripts.[38] Thus, the Mishnah informs us: "All Biblical scrolls defile the hands, except the scroll of the 'Azarah.''[39] Another statement declares: "And they corrected it (the Torah scroll of the king) in accordance with the scroll in the 'Azarah in accordance with the instruction of the Court of Seventy-One.''[40] The reference to the "scroll of the king" makes it clear that, like many other Rabbinic traditions regarding the Court of Seventy-One, it is the ideal Sanhedrin rather than the historical reality that is being described.[41] Nevertheless, the matter-of-fact, almost incidental reference to the *Sepher ha 'Azarah* is impressive evidence for the existence and function of this codex in the Temple.

This conclusion is strengthened by another passage in the Babylonian Talmud which states, "The revisers of Bible manuscripts in Jerusalem received their recompense from the income of the Temple treasury.''[42] Even more germane to our subject is the parallel text in the Palestinian Talmud, which may well be more original than the Babylonian.[43] It reads as follows:

מגיהי ספר העזרה היו נוטלין שכרן מתרומת הלשכה.

The opening words may possibly be rendered, "The revisers *of* the 'Azarah Scroll," but the reference to an ongoing process of collation make this very unlikely. The passage almost surely means, "The revisers [of Bible manuscripts] *by means of* the 'Azarah Scroll used to receive their recompense from the Temple treasury." In any event, what is significant in the two passages cited is the casual mention of manuscript revisers working in Jerusalem during the Temple period. There are also other references to the Temple scroll in Rabbinic sources that underscore its unique character.[44]

It, therefore, seems reasonable to identify the ספר העזרה, (or ספר עזרא) with the ancient, highly regarded manuscript which became the archetype for all accurate codices. The general accuracy of this manuscript and the authority of these early Masoretes endowed it with a high level of sanctity. Hence, each scribe sought to reproduce all its attributes, including minor features such as majuscule and minuscule letters, suspended and "cut off" letters (קטועה, תלויה, זעירא, רבתי), many of which arose simply through scribal accident. For the goal of each copyist was to create a facsimile of the original scroll. Slowly, the text and orthography

45

of this basic manuscript achieved general acceptance, but the process, before the invention of printing, required centuries for its completion. For every copyist was liable to produce new errors that would then be reproduced and even augmented. On the relation of the Masoretic text to the "vulgar" manuscripts in popular use, more will be said below.

The antiquity of the archetypal manuscript is attested by the fact that nearly always its text, the *Kethibh*, contains older, even archaic, grammatical forms, while the *Qere*, which preserves readings from other manuscripts collated with it, registers later forms.[45] Yet, even here, the *Qere* is not a correction of the *Kethibh*, for virtually every category of older forms found in the *Kethibh* may be parallelled by additional examples in the Masoretic text with no *Qere* on the margin.[46] Moreover, there is no consistency in the orthography of the archetypal manuscript itself, because by the time it had been chosen centuries had elapsed since the composition of the Biblical books and substantial changes in the spelling had already been introduced into it. The "Phoenician" orthography, completely *defectiva,* no longer obtained since the earliest scribes had already begun to introduce vowel letters as *matres lectionis* in substantial measure in order to help the problems of reading. On the other hand, "Mishnaic" orthography, completely *plene,* had not yet penetrated to the archetypal manuscript; therein lay its great superiority over other manuscripts among the people which were increasingly introducing *plene* spelling. Nevertheless, even in the archetype, the various orthographic systems are all to be met with. Thus we find בְּתֻלָת (Lam. 5:11) and also בְּתוּלוֹת, (Isa. 23:41), but the dominant orthographic system is intermediate: בתלות (Zech. 9:17) or בְּתוּלָת (Ezek. 44:22). The fact that the orthography of this manuscript was not made uniform serves as additional and decisive evidence that the goal of the Masoretes was not the "correction" or the "improvement" of the text, but its preservation in the form it had reached them with no change whatsoever.

In the course of their labors, the guardians of the text learned to recognize *that even the finest manuscript may contain inferior readings at certain points and that, on the other hand, manuscripts of lesser merit may well contain superior readings.*[47] Hence they concluded that in order to establish a standard text, it was essential not merely to select an accurate archetype, but also to reckon with variants in other ancient and highly esteemed codices. This led these early Masoretes to collate various manuscripts in order to choose the superior reading. In the beginning their system was very simple—they selected the reading of the majority over that of the minority. This method of dealing with the problem of variance is attested by the familiar report in the Talmud (*J. Megillah* 4,2; *Sopherim* 6,4), שלשה ספרים נמצאו בעזרה וגו', "Three manuscripts were found in the Temple precincts: the manuscript *mā'ōn,* the manuscript *za'tūtē,* and the manuscript *hū'.* In one they found . . .; in two, they found . . .; in each instance they preserved the reading of the two manuscripts and set aside the other." Obviously, there were many more than simply these three variations. They are cited here as an illustration of the procedure adopted at this early period, in which the majority reading was preserved and the minority reading was eliminated.[48]

The drawbacks of this technique became clear in time to the guardians of the text. They recognized that it was possible for an inferior reading to be preserved in a larger number of manuscripts or in the "best" codex, while the superior text might appear only in a minority or in less prestigious codices. It was therefore obvious that these questions could not be decided by majority rule. They therefore adopted another and more sophisticated method. By the side of the archetypal manuscript they selected a small number of others of high repute. From them they copied the variants they regarded as worthy of attention and noted them on the margins of the archetypal manuscript. The number of such variants was not small, reaching over a thousand. These variations were subsumed under the category of *Kethibh-Qere.* Ultimately, they include all marginal readings beside those of the earlier categories, the guides to the reader against blasphemy, obscenity, or error.

The essential character of these readings as textual variations cannot be doubted. We have already demonstrated that these readings cannot be regarded as corrections or improvements introduced by the Masoretes. On the contrary, it is possible to prove that originally our *Qere* readings constituted the "normal" text in manuscripts to be found in the hands of the masses.[49] That our *Qere* readings were originally imbedded in the text is clear from a passage like Joshua 3:16: (ק') מאדם (כ') באדם מאד הרחק where the Septuagint reads: ‌σφόδρα σφοδῶς ‌. This rendering would have been impossible unless the three words ran consecutively in the Hebrew manuscript before the translator: הרחק מאד מאד.[50]

The Qumran Scrolls supply additional evidence. In the Isaiah manuscript from Qumran 4 (4QIsa), seven passages have readings in the text identical with our Masoretic *Qere* (13:16; 49:5; 54:16; 55:13; 56:10; 65:4; 66:17).[51]

At what period were conditions ripe for this gigantic task of collating the archetype with other significant manuscripts? Moreover, when could the product of these labors be expected to attain virtually universal acceptance? It must have been an early period, when the life of the people was still normal and well organized, and there existed a recognized religious and literary center. Moreover, it would need to be an age of relatively few historical records, since there is no explicit reference in our extant sources to this massive project of textual collation. A more specific delimitation of the period will be presented below. At this point it suffices to note that this collation of textual variants that were marked on the margin of the archetypal manuscript (and copies made of it) took place before the destruction of the Second Temple (70 C.E.).[52] With the passing of time these textual readings were fused and identified with the original *Qere* notations which were also to be found on the margin (e.g., Lev. 19:22 ק' ידיו כ' ידו ; II Ki. 4:5 מוצקת ק' —כ' מיצקת).

In the period following the collation of manuscripts there were no special lists of these "new" *Kethibh-Qere* variants; at each verse the notation was written on the margin. Only two categories of *Kethibh-Qere* variants aroused special attention in the Talmud because of their anomalous character: כתיבין ולא קריין , i.e., passages where the archetype contains a word which is lacking in the other collated manuscripts and: קריין ולא כתיבין , i.e., places where a word is lacking in the archetype, but is found in the other manuscripts. Hence, only these two categories of *Kethibh-Qere* variations are explicitly mentioned in the Talmud together with other ancient Masoretic phenomena, and are described as "a tradition going back to Moses on Sinai":[53]

א״ר יצחק מקרא סופרים ועיטור סופרים וקרין ולא כתיבין וכתיבין ולא
קרין הלכה למשה מסיני.

In sum, the last stage in the development of the *Kethibh-Qere,* the registering of textual variants of value from important manuscripts, constitutes an extremely important chapter in the evolution of the Masoretic text. This category of *Kethibh-Qere,* which totals over a thousand instances, is far more numerous than the original categories which preceded it.[54]

IV.

To be sure, the archetype was not immediately or universally recognized as the ultimate authority. Undoubtedly, this text was first accepted in the official circles of normative Judaism, the scholars who were the successors to the Sopherim and the Pharisees. It was natural that members of the groups that followed Pharisaic tradition tried to procure for their own use copies of the Torah, the Prophets, and the Hagiographa that would agree with the text of the archetype or that would be exact copies of it. Failing that, they would try to have manuscripts already in their hands corrected by comparing them with the official codex in Jerusalem. Thus, Rabbi Akiba emphasized the importance of a corrected Torah scroll (*B. Pesaḥim,* 112a). We have already referred to the Talmudic passages regarding the compensation received by manuscript revisers in Jerusalem. Yet at times even scholars had to be content with "popular" manuscripts that differed from the official standard. Such was "the scroll of Rabbi Meir," some divergences of which are recorded in the Talmud.[55] Moreover, the expense and scarcity

49

of Bible texts often impelled scholars to quote Scriptures from memory, with the result that they sometimes cited passages inexactly. There would come into play the tendency to leveling, i.e., recalling the verse in the more usual and familiar form.[56] At times, a text might even have been cited that does not occur in the Bible at all! [57]

If the circles identified with normative Judaism did not always possess manuscripts that conformed to the archetype, this was far truer of those more distant from Pharisaic influence. These groups continued to use "unrevised" codices that differed from the archetype not only in orthography but also in text. These divergencies continued to multiply, consciously or unconsciously, as each copyist transcribed the text.

The Samaritans, who had become antagonists of official Judaism after the schism in the fifth or fourth century B.C.E., had a recension of the Pentateuch which was "non-Masoretic" in many respects—a multiplicity of *matres lectionis,* late forms of suffixes (like the masculine third person singular), the absence of the petrified case endings and others.[58] To be sure, the effort has been made to explain these phenomena by the assumption that at a later period the Samaritans tried to have their version agree with that of the Jews.[59] However, such a mutual influence is inconceivable in view of the deep hostility prevailing between the two communities; nor is there any echo of such an important event in the long polemic between them that continued into the Middle Ages. The divergent features of the Samaritan recension are entirely explicable if we recognize that the "popular" versions, of which the Samaritan is one, were widely circulated at every stage and that the official version in Jerusalem was created during the Second Temple period to serve as a guard and protector against such texts.

In the Diaspora, too, especially in centers like Alexandria, where linguistic assimilation held sway and where even leading scholars, like Philo, had little knowledge of Hebrew, popular, inexact manuscripts sufficed for the limited need. The Greek translations, and above all the Septuagint, are witnesses to these versions circulating in the Diaspora communities.[60] In Babylonia, where a knowledge of Hebrew was more frequently met, the same situation probably prevailed to a lesser degree.

The divergencies of Diaspora Jewry were by and large unconscious, since its members regarded themselves as loyal adherents of normative Judaism in Palestine. On the other hand, opposition sects like the Qumranites were more likely to diverge consciously from the standard text that represented the labors of the Jerusalem authorities. It is no wonder, therefore, that the Bible manuscripts and fragments of the Qumran sect contain so large a number of variations from the Masoretic text. It is thus clear that the variants in medieval Bible manuscripts and in the fragments of the Cairo Genizah are incapable of disproving the existence of an archetypal codex, without which we cannot explain the creation of a uniform, universally accepted text.[61]

The evidence from Rabbinic literature supporting the view that the selection of the archetype preceded the destruction of the Temple (70 C.E.) has already been cited.[62] This view is confirmed by Josephus who boasts to his Greek readers that *"during all the past generations* no man dared to add to them (i.e., the Scriptures) or take from them or *make any change whatever in them."*[63] This statement makes sense only if in Josephus' time (first century C.E.) the Biblical text had been fixed and universally recognized for at least several generations.

A striking parallel to the process we have outlined may be found in an account transmitted in a manuscript containing an Arabic translation of the Pentateuch that is to be found in the library at Leiden, Holland. It tells that at the time of the destruction of the Temple the priests saved the Torah scroll that was in the sanctuary and brought it to the fortress at Bether. After the fall of Bether, the Patriarchs of the house of David transferred the scroll to Bagdad, where copies were made and sent to the entire Diaspora.[64] The narrative is obviously legendary, but it would seem to preserve some authentic recollection of the time and place of origin of the text of Scripture that was accepted as holy.

This report aside, it is a fair inference that at the destruction of the Temple, the effort would be made to save the Temple archetype, or at least a copy, so as to make possible the task of national and religious reconstruction to which Rabbi Joḥanan ben Zakkai and his successors devoted themselves at Yavneh. This standard traditional text was the *basis* of Rabbi Akiba's Halakhic activity, not its *consequence*. R. Akiba perfected the method of hermeneutics based upon "amplification and limitation" (רבוי ומעוט) and the interpretation of all particles in the Torah (אתין, אכין גמין ורקין).[65] However, he was not the creator of this technique, for there is explicit evidence that Naḥum of Gimzo used it a generation earlier.[66] Rabbi Akiba's great opponent, Rabbi Ishmael, used the method of "amplification and limitation" very little, and emphasized that "the Torah speaks in the language of men."[67] Yet even he derived many laws from the *plene* or *defectiva* spelling of words in the Torah text.[68] At no time did a scholar or a student arise in the academy and point out that in his own Bible manuscript the alleged *plene* reading was spelled *defectiva,* or vice versa. It is therefore certain that by the time of Rabbi Akiba and the preceding generation a uniform text was universally accepted. Its reading and orthography were not subject to controversy, but, on the contrary, served as a common basis for the various Halakhic schools.

The selection of the archetype may be moved even earlier. We possess a great deal of information regarding Rabban Joḥanan ben Zakkai and Rabban Gamaliel of Yavneh, who flourished two generations before Rabbi Akiba. There are many reports regarding the important innovations in religious life introduced at the Council of Yavneh in 90 C.E., when Rabbi Eleazer ben Azariah replaced Rabban Gamaliel temporarily as Nasi (*bō bayōm,* "on that day"). It is inconceivable that an act as significant and far-reaching as the establishment of the official text of Scripture could have been carried out in their time without leaving an echo in our extensive sources for this period.

Several other considerations rule out the theory that the *textus receptus* was first adopted in the days of Rabbi Akiba (second century C.E.). The Church Father Origen, who lived in Caesarea during the third century, was probably the greatest Biblical scholar in the early Church. He dedicated his life to harmonizing the Septuagint, which was sacred to Christians, with the Hebrew text of his time. To achieve this purpose he compiled his gigantic work, the *Hexapla,* a work requiring phenomenal energy and patience, as well as extraordinary learning. During these early Christian centuries, when the Church Fathers carried on a vigorous polemic against Judaism, they frequently accused the Jews of having falsified the Bible and perverted the text in order to support their nefarious doctrines. Though Origen lived in close proximity to the scholars of the Mishnah, he does not refer to the fixing of the Hebrew text which is to have taken place only a few years before his time. This is all the more significant in view of the far-flung controversy between Christians and Jews and the vast number of variants between the Hebrew text and the various Greek translations. In the fourth century, Jerome followed in Origen's footsteps when he prepared the Vulgate version in harmony with the "Hebrew truth" (*Hebraica veritas*), as he called the Hebrew original. Only one conclusion may fairly be drawn from these facts—in their time the Hebrew text was already firmly established from generations past. Hence it did not occur even to the most vigorous opponents of Rabbinic Judaism to point to the recent adoption of the accepted text as proof of its illegitimacy.

This argument from silence is confirmed by positive proof. The Mishnah testifies to the existence of a *Kethibh-Qere* variant in the period of Yavneh:

בו ביום דרש ר' יהושע בן הורקנוס לא עבד איוב את הקב"ה
אלא מאהבה שנאמר הן יקטלני לו איחל ועדיין הדבר שקול לו אני
מצפה או איני מצפה ת"ל עד אגוע לא אסיר תומתי ממני מלמד
שמאהבה עשה.

"On that day Joshua ben Hyrcanus expounded, 'Job served the Holy One blessed be He out of love, as it is said, 'Indeed though

53

He slay me yet will I trust in Him' (Job 14:15). But the matter is still undecided: 'I wait for Him' (לו איחל) or 'I do not wait' (לא איחל).' Another verse teaches that Job served from love (Job 27:5): 'Until I die, I will not surrender my integrity'—proving that he served from love" (Mishnah, Sotah 5:5). Here the Tanna, who was a pupil of Rabban Johanan ben Zakkai and a member of the academy of Yavneh in the significant year 90 C.E. (בו ביום "On that day"), is in doubt with regard to the meaning of a Biblical passage because he had two readings before him: לא and לו—the exact *Kethibh-Qere* in our Masorah. If Joshua ben Hyrcanus' manuscript had only one of these readings, the question regarding Job's motivation would have been answered very simply, either positively or negatively.

Another important conclusion may be derived from this passage. The Mishnah does not refer to these readings in Job by the term *Kethibh-Qere.* As we have noted, this term was originally applied to passages in which a different word was read for the word written in the text. The variant readings which the guardians of the text later noted in the margin were not originally part of the *Kethibh-Qere* apparatus. The latter group was absorbed into the former only after a considerable elapse of time when the various types of marginal notes, (i.e., the original *Kethibh-Qere* readings, and the variants of manuscripts) were subsumed under the identical formula. That the Tanna does not call the variant readings before him in Job 13:15 by the term *Kethibh-Qere* demonstrates that this process was not yet complete in Mishnaic times. It is only in the Amoraic period, beginning with the third century C.E., that we find the term used for variant readings.[69] Thus on Ecclesiastes 9:4:

כִּי מִי אֲשֶׁר יְבָחֵר כ' יְחֻבַּר ק' אֶל כָּל הַחַיִּים

Rabbi Johanan says:

יבחר כתיב — אל כל החיים יש בטחון שכל זמן שאדם חי יש לו תקוה לחזור בתשובה מת אבדה תקותו.

"It is written יבחר—all the living have hope, for so long as a man lives there is hope that he may repent; when he dies his hope is

54

lost" (*J. Bekhorot* 9,1). There are other instances of Amoraim basing their ideas upon a *Kethibh* differing from the *Qere* or from both the *Kethibh* and the *Qere*.[70]

From this mass of evidence we may conclude that the fixing of the official text and the perfecting of this method for significant variants is to be dated in the period before the destruction of the Temple and not during the generation of Rabbi Akiba, who already found the text available for his use. In his famous statement מסורת סיג לתורה (*M. Abot* 3, 13), Rabbi Akiba uses the word *Massoret* as a generally familiar term. The various efforts that have been made to avoid the simple meaning of his utterance are unconvincing and superfluous. Rabbi Akiba makes the point that the *Massoret,* the official and traditional text of Scripture is a basic means for the observance of the Torah, especially in a period when there circulated among the people many manuscripts that were inexact either in their orthography or their readings. The term *Massoret* (an older form for *Masorah,* from the root *masar,* "hand over, transmit," distinct from the form in Ezek. 20:37) was not created by Rabbi Akiba, for the schools of Hillel and Shammai had already discussed the question as to whether יש אם למסורת or יש אם למקרא, that is to say, whether the traditional text without vowels is authoritative or the traditional reading (according to the vowels) is the guide.[71] It should be noted, too, that at times the Tannaim used as the basis of their derivation not merely the text of the Biblical verse, but the verse together with its Masoretic comment—proof that the work of the ancient Masoretes was already well advanced and highly esteemed in their time.[72]

An important source available for solving the problem has come to light in the discovery of the Dead Sea Scrolls. When the text of Isaiah I and other Biblical fragments were published, the scholarly world was astonished by their very special *plene* orthography, which is far more extreme in its use of *matres lectionis* than the most inexact non-Masoretic codices of the Middle Ages. To be sure, the spelling in the Scrolls is not consistent, and by the side of the *plene* spelling בכול, לוא, כיא, we find as well מזנים (=מאזנים),

(תלאים=) תלים, (נמצאתי=) נמצתי. We also encounter a mixture of *plene* and *defectiva* orthography, at times in the same passage, exactly as in the Masoretic text of the Bible as, for example[73]: ולוא נסתרו ולא נעדרו מלפניהם.

Though the scroll kept in the Temple in Jerusalem was all but universally accepted by the Pharisees and their followers, it is clear that its influence upon the Biblical text of this fanatically hostile sect, the Essenes, was naturally weak. In the Essenic circles each scribe and copyist added *matres lectionis* at will and in accordance with his own understanding of the text.

This natural tendency to fill out defective orthography was obviously not limited to the members of the sect. It was liable to spread more and more with the passing of time until an extreme *plene* (מלא דמלא) text would emerge. Had the process of copying and recopying manuscripts been permitted to continue without interference for several centuries, the process would have been irreversible. It would have been impossible to restore the text to its earlier form, for no Masorete would have dared to decide which *matres lectionis* were to be removed and which were to be preserved. The fact that even the later Masoretic manuscripts are in overwhelming measure written *defectiva,* in contradistinction to the far earlier Qumran Scrolls, testifies to the labors of the proto-Masoretes even before the Dead Sea Scrolls were being copied. They interrupted the "natural" process of adding vowel letters indulged in by copyists in every age. *In sum, the Qumran Scrolls which contain variations from the Masoretic text are unimpeachable testimony to the existence of this normative text.*

The recent discoveries at the Dead Sea make another important contribution to the history of the Masorah. In Wadi Muraba'at many Biblical fragments were found, dating from the revolt of Bar Kokhba (132–135 c.e.). In this newer material the Scriptural text is by and large identical with the Masoretic text, and thus diverges radically from the scrolls of the Qumran sect left behind in the caves before the destruction of the Temple.

Some scholars have sought to argue that this difference between the Qumran Scrolls and the fragments of Wadi Muraba'at supports the view that the official text was first established in the days of Rabbi Akiba, the contemporary of Bar Kokhba. They suggest that the army of the great rebel leader used the Masoretic version which had been fashioned during their own time and which had not existed in the period of the Dead Sea sectarians who preceded them by two centuries and more.[74] When subjected to analysis, however, this conclusion proves untenable. The soldiers of Bar Kokhba differed from the members of the Qumran sect not merely chronologically, but ideologically as well. Many of them were students of the academies, and they were loyal to Rabbinic teaching, whereas the Qumran sect was violently opposed to the official Pharisaic leadership. The greatness of this tragic and heroic leader did not lie in his Biblical or Rabbinic learning. This has become crystal clear from the style and orthography of his dispatches that have come to light. But even without this concrete evidence it is unlikely to the point of impossibility that in the difficult days of the Third War against Rome, Bar Kokhba's army in the field could have been equipped with the "newest edition" of Scripture which had just been created. The evidence points in the opposite direction. Unless the traditional text had long been established as sacred, it could scarcely have reached this distant and isolated refuge in the wilderness in a period of crisis. From the essentially Masoretic character of the Biblical texts in the Muraba'at caves, we may conclude that this text had been accepted as official substantially before this period and, therefore, it had been brought by the soldiers to this fortress. As for the fact that the members of the Qumran sect possessed manuscripts that varied from the Masorah, this does not prove that they preceded' the period of the early anonymous proto-Masoretes who carried on their work during the days of the Temple. The methodological principle to be invoked here is not "these after those," but "these against those." The Dead Sea sectarians, who were hostile to normative Judaism centered in Jerusalem, would not easily accept the version of Scripture originating among the *marshi'ei brit* "violators of the Covenant," because of whom they had been compelled to flee to the desolate wilderness. The fact that among the remains of the Qumranite library are substantial Biblical fragments and, above all, the text of Isaiah II, that are in basic agreement with the Masoretic version, is highly illuminating. It indicates how powerful was the impact of this accepted text even upon circles opposed to Pharisaic Judaism.

V.

We may now summarize the results of our investigation and set forth the principal steps in the development of the early or proto-Masorah. Rabbinic literature attributes to Ezra and the early scribes many features found in our Biblical text. The method of conflation, though it is not explicitly mentioned in our sources, also appears to be ancient. The antiquity of such phenomena as the dotted words,[75] the *tiqqunei Sopherim*,[76] the *'itturei Sopherim*,[77] and conflation[78] is attested by the Samaritan version of the Pentateuch, on the one hand, and the Septuagint on the other. Many of the *Qere* readings in our Masorah were independent readings in the manuscripts before the ancient translators. It is clear, however, that the *Kethibh-Qere* apparatus on the margins of manuscripts was not yet in existence at the time of the Septuagint. After the victory of the Maccabees and the rise of a strong religio-national spirit, the demand arose for a uniform and accurate text of the Scriptures, especially since so many manuscripts had been destroyed in the Antiochian persecutions a few years earlier (168–165 B.C.E.).[79] It was either during these days of spiritual renascence under the Maccabees or the period of chronic crisis during Roman rule, when the preservation of Judaism was threatened, that the leaders recognized that "it was time to act for the Lord." Anonymous scholars now arose and chose for this purpose a manuscript known to be both ancient and accurate, which was deposited in the Temple as a standard. This important act took place between the accession of Simon the Maccabean (142 B.C.E.) and the destruction of the Temple (70 C.E.), which is the *terminus non post quem.*

The discussions between the Hillelites and the Shammaites concerning אם למקרא and למסורת אם and the use by Hillel the Elder of "the seven methods of hermeneutics" make it more likely that the selection of the archetype took place in the earlier rather than in the later portion of this period. While dogmatism on this subject is not warranted, it would seem reasonable to attribute this project to the reign of Salome Alexandra (76–67 B.C.E.) who sympathized with the Pharisees and supported them, even though the Sadducees were not totally alienated from the seats of power.

This basic manuscript, like most of the scrolls of its time, already contained in it the fruit of the labors of the early scribes (*'itturim, tiqqunim,* dotted words, and conflation). The scholars were especially concerned with the public reading of Holy Writ in the synagogue. To avoid the possibility of blasphemy involved in pronouncing the Divine Name as written and obscenity, they ordained a *Qere* "to be read" to replace the word written (*Kethibh*) in the text. In addition, the *defectiva* orthography raised the two dangers of incorrect reading on the one hand, and the insertion of additional vowel letters on the other. The guardians of the official text stepped into the breach by marking the correct readings through the medium of a *plene* orthography on the margin, without touching the text proper.

These scholars learned early that one could not depend on any single manuscripts for the preservation of all the best readings. They therefore assembled a limited number of other ancient, highly regarded codices and collated the variations among them. At first, they preserved the text of the majority and set aside the minority reading. As their sophistication grew, however, they noted those variations that seemed to them to have significant value and preserved them on the margins of the standard manuscript. The *Kethibh* thus preserved the reading of the archetype, while the *Qere* is a collection of variants from other manuscripts. The collation of the variants was carried through after the choice of the archetype but before the destruction of the Temple, when its library was still intact. This model codex served as the basis for all new copies that were made and as the standard by which scribes revised existing manuscripts which were entrusted to them.

The creation of the Masoretic text did not eliminate the existence of "vulgar," inexact manuscripts, which continued to circulate among the people, particularly in those circles which were distant either in space or in outlook from normative Judaism. These groups included divergent ideological sects, like the Samaritans and the Qumranites, and Diaspora communities, as in Alexandria. These popular scrolls also continued to be used among broad segments of the people even in Palestine, including those scholars who were unable to afford the expensive, accurately revised manuscripts. These popular scrolls contained many variants, most of which were due to scribal error, yet some of which presented original and preferable readings. But the early Masoretes were concerned only with preserving the text unchanged. For them the distinction between these two types of divergencies did not exist—both represented aberrations from the standard, sacred model and hence were not incorporated into the Masoretic codices.

After the destruction of the Temple and the dissolution of the religio-national center in Jerusalem, the Halakhah became the basic instrument of expression for the Jewish spirit. As the Mishnaic sages carried on their work, they found a superb instrument available for their use—an accepted text of the Bible that they could interpret according to need. It thus became possible for them to utilize the written Torah as preserved by the Masorah to establish a holy way of life for Israel, which served as a fortress of life for the nation and as a pillar of fire to lead it during the long night of exile.

NOTES

1. Rosenmüller expressed his view on this subject in 1834 in *Vorrede zur Stereotypausgabe des AT;* Olshausen in his Commentary on Psalms in 1853; Lagarde strengthened and expanded the hypothesis in 1863. Cf., his *Anmerkungen zur griechischen Uebersetzung der Proverbien,* p. 6 ff.

2. Kennicott examined 615 manuscripts and 52 printed editions and presented his conclusions in 1776–1780. De Rossi collated 731 manuscripts and 300 printed editions. His book appeared in 1784–1788, with additions in 1798.

3. Cf., *B. Shebuot* 26a.

4. The roster of scholars who accepted Lagarde's thesis includes Noeldeke, Wellhausen, Robertson-Smith, S. R. Driver, Kuenen, Margolis. See the list in B. J. Roberts, *The OT Text and Versions* (Cardiff, Wales: 1951), cited henceforth as *OTTV.* Roberts himself seems undecided and seems to contradict himself (cf. pp. 25 ff). The opponents of the archetype hypothesis include Steuernagel, Eissfeldt, Hempel, Bentzen, Pfeiffer, Kahle, and his student, my late colleague, Alexander Sperber.

5. Cf., C. D. Ginsburg, *Introduction to a Masoretico-Critical Text of the Hebrew Bible,* pp. 780–794.

6. His important studies and books include *Der masoretische Text des AT nach der Ueberlieferung der babylonischen Juden* (Leipzig: 1907); *Masoreten des Ostens* (Leipzig: 1913); *Masoreten des Westens* (1927–30); *The Cairo Genizah* (London: 1947).

7. Cf., V. Aptowitzer, *Das Schriftwort in der rabbinischen Literatur* (Vienna: 1906; reprint edition, New York).

8. Cf., G. M. Powis-Smith, "Studies in the Masoretes," in *JAOS,* vol. 45, 1927–1928, pp. 208 ff.

9. Thus Pfeiffer (*Introduction to OT,* p. 79) assumes that Rabbi Akiba's text lacked the authority to prevent the introduction of additional variants by later scribes. Roberts (*OTTV,* p. 28) describes the "bitter and constant struggle" among the various versions circulating among the people.

10. This is essentially the view of Kahle accepted by O. Eissfeldt, *Einleitung in das AT,* p. 306; *see* Roberts *OTTV,* p. 28.

11. Cf., E. Wurthwein, *The Text of the OT* (Oxford: 1957), who adopts a more moderate position (p. 19).

12. Cf., Roberts, *OTTV,* p. 70, who attributes most of these changes to variations in the vocalization between Ben Asher and Ben Naphtali. Actually there is only one category of *Kethibh-Qere* variants dependent on the vocalization. Cf., the *Biblical Text in the Making, A Study in the Kethibh-Qere* (Philadelphia: 1937), reprinted in the present volume (and cited henceforth in this paper as *BTM*), lists 30–31. All told, there are only thirty-six examples of where the *holem* in the *Kethibh* is changed to a *qameṣ ḥatuph* because of the introduction of a *maqeph* or a change of the accent, as for example, Joshua 9:7:

אכרות־לך כ' אכרת־לך ק'.

None of the other examples of *Kethibh-Qere,* some 1,350 in number, depend upon vocalization.

13. Cf., *BTM,* chap. 2, pp. 15–28.

14. Cf., *BTM,* especially pp. 20 ff. for the detailed evidence.

15. Cf. our discussion of the *Sebirin* (*BTM,* p. 26 ff.). It is strange that the meaning of this term is apparently not clear to Roberts (*OTTV,* p. 36). He translates סביר עד in Genesis 49:13 in two ways: 1. "עד is to be expected" and 2. "על has here the significance of עד." The correct meaning of the Masoretic term is different: "There are those who believe (סבירין) it better to read עד but you, the scribe, do not make the same mistake; follow the Masoretic text and write על!"

16. The translation *kyrios,* as is well known, occurs everywhere in the Torah, the Prophets, and the Hagiographa instead of the Tetragrammaton in the Hebrew original. It is clear that the reading of the Tetragrammaton as *Adonai* had been widespread in Palestine long before it penetrated to the Diaspora. This explains the replacement of the Tetragrammaton by *Adonai* in the Qumran Isaiah Scroll I (3:17) and its opposite, the use of the Tetragrammaton instead of *Adonai* (6:11; 7:14; 9:7; 21:16). Cf., Eissfeldt in *Theologische Literaturzeitung,* vol. 74, 1949, p. 225; Kahle, *Handschriften,* pp. 63 ff.

17. Such are the usages of "I am the Lord" and "I am the Lord, your God" in Leviticus (chaps. 18–25) and in the Prophets, especially Ezekiel.

18. For possible interpretations of these facts, cf., *BTM,* p. 29, note 1, and our study, "The Social Background of Wisdom Literature" in *HUCA,* vol. 18, 1944, pp. 77–118, now accessible in Robert Gordis, *Poets, Prophets and Sages* (Bloomington, Ind., 1971).

19. The opinion of H. M. Orlinsky (cited by Albright in *JBL*, vol. 67, 1938, p. 244) that these *Quarian* are not guides to the reader but variant readings in manuscripts, is totally refuted by the fact that *in these categories the Masorah notes every instance of* defectiva *or archaic orthography without exception,* whereas with regard to the true variant readings (as will be clarified below) there are many instances over which the Masorah passes in silence, as has been pointed out above. Cf., in detail, *BTM*, p. 21, note 16. Albright himself wrote, "I am inclined to accept the basic conclusion of Gordis with regard to the purpose of the *Qere* and to the various categories that may be distinguished in it" (*ibid.*). His basic criticism was that we assign too early a period for Masoretic activity and the collation of Biblical manuscripts, and that the *Kethibh-Qere* is "in no case" to be dated before the fourth century C.E. The present paper deals in large measure with this assumption.

20. This opinion Urbach expressed in a paper read before the Second World Congress for Judaic Studies in Jerusalem, Ab 5715 (cf., *Tarbitz,* vol. 27, pp. 166 ff.). It may be added that it is possible to find a parallel in the Biblical period for his theory that the Hakhamim of the Second Temple and Mishnaic periods belong to the upper strata of society. In our paper, cited in note 18 above, we have demonstrated that the creators of Wisdom Literature were members of the upper socio-economic levels of society, as is clear from their environment and their political, economic, social, religious, and ethical ideas.

21. Cf., *Abot de Rabbi Nathan,* chap. 24:

כך אמר עזרא אם יבוא אליהו ויאמר לי מפני מה כתבת כך
אומר אני כבר נקודתי עליהם ואם יאמר לי יפה כתבת אעביר
הנקודה מעליהם.

"Thus said Ezra: If Elijah comes and says to me 'Why have you written thus?' then I shall say: 'I have already placed dots upon them.' And if he says to me: 'You have written well,' I will remove the dot from them." Older sources are found in *Sifre,* Numbers 9:10 (ed. M. Friedmann, p. 18); *M. Pesahim* 9, 2; and in Jerome's commentary on Genesis 19:33. On the usage in the Qumran Scrolls, cf. Y. Yadin *Megillat Milhemet B'nei Or biB'nei Hoshekh* (Jerusalem: 1955), p. 253; J. Licht, *Megillat Hahodayot* (Jerusalem: 1957), p. 16.

63

22. Cf.,*Mekhilta Sirata,* Ex. 15:5 (ed. Lauterbach, vol. 2, on pp. 43 ff.); *Tanḥuma Besallaḥ,* Ex. 15:7 (ed. Horeb, p. 230); *Sifre* Num. 10:35 (ed. M. Friedmann, p. 22b); Masorah on Num. 1:2, and on Psalm 106:12.

23. Cf., E. Wurthwein *op. cit.* p. 15: "We shall not go far wrong, if we regard these traditions as pointers to only a small part of a much more extensive process." We have proposed a *tiqqun Sopherim* for the difficult passage in Hosea 4:15, for a full discussion of which cf. our paper, "Studies in the Relationship of Biblical and Rabbinic Hebrew," *Louis Ginzberg Jubilee Volume* (New York: 1945, English section), pp. 195–197. Ehrlich makes a similar suggestion for Job 9:35; cf. his *Randglossen* ad loc.

24. Cf., Azariah de Rossi, *Me'or Einayim,* chap. 19, who cites R. Salomon ibn Adret, R. Joseph Albo, and the Mizrahi, who maintain this view. Cf., S. Lieberman, *Hellenism in Jewish Palestine* (New York: 1950), p. 29, notes 8 and 9; W. E. Barnes, "Ancient Corrections in the Text of the OT," *Journal of Theological Studies* (1900), vol. 1, pp. 387 ff. Apparently Roberts (p. 35) adopts this position, though he does accept the truth of the reports concerning the *'itturei Sopherim* and in another passage admits that the list of *tiqqunei Sopherim* is not complete in our sources (p. 36)!

25. Cf., S. Lieberman, *op. cit.* pp. 28–37. At the end of his discussion he concludes that the scribes changed the text only when God's honor was involved (p. 37), thus identifying himself in the vast majority of instances with the view we find preferable.

26. Characteristic for this approach are the words of Azariah de Rossi, *op. cit.* (Vilna ed.: 1866), p. 222:

וכן בכל יתר כתבי הקודש מי שלח בהם יד ונקה

"and indeed who in all the sacred writings would tamper with them and emerge guiltless?"

27. Cf., *B. Nedarim* 37b. The *'itturim* occur four times in connection with the word *'aḥar* (Gen. 18:5, 24:55, Num. 31:2, Ps. 68:26) and once in connection with the word *mispatekha* (Ps. 36:7).

28. Cf. his remarks, *s.v.,* עטר in *Arukh Hashalem* (ed., Kohut, Vienna: 1926), vol. 6, p. 189: "And it is reasonable to believe that originally the village dwellers were not exact in regard to Scripture. . . . They fell into error with these words at that time and thought that this was correct usage because this seemed plausible, but the scribes then came and removed these *vavs.*"

29. Septuagint translates with the *vav* connective in the three Penta-teuchal passages. However, this cannot be regarded as definite proof of their actual reading in view of the phenomenon of level-ing, i.e., the tendency of each translator to follow the simpler and more usual reading. The importance of this practice has not been fully recognized in textual criticism.

30. Cf., *Sifre* Num. (ed. Friedmann), p. 27:

נקוד עליו מלמעלה ומלמטה מפני שלא היה זה מקומו. ר' יהודה
אומר מפני שהוא ספר בפני עצמו.

"It is dotted above and below because this was not its original place. R. Judah says: Because it is an independent book." (The other sources *apud*, Lieberman, *op. cit.* p. 38 ff.) It is clear that R. Judah's opinion stems from the desire to negate the possibility of any change or doubt regarding the text; it is obviously homi-letic in character and offers no explanation of the "inverted *nun*" in Psalms 107. The opinion of the first Tanna is unquestionably correct.

31. The existence of this phenomenon in the Masoretic text was first pointed out by us in *BTM*, pp. 41–43, where we cited thirteen examples.

32. See the appendix to this paper.

33. On the value of the recension of the Septuagint as against the Masoretic text of Samuel, cf. S. R. Driver, *Notes on the Hebrew Text of the Books of Samuel* (Oxford: 1890), *passim* and espe-cially the important introduction; and more recently, M. S. Segal, *Sifrei Šemu'el* (Jerusalem: 1956). In his detailed introduction, which also deals with the readings of the Qumran fragments to the Septuagint and the Masorah (pp. 32–48), Segal concludes that most of the fragmentary readings agree with Septuagint against the Masorah (p. 51). Cf. also Albright, "New Light on Early Recensions of the Hebrew Bible" in BASOR, no. 140, 1955, pp. 27 ff.

34. This parallel was called to my attention many years ago by Pro-fessor Solomon L. Skoss and more recently by Professor Chaim Rabin. Cf. Arthur Jeffrey, "The Textual History of the Quran," *Journal of the Middle East Society*, 1947, pp. 35–49, which was reprinted as an appendix to his book, *The Quran as Scripture* (New York: 1952), pp. 89 ff., especially pp. 41–43, 46–48. A more detailed discussion may be found in R. Blachēré, *Introduc-tion au Coran* (Paris: 1947).

35. Some of them, like the "dotted words," are attributed in the tradition to Ezra (cf. note 36); others, as the name indicates, are associated with the Sopherim, while still others, like the inverted *nun,* the majuscules and the miniscules, are not given any attribution.

36. It should not be necessary to point out that this manuscript is not the medieval "Ezra codex" referred to in the *Masorah Parva,* an alleged copy of which was in the possession of C. D. Ginsburg.

37. Cf., *B. Sanhedrin* 21b–22a, and parallels.

38. Later tradition was unaware of the textual problems which the archetype was designed to solve. Hence, the name *Sepher ha-'Azarah* was interpreted in practical Halakhic terms. Thus Rashi (*B. Baba Batra* 14b) explains the term:

ספר עזרה. ספר שכתב משה ובו קורין בעזרה פרשת המלך בהקהל וכהן גדול ביום הכיפורים.

"The scroll, written by Moses, from which 'the law of the king' (Deut. 17:13–20) was read at the public reading of the Torah ordained for the seventh year of release (cf. Deut. 31:10–13) and from which the High Priest read on the Day of Atonement." Bertinoro, in his commentary on *M. Kelim* 15,6, interprets the phrase to mean that this reading by the High Priest was done בעזרת נשים: "in the women's court of the Temple precincts."

39. Cf. *M. Kelim* 15,6:

כל הספרים מטמאין את הידים חוץ מספר העזרה

40. Cf. *P. Sanhedrin* ii 6, 20c:

ומגיהין אותו מספר עזרה על פי בית דין של שבעים ואחד

However, *Tosefta Sanhedrin* 4,7 has a different reading:

ומגיהין אותו בבית דין של כהנים ובבית דין של לויים ובבית דין של ישראל.

"They correct it in the Court of the Priests and the Court of the Levites and the Court of the Israelites." This is not only an inferior but, indeed, a meaningless text, for a manuscript could not be corrected in a court, let alone in three courts! The reading in the *Tosefta* is obviously based on an erroneous transcription from the former text and induced by the frequent triad of Priests, Levites, and Israelites. Maimonides clearly bases himself on the reading in *P. Sanhedrin* in his statement:

ומגיהו מספר העזרה על פי בית דין של ע"א

"He corrects [the royal Bible codex] by means of the *'Azarah*

Scroll in accordance with the authority of the Court of Seventy-One" (*Yad, Hilkhot Melakhim* 3,2). The שיירי קרבן comments on the passage in *Sanhedrin*:

ונראה לי שכיון שהוא ספר ˙המוגה מכל הספרים כל הרוצה לתקן
ספרו ממנו הוא מתקן.

"It seems to me that since it (i.e., the 'Azarah Scroll) is the most
accurate of all manuscripts, whoever wishes to correct his codices,
corrects it by it."

41. For a balanced discussion of the ideal and historical elements in
    Rabbinic reports concerning the Sanhedrin, cf. Alexander Gutt-
    mann, *Rabbinic Judaism in the Making* (Detroit, 1970), pp.
    21–25.
42. Cf. *B. Kethubbot,* 106a:

מגיהי ספרים בירושלים היו נוטלין שכרן מתרומת הלשכה.

43. Cf. *P. Sheqalim,* chap. 4, p. 48a.
44. Cf. *Mishna Mo'ed Qatan* 3,4; *B. Batra,* 14b.
45. These forms are categorized and presented in *BTM,* lists 13–25,
    pp. 101–110, and in the relevant notes.
46. Cf., the introductions to each of these lists in *BTM,* in which we
    cite the passages where the text carries the archaic form with no
    corresponding *Qere,* at times *in the same context.* In other cases,
    the reading of the *Qere* occurs as the text elsewhere.
47. This basic methodological principle has not always been properly
    reckoned with, with the result that there is a wide discrepancy of
    views concerning the value of Qumran Isaiah I. To be sure, on an
    overall basis it is inferior to the Masoretic text, but in specific
    instances its readings may be preferable. We are, therefore, unable
    to accept the view of Orlinsky (*JQR,* vol. 43, p. 338) : "Its text
    is worthless to the student who wishes to get behind the Masoretic
    text."
48. Cf., I. H. Weiss, *Dor Dor Vedorshav,* vol. 4, p. 240, who suggests
    that there were special *Baraitot* and collections dealing with
    Masoretic subjects.
49. Cf., *BTM,* pp. 19–28.
50. "In the mss. before the LXX, many of our Qarian existed as
    ordinary readings" (*BTM,* p. 61).
51. Cf., M. Burrows, "Variant Readings" in *BASOR,* no. 91, 1948,
    p. 20.
52. Our view that proto-Masoretic activity was some six or seven
    centuries older than the medieval Masoretes was denied in some

quarters when first proposed. Cf., the review of *BTM* by W. F. Albright and our response in *JBL,* vol. 57, 1931, pp. 329–333. To be sure, Albright accepts our view regarding the various categories of the *Kethibh-Qere* apparatus that we have postulated, but he attributes them to the eighth century C.E. (*ibid.* p. 224). His view was followed by Roberts, *OTTV,* pp. 22, 25, 69, 85. In general, contemporary scholars have treated data from Rabbinic literature with skepticism and even with open hostility. Cf., the statements of Roberts, *op. cit.* p. 25: "Rabbi Akiba, the notorious anti-Christian," and p. 29: "the diehard traditions of the Rabbinic academies."

53. Cf., *B. Nedarim* 37b. Among the instances cited in the Babylonian Talmud, it had not been noted previously that two of the readings agree with the *Madinhae* against the *Ma'arba'e* school, as is entirely natural: Jeremiah 32:11, Ruth 2:11. There is, therefore, no need to emend the text with Rabbi Nissim; cf. *BTM,* p. 52, note 28.

54. As a result of our investigation of Masoretic lists and the editions of Baer and C. D. Ginsburg, we established 1,350 *Ketibhin veQarian,* possessing good Masoretic authority (exclusive of the Tetragrammaton). From this number we must subtract the original categories of *Kethibh-Qere* discussed above (lists 1–8), numbering 273 examples. This leaves 1,077 instances of genuine textual variations attested by the Masorah. To be sure, non-Masoretic codices contain many variations from the authentic Masoretic text, some of which are noted as *Kethibh-Qere,* especially when they are *similar in character to authentic Kethibh-Qere* examples. On the spurious *Kethibh-Qere* instances, cf. *BTM,* chap. 6.

55. See the important discussion by S. Lieberman, *Hellenism in Jewish Palestine,* chap. 1, which discusses the various manuscripts circulating among the people.

56. The material assembled by Aptowitzer requires careful investigation anew, in order to establish the different factors operating to produce variants in Rabbinic quotations. As an instance of the tendency to prefer the familiar form, cf. *B. Berakhot* 7b: רב הונא רמי כתיב לענותו וכתיב לכלותו. The first reference (לענותו) is to II Samuel 7:10; the second to I Chronicles 17:9, but here our Masoretic reading is לבלתו (with *beth*). Rab Huna, who cites this latter passage as לכלותו (with a *kaph*)

is following the more common usage (leveling) and may be citing from memory. In any event, there is no proof that this was the accepted reading in his time. Such instances can be multiplied again and again.

57. In *B. Qiddušin* 11 b, a non-existent passage is quoted: דכתיב ונתן הכסף וקם לו which is an inexact citation of Lev. 27:19: ויסף חמשית כסף ערכך עליו וקם לו. It was probably influenced by Deut. 14:26 ונתתה הכסף. The citation is graphically too distant from the Masoretic text and substantively too inexact to be a genuine textual variation; it is clearly the product of a fallible memory leveling a complex reading to a simpler one.

58. Cf. *OTTV*, p. 190.

59. Cf. P. Kahle, "Untersuchungen zur Geschichte des Pentateuch-textes" in *Theologische Studien und Kritiken*, vol. 88, 1915, p. 402; *idem, The Cairo Genizah*, pp. 49 ff.

60. Cf., W. F. Albright, "New Light on Early Recensions of the Hebrew Bible," in *BASOR*, no. 140, 1955, pp. 27 ff., whose view of divergent recensions circulating among the people is very similar to ours.

61. Kahle, who denies the existence of an archetype for the Hebrew original, maintains a similar view with regard to the Septuagint. Here, too, he denies the existence of an originally basic translation and maintains that many variants of the Greek translation were in use and that the Septuagint, as we know it today, is the result of a long development. Cf. his *Cairo Genizah*, p. 141 ff. Nevertheless, his thesis has by no means been accepted by all scholars. Thus, H. H. Rowley prefers the approach of Lagarde and Margolis that there originally was a proto-Septuagint from which the variants developed. Cf., H. M. Orlinsky, "The Proto-Septuagint Question" in *JQR*, 1943, pp. 497 ff; Roberts, *OTTV*, pp. 114 ff. If this conclusion of a uniform text is plausible with regard to the Septuagint, a translation that never pretended to be the original, it is all the more reasonable with regard to the Hebrew text. It is clear that the existence of variations in the Hebrew text does not disprove the existence of an accepted uniform text, especially when there are so many additional lines of evidence converging on this conclusion.

62. See the detailed treatment in L. Blau, *Studien zum althebräischen Buchwesen*, 1902, pp. 107 ff.

63. *Contra Apionem* ii, 42.

64. Cf., K. Steuernagel, *Lehrbuch der Einleitung in das AT,* 1912, pp. 20 ff. The legend is summarized briefly in Roberts, *OTTV,* p. 26.

65. Cf., *Tosefta Shebuot* 1, 7; *B. Pesaḥim* 22b; *Midrash Delamed-Bet Middot*; and see W. Bacher, *'Erkhei Midrash* (Tel Aviv: 5683-1923), pp. 75, 123.

66. Cf., *B. Ḥagigah* 12a. It is likely that he is to be identified with Nehemiah Ha 'Amsoni who is reported to have used the same method: דרש אתין גמין ורקין (P. *Berakhot* 9,5; M. *Sotah* 5,5; *B. Pesaḥim* 22b; *B. Kiddushin* 57a, etc.). The view of H. Hyman, *Toldot Tannaim VaAmoraim,* vol. 3, p. 928, that Nehemiah was the pupil of Rabbi Akiba is highly implausible.

67. Cf.,*Sifre,* Num. 6,3.

68. Cf.,*B. Sanhedrin* 4b:

לטטפת לטטפת לטטפות — הרי כאן ארבע דברי ר' ישמעאל.
ר' עקיבא אומר אינו צריך.

69. These *Kethibin* are cited with the term *Kethibh* by the Amoraim. We may add the following passages:

Gen. 9:21 אהלה   (*Gen. Rabbah* 36,4);
Isa. 44:24 מי אתי   (*Gen. Rabbah* 1,3;3,8);
Zech. 14:6 וקפאון   (*Pesikta Rabbati,* 39,1);
Prov. 22:20 שלשום   (*Pesikta Rabbati,* 105a);
Prov. 31:18 בליל   (*Pesikta Rabbati,* 65a).

It should be added that the term *Kethibh* is also used in a more general, non-technical sense to indicate that the orthography permits a different vocalization, "for the purpose of homiletic interpretation and not as it is vocalized by the Masorah." Cf., B. Z. Bacher *op. cit.,* pp. 210–211, who brings instances of both uses.

70. At times, the *Kethibh* occurs without the technical term being used. Frequently, however, the entire terminology . . . . כתיב וקרינן occurs; cf., *B. Erubin* 26a; *B. Yoma* 21b; *B. Menaḥot* 89b; and see the other sources indicated in *BTM,* p. 52, notes 29–32.

71. Cf., *Sifra,* Lev. 12:7; *B. Sanhderin* 4a. Bacher suggests that Rabbi Judah ben Ro'etz mentioned belonged to the generation preceding Rabbi Akiba.

72. Cf. the material gathered by L. Blau, *Masoretische Untersuchungen* (1891), who devotes a chapter (pp. 54–62) to the Midrashic interpretation of Masoretic notes.

73. The phrase occurs in *The Scrolls of Thanksgiving* (ed. J. Licht,

Jerusalem: 1957), p. 61. The other examples, which are easily amplified, are drawn from the *Isaiah Scroll*, the *Pešer of Habakkuk* and *Koheleth* fragments.

74. Cf., the discussion of P. Skehan at the Second International Congress of Orientalists held in Strassburg (August 27–September 1, 1956) and the summary by H. H. Rowley, *VT*, vol. 6, 1956, p. 445.

75. L. Blau, *Masoretische Untersuchungen*, p. 9, concludes that the use of dots was much earlier than the first century and already existed in the Temple manuscript. The Samaritan and the Septuagint both offer the full reading found in the Masoretic text.

76. In the case of all three *tiqqunei Sopherim* in the Pentateuch (Gen. 18:32; Num. 11:15; 12:12) the Septuagint has our reading. Cf., A. Rahlfs, *Septuaginta* (fifth ed., Stuttgart, 1952) *ad locum*.

77. In all three instances of *'itturei Sopherim* in the Pentateuch (Gen. 18:5; 24:55; Num. 31:2) the Septuagint renders the *vav*. However, it is not absolutely certain what their manuscript read because of the tendency to leveling. It already has been noted that the Samaritan also reads the *vav*. In Psalms 68:26 the Septuagint renders very freely, apparently in agreement with the Masorah, without a *vav*, and similarly in Psalms 36:7.

78. Septuagint reads the Masoretic text in Exodus 6:4, 16:35, 35:25f; 40:36; Leviticus 11:37. In two other passages the translation is not literal but testifies to the Masoretic reading: Genesis 27:44–45; Exodus 22:24. For details see the Hebrew original of this paper, note 70.

79. See the Second Letter in II Maccabees 2:13f.: "Besides these things, it is also told in the records and in Nehemiah's memoirs how he collected the books about the kings, the writings of the prophets, the works of David and the royal letters about sacred offerings. In like manner, Judas also collected for us the books that had been scattered because of the war and we now have them in our possession." (*New American Bible*, New York: 1970, p. 665). There is a substantial variety of views regarding the date of this letter. However, the composition of II Maccabees, which is an abridgement of the larger work of Jason of Cyrene, cannot be earlier than 125 B.C.E. or later than 50 C.E.

Appendix

Supplementary list of conflate passages in the Bible. See pages 41-43 below.

רשימה נוספת של פסוקים שבאו בהם עקבות של "צירוף החילופים"

1. בר' כז, מד, מה: עד אשר תשוב חמת אחיך עד שוב אף אחיך ממך

   א. עד אשר תשוב חמת אחיך

   ב. עד שוב אף אחיך ממך

2. שמ' כב, כד: אם כסף תלוה את עמי את העני עמך

   א. אם כסף תלוה את עמי

   ב. אם כסף תלוה את העני עמך

3. שמ' לה, כה, כו: וכל אשה חכמת לב בידיה טוו... וכל הנשים אשר נשא לבן אתנה בחכמה טוו את העזים

   א. וכל אשה חכמת לב בידיה טוו

   ב. וכל הנשים אשר נשא לבן אתנה בחכמה טוו את העזים

4. שמ' מ, לו, לז: ובהעלות הענן מעל המשכן יסעו בני ישראל בכל מסעיהם ואם לא יעלה הענן ולא יסעו עד יום העלתו

   א. ואם לא יעלה הענן ולא יסעו

   ב. ולא יסעו עד יום העלתו

5. וי' יא, לז: על כל זרע זרוע אשר יזרע

   א. על כל זרע זרוע

   ב. על כל זרע אשר יזרע

6. יהו' ג, יג: מי הירדן יכרתון המים הירדים מלמעלה ויעמדו נד אחד

   א. מי הירדן יכרתון ויעמדו נד אחד

   ב. יכרתון המים הירדים מלמעלה ויעמדו נד אחד

7. שמ"א ה, ג: והנה דגון נפל לפניו ארצה לפני ארון ה'

   א. והנה דגון נפל לפניו ארצה

   ב. והנה דגון נפל ארצה לפני ארון ה'

8. שמ"א יב, יג: ועתה הנה המלך אשר בחרתם אשר שאלתם

   א. ועתה הנה המלך אשר בחרתם

   ב. ועתה הנה המלך אשר שאלתם.

9. שמ"א יז, יג: וילכו שלשת בני ישי הגדלים הלכו אחרי שאול

א. וילכו שלשת בני ישי הגדולים אחרי שאול

ב. [ו]שלשת בני ישי הגדלים הלכו אחרי שאול

10. שמ"א יז, יג—טו: ושם שלשת בניו... לרעות את צאן אביו בית לחם

א. ושם שלשה בניו אשר הלכו למלחמה... ודוד הוא הקטן

ב. ושלשה הגדלים הלכו אחרי שאול ודוד הלך ושב מעל שאול לרעות את צאן אביו בית להם

11. שמ"ב ג, יג: כי אם לפני הביאך את מיכל

א. כי אם [ב]הביאך את מיכל

ב. לפני הביאך את מיכל

12. שמ"ב ג, לו: וכל העם הכירו וייטב בעיניהם ככל אשר עשה המלך בעיני כל העם טוב

א. וכל העם הכירו וייטב בעיניהם כל אשר עשה המלך

ב. וכל אשר עשה המלך בעיני כל העם טוב

13. שמ"ב ט, י, יא: ומפיבשת בן אדניך יאכל תמיד על שלחני... ומפיבשת אכל על שלחני כאחד מבני המלך

א. ומפיבשת בן אדניך (גרוס: אדני) יאכל תמיד על שלחני

ב. ומפיבשת אכל על שלחני כאחד מבני המלך

14. שמ"ב י, ט: ויבחר מכל בחורי בישראל (גרסת הכתיב)

א. ויבחר מכל בתורי ישראל (וכן גרסת הקרי)

ב. ויבחר מכל בחור בישראל

15. שמ"ב יב, ט: את אוריה החתי הכית... ואתו הרגת בחרב בני עמון

א. את אוריה החתי הכית בחרב ואת אשתו לקחת לך לאשה

ב. את אשתו לקחת לך לאשה ואתו הרגת בחרב בני עמון

16. שמ"ב יב, יא: חיך וחי נפשך אם אעשה

א. חיך אם אעשה

ב. חי נפשך אם אעשה

17. שמ"ב כ, יב: וירא האיש כי עמד כל העם... כאשר ראה כל הבא עליו ועמד

א. וירא האיש כי עמד כל העם ויסב את עמשא מן המסלה השדה וישלך עליו בגד

ב. ויסב את עמשא מן המסלה השדה וישלך עליו בגד כאשר ראה כל הבא עליו ועמד

18. מל"א י, כא: אין כסף לא נחשב בימי שלמה למאומה

א. אין כסף נחשב בימי שלמה למאומה

ב. כסף לא נחשב בימי שלמה למאומה

19. מל"א ז, מא—מב: והשבכות שתים... אשר על פני העמודים

א. והשבכות שתים לכסות את שתי גלות הכותרות אשר על ראש העמודים

ב. לשתי השבכות שני טורים רמנים לשבכה האחת לכסות את שתי הכותרת אשר על פני העמודים

20. מל"ב ה, יח: לדבר הזה יסלח ה' לעבדך... יסלח נא ה' לעבדך בדבר הזה

א. לדבר הזה יסלח ה' לעבדך בבוא אדני בית רמון להשתחוות שמה והוא נשען על ידי השתחויתי בית רמון

ב. בבא אדני בית רמון להשתחוות שמה והוא נשען על ידי בהשתחויתי בית רמון יסלח נא ה' לעבדך בדבר הזה

21. מל"ב ז, יג: ויען אחד מעבדיו ויאמר ויקחו נא חמשה מן הסוסים הנשארים... ונשלחה ונראה

א. חמשה מן הסוסים הנשארים הנם ככל ההמון (כ') ישראל אשר נשארו בה ונשלחה ונראה

ב. חמשה מן הסוסים אשר נשארו בה הנם ככל המון ישראל אשר תמו ונשלחה ונראה

22. יש' יז, יב—יג: ושאון לאומים כשאון מים כבירים ישאון לאמים כשאון מים רבים ישאון

א. ושאון לאומים... כבירים ישאון

ב. לאמים... רבים ישאון

23. יונה ג, ז: האדם והבהמה הבקר והצאן אל יטעמו מאומה אל ירעו ומים אל ישתו

א. האדם והבהמה... אל יטעמו מאומה ומים אל ישתו

ב. האדם והבהמה... מאומה אל ירעו ומים אל ישתו

24. יונה ד, ו: להיות צל על ראשו להציל לו מרעתו

א. להיות צל על ראשו

ב. להציל (גרוס: להצל) לו מרעתו

25. תה' יח, ז: ושועתי לפניו תבוא באזניו

א. ושועתי באזניו (וכן נוסח שמ"ב כב, ז)

ב. ושועתי לפניו תבוא

26. איוב לא, לא: אם לא אמרו מתי אהלי מי יתן מבשרו לא נשבע

א. אם אמרו מתי אהלי...

ב. לא אמרו מתי אהלי

27. דה"א ח, לב: ואף המה נגד אחיהם ישבו בירושלם עם אחיהם

א. ואף המה נגד אחיהם ישבו בירושלים

ב. ואף המה ישבו בירושלם עם אחיהם

28. דה"א י, יג: וגם לשאול באוב לדרוש

א. וגם לשאול באוב

ב. וגם באוב לדרוש

74

THE SIGNIFICANCE OF THE PARADISE MYTH

I

The story of Adam and Eve in the Garden of Eden is one of the foundation stones of human thought. Untold generations have fallen under the spell of the simple, yet mysterious beauty of the tale, and re-written it in accordance with their own philosophical and religious preconceptions. For this reason the Paradise story has been one of the last citadels to fall before the all-conquering sweep of the historical spirit and the philological method. Even modern attempts to elucidate the myth in terms of what it meant to its author and earliest readers have not succeeded in solving all the problems raised by the story: What is the nature of the Tree of Knowledge of Good and Evil? What relationship do the two trees in the Garden bear to each other? Why should God refuse man the knowledge of good and evil? Why could not Adam have eaten of the Tree of Life during his period of innocence, or even after his sin, and so have secured immortal life for himself before being expelled from the Garden of Eden? Last, what relation does the story in Genesis bear to other Adam traditions: to the fragments in Ezekiel, Job, and Psalms, and the later developments in post-biblical literature, Philo, the Apocrypha, the Midrash, the Gnostics, and the patristic writings?

Of all the problems we have enumerated, the basic one is undoubtedly the first: What is the nature of the Tree of Good and Evil? The traditional interpretation which equates it with the moral sense, the knowledge of right and wrong, has found few modern defenders except Budde.[1] Gressmann has suggested that the fruit of the Tree of Knowledge endowed its eater with magical knowledge.[2] But the two most widely accepted views are those of Wellhausen and Gunkel. Wellhausen sees in it the insight into the secrets of nature and the arts of civilization.[3] Gunkel believes that the knowledge of good and evil

---

[1] *Urgeschichte*, pp. 69 ff.

[2] *Archiv für Religionswissenschaft*, X, 351 ff.

[3] *Prolegomena* (6th ed.), pp. 297 ff.

86

represents the mature understanding of the world, which distinguishes the grownup from the child.[4]

Of the many objections to which these interpretations are open, the most telling is to be found in Gen. 2:19, which describes the naming of the animals and birds by Adam. That he could give names to all the animals scarcely implies that he needed the fruit of the Tree of Knowledge in order to gain maturity or insight into the secrets of nature, for to the ancients the name of the thing was tantamount to its very essence.[5] This conception of Adam's transcendent wisdom, which is implicit in Gen. 2:19, becomes explicit throughout the entire range of post-biblical literature.[6] Everywhere Adam is pictured as a demigod, the acme of beauty and wisdom, and by no means ignorant and immature. The eating of the Tree of Knowledge cannot therefore mark the beginning of Adam's wisdom or maturity.

Scholars have also found it difficult to understand why the Tree of Life enters into the narrative at all, and what relationship it bears to the Tree of Knowledge. Many have therefore followed Budde and Gunkel in assuming that the Paradise story in Genesis, chapters 2 and 3, is a blending of two distinct accounts of the first sin. Skinner[7] summarizes this hypothesis as follows: "On the whole, the facts seem to warrant these conclusions: of the Paradise story, two recensions existed; in one, the only tree mentioned was the Tree of Knowledge of good and evil, while the other certainly contained the Tree of Life and possibly both trees."

Skinner himself recognizes that the "evidence" for a double recension is only "more or less decisive" and even "precarious." As an instance of the full weakness of this theory, however, we may point to the second of the hypothetical recensions. If we assume that this recension contained both trees, all the problems created by the existence of two trees in our present narrative reappear: specifically, the question of the nature of the Tree of Knowledge and the relationship of the two trees.

[4] *Genesis* (2d ed., 1902), pp. 25 ff.

[5] See Ibn Ezra on Gen. 2:17, who points out "Adam [before the fall] was filled with Knowledge, ... and was a great sage."

[6] See Ginzberg, *Legends of the Jews*, I, 59–62; V, § 2, "Adam," nn. 21, 22, 27, 29, 30.

[7] *ICC*, on Genesis, pp. 52 f.

If we assume that this recension contained only one tree, the Tree of Life, of which Adam ate against God's express prohibition, another question arises: Why did not the eating of its fruits confer immortal life upon Adam and his descendants? The mytho-poetic faculty is always honest; it does not violate its own axioms. In the large number of similar stories adduced by Frazer,[8] man fails to achieve immortality only because he does not accept the message or because he refuses to eat the food of immortal life, as the case may be. Thus, in the Assyro-Babylonian myth, Adapa refuses the food of immortality and so loses the divine prerogative. The underlying theory in this and all similar tales is that had he partaken of the food of life, immortality would have been his. The question posed above is therefore unanswerable. If Adam ate of the Tree of Life, he should have become immortal. The assumption that this recension contained only the Tree of Life is thus extremely weak.

Even the first recension, which revolved about the Tree of Knowledge alone, bristles with problems which need not be detailed at length. Enough evidence has been offered to indicate that the division of the Paradise story is an unsatisfactory assumption.

An altogether different approach, based not on literary analysis but on comparative folklore, is that of Frazer.[9] Drawing upon his unrivaled knowledge of primitive tradition, he reconstructs the original story of Genesis as follows:

In the Garden of Eden there stood two trees, one the Tree of Life and the other the Tree of Death. In his benevolent goodness, God sent the snake to man with this message, "Eat not of the Tree of Death, for in the day that ye eat thereof, ye shall surely die; but eat of the Tree of Life and live forever." But the cunning serpent perverted the message, and reported that God wished man to eat of the Tree of Death and live forever. Man did so and became mortal, while the snake ate of the Tree of Life and achieved this boon for himself. Ever since that day the snake casts his skin each year and lives eternally.

Frazer's hypothesis has much to recommend it. It avoids the pitfalls of the double-recension view described above. The attitude of God toward man is friendly rather than resentful and hostile. The

[8] *Folk Lore in the Old Testament* (1-vol. ed.), pp. 15–33.   [9] *Ibid.*

two trees are integrally related to each other. Frazer is undoubtedly right in feeling that there should be a definite contrast between the two trees. Unfortunately, there is no trace of a Tree of Death in the present account of Genesis. It is impossible to explain how that simple name could have been replaced by the difficult concept of the knowledge of good and evil. Moreover, while rivers, trees, and fruits of life abound in the folklore of the world,[10] we do not hear of a Tree of Death. For these reasons we feel that Frazer's hypothesis is untenable in its present form. But one remains grateful to him for the illuminating material he has assembled.

While Frazer changes the Tree of Knowledge into the Tree of Death, Ludwig Levy[11] insists that the Tree of Knowledge is the same as the Tree of Life. He maintains that the story in Genesis actually speaks of one tree which possessed two names. In Gen. 2:9, וְעֵץ הַחַיִּים בְּתוֹךְ הַגָּן וְעֵץ הַדַּעַת טוֹב וָרָע, he interprets the Vav of וְעֵץ הַדַּעַת as a Vav Copulativum,[12] and renders: "'The Tree of Life was in the Garden, which is the Tree of Knowledge of Good and Evil." This hypothesis involves Levy in difficulties when 3:22 is reached, because there the existence of a Tree of Life as distinguished from the Tree of Knowledge cannot be explained away. He therefore assumes that this verse is a later addition, when the misinterpretation concerning the two trees had already become firmly fixed. This is not the only difficulty of his view, even if the doubtful syntactic construction of 2:9 be overlooked. If there were only one tree, that of Life-Knowledge, in the Garden, and Adam ate of its fruit, that should have conferred immortality on him and nullified God's threat of punishment. As will become clear presently, Levy has correctly understood "the Knowledge of Good and Evil," but his theory of the identity of the two trees leaves much to be desired.

II

In spite of these difficulties, we believe that it is possible to arrive at a true understanding of the Paradise story without recourse to extreme hypotheses or emendations. We should like to suggest that

[10] Wünsche, *Die Sagen vom Lebensbaum und Lebenswasser;* Frazer, *ibid.;* Skinner, *op. cit.,* pp. 58 f.

[11] *Sexualsymbolik in der biblischen Paradiesgeschichte* in *Imago,* V (1917), 16–30.

[12] See Gesenius-Kautzsch, *Hebräische Grammatik* (28th ed.), § 154.

the knowledge of good and evil is "sexual consciousness."[13] There is abundant evidence that the phrase דַּעַת טוֹב וָרָע can bear this interpretation. The verb יָדַע is used in the very next chapter and elsewhere in a sexual significance.[14] Other languages illustrate this usage as well. The Syriac ܝܺܕܰܥ, the Arabic عرف, the Assyrian lamâdu (idû), the Greek γιγνώσκειν, the Latin noscere, cognoscere, notitiam habere—all have developed the special meaning of coire, by the side of their more general significance. A study of the use of the phrase "knowing good and evil" in the Bible shows that it is used of children who still do not possess sexual consciousness, as in Deut. 1:39, Isa. 7:15 f.,[15] and of the very old, whose sex powers have decayed and who therefore no longer "know good and evil," as in II Sam. 19:36.[16]

It will therefore be granted that the phrase has the connotation of "sexual consciousness." How does it come, however, that "the knowledge of good and evil" should develop this meaning? Modern psychological research has demonstrated that "abnormal" sexual manifesta-

[13] This view has been more or less definitely suggested before, though its full bearing on the unity and significance of the story has not been realized. Ibn Ezra on 3:6 says, והאחד עץ הדעת והוא יוליד תאות המשגל, "The Tree of Knowledge causes sexual desire," and quotes the use of ירע in Gen. 4:1. Ehrlich, in both his Hebrew and his German commentary on 2:9, maintains that the phrase דעת טוב ורע has sexuelle Bedeutung. Barton (Semitic Origins, pp. 93 ff.) speaks of the fruit of the tree as an "aphrodisiac." Levy (op. cit.) gives the tree and the entire story a sexual significance. Unfortunately, Levy is led by his psychoanalytic approach to see in each element of the Paradise story an unconscious sexual motive. Thus "eat," "fruit," "apple," "knowledge," "good and evil," "Garden of Eden," "serpent," "fig leaves"—all become symbols representing the sexual act. As a result, the concrete details of the story fade into a series of veiled allusions and metaphors. He also makes no attempt to deal with the etymology of the phrase, "the knowledge of good and evil," the meaning of which, however, he has grasped clearly. The objection to his procedure has been discussed above.

[14] The passages are listed in Brown-Driver-Briggs, Lexicon, p. 394a.

[15] We should like to call attention to the following interesting detail in the Immanuel prophecy. Isaiah points to the pregnant woman and informs the king that before the child will attain "the knowledge to despise evil and choose the good," the enemies of the king will be destroyed. On the basis of our interpretation of "good and evil," as meaning "sexual consciousness," the child will attain this knowledge when he reaches puberty, about thirteen years after the prophet's sign. The prophet is speaking to Ahaz during the Syro-Ephraimitic War, 734 B.C. Thirteen years later would bring us down to 721. Samaria was destroyed in 722, a remarkable fulfilment of the prophecy that "before the child shall know to refuse the evil and choose the good, the land before the kings of which thou art affrighted shall be forsaken"! The conquest of Damascus had taken place much earlier, in 733 (Kittel, History of the Hebrews, II, 347).

[16] The ordinary interpretations of "good and evil" fail to do justice to the verse. The aged Barzilai declines to go to the king's court because "I am this day fourscore years old; can I discern between good and bad? Can thy servant taste what I eat or what I drink? Can I hear any more the voice of singing men and singing women?" On our interpretation, this verse would contain the earliest reference to the triad of "Wine, Women, and Song!"

tions, such as homosexuality, onanism, and sodomy, are often deeply ingrained in man, and must be included in the scope of sexual experience. Anthropology has found overwhelming evidence of homosexual practices among primitive peoples as well as among civilized races like the Greeks and Romans.[17] Biblical literature speaks of "unnatural sin" in Gen. 19:22, 23, and Judg. 19:22. The *Kedeshim* and *Kedeshoth*, the Temple prostitutes, are forbidden in Deut. 23:13, but they are frequently mentioned during the period of the monarchy of Judah.[18] They may have been "sodomites" as the English versions render it.

We may therefore expect that a comprehensive designation for the sexual consciousness such as "the knowledge of good and evil" would include both heterosexual and homosexual forms of experience. טוֹב would stand for good, i.e., the natural, heterosexual manifestations. רַע would express the evil, i.e., the unnatural, homosexual forms. It is well known that biblical Hebrew compensates for its limited vocabulary by the richness of the nuances of words.

This meaning of רַע meets us in Gen. 19:5, 6 in the story of Lot and his guests in Sodom. When the townspeople cry out for the strangers, "Bring them out unto us that we may know them," Lot begs them: אַל נָא אַחַי תָּרֵעוּ, "I pray you, my brethren, do not so wickedly." He offers his daughters up to their lust instead of his guests. To account for the use of תָּרֵעוּ to describe the act of pederasty, much ink has been spilt in an attempt to prove that the author does not consider the violation of virgins a crime and hence uses תָּרֵעוּ, "do wickedly," to describe the homosexual act, but not rape. Ehrlich avoids this questionable assumption by rendering תָּרֵעוּ "Seid nicht unnatürlich, begeht nicht die naturwidrige Tat." In the similar passage in Judg. 19:23 the same meaning for תָּרֵעוּ is to be assigned: "Do not act unnaturally." Other instances of this use of טוֹב and רַע are not lacking.[19] We therefore submit that, side by side with its significance of

[17] The material is summarized in Westermarck, *The Origin and Development of the Moral Ideas*, chap. xlvi, "Homosexual Love," and in Hans Licht, *Sexual Life of the Ancient Greeks*. References are met with in Aristophanes, Plato, Horace, Polybius, and other classical writers.

[18] Driver, "Deuteronomy," *ICC*, pp. 364 f. See the Authorized Version, Revised Version, and the Jewish Publication Society Version on I Kings 14:24; 15:12; 22:47; II Kings 23:7. The denunciations of the practice are to be found in Lev. 18:22, 24; 20:13; Rom. 1:26, 27.

[19] See Ehrlich on וַיַּרְא אֱלֹהִים כִּי טוֹב in Gen., chap. 1, and on זֶרַע מְרֵעִים (Isa. 1:4). To these passages we may perhaps add Isa. 14:20, where the king of Babylonia is

"ethical good and evil," דַּעַת טוֹב וָרָע possessed the special meaning of "sexual awareness, in its broadest sense, i.e., knowledge of the natural and the unnatural, the heterosexual and the homosexual impulses."

We are now able to understand the Paradise myth in its true light. God, actuated by love for his creature Adam, places him in the Garden of Eden, his own dwelling-place.[20] Man has been created in the image of God (1:27) and possesses divine wisdom, which enables him to name all the animals and birds (2:19). One more great gift God grants to Adam, the gift of eternal life, which comes to him through the partaking of the fruit of life in the Garden. Only in one respect is "man less than God": he is forbidden to eat of the Tree of Knowing Good and Evil and learn of the existence of sexual consciousness. But the snake persuades the woman that eating of it would make her and her husband equal to God, possessing the divine secret of creation, the power of calling into existence new beings, which is the distinguishing mark of God.[21] The woman succumbs to the temptation and persuades her husband to do likewise. They discover that they are naked and the world of sexual consciousness swims into their ken. When God learns of the disobedience of the human pair he metes out punishment to them. The sexual act, which he had originally denied man, now becomes the cause of human suffering. Adam can no longer be allowed to dwell in the Garden and continue to eat of the fruit of life, for then he would possess both attributes of God, immortality and the power of creation.[22] Adam and Eve are therefore expelled from the

---

described as זֶרַע מְרֵעִים, "unnatural offspring," because "thou hast destroyed thy land and thou hast slain thy people." The prophet taunts the king that he has brought destruction upon his own people instead of spreading devastation among foreign nations, as is usual with great conquerors.

[20] On Eden as the heavenly city of God see Gunkel, op. cit., pp. 30 f.

[21] So Rashi on 3:5, יוֹצְרֵי עוֹלָמוֹת, "creating worlds." Levy (op. cit.) renders Schöpfer wie die Gottheit. Passages like Gen. 1:27 and 6:2 imply a physical similarity between God and man, which makes 3:5, 22 credible statements. Human procreation represents, to the author, the counterpart of divine creation.

[22] The problem as to why Adam did not eat of the Tree of Life and thus achieve immortality before his expulsion is resolved by comparative folklore. The fruit of the tree did not possess the quality of conferring unending life upon whomsoever ate of its fruit once. Rather, one was immortal so long as one continued to eat of it. This seems to be a common characteristic of the Fruit of Life. Thus, the Germanic myth of "The Twilight of the Gods" tells that while the golden apples were within reach of the gods, they were youthful and happy. But when the giants stole the apples, the gods began to grow old and shrivel up, until Loki succeeded in bringing back the apples, whereupon the gods revived and grew young again. Gen. 3:22, פֶּן יִשְׁלַח יָדוֹ, implies that the apples are within easy reach, but not that "a single partaking of the fruit would have conferred eternal life" (against Budde, quoted by Skinner, p. 88).

Garden. Man is doomed to the hard life of the farmer, toiling in the field to wrest food from the cruel earth for himself and his family. The woman must become a mother and undergo the pain of child-birth. No longer can they enjoy the boon of eternal life. After years of toil and suffering, death awaits them with only the partial and vicarious immortality afforded by procreation. As Ibn Ezra remarks, "When Adam saw that he could not live eternally in his own person, he was compelled to perpetuate his kind, as it is written, I have 'acquired a man from the Lord.' "[23]

Far from being at variance with the other Adam traditions, the Genesis story agrees in picturing Adam as possessing transcendental wisdom and insight. Adam before his fall lacked only the power of creation through sexual experience, a gift of which he had no need so long as the boon of personal immortality was his.

The two trees are now seen to bear a close and organic relation to each other. The Tree of Life represents eternal life in the flesh; the Tree of Knowledge of Good and Evil, sexual consciousness, and the immortality which comes through the procreation of children.[24] God had given man the greater boon, but man had trespassed and seized for himself the forbidden secret, the bittersweet experience of sexual desire. Viewed from the standpoint of the race, the two trees represent two types of eternal life, personal immortality and the immortality through children. From the position of the individual, however, one is indeed the Tree of Life, while the other, the Tree of Knowledge, is the Tree of Death. The knowledge of good and evil is both a substitute for eternal life and its opposite.

It is no longer necessary to read allegories, esoteric doctrines, and later dogmas into the Paradise story to see its profundity. It represents some of man's earliest thoughts and fears and dreams concerning his life and his activity on earth. The purpose of the myth is to explain

[23] On Gen. 4:1.

[24] We must not exaggerate the primitive character of the story. Skinner (p. 52) points out that "the purely mythological phase of thought has long been outgrown." Even primitive legends, however, recognize that the procreation of children is at once a contrast to, and a substitute for, personal immortality. Frazer (*op. cit.*) quotes a tale of the Mentras, a savage tribe of the Malay Peninsula, who tell that in the early history of the world it was found that the population was increasing at an alarming rate, because there was no death. Finally, the younger brother of the first man said, "Let men die like the banana, leaving their offspring behind." Frazer (p. 30) quotes a similar tradition among the Bahnars of Western Cochin China.

why man must die and yet point out that man has a source of undying life through perpetuating his kind. It was not jealousy but benevolence that impelled God to seek to keep from man any awareness of sex. How much happier man would be, the author muses, if he possessed eternal life in his own person, instead of the secondary immortality through children, which comes to him only through the painful pleasure of sexual desire and its satisfaction, and through the hardship and pain that accompany the rearing of offspring.

In its balanced attitude toward sex, the legend is in thorough keeping with the dominant view of later Jewish thought. It recognizes the double character of the sexual impulse, its capacity for evil and sin, and its primacy as the means to immortality and the incentive to civilization.[25]

---

[25] The rabbinic attitude is reflected in these and similar statements: "Let us be grateful to our ancestors, for if they had not sinned we should never have come into the world" (Abodah Zarah 52); "Were it not for the sexual impulse, man would never build a house or marry or beget children or engage in an occupation" (Bereshith Rabbah 8:9). Cf. also Sanh. 64a for an interesting legend which describes what happened when the sexual impulse was temporarily conquered by men.

Love, Marriage, and Business in the Book of Ruth: A Chapter in Hebrew Customary Law

Ḥesed AND *Ḥokhmah* IN RUTH

For two millennia, the book of Ruth has charmed readers by its idyllic beauty. Goethe described it as *das lieblicheste kleine Ganze das uns episch und idyllisch ueberliefert worden ist.* In this charming tale, the tragedies of life are muted, being bathed in a gentle melancholy, with evil being virtually nonexistent. The *Midrash* succinctly epitomizes the book as a tribute to the practice of loving-kindness (*gemilūt ḥasādīm*).[1] The word *ḥesed* in biblical Hebrew has been rendered by a variety of terms: "goodness," "kindness," "favor," "love," and most commonly by "loving-kindness." Recently, translators have sought to approximate its essence more closely in the rendering "steadfast love."[2] As the book of Ruth makes clear, *ḥesed* includes a broad spectrum of family piety, friendship, loyalty, and love, both Divine and human. Within the confines of this small book, *ḥesed* represents the basic attribute of God in dealing with his creatures, which Naomi invokes for her daughter-in-law (1: 8) and of which she finds evidence in Boaz's kindness to Ruth (2: 20). It is the quality that Boaz praises in Ruth's turning to him rather than to younger and more attractive men (3: 10). When this loyalty is suffused by deep emotion, it becomes virtually

It is a privilege to extend warmest felicitations and best wishes to Professor Jacob M. Myers on the occasion of his sixty-eighth birthday, and to join with his colleagues, students, and admirers everywhere in paying tribute to his distinguished career as a biblical scholar and teacher. Because of Professor Myers' lifelong interest in Ruth, which found expression in his monograph *The Linguistic and Literary Form of the Book of Ruth* (Leiden, 1955) I am happy to contribute this paper to the Festschrift being issued in his honor.

identical with love, as in the formula of betrothal in Hos (Hebrew) (2: 21–22): "And I will betroth you to me forever; I will betroth you to me in righteousness and in justice, in steadfast love and in mercy. I will betroth you to me in faithfulness; and you shall know the Lord." So too, in the words of his spiritual descendant Jeremiah (Jer 2: 2): "Go and proclaim in the hearing of Jerusalem, Thus says the Lord, I remember the devotion (*ḥesed*) of your youth, your love (*'ahabhat*) as a bride, how you followed me in the wilderness, in a land unsown."[3] At its ultimate, *ḥesed* represents the blending of man's love and loyalty toward God (Hos 6: 6). It is characteristic of the gentle and relaxed atmosphere of the book of Ruth that the verb *'āhabh* does not occur; all the passion may have well dwelt in Boaz's breast. It is *ḥesed*, steadfast loyalty, faithful love, that Ruth feels for her mother-in-law, which she then manifests toward Boaz and which impels her to seek refuge under the wings of the God of Israel (2: 12).

That *ḥesed* triumphs over the tragedies of life in the book of Ruth is due to another highly prized virtue in ancient Israel, that of *ḥokhmah*. The old tradition which places the book of Ruth after Judges is of course self-explanatory. The opening phrase, as well as the entire background of the tale, associates the events with the period of the Judges.[4] However, as we have suggested elsewhere, the present position of the book within the Hagiographa is not accidental. Its precise place among the five Megillot, after the Song of Songs, is of course due to its position in the synagogue liturgy as the reading for the Feast of Shavuoth.

However, its position in the Hagiographa generally is, I believe, thoroughly justified by the fact that the Hagiographa is basically the repository of Wisdom Literature.[5] This includes both the lower, conventional *ḥokhmah*, which sought to inculcate the practical qualities needed for success in life, and the higher, speculative *ḥokhmah*, which wrestled with the ultimate issues of human existence, the purpose of creation, the goals of human life, the nature of death, the inaccessibility of truth, and—above all—the agonizing problem of evil. The book of Psalms is a great collection of religious poetry, most of which was chanted at the Temple service with musical accompaniment. Both the composition and the rendition of the Psalms in worship required a high degree of that technical skill which is *ḥokhmah*. Moreover, in point of content, many Psalms (like 37, 49, 112, 128) have close affinities with the proverbial lore of the Wisdom teachers. The Song of Songs is included, not merely because it is traditionally ascribed to King Solomon, the symbol and traditional source of Hebrew Wisdom, but because these songs, whether sung at weddings or at other celebrations, were also a branch of technical song. It may also be that the Song of Songs entered the Wisdom collection because it was regarded as an allegory of the relationship of love subsisting between God and Israel. From this point of view, it would be a *māšāl*, the basic literary genre of *ḥokhmah*, which means "allegory" and "fable" as well as "proverb." The book of Daniel, the wise interpreter of dreams, obviously is in place among the Wisdom books.

The chanting of Lamentations required a special expertise described as *ḥokhmah* (Jer 9: 16). The three closing books of the Bible, which survey history from Adam to the Persian period, are really parts of one larger work, Chronicles-Ezra-Nehemiah. It is possible that they owe their position in the Hagiographa to the fact that they serve as an appendix to the Bible as a whole. It is also possible that Chronicles (with its adjuncts) is regarded as an appendix to Psalms, since one of its principal concerns is to describe in detail the establishment of the musical guilds and priestly orders in the Temple in Jerusalem.

The books of Ruth and Esther are narratives, showing how *ḥokhmah* operates and succeeds in human affairs. They belong to the same genre as the Joseph saga in Genesis. The same kind of practical wisdom that helped Joseph rise to power and influence was utilized by Mordecai and Esther to save their people, and was displayed by Naomi and Ruth on the more limited stage of domestic affairs. Without Naomi's practical wisdom, which Ruth obeyed, the young woman would not have come to the attention of Boaz; and without his shrewdness during the transaction with the kinsman, he would not have been able to marry her.

Frequently described as an idyll, the book of Ruth is by no means a simple tale. Its apparent simplicity has often prevented a full appreciation of its high literary artistry.[6] It has also served to obscure the complexity of the problems the book contains.

THE PURPOSE AND DATE OF RUTH

There is a wide disparity of views regarding the background of the book. It has been suggested that Ruth is a polemic against the exclusion of Moabites from the community of Israel, which is enjoined in Deut 23: 4. More often, the book has been described as a tract against the campaign of Ezra and Nehemiah to exclude mixed marriages from the post-Exilic Jewish community,[7] and contrariwise, as a possible defence of their policy.[8] But nothing could be further removed from the polemic spirit than the irenic tone of our book. It is this characteristic which also rules out the possibility of its being propagandistic in any sense. It does not agitate for the enforcement of the duty of levirate marriage,[9] even if the transaction in Chapter 4 be regarded as an instance of this rite. It does not preach benevolence toward the heathens,[10] for, be it noted, Ruth accepts the faith of Naomi long before any kindness is shown her in Bethlehem. It surely cannot be construed as a protest against intermarriage or indiscriminate proselytization.[11] That the book praises the piety of Ruth[12] and her loyalty as a widow[13] may be true, but this can scarcely be regarded as its purpose. Naomi may share the honors of being the heroine of the book with Ruth,[14] but this too supplies no purpose for the book.

It has been suggested that the function of Ruth is to supplement the account in 1 Sam 22: 3, which informs us that David sought a refuge for his parents in Moab, by supplying him with a Moabite ancestry in that country.[15] But even for those, who, like the present writer, regard the genealogy at the end of the book as integral to it and possessing a good claim to authenticity, this idea plays no part in the book and hardly qualifies as its purpose. Finally, the theory, propounded a few decades ago, that we have here a liturgical text of a fertility cult centered in Bethlehem,[16] has few, if any, defenders today. By a process of elimination, we are therefore left virtually only with the view that the book of Ruth is a story told for its own sake.[17] This conclusion does not necessarily rule out the possibility that there may have been an authentic tradition of David's being partly descended from Moabite stock.

Divergences with regard to dating are of course common in all biblical research.[18] Talmudic tradition assigns the book to the authorship of Samuel.[19] It has been variously assigned to the early Monarchy,[20] to the period between David and the Exile,[21] to the days of Hezekiah,[22] to the Exilic period,[23] and to the post-Exilic age.[24] In spite of this wide disparity of views, I am convinced that the lines of evidence converge on the period from the middle of the fifth to the early fourth century B.C.E.

The testimony from language and style must be used with caution.[25] On the one hand, the classic style of the book includes such formulas as *kh y'śh Yhwh ly wkh ysyp* (1: 17) and *'qlh 'znk* (4: 4). The popular speech probably preserved such older forms as the second person singular of the imperfect with *Nun* (originally the energeticus) *tidbāqîn* (2: 8, 21), *tēd'în* (3: 18)[26] and the archaic form of the second person feminine of the perfect with *Yod*, *wyrdty* (3: 3) and *wškbty* (3: 4).[27] The Divine name *šdy* (1: 20) is ancient, but it reappears frequently in Job.

On the other hand, there are such late locutions as *wyś'w lhm nšym* (1: 4; cf 1 Chron 23: 22), where the older classic idiom was *lqḥ 'šh* (Gen 4: 4; 6: 2; 11: 14; Deut 24: 1). We may note also the use of *'syt* in the meaning "to spend (time)" (2: 19), which occurs biblically only in Eccles 6: 12 but is common in Rabbinic Hebrew, as is the root *'gn* "to be chained" (1: 13).[28]

In Mishnaic Hebrew, the *tertiae Aleph* verbs coalesce with *tertiae Yod*, under the influence of Aramaic. The orthography and vocalization of 2: 9

reflect this tendency.[29] *mrglwt* (3: 4, 7, 8, 14) occurs elsewhere only in Dan 10: 6, but the parallel form *mr'šwt* is early (Gen 28: 11, 18; 1 Sam 19: 13,16).

Elsewhere, we have called attention to the four categories of Aramaisms in biblical Hebrew and the care that must be exercised before invoking them as evidence of late dating.[30] However, it is clear that a large concentration of Aramaisms, as in Ps 139, does point to the post-Exilic period, when Hebrew writers knew and used Aramaic, the *lingua franca et scripta* of the Middle East from the sixth century B.C.E. onward. This concentration of Aramaisms does obtain in Ruth. *Hlhn*, "therefore" (1: 12), occurs in Dan 2: 6, 9; 4: 24 (*lāhēn*). The verb *tśbrnh*, "hope" (1: 13), is an Aramaism (*śbr*) occurring only in such late passages as Is 38: 18; Ps 104: 27; 119: 116, 166; and Esther 9: 1. The *Piel* (4: 7) *lqym*, "attest, confirm," is a clear Aramaism, occurring only in Ezek 13: 6, Ps 119: 28, 106; Esther 9: 21, 27, 31, 32. On the other hand, the root *lpt*, "twist turn" (3: 8), which appears in biblical Hebrew in Job 6: 18, cannot be invoked, since it occurs also in Judg 16: 29.

There is only one adequate explanation for these superficially contradictory phenomena, the occurrence of both early and late Hebrew usages in Ruth: the author was a late writer who was consciously archaizing and using colloquial speech, in order to give an antique flavor to his narrative, which he set in the period of the Judges.

Substantive considerations agree with the linguistic evidence for a post-Exilic date for Ruth. The author finds it necessary, from the vantage point of a later period *wz't pnym byśr'l* (4: 7), to explain the use of the sandal for the transfer of rights and obligations. Moreover, the period of the Judges is pictured as idyllic and peaceful, a situation radically at variance with the conditions of war, cruelty, and insecurity realistically reflected in the book of Judges. More specifically, Moab is no longer an actual enemy on the borders of Israel, as was the case during most of the pre-Exilic period, including the age of the Judges (cf Judg 3: 13 ff; 11: 15 ff; 1 Sam 12: 9).

It is admittedly difficult to fix a precise date for the book within the Second Temple period. A *terminus post quem* may be found in the fact that there is no echo of the agitation or of the activity associated with Ezra and Nehemiah, for which the date of 444 B.C.E. is generally assigned, though the problems of Ezra chronology are massive and perhaps insoluble.[31] This consideration would bring the time down to the second half of the fifth century. A *terminus ante quem* may be advanced with greater assurance. There is no echo in Ruth of the widespread upheavals in the Middle East caused by the incursion of Alexander the Great into western Asia (334 B.C.E.) and no trace of Hellenistic influence, either in style or in substance.

The book would seem to emanate from a period of relative tranquility, such as the post-Exilic Jewish community experienced under Persian suzerainty. Above all, the spirit of universalism and broad humanity which the book breathes belongs to the same spiritual climate as do the book of Jonah and the great masterpieces of wisdom literature, Job and Ecclesiastes.

As is often the case, the evidence is cumulative in character rather than decisive in detail. All in all, the most appropriate *Sitz im Leben* for the book of Ruth is the early Second Temple period, when the Jewish community enjoyed a substantial measure of autonomy under the Persian rule, about 450–350 B.C.E.

RUTH AND THE LEVIRATE

Neither the problem of the purpose of the book nor its date, important as these questions are, is crucial to understanding the narrative itself. There are, however, two major difficulties in the closing chapter which fundamentally affect our comprehension of its contents. In Rowley's words, "Unexpectedly we find Naomi possessed of land, and we are left to guess how it came into her possession, and what had happened to it during the years of her sojourn in Moab. . . . That the story of Ruth's marriage must be linked with the question of levirate marriage is generally agreed, though this is clearly not strictly a case of levirate marriage, since Boaz is not a brother-in-law or levir."[32]

It is to these two basic problems that we should like to address ourselves: the nature of the transaction involving Boaz and his unnamed kinsman, and the role of Naomi in these negotiations.

Undoubtedly, many scholars and probably most readers have linked the events in Ruth, Chapter 4, to the levirate, regarding it as a rather unorthodox instance of the rite. When, however, the details of Ruth are compared with the biblical law in Deut 25: 5–10 and with other pertinent data, it becomes clear that there is virtually no similarity between them.

In Deuteronomy, the rite is obligatory upon "brothers dwelling together." Here, both Boaz and his kinsman are such distant relatives that the possibility of the levirate does not occur to Naomi, even in the extremity in which she finds herself upon her return from Moab.

In Deuteronomy, the emphasis is upon "perpetuating the name of the dead man in Israel" by the birth of a son to his widow, and there is no reference to the transfer of property. In Ruth, the transaction revolves basically around the "redemption" of property, while the concomitant marriage and the support of Ruth and her future offspring are secondary consider-

,ations. Nor can this be dismissed as part of Boaz's strategy vis-à-vis the kinsman. For even in Boaz's official avowal of his acceptance of the obligation, the property transaction is primary, and the marriage to Ruth is secondary:

> Then Boaz said to the elders and all the people, "You are witnesses this day that I have bought from the hand of Naomi all that belonged to Elimelech and all that belonged to Chilion and to Mahlon. Also Ruth the Moabitess, the widow of Mahlon, I have bought to be my wife, to perpetuate the name of the dead in his inheritance, that the name of the dead may not be cut off from among his brethren and from the gate of his native place. You are witnesses this day" (4: 9-10)

In Deuteronomy there is a clear stigma attaching to the brother who does not fulfill his duty as a *levir*. The elders therefore seek to persuade the recalcitrant brother-in-law (vs 8). If they fail, the widow "pulls his sandal off his foot and spits in his face" (vs 9). His family is henceforth called "the household of the cast-off sandal" (vs 10). In Ruth, we have a straightforward business transaction without the shadow of any discredit falling upon the kinsman when he declines to participate.

"The pulling off of the sandal" in Deuteronomy (*wtḥlṣ n'lw*) and "the drawing off of the sandal" in Ruth (*šlp 'yš n'lw wntn lr'hw*) (4: 7), which seems at first glance to represent an identical act, are totally different in both instances.

First, a different verb is used in each instance: *ḥalaṣ* and *šalaph*. Technical terms are not used indiscriminately.

Second, in Deuteronomy, it is the widow who draws off the shoe of her recusant brother-in-law. In Ruth, it is the unwilling kinsman who draws off his own shoe and transfers it to his fellow relative who does undertake the obligation.

Third, in Deuteronomy, the widow's removal of her brother-in-law's shoe is a symbolic representation of the cutting of the link binding her to him. On the other hand, in Ruth, the act of removing one's own shoe is a general procedure, commerical in character, as is clearly indicated: "Now this was the custom in former times in Israel concerning redeeming and exchanging: to confirm a transaction, the one drew off his sandal and gave it to the other, and this was the manner of attesting in Israel" (4: 7). Evidence from such varied cultures as those of India,[33] Egypt[34] and the Nuzi texts,[35] as well as the biblical passages, Ps 60: 10; 108: 10, demonstrate that the interpretation given in Ruth is valid. The shoe symbolizes power and authority, and its use in a transaction marks the transfer of some right and obligation from one party to another.[36]

Fourth, in Deuteronomy, the woman plays a central role in the rite. In Ruth, there is no evidence that Naomi or Ruth was present at all. In fact, the reference to them in third person suggests that they are absent; they surely do not participate in the proceedings.

Fifth, that we are not dealing with the levirate, even in its broadest sense, in Ruth is clear from Boaz's statement in 3: 10: "May you be blessed by the Lord, my daughter; you have made this last kindness greater than the first, in that you have not gone after young men, whether poor or rich." In the levirate, the obligation falls upon the male relative, primarily the brother, and the woman has no freedom of choice whatsoever. Here, Boaz expresses his gratitude to Ruth for preferring him to younger and presumably more attractive swains whom she might very well have married.

Finally, these far-reaching differences between the levirate in Deuteronomy and the transaction described in Ruth become even more impressive when we seek to relate the latter to the origin and purpose of the levirate in general and to its history in Israel in particular. As is well known, the levirate is one of the most widely diffused aspects of marriage custom in primitive and ancient society, one that is to be met with in Indo-European, Semitic, and Melanesian culture areas.[37] Anthropologists have suggested that it is a survival of polyandry or that it is a consequence of ancestor worship. These factors may have played a part in the levirate in other cultures, but there is not the slightest evidence for these elements as factors in Israel.

It is possible that in some societies the levirate rite may have reflected the concept of the woman as being part of the family property, so that she is inherited by the dead man's kinsman along with his estate. This is emphatically not the case in Israel. The active role played by the woman in the levirate in Deut 25 militates against this view of the woman as a passive chattel being passed from hand to hand. The only reason for the rite assigned in Deuteronomy is "to perpetuate his brother's name in Israel" (Deut 25: 7). On the other hand, it is noteworthy that the child born to Ruth, Obed, is called the son of Boaz (4: 21) and not of Mahlon, Ruth's first husband.

There is one more general consideration that supports these arguments against identifying the transaction in Ruth with the levirate. Contemporary scholarship has legitimately veered away from postulating unilinear lines of evolution in the history of human culture and institutions. In the case of the levirate in Israel, however, a clear process of development can be traced from our earliest biblical sources to the post-talmudic period, each step being marked by a consistent tendency to contract the rite and limit its exercise until it is virtually eliminated.

The first, and indeed the only, instance in the biblical narrative of the levirate is the highly unconventional encounter of Tamar and Judah (Gen

38). The narrative, which is assigned by Higher Criticism to the J Source, and is generally dated in the ninth or eighth century B.C.E., clearly reflects a very ancient tradition. When Tamar is twice widowed of Judah's sons, Er and Onan, Judah refrains from giving his third son, Shelah, to her in marriage. Tamar then decides upon extreme measures. Disguising herself as a harlot, she waits upon the highway, encounters Judah, and becomes pregnant by him. When her pregnancy is revealed some three months later, Judah is prepared to have her publicly burned for her sin. However, she discreetly lets Judah know that he is the father of her child, to which Judah responds: "She is more righteous than I, inasmuch as I did not give her to my son Shelah" (Gen 38: 26).

There are two features in this familiar story that need to be underscored:

First, the rite of the levirate is here not limited to brothers, but extends to other kinsmen, including a father-in-law. Were this not the case, Perez and Zerah, the twins that are born her, would have been the illegitimate offspring of an incestuous union and would have been excluded from "the community of JHWH" (Deut 23: 3), instead of being honored eponymous heads of Judahite clans (1 Chron 2: 4 ff; 4: 1; 9: 4; 27: 3; Neh 11: 4 ff; Num 26: 20; Josh 7: 1; 18: 24; 22: 20). In the Middle Assyrian Laws (sec. 33), the marriage of a childless widow to her father-in-law is explicitly permitted. The extant tablets date from Tiglath Pileser I (twelfth century B.C.E.), but the laws may go back to the patriarchal period (fifteenth century B.C.E.). It is a reasonable inference that the obligation first fell upon a brother, but the lacuna in the text makes this less than certain.[38] In the Hittite Laws (sec. 193), the obligation to marry the dead man's widow falls successively upon his brother, his father, and his nephew.[39]

Second, the fulfillment of the levirate rite is obligatory, and brooks of no exception. Hence, Judah's failure to have Shelâh marry Tamar justifies Tamar's extreme measures, even if it includes an act of public immorality and sexual license which would normally be stigmatized as incest (Lev 18: 15; 20: 12). That marrying the widow is an obligation is clear in the Hittite Laws and is apparently the case also in the Middle Assyrian Laws.

The next stage of the levirate in Israel that we are able to document from our limited sources is described in Deut 25. Deuteronomy is generally dated shortly before the discovery of the Book of the Covenant in the Temple during the eighteenth year of Josiah (2 Kings 22), in the year 621.[40]

In Deuteronomy, the rite has now been considerably constricted.[41] It is now limited to "brothers dwelling together," with no hint that the obligation also falls upon other, more distant relatives. Moreover, even for the brothers, *yibbum* no longer is obligatory, though it is clearly the preferred procedure. A brother may avoid the duty, if he is willing to be exposed to a measure of public indignity and have his family carry some stigma, the severity of which we cannot judge.

The next stage in the history of the rite may be documented in Leviticus in the Holiness Code, usually assigned to the sixth century B.C.E. It takes the form of the total prohibition of the marriage of a woman to her brother-in-law (Lev 18: 16; 20: 21).

This thoroughgoing contradiction between Leviticus and Deuteronomy did not escape the vigilant eyes of the talmudic rabbis. The theological problem they solved by declaring that both ordinances were revealed simultaneously: *'rwt 'št 'ḥyk l' tglh* "the nakedness of your brother's wife you shall not uncover" (Lev 18:16) and *ybmh yb' 'lyh* "her brother-in-law shall come in to her" (Deut 25: 5) were both pronounced in one divine utterance *bdbwr 'ḥd n'mr* (*Palestinian Talmud, Nedarim*, Ch 3, 5). The legal antinomy they met by establishing the prohibition in Leviticus as the general principle, applicable during the brother's lifetime, and by declaring the levirate to be the one specific exception, applicable only when a man leaves a childless widow after his death. The Samaritans[42] and the early Qaraite authorities[43] solved the contradiction by ordaining (and permitting) the levirate only in the case of a *betrothed* woman whose husband had died, but forbidding the rite to a *married* woman. Thus, they avoided the possibility of a violation of Lev 18: 16. In the Laws of Manu, the *levir* was permitted to approach the childless widow only once, until a child was born—a different practice for meeting the same dilemma.[44]

It may be, as many scholars have maintained, that the talmudic reconciliation of both passages is in conformity with the original intent of the law and that the two passages were not opposed to each other. On the other hand, the resolution may represent a reasoned effort by the Rabbis at harmonizing two originally distinct and contradictory biblical laws which they regarded as equally binding.

A striking example of this harmonizing procedure is to be found with regard to the biblical laws of the tithe. In Num 18: 21–24, the tithe is a tax imposed upon the Israelite farmer for the exclusive benefit of the Levite. In Deut 14: 22–27, the tithe was to be spent by the farmer upon himself and his family, "in the place which God would choose to settle his name upon" (14: 14); only on the third year was the tithe to be left "at the gate," so that the landless Levite as well as the stranger, the orphan, and the widow might eat and be satisfied (Deut 14: 28–29). The clear-cut contradiction between Numbers and Deuteronomy was resolved by the rabbis through the creation of a complex system of double tithes.[45] The Jewish farmer was required to set aside two tithes each year: during the first, second, fourth, and fifth years of the sabbatical cycle, *ma'ăsēr rišōn* "the first tithe" went to the Levites and *ma'āsēr šēnī* "the second tithe" was to be consumed by the farmer and his family in Jerusalem. In the third and sixth years of the sabbatical cycle, *ma'āsēr rišōn* still went to the Levites and *ma'āsēr 'ānī* "the tithe of the poor" was to be made available to the needy.

To revert to the levirate, if the prohibitions in Leviticus are regarded as overriding the Deuteronomic levirate law, there is a clear and direct line of development of the rite from the ineluctable obligation in Genesis, through the preferred procedure in Deuteronomy, to its total prohibition in Leviticus. If, on the other hand, the prohibition in Leviticus is interpreted as being restricted to the lifetime of the brother, while the levirate remains operative after his death, the next stage in its history is to be sought in the post-biblical period.

In Rabbinic Judaism, the recognition of personal desires and the play of human likes and dislikes affecting both the brother-in-law and the widow increasingly came to the fore. The Mishnah declares: "*Yibbum* took precedence over *ḥaliṣah* in earlier times when men were concerned with fulfilling the Divine commandment. But now, that men are not concerned with fulfilling the Divine commandment, *ḥaliṣah* takes precedence over *yibbum*."[46] Undoubtedly, the rarity of polygamy, even in talmudic times, also militated strongly against the practice of *yibbum*, since most adult men were married.

All the resources of Rabbinic hermeneutics were mobilized to limit and, where possible, to prevent the consummation of the levirate.[47] On the basis of the phrase *ky yšbw 'ḥym yḥdw* (Deut 25: 5) "when brothers dwell together," the Talmud excludes half brothers on the mother's side as well as a younger brother born subsequent to the death of the widow's husband.[48] Even more revelatory of the Rabbinic attitude is the broad interpretation given the biblical phrase "*wbn 'yn lw*" (Deut 25: 8). Quite at variance with the general practice in Rabbinic exegesis, *bēn* is construed broadly to mean "child," and not merely "son," and the phrase understood "if he left no offspring." Hence, if the dead man has an illegitimate child or a daughter or a grandchild, the brother-in-law is forbidden to marry the widow.[49] Similarly, the LXX renders *bēn* in Deut 25 by *sperma*, "seed," thus encompassing both male and female offspring and limiting the rite to a totally childless widow. The LXX rendering demonstrates that this restrictive process is substantially older than the later Mishnaic limitation.

In the tenth century, the *taqqānāh* of Rabbi Gershom Ben Judah of Mainz (born 960) and his synod forbade polygamy for European Jewry, so that henceforth *ḥaliṣah* became the only permissible mode of procedure in Western countries. *Yibbum* continued to be permissible only in Muslim countries, where polygamy was not prohibited.[50]

In sum, it is clear that the transaction in Ruth cannot be integrated into any stage of the history of the levirate in Israel. We have already noted above the substantial discrepancies between the transaction of Ruth and the law in Deuteronomy. The task becomes totally impossible in the post-Exilic period, when the practice of the levirate was increasingly restricted both by law and by custom. We conclude that the marriage of Ruth to a distant kinsman cannot be regarded as an instance of *yibbum*.

THE REDEMPTION OF THE LAND

It is true that as a result of the transaction in the closing chapter of the book, Ruth is married to Boaz, and that this goal undoubtedly was uppermost in his mind. But the negotiations themselves revolve around property which belonged to Elimelech, the acquisition of which by a kinsman (*ge'ūlāh*) would entail support for the destitute feminine members of his family—his widow Naomi, and her nubile daughter-in-law Ruth.

This redemption of land was of course only one of the functions of the *gō'ēl*. The execution of blood vengeance on behalf of a murdered member of the family or clan (Num. 35: 9 ff; Deut 19: 1 ff) had been progressively restricted by the establishment of the cities of refuge. This process of attrition of the blood-avenging function was undoubtedly accelerated by the establishment of the Hebrew monarchy with its own organs of justice. What remained for the *gō'ēl* was the more pacific duty of preventing the alienation of land from the family. This function survived longer, since it did not compete with the structure of government. Yet, it too ultimately disappeared with the erosion of tribal distinctions and the later weakening of group solidarity. This process went hand in hand with the emergence of a new sense of individualism in the closing days of the Monarchy and in the Exilic and post-Exilic periods.

When the institution of land redemption was in force, a man suffering economic distress had four courses of action open to him:

First, he might seek out a kinsman and ask him to buy his landholdings directly from him, thus preventing its alienation from the family. He stood a better chance of repossessing it later if it was in the hands of a relation. Second, he might sell the land to an outsider and later appeal to a kinsman to "redeem" it by repurchase. Third, he might sell the land and later "redeem" the land from its alien owner himself. Fourth, if none of these methods was available to him, the impoverished seller could wait until the Jubilee Year, and it would revert to him without payment.

The second precedure is described in Lev 25: 25: "If your brother becomes poor, and sells part of his property, then his next of kin shall come and redeem what his brother has sold." The third procedure is described in Lev 25: 26–27: "If a man has no one to redeem it, and then himself becomes prosperous and finds sufficient means to redeem it, let him reckon the years since he sold it and pay back the overpayment to the man to whom he sold it; and he shall return to his property." The fourth possibility is set forth in Lev 25: 28: "But if he has not sufficient means to get it back for himself, then what he sold shall remain in the hands of him who bought it until the Year of Jubilee. In the Jubilee it shall be released, and he shall return to his property."

The extent to which these regulations were actually operative in character is not our present concern. In this connection, it should be noted that the Edict of *Ammisaduqa* and other Mesopotamian sources concerning the remission of debts, the freeing of slaves, and the reversion of landholdings suggest that the biblical laws may not have been merely utopian.[51]

It should be noted that only the last three procedures, all set forth in the Holiness Code in Leviticus, are, properly speaking, instances of redemption, that is to say, the restoration to its original owner of land sold to an outsider. The first procedure, which does not involve either the removal of the land from the possession of an alien purchaser or its restoration to its original owner, is not an instance of redemption, and is therefore not included in the laws of *ge'ulah* in Leviticus.

An examination of the biblical root *gā'al* makes it clear that its basic meaning is "the restoration of an object to its primal condition."[52] In the ordinances of the Jubilee (Lev 25), as has been noted, *ge'ūlāh* represents the process of restoration to the *status quo ante.* Since a kinsman was charged with this obligation, the participle *gō'ēl* develops the secondary meaning of "relative" pure and simple (Ruth 2: 20; 3: 9, 12) and is a synonym for *mōda'* (2: 1), and the verb gets the meaning "act the kinsman's role" (3: 13).

The root *gā'al* is frequently associated with the Exodus from Egypt (Ex 6: 6; 15: 13; Ps 75: 2: 77: 16: 78: 35; 106: 10), representing the return of Israel to its earlier condition of liberty. Deutero-Isaiah uses the root to describe Israel's restoration from Exile (Is 43: 1; 44; 23: 48: 20; 52: 9). It is applied to the promise of God to redeem man from death by restoring him to the status of the living (Hos 13: 14; Ps 103: 4; Lam 3: 58).

When Job curses the day of his birth (Job 3: 5), he prays: *yg'lhw ḥšk wṣlmwt,* "May darkness and gloom redeem it." There is more than a trace of irony in Job's use of the verb "redeem"; he is referring to the recapture of the day by the primordial darkness and chaos out of which the light emerged at Creation. Similarly, the *gō'ēl haddām,* "blood avenger" (Num 35; Josh 20: 3, 5; Deut 19: 8, 12; 2 Sam 14: 11), redresses the cosmic balance upset by the pouring out of innocent blood.

96

In Job's famous affirmation of faith *w'ny yd'ty g'ly ḥy*, "I know that my *Gō'ēl* lives," both nuances are to be found. Earlier he had wished that his cause could be adjudicated by an impartial arbiter (*mōkhiaḥ*, 9: 33). He then moves forward to the conviction that the witness prepared to testify on his behalf (*'ēdh, sahadh*, 16: 19) is already on hand in the heavens. In his crescendo of faith, Job now declares that he has more than an arbiter or even a witness—he has a *gō'ēl*. God is his kinsman who will defend him against injustice; he is his redeemer who will restore him to his earlier, far happier state.

The first of the four procedures outlined above is documented in our biblical sources as well, in Jer 32: 8 ff. It is clear that the transaction described in Jeremiah is not an example of land redemption, but rather of land purchase by a kinsman to keep the land of a distressed relative from being sold to an outsider. The prophet is visited by his cousin Hanamel, who says to him: *qnh n' 't śdy 'šr b'ntwt ky lk mšpṭ hg'wlh lqnwt*, "Buy for yourself my field that is in Anathoth, because the obligation-right of redemption by purchase is yours." Or, more fully in vs 8, *ky lk mšpṭ hyrsh wmšpṭ hg'wlh*, "for the right of inheritance and the obligation of redemption is yours." As a kinsman, Jeremiah has the obligation to redeem the land if it is being sold to an alien, and he has the right of inheritance after Hanamel's death. As the ensuing narrative makes clear, Jeremiah does not "redeem" the land from an outsider; he purchases it directly from Hanamel, pays him for it, and prepares the papers attesting to the sale. He does not return the field to Hanamel, which would have been the case had Jeremiah purchased it from an "outside" buyer. The term used throughout is *qānāh: qnh lk* (vs 8), *spr hmqnh* (22: 11, 12, 14). The prophet's purpose is clearly indicated in vs 15: *'wd yqnw btym wśdwt wkrmym b'rṣ hz't*, "Houses, fields, and vineyards will yet be sold in this land." The Jeremiah incident is a bona fide example of the first procedure open to a farmer threatened with loss of his land to an outsider—its sale to a kinsman.

The situation in Ruth is completely different. When Naomi and Ruth return from the fields of Moab, they are completely destitute, and therefore Ruth goes out into the fields to glean with the poor. There is not the slightest indication that Naomi possesses any land, fertile or otherwise, available for sale from the past or that she has acquired any before or since her return, as Rowley seems to imply in his statement, "Then unexpectedly we find Naomi possessed of land, and we are left to guess how it came into her possession, and what had happened to it during the years of her sojourn in Moab."[53] Rowley has evidently overlooked the clear statement that the land had belonged to Elimelech (4: 3) and his sons (4: 9). It has also been proposed that Naomi was merely the executor or the trustee for the successors to the legal heirs.[54] The idea has been advanced that Naomi had property from her own family, which Elimelech had administered during his lifetime.[55] Another suggestion is that Elimelech had willed Naomi a life contract in the property.[56] But if Naomi were a landowner, or even the administrator of land, no matter what the circumstances, she would be guilty of greed and deception in sending her foreign-born daughter-in-law to glean in the fields among the poor. To turn the force of this argument, it has been suggested that the property was too slight to support Naomi and Ruth,[57] or that Naomi was unaware that she had property,[58] but neither suggestion finds the slightest support either in the letter or in the spirit of the book— Naomi is totally destitute.

Moreover, as our analysis of the root makes clear, the term *gā'al* (4: 6) could not properly be applied to the purchase of land *from Naomi* by her kinsman. Nor, indeed, is there any indication that she receives any money in the transaction or even that she is present at the proceedings.

The crucial verse 4: 3: *ḥlqt hśdh 'šr l'ḥynw l'lymlk mkrh n'my hšbh mśdh mw'b* is rendered by LXX: "And Boaz said to the kinsman: 'The portion of the field which was our brother Elimelech's which was given to Naomi [*ē dedotai noemin*] returning out of the land of Moab.'" This rendering seeks to achieve two purposes: if offers the "explanation" that Naomi received the land as a gift, and eliminates the difficulty of her "having sold" (*mkrh*) any land. However, LXX cannot possibly represent the original Hebrew. Aside from its complete graphic divergence from MT, the sentence in LXX is grammatically defective since it has no principal clause. It cannot therefore be described as a successful solution of the substantive difficulty. The LXX rendering is, in a word, a midrash. Peshitta translates the verse: "The portion of the field of our brother Elimelech, Naomi sold me." This preserves the perfect of the verb, to be sure, but gratuitously adds an all-important pronoun and omits the remainder of the verse. Even this radical procedure does not solve the difficulties either of the text or of the incident being narrated. For obviously at this point in the proceedings Boaz has bought nothing!

How is the perfect tense of *mkrh* to be construed? Many scholars vocalize it *mōkrāh*, but the change is unnecessary. We suggest that the perfect serves to affirm the act in the present, being similar in psychological motivation to the perfect of prophetic certitude.[59] The verb *mkrh* means "she is definitely selling" (cf 4: 5). Instances of this use of the perfect in a legal-commercial context occur in the transaction between Abraham and Ephron (Gen 23: 11): *hśdh ntty lk*; and 23: 13: *ntty ksp hśdh*.

I suggest that what Naomi is disposing of is the obligation-right to redeem the land which originally had belonged to her husband and her sons. Under the pressure of the famine which finally drove him and his family out of his native land, Elimelech would surely have disposed of all his holdings before leaving for Moab. Consequently, Naomi upon her return is completely without means. In view of the death of her two sons, she is the only living heir of Elimelech. As such, she has the right to redeem the alienated property of her husband by repurchasing it from its buyers. However, lacking any resources of her own, she is unable to do so. What she therefore does is to call upon her kinsman to "redeem" the land by repurchasing it from its present owners. At first, the unnamed kinsman is willing to expend some of his financial means on the redemption, because the cost will be balanced by the increased landholdings he will henceforth possess. But Boaz then informs him that the obligation will also include the marriage and support of Ruth, with the probability that she will bear children, who will then claim the land that had originally belonged to Elimelech. The kinsman will have expended some of his money, with no permanent addition to his land holdings. He now declares himself unable to proceed with the redemption, "lest he impair his own inheritance," which he is guarding for his children. The kinsman then removes his shoe in order to confirm his transference of this obligation-right to Boaz, the next of kin. Boaz willingly accepts these obligations both vis-à-vis Elimelech's former holdings as well as vis-à-vis Ruth, undertaking her support and that of the children that will be born to her as well as of Naomi, who is part of the household (4: 16).

In order to place the transaction in perspective, it is important to recognize that by the side of the official codified family laws laid down in the Pentateuch there was a body of customary law often quite different in spirit and substance. Evidence for this customary law, affecting the status and rights of women, is growing, and the subject deserves careful study and analysis.

Our extant biblical law codes give no indication that a woman possessed such legal rights as land redemption. But the point need not be labored that in ancient times, as in our own, codified law, particularly in such areas as the rights of women, lagged behind life and custom. According to the Book of the Covenant (Ex 21: 7–11), a woman was virtually rightless, being under the power of her father until her marriage and subsequently under the authority of her husband. Any vow she took could be abrogated by her father or her husband (Num 30: 6, 9). She had no rights of inheritance, since only sons shared in the estate of their father (Deut 21: 15 ff). If a betrothed girl was caught in adultery, her execution was mandatory, with no provision for forgiveness or reconciliation with her husband (Deut 22: 20 ff). Manifestly, the penalty for a married woman could be no less (Lev 20: 10).

99

The records of biblical life that have come down to us, however, disclose that, notwithstanding these legal liabilities, women were by no means chattels in the hands of the males but vital personalities to their own right. The gallery of sharply etched, powerful characters among the women includes Sarah and Rebecca, Rachel and Leah, Deborah and Abigail, Bath-Sheba and Esther. If nothing else, the ability to make family life a heaven or a hell, to which the Proverbist refers time and again (Prov 21: 9, 19; 25: 24; 27: 15), placed substantial power in women's hands. As the Rabbinic dictum puts it, "A woman carries her weapons in her own person" (*'sh kly zynh 'lyh*).[60]

Even in codified biblical law, a few breaches in the rightlessness of women are discernible. When Zelophehad died without male issue, his daughters were given the right to inherit from him, though, to be sure, a special Divine dispensation was required (Num 27: 1–11). A widow or a divorced woman could not easily be made totally subservient to her father again, as the law of oaths makes clear (Num 30: 10).

According to customary law, as distinguished from the official codes, women enjoyed a substantially higher status. The marital tragedy of Hosea, however interpreted, makes it clear that a woman guilty of adultery could be forgiven and restored to her husband's home (Hos 1, 2, 3, esp. 2: 16 ff; 3: 3). This attitude is entirely congruent with the fact that Hosea is the first figure in history to insist on a single standard of sexual morality for both sexes: "I will not punish your daughters when they play the harlot, nor your brides when they commit adultery; for the men themselves go aside with harlots, and sacrifice with cult prostitutes, and a people without understanding shall come to ruin" (Hos 4: 14).

The "woman of valor" in Proverbs, who undoubtedly belonged to the upper levels of society, engaged in buying and selling, and did not content herself with her household duties (Prov 31: 14). Job, after his restoration, gives his daughters an inheritance "among their brothers" (Job 42: 15). The Elephantine papyri document the elaborate business activities of the redoubtable, thrice-married property owner Mibtahiah, daughter of Mahseiah.[61]

It is one of the major achievements of talmudic law that it substantially extended the rights of women, particularly in the areas of marriage, divorce, and property.[62] The final step was taken in the post-talmudic era, when the synod of Rabbi Gershom of Mainz made the consent of the wife mandatory when the husband issued a divorce.[63]

The most radical extension of women's rights, the power to initiate a divorce, has not become normative in traditional Judaism, at least not yet. But there is mounting evidence that at various periods and in different com-

munities a woman was able to demand and receive a divorce when she found
her marriage intolerable. This right seems to have been widespread in the
Elephantine Jewish colony of the fifth century B.C.E.[64] It also held true
of Palestine in at least three different periods. This is clear from a second-
century text found in Muraba'at,[65] from the Palestinian Talmud a few
centuries later,[66] and from at least three documents in the Cairo Genizah,
dating from the tenth or eleventh century.[67] This virtual equalization of
the sexes with regard to divorce, which contravenes the clear intent of Deut
24: 1, was achieved either by a special prenuptial arrangement,[68] or by the
court's compelling the husband to issue the divorce,[69] or by the rabbis'
annulling the marriage retroactively by invoking their fundamental authority in domestic law.[70]

To revert to Ruth, it is reasonable to assume, on the basis of the data
adduced, that, in the late biblical period at least, when there were no male
survivors a woman would inherit from her husband and succeed to his
rights and privileges. Naomi inherited no land from her husband and sons—
only the right to redeem the family property that her husband had sold.
Because she is unable to exercise this right, in view of her poverty, she
transfers (*mkrh*) this obligation-right to her nearest kinsman. When he
declines, Boaz, a somewhat more distant relative, accepts (*qnty*) this obligation-right, which brings him Ruth as a wife. His subsequent redemption
of the land from the original purchaser from Elimelech, is not described
in the book, because it is Ruth who is the focus of interest.

The verbs *mākhar*, "sell," and *qānāh*, "buy," must therefore carry a
special nuance of their basic meaning "sell" and "buy." In our context,
mākhar means "to transfer the obligation-right of redemption" and *qānāh*
"to accept, acquire the obligation-right of redemption." It is this power
which the kinsman transmits to Boaz by taking off his sandal and giving
it to Boaz. The practice of a buyer's taking hold of some movable object
(*m'tall'lin*) like a cloth-band or kerchief to confirm the transfer of property
(*qabbalat qinyan*, lit. "the acceptance of ownership") is operative in Rabbinic law to the present day.[71]

This special usage of the verbs *mākhar* and *qānāh* cannot now, as far as
I know, be attested elsewhere in our extant sources. The fact is perhaps
explicable by the fact that we have very few descriptions of commercial
transactions in biblical times. However, partial analogies for this usage
may be found. The verb *mākhar* is used in a noncommercial context to
"hand over to enemies" (Deut 32: 30; Judg 2: 14; 3: 8, 4: 2, 9, 10; 7; 1
Sam 12: 9; Is 50: 1; Ezek 30: 12; Ps 44: 13), a sense which embodies the
nuance of "transfer," which we postulate for Ruth 4: 3. In Mishnaic Hebrew,
the *Qal* of *qānāh* means "acquire," and the *Hiphil, hiqnah* means "to cause

to acquire—empower to acquire." Thus, *'šh hqnw lw mn hšmym* (*B. Kethubot* 82a) "Heaven gave him the power to acquire a wife," *'yn 'dm mqnh dbr šl' b' l'wlm* (*B. Baba Metzia*) "A man cannot empower the sale of something not yet in existence." *lyhwh h'rṣ wmly'h 'l šm šqnh whqnh wšlyṭ b'ylmw* (*B. Roš Hašānāh* 31a) "The earth is the Lord's and its fullness—because He acquired it and empowered its inhabitants to take possession and He rules in His world."[72] The verb *mākhar* in Ruth is equivalent to the Mishnaic *hiqnāh* "cause, empower to buy." For this meaning, we may also note the Aramaic root *zbn*, which in the *Pe'al* means "buy" and in the *Pa'el* has a causative sense, "cause to buy, hence, sell."

What we have in Ruth is therefore a classic tale from the Silver Age of biblical literature that tells a moving story of a distant and idealized past. The transaction described is not an instance of the levirate, but a genuine example of the redemption of land, which had been sold under the stress of economic want to an outsider. The land is redeemed and restored to the family by a kinsman who finds his reward in the love and devotion of the destitute woman whom he has befriended and sheltered.

NOTES

[1] Cf *Midraš Ruth Rabbah* 2: 14: "This scroll is concerned neither with the laws of purity or impurity, of permitted or forbidden actions. Why, then, was it written? To teach you how great is the reward for the practice of loving-kindness." Cf also *Midraš Leviticus Rabbah* 34: 8.

[2] Cf Nelson Glueck's well-known study, first published in German in 1927, translated into English by A. Gottschalk under the title, *Hesed in the Bible* (Cincinnati, 1967).

[3] *Ḥesed* is used for "love" even in its transitory and superficial sense, as in Hos 6: 4: *mh' 'śh lk 'prym mh' 'śh lk yhwdh wḥsdkm k'nn bqr wkṭl mškym hlk*, "What shall I do with you, O Ephraim? What shall I do with you, O Judah? Seeing that your love is like a morning cloud, like the passing dew of the morning." For *w'kaṭṭal* in MT, read the construct *ûkṭal*. On *maškîm*, lit. "rising (time), morning," cf the usage in post-biblical Hebrew: M. Bikkurim 3: 2: *wlmškym hmmwnh 'wmr*, "In the morning the official says." This usage occurs also in *Seder Olam* (ed. Marx), p. 31, and *Damascus Scroll* (S. Schechter, *Zadokite Sect*, p. 10), and see R. Gordis in *Sepher Tur-Sinai* (Jerusalem, 5720-1960), p. 158.

[4] This tradition is found in the LXX and in the versions dependent upon it and is reflected in the talmudic statement: "Samuel wrote the book bearing his name, Judges and Ruth" (B. *Bathra*, 14b).

[5] Cf R. Gordis, "The Bible as a Cultural Monument" (in L. Finkelstein, *The Jews*, New York, 1949), p. 809, now in idem, *Poets, Prophets and Sages* (Bloomington, 1970, p. 34), and in *Koheleth: The Man and His World* (New York, 1955), p. 18 f.

[6] For an excellent recent treatment of the literary motifs in Ruth, cf D. F. Rauber, "Literary Values in the Bible: The Book of Ruth," in *JBL* 89 (1970), 27–37.

[7] So Berthold and Graetz, who are followed by Bertholet, Cornill, Meinhold, Hempel, and many moderns.

[8] Suggested as a possibility by H. H. Rowley, "The Marriage of Ruth" in *The Servant*

of the Lord and Other Essays on the O.T. (London, 1952), p. 164. This important paper, rich in bibliographical references, will henceforth be cited as RMR.

⁹ So S. R. Driver, A. Kahana (*Peruš Mada'i*), *ad loc.*

¹⁰ So S. R. Driver.

¹¹ S. J. J. Slotki in Soncino Bible, *Five Megillot* (London, 1946), p. 39a.

¹² So Humbert.

¹³ So Gunkel.

¹⁴ So Haller, *Die Fünf Megillot* (Tübingen, 1940), p. 2.

¹⁵ So Budde, Oettli.

¹⁶ Cf W. E. Staples in *AJSL* (1937), 147–57.

¹⁷ So R. H. Pfeiffer, *Introduction to the OT* (New York, 1941), p. 719; O. Eissfeldt, *The OT: An Introduction* (New York, 1965), p. 480 f.

¹⁸ See the useful conspectus of views in RMR, p. 164, n. 1, and the OT Introductions of Driver, Pfeiffer, and Eissfeldt.

¹⁹ Cf B. *Baba Batra*, 14b, cited in n. 4 above.

²⁰ So Keil, Wright, Albright, and Myers.

²¹ So Wright, Oettli, Driver, Fischer, Haller, and Kaufmann.

²² So Davidson, Reuss.

²³ So Ewald, Jepsen.

²⁴ So Wellhausen, Bertholet, Cornill, Steuernagel. The fourth century is preferred by Jouon, Meinhold, Sellin, Oesterley-Robinson, Eissfeldt, Pfeiffer.

²⁵ In his careful study of the language of our book, *The Linguistic and Literary Form of the Book of Ruth* (Leiden, 1955), pp. 8–32, Jacob M. Myers concludes that Ruth belongs to the period of the early Monarchy. He categorizes the language as belonging "to the same broad category as JE in the *Pentateuch, Joshua, Judges, Samuel* and *Kings*" (p. 32). Our reasons for being unable to accept this view are indicated in the body of this paper.

²⁶ Thus, by the side of the early *tštkryn* I Sam 1: 14, note the later *tthmqyn* Jer 31: 21, and *thylyn* Is 45: 10.

²⁷ On these forms, which occur not only as *Kethibh-Qere* readings but in the MT with no variants, and the implications of this fact for the Masorah, see Gordis, *The Biblical Text in the Making* (Philadelphia, 1937), pp. 101 ff; augmented edition (New York, 1971).

²⁸ Thus *rby sm'wn š'šh šlš 'srh šnh bm'rh*, "R. Simeon, who spent thirteen years in the cave" (*Midraš Tehillim* on Ps 17: 14) and often. On *'gwnh*, lit. "chained," the technical term for a deserted wife who has not received a religious divorce (*gēt*) from her husband, cf B. *Gittin* and often.

²⁹ In spite of this usage and other linguistic phenomena adduced in the text, W. F. Albright declares "Neither vocabulary nor syntax suggests any Aramaic influence in the writer's [sc. of Ruth] Hebrew" (in his review of R. H. Pfeiffer's *Introduction to the Old Testament* in *JBL*, 61 [1942], 124). Even if Aramaic influence be discounted in this instance, the well-attested tendency of *tertiae Aleph* forms to become *tertiae Yod* in "late" OT and Middle Hebrew (cf e.g., B. Margulis in *JBL* 89 [1970], 300, n. 14) would still point to a later rather than to an earlier date for Ruth. The current tendency to deny altogether the existence of Aramaisms in biblical Hebrew is an overreaction to the earlier propensity to exaggerate their extent. It has happened in the history of biblical scholarship more than once that the pendulum has swung from one to the other extreme. What is obviously needed is a balanced position. A fuller discussion of the tendency toward *tertiae Yod* forms instead of *tertiae Aleph* would also need to reckon with the problems of Biblical orthography and the evidence of Mishnaic Hebrew.

³⁰ See our discussion of the four categories of Aramaisms, real and alleged, in *The*

Book of God and Man: A Study of Job (Chicago, 1965), pp. 161–63, 334, and "On the Methodology of Biblical Exegesis" in *JQR* vol. 61, 1970, 93–118.

[31] Cf Rowley's summary of the various views in "The Chronological Order of Ezra and Nehemiah," *op. cit.*, pp. 131–59.

[32] See RMR, p. 163.

[33] Cf R. T. H. Griffith, *The Ramayan of Valmiki* (1915), p. 265 f.

[34] Cf J. Scheftelowitz, *Archiv für Religionswissenschaft* 18 (1915), 255.

[35] Cf E. R. Lacheman in *JBL* 56 (1937), 53 ff; E. A. Speiser, in *BASOR* 77 (1940), 15 ff, who adduces Akkadian evidence and argues for the use of the shoe to validate special transactions. It may be added that the reason for the use of the shoe to confirm a transfer of property was probably a practical one. In ancient society, men possessed few movable objects that could be used to symbolize a transaction. The only article of major clothing was the garment worn by day and used as a covering by night (Ex 22: 25–27; Deut 24: 11), which could obviously not be removed in public. Hence, the sandal was used. In Rabbinic Judaism, acquisition was validated by taking hold of a scarf (*qinyān 'agabh sūdār*). This practice is still in vogue, in the validation of the Kethubbah "marriage contract" at weddings and at *mᵉkhirat ḥāmeṣ*, the fictive "sale of leaven" before Passover, the possession of which is forbidden to householders by Rabbinic law.

[36] On the other hand, the passage in Amos 2: 6: *'l-mkrm bksp ṣdyq w'bywn b'bwr n'lym* (see also 8: 6) which is often cited in this connection (so Speiser, *loc. cit.*) is not an instance of this usage. Note that the *na'alāyim* are not the instruments but the object of the evildoers' activity. It is important to note: a) the parallelism in Amos, b) the textual evidence from 1 Sam 12: 3: *w''lm 'yny bw* (cf LXX, which read *wn'lym 'nu by*), c) the Hebrew text of Ben Sira 46: 19 *kpr wn'alm* (cf *Pešitta*, "ransom and bribe" as well as d) the use of the noun *n'lmym* in the Qumran Thanksgiving Scrolls (Tablet XIII, 1.3) and Ps 26: 4; on the basis of this evidence, we have postulated a noun *na'ᵃlām*, "bribe," lit. "covering, hiding material," in all these passages. In Amos 3: 6; 8: 6, read: *'l-mkrm bksp ṣdyq w'bywn b'bwr n'lm*. Note the parallel with *ksp*. In 1 Sam 12: 3, read: *wmyd my lqhty kpr wn'lm*. In Ben Sira, read similarly: *kpr wn'lm*. See R. Gordis, "Na'alam and Other Observations on the Ain Feshka Scrolls," in *JNES* 19 (1950), 44 ff. In Ps 26: 4 and in the Thanksgiving Scrolls, the plural *n'lmym* is a synecdoche for "men of bribes"; cf the parallelism with *mty šw'*. The form *na'ᵃlām* is a *Nun*-preformative noun, derived from the *Niphal*. On this formation, cf the biblical form *naptūl* (Gen 30: 8) and see Ges.-Kautzsch, *Grammatik*, 28 ed. sec. 85, par. 49. The form is more common in Mishnaic Hebrew, as, e.g., *naḥtôm*, "baker" (B. *Baba Batra* 20b.), *nḥšwl*, "crushing wind" (B. *Baba Kamma* 116b.), cf also *nsph*, *nysoq*, *ndbkh*, and see M. H. Segal, *Diqduq Lešon Hamišnah* (Tel Aviv, 5696–1936), sec. 129. The existence of feminine *Nun*-preformative nouns in Mishnaic Hebrew such as *nibrešet* and *nibrekhet* suggests that in Ps 37: 38 *nkrth* may also be a noun meaning "destruction," similarly in Prov 15: 6 *wbtbu't rš' n'krt* "but for the income of the wicked, there is destruction" (note the Beth).

[37] On the levirate in general, cf E. Westermarck, *The History of Human Marriage* (5th ed., New York, 1922), vol. 3, pp. 207–20, 261–63. On the biblical institution, cf J. G. Frazer, *Folklore in the OT*, vol. 2, pp. 266–303; D. Jacobson, *The Social Background of the OT* (Cincinnati, 1942), pp. 290 ff; T. H. Gaster, *Myth, Legend, and Custom in OT* (New York, 1969), pp. 447 ff. For the levirate in post-biblical Judaism, cf L. M. Epstein, *Marriage Laws in the Bible and the Talmud*, (Cambridge, 1942).

[38] Cf T. J. Meek in *ANET*, p. 182, who supplies in brackets the crucial words, reading: "[If] she has no [son, her father-in-law shall marry her to the son] of his choice . . . or, if he wishes, he may give her to her father-in-law."

[39] Cf A. Goetze in *ANET* p. 196b; E. Neufeld, *The Hittite Laws* (London, 1951), p. 55. It is worth noting that there is no explicit reference here to the widow's childlessness. This is, however, probably the circumstance to which the levirate applied. On the other hand, it is possible that the levirate marriage in these Middle-East cultures was concerned not with "preserving the name of the dead man" but with economic factors, either providing for the widow's maintenance or, as would be more likely, with retaining her as property within the circle of the family. See E. M. MacDonald, *The Position of Women as Reflected in Semitic Codes of Law* (Toronto, 1931), pp. 45, 63 ff, who stresses the element of property in the levirate, as do other writers.

[40] The considerably earlier date we assign to the composition of Deuteronomy (the evidence for which we hope to present shortly) does not affect the development of the levirate discussed in the text. The later date proposed by some scholars would not militate against the relative antiquity of the rite. See also n. 41.

[41] Thus, Rowley correctly observes that Deuteronomy "reflects a limitation of something that was once wider in Israel, as is clear from the other duties of the *gō'ēl*" (RMR, p. 170).

[42] The Talmud (B. *Kiddušin*, 7b; B. *Yebamot*, 6: 1) explains that the Samaritans arrived at their conclusion by treating *ḥḥwṣh* in *l' thyh 'št-hmt ḥḥwṣh l'yš zr* (Deut 25: 5) as an adjective modifying *'št*: "hence a woman outside, not yet living in his house, i.e., a betrothed woman." They then interpret the passage to mean that this category of woman, i.e. a betrothed woman, may not be married to a stranger (but must marry her brother-in-law), but a woman "inside," living in his house, i.e., a married woman, may be taken by a stranger (and must not marry her brother-in-law). The Samaritan Targum renders *ḥḥwṣh* as *br'yth* "one outside." The Talmud interprets *ḥḥwṣh* similarly, as a reference to a betrothed woman. It therefore requires *yibbum*, *both* for an engaged and for a married woman (*B. Yeb.* 13b).

[43] So Benjamin ben Meshe of Nehawend (ca 830), Joseph ben Jacob Qirqisani (tenth century), and Elijah Bashyazi (ca 1420). Later Qaraite practice permitted the levirate only to cousins of the dead husband. Other authorities forbade the rite, even in the case of a betrothed woman. For a succinct summary of Samaritan and Qaraite views, see J. D. Eisenstein, *Osar Yisrael*, vol. 5, p. 47.

[44] Cf W. Max Müller, *The Sacred Books of the East* (1886), vol. 25, p. 335.

[45] Cf the Mishnah tractates *Ma'aserōt* and *Ma'asēr Šēni* for the detailed provisions.

[46] M. *Bekhorot* 1: 7.

[47] The great variety of views in the Talmud cannot be set forth here. For a conspectus of these views, associated with the biblical text, cf Barukh Halevi Epstein, *Torah Temimah*, (New York, 1922), vol. 5, pp. 384–404. One classic statement cited in the Babylonian and the Palestinian Talmud will suffice: (*Tosefta, Yebamot*, Ch 6; B. *Yebamot* 39b; 109a; J. *Yebamot* 13: 2). "Abba Saul says: He who marries his sister-in-law for the sake of her beauty or because of desire, or any other ulterior motive [*Tosefta*—for the sake of property], is guilty of incest and I am inclined to regard the offspring as illegitimate. The Sages say, "The Biblical statement ' her brother-in-law shall come into her' means no matter what the circumstances or the motive."

[48] B. *Baba Batra*, 109b.

[49] Cf Barukh Halevi Epstein, *op. cit.* p. 386, n. 52, who calls attention to this unusually broad interpretation of *bēn*.

[50] Levirate marriage is forbidden by the Franco-German school of Tosafists like Rabbi Jacob ben Meir Tam (1100–1171), the grandson of Rashi (1040–1105). The levirate is permitted by Rabbi Isaac ben Jacob Al-Fasi of North Africa (1013–1103), Maimonides

(1135–1204), and Rabbi Asher ben Jehiel (1250–1328), who lived in an Islamic environment.

51 For the fullest text of the *Edict of Ammisaduqa* (seventeenth century B.C.E.), cf J. J. Finkelstein in *ANET*, Supplement, (Princeton, 1969), pp. 526–28. This is the most extensive document extant dealing with the proclamation of an act of "equity" (Sumerian *nig. si. sa.*, Akkadian *mišarum*) by a Babylonian king, a practice in vogue at the accession of a king to the throne and on succeeding intervals of seven or more years. Ammisaduqa, the tenth ruler of the Hammurabi dynasty, ruled from 1641 to 1626 B.C.E. Finkelstein, who cites other, less complete references to this usage in Near Eastern texts, speaks of *mišarum* as encompassing "the remission of debts and the reversion of land-holdings to their original owners" (*op. cit.*, p. 526a). It may be noted that the Edict of Ammisaduqa is very detailed only with regard to the remission of debts, but is much less explicit on the freeing of those sold into slavery for debt. I am unable to find any reference in the Edict to the restoration of land to the original owner. Nor is there an enunciation of any cosmic religious principle, such as is set forth in Lev 25: 23.

It is noteworthy that the differences in the degree of attention given in Mesopotamia to the various features of the *mišarum* have their parallel in biblical and post-biblical experience. The principle of the remission of debts (Deut 15: 1 ff) during "the year of release" was operative as late as the Second Temple Period. Its observance created grave economic problems in the more advanced, urbanized society which required access to credit. Hence, Hillel's *taqqānāh* of the *prosbūl* (first century C.E.), (M. *Shebiith* 10: 2, 3), which utilized a legal fiction to make it possible to collect unpaid debts after the *šᵉmittāh*. On the other hand, Rabbinic tradition declares that the biblical provision for the restoration of land in the Jubilee Year was not enforced after the early exile of the Trans-Jordanian tribes of Reuben, Gad, and half of Manasseh (*Sifra, Behar* II, 3) or thereafter, during the Second Temple (B. *Arakhin*, 32b.).

52 After the paper was completed, I was pleased to find that D. Daube, in *Studies in Biblical Law* (Cambridge, 1944; reprint edition New York, 1969), pp. 39–62, who treats the role of the *gᵓēl* in detail, presents a similar interpretation of the primary meaning of the root *gāᵓal*.

53 *Op. cit.*, p. 163.

54 So E. Neufeld, *Ancient Hebrew Marriage Laws* (London, 1944), pp. 240 f.

55 So J. A. Jepsen, *Theologische Studien und Kritiken*, 108 (1937–38) 419 ff; and W. Caspari, *Neue Kirchliche Zeitschrift*, 19, (1908) 115 ff.

56 So, apparently, Rowley, *op. cit.*

57 S. M. Burrows in *JBL* 59 (1940), 448.

58 So Haller, *ad loc.*

59 So also Haller. On this usage, cf S. R. Driver, *A Treatise in the Use of the Tenses in Hebrew* (Oxford, 1892), pp. 17 f, sec. 13 f.

60 B. *Yebamot* 115a.

61 See E. Sachau, *Aramäische Papyrus und Ostraka* (Leipzig, 1911) and A. Ungnad, *Aramäische Papyrus aus Elephantine* (Leipzig, 1911) for the texts discovered earlier; and for those found later, E. G. Kraeling, *The Brooklyn Museum Papyri* (New Haven, 1953). From the extensive literature we cite M. L. Margolis, *The Elephantine Documents* (*JQR*, 12 [1912], 419–43); and B. Porten, *Archives from Elephantine* (Berkeley and Los Angeles, 1960), who treats of Mibtahiah's life and career in pp. 235–63.

62 On the content and development of talmudic law with regard to women and the family, cf L. M. Epstein, *The Jewish Marriage Contract* (New York, 1927): *Marriage Laws in the Bible and the Talmud* (Cambridge, 1942); L. Finkelstein, *Akiba: Scholar,*

Saint, and Martyr (New York, 1936), L. Finkelstein, *The Pharisees*, 3d ed. (Philadelphia, 1962), and see vol. 2, p. 837, n. 52. For the post-talmudic period, cf. A. H. Freimann, *Seder Qiddušin Unesuin* (Heb) (Jerusalem, 5705 = 1945).

[63] Salo W. Baron, *A Social and Religious History of the Jews* (New York, 1958), vol. 6, pp. 135 f.

[64] Cf B. Porten, *op. cit.*, pp. 209 f, 261 f for the divorce formula in Elephantine and its relationship to other evidence for this practice.

[55] For this as yet unpublished document, see P. Benoit, J. T. Milik, R. de Vaux, *Discoveries in the Judean Desert II* (Oxford, 1961), p. 108.

[66] Cf J. *Ketubot* 30b, v, 8; also J. *Ketubot* 31c, VII, 6; and see L. M. Epstein *The Jewish Marriage Contract* (New York, 1927), pp. 197 ff.

[67] Cf the brief discussion of these texts and their implications in M. A. Friedman, *Bıtlul Hanesuʾin ʿal pi Baqqašat Haʾišah*, "The Termination of a Marriage on the Wife's Request," in *Haʾarets*, Oct. 1, 1968, p. 19, and his more extensive treatment of the subject in *PAAJR*, 1969, pp. 29–55.

[68] This was an optional procedure practiced in Palestine, according to the Palestinian Talmud.

[69] The formula used to validate the practice was: *kwpyn ʾwtw ʿd šyʾmr rwṣh ʾny*, "The husband is placed under duress until he says 'I am willing!'" (B. *Yebamot* 106a.)

[70] The far-reaching principle laid down in the Talmud is: *kl hmqdš ʾdʿtʾ drbnn mqdš*, "Whoever marries does so by the authority and consent of the Sages." (B. *Kethubot* 3a.)

[71] Cf n. 35 above.

[72] Cf Rashi *ad loc. klwmr qwng wmqnh*, "He acquires and transmits the right to it." Jastrow: "He gave His creatures possession of His world."

MIDRASH IN THE PROPHETS

I. Until quite recently, all students of Hebrew literature assumed a wide and impassable chasm between the Bible and the literary products of post-canonical Judaism. For reasons that need not concern us here, the Bible was looked upon as the culminating point in the spiritual history of Israel; all that came after was an inferior sequel. Vivid and forceful contrasts were drawn between the noble, free-flowing spirit of the Prophets and the confined, petty legalism of the Rabbis; between the great poetry of Israel's Golden Age and the unadorned prose or artificial poetry of later periods; between the classic purity of the language of the Bible and its degenerate offspring, that graceless, hybrid idiom known as Rabbinic Hebrew.

This attitude is now rapidly being out-moded. Deeper researches have laid bare the intimate and organic connection between "Hebraism" and "Judaism." We are now becoming increasingly aware that the same spirit animates both and that the difference are to be accounted for as the normal variations in the life-history of any organism. The germ of much that is characteristically "Rabbinic" is to be sought in the Bible. Conversely, the entire course and development of Biblical ideals and institutions must be studied in the Mishnic and post-Mishnic periods.

In this paper we seek to establish one more bond of union between Hebraism and normative Judaism. We hope to prove the existence of that most characteristic genre of the Rabbis—the

Midrash—in Biblical times and its utilization by the Prophets. From such a study we hope to gain more than merely a truer exegesis of several passages, important as that is. There will emerge another aspect of the spirit and literary structure of Prophecy, as well as a recognition of the essential truth of the Talmudic dictum that makes Prophet and Scribe two links in the same, unbroken chain of tradition.

II. The Midrashic form may be analyzed into two elements, one—legend—common to all peoples, the other, restricted almost entirely to Jewish literature. Legend is the result of two complementary impulses, a poetical and narrative fancy innate in man, and an equally fundamental curiosity. Primitive man seeks to account for his environment, the sun, the moon, the rainbow, and the storm, by producing nature myths. His interest in the traditions of his race leads him to fill in the many gaps in his knowledge, in the same manner. The stories of young Abraham in Terah's idol-shop, or Alfred the Great in the old woman's hut, or George Washington and the cherry-tree, bear witness to the wide prevalence of the "personality" legend.

Legend is, as we have said, common to all nations. In the case of the Jewish people, however, it was usually subjected to a reworking before it became a typical Midrash. When the folk-tale is linked up to a *Biblical verse* in some *homiletic* fashion and a *moral lesson* is drawn for the edification of the audience, we have a full-fledged Midrash. We may call the first the expansion-element; the second, the interpretation-element. It must be added that this analysis is not always applicable. In many instances, only the first element exists; this may be called the "incomplete" as against the "complete" type of Midrash.

III. The propensity to Midrash in the Old Testament has not been altogether unnoticed, especially in the case of the Book of Chronicles. If we except certain auxiliary sources which the Chronicler may have used,[1] the book may aptly be called a Midrash to Kings. The expansion-element is evident in the large amount of additional information supplied regarding the lives of

[1] Cf. Driver: *Intr. to Literature* of O. T., 12 ed. pp. 527—533.

the Davidic kings, the institution of the Levitical choruses, and
the Temple functionaries. Scarcely less apparent is the interpretation-element. The central purpose of the Chronicler is the glori-
fication of the Temple worship and its protectors, the kings of
Judah, and to this aim the entire history is subservient.

The Midrashic character of Chronicles has been recognized by
scholars for decades. Yet the existence of Midrashim in pre-exilic
Israel and its use by the Prophets have been altogether overlooked.

IV. The difficult twelfth chapter of Hosea is a case in point.
To follow the connection and meaning in all the details is almost
impossible.[2] Yet the drift of the passage is unmistakable. The
prophecy is a comparison between the life of Jacob and that of
his descendants, and an attempt to trace their propensities to sin
and wickedness in the life-history of their ancestor.[3] The Penta-
teuchal story of Jacob's life, while not necessarily laudatory, is
far from being unfavorable to the Patriarch. In its familiar version,
it could not serve Hosea's purpose. Boldly disregarding the conventional form, the prophet interprets it in a new and unfamiliar
light, so as to bring home a moral lesson to his audience—the exact
procedure of the Darshan (homilectic preacher) to-day.

The first fragment of the Midrash meets us in v. 4:

בבטן עקב את אחיו   ובאונו שרה את האלהים

That Hosea here implies a reproach is plain by the preceding verse:
וריב לד' עם יהודה לפקד על יעקב כדרכיו, as well as by his use
of the verb עקב, which, in the two other passages where it occurs
(Gen. 27 36; Jer. 9 3), always means "attack insidiously, over-
reach." In Genesis 25 26, Jacob's seizing of Esau's heel is described non-committally as וְיָדוֹ אֹחֶזֶת בַּעֲקָב אָחִיו, Hosea, however,
uses the verb עקב with its sinister implications, the same word
used by Esau in his wrath (Gen. 27 36) ויעקבני זה פעמים. The
verse ought therefore to be rendered:

---

[2] Cf. Harper's commentary in the *ICC* series, ad loc.

[3] Cf. Harper p. 379: "Jacob's supplanting of his brother in the womb before birth indicates that fatal characteristic of the nation, which, as exhibited
again and again in its history, has now reached the point at which punishment must be administered. This reference clearly carries with it reproach."

In the womb he overreached his brother, and in his prime[4] he contended with God.

Here we have the very essence of Midrash - what we have called the interpretation-element. In the verse following, we find the other characteristic of Midrash, the expansion-element:

v. 5   וישר אל מלאך ויכל   בכה ויתחנן לו
        בית אל ימצאנו   ושם ידבר עמנו

He strove with an angel and prevailed; he wept and made supplication
*   to him;*
At Bethel he would find him; and there he would speak with him.

In Genesis we are told that the angel asked: שלחני כי עלה השחר (32 27). We find no mention of his weeping or of any promise to meet Jacob at Bethel. These details are noteworthy examples of the expansion-element in its purity. The exact connection of the verses here becomes confused,[5] but we meet with another strand of the Jacob Midrash in v. 13:

ויברח יעקב שדה ארם ויעבד ישראל באשה ובאשה שמר

And Jacob fled to the field of Aram, and Israel served for a wife and for a wife he guarded (the flocks).

Here Jacob's serving Laban for Rachel, while not inherently sinful, is contrasted with the Lord's far more exalted action in taking Israel out of Egypt under the guidance of His prophet: ובנביא העלה ה' את ישראל ממצרים ובנביא נשמר. *But by a prophet did the Lord bring Israel out of Egypt, and by a prophet was he guarded.*

This is all that is extant of this Midrash. It is idle to speculate as to whether these are quotations from an independent work utilized by Hosea or merely a Midrashic expansion written by the prophet to suit his needs at the moment. Perhaps the seemingly pointless Midrash in v. 5 would seem to favor the former alternative. Yet it does seem clear that we have here a fragment of a much larger prophecy and its accompanying Midrash. Notwithstanding the difficulties with which Hosea is replete, and our

---

[4] Cf. Ehrlich, *Randglossen* ad. loc.
[5] Cf. Ehrlich ad loc. for an ingenious attempt to restore the connection.

chapter is no exception, we have succeeded in discovering both elements of the Midrashic form in the eighth pre-Christian century.

V. Another Midrashic allusion in the Prophets is to be found in Isa 30 26: ‏והיה אור הלבנה כאור החמה ואור החמה שבעתים כאור‎ ‏שבעת הימים‎. The phrase ‏כאור שבעת הימים‎ is lacking in LXX, and so scholars from Lowth downwards have excised it as a gloss.[6] Even those scholars who accepted the phrase as genuine generally overlooked the definite article before ‏ימים‎ and rendered "seven-fold, as the light of seven days."[7]

To the writer it would seem that we have here an allusion to an ancient Midrash. The Creation story in Genesis 1 speaks of the light as having been created on the first day, while the sun, moon, and stars were created on the fourth. What was this primal light that existed before the heavenly "lights" came into existence? Speculation was rife on this point in earliest times, for we meet the answer in varying form, but with unceasing persistence, in the Apocalyptic literature, in Philo, in the Talmud, the Midrashim, and the Liturgy.[8] The light that preceded the creation was a super-natural light of marvelous effulgence and power, which the Almighty hid (‏גנז‎) because he foresaw the sinfulness of later generations. We shall content ourselves with one typical quotation from B. Hagigah 12 a:

‏אור שברא הקדוש ברוך הוא ביום הראשון אדם צופה בו מסוף‎
‏העולם ועד סופו. כיון שנסתכל הקדוש ברוך הוא בדור המבול‎
‏ובדור הפלגה וראה שמעשיהם מקולקלים עמד וגנזו. ולמי גנזו.‎
‏לצדיקים לעתיד לבא.‎

"The light that the Holy One, Blessed be He, created on the first

[6] Wade, Ehrlich, and many others. Dillmann, Delitzsch recognize the *possibility* of its being original.

[7] So Vulgate, Ibn Ezra, Ottley. Kimhi, followed by Delitzsch, interprets "the light of the seven days (sc. of the week)," a rather inept figure. Maimonides (as quoted by Kimhi ad loc.) understood it as a reference to the seven days of the dedication of Solomon's Temple, though we are told that the festivities lasted fourteen days (I Kings 8 65).

[8] The references are given in detail in L. Ginzberg: *Legends of the Jews* vol. V., notes 19, 100.

day (was so bright) that a man could see from one end of the earth to the other. But when the Holy One beheld the generation of the Flood and the generation of the Dispersion, and saw that their deeds would be corrupt, He hid it; and that for the righteous in the world to come."

Our verse seems a clear reference to this preternatural light. The phrase in question should be rendered "the light of the sun shall be sevenfold, like the light of the Seven Days (of Creation)."[9] This obvious explanation is to be found in Genesis Rabba c. 3. It also lies at the basis of the prayer recited at the Sanctification of the Moon, where our verse is paraphrased thus: ואור החמה שבעתים כאור שבעת ימי בראשית.

The long chain of Midrash is thus re-enforced by another and most important link. In this detail as well, the Bible assumes its rightful place as the fountain-head of Jewish literature. These examples of Midrash by no means exhaust this literary form in the Bible, but they are of particular significance in illustrating once again the continuity of the Jewish spirit as manifested throughout history in Prophet, Scribe and Rabbi.

[9] Since writing the above, I have discovered this interpretation in the Hebrew commentary on Isaiah Or Bahir, by S. Berman, Vilna 1903.

PSALM 9–10 — A TEXTUAL AND
EXEGETICAL STUDY

In spite of the Masoretic division there is an old tradition which links Psalm 9 and 10 together as a literary unit,[1] as is the case with Ps. 42–43. The basis for this view is the existence of an alphabetic acrostic, which appears every second verse, as in Ps. 37, with Ps. 9 containing the first half of the letters and Psalm 10, the unmistakable remnants of the remainder.

In Psalm 9 the acrostic is tolerably well preserved, each letter from Aleph to Kaph being represented in order, with the exception of the verse for *Dalet*. The second, non-alphabetic verse for *Gimel* (after v. 6) and for *Yod* (after v. 11) is also lacking in MT, but these omissions may simply be cases of misplacement, for following upon the letter *He* (v. 7) we have four verses beginning with *Vav* (vv. 8–11). One of these is needed as the non-alphabetic pendant for *He* and two are required for the letter *Vav*, leaving one in excess. This may have been the original non-alphabetic pendant for *Gimel*. It would be fatuous to insist upon a given allocation of these verses, but v. 8 would follow well upon v. 6, as its pendant, v. 9 would be equally appropriate after v. 7, and vv. 10 and 11, which manifestly belong together, would constitute *Vav* and its pendant. Similarly, v. 21 is superfluous in the present arrangement; if placed after v. 18, it would be an excellent pendant for *Yod*; note the pronoun להם (v. 21) which would

---

[1] So LXX, Vulgate, Jerome, Bar Hebraeus.

104

114

have its antecedent in רשעים and שכחי אלהים (v. 18). With these minor adjustments, the acrostic would be as well preserved as Ps. 145, where also one letter only, the *Nun*, is omitted, or Psalm 37, which lacks only the pendant verses to *Dalet*, *Ayin*,[2] and *Koph*.[3]

The situation is quite otherwise with regard to Psalm 10. Here the *Lamed* appears (v. 1) and at the close, the four concluding letters, *Koph*, *Reš*, *Šin* and *Tav* (vv. 12, 14, 16, 18): The verses for *Mem*, *Nun*, *Samekh*, *Ayin*, *Pe* and *Ṣade* have been either lost or mutilated, so that they do not appear in MT. Normally, an acrostic helps to preserve a text, but not always, as the mutilated form of the acrostic hymn in Nahum chap. 1[4] and later examples in the Jewish liturgy demonstrate.[5] The imperfect state of preservation of our acrostic is reflected in the general condition of the text. While Psalm 9 offers relatively few problems to the exegete, Psalm 10 bristles with difficulties.

Largely because of the Masoretic division, some commentators have insisted that the two sections are unrelated, in spite of the dovetailing of the acrostic. Psalm 9, it is argued, is concerned with foreign enemies of the nation (vv. 6, 9,

[2] *Ayin* occurs in v. 28c, where לעולם נשמרו is an error through haplography of the original עולים לעולם נשמדו וזרע רשעים נכרת.

[3] Only one stich of the pendant is lacking, the other having been preserved in v. 34d.

[4] Cf. e. g. G. B. Gray, *The Forms of Hebrew Poetry* (New York, 1915) and see T. H. Robinson - F. Horst, *Die zwölf Kleinen Propheten* (Tübingen, 1938), p. 157.

[5] Cf. the *Seliḥah*, אל אלהי ישראל recited in the Morning Service on Mondays and Thursdays, which still exhibits the poetic acrostic for the letters *Zayin*, *Heth*, *Teth* and *Yod* (perhaps also *He*, *Vav and Kaph*), while the rest of the present text is neither alphabetic nor poetic. The contention of I. Elbogen, *Der jüdische Gottesdienst in seiner geschichtlichen Entwicklung* (Leipzig, 1913) pp. 18, 274 f., that the acrostics might not have been complete originally rests only upon the fact that in some cases defective acrostics have survived. But as an "art-form" an incomplete acrostic defeats its goal, and Elbogen himself cites fuller forms of some of these defective acrostics in variant liturgical rites.

12), so that even when the Psalmist speaks in the singular and refers to his foes (vv. 3, 4, 5), he is identifying himself with the group. Psalm 10, on the other hand, deals with purely personal enemies, domestic evil-doers (vv. 2, 3, 7, 8). Moreover, Psalm 9 is a hymn of thanksgiving for victory; Psalm 10 is a prayer for succor yet to be achieved.

Neither of these contentions is decisive. Recent research into biblical psychology has clarified the concept of "fluid personality" which is the key to the process of "identification" of an individual with a group, be it a party vis-à-vis its opponents, or the nation as against its external enemies.[6] This fruitful insight is the key to such phenomena as the interchange of singular and plural in the Psalter, in the moving acrostic elegy in Lamentations chap. 3[7] and in Deuteronomy,[8] as well as the common shifting from first person to third in the Prophets. Lacking this key to biblical psychology, modern scholars have found these changes disconcerting and have had recourse to the unnecessary atomizing of the text.

More complex phenomena in biblical literature are also solved by recognizing the phenomenon of "fluid personality." Thus the "Servant of the Lord" in Deutero-Isaiah is described in terms that are unmistakably personal in one passage, and is then identified clearly with Israel in another.

[6] Cf. H. W. Robinson, *The Cross of the Servant — A Study in Deutero-Isaiah* (London 1926) and "The Hebrew Concept of Corporate Personality" in *Werden und Wesen des A. T.*, ed. J. Hempel, 1936, pp. 49 ff.; O. Eissfeldt, *Der Gottesknecht bei Deuterojesaia* (Halle, 1933); H. H. Rowley, *The Servant of the Lord and other Essays* (London, 1952), esp. pp. 33 ff.; 38 f.; R. Gordis, "Hosea's Marriage and Message: A New Approach" in *HUCA*, vol. 25, 1954, esp. pp. 15 ff.

[7] We hope to publish a study of this text, highly important for biblical theology, in the near future.

[8] On Steuernagel's attempt to divide Deuteronomy into two sources "Plural" and "Singular," see the witty and devastating comment of A. B. Ehrlich, *Randglossen zur hebräischen Bibel* (Leipzig, 1919), vol. II, p. 299.

All attempts to interpret the "Servant" as either individual or collective are inadequate, because he is both.[9] The same insight is the key to the understanding of the text of the opening chapters of Hosea, notably chapter 2, which identifies the prophet's personal tragedy with the Divine experience of betrayal by Israel.[10]

In view of the concept of fluid personality so richly documented in the Bible, it is not strange that the psalmist identifies his own enemies with those of his group, and, seeing his group of the "humble" and the "poor" as the authentic Israel, identifies these foes with the enemies of the nation. Moreover, it is clear that the opponents he has principally in view, שכחי אלהים, שנאים, רשעים are domestic, who attack the "poor" (דך, אביון, ענוים). There is therefore no need to emend גוים (9.6, 16) to גאים "the arrogant," in order to bring it into harmony with the other references to internal foes. In referring to "the nations" the Psalmist is invoking the aid of the God who has manifested Himself in history, judging the heathen nations by His standards of righteousness (9.9, 10) and chastising them for their sins (9.6, 16; 10.16). The implication is clear — God, who establishes justice in the world cannot suffer wickedness to triumph at home.

That Ps. 9 is basically a hymn of thanksgiving and Ps. 10 voices a plea for succor, also does not militate against the unity of the whole. The logic which dictates that God be praised for His saving acts in the past before He is implored to intervene in the present, is illustrated in such Psalms as 27 and 30. It became the standard pattern in post-biblical liturgy, as for example in the traditional *Amidah* and was codified as a principle of prayer:

---

[9] Cf. C. R. North, *The Suffering Servant in Deutero-Isaiah* (Oxford, 1948) and Rowley, *op. cit.*, pp. 3–88.

[10] Cf. our study "Hosea's Marriage and Message" in *HUCA*, vol. 25, 1954, esp. pp. 9–35.

"A man should always first set forth his praise of the Holy One, blessed be He, and then offer his prayer."[11]

Moreover, the two chapters are not as sharply demarcated between thanksgiving and petition as has been suggested. Psalm 9 contains explicit petition in vv. 14, 18–21, while Psalm 10 stresses the note of assurance of victory in vv. 14 and 16, as will be noted below.

Finally, the stylistic affinities linking the two psalms are striking. Note עתות בצרה (9.10; 10.1), ידרש, דרש = "God the avenger" (9.13; 10.4, 13) the rare דך (9.10; 10.10, 18), אנוש = "mere man" (9.20, 21; 10.18), as well as the striking similarity in phrasing in the concluding verse of each half of the acrostic: 10,17.18: תקות ענוים .... אל־ייעז אנוש :9.19, 20 תאות ענוים ... בל־יוסיף עוד לערץ אנוש.

In view of all these points of similarity and contact, it is clear that Ps. 9 and 10 constitute the two halves of a single alphabetic psalm.[12] The hymn begins with praise to the God of righteousness (9.2–5) who has revealed His saving hand in the affairs of nations (9.6, 7, 9, 8, 11, 12) and who cannot remain indifferent to the misery of the humble (9.13–15). By imposing His judgment upon the wicked (9.16–18.21) He will succor the poor from their afflictions (v. 19) and punish the wicked for their arrogance (9.20;

[11] T. Ber. 32a: לעולם יסדר אדם שבחו של הקב"ה ואחר כך יתפלל. Cf. also ibid., 34a: לעולם אל ישאל אדם צרכיו לא בג' הראשונות ולא בג' האחרונות אלא באמצעיות. The three opening Benedictions of the *Amidah* are accordingly dedicated to praise, the last three to thanksgiving; petition occurs only in the central blessings of the week-day *Amidah*.

[12] The alternatives, which some commentators have adopted, are considerably less plausible. One assumption has it that a different poet wrote Ps. 10, either because the author of Ps. 9 wrote only half an acrostic or because the second half of the original was lost. Equally unlikely is the view that 10.1–11 represents an independent poem descriptive of the wicked, which was inserted after the original section was lost, (ag. Kirkpatrick). Not only does this section contain several letters of the acrostic that can be recovered, but vv. 3 and 4 are directly cited in vv. 12 and 13.

10.1–3). For the sinner is emboldened to do evil, because he despises God, assuming that He is indifferent to injustice and will not disturb the complacent prosperity of the evil-doer nor interfere with his plots against the innocent (10.3–11). The Psalmist, however, calls upon God to arise (v. 12), knowing with the certitude of faith that the prosperity of the wicked is but temporary and that the vindication of the humble is assured (vv. 13–18).

Evidently, the lower half of the sheet containing the original Psalm in its entirety sustained considerable damage; hence the greater injury to the acrostic and the text as a whole in Ps. 10. The lower half of a ms. frequently exhibits greater physical damage. Similarly, the dittograph of Psalms 14 and 53 shows only a normal amount of variation in the opening section until שם פחדו פחד (14.5a; 53.6a) while the penultimate verse suffered substantial mutilation.[13]

Because of these difficulties, some scholars have been led to view the task as hopeless,[14] while many others have proceeded to radical emendations, excisions and transpositions in the text. We believe that it is possible to restore much of the original text, without recourse to extreme measures, though the disturbed character of the *textus receptus* makes it clear that the judicious use of emendations here is eminently justified.

A word is in order on the varied metric pattern of the Psalm. At this stage of biblical scholarship, it should not be necessary to argue against the two alternatives set forth

[13] The wide variations between 14.5 and 53.6 represent an effort to restore a text that must have become virtually illegible. That the closing verse in both recensions is identical (14.6; 53.7) indicates that it is a liturgical supplement, added after the textual damage to the previous verse had already taken place.

[14] Cf. Kittel on vv. 1–10: "Die gegebene Uebersetzung kann mehrfach nur als Versuch gelten."

by Cheyne and adopted by Briggs; the variations in meter indicate neither "the imperfect skill of the psalmist," nor "the interference of a second writer with the original poem."[15] What should have been expected *a priori* and indeed has been exhibited by biblical poetry, has now been conclusively demonstrated by Canaanite epic verse from Ugarit — a gifted poet will vary his meter, in order to avoid monotony, to heighten the interest, and to achieve a special effect.[16] Our psalmist is no exception to this principle, which is illustrated in the Song of the Sea (Ex. 15)[17] or in any other masterpiece of biblical poetry. The metric pattern of our psalm will be set forth at the end of our paper.

It should be added, however, that on the basis of the received text, it would seem that while the author used two, three and four-beat stichs, each verse is limited to distichs. There are no tristichs in Ps. 9, the better preserved half, while in Ps. 10 all the tristichs that appear in MT (vv. 3a (?) 5, 8, 9) are the result of the imperfect preservation of the text and the consequently erroneous division of verses. The only exception is the closing verse 18, the reason for which will be indicated below.

In view of the generally clear character of the text of Ps. 9, we shall preface these exegetical and textual notes on Ps. 10 with only one comment on Ps. 9, verse 7:

9.7 — On the basis of Masoretic חֳרָבוֹת, the first half of the verse is generally rendered "the enemy is destroyed, they are ruins forever" (so ICC), but the plural verb with a singular subject is difficult and the reference to enemies becoming ruins is forced. The various emendations proposed

---

[15] Cf. C. H. and E. G. Briggs, *ICC on Psalms* (New York 1906), vol. 1, p. 70.

[16] Cf. our study, "Al Mibneh Haširah Haivrit Haqedummah ("On the Structure of Ancient Hebrew Poetry") in *Sefer Hashanah Liyehudei Amerika* (5705 = 1945), pp. 136–159, particularly pp. 143 f.

[17] Here we encounter 4:4 (v. 1), 3:3 (v. 2), 5:5 (v. 4) and 2:2 (v. 9).

are far-fetched. It is preferable to vocalize חֳרָבוֹת, with *Pešita* and some Hebrew mss. The syntax, however, has not been understood, since we have here a rare form of the *casus pendens*.[18] Normally in this construction there is a suffix linking the clause to its logical subject. Thus in Ps. 103.15, אנוש כחציר ימיו the third person masculine suffix of ימיו refers back to אנוש. Here the reference is looser, the pronominal suffix being lacking; it is, however, explicit, linking חרבות with האויב. For other instances of this looser construction of the *casus pendens*, cf. *inter alia*, Jer. 44.16: הדבר אשר־דברת אלינו בשם ה' איננו שמעים אליך (בו *scil.*), Ezek. 10.11: כי המקום אשר־יפנה הראש אחריו ילכו (= אליו ילכו), Hos. 8.13: זבחי הבהבי יזבחו בשר ויאכלו (= יזבחו בשרם ויאכל).

The remainder of our verse consists of one clause, exhibiting the usual form of *casus pendens*. ערים is not "cities" but "enemy." Cf. I Sam. 28.16 ויהי ערך. The verb נתש is never used of cities, only of living things, generally of human beings (I Kings 14.15; Jer. 12.14, 17; II Chron. 7.20); and in one passage of a plant (Mic. 5.13).

For the close of the verse LXX, read μετ' ἤχου "with a noise," = מְהֻמָּה which validates the reading מַהֲמָה.

The verse is accordingly to be rendered literally:

"As for the enemy, his swords have ceased forever,
   And the foes Thou hast uprooted, the very memory has
   perished from them."

Ps. 10

1. ברחוק in MT is not to be emended to מרחוק; the *Beth* means "from" as in Hos. 7.14d; Ps. 6.8b; 18.14; 19.5a; 68.19, as, we now know, in Ugaritic, where the prefix means

---

[18] See the classic study of this construction in S. R. Driver, *A Treatise on the Use of the Tenses in Hebrew*, 3rd ed. (Oxford, 1892), pp. 264–73; esp. p. 267 for our special type of the construction.

both "in" and "from."[19] The Vss. (except *Pešita*, which clearly read the *Beth*), exhibit "levelling" when they render "from afar," not a bona fide textual variant. תְּעָלִים need not be emended to תִּתְעַלֵּם or even revocalized as תֵּעָלִים. On the secondary conjugations developing a reflexive sense, cf. וַיִּגְלַח (Gen. 41.14), תכסה (Deut. 22.12) and ברך and הלל in v. 3, on which see below.

2. בְּנַאֲוַת need not be revocalized to בִּנְאוֹת. It is best taken as an absolute, with the old *Tav* ending (cf. שפעת II Kings 9.17; חכמת Isa. 33.6; ברקת Ezek. 28.13; and also Isa. 28.16; Ps. 61.1; 74.19a; Lam. 2.18). Its absolute character has been overlooked by the Masorah, which has inserted a *Makkeph*, exactly as in Jer. 8.9 וחכמת־מה להם, which is to be rendered correctly: "The word of the Lord have they despised and wisdom is nothing to them!"[20] רשע is thus the subject of ידלק, which need not be emended to a *Niphal*. Against the rendering: "They (i. e. the rightous) are taken in the devices they (i. e. the wicked) have imagined" is the shift of subject of the two verbs. Moreover, the use of the plural suggests that the clause is an imprecation by the Psalmist: "May they be taken in the devices they have imagined!" Cf. Job 21.16; 22.18 for a similar formula: "May the counsel of. the wicked be far from me!"

3. הלל and ברך are here used reflexively (cf. note on v. 1), equivalent to the more familiar *Hithpael*, which occurs in Jer. 9.22 and Deut. 29.18, respectively. From v. 13, which

[19] Cf. J. H. Patton, *Canaanite Parallels in the Book of Psalms* (Baltimore 1944), p. 54.

[20] The usual renderings "What wisdom is in them" (AV, JPS, Moffatt, SRV), "What manner of wisdom have they" (Driver) are not borne out by the Hebrew, which would have been מה חכמה להם. The parallelism with מאסו makes it clear that here מה is the interrogative-rhetorical particle meaning "nothing," cf. *BDB*, s. v. Id, p. 553; see e. g. I Kings 12.16 as against II Sam. 20.1. חכמת is therefore to be construed as an absolute, in the sense of Divine wisdom (as in Prov. 9.10; 15.33; 30.3; Job 28.28).

is a quotation of our passage,[21] it is clear that נאץ ה' should be joined to v. 4, thus reading נאץ ה' רשע and creating the *Nun* verse in the acrostic.

This removal of the last two words does not leave a prose passage (ag. Briggs), if the caesura is placed in v. 3, after תאות, which is to be vocalized as תאותו and the *Vav* of ובצע is deleted as a dittography. נפש = "desire," cf. Deut. 21.14; 23.25; Ps. 35.25; Ezek. 16.27. בצע = "evil doer" cf. Job 27.8.

The verse then exhibits perfect synonymous parallelism in chiastic structure: a b c // c' b' a', and is to be rendered, literally:

> "The wicked boasts of his lust,
> Of his desire the evil-doer is proud."

It is worth noting that the metric problem for both vv. 3 and 4 is also solved by this slight change — the entire passage consists of 3:3 meter. See below.

4. The quotation in v. 13 makes it clear that the subject of בל-ידרש is God. The clause is therefore a quotation without a *verbum dicendi*:[22] "He says: 'God does not exact retribution.' " The sinner is voicing ancient disbelief in its most characteristic form, which did not negate the existence of Divine beings, but doubted their intervention in human affairs. Cf. e. g. Mal. 3.13–15; Ps. 14.1; Job 22.11–14; Eccl. 9.2 f.

5. יחילו "be powerful, endure," cf. Job 20.21. MT מרום

---

[21] On this widespread rhetorical device, see our study, "Quotations as a Literary Usage in Biblical, Oriental and Rabbinic Literature" in *HUCA*, vol. 22, 1949, pp. 157–219.

[22] Not an exact citation, נאץ ה' רשע appearing as נאץ רשע אלהים and בל ידרש as לא תדרש. Quotations, particularly in polemic contexts, will often not be exact; note Job's final words (42.6) where he cites the Lord's speech out of the whirlwind (38.2 f.) with minor variations. See p. 218, n. 106 of the study cited in note 21 above. Similarly, refrains are often repeated with minor variations, and are not to be levelled to uniformity, cf. e. g. Ps. 49.13, 21 and Job 28.12, 20.

is taken virtually as a predicate adjective by most commentators: "Thy judgments are too high for him, i. e., remote," but the usage remains strange. Hence the opening word is emended to מורמים "are lifted up," and is given the same nuance. The two clauses are then inverted so as to supply the *Mem* of the acrostic.

Actually its present position (after *Nun* v. 2 and before *Pe*, v. 7, and *Ayin* v. 8, see below) suggests that we have here the remnants of the *Samekh* line. For the inherently difficult מרום משפטיך read סרו משפטיך, the final *Mem* of מרום being a dittography of משפטיך and the first *Mem* an error for *Samekh*. The similarity of *Mem* and *Samekh* is noticeable in later rather than in earlier scripts, but it is very close in the Phoenician inscriptions from Athens, Piraeus, Carthage and Thugga, as well as in several Aramaic texts.[23] The confusion of these two letters is demonstrated as early as the LXX, cf. Isa. 30.4 חנס read as חנם by LXX (μάτην "in vain"). Cf. also the common talmudic לסטם "robber" from Greek λῄστης, which becomes a denominative verb מלסטם (Sanh. 72a). סרו משפטיך מנגדו means lit. "Thy judgments are turned away from before him," i. e. "He turns away from thy judgments."[24] It represents the opposite of the conduct of the saint, cf. 16.8 שויתי ה' לנגדי תמיד "I have set the Lord always before me"; Ps. 18.23: כי כל משפטיו ממשפטיך לא סרתי; and Ps. 119.120 לנגדי וחקותיו לא אסיר מני. Note the use of סור and the difference between לנגדי "before me" and מנגדו "away from him."

[23] Cf. G. A. Cooke, *Text-book of North-Semitic Inscriptions* (Oxford, 1903) Plates XII and XIII.

[24] Biblical Hebrew expresses the idea of separation, either by the removal of the person from the object or of the object from the person. Cf. Job 24.4 יטו אביונים מדרך as against Amos 2.7 יטו ודרך ענוים and see the two parallel stichs in Isa. 10.1 a, b. Cf. also Job 36.16, where הסיתך מפי-צר is a transposition for הסית צר ממך, as Tur-Sinai (*The Book of Job*, Jerusalem 1957), p. xxiii has noted.

Since stich b is the beginning of the *Samekh* verse, it seems plausible to join 4c and 5a as a separate verse. There are several additional grounds for doing so: 1) the metric pattern of the Psalm throughout (see above and the comments on vv. 8, 9) is the distich, not the tristich. 2) in v. 13, only the first two stichs of v. 4 are cited, not the third. 3) The newly constituted verse is needed as the non-alphabetic pendant for the restored *Nun* verse. Perhaps ויחילו should be read instead יחילו, by haplography from מזמותי. יפיח בהם = "he puffs at them, contemns them"; cf. והפחתם אתי, Mal. 1.13.

6. In stich b, which requires a verb, vocalize אשר as אָשׁוּר לֹא בְרָע (from the root שור "see, behold") hence, "I shall not experience any trouble." Cf. the use of its prose synonym ראה "experience" (in Num. 22.9 ואל אראה ברעתי and its frequent use in Ecclesiastes, as e. g. Eccl. 6.17 לראות במה שיהיה אחריו 3.22 לראות טובה; cf. also 1.16; 6.10; 9.9). On שור, as parallel to ראה, cf. Num. 23.9; 24.17.

7. The opening noun אלה must be deleted, thus restoring a 4:4 meter and revealing the *Pe* verse in the acrostic. Efforts to discover its original position in the Psalm have proved unsuccessful.[25] It may have entered our passage as a scribal reminiscence of the catalogue of sins in Hos. 4.2: אלה וכחש ורצח וגנב ונאף.[26] The *Vav* of ומרמות was added after the additional noun entered the text. תחת לשונו = not "on his tongue," but "under his tongue, i. e., as a delicacy," cf. Job 20.12 יכחידנה תחת לשונו.

8. Verses 8 and 9 in MT contain 3 stichs each. Since עיניו is, as most scholars have recognized, the beginning of

[25] Countless instances may be found in the commentaries of Briggs, Gunkel, Kittel and Schmidt, *inter alia*.

[26] Or it may be an error for סלה and would belong to the previous verse, cf. 9.17, 21. Undoubtedly, this musical notation fell out of the text at several other points in the psalm.

the *Ayin* in the acrostic, the six stichs are to be divided into 3 distichs of 3:3 meter. The *Ayin* follows *Pe* here in the alphabet as in Lam. chap. 2.3, 4 and in the original form of Ps. 34. On 9a, see below. חצרים has proved a *crux interpretum* from the days of the LXX which read עשירים, an impossible reading which probably arose by contrasting the righteous poor with the rich sinners, cf. Isa. 53.9 in the MT. Such emendations as כמרצחים (Schmidt) are inept and graphically distant. חצרים is an unwalled settlement (defined as such in Lev. 25.31), a peaceful village where violence is not normally expected and hence not guarded against. נקי is its parallel, meaning "innocent" in its etymological sense, "doing no harm," actually "unarmed." So Ehrlich. Cf. Prov. 1.11 נצפנה לנקי חנם and the Mishnic usage נקי מנכסיו "empty-handed," Pes. 22b). The passage emphasizes the enormity of the crime, against which no precautions have been taken. MT יצפנו is to be retained on the principle of *difficilior lectio* instead of יצפין (ag. Saadiah *apud* Ibn Ezra, and many moderns), cf. Ps. 56.7; Prov. 1.11.

9. In 9a, which belongs with 8c as an independent verse, במסתר is redundant after יארב and disrupts the three-beat meter. It is therefore to be deleted as a dittography from במסתרים in v. 8. In stich c, the two closing words, usually rendered "when he pulls him into his net" are too prosaic and likewise disturb the three-beat meter, which occurs in the entire section. ברשתו is to be attached to v. 10 with LXX, for reasons of meter and parallelism, as will be indicated below.

במשכו to be rendered, not as an infinitive construct, "when he pulls him" but as a noun "in his bag," cf. Ps. 126.6 משך הזרע "bag of seed," which is derived not from "drawing, trail" (*BDB*) but from משך = "seize," Arabic مسك I, IV, "grasp, hold." Cf. Ex. 12.21; Judg. 20.37 and

Job 40.25.[27] מֶשֶׁךְ would be one more biblical term for "trap," cf. מַלְכֹּדֶת from לכד, "capture, seize" (Job 18.8–10) and five other terms for this instrument of the hunter used by the poet. In Job 28.18 מֶשֶׁךְ = "price" not "drawing forth." On the metaplastic forms of the segolate noun מֶשֶׁךְ and מָשָׁךְ, cf. עֶצֶב (Ps. 139.24; I Chron. 4.9) and עָצָב (Gen. 3.16; Prov. 10.22; 14.23 etc.).

10. The MT is difficult both with regard to meter and to meaning. A closing stich that is longer than the opening is highly irregular if not impossible.[28] The usual views of בעצומיו = "through his strong ones" or "through his strength" are also unsatisfactory. With LXX attach the last word of v. 9 to v. 10. The MT may have arisen by an erroneous reading of the original בְּלִי־יִרְאֶה as בְּלִי־רָאָה, reproduced as בַּל־רָאָה. On the confusion of *bal* and *b^eli*, see the *Kethib-Qere* in Hos. 9.16. The *Kethib*, the *Vav* of which is to be deleted as a dittography, is to be vocalized דִּכָּה; a variant orthography for דכא (Isa. 57.15; Ps. 34.19).[29] That בעצומיו must contain a noun meaning "trap" and paralleling ברשתו was acutely recognized by Duhm, but it is not necessary to emend with him to בצמימיו (cf. Job 18.9). עצם means "close," (cf. Isa. 29.10; 33.15 and often in Mishnic Hebrew.[30]) עצומים would therefore mean "pincers, trap." The

---

[27] Cf. H. Tur-Sinai, *Halashon Vehasepher, Kerekh Halashon* (Jerusalem 5708 = 1948), pp. 383 ff.

[28] We believe that a closing stich will be longer than the opening one only at the end of a composition or of a section, or a poem composed in distichs will end in a tristich, in order to create a powerful conclusion, corresponding to a *fortissimo* in music. Cf. the evidence assembled on pp. 144 f., note 16 of the study cited in note 16 above.

[29] Cf. מורה in 9.21 which most scholars regard as an aberrant orthography for מורא. The noun may also be vocalized דְּכָה.

[30] Cf. M. Shab. 23.5, B. Kid. 32b. The root is always used in biblical, rabbinic and medieval Hebrew of closing the eyes, bringing the eyelids together. Cf. E. Ben Jehuda, *Thesaurus*, vol. 9, p. 4654a for this meaning and examples. It would therefore be most appropriate for a trap closing on its victims.

entire verse is in 3:3 meter and exhibits perfect parallelism: a b c // c' a' b':

> "In his trap the poor is brought low,
> And in his pincers the afflicted fall."

11. With most moderns, בל־דראה should be read בל־יראה.

14. The usual rendering of the first half of MT: "You deem it proper to look upon sin and iniquity" is both involved in sense and cumbersome in meter. כי אתה is to be omitted as an erroneous dittography for ראתה; note the orthography. The infinitive in לתת has its exact syntactic and semantic parallel in Ps. 92.8: "The wicked may spring up as the grass and the workers of iniquity may flourish, (להשמדם) with the result that they be destroyed forever." Similarly here, "Thou seest wrong-doing and lookest quietly upon evil, only that they may be given over into thy hand." The second half of the verse in MT is the pendant for *Resh* in the acrostic.

15. The first stich can hardly mean: "Break the arm of the wicked and the evil-doer" which is tautological, or "the arm of the wicked and (his) evil" since זרוע is always used of persons. Hence ורע is best deleted as a dittography. In stich b we expect to find a statement that the sinner will have disappeared by reason of God's retribution, not that his sin will be gone. (Cf. Job 8.18; 15.34; 18.18 ff.; 20.9 etc.) Hence read: תדרוש־רשע ובל תמצא. The second person may be impersonal, "one may seek the sinner, but not find him," cf. Prov. 19.23; 30.28; Job 7.21 and the idiomatic באכה (Gen. 10.19 etc.).[31]

17. תאות, best taken not as "desire" for which שמעת is inappropriate, but as "cry," a derivative from the exclama-

---

[31] Cf. Gesenius-Kautzsch, *Hebraeische Grammatik* (25 ed.), Leipzig, 1889, sec. 144c, for other examples of this impersonal use of the 2nd person, and see now Tur-Sinai, *op. cit.*, p. xxiv.

tion אוי; cf. Ps. 38.10 תאותי ‖ אנחתי and Jer. 17.16 יום אנוש
לא התאויתי "In the day of mortal pain, I did not cry out."
שמעת is a precative perfect, cf. *inter multa*, Ps. 4.2; 6.10;
Lam. 1.21. In stich b, לבם has been emended to לבך, but
the phrase is used of only man (Ps. 51.12; 57.18; 112.7, cf.
also Prov. 2.2), and is inappropriate to God. But if לבם is
retained, the parallelism requires a noun before it. LXX
and P accordingly render תכין as "preparation" (ἑτοιμα-
σίαν, ܬܩܢܬ). There is no need to emend to תכן or תכונת
(Schleusner). The *kâtîl* form (cf. קָצִיר, שָׁמִיר) occurs in our
root in Ps. 65.10 כי כן תכינה, which also rendered as a noun
by LXX and V. The noun means "content, substance."
Read the construct: תְּכִין לָבָּם.

18. While ערץ is usually intransitive, its transitive use,
induced by the paranomasia with ארץ, is well attested by
Isa. 2.21; Job 13.23 and by the common noun עָרִיץ lit.
"terrorizer." Stich b may be rendered in one of two ways:
"that he (i. e. the enemy) may no longer terrorize man off
the earth (*Pešita*, similarly Ehr.) or "so that mere man of
earth may no longer spread terror" (so LXX, V, etc.).
The latter idea has its parallel in the close of the first half
of the Psalm (9.20, 21) and is therefore preferable. By
ending the poem with a tristich (3:3:3), the psalmist gives a
powerful close to the hymn.[32]

Lamed

v. 1 4:3	תעלים לעתות בצרה	למה ה' תעמד ברחוק
v. 2 4:4	יתפשו במזמות זו חשבו	בגאות רשע ידלק עני
v. 3a, b–3:3	נפשו בצע ברך	כי הלל רשע על תאותו

[32] Cf. note 28 above. The same stylistic procedure is to be found in
Ps. 13, 14, 16, 18, 19, 37, 47, 53, 55, 63, 73, 90, 94, 103, 104, 111, 119,
125, 129, 140; Job, chaps. 10, 11, 19, 26.

Nun

נאץ ה' רשע   כנבה אפו בל ידרש   v. 3c, 4a–3:3

אין אלהים כל מזמותיו   וְיָחִילוּ דרכיו בכל עת   v. 4b, 5a–4:4

Samekh

סרו משפטיך מנגדו   כל צורריו יפיח בהם   v. 5b, c–3:3

אמר בלבו בל אמוט   לדר ודר אֲשֶׁר לא ברע   v. 6 4:4

Pe

פיהו מלא מרמות ותך   תחת לשונו עמל ואון   v. 7 4:4

ישב במארב חצרים   במסתרים יהרג נקי   v. 8a, b 3:3

Ayin

עיניו לחלכה יצפנו   יארב כאריה בסכה   v. 8c, 9a 3:3

יארב לחטוף עני   יחטף עני במשכו   v. 9b, c 3:3

ברשתו דַּכָּה ישח   ונפל בעצומיו חלכאים   v. 10 3:3

אמר בלבו שכח אל   הסתיר פניו בל יראה לנצח   v. 11 4:4

Koph

קומה ה' אל נשא ידך   אל תשכח עניים   v. 12 4:3

על מה נאץ רשע אלהים   אמר בלבו לא תדרש   v. 13 4:4

Reš

רָאתָה עמל וכעס תביט   לתת בידך   v. 14a, b, c 4:2

עליך יעזב חלכה   יתום אתה היית עוזר   v. 14d, e 4:4

Sin

שבר זרוע רשע   תדרוש רָשָׁע וּבַל תִּמְצָא   v. 15 3:3

ה' מלך עולם ועד   אבדו גוים מארצו   v. 16 3:3

Tav

v. 17 4:4   תָּכִין לבם תקשיב אזנך   תאות ענוים שמעת ה'
v. 18 3:3:3   בל יוסיף עוד לערץ   לשפט יתום ודך
אנוש מן־הארץ

Why, O Lord, dost Thou stand afar off,
Hiding Thyself in times of trouble?
In arrogance, the wicked pursues the poor —
May they be seized in the schemes they have concocted!

For the wicked boasts of his lust,
The evil-doer is proud of his appetite.
The wicked despises the Lord,
In his arrogance he says, "God exacts no penalty,"
"There is no God" — are all his thoughts,
While his paths prosper in every season.
Thy judgments are far removed from him,
And all his foes he contemns.
He says in his heart, "I shall not stumble,
For all time, I shall experience no trouble."
His mouth is filled with deceit and oppression,
Beneath his tongue lurk iniquity and sin.
He waits in ambush even in open villages,
In the secret places he slays the unarmed.
His eyes peer out for the afflicted,
He waits in ambush like a lion in his lair.
He lies in wait to seize the poor,
He seizes the afflicted in his trap.
Into his net the poor tumbles,
And the afflicted fall into his pincers.
He says in his heart, "God has forgotten,
He has hidden His face, He never will see."

131

Arise, Lord God, lift up Thy hand,
Forget not the humble.
Why should the wicked despise God,
Saying in his heart, "Thou dost not exact any penalty."
Thou hast indeed looked upon evil and gazed upon iniquity,
Only that they might be given over unto Thy hand.
To Thee the afflicted entrusts his all,
Of the orphan hast Thou been the Helper.
Shatter the arm of the wicked,
So that one may look for the wicked and not find him.
The Lord is King forever and ever;
The nations are destroyed from his earth.
The cry of the humble Thou must surely hear,
The contents of their hearts Thine ear must heed.
That the orphan and the weak may find justice,
And mere man, made of earth, may no longer spread terror.

CORPORATE PERSONALITY IN JOB: A NOTE ON 22:29-30

IN HIS stimulating paper on "The Sources of the Suffering Servant Idea,"[1] Professor J. Philip Hyatt follows H. W. Robinson in calling attention to the widely prevalent conception of "corporate personality" as a source for Deutero-Isaiah's thought.[2] Particularly welcome is Hyatt's emphasis upon what we may call the positive aspect of the doctrine, that not only punishment, but salvation as well, may accrue to the group from the actions of the individual.[3]

This insight, at which we arrived independently, is the key, I believe, to the enigmatic passage in Job 22:29-30, with which Eliphaz closes his fourth and last address to Job:

כִּי־הִשְׁפִּילוּ וַתֹּאמֶר גֵּוָה וְשַׁח עֵינַיִם יוֹשֵׁעַ
יְמַלֵּט אִי־נָקִי נִמְלַט בְּבֹר כַּפֶּיךָ

The difficulties scholars have encountered in this passage may be studied in detail in the commentaries. Thus verse 29 has been rendered: "If they lowered you" (Rödiger, Hitzig), or "If your ways are depressed" (Ewald,

Delitzsch, Dillmann), "You say 'Rise up,'" and He will save the humble [i.e., Job]."

Other commentators refer the promised salvation, not to Job, but to the innocent in general, but then find difficulty in ʾiy nāḳiy. They therefore emend it to ʾiš nāḳiy, "an innocent man," (Reiske, Dathe). A far-fetched attempt to extract this meaning from the Massoretic Text is to interpret it as "one unjustly condemned (but innocent)" (Rabinowitz-Abronin).

The obviously unsatisfactory character of these interpretations has led to a plethora of emendations, among the best of which are: kī hišpīl ʾōmer gaʾawāh (Duhm); kī hišpīl ʾet rām weɡēʾeh (Beer); and kī hišpīl rōmeh ɡēwoh (Hoelscher). After an extensive discussion, Driver-Gray (I.C.C., I, 198-99; II, 157-58) adopt Budde's emendation for 29a: kī hišpīl ʾelōah gaʾawāh, and in verse 30 read: yimmālēṭ ʾiš nāḳiy wattimmālēṭ bebʰōr kappekʰa. Nonetheless, they are constrained to admit that, "even as emended, the text is not a very forcibly expressed conclusion to the speech."

When, however, the entire passage is understood in terms of traditional Hebrew thought, it constitutes a powerful close to Eliphaz's address, without the need of radical emendation. Like all the Friends, Eliphaz stands four-square upon the ancient doctrine of corporate responsibility, against which Jeremiah (31:20-21) and Ezekiel (14:12 ff. and chapter 18) inveighed (cf. Job. 5:4-5; 8:15, 22; 21:19a).

---

[1] *JNES*, III (April, 1944), 79-86.

[2] Cf. Robinson's fundamental paper, "The Hebrew Conception of Corporate Personality," *Werden und Wesen des Alten Testaments* ("BZAW," Vol. LXVI [1936]), pp. 49-62). A significant development of several phases of this basic outlook will be found in Aubrey R. Johnson, *The One and the Many in the Israelite Conception of God* (Cardiff, Wales, 1942), pp. 6-17.

This idea had, as we have noted, its positive as well as its negative aspects. In addition, it was not only "vertical" but also "horizontal," that is to say, it operated in space as well as in time, so that a righteous individual could save not merely his descendants but also his contemporaries. That is the basis of Abraham's appeal to God to save Sodom for the sake of ten righteous men and Ezekiel's citing of the doctrine, to which he objects, that the presence of Noah, Daniel, and Job in a city could save it from destruction (14:14 ff.). Another case in point is Job's prayer for his friends (42:8, 10).

This doctrine never disappeared from Judaism. Even after the idea of individual responsibility was accepted, it continued in the idea that a saint could even set aside God's decree, as in Talmud Babli, *Moed Katan*, 16b: "Said the Holy One, blessed be He, 'I rule over man, but who rules over Me? The Saint, for when I issue a decree (*gōzēr gᵉzērāh*), he sets it aside.'" The same idea persisted in the widespread Jewish folk belief of the thirty-six saints whose lives glorify God's presence and preserve the world from ruin (*lamed-vav ṣaddīkīm*).⁴

It is from this standpoint of "horizontal" corporate responsibility that Eliphaz speaks. A righteous Job will not only be restored to personal safety (22:21, 23) and prosperity (22:25) but will also regain his great influence among men and with God. His mere word will suffice to save those humbled in society, and even the guilty will escape divine punishment because of Job's transcendent righteousness. On the juxtaposition of these two ideas—favor with God and man—compare Num. 32:22 ("Ye shall be free from guilt before God and Israel") and Pr. 3:4 ("and find grace and good favor in the eyes of God and man"),

for which parallels may also be adduced in Canaanite literature.⁵

Verses 28–30 now require no change in the Massoretic Text, except for the possible, though not absolutely necessary, modification of the vowels in one word. The passage now gives an excellent climax to Eliphaz's speech:

Thou shalt issue a decree⁶ and it will be ful-
    filled for thee,
And light shall shine upon thy ways.
When men are brought low,⁷ thou wilt say,
    "Rise up!"⁸
And the humble will be saved,⁹
Even the guilty¹⁰ will escape punishment,¹¹
Escaping through the cleanness of thy hands.

JEWISH THEOLOGICAL SEMINARY

⁵ Cf. the Phoenician inscription from Memphis in M. Lidzbarski, *Altsemitische Texte* (Giessen, 1907), p. 35, l. 4: *wytn lm ḥn whym lᶜn ʾlnm wbn ʾdm*, and the inscription of Yehawmilk of Byblus in *ibid.*, p. 14; cf. G. A. Cooke, *Textbook of North-Semitic Inscriptions* (Oxford, 1903), pp. 18, 24: *wttn . . . . ḥnˊlᶜn ʾlnm wlᶜn ᶜm ʾrṣ z*. I am indebted for these references to my colleague, Professor H. L. Ginsberg.

⁶ Note the root *gāzar*, "decide," used in the passage in *Moed Katan* cited above.

⁷ The *hiphil* is used intransitively (cf. *hirḥīqu* [Gen. 44:4]; *hašmēn* [Isa. 6:10]). Or, less probably, the clause may be translated, "If they cast men down, etc."

⁸ On גְרֵה as an alternative spelling for גַּאֲרָה, "pride," cf. Jer. 13:17 and Dan 4:34.

⁹ Probably to be vocalized as a *niphal*, *yiwašēᶜa* (so also Hoelscher). On the other hand, W. A. Irwin suggests in a note to me that the *hiphil* of the MT be retained, either as an indefinite subject equivalent to a passive or that "God" be understood as the subject.

¹⁰ אִי is the negative particle, common in rabbinic Hebrew and normal in Ethiopic. While "Ichabod" (I Sam. 4:21) may originally have been a theophorous name, the biblical author undoubtedly interprets it as containing the negative particle, "No-Glory" (cf. "Saying, 'Glory has departed from Israel'" [*ibid.*]). He thus testifies to the antiquity of its usage as a negative in Hebrew.

¹¹ The *piel* of the Massoretic Text does not require a change to the *niphal*, since the *piel* may be used reflexively and hence is a virtual passive. Cf. Gen. 41:14, *wayyᵉgallaḥ*; Amos 2:15 *wᵉqal bᵉraglāw lō yᵉmallēt*.

⁴ Talmud Babli, *Suk.* 45b: "The world cannot do with less than thirty-six saints who greet the Divine Presence daily."

STUDIES IN BIBLICAL
SEMANTICS AND RHETORIC

SOME EFFECTS OF PRIMITIVE THOUGHT
ON LANGUAGE

I. WORDS OF MUTUALLY OPPOSED MEANING

Students of philosophy have long been aware of the existence of a large number of roots that possess mutually opposed meanings either within the same language or in different members of the same group. This phenomenon is especially marked in the Semitic group. Medieval Hebraists like Menahem ben Saruk, Abulwalid ibn Ganah, Abraham ibn Ezra, Joseph Kara, and others[1] noticed that *berech* meant "curse" in addition to "bless"; *hesed*, "disgrace" as well as "kindness," or "darkness" besides "light." These roots of opposing meaning, even more frequent in Arabic, have served as the subject of entire works by many Arabic scholars, the most important of whom was Abu Bahr al Anbari of the tenth century.[2] Even if dubious instances be excluded from consideration, this attribute of contrasting meanings (Arabic *addad*) is so common that a very careful modern scholar has said that we have the right to postulate the opposite of any given meaning of an Arabic root if it aids in the interpretation of a passage.[3] Other Semitic languages show the same tendency, though to a lesser extent than Arabic.

At times the opposite meaning develops in different languages. The root *ʾaban* means "to be willing" in Hebrew, "to refuse" in Ethiopic; *ʿalam* means "to be hidden," "unknown," in Hebrew, "to know" in Arabic.[4]

Nor is this tendency restricted to Semitic languages. In Egyptian, examples are abundant.[5] *Ken* means "strong" and "weak," *at* "to

[1] Cf. E. Landau, *Gegensinnige Wörter im Hebräischen* (Berlin, 1896).

[2] Th. M. Redslob (*Die arabischen Wörter mit entgegengesetzten Bedeutungen* [Göttingen, 1873]) lists fifteen such works (p. 15). He also publishes a specimen of Anbari's work. The entire treatise was edited by Houtsma.

[3] Dr. S. L. Skoss, professor of Arabic at the Dropsie College, in a private conversation

[4] The examples in Landau (*op. cit., passim*) must be used with caution, as Noeldeke has observed.

[5] See Carl Abel, *Über den Gegensinn der Wörter* (Leipzig, 1884). Reprinted in hi *Wissenschaftliche Abhandlungen* (Leipzig, 1885), pp. 311–68.

hear" and "be deaf." Aryan languages likewise show considerable traces of this characteristic.[6] In German *sauber* means "clean," but it has the opposite significance in the phrase *saubere Gesellschaft*. The French *sacré* means "cursed" as well as "blessed." The Latin *clam* means "silent"; *clamare*, "to shout." The English "let" signifies "permit" and "prevent" (as in the phrase "without let or hindrance").

It was the merit of Carl Abel to have been the first modern scholar to seek the origin of this universal phenomenon.[7] Its widespread character precluded the idea that it arose from a merely accidental resemblance of sounds, or was due to varying dialects. Abel therefore proposed the following explanation. All our concepts arise out of comparison. Man develops the idea of "dark" because he sees "light"; the idea of "large" arises out of contrast with "small." Each concept is, therefore, closely linked to its opposite, so that the word which expresses any idea originally referred to it and its opposite. To quote him exactly: "The word which originally united the conception of 'strong' and 'weak,' in truth meant neither 'strong' nor 'weak,' but the relation of both, and the difference between both, which created both."[8] As for the problem how the reader knew which meaning the writer intended, Abel answers that in Egyptian various determinatives make that clear. An upright, armed figure shows that *ken* is to be taken in the sense of "strong," while a dejected, unarmed character betokens "weak." In the spoken language, Abel insists that gestures could be depended upon to make clear which of the two meanings was intended.

This interesting theory failed to convince later students of the subject. Yet Noeldeke was unduly severe when he dismissed it with the single epithet *wunderlich* ("strange"). In fact, Abel's theory impressed Sigmund Freud very favorably, and he published his own summary of Abel's essay in his *Journal für Psychoanalyse* in 1910. Nevertheless, the theory cannot be seriously defended today. When Abel wrote, a great deal of modern anthropology was not yet in existence, and practically nothing was known of the mental processes of primitive man. We were unaware of how profound was the sway of the group and how negligible the role of the individual in ancient

---

[6] Cf. Nyrop, *Das Leben der Wörter* (Leipzig, 1923), who quotes many striking examples.
[7] *Op. cit.*   [8] *Ibid.*, p. 326.

society. Abel's theory, moreover, is based too exclusively upon a priori, logical considerations and takes no account of psychological factors.[9] It is inconceivable that men could ever have used words without some definite meaning as primary. A study of extant examples of words of contrasted meanings shows that in practically every instance one meaning is basic, and the other secondary.[10] Besides, psychologists have noted that children offer many analogies to the primitive mind. If the process postulated by Abel were indeed native to it, we should meet with similar usage among children. Lastly, Abel proves too much. According to his theory, every word ought to have mutually contrasting meanings, while the truth is that, even in Arabic, the examples are an infinitesimal proportion of the vocabulary.[11]

The unsatisfactory character of Abel's theory made scholars wary of similar hypotheses. Landau treated the subject in a monograph *Gegensinnige Wörter im Hebräischen*, a work containing a great deal of solid learning but uncritical in its treatment of the material. Landau offered no explanation of the phenomena but classified the examples into a large number of abstract categories.

On the other hand, a model of scientific methodology and thorough scholarship was furnished by Noeldeke in his brilliant essay "Wörter mit Gegensinn." Before approaching the subject proper, Noeldeke excludes certain types of words as not genuine: (*a*) where the alleged opposite meanings are doubtful; (*b*) textual errors; (*c*) where the governing preposition is the source of the opposite meaning;[12] (*d*) where varying constructions create different meanings;[13] and (*e*) where originally distinct roots have coalesced in sound.[14]

[9] The same objection is advanced by Marett against Frazer's theory of magic and religion. See the former's *The Threshold of Religion* (London, 1914), p. 37.

[10] Thus the Hebrew *berech* = bless, *hesed* = kindness, *or* = light. On the other hand, there are words which occur so infrequently that it is difficult to decide which is basic, as *ᵓon* = strength, weakness.

[11] The index to Noeldeke's essay "Wörter mit Gegensinn" (*Neue Beiträge zur semitischen Sprachwissenschaft* [Strassburg, 1904], pp. 67–108) lists 185 Arabic roots. Of these, many are not true instances but are listed because they are discussed in the body of the essay. Obviously even 185 is a tiny fraction of the copious Arabic vocabulary.

[12] Thus *raghiba ʼan*, "despise," "loath"; *raghiba ʼila* or *bi*, "desire," "long for."

[13] *Zeman*, "buy"; *zammen*, "sell," in Syriac.

[14] Thus שׂכל "wisdom, sense" which goes back to the Arabic شَكَلَ has coalesced with סכל fool (Syriac סכלא) (*op. cit.*, p. 72). Noeldeke does not reckon with the close resemblance of these original Semitic roots, which can scarcely be accidental and itself deserves explanation.

He then proceeds to classify the genuine instances of Semitic words of like and opposite meaning as follows: (1) words expressing reciprocal relationships,[15] (2) words expressing the different standpoints of the speakers,[16] (3) extensions beyond the original limit of meaning,[17] (4) words meaning "cover" and "uncover,"[18] (5) words meaning "sleep" and "wake,"[19] (6) words betokening opposed emotional states,[20] (7) euphemisms,[21] (8) cacophonies,[22] (9) ironic usages, and (10 varia.

A glance at these groups suffices to show that they are by no means of the same character. Groups 2 and 9 do not really belong here, not being genuine examples of *addad*. That words can be so extended beyond their original meaning as to mean the opposite (Group 3) is not a solution but a problem. Groups 4 and 5 are merely convenient classifications. On the other hand, in Groups 7 and 8 the cause for the phenomenon of opposite meanings is suggested as inhering in the desire to avoid unpleasant expressions or divert evil influences. Had this idea been followed up, it would have led to the origin of these words of opposed meaning. Unfortunately, Noeldeke is emphatically of the opinion that no basic explanation can be found. He says:

Perhaps this entire exposition will serve to strengthen the insight that . . . . firm, universally valid laws for semasiology are much less demonstrable than in phonetics. The variegated array of human emotion, thought, and speech defies all attempts to force them into fixed formulas [p. 72].

[15] E.g., *ja'r* means both patron and client.

[16] E.g., *shim'l*, *left* means "north" to the Arab who faces Mecca in prayer (*kibla*). In Hadramaut, South Arabia, it stands for the southwest, for the same reason.

[17] Noeldeke explains that אוֹר, אוֹרְתָּא, meaning "light," is then extended to the period before the break of day, hence "night, evening." This appears forced.

[18] As Arabic احتفر.

[19] The Aramaic and Mandaic שְׁאַהְרָא, like the Arabic, سهر, also means "sleep." See Noeldeke, *op. cit.*, p. 87.

[20] As רנן "shout for joy"—also "moan" (Lam. 2:19). מרזח "revelry" (Amos 6:7); "lamentation" (Jer. 16:5).

[21] As, e.g., סַגִי נְהוֹר *lichtreich*, "seeing, light-eyed" for blind; בֵּרַכְתָּ הַשֵּׁם "blessing God" in talmudic Hebrew (*Sanh.* 58a) for cursing him. In Morocco the raven, a bird of ill omen, is called *msaoud*, "fortunate." Cf. the Greek designation for the furies as "Eumenides"—"well disposed."

[22] In Arabic شَوْهَاء, "ugly," is frequently used to describe a beautiful mare (cf. Noeldeke, *op. cit.*, p. 97). The story of the Schnorrer who tell Gutchen Rothschild in Frankfurt that Jewish girls are called *Schoenchen*, when ugly, and *Gutchen* when bad, and that she is called *Gutchen* because she is worse than ugly, is a good case in point.

With all reverence for his great authority, we feel that modern anthropology offers us the means of getting to the root not alone of this interesting linguistic phenomenon but of several others which have hitherto been taken for granted as "natural" and never subjected to investigation. Their detailed study must be prefaced by some general considerations.

Of all our debts to primitive man, language is unquestionably of outstanding importance. Not only is it likely that language is the oldest human invention[23] but it has undergone relatively little basic change. Discoveries like fire have been completely outstripped by later technological achievements; religious and moral ideas have often been modified or discarded; language, however, remains the province wherein primitive man has shown himself most highly creative and modern man essentially derivative. Modern languages have increased their vocabularies tremendously and have sloughed off and modified their inflections, but the basic structure, the linguistic "drift," has scarcely changed. Above all, the habitual forms of discourse that constitute the field of syntax have endured.

Since "language does not exist apart from culture, that is, from the socially inherited assemblage of practices and beliefs of the group,"[24] it is in primitive society that we must seek the key to many phenomena in language. The origin of words of mutually opposed meaning seems to us to inhere in two well-known elements of primitive thought.

TABOO—MANA

Modern anthropology has shown that primitive men everywhere believed that a mysterious, nonmaterial force inhered in nearly all elements of human experience. This force is usually described today by the Melanesian term "mana." Since these influences might prove harmful or dangerous, "taboo" came into being, usually defined as negative magic, i.e., abstinence from certain acts in order that undesired magical results might not follow.[25] Mana is thus the positive side of this supernatural power; taboo its negative aspect. But Marett is correct in emphasizing that taboo implies that "you must be heedful in regard to the supernatural, not that you must guard against it

---

[23] Cf. Edward Sapir, *Language* (New York, 1921).
[24] *Ibid.*, p. 142.   [25] *Encyclopaedia Britannica* (11th or 13th ed.), XXVI, 336.

absolutely, or there could be no practical religion. Under certain conditions, man may draw nigh, but it is well for him to respect those conditions."[26] Taboo means not the prohibition but rather the limitation of contact with spiritual forces.

Though mana is ubiquitous and may inhere everywhere, yet it clusters most thickly about the exceptional elements of life, the extremes of power or weakness, and the great occasions, like birth, puberty, marriage, and death. Hence it is here that taboos arise in the greatest profession. The primitive mind found it eminently reasonable that this mysterious power should manifest itself more frequently in the extraordinary and unusual aspects of existence rather than in the common and average ones.

THE POWER OF WORDS

As widely diffused as the belief in mana and the practice of taboo is the feeling that there is a particularly intimate connection between a thing and its name, a relation bordering on identity.[27] Hence to the savage mind the manipulation of names is tantamount to control over the persons and things they represent. Words are real. It is therefore to be expected that taboo includes not alone physical acts but spoken words as well.

These two primitive conceptions create *verbal taboo*. Among many savage tribes the attempt is made to keep personal names hidden from strangers and enemies. Taboos frequently occur against mentioning the names of dead or of chiefs or gods, undoubtedly because mana is taken to reside in the name as well as in the being. The universal horror of a curse, which persists to this day, derives from the same feeling that the name and the person are identical and that the malediction of the one is the misfortune of the other. It is not impossible that the royal custom of adopting a "throne name" on the accession to power originally arose out of a desire to avert the curses which might have accumulated against the king's former name.[28] It would

[26] *Op. cit.*, p. 142.

[27] Thus in Hebrew, *davar* means "thing" and "word," as does the Aramaic *miltha*. See E. B. Tylor, *Early History of Mankind* (London, 1863), pp. 123 ff.; J. G. Frazer, *The Golden Bough*, chap. vi: "Taboo and Perils of the Soul," pp. 318–418.

[28] The custom of giving throne names, which seems to have originated in Egypt, began in Judah as early as the reign of Solomon, whose personal name was Jedidiah (II Sam. 12:25). See W. F. Albright, "The Seal of Eliakim and the Later Pre-Exilic History of Judah," *Journal of Biblical Literature*, LI (1932), 85, n. 25.

seem, too, that the common custom of giving a sick person an additional name was originally a change of name, and the purpose of the ceremony was to avert the evil influences that had fastened upon the original name and its bearer. The extensive field of world superstitions, where words are taken as emblematic of good or evil, is due to the same sense of the literal potency of words.

What has not been recognized, however, is that verbal taboo is not limited to proper names or specific situations but has entered the very structure of language and profoundly influenced the meaning of words. These verbal taboos, which differ in degree rather than in essence, may be classified as follows.

1. *Ordinary euphemisms.*—In modern usage certain words are avoided because they are felt to be unpleasant. They are essentially those connected with sex and death. The repugnance we feel today to "calling a spade a spade" is the residue of a much more imperious feeling—the ancient taboo, which considered it positively dangerous to do so. Hence "die" is expressed by "pass away," "coitus" by "sleeping," in nearly all languages. Diseases, too, are not mentioned directly. In Java, smallpox is known as *lara bagus*, "pretty girl"; in modern Greek as εὐλογία; while the Arabs call leprosy "the blessed disease," and a person bitten by a serpent is described as "the sound one."[29]

2. *Ordinary cacophonisms.*—At times, however, the directly opposite process takes place. Instead of seeking to call dangerous and unpleasant things by favorable names, primitive man seeks to ward off the evil eye by describing the healthy and the beautiful in negative terms, especially when evil is spoken or contemplated of them.[30] The Arabs frequently describe a beautiful mare as "ugly." The Talmud will often replace Israel by "the enemies of Israel" in a passage describing suffering or trouble.[31] Conversely, the Dejahs of the Upper Melawie will refer to their enemies as "friends" when they invoke their death.[32]

3. *Extreme euphemisms.*—These primitive euphemisms and cacoph-

---

[29] *Wellhausen, Reste des arabischen Heidentums* (2d ed.; Berlin, 1897), p. 199.

[30] See Noeldeke, *op. cit.*, p. 91 n.; Frazer, *op. cit.*, p. 417.

[31] Cf. Babylonian Talmud, *Sukkah* 29a: "An evil sign for the *enemies of Israel*"; *Yoma* 72b: "no remnant would have remained of the *enemies of Israel*," where *Israel* is meant.

[32] Frazer, *op. cit.*, p. 72.

onies are only partial disguises. Very often there is a desire to escape from the unpleasant word as far as possible, and so refuge is had in the very opposite.[33] Instead of avoiding "death" by "pass away" "depart," etc., the speaker goes to the opposite and describes it as "life," the cemetery as "the house of life," and even mourning as "joy."[34] What better euphemism for "curse" could the Hebrew find than the word for "bless," or for weakness than the word "strength"? Similarly, to express "infamy" the Semite would use the root meaning "goodness" (*hesed*).

But usage tends to dull the figure of speech. It is soon forgotten that the word was used only figuratively in a negative meaning, and it comes to mean what originally it sought to replace.[35] Thus the Hebrew *hesed*, "grace, goodness," has an Arabic cognate meaning "envy" and an Aramaic one signifying "disgrace," a meaning which has come over into Hebrew as well. Nearly always, the original meaning persists side by side with its opposed, more recently acquired significance, and so words of like and opposite meaning arise. They are, in sum, verbal taboos, euphemisms of the ultimate degree.

Primitive taboos extended over the entire course of man's experience. We must therefore be prepared to find that sometimes we cannot isolate the source of unpleasantness or "danger" which impelled primitive men to use these extreme euphemisms. Yet it is noteworthy that, in the overwhelming majority of instances of words of opposed meaning, one of them is definitely negative and unpleasant.

For purposes of investigation we may take Noeldeke's careful list of Hebrew and Aramaic words in the essay previously quoted. Though by no means exhaustive, it can serve as a cross-section of all such examples.

After privatives and spurious examples are omitted, there remain thirty examples. In twenty-eight, we find that one of the two contrasting meanings is definitely negative:

darkness—light. Two instances.[36] The primitive fear of darkness is universal and requires no proof.

---

[33] Cf. Nyrop, *op. cit.*, p. 6: "Hier konnte auch kein abschwächender Euphemismus helfen, man muss zu einem gewaltsameren Mittel greifen, zur Antiphrase."

[34] שׂמחות is the name for the talmudic treatise on mourning.

[35] See Nyrop, *op. cit.*, p. 7: "Ein Ausdruck so häufig antiphrastisch gebraucht, dass die ursprüngliche Bedeutung dem Bewusstein so gut wie ganz entschwindet."

[36] נגהא, אור, אורתא.

blind—open-eyed, seer, etc. Four instances.[37] Diseases are ill-omened and hence avoided.

disgrace—praise, kindness. Three instances.[38]

curse mock—bless, praise.[39] Two instances.

cry, weep—laugh, sing, revel.[40] Three instances.

anger—pleasurable excitement.[41] Two instances.

excrement—food.[42] Two instances. That there is spiritual danger in physical uncleanness was a widely spread belief among the Australian aborigines in Melanesia, Polynesia, and South America. The biblical injunctions concerning personal cleanliness in Deut. 23:9–14 may have their roots in the same taboo.[43]

damage, calamity—healing.[44] One instance.

sleep—wake.[45] One instance. That sleep is a dangerous time for the soul is a universal superstition.

loathe—desire.[46] One instance.

be disturbed—be at ease.[47] One instance.

disperse—come near.[48] One instance.

folly—wisdom.[49] One instance.

strange, unknown—know, recognize.[50] One instance. The fear of strangers plays a great part in primitive taboo and has largely endured to our own day.[51] This unfortunate trait seems to have deep roots in the human soul, as modern psychology has shown.

avenge, requite—be comforted, reward.[52] Two instances.

bitter—sweet. One instance.[53]

[37] סגר נהור ,מפתחא ,מאור עינים, and ראה. For the use of euphemisms for other bodily defects as well see the writer's paper, "Studies in Hebrew Roots of Contrasted Meaning," in *JQR* (N.S.), XXVII (1936), 33–58 (nos. 9, 14, 17, 18, 20).

[38] Cf., respectively, הלל (Syriac אהלל), חסד ,נבל (as a proper name [II Sam. 25:20] derived from the Arabic "distinguished," so recognized by J. A. Montgomery in *JQR* [N.S.], XXV [January, 1935], 262).

[39] Respectively, קלס ,ברך.

[40] Respectively, שמחות ,מרזח; רנן; קתיא as the name of the treatise on mourning, אבל.

[41] פחד ,רגז.   [43] See Frazer, *op. cit.*, p. 158, n. 1, and literature there quoted.

[42] רעי ,אוכלא.   [44] אסי ,אסון ,אסר.

[45] See Frazer, *op. cit.*, pp. 36–42; שהר in Aramaic.

[46] מתאב in Amos 6:8 is taken by Noeldeke as a textual error for מתעב. Yet this is not necessary, for such opposites are common. Cf. איב, "hate"; ראב, "desire"; אהב, "love." Geiger's assumption that this is a tendencious change to avoid the unpleasant thought of God's hating the glory of Jacob (*Urschrift* [Breslau, 1857], p. 349) is unlikely in view of the large number of denunciatory passages in the Prophets. The root בחל "loathe, desire," also belongs here.

[47] רגע.   [48] קרב in קרב אליך (Isa. 65:5). Cf. נש הלאה (Gen. 19:9).

[49] סכל ,שכל, and שכלות which Noeldeke traces to different roots. See above, n. 14.

[50] נכר ,הכיר, and התנכר.

[51] Cf. Frazer (*op. cit.*, pp. 101–16) for many taboos affecting strangers.

[52] נחם and גמל.   [53] מתוק means "bitter apple." See Mishna, *Shebiith*, 3:1; 9:16.

In two instances, we cannot now establish the process by which these opposing meanings developed.[54]

Thus it becomes clear that these words include such favorite objects of taboo as night, disease, sleep, strangers, fear, anger, mourning, sorrow, and maledictions.[55] The slightest acquaintance with the universal sway of primitive taboo is sufficient to prove that many early conceptions must have been at work that we cannot longer reconstruct today.

Nor is this the only indefinite factor in the creation of these words of self-opposed meanings. Analogy, the supreme law of language, plays a tremendous role in its growth. Once the custom of using words in diametrically opposed senses begins, it is extended where the original motivation of taboo did not exist.

Thus, among many tribes and peoples, the use of substitutes for taboo words ultimately creates an entire language. The Victorian tribes of Australia have an entire "turn-tongue" which is understood by everybody but must be used among certain relatives by marriage. This substitute vocabulary was not restricted to "dangerous" themes. Among the specimens of this peculiar dialect given by Dawson is the following. "It will be warm by and by" is expressed ordinarily as *baawan kulluun;* in "turn tongue," by *qnullewa—gnatnoen tirambue.*[56]

In Laos, terms are in use for common objects, creating a sort of special language for elephant hunters. A similar practice obtains among the eaglewood searchers of Indo-China and the *gaharu* searchers of Malacca.[57] In eastern India, during the camphor-searching season, a special language called *bassa kapor* or *pantang kapur* is used not only by the members of the expeditions but by those who remain at home.[58] The process is especially clear in Celebes. "Beginning with a rule of avoiding a certain number of common words, the custom has

---

[54] גלש Hebrew "come down," has an Arabic cognate—rise, Highland (Noeldeke, *op. cit.*, p. 92, n. 4). פָּרִים and its derivatives remain difficult (*ibid.*, p. 83). Perhaps the explanation resides in the fact that there are many taboos against showing the face. Cf. Frazer, *op. cit.*, pp. 120–23.

[55] On the other hand, sexual experiences do not supply any examples. This is, however, completely explicable by the fact that, while opposites for disease, death, cursing, and hate occur (health, life, bless, love, etc.), no opposite terms can be used for sexual experience. Verbal taboos of a sexual origin cannot be expressed as extreme euphemisms, but in the ordinary way, as the Hebrew *shakhab,* "sleep," for *coire,* etc.

[56] Frazer, *op. cit.*, p. 346, and n. 1.   [57] *Ibid.*, p. 404.   [58] *Ibid.*, p. 405.

grown among people of the Malay stock till it has produced a complete language for use in the field."[59]

We cannot, therefore, expect to be able to isolate the taboo element in every instance of words of contradictory meaning. Given the evidence that taboo supplied the original impetus for their creation, the usage undoubtedly continued through the momentum of analogy.

As time goes on and animistic conceptions begin to fade, such formations become less and less frequent. Certain phases of human experience, notably death, continue to feel "unpleasant," and here euphemisms remain. By and large, however, words of contradictory meaning endure in the speech of mankind only as survivals from primitive ways of thought.

II. PLURAL OF MAJESTY

Words of like and opposite meaning do not exhaust the effects of taboo on the structure of language. Some of its effects have become so prevalent that it is assumed that they are "natural," and no explanation has been sought for them. Such a phenomenon is the plural of majesty, the use of the plural by exalted figures in speaking of themselves. Instances are innumerable. We may adduce the speech of the King of Denmark in *Hamlet:*

> Though yet of Hamlet our dear brother's death
> The memory be green, and that it us befitted
> To bear our hearts in grief, and our whole kingdom
> To be contracted in one brow of woe;
> Yet so far hath discretion fought with nature
> That we with wisest sorrow think on him
> Together with remembrance of ourselves [Act I, scene 2].

The explanation of this usage, it may be suggested, lies in the concept of taboo and mana. Marett points out that, if a man has mana, it resides in his spiritual part or "soul," and he adds that an inspired man, or a chief, which is the same thing, will even say of himself not "I" but "we two," referring to himself and his mana.[60] A missionary reports that, in response to an exhortation on his part, Australian blacks replied, "Yes, yes, we also are two; we also have a little body within the heart."[61] Codrington tells that a young native of Leper's

---

[59] *Ibid.*, p. 412.   [60] Marett, *op. cit.*, p. 137.   [61] Frazer, *op. cit.*, p. 27.

Island made his dead brother's bones into arrowheads and spoke of himself as "we two" and was much feared by the other natives because he had acquired the mana or supernatural power of his brother.[62]

All human beings possess a soul, but it is the chief or magician who is most conscious of the mysterious power or mana residing in him which is his distinguishing mark. He therefore uses the plural in talking of himself because he includes his mana. This plural becomes associated with greatness or majesty and is retained long after the basis of the usage is forgotten. Thus "the plural of majesty" and perhaps the "editorial we" may have come into being.

III. POLITE AND FAMILIAR ADDRESS

Most languages possess two types of direct address known as the "polite" and the "familiar," which have likewise been taken for granted. At present, the use of the polite address is a matter of etiquette, but, as in other elements of modern practice, there seems originally to have been much more than the mere urge of "good manners" behind it—the compulsion of taboo. Thus eating in public which is frowned upon today as improper was formerly widely prohibited. Kings, in particular, upon whose safety the welfare of their subjects depended, were forced to eat their meals in strict seclusion, so that no one would see them eat or drink.[63] Crossing one's legs is not regarded today as the most dignified of postures, but in primitive thought it was considered positively dangerous in childbirth and other crises, by races as varied as the Toumbuluhs, the Romans, the Bulgarians, and the Bavarians.[64]

Etiquette thus sometimes contains the vestigial remains of taboo. This seems to have been the case in the so-called "polite address." The clue to this usage we find in the following description of taboo and mana:

Thus kings and chiefs are possessors of great power and it is death for their subjects to address them directly. But a minister or other person of greater mana than common can approach them unharmed, and can in turn be approached by their inferiors without risk.[65]

[62] Quoted by Marett, *op. cit.*, p. 27, from Codrington, *JAI*, XIX, 216–17.

[63] Frazer, *op. cit.*, pp. 116 ff., cites the sources for this widely spread taboo.

[64] *Ibid.*, pp. 298 f.

[65] *Encyclopaedia Britannica* (13th ed.), XXVI, 338 *b*.

It follows, therefore, that people of approximately the same social level or degree of mana speak to one another, directly, through the familiar form; hence Semitic *atta*, French *tu*, German *du*, English *thou*. In addressing a superior, however, there is need to address him obliquely, so that no direct contact with the mana-charged individual takes place. This is done through "polite address," which takes one of two forms. In some languages the superior is addressed indirectly, in third person, as in the Hebrew *yomar na adoni*, "Let my lord say," or Spanish *Usted habla*. In other instances the superior is addressed in the plural, that is, tribute is paid both to him and to his mana,[66] as in the French, *vous êtes*, English, *you are*, and Old German, *Ihr seid*. At times both methods are combined as in the modern German, *Sie sind*, which is both indirect and plural. That such usages endure long after the taboo has been outgrown is entirely comprehensible if it is recalled that the direction of linguistic "drift" is laid early. The two forms of direct address show another effect of taboo on language.

IV. FIGURES OF SPEECH

From the very dawn of literature men have found aesthetic satisfaction in various figures of speech such as similes, metaphors, and epithets. All these may be described as partial displacements of the objects of discourse. Instead of calling a thing or act directly by name, we replace it by an epithet or comparison that suggests it without naming it. It is not within our province here to inquire into all the sources of the aesthetic satisfaction involved. Perhaps it is the pleasure derived from the recognition of the allusion and from the vivid perception of the image thus indirectly raised. What concerns us here is that these figures of speech or verbal displacements have striking analogies in primitive verbal taboos. It therefore seems plausible to assume that the aesthetic pleasure we derive today from figures of speech is the residue of a more concrete satisfaction of primitive man. By displacing certain words through epithets, he felt he was escaping the spiritual dangers that lurked in their use. The examples that will be adduced below are often vivid and picturesque, but they owe their origin to genuine verbal taboos and not to a desire for aesthetic charm.

[66] See above on the plural of majesty.

Thus the Namdi caution their children against mentioning the names of the members of a hunting expedition by the word, "Do not talk of birds who are in the heaven" (p. 330).[67]

Sheep are called "bleating ones" by Kirghiz women (p. 337). The dog is called "barker" or "driver away" in Madagascar, if the chief has a name that resembles the ordinary word for dog (p. 378). The fox is called "red dog" by Highland fishermen (p. 394), "long-tail" in Mecklenburg (p. 397), and "blue-foot" in Sweden (p. 397). The monkey is "the tree climber" among the Bhuisgars (p. 403). The tiger is called "grandfather," "the master of the wood," "he with the striped coat" (p. 410), and, most vivid of all, "the roaring trap" by the Karo Bataks.

The mouse is called "leg runner" in Mecklenburg (p. 397) and "small grey" in Sweden (p. 397). The wolf enjoys many descriptive epithets in Sweden, such as "golden tooth," "silent one," and "grey legs" (p. 397). The bear is no less popular. The Swedish herd girls call him "old man," "twelve men's strength" and "golden feet" (p. 397), while the Finns speak of him as "apple of the wood," "beautiful honey paw," and "the pride of the thicket" (p. 398). The snake is called "long one" by the Huzuls of the Carpathians (p. 397), "the creeping thing" by the Bengalese (p. 412), "the rope" in northern India (p. 412), and "the good lord" in Transvancore (p. 412).

Nor is the speech by epithet restricted to the names of animals. Highland fishermen on a trip avoid many ordinary words, calling a "rock" by the word for "hard," the knife, "the sharp one," the seal, the "bald beast" (p. 394). In Scotland, a church is called "bell-house" and the minister, "the man with the black quyte." Galelareese sailors on a voyage speak of the bow of their vessel as "the beak of the bird," starboard as "the sword," and larboard as "the shield" (p. 414).

In the harvest fields of Celebes the word "to run" is changed into "limp"; the foot, "the thing with which one limps"; to drink, "thrust forward the mouth"; to pass by, "nod with the head"; the gun, "the fire-producer" (p. 412). As we have seen, this avoidance of certain words is immeasurably extended by the process of analogy until complete substitute languages are created by some tribes.

It must be kept in mind that these epithets are not voluntary varia-

[67] All page references given in parenthesis refer to Frazer, *op. cit.*

tions in speech for the sake of novelty or vividness but obligatory usages, the infraction of which, it is believed, will expose the speaker and his fellows to grave danger or loss. Yet their formal identity with our figures of speech cannot be gainsaid. Frazer's remark in another connection is thus seen to have much wider significance: "What is metaphor to a modern European poet was sober earnest to his savage ancestor" (p. 34). The embellishments of figures of speech originated in verbal taboos designed to guard men against literal perils of the soul.[68]

In sum, taboo and its concepts have played an important part in the growth of language. We have sought to indicate the effect of primitive thought on such phenomena as euphemisms, words of self-contradictory meanings, the plural of majesty, the "polite" modes of address, and figures of speech generally. We thus hope to have indicated part of the profound debt that modern man owes his primitive ancestors.

---

[68] From the Greek area of culture comes interesting evidence that similes, no less than metaphors, are the results of primitive religious conceptions, though not examples of verbal taboo. Professor J. A. K. Thomson (*Studies in the Odyssey* [Oxford, 1914]) has called attention to the Homeric device of "transformations," by which the Olympian gods are compared to lower animals or other natural objects. "So in the Iliad and Odyssey we find the old way of belief asserting itself in the constant transformations of the Immortals into shapes other than their ideal or typical shapes, into the semblance of a particular hero, or an old woman, or a young girl carrying a pitcher, or a vulture or a swallow. They are not in origin an artistic device but an article of primitive religion, as indeed we all now recognize—the dreams of men who believed that the Olympian gods in battle with the Giants assumed the forms of the mean animals, and who discovered a dreadful sanctity in an oak-grove or a blackened stone" (*ibid.*, p. 4).

Thomson gives many striking illustrations of similes in Homer, the origins of which are religious rather than aesthetic. "When Thetis arose from the waters, they saw her 'like a mist.' Modern readers call this a simile because they are educated. But the audience who listened when that image of the sea-fog was first used, imagined, or half imagined, the goddess as physically bodied forth in it" (*ibid.*, p. 6). "There is, for instance, the curious simile applied to Hera and Athene marching to battle: 'they went on their way like timid doves in their going'—an almost humorously inappropriate description of two warlike goddesses stepping so daintily. Is it a merely fanciful suggestion of Mr. Cook, that the explanation may lie in the relation of these divinities to Zeus, who, as the Odyssey itself implies, was attended by sacred doves? Once doves in bodily form perhaps, they have become now only 'like unto doves in their going' " (*ibid.*, p. 7). "Once more, when the sword of Poseidon was compared to the lightning-flash, did it not pass through the mind of the hearer that the characteristic weapon of the god, the triple-pointed trident, was indeed in origin nothing else? Or was the poet who composed the simile ignorant of this?" (*ibid.*, p. 9).

A RHETORICAL USE OF INTERROGATIVE SENTENCES IN BIBLICAL HEBREW

INTERROGATIVE SENTENCES IN BIBLICAL HEBREW

A phenomenon with which students of language have long been familiar but to which little attention has been paid is the type of question that requires an affirmative answer. Perhaps because of its commonness, this construction has rarely elicited more than a note in a grammar to the effect that a negative is employed in such questions, as, for example, οὐ, ἆρ οὐ, οὐκοῦν in Greek,[1] *nonne* in Latin, *no es verdad* in Spanish, *n'est-ce pas* in French, etc. The use of the Hebrew הֲלֹא[2] and the Arabic أَلَا[3] has rightly been viewed as entirely similar.

Yet no reason has ever been advanced for this universal insertion of a negative in questions seeking an affirmative answer. Moreover, biblical usage shows in several passages a noteworthy departure from this practice. In these instances, though an affirmative answer is obviously desired by the speaker, no negative is expressed. One illustration will suffice at this point. In Jer. 31:20 we read הֲבֵן יַקִּיר לִי אֶפְרַיִם אִם יֶלֶד שַׁעֲשׁוּעִים. Here the prophet's obvious and emphatic meaning is that Ephraim *is* a darling son to the Lord. Yet the English versions render an opposite sense when they translate it literally: "Is Ephraim a darling son to me? Is he a child, etc.?" Indeed, the correct procedure would be to insert a negative and then render: "Is [not] Ephraim a darling son, etc.?"

As will become clear presently, this is by no means the only instance in biblical Hebrew where *questions seeking an affirmative reply* occur *without a negative*. Indeed, several verses have been variously emended because the existence as well as the psychologic explanation of this construction has remained unknown. Gesenius-Kautzsch-Cowley, §150*e*, says: "A few passages deserve special mention in which the use of the interrogative is altogether different from our idiom,

---

[1] Babbit, *Greek Grammar*, p. 572, 1.

[2] In the recurrent formula הֲלֹא הֵם כְּתוּבִים and elsewhere as in Gen. 29:25.

[3] Cf. Wright, *Arabic Grammar*, Vol. II, § 168, and examples there cited.

212

since it merely serves to express the conviction that the contents of
the statement are well known to the hearer and are unconditionally
admitted by him." In the citations which follow, however, questions
with a negative are indiscriminately lumped together with others
where a negative is lacking, with no attempt to distinguish or account
for the existence of these two groups.

The true meaning of this universal type of question as well as the
aberrations observed in Hebrew depend upon our establishing the
psychologic background of their formation. In the writer's opinion,
the use of a negative in questions of this character is traceable to a
piece of primitive diplomacy. From earliest times, whoever has sought
to gain the assent of his fellows to any proposition has had to contend
with a deep-seated, seemingly instinctive spirit of contrariness in his
listeners. If A wants his hearers to agree that the house is beautiful,
the bald question, "Is the house beautiful?" is calculated to arouse the
contrary assertion rather than the view he champions. Or, to put it in
psychologic terms, the ego functions far more pleasurably when it
asserts itself in opposition to its fellows than when it acquiesces in a
judgment previously uttered by another. This desire to disagree has
always been known to mankind and is reflected in countless proverbs,
anecdotes, and quips[4] which attest the universality and antiquity of
this tendency.

Therefore, at some early stage in man's rational life a resort was
had to a naïve piece of deception—the insertion of a negative into the
question. A, to gain the commendation he craves for the house in
question, asks, "Is not the house beautiful?"—a form which permits
his listeners the pleasurable function of contradicting his superficial
statement by replying, in effect: "You imply that the house is not
beautiful. On the contrary, it *is* beautiful." To revert to psychologic
terms once more, A's ego, in order to get a desired reaction from the
others, expresses the opposite of its intention so that the ego of B
will be able to assert itself freely in a contradiction, which is, in reality,
in agreement with his secret aim.

---

[4] An excellent illustration of this characteristic is to be found in a quip current among
students of the Talmud. In discussing a Mishna where two contradictory opinions are
voiced, the Gemara frequently asks: מַאי טַעְמָא דְתַנָּא קַמָּא אֶלָּא . What is the reason for the
first sage's opinion? At this point it has been asked, "Why does the Gemara never ask as
to the reason for the second sage's opinion?" The humorous rejoinder given is "The second sage's opinion offers no difficulty. He is merely contradicting what the first sage says!"

This rather naïve deceit lies at the root of the universal use of negatives in questions when an affirmative reply is wanted. It is true that the intended force of the construction is soon lost by virtue of its frequency and simplicity. Frequently the particle is stripped of its negative-interrogative meaning completely and becomes purely asseverative as in Hebrew and Arabic.[5] Nevertheless, habit and imitation, the strongest influences in speech, succeed in keeping the construction intact and all languages agree in making the negative a regular part of questions when an affirmative answer is desired.

Yet under very special circumstances this negative may be omitted in the question. When the speaker is animated by an all-powerful certainty of the truth of his contentions, so that he feels it inconceivable for anyone to differ, he can neglect this sop to the ego of his audience. In these rare moments of unshakable certitude he dares to put his questions without troubling to conciliate his hearers, convinced that he will achieve the assent he craves in spite of the feeble resistance of their egos.

This heightened emotional condition that permits of the omission of the negative is infrequent enough to have escaped the notice of students of the psychology of grammar heretofore. A priori, one would expect a fair representation of this usage in the colorful and highly emotional utterances of the prophets, and this expectation is not disappointed.

There are two main classes where questions demanding an affirmative answer dispense with the negative: (a) questions relative to the condition actually present before the eyes of the speaker and hearers and hence admitting of no denial and (b) contentions by the prophets, who, in their fiery zeal and passionate insistence upon duty, likewise feel a contradiction to be inconceivable. Both groups are well represented in the Old Testament, though examples of Group A may be gathered elsewhere. Two fish wives in a frenzied altercation will invoke the casual passer-by with some such phrase as "Do you hear what she says?" "Do you see that . . . . ?" Here the physical closeness of the incident, occurring as it does in present time, coupled with

---

[5] Thus הֲלֹא הֵם כְּתוּבִים is a synonym for הֵם כְּתוּבִים (I Kings 14:19), meaning "indeed." أَلَّا becomes a corroborative pure and simple in such oaths as أَلَّا قَبَّحَ اللّٰه وَجْهَك, "May God disfigure thy face!"

the thorough conviction of the speaker, makes it possible to omit the negative which is normally employed to insinuate the desired answer.

Biblical illustrations of this use are not lacking. Thus I Sam. 10:24, הַרְאִיתֶם אֲשֶׁר בָּחַר־בּוֹ (R. V.: "See ye him whom the Lord hath chosen, that there is none like him among all the people") should be rendered in our idiom, "Do you not see whom the Lord hath chosen?"

In I Sam. 17:25, הַרְאִיתֶם אֶת הָאִישׁ הָעֹלֶה (Jewish Publication Society version): "Have ye seen this man who is come up; surely to taunt Israel has he come up"), is likewise incorrectly rendered. Here, too, the English idiom demands the insertion of the negative: "Do you not see the man, etc.?"[6] Similarly, II Kings 6:32, הַרְאִיתֶם, and I Kings 20:13, הֲרָאִיתָ, should be translated in a manner to make plain that an affirmative answer is required even in the absence of the usual negative.

But not only of actual occurrences does this hold true. The powerful inner conviction of the biblical writers often carries them away beyond this petty device of a negative. Matters that to less fiery souls might seem dubious or at least open to discussion become unassailable verities, assured of assent even without this cajoling of the ego.

This rhetorical use in Hebrew has been entirely overlooked even when the meaning of the verse, as in Jer. 31:19, is entirely clear. To convey the force of these passages to a Western reader the insertion of "not" is emphatically necessary. We shall content ourselves with giving these passages together with a rendering and an occasional note.

Gen. 16:13b: הֲגַם הֲלֹם רָאִיתִי אַחֲרֵי רֹאִי

Without entering into any discussion of the difficult רֹאִי, it is perfectly plain that Hagar is here accounting for her daring to invoke the Lord by asking herself "Have I not even here seen Him that seeth me?"—a question to which an emphatic "Yes" is the only possible reply.

I Sam. 2:27: הֲנִגְלֹה נִגְלֵיתִי אֶל בֵּית אָבִיךָ

Here the intent of the question has been universally misunderstood. The context renders it plain that the Man of God is here seeking to

---

[6] That this question is not put to David but is a rhetorical question among the men themselves is proved by the plural הַרְאִיתֶם as well as by David's query in vs. 26, which would have no point if he had heard the words of vs. 25.

express the affirmative. The most popular expedient is to delete the first ה of הנגלה (Ehrlich, H. P. Smith, and others there quoted). The R.V. "Did I reveal myself?" is absolutely untrue to the sense of the passage. Only Nowack[7] renders it satisfactorily: "Have I [not truly] revealed myself, etc.?" That this rendering is far superior to the emendation is self-evident.

I Kings 22:3: הַיְדַעְתֶּם כִּי לָנוּ רָמֹת גִּלְעָד

Here the R.V. "Know ye that Ramoth-Gilead is ours?" is likewise inept. A somewhat colloquial translation will make the meaning of the verse clear. The king is addressing his nobles on the eve of a war, "You know, don't you, that Ramoth-Gilead is ours?" Here, too, the king's passionate utterance makes any answer except an affirmative impossible, even without his use of a negative.

Jer. 31:20: הֲבֵן יַקִּיר לִי אֶפְרַיִם אִם יֶלֶד שַׁעֲשׁוּעִים

This instance has already been discussed. The prophet's meaning is brought out only by inserting a negative in the translation: "Is not Ephraim my beloved son?"

Amos 6:2: עִבְרוּ כַלְנֵה וּרְאוּ וּלְכוּ מִשָּׁם חֲמַת רַבָּה וּרְדוּ גַת־פְּלִשְׁתִּים
הֲטוֹבִים מִן־הַמַּמְלָכוֹת הָאֵלֶּה אִם רַב גְּבוּלָם מִגְּבֻלְכֶם

Here the traditional rendering is (R.V.) "Are they (i.e., the other nations) better than these kingdoms (Israel and Judah): is their border greater than yours?" This is entirely unsatisfactory, as has long been recognized. One of the most common burdens of prophetic utterance is the physical insignificance of Israel and Judah. Deut. 7:7, Amos 9:7, Nah. 3:8, in varying form, but with equal earnestness, stress the uniqueness of Israel as conditioned only by his moral greatness, and threaten dire punishment if Israel persists in trusting to his wealth and arms. It is this doctrine which our passage seeks to inculcate. Amos calls upon "those at ease in Zion and those secure in the mountains of Samaria, the notable men," to pass through Calneh, Hamath, and Gath, which have recently been destroyed, in order to learn the lesson that strength is often merely a prelude to death. Hence with practical unanimity scholars since Geiger have sought to restore the text by inserting אַתֶּם after הֲטוֹבִים and reading גְּבֻלְכֶם מִגְּבוּלָם in-

---

[7] *Urschrift*, pp. 96 f.

stead of the Masoretic גְּבוּלָם מִגְּבֻלְכֶם.[8] The rendering of the second clause now becomes:

> Are you better than these kingdoms,
> Is your border greater than theirs?

In proposing this emendation Geiger pursued his usual theory of *tendenz* as the cause of the error, insisting that the change was purposely made in order to prevent a derogatory comparison of Israel with the Philistines. This is scarcely likely. The Bible contains other equally distasteful passages (cf. especially Amos 9:7) which have come through unscathed. Indeed, in his anxiety to make out a case for conscious tendency, Geiger sets the Septuagintal misreading of כַּלְנֵה as כָּלְנָה down to patriotism rather than to ignorance!

Yet it is indisputable that this emendation gets at the real meaning of the passage far better than the traditional view. But the emendation is rather drastic, necessitating, as it does, the insertion of an entire word and correction of two others. Fortunately the passage can be interpreted without recourse to emendation in the light of the previous discussion. If we recall the prophetic usage of omitting the negative in questions, even when an affirmative reply is expected, a negative which in other languages is obligatory, we may translate as follows:

Are they[9] [not] better than these kingdoms [Israel and Judah]?
Is [not] their border greater than yours?

$$\text{הֲזֹאת יָדַעְתָּ מִנִּי עַד מִנִּי שִׂים אָדָם עֲלֵי אָרֶץ}$$

Job 20:4, 5a: כִּי רִנְנַת רְשָׁעִים מִקָּרוֹב

Here Driver-Gray recognizes the unnecessary character of the emendation הֲלֹא for הֲזֹאת proposed by Siegfried and Duhm. The question here properly implies an affirmative answer, though the negative is omitted, and is well rendered in the Jewish Publications Society version:

> Knowest thou not this of old time,
> Since man was placed upon earth,
> That the triumph of the wicked is short?

---

[8] See on the historical difficulty Harper's full discussion, and Ehrlich's sensible comment and note at the passage, Kittel in *Biblia-Hebraica* offers an alternative emendation to מְגֻבָלִם גְּבֻלְכֶם—גְּבֻלְכֶם מִגֻּבֹלָם, which does not affect the sense.

[9] On the subject (הֵם) omitted, cf. Ewald, p. 303, *b*, 1.

STUDIES IN THE RELATIONSHIP OF BIBLICAL
AND RABBINIC HEBREW

The unity of all knowledge and of Jewish learning in particular is strikingly symbolized in the career of our great teacher, Professor Louis Ginzberg. Through his mastery of all branches of Jewish literature and cognate fields, and his brilliant use of the comparative method, he has illumined almost every phase of Jewish history, law, institutions, literature, theology and linguistics.

In its application to the field of Biblical philology, the comparative method has two aspects. One we may call the "horizontal," i. e., related to other Semitic languages and literatures, the other, the "vertical," i. e., related to later periods in the history of Hebrew language and literature. Both phases are now celebrating their thousandth anniversary. Judah ibn Koreish (10th cent.), in the *Risalah*, first laid Aramaic and Arabic under contribution for the elucidation of Biblical Hebrew. His younger contemporary Saadia (d. 942), in his *Tafsir Al-sab'ina lafẓah* utilized Rabbinic Hebrew for the same purpose.

Since their day, both aspects have been cultivated with notable results. But while material from other Semitic languages has been sedulously collected for the interpretation and emendation of the Biblical text, the resources of post-Biblical Hebrew have not been as effectively utilized.

In part, this may be due to the fact that few Biblical scholars today are familiar with the vast reaches of Talmudic and medieval Jewish literature. Doubtless, too, the theory, whether stated or implied, that later Hebrew is a "decadent" form of the language has played its part. This point of view is a formulation in philological guise of the old theological doctrine that post-Biblical Judaism represents a decline from the exalted standards of Biblical and particularly "Prophetic" religion.

Obviously this notion, whether in theological or philological dress, has no scientific value whatsoever. The Hebrew language has naturally undergone various stages of development, but an organic unity underlies them all. For all the differences among these epochs, there is no wall of demarcation between Biblical and Rabbinic Hebrew, any more than between the various periods in the life of an individual.

Moreover, it is highly hazardous to decide that a given word or usage is "late," because only fragments of ancient Hebrew literature are extant, so that the absence or rarity of a linguistic phenomenon may be purely accidental. To cite a familiar example or two, the conjunction *še* was once confidently explained as a late form, reflecting Aramaic influence (Aramaic *zi, di*) and its presence in the "Song of Songs" was held to be *prima facie* evidence of its late date. It is today recognized as part of the north-Israelite dialect, and was probably used in Southern Palestine as well. Hence its early occurrence in the Oracles of Balaam (Num. 24:3, 15),[1] the Song of Deborah (Judges 5:7), and the story of Gideon (Jud. 7:12; 8:26). The "Mishnic" word *nekhasim* "riches," is met with in such late Biblical books as Ecclesiastes (5:18, 6:2) and Chronicles (II Chr. 1:11, 12). But actually the word is considerably older, as its

[1] See W. F. Albright's highly significant study, "The Oracles of Balaam" (*JBL*, Vol. 63, 1944, pp. 207 ff., especially note 56).

etymology indicates,[2] for it occurs in Joshua 22:8! In the Hebrew text of Ben Sira (50:3) the word 'ašīăḥ "reservoir" occurs, with no Biblical parallel. Fortunately we are prevented from putting it down as late by the fact that it occurs as 'ašūăḥ on the Mesha Inscription (l. 9) almost seven hundred years earlier. Another striking case in point has recently come to light. The verb *kibbel* "receive, accept," (Job 2:10; Est. 9:27) is generally treated as a late Aramaic borrowing. Prof. W. F. Albright has now discovered the form in a Canaanite proverb in the Tel-el-Amarna Letters of the 14th century B. C. E.[3]

A word should be added on the comparative value of the "vertical" and horizontal" approaches, especially because the opposite position is generally adopted, explicitly or by implication. Parallels from other Semitic languages are highly welcome, but they can only establish a possibility or at best a likelihood for a similar use in Hebrew. On the other hand, evidence from later Hebrew literature should be regarded as at least equally strong proof, if not more so, because it proves the *actual existence* of the usage in Hebrew.[4] One *caveat* is in order. One must be certain that the late usage is not merely a citation or an imitation of a Biblical passage.

[2] Cf. Akkadian *nikâsu*, "hew down, behead," Syriac *n'khas* "slay," hence "cattle for slaughter," cf. Latin *pecunia* from *pecus*, English *fee* from Anglo-Saxon *feoh* "cattle, property."

[3] *BASOR*, No. 89, Feb. 1943, pp. 29 ff.

[4] Thus Professor Louis Ginzberg utilized Rabbinic material in his "Randglossen zum hebräischen Ben Sira" (Giessen, 1906) in *Theodor Noeldeke Festschrift*. Cf. also M. Seidel, "Ḥeker Millin" in *Debir*, vol. 1, 1923, pp. 32 ff., and *Hiqre Lashon*, (Jerusalem, 5692). H. Yallon, with his associates, has skillfully utilized Midrashic and Payyetanic sources for Biblical lexicography, in his two series of publications, *Kūntresim Le'inyene Halashon Haivrit*. Cf. e. g. J. Gumpertz in the latter journal (Marheshvan 5703), p. 19. The nineteenth century Hebrew journals like *Keren Hemed, Ha'asif*, also contain much pertinent material, that deserves to be rescued from oblivion. Jewish commentators like Ehrlich have occasionally utilized Rabbinic material as well.

In this paper, Rabbinic material will be utilized for Biblical lexicography and exegesis, principally in the field of semantics and syntax.

אִין

וְאַתֶּם עֵדַי הֲיֵשׁ אֱלוֹהַּ מִבַּלְעָדַי וְאֵין צוּר בַּל־יָדָעְתִּי

Isa. 44:8 cde is generally rendered, "And ye are My witnesses. Is•there a God beside Me? Yea, there is no Rock; I know not any," but the awkwardness of this interpretation is patent. With the interrogative *He* in stich d, we normally expect אִם in stich e (cf. Job 6:6, 5, 12 and frequently). וְאֵין is therefore corrected to וְאִם by most moderns.

The consonantal change, however, is unnecessary. Revocalized as אִין, it is a perfectly satisfactory interrogative particle, like the Aramaic אִין, ܝܢ², which occurs in Palestinian Aramaic in two usages: 1) as equivalent to "if" (Targum to Ps. 7.4 etc.) אין תימר (J. Makk. ii. 31d); and 2) as = *num* (the sign of a question where a negative reply is expected) (Targ. Job 6:6, 12).

This latter use corresponds exactly to our passage, which should be rendered:

"And ye are My witnesses, is there a God beside Me? Or any Rock, whom I do not know?"

The first use of the particle also occurs in Biblical Hebrew, in I Sam. 21:9:

וְאִין יֶשׁ־פֹּה תַחַת־יָדְךָ חֲנִית אוֹ־חָרֶב

Here the suggested change to אֵין with יֵשׁ as a pleonasm (so Kimḥi, Gesenius, Stade) is both awkward and unnecessary. The parallel of Ps. 135:17 אַף אֵין־יֶשׁ־רוּחַ בְּפִיהֶם adduced by Del. and BDB is not to the point, since the latter passage is declarative and not interrogative like the one in Samuel.

It is possible that another instance of this use occurs in Ps. 139:4:

כִּי אֵין מִלָּה בִּלְשׁוֹנִי הֵן ה' יָדַעְתָּ כֻלָּה

The usual rendering is:

> "For there is not a word in my tongue,
> But, lo, O lord, Thou knowest it altogether."

This is logically difficult, since God is described as knowing a non-existent word! A better rendering is: "When there is no word upon my lips (i. e. before the word is spoken), Thou, O, Lord, knowest it all" (Kirkpatrick). This idea, however, should have been expressed בְּטֶרֶם מִלָּה בִלְשׁוֹנִי (cf. Isa. 17:14; 28:4) and our text leaves the heart of this suggested idea unstated.

Ehrlich seeks to avoid this difficulty, by having as the antecedent of כֻלָּה not מִלָּה, but the confidence in God expressed in the entire passage, — a dubious procedure.

It may be suggested that אֵין is to be vocalized as אִין and the verse rendered:

> "If there be a word upon my tongue,
> You, Lord, know it all."

On the use of a predicate nominative after the hypothetical particle, without a copula, cf. Lev. 1:3 אִם־עוֹלָה קָרְבָּנוֹ and Dt. 25:2 וְהָיָה אִם־בִּן הַכּוֹת הָרָשָׁע.

חשב

The Masoretic text of Amos 6:5b כְּדָוִיד חָשְׁבוּ לָהֶם כְּלֵי שִׁיר is usually rendered "Like David, they invent musical instruments." This is generally regarded as unsatisfactory, since we have no reference anywhere to David's inventive proclivities.

Countless emendations have been proposed, among the most curious being Elhorst's:

כַּד וְיָד חָשְׁבוּ לָהֶם וגו' "They consider them — jug and hand!" Sellin deletes כדויד and reads מְלֵי שִׁיר; Kittel reads: כְּדָוִיד נֶחְשְׁבוּ לְהַשְׂכִּיל בְּשִׁיר. Other attempts to interpret the passage may be studied in the commentaries.

We believe that a simpler solution is at hand. In Rabbinic Hebrew חשב means "to regard highly, esteem" as e. g. Ber. 14a: במה חשבתו לזה ולא לאלוה "Why did you esteem this man above God?," and the common adjective חָשׁוּב "important, esteemed."

This meaning occurs in Isa. 13:17 and in Mal. 3:16 לְיִרְאֵי ה' וּלְחֹשְׁבֵי שְׁמוֹ "those who fear God and esteem his name."

D. Yellin (Hiqre Miqra-Isaiah, Jerusalem, 5699) so interprets Isa. 53:3: נִבְזֶה וְלֹא חֲשַׁבְנֻהוּ. We may add that נבזה should be vocalized to read נִבְזֻהוּ = נִבְזֻהָ "we despised him and esteemed him not."

If this meaning is applied to our passage, the prophet paints a sarcastic picture of the devotees of luxury, who pretend to artistic interests, like David the sweet singer of Israel:

"Who strum on the psaltery,
Like David they highly esteem[5] musical instruments."

כִּי

The few particles Hebrew possesses have had an elaborate semantic development, as the nine columns on כִּי in BDB, Lexicon, amply attest.

Nevertheless, several uses have not been clearly noted.

I In Job 39:27 אִם־עַל־פִּיךָ יַגְבִּיהַ נָשֶׁר וְכִי יָרִים קִנּוֹ, stich b is rendered "and is it that it makes its nest on high?," equivalent

---

[5] להם is an ethical dative.

וְכִי הִצִּילוּ אֶת־שֹׁמְרוֹן In Isa. 36:19 .‎6‏ וְאִם עַל פִּיךָ כִי יְרִים קְנוּ to מִיָּדִי is also rendered awkwardly, "have the gods of the nations delivered each his land . . . . and that they have delivered Samaria out of my hand?‎[7]

Actually וְכִי is here used as the *interrogative particle*, exactly like וְאִם in the second half of a double question.[8] This is especially common when a negative answer is expected, and is a frequent usage in Rabbinic Hebrew. Cf. Rosh Hashanah 9a: וכי בתשעה מתענין; Shab. 4a וכי אומרים and countless other instances. Another example in late Biblical Hebrew occurs in I Chron. 29:14 וְכִי מִי אֲנִי.

In a single question, הֲכִי occurs, exactly like הַאִם and it is not to be rendered "Is it that . . ." Cf. Job 6:22: הֲכִי אָמַרְתִּי "Did I say?" So also II Sam. 9:1 הֲכִי יֵשׁ עוֹד אֲשֶׁר נוֹתָר.[9]

II Another and distinct use of כִי as *the comparative particle* (either borrowed from the Akkadian or as a plene spelling of כְּ) is to be found in Isa. 54:9 כִּי מֵי־נֹחַ זֹאת לִי. This form of the particle is familiar on every page of the Talmud כי האי גוונא etc.

On this basis, we have explained[10] the crux in Hab. 2:5:

אַף כִּי־הַיַּיִן בֹּגֵד גֶּבֶר יָהִיר וְלֹא יִנְוֶה

The difficulties may be studied in the commentaries, and countless emendations have been proposed. We suggested the single slight change of בֹּגֵד to בַּנַּת and the verse becomes clear.

---

[6] Driver-Gray, *ICC on Job*, Vol. 2, p. 323; *BDB*, p. 472a bottom.

[7] *BDB*, ibid.

[8] On the parallel development of *ki* as *'im* in the meanings a) "if", b) as the interrogative particle and c) as an asseverative, cf. *JAOS*, vol. 63, 1943, p. 176, n. 5.

[9] In Gen. 27:36, הֲכִי may be the interrogative, added to the conjunction. The verse would then be rendered: "Is it because he is called Jacob, that he has overreached me twice?" Similarly 29:15. "Is it because you are my brother, that you must serve me for nothing?"

[10] Cf. *Horeb*, Tishri, 5695, p. 118.

We have a vivid description of the insatiable ambition of the Assyrian conqueror, whom the prophet compares to an over-flowing winepress in stich a (cf. Joel 4:13) and to death itself in stichs c and d (cf. Pr. 30:15).

The passage is to be rendered:

> Indeed, like the wine in the vat,
> The arrogant man cannot rest,
> He enlarges his desire like the grave
> And like death, is not satisfied.[11]

כ פ ר

Psalm 34:11: כְּפִירִים רָשׁוּ וְרָעֵבוּ וְדֹרְשֵׁי ה' לֹא־יַחְסְרוּ כָל־טוֹב has been generally rendered "the young lions lack and suffer hunger, while those who seek the Lord will not lack for good." In spite of the figurative use of "lions" for "sinners" elsewhere (Ps. 17:12; 35:17; 57:5; Job 4:10 f.) this interpretation is not satisfactory. Lions can scarcely be described as becoming poor (רָשׁוּ) and most authorities have felt the need of a contrast with stich b. The LXX, Vulgate and Pešita have boldly inter-preted כְּפִירִים as "rich." Some moderns have suggested כַּבִּירִים "mighty," but this is no true contrast to דֹרְשֵׁי ה'.

The emendation כֹּפְרִים from the root כפר, Arabic كافر "disbelieve, be a heretic," is rejected by Delitzsch and Chajes on the ground that this meaning is post-Biblical.

---

[11] Albright has recently suggested an emended text based on his Ugaritic studies, (*BASOR*, Oct. 1943, no. 91, p. 40). He reads: אף כי יהיר כהיון נבר בגד לא ינוה which he renders:

> "Even though he be as crafty as Hiyyun,
> A faithless man shall not succeed."

While the proposed text is thoroughly idiomatic Hebrew, it unfortunately requires an extensive rearrangement of several words, and does not link itself with the rest of the verse.

On the basis of the considerations advanced above, it is clear that this is no decisive reason for rejecting this interpretation. Moreover, there is no need to modify the vocalization. כְּפִירִים is probably the plural of the *kâtīl* form כָּפִיר, the active participle, cf. פָּלִיט, עָרִיץ, נָבִיא, פָּרִיץ. In at least one instance, this form occurs with *Kāmes* reduced to *sheva*, נְצִיב "governor," so that the singular may be כְּפִיר.[12]

לֹא

The difficulties of the crux Hos. 10:9: לֹא־תַשִּׂינֵם בַּגִּבְעָה מִלְחָמָה עַל־בְּנֵי עַלְוָה are heightened by the negative particle לֹא. Though the precise sense of the passage eludes us today, it is clear that לֹא is here used interrogatively (=הֲלוֹא) and is therefore equivalent to an emphatic declarative. This use of לֹא is frequent in Rabbinic Hebrew. A few random examples may be cited: Thus the Vilna Talmud edition of Aboth de R. Nathan 6:2 reads:

אמר מי חקק אבן זו אמרו לא המים שתדיר נופלין עליה בכל יום

Schechter's edition (Vienna, 1887) reads אמרו לו המים וגו' (Version A, p. 28). Critical question aside, it is clear that both readings are identical in meaning and are idiomatic Hebrew:

"He said, 'Who has hewn out this rock?' They replied, 'Indeed the waters that fall upon it continually.'" The declarative use of לֹא is especially clear from these passages in *Midrash Tanḥuma*, particularly from the parallel opening and closing clauses. (*Tsav, beg.*, ed. Buber, vol. 3, p. 12.)

(1   אמר הקדוש ברוך הוא אלו הייתי מבקש קרבן לא הייתי
אומר למיכאל שהוא אצלי להקריב קרבן . . . .

(2   מה הקריב אברהם לפניו לא איל אחד

---

[12] Cf. J. Barth, *Nominalbildung in den semitischen Sprachen* (Leipzig, 1889), Sec. 125e, p. 184.

3) אמר לו הקדוש ברוך הוא רשע אם הייתי מבקש קרבן הייתי
אומר למיכאל ולגבריאל והיו מקריבין לי

The passage in Hosea is accordingly to be rendered somewhat
as follows:

"Surely (lit. will not) a war as in Gibeah will overtake the
evil-doers."

This usage occurs also in another passage in Hosea (11:5),
where the parallel stich is in the declarative:

לֹא יָשׁוּב אֶל־אֶרֶץ מִצְרַיִם וְאַשּׁוּר הוּא מַלְכּוֹ

The verse is to be interpreted:

"He will surely (lit. will he not?) return to Egypt, and Assur
will be king over him."

It may be added that Hosea has a fondness for introducing
questions without the interrogative *He*, where the inflection is
the only clue to his meaning (4:16; 13:14).

This interrogative-emphatic use of לֹא may lie at the basis of
the difficult passage, Isa. 7:23–25, which is obviously a distinct
literary unit, being introduced by וְהָיָה, like the fragment
vv. 21–22. In vv. 23 and 24, the prophet declares that the
choice vinelands will be exposed to brambles and thorns. V. 25b
elaborates on the same picture of desolation by describing the
terraced hillsides as becoming grazing lands for cattle.

In this consistent picture, v. 25a seems to offer great diffi-
culty וְכֹל הֶהָרִים אֲשֶׁר בַּמַּעְדֵּר יֵעָדֵרוּן לֹא תָבוֹא שָׁמָּה יִרְאַת שָׁמִיר
וָשָׁיִת. For if תָבוֹא be taken as the 3rd person fem. and יִרְאַת as
its subject (so AV) it would contradict vv. 23, 24 and 25b, by
declaring that "no fear of brambles and thorns would come
there."

Practically all commentators are therefore driven to construe
תָבוֹא as 2nd per. masc. and render, "Thou shalt not come
thither out of fear of brambles and thorns." This, in spite of

the fact, noted by Gray (ICC, *Isaiah*, p. 140 f.) that "the change to second person singular is without apparent reason," and there is no *Mem causae* before יִרְאַת. The text is therefore regarded as corrupt by many moderns, who emend variously, as e. g. יָבוֹא (Duhm, Ehrlich, who also reads מִיִרְאַת), לֹא and וְרָאִיתָ for לֹא and יִרְאַת (Kennedy) etc.

The reading of LXX is cited by Gray (p. 141) as possible evidence of another text: καὶ οὐ μὴ ἐπέλθῃ ἐκεῖ φόβος. ἔσται γὰρ ἀπὸ τῆς χέρσου καὶ ἀκάνθης εἰς βόσκημα προβάτου καὶ εἰς καταπάτημα βοός (= Fear shall not come thither; for from the barren land and thorn it shall be for the feeding of a sheep and the treading of an ox.) Actually, LXX read the Masoretic text in the first half, understood יִרְאַת as an absolute noun, subject of תבוא and read וְהָיָה as יִהְיֶה. Its text read וְלֹא תָבוֹא שָׁמָּה יִרְאַת|שָׁמִיר וָשַׁיִת יִהְיֶה לְמִשְׁלַח, but this is not particularly helpful, except to attest to the Masoretic text.

The difficulty of the MT is easily obviated, if the inter-rogative-declarative use of לֹא is recognized here. The verse may be translated: "As for all the hills now being dug with the mattock, surely (lit. will not) the fear of brambles and thorns will come there, and they shall be used for the grazing of oxen and the trampling of sheep." The entire passage, vv. 23–25, thus paints a consistent picture of ultimate desolation.

סחף

Graetz's well-known emendation of סְפִיחֶיהָ to סְחִיפָה (Job 14:19) (cf. Pr. 28:3 מָטָר סֹחֵף) is accepted by Budde, Beer and most moderns. It is, however, dubbed "precarious" by Driver-Gray (Vol. II, p. 94) because there is no evidence that סחף, meaning "to throw down" in Syriac, would of itself mean a "cloud-burst" or "flood."

We may cite, however, the Talmudic idiom נסתחפה שדך

"your field has been flooded," to substantiate the emendation and the required meaning of the root.

It is possible that סְפִיחֶיהָ should be emended into סְחִיפְיָה "a mighty flood," the Divine name being used as an intensive, cf. שַׁלְהָבָתְיָה (Song 8:6), מַאְפֵּלְיָה (Jer. 2:31).

ס כ ן

Under this caption, the Lexicons distinguish several distinct roots: 1) "be of use, service" (Job 15:3), "be accustomed" Num. 22:30), whence "steward, servant" (Isa. 22:15; I Ki. 1:2) and *perhaps* מִסְכְּנוֹת (Ex. 1:11) "storage cities and 2) "incur danger" (Ecc. 10:9). Probably related only externally are 3) "be poor," (Dt. 8:9, Ecc. 4:13, 15; 9:15 f. and probably Isa. 40:20), apparently a loan-word from the Akkadian *muškênu*, and 4) שֹׂכִין, Pr. 23:2 (late Hebrew סַכִּין, Arabic سكّين, regarded by Noeldeke and Fraenkel as an Aramaic loan-word from an unknown root.

None of these meanings are satisfactory in several passages: Job 22:21 reads: הַסְכָּן־נָא עִמּוֹ וּשְׁלָם בָּהֶם תְּבוֹאָתְךָ טוֹבָה. Here הַסְכֶּן is generally derived from meaning 1 and rendered "show harmony with Him," (BDB) or "acquaint yourself with Him (JPS) and be at peace." Aside from the strained meaning of the verb, the plural pronoun בָּהֶם in stich b is difficult.

We suggest that we have here another distinct root סכן (5), which is to be regarded as a metaplastic form of the common Rabbinic root סכם (הִסְכִּים = "agree") like שָׂטַם ‖ שָׂטַן.

Our passage may now be rendered simply:

> Agree with Him and make peace,
> Through these acts, good will overtake thee.

The use of the plural בָּהֶם otherwise inexplicable, is now clear. *Biblical Hebrew uses a plural pronoun to refer to a single act or thing, if it is expressed by two distinct terms in one passage.*

This principle is clearly indicated by another passage in Job (13:20 f.):

אַךְ־שְׁתַּיִם אַל־תַּעַשׂ עִמָּדִי אָז מִפָּנֶיךָ לֹא אֶסָּתֵר

כַּפְּךָ מֵעָלַי הַרְחַק וְאֵמָתְךָ אַל־תְּבַעֲתַנִּי

Here God's removing His hand and His desisting from frightening Job are obviously identical, yet the poet refers to them as שתים, two acts! So, too, in our passage הסכן and שלם are parallel in construction and identical in meaning, but they are referred to by the plural pronoun בָּהֶם.

This usage in Biblical syntax explains several Biblical passages that have hitherto been unclear and in some instances been subjected to emendation. Thus Ez. 18:26: בְּשׁוּב צַדִּיק מִצִּדְקָתוֹ וְעָשָׂה עָוֶל וּמֵת עֲלֵיהֶם. Here 'alēhĕm refers to בְּשׁוּב צַדִּיק and וְעָשָׂה עָוֶל, though they are identical in meaning. The same construction occurs also in Ez. 33:18, 19:

בְּשׁוּב צַדִּיק מִצִּדְקָתוֹ וְעָשָׂה עָוֶל . . . .

וּבְשׁוּב רָשָׁע מֵרִשְׁעָתוֹ וְעָשָׂה מִשְׁפָּט וּצְדָקָה עֲלֵיהֶם הוּא יִחְיֶה

In Zech. 2:6, 7:

וְהָיְתָה חֶבֶל הַיָּם נְוֹת כְּרֹת רֹעִים וְגִדְרוֹת צֹאן

וְהָיָה חֶבֶל לִשְׁאֵרִית בֵּית יְהוּדָה עֲלֵיהֶם יִרְעוּן

עֲלֵיהֶם is generally emended into עַל הַיָּם (Wellhausen, Oort, Marti, Driver, J. M. P. Smith), עֲגֵלִים (Bachmann) or עָלָיו הֵם (Van Hoonacker). Here no change is required; עֲלֵיהֶם refers back to כְּרֹת רֹעִים and גִּדְרוֹת צֹאן, and the passage is to be rendered:

The sea district will become
Pastures for shepherds and sheep enclosures,
And the district will belong
To the remnant of the house of Judah.
Upon them (the pastures and enclosures) they will feed, etc.

170

This use of the plural pronoun in referring to two parallel
antecedents is the clue to Isa. 49:14:

הֲתִשְׁכַּח אִשָּׁה עוּלָהּ מֵרַחֵם בֶּן־בִּטְנָהּ
גַּם אֵלֶּה תִשְׁכַּחְנָה וְאָנֹכִי לֹא אֶשְׁכָּחֵךְ

Here אֵלֶּה has no antecedent in the MT and שכח is construed with a Mem, מֵרַחֵם which is impossible. The various
emendations proposed fall away if מרחם is recognized as a
noun, meaning "woman, mother." Cf. רַחַם Ju. 5:30, רחם in
Mesha Inscription (l. 17), and in Ugaritic.

Its vocalization may be מְרַחָם cf. קְדָשׁ, מִקְדָשׁ; דֶּרֶךְ, מִדְרָךְ,
etc. Perhaps the word occurs in the enigmatic verse Ps. 110:3.
At all events, our verse now exhibits perfect parallelism:

> "Can a woman forget her sucking child,
> A mother, the offspring of her womb?
> Yea, these may forget,
> But I will not forget thee!

Another difficult passage containing סכן is Job 22:2: הֲלְאֵל
יִסְכָּן־גָּבֶר כִּי־יִסְכֹּן עָלֵימוֹ מַשְׂכִּיל. It is usually rendered as
follows:

> "Can a man be profitable to God?
> Indeed, a righteous man benefits himself alone!
> (Driver-Gray)

This question-and-answer construction is harsh. An alternative rendering of stich b is:

> "Or can a man that is wise also be profitable unto Him?"
> (JPS)

Even this is difficult, since *or* is not expressed, כִּי is left
untranslated and the entire idea is prolix.

It appears that the passage exhibits a paronomasia, playing

on two meanings of סכן, "serve" (as in Job 15:3) and "agree" (as in Job 22:21):

> "Is a man useful to God,
> "When a righteous man agrees with Him? (i. e. fulfills God's
> will)"

This is precisely the meaning of Job 34:9, which is unquestionably based on our passage:

כִּי־אָמַר לֹא יִסְכָּן־גָּבֶר בִּרְצֹתוֹ עִם־אֱלֹהִים

This is correctly rendered by JPS:

> "It profiteth a man nothing, that he should be in accord
> with God!"

בִּרְצֹתוֹ thus testifies to the meaning of סכן in 22:26!

This meaning סכן = "agree," rather than "be useful," may also be the basis of Ps. 139:3 וְכָל דְּרָכַי הִסְכַּנְתָּה, "with all my ways you are familiar," exactly as ידע "know" means "to favor, look with approval upon" (Am. 3:2; Ps. 1:6). The root סכן V "agree" would thus govern עם (Job 22:11), אל = על (Job 22:2) and the direct accusative (Ps. 139:3).

סתר

While the common Biblical root סתר means "hide, conceal," Rabbinic Hebrew uses a homonym meaning "destroy, upset," as in the Mishnah Shab. 7:2 הבונה והסותר and the familiar proverb: (Meg. 31b and elsewhere) סתירת זקנים בנין "When elders destroy, they are really building."

"The Arabic and Ethiopic šatara, "lacerate," Akkadian šatâru II "tear down" and Sabean שתר "destroy," all indicate that the sibilant in this root was originally a Sin. Cf. I Sam. 5:9: וַיִּשָּׂתְרוּ לָהֶם עֳפָלִים (כ׳) "tumors broke out in them." The change in orthography to *Samekh* already occurs in Biblical Aramaic (Ez. 5:12).

It has not been noted that this root occurs also in Biblical Hebrew. The meaning "destroy" is far more appropriate than the usual rendering "be hidden:" וְאָבְדָה חָכְמַת חֲכָמָיו וּבִינַת נְבוֹנָיו תִּסְתַּתָּר. (Isa. 29:14)

"The wisdom of their sages shall perish and the understanding of their wise men shall be destroyed." For the parallel of אבד and סתר cf. אבד and נצת (Jer. 9:11) and אבד and כרת (Jer. 7:28).

עון

In II Sam. 16:12, אוּלַי יִרְאָה ה' בעוני (כ') בְּעֵינִי ק', it is generally recognized that the Qere is impossible. Most commentators emend the Kethib to בְּעָנְיִ on the basis of LXX and Vulgate.

The Kethib, however, which is to be vocalized בַּעֲוֹנִי, as we have pointed out elsewhere,[13] is to be preferred. The suffix is an objective genitive, like חֲמָסִי (Gen. 16:5) "the wrong done to me." Driver argues that only חָמָס and not עָוֹן could be used in this sense of "injury, offense."

However, this use of עון occurs in Medieval Hebrew in a passage which is not a reminiscence of our verse. In the "Rule of Asher ben Jehiel,"[14] the text reads:

ותכנע לפניו לבקש ממנו מחילה
אל יגבה לבך לאמר יש לי עון ממנו

Abrahams translates the last clause freely, but correctly "I am the injured party."[14] Literally, of course, it means" I have suffered a wrong from him."

Our Biblical passage is to be rendered "Perhaps the Lord will see the wrong done me."

[13] Cf. *The Biblical Text in the Making* (Phila. 1937), p. 148 and n. 473.
[14] I. Abrahams, *Hebrew Ethical Wills* (Phila. 1926), vol. 1, p. 122.

עצב

In Zech. 11:16: כִּי הִנֵּה־אָנֹכִי מֵקִים רֹעֶה בָּאָרֶץ הַנִּכְחָדוֹת
לֹא־יִפְקֹד הַנַּעַר לֹא יְבַקֵּשׁ וְהַנִּשְׁבֶּרֶת לֹא יְרַפֵּא הַנִּצָּבָה לֹא יְכַלְכֵּל
וּבְשַׂר הַבְּרִיאָה יֹאכַל וּפַרְסֵיהֶן יְפָרֵק. The Masoretic text is rendered by JPS, "For lo, I will raise up a shepherd in the land,
who will not think of those that are cut off, neither will he seek
those that are young, nor heal that which is broken; neither
will he feed that which standeth still, but he will eat the flesh
of the fat and will break their hoofs in pieces."

The several difficulties are obvious. הַנַּעַר cannot mean "the
young" and has been emended into הַנַּחַת or הַנֶּעְדָּרָה (Oort),
the latter occurring in a similar context in Ez. 34:4. That some
such meaning is required is clear, besides being attested by the
Versions (LXX, P, V, Targum), so that the suggestion הַנֹּעָה
"one wandering off" (ICC) easily commends itself.

But another problem still remains. "He will not feed the
one standing still" is meaningless. Nowack's proposed הַנַּחְלָה
"the ill one," Harper and Kennedy's הָרְעֵבָה are both too distant graphically from הַנִּצָּבָה.

A simpler expedient is at hand. We suggest that הנצבה has
elided the Ayin and=הַנֶּעְצָבָה "the injured one," as in Ecc.
10:9 מַסִּיעַ אֲבָנִים יֵעָצֵב בָּהֶם, "he who removes rocks will be
hurt by them." On the development of meaning, from עצב
"grieve, sorrow" to "physical injury," we may compare צַעַר
"grief" and the Rabbinic use המצטער פטור מן הסוכה (Suk. 26a)
"he who feels physically uncomfortable is exempt from sitting
in the Sukkah."

On the absence of an Ayin in the Masoretic text, cp. inter
alia Am. 8:8 Kethib ונשקה, Qere וְנִשְׁקְעָה and Jos. 15:29 בַּעֲלָה
by the side of בָּלָה Jos. 19:3, as well as such likely examples
as Isa. 53:9 עֹשִׂי רָע=עָשִׁיר; Mi. 1:10 בְּכוֹ=בְּעַכּוֹ;

Neh. 5:2 רַבִּים=עֲרָבִים and רוּת=רְעוּת. Other instances, many of which must be taken with caution, are given in F. Delitzsch, *Schreib- und Lese-fehler*, sec. 16 and J. Kennedy, *An Aid to the Textual Amendment of the O. T.*, p. 27.

The Pilpel of כּוּל=כִּלְכֵּל means basically "sustain, maintain," hence a) "nourish, feed" (Gen. 45:11; 50:21 and elsewhere), and b) "sustain a cause, manage affairs" as in Ps. 112:5: יְכַלְכֵּל דְּבָרָיו בְּמִשְׁפָּט. Particularly apposite to our passage are Pr. 18:14: רוּחַ אִישׁ יְכַלְכֵּל מַחֲלֵהוּ, "A man's spirit causes him to endure sickness," and the classic phrase of the *Amidah*: מְכַלְכֵּל חַיִּים בְּחֶסֶד, "He sustains the living in loving-kindness."

Our passage may now be rendered:

"For lo, I will raise up a shepherd in the land, who will not think of the one cut off,

Nor will he seek the one wandered off, nor will he heal the one maimed,

Neither will he sustain the one that is injured,

But he will eat the flesh of the fat, and will break their hoofs in pieces."

ק שׁ ה

The book of Job is replete with the language of legal controversy and argumentation, as e. g. *rībh*, *šōfēt*, *hōkhīāḥ* (pass.). It should be noted that several of the terms find their analogies in the technical terms of Talmudic debate.

Thus in Job 15:2 דַּעַת רוּחַ does not mean "windy knowledge" (JPS) but "foolish opinion," cf. דַּעַת יָחִיד="single opinion" etc. as Ehrlich has recognized. We may add also דֵּעַ (Job 32:7, 10)=opinion.

In Job 13:22 and 37:5, 32 הֲשִׁיבֵנִי is generally taken as an elipsis for הֲשִׁיבֵנִי דָבָר as in II Sam. 3:11. Doubtless the idiom originated in this manner, but in láter Hebrew הֵשִׁיב alone means "to answer." This is clear from II Chron. 10:16 וַיָּשִׁיבוּ הָעָם אֶת הַמֶּלֶךְ as against its earlier parallel in I Ki. 12:16: וַיָּשִׁיבוּ הָעָם אֶת הַמֶּלֶךְ דָּבָר. Note particularly Job 20:2 where יְשִׁיבוּנִי must mean "cause me to answer." This usage of השיב, התיב is common in Talmudic Hebrew and Aramaic.

In Job 9:4 מִי הִקְשָׁה אֵלָיו וַיִּשְׁלָם is taken to mean "who has hardened his heart against him and escaped safely?" (Rashi, Ibn Ezra, Driver-Gray). While the elipsis הקשה for הקשה לב occurs in one passage (Ex. 13:15), our context refers not to obstinacy, but to arguing with God, cf. v. 3: אִם יַחְפֹּץ לָרִיב עִמּוֹ. הִקְשָׁה is therefore better taken in the Talmudic sense, "ask a question, argue" as e. g. Hor. 3a חריף ומקשה "acute in argumentation," and often.

Our passage should then be rendered:

However wise or mighty one may be,
Who has ever argued with Him and emerged unscathed?

שיר

In Amos 8:3a וְהֵילִילוּ שִׁירוֹת הֵיכָל, the Masoretic text is usually rendered, "The songs of the palace shall be wailings on that day." This translation disguises, but does not solve, the difficulty in the Hebrew, which says: "The songs shall wail on that day." In connection with this interpretation, Harper (ICC, p. 180) justly remarks that "the present text yields no sense." Accordingly the passage has been generally emended to read שָׁרוֹת "singers," (Oort, Nowack, Marti, Harper, Kittel, Sellin).

No change, however, is required. שִׁירוֹת is to be understood in the meaning "walls." This word occurs in a variety of forms:

שׁוּר (Gen. 49:22; II Sam. 22:30); שָׂרָה (in עָלוּ בְּשָׁרוֹתֶיהָ Jer.
5:10; so Vss., most commentators); late Hebrew שׁוּרָה "wall,
row" (cf. Job 24:11).

A by-form שׁוּרָה ‖ שִׁירָה is quite likely, cf. such parallel forms
as: צִירִים Isa. 45:16 parallel to צוּרָה; שִׁיחָה Ps. 57:7; 119:85
parallel to שׁוּחָה Jer. 2:6; 18:20, etc.

Actually a clue to the correct interpretation has long been
available in the LXX rendering τα φατνώματα "panels, com-
partments of ceiling." This has been variously explained as
representing קוֹרוֹת (Riedel), סְפֻנִים (Valeton), קִירוֹת (Tychsen),
and שׁוּרוֹת (Dahl, Schleusner).

That this suggestion in LXX has generally been overlooked
is probably due to the fact that the meaning still remained
obscure. However, the prophet's figure is strikingly illustrated
by a beautiful passage in the Midrash *Ekhah Zuta* 1:2 (ed.
Buber, p. 53):

למה נשתנה בוכה בלילה מבוכה ביום שהבוכה
בלילה כותלי הבית ומזלי רקיע נושאים עמו קינה

"Why is he who weeps at night different from him who weeps
by day? When a man weeps by night, *the walls of the house*
and the planets in the heavens weep with him."

Our passage may therefore be rendered literally, "The walls
of the palace will wail on that day."

שער

In Deut. 32:17, the accepted rendering of stich d לֹא שְׂעָרוּם
אֲבוֹתֵיכֶם, "which your fathers dreaded not,"[15] derives the verb
from שער "bristle with horror" (Jer. 2:12; Ez. 27:35; 32:10).

15 So Rashi, Ibn Ezra, English Versions; Driver, *ICC* ad loc., p. 363.

Yet this verb never occurs with the accusative personae, being a denominative verb.

The parallelism with יָדְעוּם and LXX ᾔδεισαν has suggested to some scholars the more appropriate meaning "be acquainted with" (Arabic شعر "perceive," Aramaic סְעַר "visit," perceive)[16].

This verb however, would be a hapax legomenon, not only in Biblical, but in all Hebrew literature.

Rabbinic Hebrew offers another suggestion, the common root שָׁעַר "estimate, calculate, appraise." This is actually suggested in the Midrash:[17]

לא שערום אבותיכם לידע אם יש בהם צורך אם לא

"Your ancestors never appraised them, to know whether there was any need of them or not."

The passage requires a somewhat more generalized meaning — "consider, conceive."

> "They sacrifice to demons, no-gods,
> Gods they did not know,
> New ones, recently arrived,
> Whom your ancestors never conceived of."

Katul — a nomen agentis

Shortly before his death, V. Aptowitzer[18] published an interesting interpretation of one of the most troublesome passages in Rabbinic literature: טוב שבגויים הרוג (Mekhilta Beshallah, sec. 1, end; J. Kiddushin end; Sopherim sec. 15). Ordinarily the passage is rendered literally, "The best of the Gentiles —

---

[16] Barth, *Etymologische Studien*, p. 87; Perles, *Analecten*, p. 75.
[17] *Pes. Zutr.* ad loc. (ed. Buber, p. 114); *Yalkut Shimeoni*, Deut. sec. 845.
[18] In the Palestinian newspaper "Ha-aretz," 21 Adar, 5700.

kill him!" and it has naturally been exploited by antisemites for centuries.

Aptowitzer construed הרוג not as imperative הֲרוֹג but as a *nomen agentis*, הָרוֹג "killer," like the Biblical בָּחוֹן Jer. 6:27; עָשׁוֹק 22:3; בָּגוֹדָה 3:27; and such Mishnic forms as לקוח, כרוז, מסור.

To buttress his view, he noted that in the adjacent passages, descriptions of all kinds appear: רוב ממזרים פקחים, כשר שבטבחים שותפו של עמלק, etc. The only example of an imperative in the entire passage הטוב שבנחשים רצוץ את מוחו has a direct object, so that we should have expected a form like הרגהו, were it a verb.

Whether this interesting interpretation of the Talmudic passage be regarded as convincing or not, it is certain that הרוג as a *nomen agentis* occurs in the Bible, except that it is vocalized in the alternate *Kătūl* form, a fact Aptowitzer overlooked. This form of the *nomen agentis* occurs also in אַהֲבַת רֵעַ "loving a paramour" (Ho. 3:1); Ps. 137:8 הַשְּׁדוּדָה "Babylon the despoiler," הַתֵּלִּים "mockers" (Job 17:2).

In Hos. 4:17 חֲבוּר עֲצַבִּים is emended by Sellin to חוֹבֵר, who renders "creating a spell, bringing life into dead images." Whether the phrase be interpreted in this fashion, or simply as "joiner, fashioner of idols," (cf. Dt. 18:11; Isa. 44:11) the change is unnecessary, the *kătul* form being the *nomen agentis*. Similarly LXX renders רָצוּץ and עָשׁוֹק in Hos. 5:11 by active participles, but they may well have read the *kătul* forms of MT and there is no evidence that they read רוֹצֵץ and עוֹשֵׁק (against Sellin).

The passage in question is Isa. 27:7 הַכְּמַכַּת מַכֵּהוּ הִכָּהוּ אִם כְּהֶרֶג הֲרֻגָיו הֹרָג. Here הֲרֻגָיו is emended to הֹרְגָיו to make it parallel to מַכֵּהוּ (BH Kittel, ad loc.). When הֲרֻגָיו is recognized as the *nomen agentis*, no change is required, and the

Masoretic text means: "Has he been killed like the killing of his killers? (i. e. has he suffered the same fate as his would-be destroyers?)"

A Possible Tikkun Sopherim

In Hos. 4:15, we read:

אִם־זֹנֶה אַתָּה יִשְׂרָאֵל אַל־יֶאְשַׁם יְהוּדָה
וְאַל־תָּבֹאוּ הַגִּלְגָּל וְאַל־תַּעֲלוּ בֵּית אָוֶן וְאַל־תִּשָּׁבְעוּ חַי ה'

This verse is generally taken to be a plea addressed by the prophet to Judah not to follow the evil example of Israel. But if that were its intent, Judah should have been directly addressed in second person:

אִם זֹנֶה יִשְׂרָאֵל אַל תֶּאְשַׁם יְהוּדָה .

"If Israel plays the harlot, do not you be guilty, O Judah!"

Moreover, the references to the shrines of Gilgal and Beth-El imply that it is Israel that is being addressed (cf. Hos. 12:12; Am. 4:4).

It may therefore be suggested that in יהודה we have a virtual תקון סופרים like מְנַשֶּׁה for מֹשֶׁה in Judges 18:30. The text read originally אַל־יֶאְשַׁם יהוה. The purpose of this tendencious change would obviously be to avoid an unpleasant reference to the Deity: "let not the Lord be held guilty," even though the allegation is denied. For a similar procedure, cf. the *Tikkun* לֹא נָמוּת for לֹא יָמוּת (Hab. 1:12), where even the denial of God's mortality is held to be unworthy and hence the text is changed.[19]

The insertion of a *Daled* into the Tetragrammaton is a very

---

[19] Mekhilta Shirata on Ex. 15:5 (ed. Lauterbach, vol. 2, p. 43 f.); Tanḥuma, Beshallaḥ on Ex. 15:7 (ed. Horeb, p. 230); Sifre, Numb. 10:35 (ed. Friedmann, p. 22b); Masorah ad Num. 1:1; Ps. 106:12.

easy way of modifying the text. Rabbinic sources are familiar
with the device of suspended letters to correct an *error* of omission in writing the Divine name. Cf. Sopherim 5:4 (ed. Higger,
p. 154): הַכּוֹתֵב אֶת הַשֵּׁם וְטָעָה אוֹת אֶחָד יִתְלֶנָה מִלְמַעְלָה. In fact,
the possibility of confusing "Judah" and the Tetragrammaton
is explicitly recognized and discussed in detail (Sopherim 5:2–4,
ed. Higger, pp. 151 ff.). Cf. 5:2:

הכותב יהודה ולא נתן בו דלת יתלנה מלמעלה

הכותב את השם וכתב יהודה וגו'

היה צריך לכתוב יהודה ונתכוון וכתב את השם

In our passage, of course, the change was conscious, but later
forgotten. It is well known that the Rabbinic sources give
various rubrics of *Tikkune Sopherim*, differing in number and
identity, and there is no ground for assuming that any one is
exhaustive.[20]

The writer is grateful to Professor Marx for recalling in this
connection the widespread usage in medieval texts, which print
אלהים with a Daled as אלדים, in order to avoid writing the
Divine name.[21]

The prophet's meaning is clear and the two halves of the
verse now have a close connection. If the people insist on worshipping Baal, let them not identify him with the God of Israel.
Let them cease making pilgrimages to the Lord's sacred shrines,
Gilgal and Beth-el, and stop invoking His name. On this well-
known prophetic hostility to the religious syncretism practiced
by the people, cf. *inter alia* I Ki. 18:21; Hos. 2:18.

[20] The Sifre lists 7 examples, the Mekhilta 11; the Tanḥuma 13; the Masorah 15 or 18.
[21] E. g. in the 1st Roman Maḥzor (Soncino 1485), which prints the Divine
name with Daled consistently.

The passage is to be rendered:

> "If you, Israel, play the harlot,
> Let not the Lord be involved (lit. be held guilty),
> Do not come to Gilgal,
> Nor go to Beth-el
> Nor swear 'as the Lord liveth'."

If this view of the passage is adopted, the verse will prove highly significant for the history of Jewish religious thought, and deserves far more extended treatment than can be given here. It serves as a striking illustration of the thesis advanced by Professor Gershom G. Sholem[22] that there are three main stages in monotheistic religion: a) the *primitive*, when the communion of God and the worshipper is immediate and no abyss exists between them; b) the *creative*, when the consciousness develops of the transcendence of God, so that the distance between God and man is acutely felt as absolute and c) the *mystical*, which Sholem calls the "romantic" period, when the attempt is made to close the gap by evolving new means of communion and reestablishing unity between man and his Maker. Thus the third stage reverts to the first or mythical level, but with significant differences. At all events, the first · and third periods are mutually illuminating.

The idea that God Himself may be "guilty" because of human sin and be in need of atonement is well-known from the Kabbalah. Our passage would thus be expressing this idea that God becomes involved in man's wrong-doing, on a considerably less sophisticated level, as is to be expected. It should be noted that adumbrations of this doctrine exist in Talmudic

---

[22] In *Major Trends in Jewish Mysticism* (Jerusalem, 1941), pp. 7–10.

literature. Cf. e. g. (Bereshit Rabbah 6:4): אמר הקב"ה הביאו
כפרה עלי שמיעטתי את הירח, "Said the Holy One, blessed be
He, 'Bring atonement for Me, because I reduced the size of the
moon'." (A slightly varying text in B. Shevuot 9a; Hullin 60b.)
The fruitful and fundamental Rabbinic concept of *Ḥillul Hashem*
is also closely related, implying that God's name (i. e. His
essence) is violated by man's misdoing.

Even the Bible exhibits similar ideas, as for example in the
belief that God shares in the suffering of Israel (Isa. 63:9):
בְּכָל־צָרָתָם לוֹ (ק') צָר and in the common idea that His name
would be profaned by calamities coming upon the Jewish people
(e. g. Ezek. 20:9, 14, 22; cf. Num. 14:16 ff.; Deut. 32:27 for a
similar idea in the simplest possible terms).

Ecc. 8:2: אֲנִי פִּי־מֶלֶךְ שְׁמֹר וְעַל־דִּבְרַת שְׁבוּעַת אֱלֹהִים

The pronoun אֲנִי in this position is very difficult, and without
analogy in Biblical literature. Many scholars supply אָמַרְתִּי
before (Keil, Ginsburg, Delitzsch, Wright, Siegfried), but the
loss of an entire word is not likely. Wildeboer emends אני to
בְּנִי. But this term, common in Prov. 1–9, and in Rabbinic
literature, does not occur in Ecclesiastes proper, 12:12 being
part of the Epilogue.

An interesting parallel to the usage in our passage, of the
first pronoun without a verb, occurs in B. Kid. 44a:

אמר רב נחמן בר יצחק אנא לא רב אבין ברבי חייא ולא רבי
אבין בר כהנא אלא רב אבין סתם.

R. Nahman ben Isaac said:

"I *report this tradition*, not in the name of R. Abin ben Hiyya
or R. Abin bar Kahana, but simply in the name of R. Abin
(without a patronymic)."

So in our passage, a verb must be understood "I declare,
'observe the word of the king'," etc.

LIST OF PASSAGES INTERPRETED

Gen. 27:36; 29:15.
Deut. 32:17.
I Sam. 21:9.
II Sam. 9:1; 16:12.
Isa. 7:25; 13:17; 27:7; 29:14; 36:19; 44:8; 49:14; 53:3; 54:9.
Ez. 18:26; 33:18, 19.
Hos. 3:1; 4:15; 10:7; 11:5.
Amos 6:5; 8:3.
Hab. 2:5.
Zech. 2:6, 7; 11:16.
Mal. 3:16.
Ps. 34:11; 137:8; 139:3; 139:4.
Job 6:22; 9:4; 13:20; 14:19; 15:2; 22:2; 22:21; 39:27.
Ecc. 8:2.
I Chr. 29:14.

STUDIES IN HEBREW ROOTS OF CONTRASTED MEANINGS

SEMITISTS have long been aware of the existence of a considerable number of words possessing mutually contradictory meanings. This phenomenon (*Addad*) is especially common in Arabic, but is by no means lacking in Hebrew. In fact, mediaeval Hebraists: Menahem ben Saruk, Abulwalid ibn Ganah, Abraham ibn Ezra, Joseph Kara, and others, noted individual instances of this usage, like *berek* "bless" and "curse," and many others.

In modern times, attempts were made to discover the cause, but without great success.[1] Whatever the validity of the explanations, the existence of the phenomenon itself is beyond dispute. In a learned monograph, Landau[2] collected a great deal of Hebrew material, much of which was however dubious or irrelevant. Noeldeke was constrained to note the uncritical character of Landau's work. In a masterly essay,[3] the great Semitic scholar presented a much smaller number of Hebrew examples, but did not pretend to exhaust all instances of this usage. Other scholars have occasionally suggested additional examples, the most recent being M. Seidel.[4]

---

[1] A critique of the theories advanced, and a new approach to the problem is attempted by the writer in his essay "Some Effects of Primitive Thought on Language", which will be published in the *American Journal of Semitic Languages*.

[2] *Gegensinnige Wörter im Hebräischen*.

[3] "Wörter mit Gegensinn" in *Neue Beiträge zur semitischen Sprachwissenschaft*, pp. 68–108.

[4] In a Hebrew monograph, *Hiqre Lashon* (Jerusalem, 1935).

33

In this paper, we wish to propose some hitherto unrecognized roots with contrasted meanings, which prove of value for biblical exegesis (nos. 1–6) or for Hebrew etymology generally (nos. 7–28). For the sake of completeness, we have included all roots not noted by Noeldeke, even if they have been discussed elsewhere.

1. אפק

This verb which occurs half a dozen times in the Bible is generally understood to mean: "control, restrain one's feelings." This meaning it undoubtedly has in Gen. 43.31, Isa. 64.11 and Esther 5.10. However, this significance does not suit the other passages as well, and so the lexicons seek to give it a more general meaning: "hold, be strong"[5], based on the Arabic roots 'afiḳa and fa'ḳa, "excel," "surpass." Even these meanings are of little value for the Hebrew root, as a consideration of some difficult passages makes evident:

I Sam. 13.12 ואמר עתה ירדו פלשתים אלי הגלגל ופני ה' לא חליתי ואתאפק ואעלה העלה

Saul apologizes for having offered the sacrifice without waiting for Samuel. All the versions and commentators have seen the difficulty, but have had no recourse except to interpret "I forced myself and offered up the sacrifice."[6] What Saul undoubtedly means is: "I could not control myself any longer and I offered up the sacrifice." We should like to suggest that the verb התאפק actually possesses this meaning. It would mean "restrain one's feelings" and also its opposite, "give vent to one's feelings," "pour forth one's feelings, express oneself." To this second meaning, the

[5] See BDB, s. v.
[6] So LXX, Vul., Pesh., Modern Versions, etc.

Arabic roots would be genuinely cognate.[7] Moreover, Noeldeke has shown the close affinity between *Hamza* and *primae Nun* roots.[8] Thus אפק and נפק would be related, the latter being the common Aramaic root for "go out." The relationship between the two roots is borne out by the Syriac *'afaḳa* "canal, sewer," which Payne-Smith places under the root *nefaḳ*. Hence התאפק would have the significance "let loose one's feelings, pour forth one's emotions." This gives excellent sense in our passage: "And I said, 'Now will the Philistines come down upon me to Gilgal, and I have not entreated the favor of the Lord.' So I lost control of myself and offered the sacrifice."

Isa. 63.15 הבט משמים וראה מזבל קדשך ותפארתך

איה קנאתך וגבורתיך המון מעיך ורחמיך אלי התאפקו

Stich d has always been difficult because of its last two words. Not only does the preposition אלי fail to suit התאפק in the sense of "refrain, restrain oneself," but the connection with the rest of the verse is by no means smooth. The last few words have been taken as an independent clause by some interpreters, either with declarative or interrogative force:

Where is thy zeal and thy strength, the sounding of thy bowels and thy mercies toward me? Are they restrained?[9]

Where . . . . mercies? They are restrained against me.[10]

[7] *Fa'ḳa*, I, means: to surpass, overcome; hiccough; (spirit) to pass forth, die; IV, recover (from illness), awake (from sleep); *'afaḳa*, go heedlessly, excel: all of which have the sense of external movement or expression.

[8] In *Neue Beiträge zur semitischen Sprachwissenschaft*, pp. 179–206. Compare below the root אצל as parallel to נצל.

[9] So A. V.

[10] So Vulgate, Joseph Kara, Rashi, Ibn Ezra, Kimhi.

187

Others have preferred to construe the last words as a subordinate clause—Where is . . . . the sounding of thy mercies, that they are restrained toward me?[11]

Though this is a preferable construction, the difficulty of התאפק with אל remains. Most moderns therefore emend the words into אל נא תתאפק or delete them from the text.[12]

On the strength of the meaning advanced above, the difficulties of the masoretic text disappear. התאפק means "express one's emotions" and the stichs are to be rendered:

Where is thy zeal and thy strength,

The abundance of thy pity and mercies, that were poured out toward me?

Gen. 45.1   ולא יכל יוסף להתאפק לכל הנצבים עליו ויקרא הוציאו
כל איש מעלי ולא עמד איש אתו בהתודע יוסף אל אחיו

The accepted rendering is: "And Joseph could not refrain himself before all them that stood by him, and he cried, 'Cause every man to go out from me.' And there stood no man with him when Joseph made himself known to his brothers."

In this rendering לכל הנצבים עליו is meaningless—"Joseph could not refrain himself, and he cried, etc." would be all that is required. The bystanders were preventing,. not his self-control, but his revealing himself to his brothers, as the second half of the verse clearly indicates.

Ehrlich feels the difficulty and renders "And Joseph was unable to control himself as he should have controlled himself, because of those standing near him"[13]—which is awkward and not in the text.

---

[11] So LXX, and Jewish Version. This construction is followed by Peshitta which renders דאתהפכו עלי reading or interpreting (?) אלי התהפכו.

[12] So Ehrlich ad loc.

[13] In *Miqra Kipsheshuto*, ad loc.

In our view, the passage is clear and unforced:

The pathetic and manly appeal of Judah has broken down Joseph's haughty reserve. "And Joseph could not give vent to his emotions before all them that stood by him, and he cried, 'Cause every man to go out from me.' And there stood no man with him when Joseph made himself known to his brothers."[13a]

Isa. 42.14   החשיתי מעולם אחריש אתאפק כיולדה אפעה אשם ואשאף
יחד

The best English rendering of this verse is:

> "I have long time held my peace
> I have been still, and refrained myself;
> Now will I cry like a travailing woman,
> Gasping and panting at once."[14]

This translation glosses over all the difficulties of the original. There is no word for "now" in the Hebrew. On the contrary, the transition from the silence of the past to the present excitement is extremely abrupt.

Rhythmically, too, this rendering is unsatisfactory, as it yields two stichs, the first of four long words, the second of five, (or, two and three).

We are unable to remove the abrupt transition, but believe that by taking אתאפק in the sense of "express one's

---

[13a] After this paper was read at the Society of Biblical Exegesis, Dr. A. S. Halkin kindly called our attention to the fact that Saadia renders this word in his Bible translation by יתרפק (=treat with kindness). He approximates our meaning more closely in his alternative rendering יתחרך (=be moved, stirred). See the text and notes of the translation (ed. J. Derenbourg, *Oeuvres Complètes de Saadia*, vol. I, p. 71).

[14] Jewish Version and most moderns. Lagarde reads מֵעַוְלָם, "because of their sin". LXX and Itala take the first two words interrogatively and render, "Will I be silent forever?" as though the text read הַלְעוֹלָם.

feelings," we get three stichs of three beats each, which is
the dominant rhythm of the entire section:

החשיתי מעולם אחריש

אתאפק כיולדה אפעה   אשם ואשאף יחד

I have - been-silént, long-tíme, held-my-peáce,

Now - I shall - expréss - myself, I-shall- cŕy like -a-
tra-vailing-womán

Gaspíng and - pantíng at-oncé.

2. חדל

This Hebrew root is frequently used in the meaning
"cease."[15] In some striking passages, notably the beautiful
and enigmatic 49th Psalm, this meaning proves inadequate.

Ps. 49.9

לא יתן לאלהים כפרו	8. אח לא פדה יפדה איש
וחדל לעולם	9. ויקר פדיון נפשם
לא יראה השחת	10. ויחי עוד לנצח

The general sense of the passage is clear. A man cannot
redeem his fellow-man from death, by paying ransom to
God. Unfortunately, v. 9, especially stich b, seems to interfere with the connection of 8 and 10. Most commentators
are therefore compelled to assume that v. 9 is a parenthesis,
between the main clause in v. 8 and the result clauses of
v. 10. Accordingly they render:

No man can by any means redeem his brother
Nor give God his ransom
(For the ransom of their soul is precious
And it ceaseth for ever)

---

[15] It has no Semitic analogue except the Sabean חדל, be negligent.
See Brown-Driver-Briggs, s. v.

That he should still live for ever

And not see corruption.[16]

To avoid this recourse to the awkward parenthesis, Chajes[17] suggests that וחדל לעולם is an error for וחי עד לעולם and that the entire stich was a doublet and ought to be deleted.

We believe that no such radical procedure is necessary. A glance at the passage reveals two facts. Stich 9a is a perfect parallel to 8a and to 8b, and לעולם of 8b is strikingly similar to 10a and 10b. Can וחדל be made parallel to ויחי? We believe it can, if, in addition to its usual meaning "cease," it be given the opposite meaning: "continue, endure." This sense occurs in the metathized Arabic analogue ḥalada, "abide, continue,"[18] frequently used in the Koran of the righteous in Paradise. It occurs in the Hebrew חָלֶד "world."

Vv. 8a, 8b, and 9a now will constitute the main clause and 9b, 10a, 10b, the result clause. The only change required is וחדל into וְיֶחְדַל, so as to make it parallel to ויחי and יראה.[19]

---

[16] So A. V.; similarly R. V., Jewish Version. Delitzsch in his *Kommentar*, (4th ed., p. 385) recognizes the awkwardness of this parenthesis, which he adopts, as does Ehrlich. The renderings of חדל by LXX ἐκοπίασεν V, *laborabit* (error for *laboravit?*) Peshitta לאי (=grew weary) are strange.

[17] Hebrew commentary to Psalms ad loc.

[18] Metathesis is no new phenomenon in Hebrew, as elementary instances like כשב, כבש; שמלה, שלמה, קהלה and להקה attest. See also Barth, *Etymologische Studien*, pp. 1–14, for other suggested examples.

[19] Instances of confusion between *Vav, Yod* and *Mem* are given by Delitzsch, Schreib und Lesefehler, pp. 120, 121, though with more enthusiasm than caution. The loss of a *Yod* is not an unusual phenomenon among scribal errors. Cf. ותתצב for ותתיצב (Ex. 2.4). Or ויחדל may have become וחדל in another manner. The suffix of נפשם is the only plural in the entire section. Perhaps נפשם וחדל is an error for נפשו ויחדל, the masoretic reading having been formed by the blurring and joining of the two *Vavs* into *Mem* and the lengthening of the *Yod* into *Vav*.

191

It is worthy of note that we now have restored the
tristich rhythm that characterizes v. 11 and 12. The passage is now to be rendered:

> "A man cannot redeem his brother,
> And cannot give God his ransom,
> For the redemption of his soul is too dear,
> That he should endure forever,
> And live on to eternity,
> And never see the grave.
> For he sees that wise men die,
> Together the fool and the brutish soul perish,
> And must leave their wealth to others."

This meaning of וחדל, "continue, endure," serves in other
passages as well:

Isa. 38.11 יושבי חדל need not be emended into חלד.[20] Both
forms would be metathetic variants like כבש, כשב, etc.

Job 10.20   הלוא מעט ימי יחדל (כ') וחדל (ק')   ישית (כ') ושית (ק')
ממני ואבלינה מעט

In this verse, the *Kere*, which construes וחדל and ושית
as imperatives, is highly awkward, and even the masoretic
accents follow the *Kethib* rather than the *Kere*, an unusual
procedure, which to our knowledge occurs only in one
other passage, Eccl. 9.4.

On the other hand, the original LXX reading ὁ χρονος
τοῦ βιου μου and the Peshitta יומתא דחיי has been taken
by a long catena of scholars to go back to יְמֵי חָלְדִי.[21] The
recognition of חָדְל in the sense advanced above makes the
consonantal change unnecessary. It is merely necessary to
re-vocalize ימי יחדל ישית as יְמֵי חָדְלִי שִׁית and render:

> Are not the days of my life few,
> Leave me in peace, that I may brighten a little.

[20] So BDB *Lexicon*, s. v.
[21] See *ICC* on Job, vol. 2, p. 65.

Moreover, even this slight change can be dispensed with. The masoretic text can be retained and given an unforced and natural sense, if יֶחְדָּל be understood in the sense of survive, continue:

Indeed but little[22] will my days continue,
Let him leave me in peace that I may brighten a little.

Job 14.6   שעה מעליו ויחדל עד ירצה כשכיר יומו

The commonly accepted rendering is:

Turn away from him, that he may rest,
Till he shall accomplish, as a hireling, his day.

Driver-Gray recognize that there is insufficient warrant for חדל = cease (from labor), i. e., rest.[23] They therefore follow Budde, Beer, Ehrlich and Stickel, and read וַחֲדָל as an imperative "and forbear."

The emendation, aside from making the first stich somewhat redundant, is unnecessary. In the light of our discussion, the passage may be rendered:

Turn away from him, that he may survive,
Until he accomplish, like a hireling, his day.

3. חפה

The Hebrew root occurs in the sense of "cover" in II Kings 17.9, Ps. 68.13 and in II Chronicles, chap. 3 passim.[24] This meaning is paralleled by the Arabic cognate *ḥafa* (undotted *Ḥa*) "hide, be hidden."

---

[22] The adverbial use of מעט is well attested. See BDB, s. v. I, d. Our own verse contains the use of מעט as an adverb of time.

The use of a singular verb after a plural verb occurs frequently. Cf. J. Meyouhas in the Hebrew quarterly *Leshonenu*, Tishri, 1929, p. 145 ff.

[23] I Sam. 2, וּרְעֵבִים חָדֵלוּ does not mean "the hungry have found rest", nor need it be emended to וּרְעֵבִים חָדְלוּ עָבַד. Its meaning is "the hungry cease, i. e., being hungry". So Jewish Version.

[24] Esth. 7.8, ופני המן חפו "they covered Haman's face" is difficult.

The root also occurs frequently in descriptions of grief
as in the phrase חפוי ראש.[25] Without scrutiny, it has been
rendered "covered the head." Thus II Sam. 15.30 is
translated by the Jewish version: "And David went up by
the ascent of the Mount of Olives, and wept as he went up,
and he had his head covered, and went barefoot; all the
people that were with him covered every man his head."[26]
In accordance with this universally accepted view, Benzinger
describes the covering of the head as a mourning custom.[27]

This rendering is however highly questionable. Mourning rites usually arise as a striking change from normal
practice, and it is well known that Semites ordinarily
walked about turbaned. Covering the head would therefore scarcely be a mourning rite. This is proved conclusively
by Ezek. 24.17, where the prophet is commanded by the
Lord to avoid any demonstrations of grief for the loss that
will overtake him:

"Sigh in silence, make no mourning for the dead, bind
thy headtire upon thee, and put thy shoes upon thy feet,
and cover not thine upper lip, and eat not the bread of
men."

So too the priests are forbidden to unbind the head (פרע
ראש) Lev. 10.6, 21.10, an act which is commanded for the
leper (Lev. 13.46) and the accused woman (Num. 5.18).[27a]

[25] II Sam. 15.30; Jer. 14.34; Esth. 6.12.
[26] Thus all versions and commentators, Rashi, following Targum,
explains: מכורך כדרך האבלים.
[27] Benzinger, Hebräische Archäologie (1st ed., p. 165). In 3rd ed.,
p. 134, he says that mourners were either bareheaded or with covered
heads!
[27a] That פרע ראש means "unbind the head" is the universally accepted
view today, but not the traditional Jewish interpretation, which takes
it to mean "let the hair grow long" (so Rashi, Ibn Ezra doubtfully, on
Lev. 10.6). This is based on the interpretation of Sifra ad loc.: אל תפרעו אל
תנדלו פרע יכול אל תפרעו מן הכובע נאמר כאן פרע ונאמר להלן פרע מה פריעה
האמורה להלן נידול שער אף פריעה האמורה כאן נידול שער.
According to Malbim, Hatorah V'hamitzvah, (p. 100a), the passage
invoked by the Sifra to prove that the idiom means "let hair grow" is

It thus becomes clear that leaving the head uncovered was a mark of grief, like walking barefoot. Moreover, the custom of putting dust or ashes upon the head (Josh. 26.28, II Sam. 1.2 and often) could take place only if the mourner's head was uncovered.

It remains to point out that this meaning of חפה "uncover" has ample etymological warrant. The Arabic *ḥafa* (dotted *Ha, tertiae Ya*) is common in the sense of "uncover, reveal,"[28] as well as its opposite meaning. In addition there is an Arabic root *ḥafa* with undotted *Ha* meaning "go barefoot." So too the Hebrew root יחף "barefoot" would seem to be cognate to חפה. The Syriac noun חפיותא means *nudipeditas*, thus exhibiting the meaning "uncover."[29]

We therefore propose that the phrase חפוי ראש be rendered, wherever it occurs, "with head uncovered."

4. חפש

The root חפש meaning "free" occurs in a variety of forms, חָפְשִׁי, חָפְשָׁה, חֹפֶשׁ.

In II Kings 15.5 = II Chron. 26.21 we are told that Uzziah was stricken with leprosy and "he dwelt in בית

Ex. 44.20 וּפָרַע לֹא יְשַׁלֵּחוּ. According to Epstein, *Torah Temimah* to Lev. 10.6 the passage is Num. 6.5 גִּדֵּל פָּרַע. In both passages, however, the noun פָּרַע means "locks" and the sense of "let grow" inheres in the verbs used, שלח, גדל respectively.

That the verb פָּרַע means "uncover" is clear from Num. 5.18, וּפָרַע אֶת רֹאשׁ הָאִשָּׁה.

This interpretation is quoted in the Sifra on Lev. 10.6, and is maintained by R. Akiba (Sifra on 13.45). It seems to have been abandoned reluctantly by Ibn Ezra (on Lev. 10.6), only because of the weight of tradition.

The mourning rite of covering the upper lip (Micah 3.7; Ezek. 24.17, 22; Lev. 13.45) refers to the covering of the beard, which ordinarily was exposed to view (see Brown-Driver-Briggs, s. v. עטה, and literature there quoted).

[28] See Noeldeke, op. cit., p. 85.
[29] Payne Smith, *Thesaurus Syriacus*, s. v. ܚܦ.

החפשית.‏"[30] This is rendered "a house set apart,"[31] or "a house of freedom or separateness."[32]

The idea of freedom in connection with a leper's house is rather farfetched. The term we expect is one expressing the idea of confinement: like בית הכלא or imprisonment, בית האסורים.

If חפש be recognized as a root of mutually contradictory meaning, it would signify (a) freedom and (b)confinement. In our passage it would mean "an enclosed house, a house of confinement."

5. כסה (כסא)

The noun כָּסֶה which occurs in Ps. 81.4[33] was taken by the Talmud to mean the New Year's festival: "Which festival is it on which the moon is covered? Say that is Rosh Hashanah" (Bezah 16a). Yet there is difficulty in assuming that the New Moon, which has just appeared, is described as covered.[34]

The modern view, on the other hand, is that the word means "the full moon," based upon the Syriac ܟܣܐ Kes'a, which possesses this meaning, and usually refers to the 15th of Tishri and the Feast of Tabernacles. But that the full moon should be described as "hidden" is manifestly impossible. Delitzsch therefore suggests the Assyrian kuseu "head-dress, train (of the moon-god)" as its derivation, though this is disputed by Brockelmann.[35]

---

[30] In Chronicles the Kethib is החפשות.
[31] So the English versions.
[32] BDB Lexicon, s. v.
[33] And in Prov. 7.20, הכסא.
[34] Rashi's comment at both passages "hidden from those far away" shows a recognition of the difficulty.
[35] See BDB, s. v.

If, however, we recall how common words meaning both "cover" and "reveal"[35a] are, we may perhaps postulate for כָּסָא the meaning, "the uncovered, revealed moon," and thus have an unforced derivation for the word.

6. שאל

The Hebrew verb שאל is ordinarily taken to mean only "inquire". The Assyrian cognate has however the opposite meaning "decide, command". In his suggestive Hebrew monograph, *Hiqre Lashon* (Jersualem, 1932, pp. 44 ff.), Dr. M. Seidel calls attention to the common salutation of the Elephantine papyri אלהא ישאל שלמך which he takes to mean "May God decide peace for you".

This meaning also occurs in at least one biblical passage:

Dan. 4.14 בגזרת עירין פתגמא ומאמר קדישין שאלתא which is to be rendered, "By the decree of the watchers is the decision, and by the word of the Holy ones, the command."

The mediaeval Hebrew work *Sheeltoth of Rab Aha of Shabha* means not *Questiones* but *Responsa*.[36]

If this meaning for שאל be recognized, we have a basis for the etymology of שְׁאוֹל not as the "place of inquiry" but "the place of decision."[37]

Seidel also suggests this meaning for the Hebrew root in Isa. 45.11, where we cannot follow him, and in Micah 7.3: הַשַּׂר שׁוֹאֵל וְהַשֹּׁפֵט בְּשִׁלּוּם which he plausibly renders:

"The lord decides, and the judge (decides) for a bribe."

[35a] Noeldeke devotes a special section to these words, op. cit., pp. 84–85.

[36] See Mendelssohn, *REJ*, vol. 32, pp. 55–62, "Sheilta et sheal".

[37] So Jeremias, *Leben n. d. Tode*, p. 109, with insufficient warrant; Albright, "The Etymology of Sheol," *AJSL*, vol. 34, p. 210. Other suggestions in BDB 982b.

7. און

The Hebrew root occurs in two forms: a) אָוֶן meaning "trouble, sorrow, wickedness," with an Arabic cognate آنَ 'a'na mediae Ya—"be fatigued, tired"; and b) אוֹן vigor, strength,[38] with an Arabic cognate 'a 'na آنَ mediae Waw—"be at rest".

Here again, the two Arabic verbs, like the Hebrew root, seem differentiations of the same root, which developed mutually contrasting meanings. As a matter of fact, the roots are used interchangeably in Arabic (Lane, p. 129, column 1).

8. יאב—איב—אהב

It is well known that there is a close relationship between verbs *primae Yod* and *mediae Yod-Vav* on the one hand[39] and verbs *mediae Vav-Yod* and *mediae He* on the other.[40]

Thus אהב "love" and איב "hate" may be differentiations of the same root with contradictory meanings. Moreover, איב possesses a metathetic form of opposite meaning as well, יאב "desire, long for" (Ps. 119.131).

9. אלם

The adjective אִלֵּם is usually derived from the verb "bind" (Gen. 37.7) in the sense of "bound, unable to speak".[41]

It is noteworthy, however, that roots meaning "bind" usually develop the sense of "strength" rather than "weakness". The Arabic *ḥazaḳa* "bind" has the common Hebrew

---

[38] The second meaning includes "wealth", i. e., which is achieved by vigor. This development of meaning occurs in חַיִל, כֹּחַ as well. The noun הוֹן also seems related to אוֹן.

[39] Cf. בוש, יבש (*Hiphil* הוֹבִישׁ); נוק, ינק, (Ex. 2.9, וַתְּנִיקֵהוּ), סוד, יסד בְּהִוָּסְדָם Ps. 31.14).

[40] Cf. בוש, בהת; רוץ רהט; קהל, קול, כול. See Zimmermann, in *JBL*, 1931, pp. 311–12.

[41] Cf. BDB *Lexicon*, p. 47b.

חֹזֶק as its cognate. אֵלִים itself means "strong" in Aramaic.[42] The Assyrian *almattu*, in addition to the meaning "widow", (on which see below), has the significance of "fortress". This may be derived from the idea of "enclosed, bound place," but the sense of "strong" is clear in the epithet *almanu* applied to a god.[42a]

The common tendency to employ euphemisms for physical defects and diseases is well known. We may quote Wetzstein's statement: "In general, in the case of every Semitic term for physical or moral evil, we may assume a priori that it is a euphemism." As one of countless instances, a man bitten by a snake is called *salim*, "the sound one," in Arabic.[43]

We should therefore like to suggest that אֵלֶם is a euphemism of contrasted meaning, "the strong one" being an epithet for "the mute". Perhaps the Arabic root *'alima* "be in pain" was originally a circumlocution, meaning "be sound, strong". See also nos. 14, 17, 18, 20.

10. אלמן—אשכל

The Hebrew noun אֶשְׁכֹּל "cluster" has never been satisfactorily traced back to a root. The natural procedure would be to assume שׁכל as the root with preformative *Aleph*.[44] This is favored by the striking similarity of the cognates of אֶשְׁכֹּל and שְׁכֹל in Aramaic and Arabic.[45]

[42] Compare the common talmudic phrase כל דאלים גבר (Giṭ. 60b and often) "Who is stronger wins". As a verb it occurs in the *Peal*, *Pael*, *Ithpaal*, in this significance. Cf. Jastrow, *Dictionary*, 71a, b, for many examples of the uses.

[42a] Delitzsch, *Assyrisches Wörterbuch*, p. 34.

[43] Cf. Wellhausen, *Reste arabischen Heidentums*, p. 199. Many interesting examples are given by D. Wetzstein in Delitzsch's *Kommentar zu Psalmen*, 4th ed., pp. 883 ff.

[44] So Gesenius, Mühlau—Völck, s. v.

[45] Hebrew, אשכל; Aramaic אתכלא; Arabic *'ithka'l*[un]; Hebrew שכל; Syriac *thekhel*; Aramaic תכל, תכול; Arabic *thakila*.

Nevertheless, no suitable etymology has been discovered for the root.[46] We should like to suggest that שכל possesses mutually contradictory meanings: a) be joined, attached —whence אֶשְׁכֹּל cluster; b) be separated, deserted, whence שְׁכוֹל "bereavement".

A similar process of thought may lie at the root of אַלְמָן (Jer. 51.5) "widower, forsaken" and the common אַלְמָנָה, "widow", for which no satisfactory origin has been proposed.[47]

It would seem that אלם likewise has opposed meanings: a) bind, attach—whence אֲלֻמָּה sheaf; b) sever, be deserted, bereaved—whence אַלְמָן widow, widower.

11. אצל

The common preposition "near" is plausibly associated by Wright[48] and Brown-Driver-Briggs with the Arabic waṣala, "join". However it should be noted that the Hebrew root has mutually contradictory meanings:

a) אצל "join" whence אֵצֶל near, אָצִיל, joint.

b) אָצַל "remove, withhold (Eccl. 2.10 and elsewhere) cognate to נָצַל, "remove, save," primae Nun and primae Aleph being closely related.[49] From the verb is derived the noun אָצִיל "end of earth" (Isa. 41.9, Jer. 6.22), and "noble lord"[50] (Ex. 24.11), as removed, distinguished from the people.

---

[46] See BDB, p. 79a.

[47] There is an Assyrian parallel almattu. See Delitzsch, in Zimmern, Babylonische Busspsalmen, p. 114; Prolegomena, p. 45 and Assyrisches Wörterbuch, p. 34. The Aramaic ארמלתא would also go back to אלם with affixed Resh. Cf. שַׁרְבִיט from שבט, etc.

[48] Semitic Grammar, p. 71.

[49] See note 8.

[50] The noun פִּנָּה (Judg. 20.2; I Sam. 14.38; Isa. 19.13; Zech. 10.4) also has both meanings, "corner, end" and "lord".

12. בחל

This verb meaning "loathe" occurs in Zech. 11.8 and in the Syriac cognate בחל.[51] The root also has the opposite significance, as in the Neo-Syriac בחל, envy; Arabic *baḥila*, be avaricious. This occurs in biblical Hebrew as well, in the *Kethib* of Prov. 20.21:

נחלה מבחלת בראשונה   ואחריתה לא תבורך

"as inheritance gotten by greed in the beginning will not be blessed at the end."

13. בקק

This root is inexplicably omitted by Noeldeke and Landau, though it is a clear cut example of *addad*:

1) be luxuriant—Hos. 10.1, גֶּפֶן בֹּקֵק—luxuriant vine; and 2) be empty, waste, as, e. g., Isa. 24.3 הִבּוֹק תִּבּוֹק הָאָרֶץ "the earth shall be laid waste."

The Arabic preserves the first significance in its cognate *baḳḳa*, "be luxuriant, abundant" (children, herbage, gnats).

The derivation of the second meaning from an Arabic *baḳḳa*, "make a gurgling noise (of a mug dipped in water, or emptied in water)"[52] and hence "empty", seems far-fetched. It is most likely an opposite development from the first meaning.

14. חגר

The mishnic Hebrew word חִגֵּר,[53] "lame", is ordinarily derived from the idea of חָגַר, bind, gird, and taken to mean "bound, tied, hence lame", like אִלֵּם.[54] On the basis of our

---

[51] See BDB, s. v. Geiger (*Urschrift*, p. 27) denies that the Syriac verb has this meaning, but overlooks the adjective בחיל "causing disgust". Cf. Payne-Smith, s. v.

[52] So BDB, p. 132b.

[53] E. g., in Mishna Peah 8.9, Sanh. 8.4 and frequently.

[54] So Jastrow, s. v.

remarks under אלם, it seems plausible to assume a euphemism in this instance as well. חגר means "bind", hence
"strong, sound", and is used to describe a physical defect
per antiphrasin. See also nos. 17, 18, 20.

15. חלף

The root חלף means "pass on, pass away" in the majority
of passages where it occurs. In Ps. 90.5, 6, however, this
meaning is inadequate. In accordance with the require-
ments of the passage, the latter verse is rendered:

In the morning it flourisheth and groweth up,
In the evening it is cut down and withereth.[55]

This significance for חלף is arrived at by positing the
sense of "come on anew, sprout again."[56] The thought of
the Psalmist is not, however, that man sprouts once again,
but that man flourishes only a short time. The sense of
repetition, which is basic to the ordinary meaning of חלף,
has no place at all in this passage. It seems advisable
therefore to assume with Bermann[57] that חלף possesses
contradictory meanings; (a) pass away, be destroyed, as
in Isa. 2.18; Ps. 102.27b; and (b) grow, flourish (in the
Kal); plant, cause to grow (in the *Hiphil*).

This meaning gives excellent sense in the following passages: Isa. 9.9 לבנים נפלו וגזית נבנה שקמים גדעו וארזים נחליף

In stich a the idea of replacement is *implied*, but not
expressed by the verb נבנה. Similarly נחליף does not mean

55 So Jewish Version, following Gesenius, A. V., Delitzsch, Hitzig,
Cheyne, etc.

56 So BDB, s. v. sec. 2.

57 S. P. Bermann's learned and suggestive Hebrew commentary on
Isaiah (Vilna, 1903) is unfortunately too little known. I have called
attention to it elsewhere, cf. *JBL*, vol. XLIX, 1930, p. 442, n. 9. On
our root see Bermann on Isa. 9.9.

"we shall put in their place" but "we shall plant," parallel to "we shall build".

"The bricks are fallen, but we shall build with hewn stones.

The sycamores are cut down, but we shall plant cedars."

כי יש לעץ תקוה אם יכרת ועוד יחליף וינקתו לא תחדל   Job 14.7

Here stich b is rendered correctly

"If it be cut down, it will sprout again."

Perhaps the phrase יחליפו כח Isa. 40.31, 41.1, means not "change for the better; renew strength", but "grow new strength".   In Ps. 129.6 שקדמת שלף יבש the difficult verb is emended by Van Ortenberg into שָׁחֲלַף, by Wellhausen and Duhm into חָלַף, and then rendered "before it sprouts, it shrivels up."

16. מלל

The noun מְלִילָה (Deut. 23.26) "ear of corn" is usually derived from מלל (Prov. 6.13) "rub, scrape (with feet)" and is taken to refer to "scraped, parched ears of grain".

It is true that the word occurs in mishnic Hebrew in the sense of "parched ears" (Maaseroth 4.5; Tos. Betz. 1.20; Tos. Terumot 3.18).

In the passage in Deuteronomy, however, it refers to ears on the stalk, that can scarcely be described as parched. Moreover, the parallel in v. 25 speaks of grapes (ענבים) without description or limitation of any kind.   It seems plausible therefore to associate מלילות with the root מלל meaning "languish, wither, fade" (Ps. 90.6; Job 14.2 and elsewhere) and to assume an opposite meaning, "bud, blossom, grow".   מְלִילָה would thus mean "ear of grain".

The same growth of meaning is apparent in חלף: a) pass away, perish; and b) spring forth, blossom.   See above.

17. סנורים

The intensive plural meaning "blindness" (Gen. 19.11; II Kings 6.18) has proved etymologically difficult. Perhaps Wetzstein's derivation from נור "light" *per antiphrasin*[58] may be supported by the common talmudic euphemisms for "blind" סני נהורא "rich in light"[59]; מאור עינים, light of the eyes[60]; and the late term רואה "seer".[61]

However, Prof. Montgomery has kindly called our attention to his very plausible derivation of this word from the root ברר "be clear, bright", based on the fact that in the Orient the sun often produces blindness, or from the dazzling sensation in certain optical diseases.[61a] He adduces the talmudic *shabriri* used in the magical formula against blindness (Pes. 112a; 'Ab. Zarah 12b). This equation is greatly strengthened by the fact that שברידיא occurs in the Talmud in the sense of "blindness,"[61b] and is actually the rendering of סנורים in the Aramaic Targums in Genesis and Kings.

18. עור

The Semitic root עור in the meaning of "blind"[62] has never received a satisfactory etymology. Gesenius[63] derives it from Arabic *gha'run*, cave, and gives the verb the sense of "dig". Halévy[64] compares עיר "skin" and defines blindness

[58] In Delitzsch, *Kommentar zu Psalmen*, p. 886.
[59] Ber. 58a and often.
[60] Ḥag. 5b.
[61] Cf. the blind Karaite teacher Joseph ben Abraham al Bassir, *Haroeh* of the 11th century.
[61a] Cf. J. A. Montgomery, *Aramaic Incantation Texts From Nippur*, p. 93.
[61b] Kohut, *Aruch*, vol. 7, p. 20; Jastrow, s. v.
[62] It occurs in Aramaic, Arabic and Ethiopic as well as in Hebrew.
[63] *Thesaurus*, s. v.
[64] *REJ*, vol. XI, p. 67.

as a cataract. It is obvious that both these derivations are very forced.

We should like to suggest that עִוֵּר is originally a euphemism which meant "wide awake". This is a highly frequent Semitic root, עור, very common in biblical and post-biblical Hebrew. Such expressions for physical defects are part of primitive taboo and widely spread. We may compare רואה מאור עינים, סגי נהור used in Jewish literature for "blind". These euphemisms came into use after it had been forgotten that עור itself was a euphemism.[65] See also no. 17.

19. עזב

This Hebrew root in the meaning "leave, forsake," is well known. However, it has several cognates, which would give it a contrary meaning; the Sabean עדֿב means "restore"; Assyrian *ušezib*, and Aramaic שיזיב, "rescue, save". These support the assumption that the Hebrew root has the opposite significance of "assist, strengthen" as well. This meaning is of service to several passages, as some of the mediaeval Hebrew lexicographers have recognized.

Ex. 23.5 וחדלת מעזוב לו עזב תעזב עמו has a play on the two meanings: "Thou shalt forbear to desert him, thou shalt surely assist him."

Jer. 49.25 איך לא עזבה עיר תהלת is well rendered in the Jewish version: "How is the city of praise left unrepaired."

Nehem. 3.8 ויעזבו ירושלים עד החמה הרחבה is to be rendered: "They restored Jerusalem to the broad wall."

---

[65] Euphemisms often lose their potency and new ones replace them. Cf. the English "undertaker", originally meaning a contractor, later used as a euphemism for those engaged in burials. This is later forgotten and new circumlocutions come into existence, such as "mortician", "funeral director", etc.

It is only this meaning that can account for the proper name עֲזוּבָה (I Kings 22.42; II Chron. 20.31; I Chron. 2.18, 19). No Hebrew parent would name his child "forsaken". On the contrary, if interpreted "aided, strengthened," it has analogies in such names as יחזקאל, חזקיהו, עודד, ישעיה, etc.

20. פסח

For this combination of consonants, BDB[66] assumes two roots: a) pass, spring over—whence פָּסַח; and b) limp, whence פִּסֵּחַ, lame, and the proper names פֶּסַח.[67] That a child would be named by his parents as "lame, limper" is unlikely. As a matter of fact, there is no need of assuming two distinct roots. פָּסַח means "leap, dance, spring.[68] *Per antiphrasin*, the lame person is described as "the dancer, the leaper", especially since the walk of one who is lame is jerky and uneven. The full form of the proper name, which is post-exilic and therefore lacks its theophorous element, is פְּסַחְיָה, and means "the Lord passes over, the Lord spares" (cf. Ex. 12.13, 27).[69]

It thus becomes apparent that the various bodily defects (nos. 9, 14, 17, 18) are described in Hebrew by words of opposite meaning.

21. קלס

This root, which occurs exclusively in the sense of "mock" in the Bible and in Ben Sira (11.4) is used in post-biblical Hebrew and in Syriac in the opposed significance of "praise, extol". This must be a very ancient and well-established

---

[66] P. 820.

[67] It occurs in Ezra 2.49; Nehem. 3.6; 7.51; I Chron. 4.12.

[68] And secondarily, "protect, save", as in Isa. 31.5. This meaning is probably based on the Passover story.

[69] Cf. personal names with roots רחם, ישע like, ירחמאל, הושע, ישעיהו.

meaning, for nowhere in rabbinic literature is the question as to its meaning raised, and it is frequently referred to the Lord, as in Lev. Rab., sec. 30, ונקלס לקב״ה, and in the traditional Sabbath Morning Prayer לְעַלָּה וּלְקַלֵּס—וּבְמַקְהֵלוֹת "to exalt and praise the Lord."

22. רגע

This verb occurs in biblical Hebrew in two contradictory meanings: a) disturb; b) be at rest, repose. It is usually assumed that there are two original roots. Barth[70] derives the first from Arabic *ra'aja*, disturb, by metathesis, which BDB accepts. The second is usually derived from Arabic *raja'a*, return, which is forced to give the sense of "return, to rest, therefore to rest". Noeldeke likewise assumes two distinct roots.[71]

The common tendency to use words in mutually contrasted meanings makes it not unlikely that we have here one root meaning both "disturb" and "rest".

23. רפה—רפא

It is merely necessary to note that the two roots meaning "sink, weaken—heal, strengthen," are not always kept apart in the masoretic text.[72]

Perhaps they constitute a single root, differentiated into the two contradictory meanings: a) grow weak; b) make strong. רְפָאִים *Giants* is usually derived from the first meaning and interpreted as "extinct and powerless"[73] or "vaguely known, hence weak".[74] Yet the constant emphasis in the Bible is upon their size and power (Deut. 2.10, 11, 20; 3.11).

[70] *Etymologische Studien*, p. 8.
[71] Op. cit. See רגע in Index.
[72] Ezek. 24.7,8 וְנִרְפְּאוּ; Jer. 17.11 הָרְפָּה; Jer. 8.11 וַיְרַפְּאוּ are ל״י forms though they mean "heal".
[73] So Driver, *ICC*, on Deut. 2.11.
[74] So Schwally, *ZATW*, 1891, p. 127 ff.

We therefore prefer to assume that רפאים may mean "strong men". It may be derived from the meaning, b) "make strong, heal", or it may be a cacophony "weak ones", due to a desire to avoid describing them as "strong".

24. שחר

Brown-Driver-Briggs *Lexicon* assumes three roots: a) be black, as in שָׁחוֹר and its derivatives; b) the dawn as in שַׁחַר; and c) שִׁיחוֹר a name for the Nile.[75]

This is unnecessary. We have here another instance of a root uniting the contrary meanings of "blackness" and "dawn, light", like אור, נגהא, אורתא[76] which mean "evening, night" as well as "light".[76a]

It is not unlikely that the primitive fear of darkness is at the bottom of these words of mutually contradictory meaning.

שִׁיחוֹר means "the black river".

It is tempting to consider the root צחר as related to שחר in its meaning of "dawn, light". It occurs as a noun in the phrase צמר צחר (Ezek. 27.18) and as an adjective in the phrase אתנת צחרת (Judg. 5.10). It is best rendered "light colored" (of wool) rather than "tawny, reddish", as most moderns interpret after the Arabic.

25. סכל—שכל

That the Hebrew roots סכל—שכל occur in the opposing significances of "wise" (מַשְׂכִּיל, הִשְׂכִּיל, שֵׂכָל) and foolish (שִׂכְלוּת, סִכְלוּת, סַכְלוּת, Eccl. 2.3,12,13; 7.25; 10.1,31, סָכָל,

---

[75] Pp. 1007a, 1009b.

[76] Cf. Noeldeke, op. cit., p. 83, and the talmudic lexicons for examples.

[76a] Perhaps a similar connection exists between Latin *nox, lux*; German *Nacht, Licht*, and English *night, light*.

סָכָל) is well known. It is usually assumed with Noeldeke (op. cit., p. 72) that this resemblance is accidental, and that the root שכל wise (Arabic *sakala*) has coalesced at times with the root סכל "fool".

Noeldeke claims that in Aramaic, as a rule, the two roots are distinct in use. The evidence from Payne-Smith does not bear out this assertion. The *Peal* of סכל is little used, but its meaning is "foolish"; its passive, the *Ethpeel*, means "be known, understood." The *Pael* means, "teach, make understand" but also "lead to folly" (Isa. 44.25). The *Ethpael* means "know, understand". The *Aphel* means "make foolish, lead wickedly" but also "teach understanding". It therefore seems that we have a single root, which has been partially differentiated in Hebrew and Syriac.

26. שתם

This *hapax legomenon* occurs only in the Balaam prophecies in the phrase הגבר שְׁתָם העין Num. 24.3,15. This descriptive epithet of the prophet becomes clear by reference to 24.4, נפל וגלוי עינים. It means "open-eyed—i. e., [gifted with miraculous vision."

There is no good reason for doubting the existence of this root in this same meaning, as does Gray. The verb occurs in the sense of "open (a vessel)" in both mishnic Hebrew (Mishna 'Ab. Zarah 5.3) and Aramaic (Yer. 'Ab. Zarah V, 44d), and in several nominal derivatives, שְׁתָם, שְׁתָם (see Jastrow, p. 1639).

It is true that no satisfactory etymology has yet been proposed. Perhaps שתם is related to סתם, which means "closed". As a word of opposite meaning שתם would also mean "opened".

שתר .27

The *hapax legomenon* in (כ') וַיִּשָּׂתְרוּ לָהֶם עֳפָלִים I Sam. 5.9
is variously derived, but not altogether adequately. The
Arabic, *shatira*, "have cracked eyelids or lips", is not very
helpful, nor are the Assyrian *satâru*, Syriac and biblical
Aramaic סְתַר, and late Hebrew סָתַר[77] which means "destroy".

It seems best to take שָׁתַר as equivalent to סָתַר, which
means primarily "hide". As a word of opposite meaning,
it would mean "disclose, make apparent, cause to appear".
The phrase means "and emerods broke out upon them".

תאב .28

In one passage Am. 6.8, the meaning "loathe" is required
for תאב. Since Geiger[78] it has been generally assumed
that תאב is an error, or an intentional change for תעב.

Nevertheless, תאב may well be a parallel form to תעב,
like גאל, געל, "pollute". It would have both meanings—
"yearn" and "loathe". These contrasted meanings exist
in בחל and אהב—איב and are entirely in consonance with
primitive verbal taboos.

[77] We believe that this meaning of סתר ="destroy" occurs in Isa.
29.14 ואבדה חכמת חכמיו ובינת נבוניו תסתתר "and the understanding of the
wise will be destroyed."

[78] *Urschrift*, p. 349.

The Asseverative Kaph in Ugaritic and Hebrew

The prefixed Kaph occurs in a number of Biblical passages where it cannot be given the usual meaning of " like," for example Neh. 7:2: *ki hu' ke' iš 'emeth*. David Kimhi describes this Kaph as *Kaph ha'amittuth*, it being used to emphasize the word or the phrase modified.[1] Later grammarians rendered this as *Kaph veritatis*.

Modern scholars have generally dismissed this view. Gesenius-Kautzsch declares such a pleonasm as " natürlich undenkbar," and renders the passage cited from Nehemiah as: " he was a kind of faithful man." [2] The Oxford Lexicon, declares: " In these passages, *kaph* is used to compare an object with the class to which it belongs. Thus ' he was a veritable, or ideal, faithful man.' " [3]

Aside from the complicated process of interpretation involved in these views, which can scarcely be applied, for example, to such passages as Num. 11:1, we believe that the existence of an asseverative Kaph in Hebrew may be validated on four grounds: (A) a closely related usage in Ugaritic, (B) the parallel use of *ki* in Biblical Hebrew, (C) some petrified forms in Biblical and Mishnic Hebrew, and (D) the better exegesis afforded several Biblical passages.

A. In the Ugaritic inscriptions, Prof. H. L. Ginsberg noticed the particle *ki*, where its only possible use could be as an emphatic,[4] as e. g. *ktṣḥ* (II AB 2, 29), *ktl'akn* (ibid. 4-5, 104) *kyṣḥ* (ibid., 53), etc. The verb strengthened by this *k* stands as a rule at the end of the clause in Ugaritic, as e. g.: *hlk b'l 'ttrt kt'n*—"Asherah eyes the going of Ba al " ; *ksp 'a[t]trt kt'n*, " Asherah sees the silver " ; *'Il 'attm kypt*," Il seduces two women." Ginsberg naturally identified this Ugaritic article with the Hebrew vocable *ki*, which is used

emphatically at the end of the clause in such passages as: Gen. 18:20; Ps. 49:16; 118:10; Lam. 3:22.

B. The use of *ki* in Biblical Hebrew as a demonstrative or emphatic particle is, however, by no means limited to this position, for it occurs at the very opening of a sentence or a clause, and even at the beginning of a literary unit, like the Arabic *'inna*.[5] We may compare: Num. 23:23; Isa. 15:1; Amos 3:7; Prov. 30:2; Job 5:2; 28:1; Ecc. 7:7.

It has not been observed that the Ugaritic parallels may well point to the proclitic *Kaph* rather than to the *ki* of asseveration as a separate word. The Ugaritic texts often, though not always, use dividers to separate words from one another. " The divider is not uncommonly placed after the conjunction *ω* and after prepositions." [6] Generally, Ugaritic practice coincides with Hebrew usage in regarding the *preposition k* (= " like ") as a proclitic, and hence it does not separate it from the word it modifies, while *km* (= Heb. *kemo*) is treated as a word—hence *klb* but *km. lb.* "like a heart." On the other hand, the *conjunction k* (= Heb. *ki*) does occur with the word-divider, though not invariably, since the word-divider is not consistently employed in our texts.[7] Nevertheless, in all extant uses of *k* as an emphatic, it

---

[1] Commentary—on Jos. 3:4; I Sam. 9:13; Hos. 5:10; *Michlol* (ed. Lyck) p. 45a; Lexicon, s. v. *yom*.

[2] Gesenius-Kautzsch, *Hebraische Grammatik* (25 ed.) c. 118, 6d.

[3] BDB, *Lexicon*, P. 454 a.

[4] Cf. his " Notes on ' The Birth of the Gracious and Beautiful Gods,' " *JRAS*, Jan. 1935, p. 56. The text was originally published by Ch. Virolleaud in *Syria*, Vol. IV, pp. 128-151. Cf. also C. H. Gordon, *Ugaritic Grammar* (Rome 1940), p. 54.

[5] Cf. BDB, p. 472b, and the spirited defence of this use of *ki* by David Yellin in his Hebrew works, *Hiqre Miqra*, *Job* (Jerusalem 1927), on 5:2 and 28:1, and *Isaiah* (Jerusalem 1939) pp. 104 f.

It may be added here that the Hebrew *'im* and *ki* possess the same variety of meanings; a) " if ": Gen. 18:26; cf. Gen. 38:16, and see BDB, s. v. *ki* 2b. b) As an interrogative sign: Job 6:22 *hakhi 'amarti* parallel exactly to *ha'im*. This usage is very frequent in Mishnic Hebrew, cf. *B. Rosh Hashanah* 9a, *Vekhi betiš'a mith'anim*, " Do we fast on the ninth? " c) The asseverative use: Job 14:5; 17:13, 16.

[6] Gordon, op. cit. p. 17.

[7] Prof. H. L. Ginsberg has kindly called my attention, in a private communication, to the two hippiatric texts, Nos. 53 and 54 in Bauer's edition. In the first, only one example of the conjunction *k* is preserved and it is joined to the verb. In 54, most of the instances of the conjunction *k* are preserved, and with only one certain exception, they are all separated from the following words by word-dividers.

is never separated from its verb. This creates a presumption, though not a certainty, that the emphatic *k* is a proclitic and not a distinct word, and hence equivalent to the Hebrew prefix and not to the vocable.

At all events, it is clear that *k* and *ki* are closely related to each other, it being possible that they are originally orthographic variants of the same particle. Thus in late unvocalized texts, the plene *ki* is frequently written for the defective k = "like" in the Talmud, as *ki ribhda'* "like a patch" (B. Baba Kamma 98a). Though the process of primitive thought by which the particle *ki* becomes an asseverative escapes us today, we may adduce the analogy of the Arabic proclitic *la* meaning "indeed, verily."

C. In addition, Hebrew exhibits some petrified forms with prefixed Kaph, which may have lost its asseverative force because of frequent use.

Such is the substantive *kim'at* "a few, slight." Cf. Isa. 1:9: *sarid kim'at* "a little remnant." Also Ps. 105:12 = I Chr. 16:19; Pr. 10:20; Isa. 26:20; Ezra 9:8.

Common in Mishnic Hebrew are such forms as *k*e*sabhur* "he thinks" (B. Gittin 56b and often) and *kim*e*dummeh 'ani* "it seems to me" (B. Menahot 18a and often). We may perhaps also adduce the Mishnah (Shab. 2:5) *k*e*has 'al hanner* "He who seeks to save the lamp."

D. These exceptional forms aside, the best evidence for this use of the asseverative Kaph is to be found in the better exegesis it affords for the Biblical passages now to be cited. For in many instances, notably Num. 11:1; Isa. 29:2; Obad 1:11; Lam. 1:20; Neh. 7:2, we require a heightening of the emphasis and not its weakening, which is the consequence of the usual view.

Num. 11:1 *K*e*mith'onenim ra'* not "and the people were as murmurers" (JV) but "and the people were indeed complaining."

Isa. 10:13 On the basis of the Kethib, *k*e*'abbir*, the final stich is usually rendered, "I shall bring low, like a mighty one, the inhabitants." It seems preferable to interpret, "I shall bring low even the mightiest of the inhabitants."

Isa. 29:2c. Render: "I shall afflict Ariel, and there will be wailing and lamentation, and it shall indeed be an Ariel (= hearth of God?)."

Hosea 4:4c. This crux has been emended count-

less times. In the next verse, the direct address and the reference to *Nabhi* would indicate that *kohen* is in the vocative. It has been suggested, therefore, to read: *ve amm*e*kha kim*e*ribhai kohen.* But to translate it, "Your people are *like* those who quarrel with Me, O priest," is very weak. A far more striking rendering is, "Your people are surely my foes, O priest."

Hosea 5:10. The rendering: "The princes of Judah are like them that remove landmarks" (JV) leaves unexpressed the sins of which they are accused. If the Kaph be recognized as asseverative, a far more direct rendering emerges: "The princes are surely removers of landmarks," violators of the Divine injunction to respect boundaries.

Ob. 1:11e. Not, "Thou wast indeed as one of them." The prophet is castigating Edom for participating in the destruction of Jerusalem. (Cf. Ez. 35:2-15; Lam. 4:21-2.) The clause is unquestionably to be rendered: "You were indeed one of them."

Ps. 119:9b. The verb *šamar* in the sense "keep observe," is always construed with a direct object. The JV renders: "Wherewith shall a young man keep his way pure, by taking heed thereto, according to Thy word." It may be better to render simply: "Indeed, by keeping Thy Word."

Ps. 122:3. This verse is generally given as "Jerusalem, thou art builded as a city compact together." There seems to be no point to the comparison. It appears preferable to translate "O Jerusalem, thou art built, indeed a city compact together."

Pr. 16:27b. "On his lips is truly a burning fire," is a more vivid rendering than "On his lips is a a burning fire."

Job 3:5c. The final stich of this verse has alway occasioned great difficulty, largely because of th Kaph. Most moderns have accepted the suggestio of Dillmann and Stade to read: *Y*e*bha'athuh kamrirei yom*, from the Syriac root *k*e*mar* "b black," rendering—"let the blacknesses of the da affright it." But this emendation suffers fron several drawbacks. Not only would we expec "the blacknesses of the night," rather than "o the day," but the emendation creates a hapa legomenon in this sense. Even more decisive i the fact that the change ignores the use of *merir* in Deut. 32:24, where it is parallel with *Behemo* the primordial monster (—*Leviathan* in Job 3 : 8) and with *Rešeph,* the North-Semitic deity whom the Phoenicians pictured with the lightning bolt or as the Fire-God.[8] Cf. Hab. 3 : 5, Ps. 78 : 48 ; Job 5 : 7; Cant. 8 : 6. It therefore seems highly reasonable to assume that *meriri* is also a mythological term, probably representing a type of demon, as Rashi recognized long ago.[9] The passage in Deuteronomy is therefore to be rendered :

Consumed by Hunger and warred upon by *Reseph,*
The devastation of *Meriri* and the death of *Behemot,*
And the wrath of creeping things will I send upon them.

When the asseverative character of the Kaph is recognized, the passage in Job receives a natural and forceful meaning :

May the demons of the day surely affright it.

Lam. 1: 20. "Without, the sword bereaved, within, there was death" is far more vivid than "at home there is the like of death" (JV).

Ecc. 10: 5. The second half of the verse is usually rendered "like an error proceeding from a ruler," and then it is connected with the next verse, which is regarded as the object of *ra'ithi.* This view, though possible, does not commend itself upon closer examination. In the first instance, v. 6, like vv. 7-8, 9 is a typical *mašal* in form, and hence a complete and independent literary unit. Besides, vv. 6, 7 which express dissatisfaction with unreasonable social conditions, do not have anything in common with v. 5, which is concerned with the ruler.

It therefore seems better to connect v. 5 with v. 4 rather than vv. 6, 7. There is no need, Koheleth

says, to surrender one's position when the ruler's anger rises against one, because great offences can be allayed by "healing" (bribery?) and rulers, too, are guilty of grave mistakes. The Kaph is to be regarded as asseverative and the verse can then be rendered :

I have seen an evil under the sun, indeed an error proceeding from the ruler.

Neh. 7: 2. The verse cannot mean, as it is usually taken, "he was a sort of good man, etc." Nehemiah wishes to emphasize that "he was truly a faithful man."

The results from this study may be given in statistical form. Like the Ugaritic particle *ki,* the Hebrew particle of asseveration is used at the end of the clause (12 instances).[10] Generally, too, it is in the predicate, with the direct object (3 cases), or with the predicate nominative (7 cases). In three cases it occurs with the subject.

Naturally, not all the passages cited will carry the same degree of conviction. Yet these conclusions seem valid :

1. Biblical Hebrew uses the proclitic Kaph as well as the vocable *ki* for asseverative purposes, the former generally at the end, the latter either at the beginning or the end of the clause. The former is used before substantives, the latter to modify verbs or an entire clause.

2. Ugaritic likewise possessed an asseverative of the same type, there being a presumption in favor of the view that it was the proclitic Kaph rather than the vocable *ki.*

---

[8] Cf. inter alia, M. J. Lagrange, *Etudes sur les Regions Sémitiques* (Paris, 1903), pp. 91, 388; G. A. Cooke, *Textbook of North-Semitic Inscriptions* (London 1903) p. 56 f.
[9] Commentary on Job 3 : 5.

[10] The only apparent exception is Ecc. 10: 5; where *šegagah* introduces a subordinate clause; at the same time, it is in apposition to *ra'ah* and is thus at the end of the main clause.

NOTE ON GENERAL CONDITIONAL SENTENCES
IN HEBREW

GENESIS 4 15 לָכֵן כָּל הֹרֵג קַיִן שִׁבְעָתַיִם יֻקָּם has always remained a difficulty syntactically, at best only partially understood. It has been almost universally conceded[1] that יֻקָּם cannot
have הֹרֵג קַיִן as subject, for the Kal passive of נקם[2] has the meaning "to be avenged"[3] and not "have vengeance visited upon one."
Therefore two subjects for the word in question have been suggested: (1) Cain, (2) the murder. Whichever alternative we adopt,
הֹרֵג קַיִן remains without a verb, and several explanations of its
construction are current.

According to one view[4] כָּל הֹרֵג קַיִן is a casus pendens, similar to
such instances as (1 Samuel 3 11) כָּל שֹׁמְעוֹ תְּצִלֶּינָה שְׁתֵּי אָזְנָיו or
(Psalms 103 15) אֱנוֹשׁ כֶּחָצִיר יָמָיו.
This comparison is, however, erroneous as will be plain upon
examination of the nature of the casus pendens. In the genuine
instances there is always a word in the clause referring back to the
suspended phrase. For example in כָּל שֹׁמְעוֹ תְּצִלֶּינָה שְׁתֵּי אָזְנָיו, the
suffix of אָזְנָיו harks back to כָּל שֹׁמְעוֹ. In אֱנוֹשׁ כֶּחָצִיר יָמָיו, the suffix

---

[1] But cf. Brown-Driver-Briggs, p. 668a, who renders "vengeance be taken."
[2] Not the *Hophal*, as maintained by Delitzsch, Tuch, Brown-Driver-
Briggs and others.
[3] So nearly all the commentators: Tuch, Delitzsch, Skinner et al.
[4] Adopted by Skinner, Spurrell. See Gesenius-Kautzsch-Cowley 116 w.

of יָמָיו links the clause up with אֱנוֹשׁ. This will be found to be the universal characteristic of the casus pendens, indeed its essential feature. Only in this way does אֱנוֹשׁ remain the logical and emphatic subject of כֶּחָצִיר יָמָיו. In our case, then, no casus pendens exists, as there is no connecting link with the introductory phrase כָּל הֹרֵג קַיִן to be found anywhere in the words שִׁבְעָתַיִם יֻקָּם.

The other view, maintained by Koenig,[5] offers no explanation whatever of the suspended participle, and contents itself with remarking: "Das Subjekt des Partizipialsatzes ist nicht identisch mit einem Satzteil des untergeordneten Satzes." How the participle is to be construed is left unexplained. Koenig adduces several other examples: Numbers 35 30, כָּל מַכֵּה נֶפֶשׁ לְפִי עֵדִים יִרְצַח אֶת הָרֹצֵחַ, Joshua 2 18, Proverbs 17 14, Job 41 18, where the same condition obtains as in Genesis 4 15. Besides we may also add 1 Samuel 2 13 כָּל־אִישׁ זֹבֵחַ זֶבַח וּבָא נַעַר הַכֹּהֵן which differs only in the use of the Vav.

The failure to find an explanation for these constructions is due to the erroneous conception that Biblical grammar is identical with Hebrew grammar, and the consequent failure to employ the rich stores of later Hebrew. Without doubt Biblical Hebrew should be viewed as one phase in the long history of the Hebrew language, each stage of which is intimately bound up with every other. Instead it is too often set apart and thus it suffers the consequences of its "splendid isolation".

The true explanation of the seemingly independent participle, somewhat approximated by Koenig and Delitzsch,[6] is that we are here dealing with *another variety of the conditional sentence*, perfectly legitimate and explicable when its origin is taken into account. It is well known that in order to express hypothetically general truths borne out by experience Biblical usage prefers the perfect, as in Proverbs 18 20, מָצָא אִשָּׁה מָצָא טוֹב. Yet this form is by no means exclusive. The participle, long before it emerges completely as an

---

[5] Koenig: *Lehrgebäude* II, 2, 412s, who indeed quotes several Mishnic examples.

[6] Delitzsch on Genesis 415 (English translation vol. I p. 188) already speaks of it as a *virtually hypothetical protasis* (quicumque si quispiam).

actual present tense, as in later Hebrew, begins to be felt as a verbal form. It is applied to the statement of general truths, at first purely nominally, but eventually more and more as a verb. Thus by the side of מצא אשה מצא טוב, Hebrew syntax may say (Proverbs 13 3) נֹצֵר פִּיו שֹׁמֵר נַפְשׁוֹ. This originally meant "The guardian of his mouth is the saviour of his life" (purely nominal), and then was taken to mean "he who guards his mouth saves his life" (verbal). Eventually it is felt as a pure condition: "if one guards his mouth, he saves his life." Of the same type are Proverbs 13 13, 20 *Kere*, 24 etc.

From this class of conditional sentence, where the subject of the protasis is identical with that of the apodosis, it is merely one step to the use of a different subject in the apodosis.

That the use of the participle is on a plane with the use of the perfect, is demonstrated by the following Mishnah in Peah 3, 5:

לקח זה צפונו וזה דרומו זה נותן פאה לעצמו וזה נותן פאה לעצמו.
המוכר קלחי אילן בתוך שדהו נותן פאה מכל אחד ואחד.

"If one took the north end of the tree, and the other the south, each one gives *Peah*[7] for himself.

"If one sells stalks of a tree in the midst of his field, the *buyer* gives *Peah* from each one."

Two observations will here suffice:

(1) The two conditional sentences are obviously similar in intent, yet in the first section we find the perfect used, while the second uses the participle.

(2) What appears absolutely conclusive of the conditional nature of the second sentence is the fact that we have a most important change of subject. As Bertinoro points out, it is not the seller (המוכר) but the buyer (הלוקח) who is the subject of נותן פאה. Here a word=for=word translation of the clause ("the seller of stalks of a tree in the midst of his field, gives Peah from each one") gives us the very opposite of the intent of the Mishnah! What is more, in order to obtain הלוקח as the subject of נותן פאה, we are compelled to recognize in המוכר an *actual* protasis.

[7] Cf. Leviticus 19 9 and 23 22 for the Biblical injunction.

216

One more illustration where positive danger of error lurks and where nevertheless the participle is chosen in the protasis is afforded by Mishnah Demai 7, 1:

המזמין את חבירו שיאכל עמו והוא אינו מאמינו על המעשרות אומר וגו׳.

"If one invites his friend to eat with him, though he (sc. the friend) does not trust him in regard to tithes, the *guest* must say etc.)"

Here, too, failure to recognize the conditional force of המזמין would make it the subject of אומר, whereas the intent of the Mishnah is that the *guest* pronounce the formula (so Maimonides, Heller, et al.). Again we are compelled to assume an actual protasis and apodosis to extract any meaning from the construction of the Mishnah.

The explanation of the syntax of Genesis 4 15 and the analogous examples is now clear. We are dealing with genuine conditional sentences, with the participle as the protasis, where the change of subject is as regular as in any other type of condition.

Genesis 4 15 is to be translated literally: "If anyone kill Cain, he (sc. Cain) will be avenged sevenfold."

I Samuel 2 13: "If any man offered sacrifice, the priest's servant would come etc."

Numbers 35 30: "If anyone kill a soul, only by witnesses shall the murderer be killed."

Joshua 2 18: "Behold when we come into the land, you shall bind etc."

Proverbs 17 13: "If one returns evil for good, evil shall not depart from his house."

Job 41 18: "If one lay at him with the sword, it will not hold."

SOME HITHERTO UNRECOGNIZED MEANINGS
OF THE VERB *SHUB*

IN the standard Biblical lexicons, the Hebrew verb שׁוּב and its derivatives are given these principal meanings (a). return, literal and figurative, and (b). restore, refresh.[1] Now the very frequency with which this verb occurs in the Bible has tended to discourage any careful study, in spite of the fact that in a large number of passages, these accepted meanings are inadequate. We shall here attempt to study the semantics of *shub* and then apply the result to various passages in the Bible. In some instances, the interpretation will have been anticipated or will be opposed, but it is hoped that a firmer basis for the exegesis of *shub* will be available.

The starting point for our inquiry is the acute observation of that master of Biblical Hebrew, Arnold B. Ehrlich. He[2] lays down the following law of language: "Im Hebräischen kann irgendein Verbum gebraucht werden, nicht nur seine eigene Handlung, sondern auch das Unterlassen, oder Verhüten einer entgegengesetzten Handlung, zu bezeichnen."

"In Hebrew, any verb maybe used to describe not merely its own action, but also the omission or prevention of an opposite action." In other words a verb may designate the negative of its opposite meaning.

[1] Ps. 19 8, 23 3.
[2] *Randglossen zur hebräischen Bibel*, Vol. I, p. 192.

He proceeds to illustrate. In Ex. 1 17, 22 *vatehayyenah, tehayyun*, the verb does not mean "make live",[3] but the negative of its opposite, that is "not kill, let live." In Gen. 38 23, *tikkah lah* the verb does not mean "let her take it," for Tamar already has the pledge, but "let her not give it, i. e. let her keep it." "Another striking illustration is to be found in the use *senu'ah* for the less favored wife,[4] which does not mean "hated" but "unloved wife".

That this transfer of meaning is largely unconscious goes without saying. The psychology of language still awaits the Semitic investigator. But that this entire process, predicated by Ehrlich, is not a figment of his imagination, is proved by a very striking instance in Mishnaic Hebrew, where the strict legal character of the passage precludes any divergence of meaning, and where the workimg of this process is clear and undisguised. In *Kethuboth* 3 4 [5] we read הָאוֹנֵס נוֹתֵן מִיָד הַמְפַתֶּה לִכְשֶׁיּוֹצִיא. Literally rendered this would mean—"The violator must pay at once, the seducer when he sends her out, i. e., divorces her." But that would contradict the plain inference of Ex. 22 16 which gives the father the right to decide whether he is to accept a fine or let his daughter be married to the seducer. Bertinoro therefore is very explicit: " 'If he sends her out' means, 'if he does not take her in, that is, does not marry her'." The passage therefore means "The seducer must pay if he does not marry her." Here is without doubt the clearest instance of the truth of the principle enunciated by Ehrlich.

He applies the same principle to the verb *shub*. *Shub* means primarily: "return, come back".—Its opposite is "go forward"—the negative of the opposite: "not to go forward, halt, stop". It is in this sense that he interprets these passages in the Bible:—

---

[3] As it does in Job 33 4.

[4] Gen. 29 31; Deut. 21 15.

[5] On the basis of Ex. 22 15 16, which specifies that a seducer must either marry his victim or pay a fine, and Deut. 22 28, which lays down the law that he who violates a woman must pay 50 pieces of silver to the father and must marry the girl, Rabbinic law establishes two categories *hamfatteh*, the seducer and *ha'ones*, the one who violates a woman. In the Mishnah, the various distinctions between these two malefactors are given.

Ex. 14 2 he renders: that they halt and camp before Pi-hahiroth.

Num. 10 36 he renders: "Halt O Yahveh, the myriads of the thousands of Israel!"[6]

Cant. 7 1 he translates "Stay, stay, O Shulammite, stay stay, that we may look upon thee"—a rendering that seems far superior to the commonly accepted one.

From the discussion thus far, we have derived that the verb *shub* may have the meaning "to stop, halt". Yet this is only the starting point of a whole series of meanings, each differing from the preceding by a slight shade, and all enclosed within the same periphery of meaning. We have seen how the verb meaning "to return" may develop the meaning "to stop". Now the change from literal to figurative is exceedingly common,[7] so that we may plausibly predicate the meaning b) to rest. An obvious extension in meaning is c) "be quiet, be silent". From it d) "to be at ease, be secure, confident", is a natural outgrowth.

Now we are not compelled to resort to the unaided imagination for these meanings, because the device of parallelism permits us to observe all these meanings as essentially similar and related to one another. The key passage is Is. 30 15.

Here we find the verb *shub* parallel to *nahath*, *hashket*, and *bithah*. The meaning b) "to rest" lies at the bottom of *nuah*; the meaning c) to be quiet, silent is common to *shakat*, as we shall see presently, and d) to be confident, at ease, is basic in *batah*. Moreover a study of the use of these and similar verbs show how many of them possess several of the meanings here assigned to *shub*.

---

[6] שׁוּבָה is rendered "return" by LXX, Vulgate, Onkelos, Fragment Targum, AV, and most modern authorities. Ehrlich is preceded by a long line of authorities who take it in the meaning of "rest". Menahem ben Saruk and Rashi, operating with the bi-literal theory, apparently identify ישׁב and שׁוב (See Rashi ad loc.) Yet Hayyug, the father of the tri-literal theory, and Ibn Ezra likewise derive shub from the idea of rest. In modern times, Berman in his Hebrew commentary "*Or Bahir*", p. 171 note 15, and Ehrlich interpret it likewise as "rest".

[7] The verb *shub* in the Hiphil means "to bring back" and "to restore". Cf. *heshib abedah* Ex. 23 4 and *heshib nefesh* Ps. 19 8.

Meanings

Root	A. Stop, halt	B. Rest do nothing	C. Be quiet, silent	D. Be at ease, confident
Nuah	Is. 7 2 *nahah aram*	Passim. Ex. 20 11	1 Sam. 25 9 *vayanuhu* Ecc. 9 17 *nahath*	Ecc. 4 6 *nahath*
shakat		Passim.	Is. 62 1 Parallel to *hashah*	Ez. 16 49
hashah		1 Kgs 22 3 "inactive"	Passim.	
batah		Cf. Arabic بطح VII "lie extend- ed on ground"		Amos. 6 1 and Passim
shalah			2 Sam. 3 27 *basheli* "quietly"	Passim
'amad	Josh. 10 12	2 Chron. 20 17	Num. 9 8; Job. 32 16	

It is interesting that this connection of ideas may be traced in Aryan languages as well. A few English verbs with their ramifications of meaning, some of which are now obsolete, may be given.

Meanings

Verb	A. Stop, halt	B. Rest, do nothing	C. Be quiet, silent	D. Be confident
Stay	Stop[8]	rest[9]		rely[10]
Rest		cessation from activity	silence (Music)	trust, rely[11]
Quiet (Quiescent)	not moving	dormant resting	silent (grammar)	

In view of this close and intimate connection subsisting between these various meanings, we believe it probable that *shub* may be

[8] "She would command the hasty sun to stay"—Spencer.
[9] "I stay here on my bow"—Shakespeare.
[10] "Trust in oppression and perverseness, and stay thereon"—AV, Is. 30 12.
[11] "On him I rested after long debate,
    And, not without considering, fixed my fate"—Dryden.

credited with the following meanings a) halt, b) to rest, c) be quiet, d) be confident, secure.

It now remains to describe the various passages where these meanings are to be utilized. Reference has already been make to

A. *The Meaning "stop, halt"*

in three passages Ex. 14 2, Num. 11 36 and Cant. 7 1.

B. *The Meaning "be at rest".*

Is. 30 15: It is obvious that the interpretation of שׁוּבָה in the sense of "returning, repentance"[12] does not suit the context. The prophet is urging, not repentance, but full-hearted confidence in the Lord, which expresses itself in desisting from human activity. The proposed emendations בְּשֶׁבֶת[13] בְּשָׁבָה[14] are unnecessary in view of the considerations advanced above. As a derivative of שׁוּב, שׁוּבָה can well mean "rest",[15] and the verse is to be translated as follows:—

> In rest and in repose shall ye be saved,
> In quietness and confidence shall be your strength.

Jer. 30 10: The ancient versions interpret וְשָׁב in the sense of "return"[16] while most modern interpreters[17] prefer to render "And Jacob shall once more be quiet etc." This, unfortunately, tends to destroy the double parallelism of the verse, which is now possible by translating:

> And Jacob shall rest and be quiet,
> And be at ease, with none to disturb him.

Hos. 14 8: The common rendering: "They that dwell in his shadow shall return",[18] gives no satisfactory meaning. LXX and Targum, followed by Kimhi, render, "They will return and dwell under his shadow", but this implies a tacit emendation to *yashubu*

[12] So LXX, Vulgate, Targum, AV, RV, Cambridge Bible.
[13] Oort. *Emendationes*, ad loc.
[14] Ehrlich, JPSV version—"sitting still."
[15] So Rashi, Ibn Ezra, Berman—see above.
[16] So LXX, V, T, AV.
[17] So Ehrlich. JPSV etc.
[18] So V, AV, most commentaries, JPSV.

veyeshbu besillo". Both interpretations are, however, inadmissible, because no return can here be intended, for 6 and 7 that precede are descriptions of the idyllic conditions of the future, of which v. 8 is a continuation. A more suitable rendering would be:

"They that dwell in his shadow will have peace etc."

Jer. 4 1; The best interpretation of the first half of this difficult verse is: "If you will return, O Israel, saith the Lord, return to me". (V, AV, JPS) but the tautology is obvious. It is evident that *tashub* cannot have the same significance in both protasis and apodosis, if it is to make sense. Like all the prophets, Jeremiah likes to play on words.[19] We must assign to the first *tashub*, the meaning "rest" and a voluntative force.[20] We then achieve a fine chiastic structure with stich b) and c), and a) and d) parallel to each other.

"If you wish to find rest, O Israel, saith the Lord, you will return to me; and if you remove your abominations from before me, you shall not wander." An alternative rendering is proposed below.[21]

Ezek. 38 8: The usual rendering is: "restored from the sword" (LXX, V, Tar, AV, JPSV). Perhaps it may be translated:

"In the end of days thou shalt come again to the land,
That is at rest from the sword,
Gathered from many peoples."[22]

---

[19] Indeed we have one such play on *shub* in Jer. 8 4. Cf. Ewald *ad loc.*

[20] Whereas in Latin, voluntative verbs are usually distinguished in form, in Hebrew they are to be told only from the context (Gesenius-Kautzsch, *Grammatik*, 28 ed. p. 305—308). Cf. Micah 5 4 which is best taken to mean "when he will *want to* come to our land." Ps. 40 6 if I *wished to* declare, etc." Ps. 69 5 "they that *would* destroy me are mighty," Ps. 78 34. "If he *wished to* slay them, etc."

[21] Kimhi assigns the meaning of "rest" to the second *tashub*, but overlooks the difficulty of *elai tashub*. Yet the LXX seems to have read *elai* before *n'um adonai*. If this is the older reading, the rendering is even more to be preferred:

If you return to me, saith the Lord, you shall find rest, And if you remove your abominations from before me, you shall not wander.

[22] Perhaps such Biblical names as *Shobab, Meshobab* may be interpreted similarly. They cannot mean "backsliding, apostate", nor even "restored." Children at birth can scarcely be described as "restored." It seems prefer-

2 Sam. 8 3: The parallel passage is 1 Ch. 18 3 reads לְהַצִּיב יָדוֹ and many scholars emend our passage accordingly[23]. The rendering of the LXX (ἐπιστῆσαι set up his hand) and V (*ut dominaretur,*— "that he might rule") are assumed to substantiate the reading of Chronicles. That these versions may well be derived from M. T. will become clear presently. Moreover, the reading of Targum, לְאַשְׁנָאָה תְּחוּמֵיהּ is the normal rendering of לְהָשִׁיג יָדוֹ[24] and would thus seem to substantiate the Shin rather than the Sade,—hence להשיב rather than להציב. The phrase *heshib yad* is, as is well known, very common. If *shub* means "rest", *heshib* would mean "make rest, place," exactly like *nuah, hinniah.* The phrase would therefore mean—to put down one's hand, to establish one's dominion", the precise translation of LXX and V.

Is. 1 25; Jer. 6 9; Ezek. 20 22; 58 12; Amos 1 8; Zech. 13 7; Ps. 81 15: *heshib yad.* This common prophetic phrase has been variously given: "turn my hand"[25] "bring my hand again"[26] "bring my hand upon thee again and again"[27] and "turn back"[28]. Now the idea of repetition which is implied in the current meaning of *shub* can be applied with difficulty, if at all, to Is. 1 25; Ezek. 20 22. In these passages some grounds may be found, to interpret "the return of God's hand". On the other hand, the idea of repetition is emphatically ruled out in the other passages. Indeed, the fundamental implication of the phrase is the coercive and violent character of the act. We are therefore unable to interpret this phrase from the ordinarily accepted meanings of *shub.* But if we assume the meaning of *shub* as "rest" we get a completely unforced and natural meaning—"let God's hand rest on", "let one feel God's power." It is not very different from Ezek. 37 11: "The hand of the Lord was upon me."

---

able to interpret these names as meaning "peace, rest." Cf. Shallum, Shelomoh, Shelemiah, Noah.

[23] Oört: Emendationes ad loc., Delitzsch: Schreib- und Lesefehler, sec. 141.

[24] Cf. Targum to Hos. 5 10 and Kimhi *ad loc.* Cf. Ehrlich on 2 Sam. 8 3.

[25] AV, RV, JPS to Is. 1 25; V, T, LXX to Jer. 6 9.

[26] RV margin to Is. 1 25, JPSV to Jer. 6 9.

[27] Rashi, Kimhi passim.

[28] AV to Jer. 6 9.

C. *The Meaning "be silent"*

Prov. 25 10: The usual meaning given to the last clause is "and thy infamy turn not away"—but this has no philological warrant. "Turn away" would be *tasur*.

The Vulgate renders: *et exprobrare non cesset*,—"he will not cease to reprove thee". This is closer to our rendering:

> "Lest he that heareth thee revile thee,
> And thy infamy become not quiet."

Job 6 29: The translation "return" (LXX, V, Tar, AV), even in the sense of "return to judge me", (V, Rashi) is meaningless. If we interpret *shubu* to mean "be silent", the verse makes excellent context. Before launching on his long lament on his sufferings, Job urges his friends to remain silent and listen. It seems to have been part of the rhetorical introduction in Semitic poetry, to ask for the silent attention of the listeners, as we find similar exhortations in Job 21 3; 34 2; and 36 2. Our verse may be translated somewhat as follows:

> Be silent, I pray, let there be no injustice,
> Be silent, my cause still is righteous.

D. *The Meaning "trust, be secure, confident"*

Prov. 1 32: The word מְשׁוּבָה occurs only here outside of the Prophets. It does not mean "backsliding" or "waywardness" in our passage. The verse manifests a perfect parallelism and מְשׁוּבַת is parallel to שַׁלְוַת. The author wishes to express the idea that the self-assurance of fools, which leads them to despise wisdom, will be their downfall, while the wise will finally achieve contentment. It is highly significant that corresponding to מֹשׁובה, and שׁלוה in our verse, the next has יִשְׁכָּן־בֶּטַח and שַׁאֲנָן. Our verse reads:—

> For the assurance of the thoughtless will slay them
> And the confidence of fools will destroy them;
> But whoso hearkens to me shall dwell safely,
> And shall be quiet from fear of evil.

Jer. 8 6b: The last two stichs occasion great difficulty, even if the unexpected plural of *bimrusatham* be discounted or emended. The renderings "every one turned to his course", or "turneth in his course" are not satisfactory. We may perhaps render:

> No man repents of his wickedness,
> Saying, what have I done.
> Each one trusts in his speed,
> Like a horse fleet in battle.

Jer. 49 4: This oracle against Ammon is very difficult. Ehrlich objects to *hashobebah*, as being inapplicable to Ammon, who never stood in a close relation to the Lord, as did Israel, and was never expected to abide by His teaching. He therefore reads *hasha'ananah* as a parallel to *habotehah*. But this very sense is inherent in the textus receptus if our meaning of *shub* be adopted:

> Why dost thou glory in thy valleys,
> Thy flowing valley, O over-confident daughter?
> Who trusteth in her treasures,
> Saying, "Who can come nigh unto me!"

Is. 47 10: That the Polel and the Hiphil may have the same meaning has already been shown by a comparison of Ps. 23 2 and Ps. 19 7. *Shobebathek* is therefore to be taken as the causative of "be confident", that is, "made you confident". The triple parallelism of the verse emerges clearly:

> Thou hast been secure in thy wickedness (or, by a slight change, knowledge):
>> Thou hast said—No one seeth me.
>> Thy wisdom and thy knowledge—
>> This has made thee confident,
>> Thou hast said in thy heart
>> "I am—and there is none beside me."

Job 34 36: This verse, which has suffered a plethora of emendations and interpretations from the ancient versions down to our own day[29], still remains a crux.—Perhaps תשבת may be taken in the same sense as משובה above "trust, confidence" and vocalized תְּשֻׁבָתוֹ. The translation would be:

> "Would that Job be tried to the end,
> Because of his trust in wicked men."

Hos. 12 7: All authorities take the first stich to mean "Thou

---

[29] The LXX read: *al tishboth ke'anshei aven*; Vul. read: *al tishboth me'anshei aven*; Rashi: So that it might be an answer to wicked men; JPSV: Because of his answering like wicked men; AV: Because of his answer for wicked men.

13

shalt return unto thy God"—but that is impossible because of the
prefix Beth. The verse is to be rendered:—

> Thou shalt trust in thy God,
> Keep mercy and justice,
> And wait for thy God continually.

We have come to the end of our task. By predicating the
meanings a) stop, b) rest, c) be quiet, and d) be secure, trusting, for
the verb שׁוּב, we hope to have cast some light on several passages that have thus far defied interpretation.

LIST OF THE PASSAGES EXPLAINED

Ex.	14 2	Ezek.	20 22
Num.	10 36		38 8
2 Sam.	8 3		58 12
Is.	1 25	Hos.	12 7
	30 15		14 8
	47 10	Amos	1 8
Jer.	4 1	Zech.	13 7
	6 9	Ps.	81 15
	8 6	Prov.	1 32
	30 10		25 10
	49 4	Cant.	7 1

QOHELETH STUDIES

THE ORIGINAL LANGUAGE OF QOHELET

IF QOHELET were alive today, he might derive some ironic satisfaction from the fact that every feature of his fascinating book has perplexed his readers. Scholars have been divided on the integrity of the text, the extent of interpolation in the book, its date and authorship, its message and standpoint. Now, the last step has been taken, and the original language of the book has been called into question.

A quarter of a century ago, F. C. Burkitt ventured to express "a feeling," which he confessed he could not validate, that Qohelet might be a translation. "If it be a translation, it is naturally a translation of the Aramaic."[1] That Qohelet might be an "adaptation of a work in some other language, probably Indo-Germanic," was a view advanced by D. S. Margoliouth two decades earlier.[2] In line with this approach, Margoliouth had laboriously reconstructed a Hebrew text for Ben Sira on the basis of the Greek and Syriac versions.[3] In spite of his ingenuity, the Genizah text discovered thereafter did not agree with his retroversion in a single verse out of several hundreds.

[1] "Is Ecclesiastes a Translation?" *JTHS*, vol. 23, 1921, pp. 23–6. The reference in Dr. Zimmermann's article should be corrected accordingly.

[2] *JE*, art. Ecclesiastes, vol. V. p. 31.

[3] *An Essay on the Place of Ecclesiasticus in Semitic Literature*, (Oxford, 1890).

His attempt thus provided a useful object-lesson in the precariousness of the entire procedure.

The tentative suggestion of Margoliouth and Burkitt has now been adopted by Zimmermann[4] who seeks to demonstrate the hypothesis. Brushing all hesitation aside, he finally declares that "the thesis of Qohelet's translation is unmistakably indicated and that he who wishes to expound Qohelet must give his attention to the reconstruction of the Aramaic original." (p. 45) If this view is sound, all previous exegetical and critical studies of Qohelet must go into the discard, and all future research must begin with the new hypothesis as basic. The issue is too important to be ignored; it must either be accepted or disproved.

Zimmermann prefaces his detailed proof by two general considerations. First, Ben Sira is, by general consent, later in origin than Qohelet, and yet it shows far less evidence of a "decadent" Hebrew style and of the use of Aramaisms and New Hebrew constructions (p. 17). Second, the book is written in a difficult style; many of the proverbs lack "crispness;" and many verses and half verses are obscure (p. 18).

Neither of these two arguments stands up under analysis. Ben Sira is written in the form of poetry rather than in prose and therefore naturally seeks to approximate the earlier, classical style. This tendency is particularly pronounced in Ben Sira, who is quite frankly imitative of Scriptures (cf. Eccl. 24.30) so that his verses are often a mosaic of Biblical phrases. Thus the older sections of the Jewish liturgy, such as *nishmat*, *yotzer 'or*, *'ahavah rabbah* and the *Amidah* are surely later than the book of Esther, and are roughly contemporaneous with the Mishnah. Yet

---

[4] "The Aramaic Provenance of Qohelet" *JQR*, vol. 35, No. 1, July 1945, pp. 17–45. All page references without source in our discussion refer to this paper.

being poetical in form and reminiscent of Biblical phraseology, they contain far fewer Aramaisms and new Hebrew
constructions than either *Esther* or the *Mishnah*. It may be
added, in passing, that the conception of a "decadent"
Hebrew is completely unscientific and would be best
abandoned altogether.

As for the second argument, that the style is difficult
and the sayings lack "crispness," this is largely a subjective judgment. But even if it be granted, there is no need
to dismiss the obvious explanation that style is a reflection
of the man, and that of two contemporaries, one may
write lucidly and simply and the other in involved and
complicated fashion. Actually, the examples of simple
style that Zimmermann adduces from contemporaries of
Qohelet are rather remarkable. (p. 18). Job, Psalms and
Proverbs are not precisely beginner's Hebrew!

There is a more fundamental objection, however, to the
widely-held theory that a difficult text *ipso facto* presupposes a translation from another language.[5] A translator faced by a difficult original may misread it, because
he lacks an adequate knowledge of the vocabulary and
misconstrues the grammar. He may tacitly emend the
text, read irrelevant matters into it and generally fail to
penetrate its meaning. But ultimately he decides upon

---

[5] Abraham Ibn Ezra suggests that Job is a translation (cf. his commentary on 2.11: הקרוב אלי כי הוא ספר מתורגם על כן הוא קשה בפירוש
כדרך כל ספר מתורגם. Thomas Carlyle says, "Biblical critics seem
agreed that our own book of Job was written in that (i. e. Arab) region
of the world. I call that, apart from all theories about it, one of the
grandest things ever written with pen. One feels indeed as if it were
not Hebrew; such a noble universality different from noble patriotism
or sectarianism reigns in it." (Quotation from *Heroes and Hero Worship*
(chapter on "The Hero As Prophet") The motive for Carlyle's opinion is scarcely to be regarded as objective, yet it is to be met with in
the work of far better scholars than the Scotch sage. R. H. Pfeiffer,
Introduction to the Old Testament, New York, 1941, pp. 670, 678–83,
assumes an "Edomite" original for Job.

some view of the passage, which he then expresses in his
idiom. His version may be incorrect, but it will be clear
and intelligible, far more so than the original, all the difficulties and alternatives of which will have been ignored or
obscured in the process. One has only to compare a difficult
verse in the Hebrew of *Hosea*, *Ezekiel* or *Job* with any
English version to see how the manifold difficulties of the
Hebrew "disappear" in the smooth English renderings.

*Other things being equal, it may therefore be maintained
that a difficult text may be presumed to be the original rather
than a translation.* In general, the translation hypothesis
may be described as visiting the sins, real or imaginary, of
the author, upon an unlucky translator. To him no folly
or stupidity is deemed impossible. Thus, Dr. Zimmermann
asks us to believe that in 9.1 the "translator slipped,
thoughtlessly incorporating the Aramaic עֲבָדֵיהָם into the
text instead of the usual מעשה" (p. 20). But the word
מעשה occurs in the book sixteen times before this passage,
and four times thereafter, all within 222 verses. This
would be a remarkable lapse of memory, since the translator had rendered it correctly in the verse immediately
preceding and had then rapidly recovered, nine verses
later.

Perhaps the most striking example of the difficulties
created by a "simple" explanation is to be found in Doctor
Zimmermann's procedure (pp. 41 f.) with 10.15: עָמֵל
הַכְּסִילִים תְּיַגְּעֶנּוּ אֲשֶׁר לֹא־יָדַע לָלֶכֶת אֶל־עִיר. He confesses that he
cannot solve the last part of the verse, but undertakes to
explain the changes of gender and number in the first half.
The Aramaic read טרחותא דשטיא תשלהינה. The translator
rendered טרחותא by עמל. The next moment, in translating
תשלהינה, he forgot that his Hebrew read עמל, a masculine
noun, and so he mechanically wrote the verb in the feminine
תיגע. But his lapses were not yet at an end. He misread

234

דשטיא as a plural and rendered it הכסילים, but, at the very next word, forgot that he had rendered it thus and recognized it as a singular, hence the singular suffix in תיגענו.

That the passage is difficult is clear. That this explanation meets the situation seems considerably less certain. This illustration is only one of many indicating the depths of stupidity and incompetence which must be assumed for the translator, who, judging by Chapter XII, was not as inept as the theory cheerfully assumes.

II

Doctor Zimmermann stakes his case on what he calls "the clearest proof," namely instances of alleged mistranslation, of which he adduces five striking examples (p. 23).

His first instance is 1.5 וְזָרַח הַשֶּׁמֶשׁ וּבָא הַשָּׁמֶשׁ וְאֶל־מְקוֹמוֹ שׁוֹאֵף זוֹרֵחַ הוּא שָׁם. Zimmermann argues that שוֹאֵף is meaningless and that the Aramaic original read תאב, ולאתריה תאב being the participle of תוב "return." It should have been given as שָׁב, but the translator mistook it as the participle from תאב "desire, long for" and hence rendered שוֹאֵף.

Not only does the solution bristle with difficulties, but what is more, the problem itself is unreal. If the translator was likely to misread תאב as "desire," he had a far more natural occasion to do so two verses later in v. 7 where the Hebrew reads: הֵם שָׁבִים לָלָכֶת. Here the existence of an apparent complementary infinitive might conceivably have led an unwary translator to render אנון תאבין למיזל as "they desire to go." If he failed to err here, he could not possibly have gone astray in v. 5.

Moreover, the problem posed is imaginary. Dr. Zimmermann's procedure here destroys one of the most characteristic phrases of the book. The conception of the sun racing across the sky from morning to night is, of course,

familiar to all readers of Semitic and Greek literature. But
each poet would infuse his own emotion into the scene.
The Psalmist, expressing the joy of life induced by his
faith in God, speaks of the sun as "rejoicing like a strong
man to run his course" (Ps. 19.6). Qohelet, lacking such
faith, is depressed by the monotonous repetition of natural
phenomena and by man's helplessness in the world. He
pictures the sun as out of breath, exhausted by his course
across the heavens, which he must repeat the next day:
"The sun rises and the sun sets, breathlessly rushing (lit.
panting) toward the place when it is to rise again."[6] That
Qohelet possessed genuine poetic gifts of a high order and
was capable of strikingly original figures is clear from the
unforgettable "Allegory of Old Age" in Chap. 12 and from
dozens of other passages, including the majestic opening
section in which this verse occurs.

Dr. Zimmermann argues that in 7.5, טוֹב לִשְׁמֹעַ גַּעֲרַת חָכָם
שִׁיר, מֵאִישׁ שֹׁמֵעַ שִׁיר כְּסִילִים is not quite suitable and that it
presupposes the Aramaic שבחא or תושבחתא, meaning both
"song," and "praise." But the existence of both these
meanings in the same root in Aramaic should have indicated
to him that an easy semantic development links both
meanings. Cf. the English idiom "to sing one's praises"
and the passage in the old prayer *Yishtabaḥ* שִׁיר ושבחה הלל
זמרה. That Qohelet should use שִׁיר in the meaning of
"praise" is particularly easy to understand, since he undoubtedly knew Aramaic and used the language considerably. At most, we have an Aramaism here, but even
that is not certain.

In 6.2 the clause וְאֵינֶנּוּ חָסֵר לְנַפְשׁוֹ מִכֹּל אֲשֶׁר־יִתְאַוֶּה is regarded
by Dr. Zimmermann as a contradiction, "which commen-

---

[6] Cf. the writer's *The Wisdom of Ecclesiastes* (New York, 1945),
which contains a new version, from which this and other renderings in
the paper are cited.

tators pass off with but brief notation." (p. 24). The
reason is obvious — there is no genuine difficulty. The
verse is to be rendered, "Here is a man whom God gives
wealth, means and position, so that he lacks nothing he
can possibly desire. Yet God does not let him enjoy it,
for some stranger is destined to consume it — this is vanity,
an evil plague."

In discussing 7.20 כִּי אָדָם אֵין צַדִּיק בָּאָרֶץ אֲשֶׁר יַעֲשֶׂה־טּוֹב וְלֹא
יֶחֱטָא, Dr. Zimmermann cites a Midrashic comment to
prove that צדיק anticipates the clause אשר יעשה טוב. He
therefore suggests that צדיק is an erroneous rendering of
the Aramaic זכי and that the passage originally read,
"no man succeeds on earth in doing good without evil."
Dr. Zimmermann gives us the Aramaic of part of the verse
דנברא לא זכי בארעא וגו' but forbears to cite the rest. But
there is the rub. The remainder would have been למעבד טבא,
but in that event the Hebrew would have read לעשות טוב
not אשר יעשה טוב. Actually there is no more difficulty in
צדיק "anticipating" אשר יעשה טוב than in אשר יעשה טוב
"anticipating" ולא יחטא. Besides, the Aramaic of the
Targum, the Talmud and the Midrash expresses "succeed"
exclusively by the verb אצלח and never by זכי.[7]

In 10.17 בִּנְבוּרָה וְלֹא בַּשְׁתִי, Dr. Zimmermann suggests that
בגבורה represents an erroneous rendering of the Eastern
Aramaic ܒܚܘܣܢܐ meaning "in moderation." It is of course
an open question as to what Aramaic dialect the original
may be presumed to have used, a question that Dr. Zimmermann himself finds it impossible to decide[8] (p. 39). But

---

[7] אצלח is used absolutely by Onkelos on Gen. 39.2, Num. 14.41, with
a noun obj. (דרך) in Gen. 24.21, 40, 42, 56; Deut. 28.29, with a clause
as object in Gen. 39.3, 23, with a complementary infinitive in Deut.
32:15 אצלח תקוף (Jerusalem Targum reads אצלחו תקוף) and absolutely
by the Targum on I Kings 1.34.

[8] The inconsistency in the spelling of the determinate and the
feminine suffix (*He* or *Aleph*) throughout the proposed Aramaic does

even if this meaning be accepted for our passage, the semantic development is clear without this hypothesis of a mistranslation. "Strength" would develop the meaning of "self-control" as naturally in Hebrew as in Aramaic. For the juxtaposition of the two ideas, note Prov. 16.32 וּמֹשֵׁל בְּרוּחוֹ מִלֹּכֵד עִיר "one who rules over his spirit is better than he who takes a city" and the Mishnah *Abot* 4.1 איזהו גבור הכובש את יצרו "Who is mighty? He who subdues his passions." It is, moreover, by no means ruled out that בגבורה is an Aramaism, if this meaning of the word be adopted here.

In 5.17 הִנֵּה אֲשֶׁר־רָאִיתִי אָנִי טוֹב אֲשֶׁר־יָפֶה, the contention that הנה is an error for הא = "this" is also untenable. Dr. Zimmerman's Aramaic הא דחזי אנא דטב would be הנה אשר ראיתי אני אשר טוב, but the אשר after אני is lacking in our text. Thus the theory of translation creates a new difficulty. The problem is however illusory. It is incredible that the translator of so many difficult passages in which Qoheleth abounds, should not know the meaning of הא. Obviously 2.24 נם זה ראיתי proves nothing. Qohelet was a literary craftsman, who would naturally use variation in his style.

Even more strikingly inadequate is Dr. Zimmermann's treatment of 12.13. He asserts that כִּי־זֶה כָּל־הָאָדָם is a mis-

---

not cease to be an inconsistency, merely because the writer cannot reach a definite conclusion as "to what form or dialect the antecedent Aramaic consisted of" (Zimmermann, p. 39 note 3). This conclusion that it is "probably Eastern Aramaic" creates a whole series of new critical problems; where the book was written and where the Epilogue was added (12.9–14); how it reached Palestine, and was accepted as canonical (without this assumption the likelihood of its being regarded as worthy of translation is very slight, cf. the Septuagint and the Apocryphal books); how it was (mis)translated and became widely known (cf. Ben Sira's linguistic reminiscences of Qohelet); and how all this activity can be compressed within a century or two. There is also a question as to why an author living outside of Palestine and writing in Aramaic would assume the guise of Solomon, even as a literary device.

translation of the original "because He is the Judge of all man." But that could only have been expressed in Aramaic by כִּי דָיָן כָּל אֱנָשָׁא הוּא and this pronoun is lacking. Actually the verse is perfectly clear as it stands, and means "for that is man's whole duty." This characteristic Hebrew construction occurs *inter alia* in Isa. 28.12 זֹאת הַמְּנוּחָה הַנִּיחוּ לֶעָיֵף; "This is the secret of rest — give peace to the weary."

III

The instances discussed above are those which Dr. Zimmermann regards as the strongest evidence for his thesis. If they fall away, the theory loses its basic support.

He then advances (p. 27) "other examples which only admit, however, of a good *probability* for the translation hypothesis." (italics his) "The Hebrew is capable of explanation" he admits, — "but with a good deal of difficulty, as I believe." Here the difficulties of the accepted view are exaggerated, and the proposals advanced are not infrequently less plausible than other suggestions made. Since these instances are regarded as less significant by the author himself, we may treat them more briefly.

In 5.6 כִּי בְרֹב חֲלֹמוֹת וַהֲבָלִים וּדְבָרִים הַרְבֵּה כִּי אֶת־הָאֱלֹהִים יְרָא the second כִּי in the MT is difficult. It may be an error or represent a syntactic usage not clear to us to day. Dr. Zimmermann suggests that the original ran: דבשניאותא דחלמין והבלין ומלין שגין די לאלהא דחל, "because in the multitude of dreams, vanities and talk, persons *err*; have reverence for that which belongs to God." (p. 27).

Now no one who is familiar with the language would call די לאלהא דחל a smooth Aramaic locution for "have reverence for that which belongs to God," nor, for that matter is it smooth in English! The suggested meaning of the verse is far inferior to the generally accepted sense

of the Hebrew, which we have rendered somewhat freely,
"After all the dreams, follies and idle chatter, this remains
— fear God!"

In 7.29 the clause וְהָמָּה בִקְשׁוּ חִשְּׁבֹנוֹת רַבִּים is regarded as
difficult and an error for חושבנין שנין "erring schemes." This
would incidentally require an *aphel* חושבנין משנין, unless we
assume a transferred epithet. But there is no problem here
at all. Qohelet wishes to express the idea that the simple
·and straightforward nature of man has been corrupted by
his complicated schemes and calculations: "Besides, note
this that I have learnt; God has made man straightforward,
but they sought out many inventions."

In 5.12, 15, the Hebrew phrase רָעָה חוֹלָה is far superior
to an assumed Aramaic בישה בישה "a very great evil." It
may be added that this is by no means identical with the
Aramaic *bish*, *bish*, "very bad."

In 5.16 גַּם כָּל־יָמָיו בַּחֹשֶׁךְ יֹאכֵל is a vivid picture of the senseless parsimony of the rich man who fails to take advantage
of the comforts of life available to him. Thus among the
fellahin and bedouins of Palestine thel amp must burn
continually. To say "he sleeps in the dark," is to express
the ultimate in poverty. (Cf. S. Benzinger, *Hebraische
Archäologie*, 2nd ed. p. 97). On the other hand, a light at
night is a symbol of a cheerful, well-conducted household.
Cf. Jer. 25.10 אוֹר רֵחַיִם וְאוֹר הַנֵּר. In our passage of course,
the reference is to the stinginess of the rich man who
conducts himself like a beggar. But even if one sees in the
word "darkness" a metaphoric allusion to bitterness and
trouble, there is no proof of a mistranslation of the Aramaic
בקבלא, which means both "complaint" and "darkness."
The association of "darkness" and "sorrow" needs no documentation. Cf. *inter alia* Isa. 9.1 and for the reverse,
Esth. 8.16.

The second half of this verse וְכָעַס הַרְבֵּה וְחָלְיוֹ וָקָצֶף undeniably offers some syntactic problems. Perhaps the simplest procedure is to delete the second *Vav* of וחליו as a dittography. It is, however, possible to regard the suffixed noun as an elliptical form virtually equivalent to וְחָלִי לוֹ = "he has pain," Cf. Gen. 22.24 וּפִילַגְשׁוֹ וּשְׁמוֹ רְאוּמָה = "he had a concubine, named *Re'umah*;" Num. 12.6 אִם יִהְיֶה נְבִיאֲכֶם ה' = "If ye have a prophet of God" and especially Ps. 115.7 יְדֵיהֶם וְלֹא יְמִישׁוּן רַגְלֵיהֶם וְלֹא יְהַלֵּכוּ = יָדַיִם (אָזְנַיִם לָהֶם . . . אַף לָהֶם . . . רַגְלַיִם לָהֶם (cf. v. 6 לָהֶם) "They have hands . . . . . they have feet." Our passage may accordingly be rendered, "All his days he eats in the dark and he has much grief, sickness and anger."

Nevertheless, whether or not any of these suggestions are accepted, the presumed Aramaic solves nothing. It has apparently escaped Dr. Zimmermann's notice that in his text אַף כל יומוהי בקבלא אכל ורגז שׁניא ובישׁה (sic) וקצפא the last three nouns are syntactically unrelated to the verse. On the basis of his rendering, "Because all his days he eats in complaint, much annoyance, malaise, and anger," the Aramaic should have been ברגז שׁניא, בבישׁא ובקצפא.

In 7.12 כִּי בְּצֵל הַחָכְמָה בְּצֵל הַכָּסֶף is assumed to be a mistranslation of דְבַטְלָא חוּכְמְתָה בְּטֵל כַּסְפָּא. But in a conditional sentence, with two different subjects being used with the participles, a conjunction like אִי "if" should have been employed in the protasis.

9.1–2 contains the very difficult phrase הַכֹּל לִפְנֵיהֶם. The Aramaic is assumed (p. 31) to have been כלא קדמיהם כלא (doubtless a graphic error for כְּלָא קֳדָמֵיהוֹן כְּלָא), which should have been given as בְּאַיִן לִפְנֵיהֶם הַכֹּל. I confess that both the Aramaic and the suggested Hebrew of Dr. Zimmermann seem incomprehensible to me in this context. The MT is immeasurably to be preferred and the verse rendered, "Men can be certain of neither God's love nor His hate — anything may happen to them."

The familiar verse 11.1 שְׁלַח לַחְמְךָ עַל־פְּנֵי הַמָּיִם כִּי־בְרֹב הַיָּמִים
תִּמְצָאֶנּוּ is referred back to a confusion of the Aramaic פרס I
meaning "spread out" hence "sail," and פרס II break
(bread). Dr. Zimmermann renders "Set your sail upon
the waters for after many days you will find it." Aside
from the fact that the difficulty is not genuine, he does not
notice that תמצאנו now has no antecedent either in grammar
or in thought.

In the famous 12.1 וּזְכֹר אֶת־בּוֹרְאֶיךָ he suggests the reading
בריך "your health" as original, an extremely prosaic reading
for this poetic passage. Actually, as we have shown elsewhere, the Masoretic text is both correct and authentic.
Qohelet who declares again and again that the only sensible
goal for man is "joy," exhorts the youth to remember God
and fulfill His will, by enjoying life while he is young and
vigorous. The thought and the mode of expression are
parallelled elsewhere in Qohelet, in Ben Sira and in Rabbinical literature.[9] Only one striking parallel may be cited
here, the statement of the Babylonian scholar Rab (3 cent.
C. E.): עתיד כל אדם ליתן דין וחשבון על כל מה שראתה עינו ולא
אכל "Every man must render an account before God for
all the good things he beheld and did not enjoy" (Jerusalem
Talmud, Kiddushin, end).

In 5.5 המלאך need not be a mistranslation of שליחא. It is
by no means certain that the reference is to the human
messenger who collects pledges for the Temple. It has been
referred by some commentators to the angel at the Divine
assize. But even the former use is characteristically
Hebrew, and is found in the contemporaneous Hebrew of
Malachi (2.7), referring to the priest as the emissary of
God on earth: כִּי מַלְאַךְ ה'־צְבָאוֹת הוּא.

---

[9] Cf. our study, pp. 30–32, and the literature cited there on p. 81,
for a fuller discussion of this important element in Qoheleth's thought.

The first part of 3.15 is perfectly explicable as it stands, without recourse to the translation-hypothesis. The verse may be given, "What has been, already exists, and what is still to be, has already been, and God always seeks to repeat what has gone by."

Verses 4.16, 17 constitute one of the most difficult passages in the book, since they refer to a historical event not now identifiable. Various solutions have been proposed, none completely satisfactory. Nor is the translation-hypothesis an improvement. Without a detailed discussion, it may be pointed .out that Dr. Zimmermann has not proved that טליא תנינא the "original" for הַיֶּלֶד הַשֵּׁנִי could mean "crown prince." The Syriac תנינא למלכא is quite another matter. If this be evidence, then the Hebrew הילד השני could itself mean "crown prince, viceroy." Cf. מִשְׁנֶה (Gen. 41.43; II Chron. 35.24) and the identical phrase מִשְׁנָה לַמֶּלֶךְ (Esth. 10.3) or מִשְׁנֵה הַמֶּלֶךְ (II Chron. 28.7).

In 7.10 we feel that the MT מֶה הָיָה "What has happened" is superior to the suggested מה הוא. In 6.10 it is suggested that וְנוֹדַע is an error for וחכים that should have been given as וְחָכָם. That the translator could fail to recognize the word which he renders correctly as חָכָם innumerable times in the book is inconceivable. Besides, the entire assumption is unnecessary, as is clear from the commentaries. We have treated אֲשֶׁר־הוּא אָדָם as an instance of "anticipation," logically the subject of שֶׁתַּקִּיף מִמֶּנּוּ. וְלֹא־יוּכַל לָדִין עִם [10] The entire verse means: "What has been, has already been

---

[10] On this usage of "anticipation," common in classical languages as well, cf. Gen. 1.4 וַיַּרְא אֱלֹהִים אֶת הָאוֹר כִּי טוֹב and Ehrlich ad loc. and on Job 1.8. Also our "Note on Josh. 22.34" (*AJSL*, July 1931, pp. 287 f.) which calls attention to this same usage in that verse. For an example of "anticipation" after the verb יָדַע, cf. Num. 32.23 וּדְעוּ חַטַּאתְכֶם אֲשֶׁר תִּמְצָא אֶתְכֶם = "Know that your sin will overtake you." For the use of the Vav after the anticipated subject, cf. Gen. 6.1 וַיַּרְא אֱלֹהִים אֶת־הָאָרֶץ וְהִנֵּה נִשְׁחָתָה — "And God saw that the earth was corrupted." Other instances occur in Gen. 8.13 and Deut. 8.18.

determined, and it is known that man cannot argue with One mightier than himself."

In his discussion of the meaning of the enigmatic verse 5.8 וְיִתְרוֹן אֶרֶץ בַּכֹּל הִיא מֶלֶךְ לְשָׂדֶה נֶעֱבָד, Dr. Zimmermann accepts what we regard as the best interpretation of stich b. However, there is no need to assume a retroversion from the Aramaic. We have rendered the second half of the verse exactly as he does, on the basis of the Hebrew: "The advantage of land is paramount, even a king is subject to the soil." "To be subject, dependent" would be expressed in Hebrew by נעבד which corresponds to the Aramaic משתעבד.

In 2.16 בְּשֶׁכְּבָר הַיָּמִים הַבָּאִים, the assumption of an Aramaic original does not meet the problem. Dr. Zimmermann suggests דכבר יומיא אתין כלא מתנשי which he translates "because days *already have* past and everything *was* forgotten (italics his). In the first instance, a mechanical translator, or for that matter, a capable one, would have rendered דכבר by שֶׁכְּבָר. The difficulty of the Bet in בְּשֶׁכְּבָר, which is the essence of the problem, is thus left unsolved. Second, Dr. Zimmermann's English version inserts the word "and," which does not exist either in his Aramaic or in the Hebrew. Third, Qohelet is not referring to the past, but to a general law of experience. He would therefore use the participle-present, exactly as in our Hebrew, not the perfect.

The difficult Hebrew phrase בשכבר הימים הבאים may be explained in several ways. Either בְּשֶׁ is a late preposition meaning here "inasmuch as." It occurs also in Jonah 1.7 בְּשֶׁלְּמִי הָרָעָה הַזֹּאת לָנוּ in another shade of meaning. The words הימים הבאים would then be an accusative of time (= "in the coming days"). Or the phrase בשכבר הימים הבאים may be equivalent to שכבר בימים הבאים. This transfer of a preposition in a phrase has its analogies in such passages as Isa. 10.2 לְהַטּוֹת מִדִּין דַּלִּים =

אִם־אָמְנַע חֵפֶץ=אִם־אָמְנַע מַחְפֵּץ דַּלִּים Job 31.16 ;לִהְטוֹת דִּין מַדְּלִים מַדְּלִים. At all events, it is clear that Dr. Zimmermann's theory overlooks the central difficulty. The passage is to be rendered: "For the wise man is no more remembered than the fool, for already in the days that follow everything is forgotten. Yet how can the wise man die like the fool!"

In 3.14 כֹל אֲשֶׁר יַעֲשֶׂה הָאֱלֹהִים, the Hebrew imperfect can mean either "does" or "may do" without recourse to any Aramaic.

In several other passages the proposed exegesis is not convincing. In 9.3 there is no need to refer הַמֵּתִים to the Aramaic מִיתָא from אֲתָא: "His back is turned on the events to come." (p. 42) Qohelet's thought is perfectly clear: "This is the root of the evil in all that happens under the sun — that one fate comes to all. Therefore men's minds are filled with evil and there is madness in their hearts while they live, for they know that afterwards they are off to the dead!" In 8.8 אֵין מִשְׁלַחַת בַּמִּלְחָמָה, can hardly mean "one cannot lay aside one's armor."

IV

A principal element in Dr. Zimmermann's line of proof is the inexact status of nouns in Qohelet (pp. 20–23). He insists that the article is employed where classical Hebrew use does not require it and that it is lacking where it is needed. As is well-known, the determinate status in most Aramaic dialects ultimately lost its specific force and became identical in meaning with the absolute status. He therefore assumes that the translator of the Aramaic, encountering a noun with a final *Aleph* or *He*, frequently failed to note accurately whether it was determinate or indeterminate in meaning.

Here several observations are in order:

1. Many of the passages in Qohelet are general statements, expressing some fundamental truth. In that event,
Hebrew may use a noun in either the determinate or the
indeterminate state.[11] Cf. out of many similar passages,
Ex. 22.19 זֹבֵחַ לָאֱלֹהִים יָחֳרָם; Prov. 20–5, 8 and *passim* for the
indeterminate use; and for the determinate use Ex. 22.30.
(לְכָלֶב); I Sam. 16.7 הָאָדָם יִרְאֶה לַעֵינַיִם; Job 2.5 (לְאִישׁ); Prov.
20.3 (לְאִישׁ). Hence Qohelet's use of the article in 5.18 הָאָדָם
10.15 הכסילים; 10.19, הכסף, for general statements is not
irregular. Even the fluctuation in usage has its parallel in
a passage like Ex. 23.9: וְגֵר לֹא תִלְחָץ . . . וְאַתֶּם יְדַעְתֶּם אֶת
נֶפֶשׁ הַגֵּר, since both usages are legitimate. Hence too, the
Kethib-Qere variation in 10.20 הכנפים כ' — כְּנָפַיִם ק'. In the
case of Qohelet, as will be noted below, an additional
factor is significant.

2. The fluctuating use of the article becomes increasingly
common in Mishnic Hebrew. Cf. the very old Wedding
Benedictions, which are quoted in the Talmud (B. Ketubot
8a), the last of which reads ברוך אתה ה' משמח חתן עם הכלה,
while the one preceding ends with the phrase משמח חתן וכלה.
Cf. also האומנין קורין (Ber. 2.4) but מתפלל אדם (ibid. 4.3),
the expression יצר טוב, by the side of יצר הרע (exclusively),
and such a form as החבית מרותחת (Abodah Zarah 4.10) with
the variants החבית המרותחת (Munich ms.) and חבית מרותחת
(Kaufmann ms. and Cambridge ms. edited by W. H.
Lowe).

3. In a passage like 9.9 רְאֵה חַיִּים עִם אִשָּׁה אֲשֶׁר אָהַבְתָּ, the
absence of the article may represent a different nuance of

---

[11] On the use of the definite article in Biblical Hebrew, cf. Gesenius-
Kautzsch, *Hebräische Grammatik*, sec. 126. On the Mishnic use, cf.
M. H. Segal, *Dikduk Leshon Hamishnah* (Tel Aviv 1936) pp. 53–6,
especially sec. 82, 83, 85, 87.

meaning. Qohelet is not an apologist for marriage; he himself was almost surely a bachelor.[12] In 8.1 מִי כְּהֶחָכָם there are problems connected with the text. Thus, it has been suggested to read מִי כֹה חָכָם.

4. Most significantly, Dr. Zimmermann's thesis breaks down when we examine a passage like 10.20 in detail: כי עוף השמים יוליך את הקול ובעל הכנפים יגיד דבר. Here we are ·asked to believe that the translator rendered שמיא by השמים, קלא by הקול, נדפיא by הכנפים, but insisted on rendering מלתא by דבר! We cannot believe that a translator, whose skill in transmitting subtle and original ideas is reflected on every page, could be blind to so obvious an element of Aramaic and Hebrew style.

V

Are the results of Dr. Zimmermann's study and our critique purely negative? We do not think so. Actually, Dr. Zimmermann's has made a positive contribution by his study of the use of the article, for he has helped to supply the evidence to demonstrate that *Qohelet was written in Hebrew, by a writer who, like all his contemporaries, knew Aramaic and probably used it freely in daily life.* A translator is always conscious of the distinctions between the two languages on which he is engaged, for that is the essence of his task. But a creative writer, familiar with two closely related tongues, and struggling to express his original thought, might unconsciously employ a word or even a usage from the other language. In other words, the *fluctuations* in the use or absence of the article prove the existence, not of a translation, but of a Hebrew original, written by an author who was familiar with Aramaic and

[12] Cf. our study, p. 14.

hence might at times use the determinate or the indeterminate form indiscriminately. He would be encouraged in this tendency because he was so largely concerned with general truths, which may be expressed in either form.

So too, not a translator, but a Hebrew writer familiar with Aramaic, might use the Aramaic עֲבָדֵיהֶם in a single passage (9.1) while using מעשה freely elsewhere, or any of the many Aramaisms in Qohelet that have long been noted and to which Dr. Zimmermann has added a few additional examples.[13] All these phenomena are natural in the Hebrew of a post-exilic Jewish author, whose style begins to manifest the traits of Mishnic Hebrew.

In conclusion, a reconsideration of the evidence clearly demonstrates that the book of the Hebrew sage, Qohelet, was originally written in Hebrew.

---

[13] A few comments on these examples are in order. While the development of חֵפֶץ 5.7, "matter, thing," *may* have been induced by the Aramaic צְבוּ from the root צב׳, the identical semantic development occurs in the Arabic شَاﺀ "thing" from شِى "desire." The particles cited on p. 20 are not necessarily a translator's reproduction of the Aramaic. Similar forms, doubtless influenced by the Aramaic, occur in the Hebrew of Jonah (1.7). בשלמי, Song of Songs (1.7) שלמה. The Aramaism רע על (2.17) is parallelled by the idiom in Esther 1.19 אם על טוב הַמֶּלֶךְ , and is no proof of mistranslation.

THE TRANSLATION-THEORY OF QOHELET
RE-EXAMINED

FOR the past few years, a discussion has been carried on in the pages of this journal regarding an alleged Aramaic original for the Hebrew text of *Ecclessiastes*. In 1945, Dr. Frank Zimmermann suggested that the Hebrew was a translation of a lost Aramaic original and offered evidence to substantiate this view.[1] In 1946 the present writer subjected the suggested proofs to critical examination and concluded that the thesis had not been demonstrated.[2] Most recently the Nestor of American biblical scholarship, Prof. Charles C. Torrey has entered the discussion with a characteristically stimulating paper, in which he espouses the Aramaic origin of Qohelet.[3]

Quite properly, Dr. Torrey calls attention to the subjective factors that enter into any such discussion, pointing out that "such revelations are unwelcome" (p. 152) and that "every such undertaking (i. e. to prove an original in another language) has the presumption against it" (p. 152). This is undoubtedly true, but he overlooks a parallel fact, that subjective attitudes enter into the thinking of the protagonists of a translation-theory no less than in that of its opponents! Thus Prof. Torrey has been a persistent advocate of this theory with regard to the *Gospels*,[4] *Daniel*,[5] *Esther*[6] and now *Qohelet*. In favor of the assumption of an Aramaic origin for the Gospels, is the undoubted fact that the spoken tongue of Palestinian Jewry in the age of Jesus and his disciples was Aramaic. Yet even here the theory has commanded

[1] "The Aramaic Provenance of Qoheleth," *JQR*, 1945, vol 36, pp. 17–45.

[2] "The Original Language of Qohelet" *JQR*, 1946, vol. 57, pp. 67–84.

[3] "The Question of the Original Language of Qoheleth" *JQR*, vol 39. 1948, pp. 151–60. The page numbers in parenthesis given in our text after quotations are to the three papers cited in thèse notes 1,2 and 3.

[4] Cf. *The Composition and Date of Acts* (Cambridge, Mass., 1916): *The Four Gospels*, New York, 1933); *Our Translated Gospels*, (New York, 1936); *Documents of the Primitive Church* (New York, 1941.)

[5] Torrey suggested the Aramaic origin of Daniel 1.1–2.4 as long ago as 1909; cf. the references in his paper cited above, p. 152, n. l. The Aramaic origin of Daniel chap. 8–12 (except 9.4–20) has been maintained by Zimmermann, *JBL*, 1938, vol. 57; pp. 255–72; idem 1939, pp.349 –54 and most recently by H. L. Ginsberg, *Studies in Daniel* (New York, 1948) pp. 41–61.

[6] Cf. "The Older Book of Esther" in *H Th R*, 1944, vol. 37, especially pp. 33–38.

103

far less than universal assent among scholars.[7] In favor of a translation-hypothesis for the Hebrew of Daniel, there is the actual existence of an Aramaic original text in chap. 2–7, aside from the outlandish Hebrew of chap. 8–12. As for Dr. Torrey's theory that the masoretic book of Esther is also a translation of the Aramaic, the argument is, as always, brilliantly presented, but it must be confessed, it has not convinced all students.[8]

[7] Cf H. J. Cadbury in *The Haverford Symposium on Archaeology and the Bible* (New Haven, 1938) pp. 92 f.: "The published examples of Torrey do not often agree with those of earlier scholars who sought evidence for the same thesis. They have convinced more Semitists than Hellenists. Many would concede occasional influence of Semitic idiom upon the Greek of these volumes without assuming the continuous effect of any translated source." See also Merril M. Parvis in *The Study of the Bible Today and Tomorrow* (Chicago, 1947) pp. 66, who summarizes "four facts" that "have thus far weighed heavily against" the theory of a Semitic original of the Gospels. On the limited extent to which Palestinian Jewry spoke Greek, cf. the judicious remarks of G. F. Moore, *Judaism* (Cambridge, 1930) Vol III (Notes), pp. 53 f., but also the material collected in S. Lieberman's, *Greek in Jewish Palestine* (New York, 1942), esp. pp. 1–67.

[8] It may be of interest to indicate some of the reasons for this hesitation. Torrey's paper presents several theses, a) that the Greek versions of Esther are based on Aramaic versions of the story, b) that the longer Aramaic form now extant in two Greek versions, is the original, and our present Hebrew book of Esther a contraction, and c) that this present Hebrew has been translated from the Aramaic. The evidence for a) seems entirely convincing, 5.11 f. in the Greek being particularly telling, especially since Aramaic versions of the Book of Esther were exceedingly popular, cf. P. Churgin, *Targum Kethubim* (New York, 1945) pp. 189–234. b) does not seem likely, the plus in the Greek bearing all the earmarks of midrashic embellishments, such as are encountered in the *Targum Sheni* and the *Midrash on Esther*; cf. L. Ginzberg, *Legends of the Jews*, vol. IV, pp. 363–448 and vol. VI, pp. 451–483 for the aggadic sources.

With regard to c, Torrey's ingenious "restoration" of the Aramaic original of Esther 1.22 וּמְדַבֵּר כָּל לָשֵׁן בִּלְשׁוֹן עַמּוֹ as וּמְדַבֵּר בְּלִשָׁן עַמֵּהּ, "ruler over every tongue of his family" is not quite parallel to the Syriac version of I Tim. 3.4 וּמְדַבֵּר בֵּיתֵהּ שַׁפִּיר, "one that ruleth well his own house."

As for Esth. 7.4 כִּי אֵין הַצָּר שֹׁוֶה בְּנֵזֶק הַמֶּלֶךְ, the meanings which Torrey attributes to the Aramaic "original" מְעִיקָא, "oppressor" and "distress," both inhere in the Hebrew צָר, as Torrey himself recognizes! Why אִישׁ צָר in v. 6 rules out the meaning of "distress' for צָר in v. 4 is difficult to see. In 7.4, אִלּוּ is cited as the Aramaic particle "occurring in only one other place in the Hebrew Bible, Eccl. 6.6." But aside from לוּ in the meaning of "if," without optative force in. Gen. 50,13,

With regard to Qohelet, Prof. Torrey declares, "I find myself generally in agreement with Gordis in the details of his criticism of Zimmermann" but, he then proceeds to add, "it is to be objected that he deals with the weakest points, and hardly touches the matters which are of major importance" (p. 152).

This last statement is unfortunately not altogether accurate, as a summary of the facts will make clear. Zimmermann's paper begins with a brief reference to the Aramaisms of Qohelet which have long been a commonplace of exegesis (pp. 19 f.), after which he devotes two pages to "the inexact status of nouns" in Qohelet (pp. 19–23). The bulk of the paper (pp. 23–38) is devoted to alleged "mistranslations," the confusion of הוּא and הָיָא and *quid pro quo* renderings. A few other arguments, regarding confusion of tenses, grammatical difficulties, and a theory of the name Qohelet as a cryptogram, round out the paper (pp. 38–45).

Obviously the burden of the argument, quantitatively and qualitatively, lies in the "mistranslations," as Zimmermann explicitly recognizes.[9] Zimmermann's proofs consist of seven passages (1.5; 7.5; 6.2; 7.20; 10.17; 5.17; 12.13), which he regards as his strongest. He then submits a number of "other examples, which" he observes, "only admit, however, of a good *probability* for the translation hypothesis. In the nine instances following 5.6; 7.29; 5.12; 5.16; 7.12; 9.1–2; 11.1; 12.1; 5.5, it should be stated that the Hebrew is capable of 'explanation' — but with a good deal of difficulty, as I believe." Of these seventeen passages adduced by Zimmermann, we discussed *all seventeen* (pp. 71–81). In addition, we dealt with three out of the four alleged instances of "confusion of הוּא and הָיָא.[10] Finally, our paper also discussed six of the supplementary fifteen passages adduced by Zimmermann, which we regarded as the most significant.[11]

As for the effectiveness of our analysis, the following data are perti-

Deut. 32:29; Judg. 8.19; 13.23, I Sam. 14.30; II Sam. 19.7, אִלּוּ is extremely frequent in mishnic Hebrew (cf. *inter alia* M. Keth. 15.5; אִלּוּ הָיִיתָ יוֹדֵעַ Nazir 5.4; אִלּוּ הָיִיתִי חַיָּב 13.8 ;אִלּוּ אֲנִי פְסַקְתִּי. Hence אִלּוּ cannot be invoked as *proof* of translation. Nor do the other instances adduced suffice, it seems to us, to demonstrate beyond question the thesis that our present Hebrew book of Esther is a translation from the Aramaic.

[9] "The clearest proof of an underlying translation is to be found in mistranslation." (p. 23).

[10] Out of 3.15; 4.16; 7.10; 6.10, only 4.16 was not discussed by us. Dr. Torrey does not refer to it either.

[11] These passages are 4.15_ 5.8; 2.16; 4.1 = 11.4; 9.3; 8.8.

nent. Of the seventeen basic passages proposed by Zimmermann, all of which we had discussed, Dr. Torrey passes fourteen over in silence, taking up for renewed discussion only three (12.13; 7.5; 5,17), besides the instances of alleged confussion of הוּא and הֵנָּ. Nor does he revert to any of the six passages we had selected for discussion out of Zimmermann's supplementary fifteen, and of the remaining nine, which we had passed over as minor, Dr. Torrey re-introduces only one (3.21).

In view of all this, one can hardly agree with Dr. Torrey that we "have dealt only with the weakest points and hardly touched the matters which are of major importance." Nonetheless, a scientific question may be reopened at any time and there is surely value in re-examining the testimony now advanced by Prof. Torrey.

II

At the very outset, he rests his case on what he calls "the fact of basal importance, outweighing any and all separate items of proof . . . the distinct impression of Aramaic made by the language of the book, in every part. There can be no question as to this, and the general impression which is made has no true parallel in Hebrew literature" (p. 153). With all the deference due Professor Torrey's extraordinary learning, this judgment still remains the height of subjectivity. An impression is not proof. Probably the reason for Dr. Torrey's impression is that he has read Qohelet with classic biblical Hebrew in mind. If he had set Qohelet against the background of mishnic Hebrew, he would have recognized its authentic Hebrew character, of it is the Hebrew of the mishnic period which is the truest source of the style of Qohelet, as has been recognized by all scholars since Delitzsch.

It is not necessary at this date to recall that mishnic Hebrew represents an authentic stage in the development of the Hebrew language, while including many resemblances to Aramaic in vocabulary and syntax, owing to the fact that Aramaic was spoken among Jews, while Hebrew remained the literary tongue and "the speech of scholars."[12]

The language of Qohelet, the latest of the biblical writers in point of style and grammar,[13] marks the transition between biblical and mishnic Hebrew. We should be the last to deny that Qohelet has an individual style, reflecting a unique personality, but that it is un-

[12] Cf. M. H. Segal, *Dikduk Leshon Hamishnah* (Tel Aviv, 5696) pp. 1–17, esp. pp. 4, 5, 16.
[13] *Op. cit.* p. 1.

Hebrew on that account, we are unable to grant. At all events, here
are two diametrically opposite "impressions" — they are hardly objective proofs.

Dr. Torrey then takes up a few examples of "Aramaic idiom in
Hebrew dress." In 8.17 בְּשֶׁל אֲשֶׁר יַעֲמֹל הָאָדָם is regarded as a clumsy,
artificial reproduction of the Aramaic בדיל די and rendered: "Because
the man labors." But the construction has its analogy in two perfectly
clear contexts, in Jonah 1.8 בַּאֲשֶׁר לְמִי הָרָעָה הַזֹּאת לָנוּ "For the sake
of whom has this evil come upon us" and even more closely in 1.12
כִּי בְּשֶׁלִּי הַסַּעַר הַגָּדוֹל הַזֶּה עֲלֵיכֶם "For my sake, on my account, this great
storm has come upon you." Hence the idiom in Qohelet means "for
the sake of which, on account of which," and the verse is to be rendered
literally: "I saw that a man cannot discover all the work that is done
under the sun, *for the sake of which* a man may labor to seek it out,
yet he shall not find it." If the phrase be rendered "because," a clumsy
locution emerges, as in the Jewish Version: "Because *though* a man
labor, etc.," for there is no basis for "though" in the text. But even this
sense "because" is derived from the literal meaning, "on account of
the fact that=seeing that a man labors." Yet whatever the exegesis
of the passage, the Aramaic background of the phrase is entirely
natural for a writer familiar with Aramaic as well as Hebrew. It is
far from sufficient to prove a translation.

In 5.15 כָּל עֻמַּת שֶׁבָּא כֵּן יֵלֵךְ is dismissed as "not Hebrew" (p. 154),
but regarded as a literal translation of the Aramaic phrase כל קבל די.
It may be pointed out that, even if this be true, the Hebrew phrase,
far from being a mechanical retroversion of the Aramaic, would reflect
a profound knowledge of Hebrew. Actually, the entire assumption is
uncalled for. In view of the common use of לְעֻמַּת throughout the
Bible, particularly, though not exclusively, in the later books and in
Qoheleth itself (as e. g. Ex. 25.27; 28.27. Lev. 3.9; II Sam. 16.13;
Ezek. 1.20; 38.18; 40.18; 42.7; 45.6 f.; 48.13 Nehem. 12.24; I Chron.
24.31; 26.16; Eccl. 7.14) and the additional prepositional form מִלְּעֻמַּת
(I Kings 7.20), there is no reason for doubting that כל־עמת is excellent
Hebrew. It is probably to be vocalized כְּלְעֻמַּת, as was suggested long
ago.[14] Our present vocalization may have been induced by the familiar
Aramaic idiom, incidentally not the only example of Aramaic influence

---

[14] So Lambert in *REJ*, vol. 31, p. 47; Rahlfs, in *Theologische Literaturzeitung* 1896, p. 587. Here, as so often, modern scholarship has been
anticipated by medieval Jewish authorities. Thus Ibn Janah makes
the same point: עיקרו לעמת והכ״ף נוספת אלא שנכתב בשתי מלים.

in the vocalization. At most, however, we have an Aramaism due to familiarity with the language, not a translation.

Even less convincing is Dr. Torrey's insistence "that חֵפֶץ, used four times in Qohelet for 'matter, affair' (3.1, 17.5, 7 and 8.6) represents an equally clear suggestion of translation, to be explained by the Aramaic צְבוּ 'thing' properly 'wish, desire,' . . . and genuine Hebrew knows no such use of חֵפֶץ" (p. 154). The evidence here should make us much more cautious, for the semantic development from חֵפֶץ "wish, desire" to חֵפֶץ, "thing" has a perfect parallel in the Arabic verb شا "wish, desire," from which the noun شي "thing" is derived. We may also adduce the French *chose* "thing" from *choisir* "choose" as a similar development.

Actually the semantics of the Hebrew root has three stages: 1) חֵפֶץ "wish, desire," 2) חֵפֶץ "object of will, hence affair, matter" and 3) finally חֵפֶץ "object of desire, hence, thing." *Actually in Qohelet the word does not yet mean "thing," but still retains its volitional nuance,* and means "phenomenon, pursuit, activity, affair," very similar in meaning to the later Hebrew עֵסֶק, as is clear from the context in each of the passages where חֵפֶץ occurs:

Eccl. 3.1 f. Everything has its appointed time, and there is a season for every event (חֵפֶץ) under the sky.
There is a time to be born and a time to die,
A time to plant and a time to uproot,
A time to kill and a time to heal,
A time to wreck and a time to build.

Eccl. 3.17. I said to myself, "Both the righteous and the wicked God will judge, for there is a proper time for everything (חֵפֶץ) and every deed — over there!"

Eccl. 5.7 If you observe the despoiling of the poor and the perversion of justice and right in the State, do not be astonished at the fact (חֵפֶץ), for each guardian of the law is higher than the next, and there are still higher ones above them!

Eccl. 8.5,6 He who keeps his command will experience no trouble, for a wise mind will know the proper time. For everything (חֵפֶץ) has its proper time, man's evil being so widespread.

Moreover, this meaning of חֵפֶץ "activity, affair" does occur elsewhere in biblical Hebrew, cf. Isa. 58.3 הֵן בְּיוֹם צֹמְכֶם תִּמְצְאוּ חֵפֶץ *ibid* 58.13 אִם תָּשִׁיב מִשַּׁבָּת רַגְלֶךָ עֲשׂוֹת חֲפָצֶךָ בְּיוֹם קָדְשִׁי וְכִבַּדְתּוֹ מֵעֲשׂוֹת

דְּרָכֶיךָ מִמְצוֹא חֶפְצְךָ וְדַבֵּר דָּבָר. The clause עֲשׂוֹת חֵפֶץ and מָצָא חֵפֶץ
are correctly rendered "pursue thy business" or "do thy affairs."[15]
Finally, the third meaning of חפץ as "object, thing" is extremely
common in mishnic Hebrew. From the numerous examples, these
may be cited here: Ned. 3.1 היה מוכר חפץ B. M. 4.10 לא יאמר לו
בכמה חפץ זה. As we should expect, Qohelet's use stands midway
between the classic biblical and the mishnic meanings.

Prof. Torrey declares that "one or two common Aramaic words
appear in *Qohelet* in a way that suggests mere carelessness, for they
are out of place in the Hebrew text" (p. 154), and he cites וַעֲבָדֵיהֶם
in 9.1 and יְהוּא in 11.3 as instances. But וַעֲבָדֵיהֶם is not an Aramaic
word;; the Aramaic would have been וַעֲבָדֵיהוֹן. Once again it is the
vocalization (the *Kames* under the *Bet*) which makes it an *Aramaism,
in Hebrew*. If it were, as Torrey says, a "momentary lapse," the Aramaic
form would have been retained.

The verb יְהוּא in 11.3 is confessedly an anomaly, but it does not
follow that this is the Aramaic יְהֵוֹא "which the translator let slip by."
Dr. Torrey asks "Is there any other plausible way of explaining the
case?" (p. 155). A suggestion may be offered. During the early history
of the transmission of the biblical text, various means were employed
to preserve variant readings. This was one of the functions of the
Kethib-Qere formula.[16] Before this device was utilized for this purpose,
another method was employed, the combination of two variants into a
conflate text. As one instance of use of may, we cite Jos. 2.7 — וַיְהִי
אַחֲרֵי כַּאֲשֶׁר יָצְאוּ הָרֹדְפִים אַחֲרֵיהֶם which is a conflate of two readings:
a) וַיְהִי כַּאֲשֶׁר יָצְאוּ הָרֹדְפִים and b) וַיְהִי אַחֲרֵי אֲשֶׁר יָצְאוּ הָרֹדְפִים
The Ketib of Eccl. 6.10 וְלֹא יוּכַל לָדִין עִם שֶׁהַתְקִיף מִמֶּנּוּ offers another
instance of a conflate of two readings: a) וְלֹא יוּכַל לָדִין עִם שֶׁתַּקִּיף
מִמֶּנּוּ and b) וְלֹא יוּכַל לָדִין עִם הַתַּקִּיף מִמֶּנּוּ. Many more instnces occur
in the biblical text.[17]

---

[15] So Delitzsch, Jewish Version, BDB, *Lexicon*, s. v. This meaning,
too, inheres in Isa. 53.10 חֵפֶץ ה' בְּיָדוֹ יִצְלָח "the cause (or business)
of the Lord will prosper in his hand" (BDB) and in Prov. 31.13 וַתַּעַשׂ
בְּחֵפֶץ כַּפֶּיהָ to be rendered not "she worketh willingly with her hands"
but "she worketh in the business of her hands" (Hitzig, BDB *ad loc.*),
or "her hands are at work in business."
[16] Cf. the writer's study *The Biblical Text in the Making* (Phila. 1937)
especially pp. 40–54.
[17] Cf. the work cited above in n. 16, especially pp. 40–43, where
attention was first called to the use of conflation as a device for preserving variants. Several years later, some additional instances were
suggested by Zimmermann in *JQR*, vol. 34 pp. 459 ff. We plan to

In view of the abundant evidence for this practice, it may be suggested that in 11.3, שָׁם יְהוּא of the Masoretic text represents a conflate of a) שָׁם הוּא and b) שָׁם יְהְיֶה.[18]

Conflation may explain the usage in 3.21 לְמַטָּה לָאָרֶץ, if, with Torrey (p. 159) and Zimmermann, we were to agree that the Aramaic text read לְאַרְע, "which the translator did not know how to take" (!) and "hence he put down the doublet למטה לארץ." But if this be a doublet, it can as well be a conflate *in the original Hebrew*, with one text reading לְמַטָּה and the other לָאָרֶץ. As a matter of fact, we do not find the double phrase "spoiling the verse"; the longer phrase serves to give the close of the verse greater emphasis.[19]

With regard to the aberrant use and absence of the article in *Ecclesiastes*, we have pointed out that the usage is not as irregular as assumed by Zimmermann and that it follows largely the rules of classical Hebrew syntax, especially as modified by the freer usage of Mishnic Hebrew (pp. 81–3). Dr. Torrey would seem to agree when he says: "Probably only a part of the examples listed by him (i. e by Zimmermann) could be classed as mistakes" (p. 155). Nonetheless, he discusses a few alleged instances of Aramaic influence on the use or absence of the article.

The passage in 3.17 עֵת לְכָל־חֵפֶץ וְעַל כָּל־הַמַּעֲשֶׂה שָׁם is difficult, not, however, because of the article in הַמַּעֲשֶׂה but rather because of the change from the preposition *Lamed* to עַל, which remains harsh. It will be conceded, we believe, that the reading: עֵת לְכָל חֵפֶץ וְעַל כָּל נַעֲשָׂה שָׁם which is the "correct translation of Dr. Torrey's suggested וְעַל כָּל עֲבְדָא תַמָּן is not elegant classical Hebrew either. As far as the article in הַמַּעֲשֶׂה is concerned, it may have been induced by כָּל, which tends to take a determined noun.

In 9.9, רְאֵה חַיִּים עִם־אִשָּׁה אֲשֶׁר־אָהַבְתָּ is an unusual construction, to be sure. But the undetermined noun אִשָּׁה may not mean "wife" but "woman," as many commentators have believed.[20] Qohelet is not

---

add new material on the early history of the preservation of the biblical text in the near future.

[18] Another explanation may perhaps be suggested. The conflate may be הוּא with * יהוא from the verb הוה הוא "fall," which occurs in Job 37.6 in the meaning "fall" כִּי לַשֶּׁלַג יֹאמַר הֱוֵא אָרֶץ "To the snow he says, 'Fall to the ground'." On this root, so important for the Divine name JHVH, cf. *inter alia*, BDB, p. 217b; Koenig, *Woerterbuch*, p. 76 and most recently, W. F. Albright in *JBL*, vol. 67, 1948, p. 379.

[19] On the varied use of longer stichs at the end of biblical poems, cf. "Al Mibneh Hashirah Ha'ivrit Hakkedummah" in *Sefer Hashanah Liyehudei America*, 5705 (1945) New York, 1945), especially pp. 144 ff.

opposing marriage, nor advocating it; he is merely urging the joys of feminine companionship, of which he was deeply conscious, as the bitter denunciation in 7.26 ff. demonstrates.

III

These examples discussed above "might well," Dr. Torrey says "suffice to settle the question" (p. 156). Nevertheless he adds a few additional instances of "mistranslation." In 12.13 כִּי־זֶה כָּל־הָאָדָם is equated by Zimmermann with כְּדִי דַּין כָּל אֱנָשָׁא, which was misread as כְּדִי דִין כָּל אֱנָשָׁא. Torrey tacitly admits our contention that this is impossible Aramaic, because the copula הוא (or איתוהי) would have been required at the end of the clause. Torrey continues, however, to posit Zimmermann's reading, with the copula added. He must then add to the original assumption of a misinterpretation of דִּין the additional one that the copula was dropped by the translator.

Actually, as was pointed out (p. 75) the difficulty of the Hebrew text is not a real one. The pregnant construction of the predicate nominative in the text is a characteristic Hebrew usage. כִּי זֶה כָּל הָאָדָם. means "this is the whole duty of man," exactly as Gen. 37.20 וְנִרְאֶה מַה יִּהְיוּ חֲלֹמֹתָיו "We shall see what will be the end of his dreams," or Isa. 28.12 זֹאת הַמְּנוּחָה הָנִיחוּ לֶעָיֵף means "This is the *essence* of rest — give rest to the weary." Cf. also Ps. 120.6 אֲנִי שָׁלוֹם "lit., I am peace, i. e. I am *for* peace"[20]; Ps. 109.4 וַאֲנִי תְפִלָּה "I am *in the mood of* prayer, lit. I am prayer"; Job 8.9, כִּי תְמוֹל אֲנַחְנוּ "our life is *as brief as* yesterday, lit. we are yesterday;" Ps. 36.7 מִשְׁפָּטֶיךָ תְּהוֹם רַבָּה "Thy judgments are *as deep as* the great abyss," Job 5.25 שָׁלוֹם אָהֳלֶךָ 'thy tent is *at* peace," etc. Job 29.15 עֵינַיִם הָיִיתִי לַעִוֵּר "Eyes was I to the blind," (contrast the prose usage in Num. 10.31 וְהָיִיתָ לָּנוּ לְעֵינָיִם "Thou shalt be for us as eyes.") Cf. also Gen. 11.1; Ex. 17.12; Isa. 5.12; Ps. 45.9; Ezra 10.13.[21]

[20] So Ginsburg, Barton, Ehrlich and others. This is based not only on grammatical grounds, but on the entire standpoint of Qohelet, who was almost surely unmarried, and whose attitude in 7.26–28 is thus not a contradiction to 9.7. Some adduce also the analogy of the "Babylonian Qoheleth" (marḥi-tum — "*a* wife").

[21] Cf. Gesenius-Kautzsch, *Hebräische Grammatik* (28 ed.), sec. 141, l., e., note 1: Dass jedoch die Sprache — namentlich der Dichter — auch die kühnsten Verbindungen nicht scheut, um die unbedingte Zusammengehörigkeit des Subjekts und des Prädikatsbegriffes recht nachdrücklich zu betonen.

In 7.5 שִׁיר in the meaning of "praise" does not presuppose an Aramaic original תשבחתא, as was already indicated (p. 72). In restating this point, we may add to the usage of the *Yištabaḥ prayer already cited* (שיר ושבחה הלל וזמרה,) the Biblical usage of שִׁיר parallel to תְּהִלָּה in Isa. 42.10; Ps. 149.1.

Zimmermann's explanation of 5.17 הִנֵּה אֲשֶׁר רָאִיתִי אָנִי טוֹב אֲשֶׁר יָפֶה by הָא דְחָזֵא אֲנָא דְטָב (p. 26) failed to solve the difficulty altogether, indeed created a new one, as we pointed out (p. 34). Undeniably, Dr. Torrey improves it by suggesting that טָב was an adverb, reading הָא דְחָזֵא אֲנָא טָב "That which I have well understood that" (p. 158).[22] Actually, however the Hebrew stands in no need of explanation. טוֹב אֲשֶׁר יָפֶה which some scholars[23] have explained as a Graecism (κάλον καγαθόν), has its authentic Hebrew analogue in עָוֹן אֲשֶׁר חֵטְא (Hos. 12.9).[24]

Dr. Torrey repeats Zimmermann's argument that הוּא and הָוָא are confused in 3.15 (p. 33) and 7.10 (p. 35). Even if the contention were granted that the two vocables have been transposed, they are sufficiently close in Hebrew to explain the error. But this assumption may legitimately be questioned, since exegesis is an art and not a science. We feel that both passages are in no need of emendation. The verse 3.15 emphasizes the identity of past and present in stich a, and of future and past in stich b, thus utilizing biblical parallelism to emphasize the repetitiousness of events. The verse may be rendered "What has been, already exists, and what is still to be, has already been, and God always seeks to repeat what has gone by." In 7.10 מֶה הָיָה "What has happened?" is perfectly satisfactory, in fact superior to Zimmermann's reading מה הוא "How is it?"

IV

One aspect of Zimmermann's argument was not discussed in our paper, his ingenious idea that קֹהֶלֶת is a Hebrew rendering of an Aramaic כָּנְשָׁה which has the same numerical value of 375 by *gematria*, as שְׁלֹמֹה. We felt that it was a *curiosum*, to be set by the side of Jastrow's suggestion that the roots קהל "gather" and שלם "complete" are nearly

---

[22] Actually, Zimmermann's Aramaic should have been הָא דחזית אנא rather than the participle דְחָזֵא, which would have yielded רואה אני in the Hebrew.

[23] So Graetz, Plumptre, Wildeboer and Siegfried.

[24] So Delitzsch, Wright, McNeil, König, Barton.

synonymous and that *Tav* and *He* are the two feminine endings, so that קהלת and שלמה are virtually equivalent![25]

For those who cannot share Dr. Torrey's opinion that this cryptogram is "convincing," it may be recalled that masculine proper names in the form of feminine participles occur elsewhere in post-exilic biblical Hebrew, e. g. סֹפֶרֶת (Ezra 2.55; Neh. 7.57); פֹּכֶרֶת הַצְּבָיִם (Ezra 2.57; Neh. 7.59), especially when they retain the sense of functionary or official. This is the case with קֹהֶלֶת which means "speaker." Note that the participle comes with the article in 12.8 and in 7.27 (where the text should read אָמַר הַקֹּהֶלֶת), and is feminine in form, like the Arabic *bā'kira* "inspector" *ḫa'lifa* "successor."

If the author really wished to imply that Solomon was the real author, the cryptogram was hardly the most direct way to do so. Actually, Qohelet is not attempting to deceive the reader. In ch. 1, and 2, he takes on the role of the great king, who was famous for wisdom and wealth, in order to carry out his experiment with these two outstanding goals of human striving. Thereafter this literary disguise is laid aside, not to be resumed again.[26] Qohelet is not a pseudepigraph, but a *nom de plume*.

Two more general considerations may also be discussed. We should have liked to have Prof. Torrey's reaction to our contention that "other things being equal, it may therefore be maintained that a difficult text may be presumed to be the original rather than a translation" (p. 20), because though the translator may misinterpret his original, and do violence to its vocabulary and syntax, he ultimately does decide upon some view of the passage, which he expresses in his idiom clearly and grammatically, if incorrectly. All the difficulties in the Hebrew of Hosea and Job, for example, disappear in the English versions. *The difficulties of style in Qohelet are therefore an argument for its original Hebrew character, rather than the reverse.*

Nor is this all. The assumed translator of *Ecclesiastes*, was not a tyro, if we note the rhythmic power of chap. 3, and the moving poetry

---

[25] M. Jastrow *A Gentle Cynic* (Phila. 1919) pp. 68 f.

[26] Cf. the insight of the Midrash into the motive for taking up this role: אלו אחר אמר הבל הבלים הייתי אומר זה שלא קנה ב' פרוטות מימיו הוא פירת בממונו של עולם אבל שלמה שכתוב בו אין כסף לא נחשב בימי שלמה למאומה (מלכים א',ו', כא) לזה נאה לומר הבל הבלים (Qoheleth Rabbah 3.11). "If some one else were to say 'vanity of vanities,' I would reply! This beggar who never owned two-pence presumes to despise all the wealth of the world, but Solomon, of whom it is said 'Silver was of no account in the days of Solomon' (I Kings 10.21) can say with propriety 'Vanity of vanities!'" Cf. other midrashic examples *ad loc.*

of chap. 12, not to speak of countless other passages of great eloquence.
Is it not rather strange to find not a single instance of mistranslation
in the difficult "Allegory of Old Age" (12.1–8), and yet to saddle the
translator with such ignorance as not to know that הוא may mean
both "he" and "was" in Aramaic?

Dr. Torrey advances one general argument in favor of the Aramaic
origin of Qohelet: "The unorthodox religious philosophy of Qohelet
is much more likely to have been composed in Aramaic, for popular
consumption, than in Hebrew. On the other hand, when there arose
a wish to preserve the book as a specimen of Solomonic wisdom, its
translation into Hebrew would be the only natural proceeding" (p. 156).
But an at least equally logical case can be made out for the opposite assumption. If the author were anxious to attribute his book to Solomon,
he would surely have written it in Hebrew rather than in Aramaic,
which would at once stamp it as unauthentic, since the Book of Kings
makes it clear that Solomon spoke Hebrew.

We have treated all the points raised by Dr. Torrey in his paper.[27]

[27] The writer was informed that Dr. Zimmermann had, in reply to
my first paper, written a lengthy rejoinder, scheduled to appear in
JQR. It was, however, only after the present paper was completed,
that the text of his article was made available to me. Since I share
the feeling of Dr. Torrey that the discussion of this hypothesis is likely
to be carried on "with no great eagerness on either side" (p. 160)
I do not feel it necessary to add an extended reply to this rejoinder,
especially with regard to the many reflections on my competence,
which are advanced with more vigor than subtlety, and with a happy
unawareness that so distinguished a Semitist as Dr. Torrey found my
analysis of Zimmermann's arguments so far from inept as to concede
his general agreement with it (see below).

Nor would it be difficult to call attention to the misinterpretations,
irrelevancies, errors and lapses in logic, in which Dr. Zimmermann's
second paper abounds, as well as his curious habit of ignoring the core
of an argument and fastening upon some peripheral detail. Thus again
and again, he fails to note that his suggested Aramaic "solves" (whether
well or poorly is subject to discussion) *some minor or non-existent
difficulty in a given passage, but leaves the real difficulty untouched.*

Thus to cite a few examples from Dr. Zimmermann's second paper,
in 2.16 the Aramaic דְּכָר which is again offered as the original, still
does not explain the double preposition in the Hebrew בְּשֶׁכְּבָר. In 5.6
the problem הַרְבֵּה is imaginary; the real difficulty lies in כִּי, which his
"retroversion" does not affect. In 9.3 אַחֲרָיו is a preposition with
petrified suffix and means "afterwards," cf. יַחְדָּו and אַחֲרָיו in Neh.
3.16, 17, 18, 20, 21, 22, 23 and *passim*. In 5.16, the proposed Aramaic

It may be well to restate our conclusion. Most of the phenomena in Qohelet may be explained equally well, or better, without the as-

"retroversion" כל יומוהי בקבלא אכל ורגז שניא ובישה וקצפא is still ungrammatical. The passages in Dan. 2.12; 3.2, 13, 21, which Zimmermann adduces, are not apposite, since the verb אכל, *which separates* בקבלא *and* רגז sets this proposed text apart from the *'unbroken'* *series of nouns* in the verses in Daniel, all governed by the preposition used with the first, as e. g. 3.2 לאחשדרפניא סגניא ופחותא, etc.

In 12.13, his printed paper offered the Aramaic דִיַן for זֶה. In discussing this passage, I revocalized it as דִיָן כָּל אֱנָשָׁא. But Dr. Zimmermann is merciless in his criticism! In the text of his second paper before us, he therefore says: "Incidentally, my דִיַן was misvocalized as דִיָן in his (i. e. Gordis') copying." It must have come as a shock to find Prof. Torrey equally "guilty" of "misvocalizing" the noun as דִיָן with a *kameṣ* under the *Yod* (p. 158). In view of Dr. Zimmermann's frequently proffered "information" on Aramaic in the paper, one has a right to expect him to reckon with at least the elements of Aramaic phonetics; the *kameṣ* is, of course, a permanent vowel, retained even in the construct and with suffixes. Any of the Aramaic grammars he cites could easily have oriented him. I add a reference to Wm. B. Stevenson, *Grammar of Palestinian-Jewish Aramaic* (Oxford, 1924) pp. 28, 30.

As against Dr. Zimmermann's untenable and unnecessary contention that שׁוֹאֵף in 1.5 is an error for תָּאֵב meaning "returns," which the translator took to mean "desires, longs for", I had pointed out that in the succeeding verses, 6 and 7, the alleged Aramaic verb תוב is correctly "rendered" by שׁוב, where the "error" would have been far more natural. To bolster his point, however, Dr. Zimmermann delivers himself of a highly astonishing statement. In the text of his second paper before us, we read, "There is other *evidence* (italics ours) that the translator did not read through the book *first* (*italics his*) before beginning his translation"(!). How conceivable is it that any translator would begin his arduous task without first reading through his text? But there is a still more searching question: — *If he did not read the book through first how could he decide that it was worthwhile translating?*

In both papers I have discussed all the most striking arguments advanced in favor of a translation-hypothesis. If some points have not been covered, it has not been, as Dr. Zimmermann alleges, because they are unanswerable, but rather because they are the least weighty and I was mindful of the limitations of space and the reader's patience. Nor can I enter here into a thorough philological and exegetical discussion of many passages, to which the writer has devoted considerable attention in his recently completed *Commentary on Ecclesiastes*.

All in all, the best refutation of Dr. Zimmermann is supplied by Dr. Torrey's paper! For Dr. Torrey's discussion, which undertakes to

sumption of an Aramaic original. Some of them remain equally difficult whether or not that theory be adopted. It therefore follows that the hypothesis is unnecessary and, in terms of scientific method, is unproved. In William of Occam's classic formulation, *essentia non sunt multiplicanda praeter necessitatem.*

To the extent that the evidence is at all significant, it underscores the fact that Qoheleth was written in Hebrew by a writer, who, like all his contemporaries, knew Aramaic and probably used it freely in daily life. The natural consequence is that his style exhibits a relatively large number of Aramaisms and other characteristics that foreshadow mishnic Hebrew. As for the theory that the Hebrew Qohelet is a translation of a non-existent Aramaic original, it may be said, *quod demonstrandum erat etiam-nunc demonstrandum est.*

support only a small fraction of Dr. Zimmermann's "proofs," as I have indicated in the opening section of the present paper, coupled with his statement that he finds himself "generally in agreement with Gordis in the details of his criticism" (p. 152) constitutes a significant admission of the weakness of the arguments which Dr. Zimmermann presents so heatedly.

Dr. Zimmermann's paper may be summarized as a repetition of the same contentions previously advanced, but with considerably greater intensity.

It is noteworthy that Dr. Torrey's expressed hope that new proofs for the translation-hypothesis would be forthcoming (p. 160), is not fulfilled in Dr. Zimmermann's second paper, which advances no new evidence, in spite of its greater length than its first paper.

Until new and considerably more decisive proof is adduced in favor of the suggestion, few fruitful results will emerge from continuing this discussion. The interested reader would be well advised, after reading Dr. Zimmermann's second rejoinder, to consult the relevant material on each point in the earlier articles by all the writers, in order to decide the merits of the case.

KOHELETH — HEBREW OR ARAMAIC?

B EFORE beginning the discussion of our theme, a personal word will perhaps be pardoned. The theory of the Aramaic origin of Koheleth was first seriously proposed by Dr. Frank Zimmermann, who is one of my oldest friends, has been supported by Professor C. C. Torrey, and most recently, has been vigorously defended by Professor H. L. Ginsberg, my distinguished colleague.[1] If, nonetheless, I set forth my objections with regard to their conclusions, it is in a spirit which I know they will understand — *amicus Plato sed magis amica veritas*. Only a careful analysis of the data can help advance the cause of learning.

It need scarcely be pointed out, inasmuch as the Hebrew text of Koheleth is extant and the Aramaic is not, that the idea that Koheleth wrote in Aramaic is a theory and not a fact, the evidence for which needs to be examined, in order to determine whether it is certain, probable, possible, or unlikely. Our own view has been that no incontrovertible proof has been advanced in favor of the theory, and that on the contrary, there are some fundamental considerations which militate against it, several of which have not hitherto been set forth.

II

Throughout the history of this discussion, the same pattern may be discerned. The number of proof-passages continues to grow less,[2] while even of those which are repeated, many rest upon a disregard of the

---

[1] The various recent treatments of the subject, in chronological order, are: — F. Zimmermann, "The Aramaic Provenance of Qoheleth" in *JQR*, vol. 36, 1945, pp. 17–45 (=APQ); R. Gordis, "The Original Language of Qoheleth" in *JQR*, vol. 37, 1946, pp. 67–84 (=OLQ); C. C. Torrey, "The Question of the Original Language of Qoheleth," vol. 39, 1948, pp. 151–60 (=QOLQ); F. Zimmermann, "The Question of Hebrew in Qoheleth," *JQR*, 1949, vol. 40, pp. 79–102 (=QHQ); R. Gordis, "The Translation-Theory of Qoheleth Re-examined" in *JQR*, vol. 40, 1949, pp. 103–116 (=TTQR); H. L. Ginsberg, *Studies in Koheleth* (New York, 1950) (=SK) following his earlier *Studies in Daniel* (New York, 1948) (=SD). This bibliography should now be supplemented by our full-length study and commentary, *Koheleth — The Man and His World* (New York, 1951), cited below as KMW; cf. esp. pp. 59–62, 362–66. Finally, we may add the judgment of Prof. W. F. Albright expressed in his review of the last-named work, published in *The Jewish Frontier*, Jan. 1952, pp. 30 ff. ("This position which he (i. e. Gordis) holds against the theory of Zimmermann and H. L. Ginsberg that Koheleth is a translation from a lost Aramaic original appears sound to the reviewer."

[2] Thus the evidence originally advanced in APQ was criticized in OLQ with at

93

263

evidence advanced or upon an uŋwillingness to evaluate the criticism fairly.

Thus of the seventeen examples of mis-translation proposed in APQ, SK refers only to seven, passing over ten in complete silence.[3]

We may begin with the arguments previously advanced, and now restated, with or without modification. SK declares that "the enormous proportions of Aramaisms and the utterly erratic use of the article *is* decisive" (p. 18). That the use of the article is far from erratic and almost always explicable in terms of Biblical and Mishnic syntax, was clearly indicated in QLQ, pp. 81–83 and the evidence there adduced has never been disputed, merely ignored. The few irregularities that remain are precisely what we should expect from an author who wrote in Hebrew but was familiar with Aramaic, in which the emphatic state was rapidly crowding out the absolute state. The same fluctuations are therefore to be found in Mishnic Hebrew. As for the Aramaisms in Koheleth, which are certainly evident but are far from "enormous," practically all of those listed in APQ, *ḥēfeṣ*, *lᵉbhad*, *raʿ* *ʿal*, *kᵉše*, *bᵉṣel*, *kilʿūmath*, *sōph*, and many others are common in Mishnic Hebrew, as was indicated by Delitzsch and Wright long ago.[4] If the Aramaisms in Koheleth are decisive, the next logical step would be to prove that the

---

least sufficient cogency for Professor Torrey to confess, "I find myself generally in agreement with Gordis on the details of his criticism." But then he added, "But he hardly touches the matters which are of major importance." However, as was pointed out in TTQR, this last statement was not accurate, since everyone of the 17 passages adduced in APQ as constituting "the strongest evidence for the theory or admitting of a *good* probability" in the opinion of the author, were dealt with in OLQ, besides 3 out of the 4 instances of alleged confusion of *hū'* and *hawā* and 6 out of the supplementary passages which had the greatest degree of force. As for the effectiveness of the rejoinder, it is noteworthy that Dr. Torrey passes over 14 of the 17 instances in silence, as well as the "alleged confusion" of *hu'* and *hawā*. Similarly, he does not revert to any of the 6 supplementary passages discussed and reintroduces only one of the others, namely 3 21.

On the other hand, Torrey argues at length that *ḥēfeṣ* is a retroversion of the Aramaic צְבוּ "thing" from צבי "desire." The evidence was presented in TTQR that the noun in Koheleth has the meaning "phenomenon, pursuit, activity, affair" (Eccles 3 1, 17; 5 1; 8 6), thus still retaining its volitional nuance, which is derived from the root *ḥāfēṣ*, "desire." Moreover, the semantic development is attested by the Arabic شئ "thing" from *šā'ā* "desire." Thus *ḥēfeṣ* in Koheleth stands midway between the Biblical meaning "wish" and the Mishnic meaning "thing, object." Moreover, this meaning occurs in the late Biblical Hebrew of Isa 53 3, 13 and Prov 31 13 as well. In sum, Koheleth's usage is in thorough harmony with the Hebrew of his contemporaries. SK does not even refer to this entire subject any longer.

[3] He defends 1 5; 7 5; 10 17; 12 13 and passes over 6 2; 7 20 and 5 17 of the "strongest" examples in APQ; of the less convincing passages, he reaffirms 7 12; 9 1–2 (doubtfully); 12 1 and 5 5, while saying nothing about 5 6, 16; 7 20; 11 1. Nor does he discuss 4 16, 17.

[4] Delitzsch's list is translated and amplified in C. H. H. Wright, *Book of Koheleth* (London 1883), pp. 490–500.

Mishnah is a translation from the Aramaic! This should be an even easier task, since over and beyond the Aramaisms in ·*Koheleth*, it contains many more, including the *īn* ending for masculine plurals and the coalescence of *tertiae alephˎ* and *tertiae yod* verbs.

Much of the evidence of alleged mistranslations restated in SK depends upon ignoring the force of the contrary arguments. In 3 17 כי עת לכל חפץ ועל כל המעשה שם the real difficulty lies, not in the fluctuation of the article, but in the change in preposition from *lamed* to *'al*. Here the translation hypothesis, as so often, leaves the situation unchanged. On the other hand, a possible explanation was adduced in TTQR (p. 110).

With regard to *šir* in 7 5, we are categorically told in SK (p. 20) "No other instance of *šir* 'praise' is known." This in the face of such Biblical passages as Isa 42 10; Jer 20 3 and Ps 149 1 where *šir* is parallel to *tehillah* and *hallel* "praise" (cf. also II Chron 5 13).

In addition, we may cite the old Morning Prayer *Yištabaḥ*, which reads *šir uš*ᵉ*bāḥāh hallēl v*ᵉ*zimrāh 'ōz umemšālāh*. This part of the traditional service is called *Birkat hašir* in the Mishnah and is explained by Rabbi Samuel ben Meir as meaning *Birkat hašebhaḥ*![5] Actually, it should not be necessary to cite such passages or Exod 15 1; Ps 96 1; 105 2; I Chron 16 6, in order to illustrate the natural semantic development of "song" to "praise."

That Koheleth wished to express the idea of "moderation" in 10 17c בגבורה ולא בשתי is an interesting suggestion, though not the only possible view of this passage. But it cannot be maintained dogmatically that the Hebrew is an erroneous translation of Aramaic, in view of the fact that the Hebrew text gives a thoroughly satisfactory sense. In fact, the argument in APQ and SK that what is required instead of *big*ᵉ*bhūrāh* is a Hebrew equivalent to an alleged Aramaic *beḥusānā* "in moderation" faces one difficulty which has been overlooked — that of finding a Hebrew equivalent for "moderation," for which I invite suggestions! Even modern Hebrew dictionaries propose only such neologisms as *hith'app'kūth, histapp*ᵉ*kūth, m*ᵉ*thīnūth, yišubh*,[6] none of which has the exact meaning required.

In Biblical Hebrew, this idea could hardly have been expressed better than by the noun *big*ᵉ*bhūrāh*. The semantic relationship of "strength" and "self-control" is well attested by such passages as Prov 16 32: "Better is he who is long-suffering than a mighty man (*gibbōr*),

[5] Cf. the Mishnah (Pes. 10:7) ואומר עליו ברכת השיר and the comments *ad loc.* of Samuel ben Meir, Maimonides and Mordecai. See also Eliezer Levi, *Yesodot Hatefillah* (Tel Aviv, 1946), p. 121. On this explicit meaning of "praise" for *šir*, cf. Samuel ben Meir ad B. Pes. 118a: חו היא ברכת השיר במתניתין כלומר ברכת השבח. Brown-Driver-Briggs, *Lexicon* defines the root *zāmar* as "sing in praise of God."

[6] Cf. Efros-Kaufman-Silk, *English Hebrew Dictionary* (Tel Aviv 1929), p. 431.

and he who controls his spirit than he who captures a city," and *Mishnah Abot* 4 1 "Who is mighty (*gibbōr*)? He who controls his impulses." Perhaps even more apposite is the Biblical verb *hitha'ppeq* "control oneself" which is derived from the root *'āfaq* "hold, be strong," its cognates being the Akkadian *'epêqu* "solid, strong" and the Arabic *'afiqa* "surpass, excel."[7] Some such juxtaposition of "strength" and "self-control" seems to underlie Isaiah's bitter indictment (5 21): "Woe to those who are brave (*gibbōrīm*) for drinking wine and men of valor in mixing strong drink."

With regard to 12 13c כי זה כל האדם, APQ originally suggested (p. 26) that the Aramaic read דין כל אנשא, meaning "he is the judge of all men." This was shown to be impossible as a clause in Aramaic without a copula (OLQ p. 75). QOLQ accordingly suggested an Aramaic text כדי דין כל אנשא הוא (or איתוהי) but that left the copula unaccounted for in the translation! SK now proposes (p. 22) as the Aramaic original די ידין כל אנש meaning "who will judge every man." Through haplography, this was then written as די דין כל אנש and the verb was then mistaken by the translator for the demonstrative *den*, hence our present Hebrew text. Aside from the necessity of making this secondary assumption of an inner Aramaic error, the theory now develops other difficulties — the clause is too far from the assumed antecedent, for the Aramaic would be something like לאלהא דחל ופקודוהי נטור די ידין כל אנש, "Fear God and keep His commandments who will judge every man." Secondly, *ki* in the Hebrew text is still unexplained.

The Hebrew text, on the other hand, is a comprehensible breviloquence perfectly appropriate to the context: "The end of the matter, everything has been heard. Fear God and keep His commandments, for this is the whole duty of man!" On this type of clause cf. Isa 28 12 זאת המנוחה הניחו לעיף וזאת המרגעה "This is the secret of rest; bring rest to the weary, and this the secret of repose." On the idea of the passage, we may cite Job chapter 28, which, after indicating that the transcendent Wisdom is beyond man, concludes: "But to man he has said, fear of the Lord is wisdom, and avoiding evil is understanding." Finally, both the form and content of our passage are paralleled in Matt 7 12: "Therefore, all things whatsoever ye would that men should do to you, do ye even so to them, for this is the Law and the Prophets." Another instance of this typically Hebrew usage probably occurs in Mic 5 4: והיה זה שלום.

SK declares "We can only feel sorry for anyone who still feels that Eccles 3 15 is satisfactory as it stands, or that *hū'* and *hāyā* were miscopied in the Hebrew" (p. 23). Nevertheless, we can only reiterate our

---

[7] Cf. the Lexicons of Brown-Driver-Briggs and Koehler-Baumgartner, s. v. Onkelos renders *hith'appeq* by *ḥasan* (Gen 43 31; 45 1).

conviction that Koheleth was seeking to express the philosophic concept
of the identity of past and present in stich a and the future and past
in stich d. The former idea Koheleth expresses again, from another
point of view, in 7 10, the latter thought in 1 9. It should be remembered
that Koheleth was seeking to express these concepts in a language
which, for a long time after his age, lacked the terminology required.
Hence he had no alternative but to use the verb for "being." We still
doubt that מה שהוא, proposed by APQ and SK means "that which is"
either in 7 15 or 6 10.

It may be added that the complexity of the Hebrew tenses should
guard us against undue assurance as to how a Hebrew writer would
express past, present and future.[8]

Undoubtedly יְהוּא in 11 2 is an anomaly. SK insists that this is an
Aramaic word left untranslated in the text,[9] and that no satisfactory
alternative explanation has been offered. Why so simple a word should
have been left untranslated, we are forbidden to inquire. Nonetheless,
we still feel that the form may well represent a conflate of two readings:
שָׁם יְהְיֶה and שָׁם הוּא, a practice which has many analogies in the Biblical text[10] and occurs in Koheleth itself in the Kethib of 6 10.[11] Various
anomalous forms in the Masoretic text are perhaps also to be explained
as conflations.[12]

III

Exegesis is a field where tastes will differ and thus one can only
register one's views. SK regards the clause "Remember thy Creator in
the days of thy youth" (12 1) as "mysterious" (p. 21). In the light of
Koheleth's basic outlook that the enjoyment of life is God's supreme

[8] Cf. such studies as S. R. Driver, *Hebrew Tenses* (3rd ed., Oxford, 1892) and G. R.
Driver, *Problems of the Hebrew Verbal System* (Edinburgh 1936) for illustrations of the
problems involved.

[9] That untranslated Aramaic words remain in the Hebrew text of Daniel is maintained in SD, page 50. The present Hebrew text is alleged to contain 3 untranslated
Aramaic words. However, of these תנתן (Dan 8 12) requires an additional emendation
in order to be fitted into the context; הֶמֶלֶךְ (Dan. 9 1) is regarded by Montgomery as
an erroneous vocalization of a Syriac idiom (cf. *ICC, ad loc.*) while יעמדנה in 8 22 as a
3rd person feminine plural imperfect has its analogy in Gen 30 38 and I Sam 6 12, as
was recognized long ago by the Masorah and is validated by Akkadian, Western
Aramaic, Arabic and Ethiopic.

[10] Cf. Gordis, *Biblical Text in the Making* (Phila. 1937), pp. 40–43 for a long list
of examples, which were supplemented in part by Zimmermann in *JQR*, vol. 34, 1943,
pp. 459 ff., and to which other examples may still be added.

[11] The reading עם שהתקיף ממנו is a conflate of a) עם שתקיף ממנו and b) עם התקיף ממנו.

[12] Thus הִתְפָּקְדוּ (Num 1 47; 2 33; 26 62; I Kings 20 27) is probably a Hithpael-Hophal
conflate. Note also הַטְּמֵאָה (Deut 24 4), הַכָּבֵס (Lev 13 55); הָדְשָׁנָה (Isa 34 6); נֶאֶלוּ
(Lam 4 14). Perles explains Lam 3 22 כי לא תמנו חסדי ה' as a conflate of תַּמּוּ and נֶּמְנוּ.

command for man (2 24 f.; 3 21; 5 17 ff.; 8 15; 9 7 ff.) one can only wonder how these involved interpretations given on p. 5, note 4 can seem attractive. As to the idea that God judges man for the pleasures he has neglected in life, that is explicitly stated in 11 9 where the Vav in *v⁰da'* is adversative, not connective, as verse 10 indicates: "Rejoice, young man, in your youth, and let your heart give you joy in the time of your vigor, and walk in the ways of your heart and according to the desires of your eyes, and know that for all these God will bring you into judgment. Remove vexation from your heart and turn aside sorrow from your flesh, for youth and vigor are only a breath." Particularly apposite is the statement of the Babylonian Sage Rab, which is not based on our passage: עתיד כל אדם ליתן דין וחשבון על כל מה שראת עינו ולא אכל "Each man is destined to give an account for all the joys his eyes beheld and did not enjoy." (J. Kiddushin, end).

One of the most attractive proposals in SK is the suggestion (p. 22) based on APQ, that the difficult phrase in 7 12 בצל החכמה בצל הכסף goes back to an Aramaic בטלת חכמתא בטל כספא. Curiously enough, a scholar who was not thinking of an Aramaic original for Koheleth at all, proposed more than a dozen years ago that the Hebrew text be emended to read כי בטלה חכמה בטל כסף, a proposal which requires the change of only one letter.[13] If this meaning for the passage is desired, we are accordingly not compelled to fall back upon the theory of an Aramaic translation of the book.

However, this view of the passage has drawbacks which have been overlooked. The "translator" was familiar with the verb *baṭal* and rendered it correctly in the far more difficult poetic passage in 12 3. Indeed, the consonants *ṭl* occurred twice in the latter text, which must have read ובטלא טחנתא מטל דאתמעטא. Unerringly he rendered them the first time as ובטלו and the second as the conjunction *ki*, while in our simpler context he twice missed the verb completely. Nor was he deterred from reading בטלת in 7 12 as the construct of a feminine noun, by the fact that the word for "shadow" is masculine in Aramaic and Syriac, and a feminine noun is non-existent!

We must also confess that the meaning of the reconstructed text is not altogether clear. What does it mean to say: "When the wisdom goes, the money goes, too." Does it mean that when a mental aberration temporarily takes hold of a man, he loses his money? This idea is not likely to have been expressed by the verb *bāṭal*, which means "cease for good, come to an end permanently."[14] Thus the Mishnah Abot 5:19

---

[13] Dr. Harris Hirschberg, who was kind enough to send me some notes on *Koheleth* which he had written before 1936–40.

[14] Cf. Ben Jehuda, s. v. who defines *baṭal* as חדל, נפסק, לא היה יותר בעולם. Similarly Jastrow, for the first meaning of the root. The other meaning of the verb *baṭal* is "cease, rest from labor, be idle," (cf. Jastrow, *ad loc.*). The semantics of the root parallels that

בטל דבר בטלה אהבה "When the motive for love ceases to exist, love ends";
Ibid. 5:21 עבר ובטל מן העולם "he passed away and disappeared from the
world," Ket. 103b בטלה קדושה "sanctity of life ceased"; Sot. 9:1 משבטלה
סנהדרין בטל השיר "from the time the Sanhedrin ceased to be, singing
ended." Or is Koheleth trying to say that where there is no wisdom,
money disappears? That would have been expressed by some such
phrase as אם אין בינה אין דעת, cf. Mishnah Abot 3 17: אם אין חכמה אין כסף
אם אין דעת אין בינה אם אין קמח אין תורה אם אין תורה אין קמח "Where there is
no understanding, there is no knowledge. Where there is no knowledge,
there is no understanding. Where there is no flour, there is no Torah.
Where there is no Torah, there is no flour." Be this as it may, the
assumption of an Aramaic translation is not indispensable to solving
the problem of the text.

In 10 15 the difficult clause עמל הכסילים תיגענו was explained in APQ
as going back to an Aramaic original טרחותא דשטיא תשלהינה as follows:
The translator rendered the Aramaic feminine noun *ṭarḥûtha* by the
Hebrew masculine noun *ʿāmāl*. The next moment he forgot that he
had written *ʿamal* and rendered the verb in the feminine to agree with
the Aramaic. Simultaneously he made another error by misreading
šatya as a plural and hence rendered it by *hakkᵉsîlîm*, but immediately
he forgot that he had written a plural and recognized it as a singular,
and hence he added the singular suffix in *tᵉyaggᵉenū*.

To strengthen this extraordinary hypothesis, SK (p. 24) offers
וּזְרֹעִים מִמֶּנּוּ יַעֲמֹדוּ in Dan 11 31 as a parallel. This clause, it is maintained, goes back to an Aramaic original ודרעין מנה יקומון and should
have been translated וזרעת ממנו תעמדנה (SD p. 48). One may grant the
translation-theory for Daniel, and yet fail to see how this passage
parallels the verse in Koheleth. All that took place is that the alleged
translator of Daniel rendered *vᵉdārᵉîn* by וזרעים instead of וזרועות and
then followed through correctly by putting the verb in the third person
masculine plural.[15] The clause in Daniel does not bear the slightest

of the Biblical *šabat*, a) *qal* "cease," Gen 8 22; Josh 5 12, *hiphil* "destroy," Hos 2 13;
Jer 7 34; II Kings 23 5, 11 and b) "rest," Gen 2 2; Exod 23 12, etc.

[15] It may be added that the proposed meaning for the noun in Dan 11 15, 22, 31,
"forces," while perfectly possible, is without parallel elsewhere. The writer of Daniel
may therefore have felt free to ignore the usual *zeroʿot* "arms" and fluctuated between
זרעים and זרועות. On this usage with other nouns, see below in the text. That *zeroʿim*
is not the invention of the author or translator of Daniel is clear from *zᵉroʿei* Gen 49 24,
uzᵉroʿai Isa 51 5 and *zᵉroāv* II Kings 9 24.

It may be added that there is good ground for doubting that any error was committed here at all by the use of the masculine plural verb *yaʿᵃmōdū*. If *zeroʿim* is masculine, the verb is perfectly in order. But even if the writer construes it as a feminine,
the use of a masculine plural verb after a feminine plural subject has ample warrant
in Biblical Hebrew (cf. Isa 49 11; Hos 14 1; Ps 11 4; Cant 6 9; Esther 1 20) while in
Mishnic Hebrew the feminine plural form *tiktōlnāh* has been entirely crowded out by
the masculine plural.

resemblance to our passage, where the presumed error in reading the Aramaic is compounded by two lapses of memory, all within three words!

The difficulties of syntax in the Hebrew text of Eccles 10 15 might well have been resolved in much simpler fashion by assuming that '*āmāl* is common in gender like many other nouns[16] and that the mem of *hakk*e*sīlīm* is a scribal error to be deleted. Or it might have been regarded as the enclitic *mem*, which Dr. Ginsberg has proposed for a good number of Biblical passages.[17]

IV

In 2 5, we are informed (SK p. 24), the plural ending *īm* of *pardēsīm* is evidence of an error in translating from the Aramaic because Rabbinic Hebrew uses *pardēsōt*. We are unable to follow the argument at all. In the first instance, it is not true that *pardēsīm* does not occur in Rabbinic Hebrew[18] or even that it is limited to reminiscences of our verse.[19] Moreover, even if Rabbinic Hebrew showed no examples of the *īm* plural of the noun, it would not place the form in Koheleth under suspicion. For Biblical Hebrew knows of many masculine nouns with plurals in *ōth* as well as *īm*, as e. g. Esther 6 1 *zikhrōnōth* and Job 13 12 *zikhrōneikhem*, *m*e*ōrōth* (Gen 1 14) and *m*e*orei* (Ezek 32 8).[20] In Mishnic Hebrew the tendency to *ōth* plurals grows, cf. *midbārōth*, *īlanōth*, *ḥayyālōth* (by the side of *ḥayyālīm*), '*inyānōth* (Shabbat 61a); *piqdōnōth*, *ma'akhālōth*, '*ayārōth* from Biblical Hebrew '*ārīm*, etc.[21] Perhaps the most striking examples where Rabbinic Hebrew replaces the *īm* ending by *ōth* is afforded by the Biblical phrase *aseret haddebārim* (Exod 34 28) which Rabbinic Hebrew reproduces as עֲשֶׂרֶת הַדְּבָרוֹת.[22]

In sum, Koheleth can very well use *pardēsīm* where later Hebrew prefers *pardēsōth*, and once again, as in the case of *ḥēfeṣ*, he will be reflecting a stage earlier than Mishnic Hebrew.

---

[16] Cf. *ḳōs*, *šabbat*, *derekh*, *šemeš*, *maḥaneh*, etc. Note particularly *hāmōn* which is masculine except in Job 31 34 and in Eccles 5 7, where תְּבוּאָה is to be read לֹא תְּבוֹאֶהוּ lit. "it will not reach him."

[17] As for example in Isa 10 1b where he emends ומכתבים עמל כתבו to read וּמְכַתְּבִים) עָמָל.

[18] Thus in B. Pes. 56a the editions vary between בניהן ובפרדסותיהן and בניהן ובפרדסיהן.

[19] Thus in Tos. Pes. II (III) 1 and B. Men. 71a the reading is בנגותיהן ובפרדסותיהן proving that the phrase is not a reminiscence or a citation of Koheleth's גנות ופרדסים.

[20] Cf. Ges.-Kautzsch, sec. 87,4.

[21] Cf. M. H. Segal, *Dikduk Leshon Hamishnah* p. 94g.

[22] That this is the correct vocalization of the plene spelling דיברות is clear from the masculine gender of the numeral and the *Mekilta* on Exod 12 21 (ed. Lauterbach, vol. I, p. 82): מה נשתנה הדבר הזה מכל הדיברות שבתורה.

With regard to Eccles 1 5, it is good to have the recognition of SK
(p. 26) oblique though it be, that the Aramaic *ta'eb* proposed by APQ
is impossible, and that the Hebrew *šō'ēph* is appropriate to the context,
as we have consistently maintained. We do not share his opinion that
the use of the participle in *šō'ēph* and the absence of the relative before
zōreāḥ constitute difficulties which require the assumption of an Aramaic
original, especially since the theory must make the additional assumption that the Aramaic text suffered haplography before being rendered
in Hebrew and that what fell out is precisely the relative we require!
The use of the participle "to describe daily occurrences" is thoroughly
normal for the Hebrew of Koheleth, as this very passage illustrates
with no fewer than 8 examples in verses 6 and 7. As for the absence of
the relative, this was rendered necessary by the rhythmic character of
the passage, which any reader of the Hebrew can recognize and which
explains the word-order as well. This fact has apparently been overlooked by SK, whose proposed prose reading is accordingly unacceptable. Actually, the entire opening section, verses 2–8, consists of
four-beat and three-beat stichs as follows:

v. 2	4:4	v. 6	4:4:4
3	4:3	7	4:3//4:3
4	4:3	8	3:3//3:3
5	4:4		

In prose, too, *'ašer* may be omitted. Exod 18 20 is particularly instruc-
tive in this respect.[23]

With regard to Eccles 6 12 כצל ויעשם and 8 13 ולא יאריך ימים כצל, SK
informs us that "some exegetical acrobats may argue that the comparison of man's days with the shadow was precisely what Koheleth
wished to express" (p. 29). The Psalmist in three passages (102 12;
109 23; 144 4, the author of Job in two (8 9; 14 2) and the Chronicler
in another (I Chron 29 15) as well as the alleged copyist, all engaged in
the "exegetical acrobatics" of comparing the fleeting character of life
to a shadow, a practice in which they were abetted by the Midrash.[24]
The reader need scarcely be reminded that a basic theme in Koheleth
is the evanescent character of man's life on earth, a thought which
motivates his insistence upon joy as the Divine imperative.

Actually, the theory of SK requires three assumptions 1) that the

---

[23] Note the two clauses: את הדרך ילכו בה ואת המעשה אשר יעשון. On Ehrlich's attractive
view that Eccles 1 14 is the continuation of the predicate of v. 14 (cf. *Randglossen ad
loc.*), *'ašer* must be understood twice in the verse, after *meʿuvvāth* and after *veḥesrōn*.

[24] Cf. *inter alia* Eccles Rab. 1 2: אם כצלו של כותל יש בו ממש אם כצלו של דקל יש בו ממש
"If man's life be like the shadow of a wall or of a palm-tree, it has some substance";
Gen. Rabb. sec. 96 כעופא דעבר וטוליה עבר עמיה "like a bird passing and its shadow passes
with it."

Aramaic read מטל די 2) that this common conjunction, which must
have occurred dozens of times in the book, (wherever we now read *ki*
and, at times, *'ašer*) was correctly rendered everywhere, except in these
two passages, where it was derived from *ṭelālā* or *ṭūlā*, the word for
"shadow," precisely where it makes excellent sense in that meaning,
and 3) that in the Aramaic original מטל די was first corrupted into
כטל די which was then rendered *kaṣel 'ašer*. To be sure, SK suggests
the alternative possibility that the *kaph* may have supplanted the *mem*
in the Hebrew translation. But this is impossible, for no translator
could have rendered *meṭol di* into *miṣṣel* either in 6 12 or 8 13. Finally,
SK has failed to explain what is to be done with the verb *veya'asēm* in
6 12. The theory is as difficult as it is unnecessary.

In 8 8 SK makes the ingenious suggestion that *bammilḥāmāh* is a
translation of the Aramaic בקרבא which was garbled from בקברא. Hence
he translates the phrase "neither is there any release in the grave"
(p. 30). He then demands to know, "Is there any other probable explanation?" The difficulty of the passage, however, lies not in *bammilḥāmāh*, but in *mišlaḥat*, which has been rendered variously as 1) "dis-
charge" (LXX) 2) "furlough" (Bar. Del. Moffat) 3) "escape" (*Pešita*,
Levy) 4) "weapons" (*Midrash*, Ehrlich). We prefer to render *mišlaḥat*
as "control," like *mišlōaḥ yād* in Isa 11 14, which is parallel to *mišma'at*.
This latter word occurs in the *Mesha Inscription* (line 28) כי כל דיבון
משמעת lit. "for all Daibon was obedience."[25] The parallelism in *Koheleth*
is now excellent: "There is no rule over the day of death, and no
control over the outcome of war."

The treatment of Eccles 5 5 *liphenei hammalākh* as the Hebrew
rendering of an erroneous Aramaic text is clever, but the difficulty which
SK finds in the phrase "before the messenger" seems to us exaggerated.
His solution is particularly complicated, assuming 1) an error in the
Aramaic 2) a conflate text consisting both of the error and the right
reading in the Aramaic and 3) the translation of its conflated text.

The argument in APQ that the name "Koheleth" goes back to an
Aramaic word which is numerically the equivalent of כנש"ה is con-
vincingly refuted by SK, who calls attention to the late date of the
isopsephic usage in Hebrew, which attaches a numerical significance to
the letters in the alphabet. Instead, SK suggests that the original text
contained the Aramaic masculine participle with Aleph, the emphatic
ending, קֳהֵלָא, which was mistaken by the translator for the feminine,
hence קהלת. Once again, however, the hapless translator suffered an
instantaneous amnesia; within two words, he both mistook the gender
of the noun and rendered the Aleph as the sign of the feminine, hence
קהלת, and then recovered sufficiently to translate the adjoining verb

---

[25] Cf. G. A. Cooke, *Textbook of North-Semitic Inscriptions* (Oxford 1903), p. 14.

correctly in the masculine, אמר (ה)קהלת and this strange attack came upon him three times — 1 12; 7 27; 12 8!

That is not all. Twice, in 12 8 and in 7 27 (where the word-division should also be אמר הקהלת), the translator exhibits a truly remarkable technique of being right and wrong in the same instant. Thus he recognizes the emphatic Aleph of the alleged original Aramaic participle, hence the definite article in the Hebrew, and at the same time fails to recognize it, hence the feminine ending Tav!

Aside from this set of assumptions for the translator, it is open to question whether the Aramaic קהלא is better than the Hebrew קהלת. First is the fact that the root does not occur in Jewish Aramaic, whether Palestinian or Babylonian. Its use in Syriac does not disprove the fact that its occurrence in our book would make it a hapax legomenon in Aramaic. Second, the use of the feminine participle for males is attested by such late Biblical Hebrew proper names as סֹפֶרֶת (Ezra 2 55; Neh 7 57) and פֹּכֶרֶת הַצְּבָאִים (Ezra 2 57; Neh 7 59), both of which apparently retain some sense of function — respectively "scribe" and "binder of the gazelles." The "feminine of office" is common in Arabic cf. *ba'kīra* "inspector" and *ḥa'līfa* "successor, caliph." As for the use of the *qal* participle instead of the *hiphil* which is used in other tenses, this is validated by the use of the *qal* participle for other verbs otherwise used in derived conjugations, cf. דָּבָר from דִּבֵּר, כָּזָב from כִּזֵּב etc.

The meaning of "Koheleth" is apparently "speaker" or "convener." It does remain somewhat unclear, but there is no ground for assuming an Aramaic original, which does not contribute to dissipating the mystery.

In Eccles 10 20, we are told, the place of במדע was originally occupied by another word, "certainly in the Aramaic, perhaps even in the Hebrew," and the reading במרבעך "on thy couch" is proposed. SK recognizes that this noun is used exclusively of cattle, but regards this as "hardly a fatal objection." Through the crowding of the *resh* and the *bet*, the *bet* was lost, and the *resh* became a *daled*.

Ingenious as this suggestion is, we do not share the certainty of SK about it. On the contrary, any one of the three following views seems to us more plausible: 1) read בְּמַצָּעֶךָ "thy couch" (Perles, Ehr.) 2) render מַדָּע as "study chamber," on which cf. Targum on Ps 68 13 מלכותא עם חיליהון אטלטלו מן פלטריהון וחכימיא אטלטלו מן מדעיהון "The kings with their hosts were removed from their palaces, and the wise men taken from their study chambers."[26] 3) render with most commentators מַדָּע as "thought, mind," its most natural meaning. Levy points out that the thought-sequence is as follows: "A king is not to be cursed even in thought, while a rich man, whose power is less extensive (and

---

[26] Proposed by M. Seidel in the Hebrew journal *Debir* (Berlin, 1923) vol. 1, p. 33.

whose spies are less ubiquitous) must not be cursed, even in the privacy of one's bed chamber." This is especially true, since what is in one's mind may emerge in sleep.

A valuable contribution toward the Wisdom background of Koheleth is presented by SK, on p. 34, who, with characteristic erudition, cites the series of king-gnomes from the Aramaic *Ahiqar Papyrus* of Elephantine. This passage, like Eccles 8 1 ff., counsels the courtier how to behave in the presence of a king, and how to react to his whims and passions. Both passages undoubtedly reflect a characteristic aspect of Oriental wisdom, which was greatly concerned with training its youthful charges as to their proper relationship to their superiors.[27] The general parallelism in thought is therefore quite clear, but SK seeks to utilize line 101 of the *Ahikar text* in order to correct Eccles 8 2. This line, as restored, reads in part as follows: חזי קדמתך מנדעם קשה [על א[נפי מ]לך] אל תקום!

This is rendered by SK: "Look before thee: Something harsh (=a harsh expression) on the face of the king means 'Stand (=tarry) not.' " The suggestion is then made that the first five letters of Eccles 8 2 אני פי מלך represent an Aramaic אנפי "the face of" and this emendation, we are told, is unavoidable. This is not all. In order to fit the emendation into the passage in *Koheleth*, the words אל תבהל of verse 3 are attached to verse 2 and מפניו תלך is emended into בפני מלך. This emended and amplified passage is then rendered: "Heed the face of the king, and in the matter of an oath to God be not hasty."

Now, obviously there is no relationship, either in form or content, between the two halves of the gnome. Nor is Prov 24 21 ירא אלהים בני ומלך, which SK cites, at all similar, for this latter passage urges showing proper reverence for both God and king. In this proposed passage of Koheleth, on the other hand, stich *a* urges us to scrutinize the king's face for signs of his possible displeasure, while stich *b* urges us not to take an oath to God too hastily.

The Masoretic text of Eccles 8 2, on the other hand, is eminently satisfactory as it stands with regard to subject-matter. It urges obedience to the king because of the oath of fealty sworn to him (2 5) and because of his power (vs. 3c–4). With regard to the difficult opening pronoun of verse 2, *'ani*, it is far simpler either to emend it to *bᵉni* (so Wildeboer).[28] We prefer to render "I say," supplying a verb of speaking before the subject. This usage has a precise parallel in Rabbinic literature: אמר רבי נחמן אנא לא רב אבין בר חייא ולא רב אבין בר כהנא אלא רב אבין סתם

---

[27] Cf. J. Fichtner, *Die altorientalische Weisheit in ihrer israelitisch-juedischen Auspraegung* (Giessen, 1933), p. 21; Gordis, "Social Background of Wisdom Literature" in *HUCA*, 1944, p. 93 f.

[28] Other, less likely, suggestions have been to delete אני as a dittography of ישנא, to insert אמרתי (Del. Wr. Sieg. Haupt) or to emend it to את (Euringer, Barton).

(B. Kiddushin 44a). "Rab Nachman said: '*I am quoting* not Rab Abin, the son of Rabbi Ḥiyya, nor Rab Abin the son of Kahana, but Rab Abin without a patronymic.' " Other Biblical examples of the use of a substantive before a quotation with no *verbum dicendi* expressed occur in Hos 12 9 (*'ephraim*) and Jer 50 7 (*JHVH*).[29] The *Ahiqar* passage is certainly apposite for Koheleth as a whole, but it was not transcribed in our passage, and cannot be utilized to correct the Masoretic reading.[30]

As SK anticipated (page 26), we cannot agree that *hū'* in Eccles 9 15 is difficult. The use of the pronoun in Koheleth, even where no emphasis is intended, is common (2 1, 11, 12, 13 etc. 17 26 etc.). Moreover, it may well be that the author meant to convey the idea that the poor man alone possessed the requisite wisdom for saving the city, so that the pronoun does add some emphasis to the passage.

In 12 9 the Aramaic text which is proposed, and the sense derived from it, seem to us inferior to the Hebrew. The Epilogist is not saying merely that Koheleth was wise — he is giving us the significant information that Koheleth was a *Ḥakam*, a professional Wisdom teacher, whose activity was not limited to his pupils, but extended to the people as a whole through the composition and collection of Wisdom apothegms.[31]

The failure to reckon with the social background of Wisdom literature in general and in Koheleth in particular, leads SK (p. 36) to object to 10 6, in which *sekhel* "folly" and *'ašīrīm* "the rich" are treated as opposites. It is therefore proposed that נתן הסכל goes back to the Aramaic יהיב סכלא which is an error for the presumed original יתיב מסכנא. Thus we must make a second assumption of an inner Aramaic error.

It is difficult to see why an error in the Aramaic from מסכנא to סכלא is easier to assume than an error in the Hebrew from מסכן to סכל! But there is an even more important objection to this hypothesis. The identification of wisdom with wealth is precisely what we would expect of the upper-class outlook of Wisdom, from the literature of which the present verse is being cited.[32] As one instance out of many, reflecting this standpoint in Oriental Wisdom, we may cite the Egyptian "Admonitions of a Prophet" (end of the Old Kingdom). In the First Poem the author laments:

> "Nay, but poor men now possess fine things.
> He who once made for himself no sandals, now possesses riches."

[29] On this usage cf. Gordis, "Quotations as a Literary Usage in Biblical, Rabbinic and Oriental Literature," *HUCA*, 1949, pp. 173–76..

[30] To give one instance, the phrase ותהך בלא יומך *Ahiqar*, line 102, is the same idiom we meet in Eccles 7 17 תמות בלא עתך and in Job 15 32 בלא יומו תמלא.

[31] Cf. KMW, pp. 76 f., 339 ff.

[32] Cf. Gordis in "The Social Background of Wisdom Literature," *HUCA*, 1944 *passim*, for some striking illustrations.

Even more apposite for the contrast in our verse are the following lines from the Second Poem of the same composition:

"Behold, a thing hath been done that hath not happened aforetimes. It is come to this that the king hath been taken away by *poor men*."

"Behold it is come to this that the land is despoiled of the kingship by a few *senseless people*."[32a] (Italics ours.)

The same background is reflected in the Biblical Wisdom Psalm 37. Thus v. 25 stoutly denies that the virtuous are ever in need, and verse 21 chooses as the type of the sinner the borrower who does not repay his loan, while the type of the righteous is the generous lender! On the other hand, the opposite emphasis, which identifies the poor with the righteous is far more prevalent in the Bible. It is expressed frequently in the Psalms. A striking illustration occurs in Isa 53 9 where $r^e\check{s}\bar{a}'\bar{\imath}m$ "wicked" is parallel to '$\bar{a}\check{s}\bar{\imath}r$. Whether '$\bar{a}\check{s}\bar{\imath}r$ emanated from the prophet or is a change due to an editor for an original '$\bar{o}sei\ r\bar{a}'$ is immaterial for our purposes here. The social cleavages and attitudes were genuine enough. This viewpoint is familiar, too, in the Gospels and in Rabbinic literature.[32b]

V

This discussion in detail of each passage presented in SK should serve to make it clear that while there is room for differences of opinion, the so-called cases of mistranslation from an assumed Aramaic are a) either capable of an alternative explanation, often simpler and more plausible, or b) the real difficulty remains unsolved by the theory.

Beyond these details, however, which are a tribute to the ingenuity of scholars, there are several more general considerations militating against the theory. SK attacks the view that "translations are always smooth, that a translator does not translate the same phrase once correctly and once otherwise, and that no translator could have been guilty of such 'stupidity'" (p. 38). A straw man is always easy to demolish. It was not maintained that translations are *always* smooth, but only that they are, other things being equal, smoother than the original.[33] That is to say, a good translator will produce a smooth trans-

---

[32a] Cf. A. Erman, *Literature of the Ancient Egyptians* (tr. Blackman), (London 1927), pp. 95, 100, 101.

[32b] Cf. the New Testament passages Mark 10 23-27; James 5 1-6 and for Rabbinic literature cf. *Midrash Shemot Rabbah* on Exod 22 24 *inter alia*.

[33] Even in the three phrases SK quotes from the Septuagint of Hosea, the LXX of Hos 11 9 may not transmit the correct sense of the Hebrew, but it is smooth Greek. As for the literal rendering of the emphatic infinitive absolute 1 2; 1 6, this Hebrew construction was so unique that the Aramaic Targums also render it literally. Moreover, it is not enough to berate the LXX. It would be necessary to *compare* the Septu-

lation because he will solve the problems of the text in one way or another, incorporating his solution into his translation. Nothing in the broadside of SK (p. 33–39) disposes of this contention.

What is indisputable is that the Hebrew of Koheleth is *good* Hebrew, intermediate between Biblical and Mishnic style. It is to damn it with faint praise to declare, as does SK, "that the Hebrew of Koheleth is less outlandish than that of Daniel chaps. 8–12" (p. 17). It remains remarkable that the ingenuity of the translation-advocates has not disclosed any examples of error in a passage like Eccles 12 1–8, which is both impressive and difficult, while the translator is assumed to be inept in a dozen simpler passages.

Nor is it merely that he is being charged with errors, but rather, as was indicated above, with the inability to remember what he is doing within the same phrase, often within two or three words! This is proposed for 10 15, as has been noted above, and three times for the phrase *'āmar (ha) Kōhelet.* Another case in point is afforded by 10 20, where the "translator" is assumed to have reproduced the definite article correctly for the emphatic state of the Aramaic two or three times [*haššamayim, hakkōl, hakkᵉnāfayim (Qere)*] and failed to recognize it in the same verse once or twice [*dābhār, kᵉnāfayim (kethib)*]. If the Hebrew of Daniel is a translation, the Hebrew of Koheleth sssuredly is not.

Additional evidence of the skill and knowledge of the "translator" is afforded by the fact that whenever a reminiscence of another Biblical passage occurs, he catches it unerringly and renders it in thorough conformity with the Hebrew original and that, without benefit of lexicon or concordance.[34]

Or is there a simpler explanation for the agreement — simply that Koheleth, writing in Hebrew, knew the Hebrew Bible? Especially since he does not merely reproduce the Biblical passages, but uses them creatively, at times in a sense varying from his source.[35]

Another important consideration, hitherto overlooked, in favor of a Hebrew original, is the existence of unmistakably rhythmic passages in *Koheleth*, marked by regular meter.[36] The many proverbs cited in the book are characterized by parallelism, often by regular rhythm.[37] In rising from prose to poetry, and reverting back to prose, Koheleth follows a practice familiar elsewhere in the Bible and characteristic of

agint of Hosea with the Hebrew original in order to determine the relative smoothness of the two texts.

[34] Cf. Eccles 12 7 with Gen 3 19; Eccles 3 14 with Deut 4 2 and 13 1; Eccles 5 3 f. with Deut 23 22 f.; Eccles 7 20 with I Kings 4 46 and perhaps Eccles 5 5 with Lev 5 4.

[35] Cf. KMW, chap. V for details.

[36] Such passages in Koheleth are 1 2 ff.; 3 1 ff,; 3 1–8; and particularly 9 8 ff. and 11 7—12 8.

[37] Cf. the proverbs 1 18; 4 5 f.; 5 9 and the collections in chap. 7 and 10.

Oriental Wisdom literature generally. That the translator, who generally is capable of the greatest *gaucheries*, none the less recognized the meter and translated the Aramaic into regular metric form is unlikely to the point of impossibility, especially since, as a rule, poetry in translation emerges as prose. It is far simpler to regard the Hebrew as the original language of the author, who used prose and poetry *ad libitum* and with marked success.

Even more striking is the evidence from assonances which are all the more remarkable because of the general resemblances of Hebrew and Aramaic. Thus one cannot draw conclusive evidence from a passage like 7 26 ממות מר אני ומצא where the Aramaic would transmit the same effect of the *mems* in the last two words (ממותא מרירא) but the *mem* of ומצא would disappear in the Aramaic (אנא ושכח).

On the other hand, in at least three other passages, the paronomasia exists only in the Hebrew and not in the Aramaic, proof that Hebrew is the original. In 7 1 — טוב משמן שם טוב, the play on *šēm* and *šemen* is lost in the Aramaic, where *šum* "name" and *mešaḥ*,[38] Syriac *mušḥa* "oil" bear no resemblance to each other. Moreover, the balancing of *ṭobh šem* and *šemen ṭobh* bears the stamp of originality. Similarly in 7 6 the play כקול הסירים תחת הסיר "like the sound of thorns under the pot" also presupposes a Hebrew original, for *sīr* does not occur in Aramaic in the meaning of "pot."[39] In 9 5 ואין להם עוד שכר כי נשכח זכרם there is a paronomasia in *sākhār* and *zekher*,[40] which the respective Aramaic equivalents *'agar* and *dukhrān* lack completely.

There is another general consideration which militates against the translation hypothesis. SK (p. 39) assumes that the Aramaic of *Koheleth* was translated into Hebrew nearly simultaneously with the rendition of the Hebrew Ben Sira into Greek (approximately 132 B. C. E.). As is generally recognized, Ben Sira's dependence upon *Koheleth* is not open to question.[41] It would therefore follow that Ben Sira used the Aramaic text of Koheleth, the only one then extant. In that event, it is remark-

---

[38] The exclusive literal rendering of *šemen* in Onkelos is *mešaḥ* (as e. g. Gen 28 18; 35 14; Exod 25 6, etc.); cf. Brederek, *Konkordanz*, p. 124.

[39] The common Hebrew noun *sīr* "pot" is rendered *dūd* almost exclusively by the Targumim (Exod 16 3; 27 3; 38 37 Jonathan; I Kings 7 45; II Kings 4 38 ff.; 25 14; Jer 1 13; 52 18 f.; Ezek 11 3, 7, 11; 24 6; Mic 3 3; Zech 14 20 f.; Ps 108 10; Job 11 23; II Chron 4 16), by פסכתירא (=Greek *psychther*) in Onkelos on Exod 27 3; 38 3; once by כיורא (II Chron 4 11) and once by קדר in II Chron 35 13. In our passage, Targum necessarily obliterates the paronomasia, rendering the first *sīr* by *kubba*, the second by *dūdā*.

[40] I. M. Casanowicz, *Paronomasia in O.T.* (Boston 1894), p. 78 notes that Koheleth uses *sākhār* rather than the common *ḥelēf* or *yithrōn* for this very purpose.

[41] Cf. *SK* p. 43 n. 6 who cites Noeldeke *ZATW* vol. 20, p. 90 ff.; Barton *Ecclesiastes* (ICC), p. 54–56. Our own investigation, for which see KMW, pp. 46–9; and the corresponding notes, eliminates many of the so-called parallels but leaves an indisputable minimum, which suffices to prove the dependence of Ben Sira on Koheleth.

able that Ben Sira was able to translate his reminiscences or citations from the Aramaic of *Koheleth* into a Hebrew which so closely resembles the independent translation of Koheleth into Hebrew, which was later produced by another hand![42]

If we seek to avoid this long arm of coincidence by the more natural assumption that the Aramaic *Koheleth* was translated into Hebrew *before* Ben Sira utilized it, then we face another difficulty. Koheleth cannot be dated earlier than the third century. All evidence points to its having been written approximately 275–250 B. C. E.[43] The assumption of an Aramaic original for Koheleth must therefore assume a) the writing of the book b) its dissemination and popularity c) its supplementation by one Epilogist, or successively, by two d) its translation into Hebrew e) the wide dissemination of the Hebrew version f) its acceptance into the Biblical canon, and g) consequently, its utilization by Ben Sira — all seven stages within five, or at most, seven decades.

In the very nature of things, it is next to impossible to prove that a book is *not* a translation, especially when the two languages are as close as Aramaic and post-Exilic Hebrew. Yet several cogent arguments against the translation-hypothesis have, we feel, been adduced, aside from the refutation of the proffered evidence. Basically, the burden of proof rests with the proponents of the theory. In all honesty, we do not feel that they have proved their case. All the evidence, internal and external, buttresses the view that Koheleth was written in the third century B. C. E. by a Sage in Jerusalem, who, like his rabbinical successors, knew Aramaic and wrote in Hebrew.

[42] Cf. Eccles 4 7 and 6 2 with B. S. 14 4; Eccles 3 7 with B. S. 39 16; Eccles 3 15 with B. S. 5 3; Eccles 8 1 with B. S. 13 24; Eccles 7 16 with B. S. 32 4 (35 4); Eccles 11 6, 9 with B. S. 26 19 f.; Eccles 7 26 with B. S. 26 23; Eccles 8 5 with B. S. 15 15. See *op. cit.* chap. V for a discussion of Ben Sira's use of Koheleth.

[43] Our grounds are indicated in *op. cit* chap. VIII. SK accepts the same general date. Cf. *op. cit.*, pages 40 ff.

WAS KOHELETH A PHOENICIAN?

SOME OBSERVATIONS ON METHODS IN RESEARCH

I.

IN spite of the tremendous strides taken by biblical scholarship in our day, it has at times disregarded some basic canons of scientific research. Envying the certitude and exactness of the natural sciences, at least as it appears to outsiders, biblical scholars have sometimes forgotten that the phenomena with which the literary and historical disciplines are concerned are far more complex than those of the natural world and that unilinear explanations can therefore rarely be true. Moreover, the conclusions of scholarship cannot be tested experimentally in the laboratory. Dogmatism is therefore particularly unjustified in these fields and humility is more than a moral virtue — it is an indispensable trait of the truly scientific spirit.

These basic principles of method, which are particularly relevant with regard to the book of *Koheleth,* need to be restated:

A. *The prevalence of multiple factors in historical phenomena must be kept in mind.* The author of *Koheleth* is a complex personality. On the one hand he is the heir of pre-exilic Hebrew religion, as taught pre-eminently in the Torah and the Prophets. He is primarily a devotee and practitioner of *Hokmah*, with its own rich tradition transcending the Hebrew national ethos. He is also the contemporary of the "proto-Pharisaic" stage in the history of Judaism, with the basic ideas of which, such as that of judgment in the after-life, he is familiar (3 17 ff.; 9 2 ff.). He has also absorbed some widely diffused Greek ideas, like the doctrine of the "four elements" (1 2 ff.) and the "golden mean" (7 16–18), besides being influenced by the more general skeptical temper of the Greek way of life. Finally, he is no mere echo of his background, but an original, richly endowed spirit. Hence it is a distortion to demand documentation at each point in his book through parallels in other cultures and to interpret his meaning exclusively in terms of other writers.

The style of Koheleth reflects the complexity of his background and personality. This book exhibits: a) many affinities with classical Hebrew, b) many points of contact with the mishnic era of the language, of which it constitutes an early stage, c) countless instances of the

103

powerful influences of Aramaic, which was the spoken language of his environment, and d) unique modes of expression for his special ideas. In part, he uses the accepted religious vocabulary of his day as a vehicle for his own unconventional ideas. In part, he is a pioneer in the attempt to use Hebrew for quasi-philosophic purposes, to express such ideas as "past," "present," "future," "recurrence," "moderation," etc.[1]

B. *The comparative method, which has proved so fruitful in contemporary Semitic and biblical studies has two aspects, not one.* The discoveries of vast amounts of epigraphic material from the surrounding cultures of the Fertile Crescent, Sumerian, Akkadian, Syrian, and Egyptian, as well as the remains of Hurrian and Hittite civilization, have naturally absorbed the energies of scholars eager to illumine biblical life and thought through parallels. However, this "horizontal" aspect of the comparative method, i. e., through space, has obscured the "vertical" aspect, i. e., through time, namely, the light shed on Hebrew life and thought by the later phases of Jewish religious and cultural development. The Hebrew Scriptures were written by a people which remained a recognizable religio-cultural-ethnic group for centuries, with an unbroken literary tradition. The Hebrew language never became extinct.

For various reasons, the methodological error is made of ignoring or belittling the evidence from post-biblical Hebrew sources in favor of alleged parallels from non-Hebrew cultures, emanating from other geographical milieus and ethnic groups. This, in spite of the fact that the evidence adduced from the "vertical aspect," is, other things being equal, at least as significant as that of the "horizontal aspect," if not more so. For in the case of material emanating from non-Hebrew sources, the problem still remains (though it is often disregarded) of explaining when and how the contacts were established by the peoples involved and what were the avenues for the transmission of culture.[2]

C. *There is need to distinguish carefully between parallels and borrowings* when the two cultures are as similar in background and character as are the various peoples of the ancient Semitic world. This becomes a more essential, and more difficult procedure, when the peoples involved have an even closer physical and spiritual relationship, because they emanate from the same area, speak practically the same language and share a similar background, as e. g., the members of the Northwest-Semitic culture-sphere. Here mere resemblance is insufficient to prove borrowing; it may simply reflect an independent, parallel development of elements going back to a common inheritance. Only an unusual

---

[1] Cf. the author's *Koheleth — The Man and His World* (=*KMW*; 1st ed., New York, 1951), chaps. XI–XIII.

[2] Cf. the author's observations on the subject in the *Louis Ginzberg Jubilee Volumes* (English Volume; New York, 1946) pp. 173 ff.

combination or a special sequence of factors can serve to demonstrate direct dependency.[3]

Careful adherence to all these canons of methodology is necessary if we are to achieve results of abiding value in biblical research.

II.

These observations are in order in connection with the most recently propounded theory on *Ecclesiastes*. In 1947, Prof. C. H. Gordon tentatively suggested that Koheleth might contain Phoenician influence, basing himself on three alleged parallels.[4] This suggestion was expanded into a monograph by Father M. J. Dahood in his *Canaanite-Phoenician Influence in Qoheleth*.[5] His thesis is that Koheleth wrote in Hebrew, not in Aramaic, that he employs Phoenician orthography and betrays strong Canaanite-Phoenician literary influence and that he was a resident of a Phoenician city.[6] This last assumption is based on some alleged "historical and social allusions" in the book.

Dahood's treatment is refreshingly free from the dogmatism and the unilinear theorizing which have affected much contemporary research. He recognizes the existence of Aramaisms and rabbinic locutions in the text and joins the virtually unanimous group of scholars, who reject the theory of an Aramaic original for Koheleth.[7] However, Dahood fails to recognize the importance of "the vertical aspect" of the comparative method, for he postulates Phoenician influence in countless instances, where the Hebrew literary tradition offers a thoroughly satisfactory explanation. As a result, his theory, we believe, fails to carry conviction.

Dahood's first argument is that the book exhibits some examples of

---

[3] Thus a historian of medieval literature rightly warns against "the unsound methodological principle that authorship may be determined on the basis of stylistic and ideological similarities, even when these are superficial . . . Similarities in style or in ideas are overriding only when they are so individualistic that not other person could conceivably have possessed them . . . In any period, similar views are held by many persons, even though their number, as in the case of heretics, may be comparatively small. Likewise, the most individualistic literary style will contain expressions, phrases, idioms, and technical terms which may be found in the writings of contemporaries." (Ellis Rivkin, *Leon da Modena and the Kol Sakhal* [Cincinnati, 1952] p. 118).

[4] Cf. his *Ugaritic Literature* (Rome, 1947), p. 123. The passages are Eccles 4 2, 7 12, 28. See our discussion of his view in *KMW*, p. 362, n. 47.

[5] Published in *Biblica*, XXXIII (1952), 30–52, 191–221, and subsequently appearing as a separate (Rome, 1952).

[6] Cf. *op. cit.*, pp. 3, 5, 39.

[7] These include, in addition to the present writer (for the bibliography see *KMW*, p. 364, n. 12), W. F. Albright (*Jewish Frontier* [Jan. 1952], pp. 30 ff.); H. H. Rowley (*Judaism*, I [1952], 279); O. S. Rankin, (*Book List of the Society for O. T. Study* [1952], p. 32); R. Marcus (*Jewish Social Studies* [1953], p. 174); E. Hammershaimb (*Vetus Testamentum*, II [1951], 237 f.).

"Phoenician" orthography, i. e., spelling marked by few or no vowel letters. It is an important question in the history of Hebrew orthography whether the introduction of *matres lectionis* was a process or an event. The older view held that this defective orthography was gradually modified by scribes, who inserted *matres lectionis* first at the end of words, where the need was greatest, and later within words. More recently, it has been maintained on the basis of epigraphic material, that the introduction of final vowel letters was a sudden change in Hebrew orthography, which took place in the ninth century under the influence of Aramaic, when the Syrian states attained hegemony in Western Asia.[8]

Whatever the genesis and tempo of the process, however, it is clear that in the post-exilic period, biblical codices exhibited all varieties of orthography, defective, *plene* and mixed, and the process of adding *matres lectionis* was still going on. The early conservers of the biblical text, who may fairly be called Massoretes, and *whose work began before the destruction of the Temple* (70 C. E.)[9] sought to stem the tide by selecting a few ancient and accurate manuscripts as the basis of the *textus receptus*. But even these official codices already exhibited all varieties of spelling, which the official guardians of the text could not and did not eliminate, for their function was to preserve the status quo, not to engage in text-critical labors. While a few preferred "massoretic" MSS established the norm, other "non-official" codices circulated freely in the Middle Ages and continued to show increasing numbers of added vowel-letters and outright errors, variants registered by Kennicott, de Rossi and C. D. Ginsburg.

When the far older biblical MSS of the Qumran caves came to light, biblical scholars were astonished by the *plene* orthography they exhibited. In fact, the extreme *plene* orthography was used by some scholars as an argument for the medieval provenance of the Scrolls. The true implication of the spelling of the Qumran Scrolls, vis-à-vis the MT, was not fully realized. The newly discovered Scrolls demonstrate that the wholesale introduction of vowel letters, which was intended to ease the problem of reading a consonantal text in the absence of vowel signs, had begun centuries before the medieval era. The Scrolls thus bore indirect, but

---

[8] Cf. F. M. Cross and D. N. Freedman, *Early Hebrew Orthography, A Study of the Epigraphic Evidence* (New Haven, 1952), pp. 58 ff.

[9] This view of the antiquity of the earliest massoretic activity was first presented nearly two decades ago by the present writer in *The Biblical Text in the Making, A Study of the Kethib-Qere* (=*BTM*; Philadelphia, 1937), pp. 29–54. While the theory there proposed on the nature and categories of the Kethib-Qere variants was widely accepted, the conception of proto-massoretic activity in the early Christian centuries was opposed as running counter to generally accepted notions. Today, a re-examination of the question is urgently called for, both because of additional material in rabbinic sources, hitherto overlooked, and the important implications of the Qumran biblical scrolls. We hope to present the subject *de novo* in the near future.

impressive, witness to the antiquity of the Massorah. For it was to counteract the peril of indiscriminate variations being inserted *ad libidinem* by scribes, that the authorities of the Synagogue set up "text proof-readers" (מניהי ספרים) in the Temple, who used the ancient codices deposited there as their model for correcting biblical MSS.[10] In other words, the extreme *plene* spelling of most MSS such as the Qumran Scrolls compelled the taking of measures to safeguard the text. *The relative paucity of scripta plena in the MT can be explained in no other way except by recognizing that there must have been an unbroken massoretic tradition going back to pre-Christian times.* Without such a tradition, the process of introducing *matres lectionis* and errors would have continued apace in the six centuries intervening between the Qumran Scrolls on the one hand, and the schools of the *Ma'arbae* and the *Madinḥae* or the traditions of Ben Asher and Ben Naphtali on the other. The process would have been so far advanced as to be beyond the power of the medieval Massoretes to reverse and correct. The Qumran Scrolls, which emanated from sectarian circles far removed from the center of normative Judaism, belong to the large number of "unofficial" codices, which were copied and circulated among the people. These MSS exhibited many variations, such as aberrant orthography and downright scribal errors, which the official guardians of the text sought to counteract through the creation and preservation of a *textus receptus*.

Yet even the Qumran Scrolls are not consistent in their orthography.[11] The extravagantly *plene*-spelling of these Scrolls is now a commonplace (as e. g. בכול, לוא, כיא) but the *aleph* is frequently lacking.[12] The contemporary character of both the *plene* and *defectiva* is also attested

[10] Note the casual, and therefore all the more trustworthy testimony of the Talmud, B. Kethubbot 106a: מניהי ספרים היו נוטלין שכרן מתרומת הלשכה "The revisers of the Torah Scrolls received their payment from the income of the Temple." See also the ancient tradition reported in Midrash Sifre, Deut sec. 356; Y. Taanit, IV 68a; Sopherim, 6.4: שלשה ספרים נמצאו בעזרה "Three Scrolls were found in the Temple court, etc.," which describes a collation of variants in these scrolls and the adoption of the majority reading. There is no reason for assuming that these were the only variations and this the only act of collation, but the existence of this type of activity in early rabbinic times cannot be gainsaid. The rabbinical traditions of *tiqqūnē sōpherīm* and *'ittūrē sōpherīm*, which testify to changes actually introduced into the text, are also very ancient. So, too, the use of conflates in MT was first noted in *BTM*, pp. 41–43 as a proto-massoretic device for registering and preserving variants. The examples cited there can be expanded substantially. The use of dots on doubtful words, which is ascribed to Ezra (*Abot de Rabbi Nathan*, chap. 34), is also an ancient text-critical technique that argues organized "massoretic" activity. That the Kethib-Qere formula, which originally arose as a guide to the readers, subsequently was utilized to preserve variants, is demonstrated in *BTM*, pp. 40–66.

[11] Cf. J. Muilenburg, "A Qoheleth Scroll from Qumran" in *BASOR*, No. 135 (Oct. 1954), pp. 23 ff., who summarizes the facts as follows: "4 Q uses *plena* less frequently than DSIa, to which it is paleographically kin, but more often than MT."

[12] Cf. in DSIa and the Habbakuk Commentary תלים for תלאים, מזנים for מאזנים, נמצאתי for נמצאתי. In the Koheleth Scroll, cf. מרשתו for מראשיתו (7 8).

for the second century C. E. in the bill of sale recently published by
J. T. Milik,[13] where the wife's name is written defective on l. 12 by the
scribe (שלם) and *plene* by the lady herself (שלום) on l. 16 of the same
document.

The MT of Koheleth exhibits the same variations in orthography.
To argue from the real or alleged defective spellings in the MT of
Koheleth for a Phoenician provenance or even Phoenician influence for
the book is completely unjustified.

As a matter of fact, many of the alleged instances of variants in
manuscripts or among the Versions are not orthographic at all, but are
syntactic in character. Thus after the relative '*ᵃšer* or *še*, the verb
may occur in the singular (1 10, 13, 16, 2 9, 4 16) either because the
antecedent *kōl* is construed as a singular or because '*ᵃšer* is treated
as a virtual relative pronoun singular. Thus subordinate clauses often
do not carry through grammatical agreement, cf. Lam 3 1 '*ᵃni haggeber
rā'â* '*ᵒnî* (for '*ᵃšer ra'îtî*) and the universal formula in rabbinic benedictions, as in the *Passover Haggadah: bārûk 'attâ 'ᵃdonay 'ᵃšer gᵉ'ālānû*.
The fact that one or another of the Versions renders the verb in the
plural *ad sensum*, taking *kōl* as a plural, or that a medieval scribe may
do likewise, hardly proves a "Phoenician" orthography and provenance
for the book.

In general, Dahood overlooks the phenomenon of "levelling," by
which a translator seeks to make his text intelligible, eliminating unusual
forms. Thus for MT 2 7 ובני בית היה לי, he notes three MSS
Kennicott and de Rossi, as well as LXX and Peshitta (S), which offer היו
(p. 8). He ignores the fact that no translator can possibly render the
verb except as a plural and that three medieval MSS might well write the
same form as an aberration from the MT in the direction of the normal!
Whether the masculine singular verb is being used in neuter fashion[14]
or is the result of attraction to בית,[15] or is a very ancient scribal error,
is irrelevant for our purpose.

Levelling and not Phoenician orthography also explains how the
characteristic demonstrative זה (2 2, 24) was changed by seven MSS
to זאת and by seven others to זו. The former represents the classical
biblical form of the demonstrative, the latter the usual mishnic form.
Koheleth thus exhibits the intermediate stage, as he does in the semantics
of *ḥēpeṣ*.[16]

The defective spelling את for '*attâ*, which occurs eight times in the

---

[13] Cf. *Revue Biblique*, LXI (1954), pp. 182 ff.

[14] Cf. Gen 15 17 ועלטה היה; Exod 12 49 תורה אחת יהיה.

[15] Cf. *G-K*, König, Barton *ad loc*.

[16] *Ḥēpeṣ*, which in earlier Hebrew means "desire, wish," retains its voluntative
force in Eccles (3 1, 17, 5 7, 8 6) and means "phenomenon, activity," while in mishnic
Hebrew it means "object, thing." Cf. *KMW*, p. 364, n. 13.

MT,[17] once in Koheleth (7 22), cannot fairly be invoked (p. 11) as evidence of a Phoenician origin of *Ecclesiastes*, unless we are prepared to argue the same for *Numbers, Deuteronomy, Samuel, Ezekiel, Psalms, Job* and *Nehemiah*.

In 7 24 מה שהיה, LXX and S read מְשֶׁהָיָה. But the omission of the *he* as a final letter occurs in Exod 4 2 (מזה *Kethib*; מַה זֶּה *Qere*) Isa 3 15 (מלכם *Kethib*; מַה לָּכֶם *Qere*) Ezek 8 6 (מהם *Kethib*; מָה הֵם *Qere*). There are several dozen instances of vowel letters, (א,ה,ו,י) missing at the end of words in the *Kethib*, but supplied by the *Qere*, as a guide to the reader, since the danger of an erroneous reading was greatest there.[18] There are, of course, many other instances when the Ancient Versions, medieval scribes and modern scholars have either supplied vowel letters at the end or words or deleted them.[19] The basic truth is that the existence of so-called "Phoenician" orthography along with mixed and *plene* spelling is no evidence of Phoenician influence.

III.

The various other phenomena in morphology, syntax, and vocabulary, which Dahood assembles, are equally inconclusive for a Phoenician origin, or even for Phoenician influence. They are thoroughly explicable in terms of the various elements of Koheleth's style: a) biblical b) proto-mishnic and c) Aramaic influence. In all these instances, Dahood's overlooking or disregarding inner Hebrew analogies in favor of Phoenician or Punic parallels illustrates the methodological error discussed above.

A. *Authentic Biblical Style*. Biblical Hebrew exhibits many examples of the phenomenon of the non-syncopation of the article, which is met in Koheleth (6 10; 8 1; 10 3). The noun *mišlaḥat* (8 8) is surprisingly described as "an uncommon formation in Hebrew" (p. 17), occurring only in Ps 78 49. But at random one thinks of *miṣnepet, mipleṣet, miš'eret, miš'enet*; the exact vocalization (a *pataḥ* because of the guttural) occurs in *mirqaḥat, mišma'at* and *mirša'at*. The conjunction *gam 'im* (8 17) needs

[17] Dahood (p. 11) is in error in declaring that את occurs five times, always as a *Kethib*, with אתה as the *Qere*. In addition to these five instances, I Sam 24 19; Ps 6 14; Job 1 10; Eccles 7 22; Neh 9 6, the defective spelling occurs without a *Qere* in Num 11 15; Deut 5 24; Exod 28 14. See *BTM*, p. 101. Note also Ps 74 6 (ועת *Kethib*, ועתה *Qere*) and Ps 90 8 (שת *Kethib*, שתה *Qere*).

[18] Cf. *BTM*, pp. 31 ff., and see pp. 95–97 for several dozen instances of vowel letters missing at the end of words in the *Kethib* but supplied in the *Qere*.

[19] Cf. F. Delitzsch, Oort and Kennedy on textual emendations. Thus we have suggested (*KMW ad loc.*) that in 2 2 Peshitta may have read מהלל as מַה הִלָּלוּ. In Isa 57 21 וּמֵעוֹלָם was read by LXX as וּמְעָלִים, both readings going back to ומעלם.

no Phoenician parallel אף אם CIS 3.6), in view of the common biblical locution *gam kî* (cf. Ps 23 4).

Similarly, the infinitive absolute with a pronominal subject (*weśabbē-'aḥ 'anî* 4 2) has parallels, not only in Esther 4 2, as Dahood avers, but also in Lev 6 7, Deut 15 2, and is thus authentically Hebrew. Its occurrence in Northwest-Semitic, as in the Azitawadd Inscription,[20] underscores the linguistic affinities of Hebrew. So too, the infinitive consecutive (4 17, 8 9, 9 11, 12 10) is neither Phoenician, nor, in its origins, late, occurring as it does in Gen 41 43 and elsewhere. Its higher frequency in *Koheleth* is what is to be expected in a later book (cf. Esther 2 3).

In 9 4 the *lamed* of *lekeleb* is the *Lamed emphaticus*, like the Arabic *la*, Akkadian *lu*; it occurs in Isa 32 1 *ûleśārîm*; Ps 32 6 *leśeṭep*; II Chron 7 21 *lekol*. That *hakkesîlîm* in 10 15 may exhibit the enclitic *mem* is a plausible suggestion by Dahood, that we had advanced independently.[21] But the usage occurs in authentic Hebrew passages, like Isa 10 1, as proposed by H. L. Ginsberg.[22] In 9 15 *hû'* is emphatic: "*this* poor man was able to save the city."[23]

It is alleged (p. 29) that in 4 2, 7 26, the third person pronoun is used as a copula in a subordinate clause. Actually, both in these passages, as well as in the Phoenician examples adduced (e. g. בשנת ... אש הא שת CIS 93.1–2), the pronoun is not a copula at all, but the subject of the clause. Moreover, examples of the use of the pronoun as a virtual copula are authentically Hebrew, cf. Deut 4 39: והשבת אל לבבך כי ה' הוא האלהים.

In 7 8, *'erek rûaḥ* is not a Phoenicism, but excellent Hebrew, meaning "patience," as *qōṣer rûaḥ* in Exod 6 9 means "impatience." The phrase has a different nuance from *'erek 'appayim*. The former is a human trait; the latter is an attribute of God, who is able to sustain the wrongdoing of men, until the hour of repentance or of doom.

B. *Mishnic Hebrew:* The preference for the masculine plural suffix הם over the feminine (p. 14) 2 6, 10, 10 9, 11 8, 12 9), already frequent in biblical Hebrew, became absolute in rabbinic Hebrew. The demonstrative זו which occurs eight times in the Bible, six in Koheleth (p. 15) is the normal form in mishnic Hebrew (זו).[24] To describe the relative *śe* as "not normal Hebrew" (p. 16) argues a very limited view of the history and extent of the language. Actually the form crowds out *'aśer* completely in rabbinic Hebrew. Koheleth's use of *'aśer* 89 times and *śe* 67 times once again stands midway between classic biblical and mishnic Hebrew.[25]

---

[20] Cf. Text C, l. 3 of the Karatepe Inscriptions יחו אנך; l. 20 ירדם אנך ישבם אנך.

[21] Suggested by the present writer in "Qoheleth — Hebrew or Aramaic" in *JBL* LXXI (1952), p. 100.

[22] When he reads *ûmiktebê-m 'āmāl kittēbû*.

[23] See *KMW ad loc.* in the commentary.

[24] See above.   [25] See n. 16 above.

'ᵃden (4 3) and 'ᵃdenâ (4 2) are the older orthography of the common mishnic adverb 'ᵃdayin. The biblical text exhibits many instances of the diphthong *ay* written *defectiva*, as in the familiar ירשלם, and II Sam 3 2 (*Kethib* אבינל; *Qere* אביניל); II Kings 14 2 (*Kethib* יהועדין, *Qere* יהועדן).²⁶

The variations in the use of the article in Koheleth are by no means erratic and are explicable in terms of biblical and mishnic usage, as has been demonstrated elsewhere.²⁷

mî, as the indefinite pronoun is illustrated on almost every page of rabbinic literature, as are the nouns *kad* "jug, pitcher," *šûq* "market-place,"²⁸ *šēm* "good name" and the conjunction '*illû* "if."²⁹ The occurrence of the conjunction in the Aḥiram Inscription, like that of the infinitive absolute with pronominal subject, is interesting, but it is incapable of replacing the biblical and post-biblical instances in Hebrew itself, as the genuine source and parallel for the usage.

C. *Aramaisms.* These include the noun *rᵉ'ût* (1 14 and often), the preposition '*al-dibrat* (3 18, 7 14, 8 2), which occurs also in Ps 110 4 and the conjunction *kol-'ummat* (5 15). In 7 17 *bᵉlō' 'ittekā* has an Aramaic analogy.³⁰ The identical noun, is, however, met with in the Hebrew of Job 22 16: '*ᵃšer qummᵉtū wᵉlō' 'ēt*, not in the Aramaic.

The high frequency of Aramaisms in *Koheleth* has, of course, long been known. There is a growing recognition that so-called "Aramaisms" fall into several categories:

a) Words indigenous to the Northwest-Semitic vocabulary, and hence common to both Hebrew and Aramaic. Some of these became frequent in Aramaic and fell into disuse in Hebrew, except in poetic style, and therefore superficially appear as "Aramaisms."

b) Words that entered Hebrew during the First Temple period, especially in the North, where there was close contact with the Syrians.³¹

c) Words entering Hebrew during post-exilic days, when Aramaic became the *lingua franca* of the Near East.

Koheleth may well exhibit all three varieties, with the third group especially well represented.

²⁶ Cf. *BTM*, p. 100 for many more instances and *KMW*, p. 229.
²⁷ Cf. the literature cited in *KMW*, p. 364, n. 12; Dahood's statement that this evidence "has been effectively refuted by Zimmerman," is entirely incomprehensible to the present writer.
²⁸ The noun occurs also in Cant 3 2, 8 1 and is of course common in Arabic *suq*.
²⁹ It occurs in Esther 7 4 and in unassimilated form in Ezek 3 6b (reading '*im lū*' with Ewald).
³⁰ Cf. the *Aḥikar papyrus*, 54 (133446e) l. 8, ותהך בלא ביומיך in E. Sachau, *Aramäische Papyrus und Ostraka aus Elephantine* (Leipzig, 1911) pp. 163 ff.
³¹ The characteristic term רְעוּת probably belongs to the second category. Cf. *KMW*, pp. 201 f. for a discussion of biblical Aramaisms.

IV.

In several instances, the suggested interpretation that is used to bolster the theory of Phoenician influence is open to question. Thus Dahood (p. 27) argues that *lammâ* (5 15, 7 16, 17) is better taken as "lest" and he adduces the Phoenician conjunction לם as a parallel. On purely exegetical grounds, we feel that the rendering "why" is to be preferred.[32] The use of a question instead of a statement at the end of a discussion is a charming mark of Koheleth's style, adding a touch of liveliness and the unexpected to the text. Additional instances of this use of an interrogative clause as a climax, occur in 2 6, 3 22, 5 15, 6 6, 12, and 10 14.

The clause in 1 5 *zōrēᵃḥ hû' šām* is described (p. 28) as "difficult to defend," because of the absence of the relative, for which he finds Phoenician parallels, e. g. בת אבא בל תבאן in *Arslan Tash* 5 f., "The house (which) I enter you must not enter." Ginsberg, incidentally, used the same passage in *Koheleth* in his attempt to prove an Aramaic original. Neither view is tenable. We have shown that the entire passage 1 2–9 is in rhythmic prose, with 4:4 as the dominant meter.[33] In verse, the relative is frequently omitted, for reasons of scansion, cf. Job 3 2: יאבד יום (אשר) אולד בו ולילה (אשר) אמר. Even in prose, the relative is omitted at times cf. Isa 6 6: ובידו רצפה (אשר) במלקחים לקח מעל המזבח.

That אדם is used 49 times to 7 uses of איש needs no explanation. Koheleth is speaking of "man" in the generic sense of "mankind."

The emendations proposed for 2 15 אז יותר, reading (אי זה יותר) and 6 10 (אדם הוא אשר, reading *'ašrēhû 'ādām*) are far inferior to the MT. Nor does *bammilḥāmâ* in 8 1 require reading a new *hapax legomenon* מלחם "cleverness." If it did, the Ugaritic parallel *m-l-ḥ* "sharp (knife)" could be well replaced by the mishnic Hebrew ממולח which means "sharp, clever."[34]

For *ba'ᵃlê 'ᵃsuppōt* "masters of assemblies" in 12 11, Dahood (pp. 49 f.) suggests that the Phoenician vocable בנאספת which occurs in the *Kranzinschrift* from Piraeus of 96 B. C. E.[35] should be read as בן אספת "(lit.) sons, i. e., members of the assembly." He also cites the feminine proper name אספת, which occurs in a bilingual third century inscription.

---

[32] So AV, RV, RSV and our translation in *KMW*.

[33] Cf. *KMW*, p. 193 for a full discussion of the meter.

[34] Cf. B. Kiddushin 29b: זריז וממולח. This root may be the key to the etymology of the name of the legendary creature in the Midrash, *mlḥm* (="the clever one") which refused to eat of the fruit of the Tree of Knowledge which Eve offered, and therefore escaped the universal doom of mortality (*Alphabet of Ben Sira*, Tav).

[35] Cf. Lidzbarski, p. 52; G. A. Cooke, *Text-Book of North-Semitic Inscriptions* (Oxford, 1903), pp. 94 ff.

Since it is, however, transliterated Ασεπι, it is not morphologically identical with the biblical *'ᵃsuppōt*, but is closer to the very common mishnic Hebrew noun אסיפה "gathering."[36]

That *hammal'āk* in 5 5 refers to "the priest" is one of several views proposed. It is, however, by no means likely that the word is to be understood as referring to "a messenger sent out by the high priest from Jerusalem to the outlying Jewish communities to oversee the fulfilment of vows" (p. 39). There is no evidence of such an institution in existence in post-exilic or rabbinic Judaism. This unproved assumption is then extended by the additional conclusion that Koheleth was therefore "not a resident of Jerusalem, but presumably an inhabitant of a Phoenician city." The term מלאך which is applied elsewhere in OT both to priests and to prophets (Hag 1 13; Mal 3 1) is most plausibly to be taken as the Temple emissary coming to collect unpaid pledges. It is in Jerusalem and its environs that we might expect the practice of having a Temple emissary go about to collect pledges for the sanctuary.

Koheleth may indeed be using the term with a sarcastic overtone. There is grave danger in underestimating the uniqueness of Koheleth's style, particularly in overlooking the nuances in which the book abounds.

Moreover, the assumption that Koheleth lived in a Phoenician city requires the completely gratuitous deletion of the phrases *melek bîrūšālayim* in 1 1, *'al yiśrā'ēl bîrūšālayim* in 1 12, *'al yᵉrūšālayim* in 1 16 and *bîrūšālayim* in 2 7. It is not merely that all these passages are vouched for by the Versions. More significantly, their deletion would destroy the entire point of the "Twin Experiment" with wisdom and wealth, which Koheleth undertakes and for the sake of which he adopts, in this passage only, the role of King Solomon, for both of which Solomon was famous.[37] That was recognized clearly by the Midrash which comments, "If someone else (but Solomon) had said, 'Vanity of vanities', I should answer 'This fellow, who never owned two cents, despises all the wealth of the world!' "[38]

That idea too, is most probably the meaning of 2 12, which we have accordingly rendered, "For of what value is a man coming after the king, who can only repeat what (lit. with what) he has already done.[39] The Egyptian *Instruction for King Merikere* offers a striking parallel both in form and content: "I would fain see a brave man (a reference to his son and successor) that equaleth me therein and that doeth more than I have done."[40]

[36] Cf. e. g. Y Taanit, 64c.

[37] Cf. *KMW*, pp. 40 f., 138, 199.

[38] Cf. Midrash. Koh. Rabba on 3 11: אלו אמר אחר הבל הבלים הייתי אומר זה שלא קנה ב' פרוטות מימיו הוא מגנה ממונו של עולם.

[39] Cf. *KMW*, pp. 210 f.

[40] Cf. A. Erman, *The Literature of the Ancient Egyptians* (trans. by A. M. Blackman; New York, 1927), p. 80.

The recognition of the force of the entire passage 1 12—2 26 not only safeguards the references to Jerusalem in MT, but rules out the recently proposed renderings of *melek* as "counsellor" based on the Phoenician and as "possessor" for which Arabic has been laid under contribution. *melek 'al yiśrā'ēl bîrūšālayim* (1 12) means simply "king over Israel in Jerusalem," as has previously been suspected.

V.

Our inability to accept Dahood's theory does not deny its heuristic value. He has helped confirm the untenability of the "Aramaic-origin" theory, by underscoring the fact that Koheleth wrote in Hebrew. His study has revealed some interesting *parallels* between Phoenician and Punic on the one hand and biblical Hebrew in general, on the other. This is a situation to be expected in view of the close kinship of both languages and literatures, and Dahood has put us in his debt by adducing some instances of such *parallels*, though much of his material is not to be accepted uncritically. On the other hand, we do not find evidence of specific *influence* from Phoenician on the orthography, morphology and syntax of Koheleth. Nor are there any substantial historic or social allusions in the book which suggest that Koheleth was a resident of Phoenicia.

All in all, the value of the parallels lies largely in the field of exegesis. These include the Ugaritic *bnt hll snnt* "daughters of joyful noise, swallows"[41] for *bᵉnōt haššîr* in 12 4, in the meaning "daughters of song, songstresses," an epithet for "birds." The juxtaposition of two such rare verbs as *mkk* and *dlp* in 10 17 is paralleled in our Ugaritic texts.[42] Such parallels do not prove Canaanite influence, but they do lend welcome additional support for the authentic Hebrew character of *Koheleth*, if any were still needed.

Other parallels are interesting, even if they do not appreciably add to our understanding of the biblical text. Such are the Canaanite parallels to *šemen rōqē'ᵃḥ* (10 1), *ba'al kᵉnāpayim* (10 20) and *gullat hazzāhāb* (12 6).

In conclusion, the theory of Phoenician influence in *Koheleth*, like the hypothesis of an Aramaic original, has the undoubted appeal of novelty. The theory cannot, however, be demonstrated before the bar of truth.

---

[41] Cf. III A B, A 17, a parallel admitted by Ginsberg, *JAOS*, LXX (1950), pp. 158 f.

[42] Cf. H. L. Ginsberg, in *BASOR*, No. 72 (1931), pp. 13 ff.

QOHELETH AND QUMRAN - A STUDY OF STYLE

In spite of the warning embodied by the Biblical sage Qoheleth in his utterance, " There is nothing new under the sun, " the past decade and a half has seen the emergence of several strikingly novel views with regard to the original language and provenance of the Biblical book.

Fifteen years ago the theory was propounded by one scholar and then vigorously defended by another, that our present text is a translation of an alleged Aramaic original, no longer extant. The present writer subjected the theory to critical analysis in a series of papers and found it totally unconvincing, (¹) a position subsequently accepted by virtually all scholars except the active proponents of the Aramaic-translation theory. Recent discoveries of Hebrew fragments of Qoheleth in Qumran have offered perhaps the final and devastating blow to the theory. Writing in *Biblica*, Father Mitchell J. Dahood (²) has cited a paragraph from an earlier paper of mine (³) which summarizes the negative verdict of scholars on the Aramaic-translation hypothesis:

" The book of Qoheleth was written about 275-250 B.C.E. and now we have the existence of manuscripts of the book among these sectarians about a century and a half later. It is impossible to believe that this short space of time could have been sufficient for all the steps in the process that must be assumed by the translation theory — the book could be written in Aramaic, become widespread and popular, be translated into Hebrew, become accepted as Scripture, not only in normative Judaism but even among these sectarians,

(¹) For a fuller discussion of this question see GORDIS, *Koheleth. The Man and His World* (New York 1951) Chap. 7 (cited hereafter as KMW); a full bibliography will be found there, p. 364, note 12.

(²) " Qoheleth and Recent Discoveries " in *Biblica* Vol. 39, (1958) pp. 302-318, cited thereafter as QRD.

(³) " The Significance of the Dead Sea Scrolls " in *Jewish Frontier*, Apr. 1957, p. 22.

whose deep faith was at the farthest possible remove from the Biblical sceptic, and be recopied in their scriptorium for their use. The Biblical book of Qoheleth was written in Hebrew ".

While there is, therefore, virtual unanimity with regard to the original Hebrew character of the book, Father Dahood himself proposed the theory that Qoheleth betrays strong Canaanite-Phoenician influence and was the resident of a Phoenician city [1]. In support of his theory, he offered alleged parallels in orthography, morphology and syntax from Ugaritic and Phoenician sources, which he presented with great urbanity and a refreshing lack of dogmatism. A careful examination of his evidence made it clear to the present writer that the material adduced failed to demonstrate that the theory was either convincing or necessary [2]. Father Dahood has now again reiterated his view regarding the Phoenician origin of Qoheleth and offered new support for his theory [3].

Unfortunately, his argumentation continues to ignore the three methodological canons set forth in our earlier paper [4]. In particular, it should be kept in mind that the comparative method has two aspects, not one. In addition to the " horizontal aspect ", which compares Hebrew material with parallels in the cultures of the surrounding peoples, Sumerian, Akkadian, Syrian, Egyptian, as well as the older remains of Hurrian and Hittite, there is the " vertical aspect ", which utilizes the light shed on Hebrew life and thought by later stages in Jewish religious and cultural development. It cannot be too strongly emphasized that no Iron Curtain may legitimately be interposed within the various stages of religious and cultural development of Judaism or in the continuity of Hebrew literature from the Bible through the Apocrypha to Rabbinic literature, or in the linguistic history and evolution of the Hebrew language. If, therefore, post-Biblical Hebrew sheds light upon a Biblical usage, it should be accorded *at least the same weight* as alleged parallels from a foreign culture, which emanate from a different geographical milieu. This is particularly true, if there is an extensive time-lag between the two docu-

[1] " Canaanite-Phoenician Influence in Qoheleth ", published in *Biblica*, Vol. 33, (1952) pp. 3-52, 191-221, and subsequently as a separate (Rome, 1952). Cf. pp. 3, 5, 39.

[2] " Was Koheleth a Phoenician? " *JBL* Vol. 74, 1955, pp. 103 ff.

[3] " Qoheleth and Recent Discoveries " in *Biblica*, Vol. 39, 1958, pp. 302 ff.

[4] Cf. note 2 above.

ments in question and there is no evidence of any direct channel of communication and influence.

Moreover, it is essential to distinguish between parallels and borrowing. Mere resemblances do not demonstrate direct borrowing unless there be some unique factor, such as an unexpected sequence of material or some other unusual element in the situation. The basic similarity of the human spirit, particularly as manifested within the same culture-sphere, should make us wary against assuming borrowings where a indigenous development may be postulated.

Thus, the evidence adduced in QRD under the heading of orthography seems to us to be totally lacking in cogency. That LXX read the difficult MT בָּשְׁתִּי in 10:17 as בֹּשֶׁת or MT מַאֲרִיךְ in 8:12 as מֵאָרֵךְ, demonstrates only that their Hebrew manuscript was *defectiva* at these points, while the manuscript which was chosen as the basis of the Massoretic text was *plene*. (¹) The existence of the MT in all essentials may now be confidently traced to a period before the destruction of the Temple on the basis of the evidence, both direct and indirect, afforded by the Qumran Scrolls and by the testimony of Rabbinic literature, much too long neglected. (²) Our present Masoretic text contains countless instances of the extreme *defectiva* spelling (" Phoenician ") and of the extreme *plene* spelling characteristic of later rabbinic texts, which the medieval Masoretes called חסר or חסר דחסר and מלא or מלא דמלא respectively. Generally, MT exhibits blending of the two orthographic modes. Thus we find both modes in the text, בְּתֻלֹת (Lam 5:11) and בְּתוּלוֹת while בְּתֻלוֹת (Zec. 9:17) is the most usual. The Qumran Scrolls themselves manifest all these orthographic varieties in the same text, some of the documents spelling even the same word differently within a few lines of each other,

---

(¹) In view of the fact that only a *Yod* is involved in these cases, it is possible that the manuscript before the Greek translators may simply have been blurred and indistinct, so that a single letter, and a small one to boot, may have been overlooked.

(²) The evidence from rabbinic sources was adduced nearly three decades ago in R. GORDIS, *The Biblical Text in the Making* (Philadelphia, Pa. 1931), esp. pp. 29-54. The bearing of the Qumran discoveries and of the rabbinic sources on the origins of Masoretic activity is treated in our paper, " Qadmutah shel Hammasoret Le'or Hammegillot Haggenuzot vesafrut Hazal " (" The Origins of the Masorah in the Light of the Qumran Scrolls and Rabbinical Literature ") in *Tarbiz*, Vol 27, 1958 Hebrew text, pp. 446-69; English summary, pp. III-VI.

as we have already pointed out. (¹)   Now, the Qumran fragment of *Ecc.* 6:8 apparently writes כמה for the Masoretic כימה. Even if we do not assume a simple scribal error in the Qumran manuscript, the *defectiva* spelling here would simply be one more example of the older, thoroughly indigenous Hebrew orthography.   It certainly does not demonstrate a North Syrian original or influence for the Biblical book.

To argue that the form מְאַת in 8:12 represents the Phoenician absolute state for the Biblical מֵאָה ignores the examples of dozens of cases in Biblical Hebrew where the old *at* ending for the feminine absolute is preserved in the text, cf. דַּעַת חָכְמַת (*Isa* 33:6), פּוֹרַת (²), at times without the Masoretes grasping the character of the form. (³) In any event, " Phoenician spelling " is no evidence of a Phoenician origin, for the former term refers to a mode of orthography common to all North-west Semitic and the latter refers to a specific geographic locale.

Many more of the passages cited in QRD depend on a proposed exegesis which, quite independently of the alleged Ugaritic parallels, seem to us to be inferior to alternative interpretations.   Such are the renderings of יָחוּשׁ (2:25) as " enjoy; " of מַר (7:26) as " strong " and מַדָּע (10:20) as " messenger, " which should be studied in the light of the entire extant literature. (⁴)   Here there is no need for argument, for exegesis is an art.   To be sure, it rests upon a variety of scientific disciplines, such as grammar, etymology and semantics, but it is the tact and insight of the commentator that is decisive.

(¹) Cf. the different orthographies of *lo'* in the same line of the *Thanksgiving Hymn*, 1, line 25: ולא נסתרו ולא נעדרו מפניכה ed. Jacob LICHT, *Megillot Hahodayot* (Jerusalem 5717) p. 59. In the 2nd Century bill of sale published by J. T. MILIK (*Revue Biblique*, LXI, 1954, pp. 182ff.) the wife's name is written *defectiva* by the scribe on l. 12 שלם, and *plene* in her own signature, שלום on l. 16.

(²) Cf. GESENIUS-KAUTZSCH, *Hebräische Grammatik*, 28 ed. (Leipzig 1889) sec. 80, for Biblical examples, and הבמת זאת (*Mesha Inscription* l. 3) המסלת (*ibid.* l. 26)

(³) Thus *Jer.* 8:9 הִנֵּה בִדְבַר ה' מָאָסוּ וְחָכְמַת־מֶה לָהֶם is to be rendered: " Behold the word of the Lord they have despised and Wisdom is nothing to them ".   Wisdom is the supernal, Divine Wisdom, cf. *Job.* 28:12,20, which is praised in *Proverbs* Chap. 8. The Makkeph in stich b treats חכמת as a construct instead of an absolute.

(⁴) Our own summary and conclusions on these various passages are to be found in *KMW ad loc.*

We see no need for invoking Phoenician parallels for revocalizing
וְתֻפַּר הָאֲבִיּוֹנָה (12:5) as וְתֻפַּר. In 9:5, וּמָצָא is an example of the authentic Hebrew impersonal construction, cf. וַיֹּאמֶר לְיוֹסֵף   (Gen. 48:1);
וַיֻּגַּד לְיַעֲקֹב (ibid. 48:2), and there is no need of postulating an obsoiete
Qal passive here in order to create a parallel with Ugaritic.

In 10:6, נָתַן הַסֶּכֶל בַּמְּרוֹמִים רַבִּים וַעֲשִׁירִים בַּשֵּׁפֶל יֵשֵׁבוּ the contrast
of the rich with the fools is thoroughly explicable within the frame-
work of the social background of Wisdom literature. In an extended
study, (¹) we have demonstrated the upper-class origin of Oriental
and Biblical Wisdom, which accordingly reflected their viewpoint
on social, political, cultural and religious issues. For this class, wisdom and wealth went hand in hand and folly and riches were opposites.

In several cases, what QRD describes as unique, is true only if
we artificially limit the scope and content of the Hebrew language to
the Biblical period. Thus the suffix on the noun ʿōlām (12:5) is no
hapax legomenon in Hebrew. It occurs time and again in Rabbinic
literature, cf. יש קונה עולמו בשעה אחת (Abodah Zarah 6:b) " A man
may acquire eternal life in one instant. "

In commenting on the view that the infinitive absolute with a
subject (Ecc. 4:2 וְשַׁבֵּחַ) is a Phoenician borrowing, we called attention
to the existence of Hebrew parallels in earlier texts, such as Lev. 6:7
שָׁמוֹט כָּל בַּעַל מַשֵּׁה יָדוֹ Deut. 15:2 and הַקְרֵב אַתָּה בְּנֵי אַהֲרֹ֜י as well as the
later Esther 9:1 וְנַהֲפוֹךְ הוּא. (²) In his zeal to correct my " errors ",
QRD objects that in these earlier Biblical parallels the subject of the
infinitive is a noun and not a pronoun, but he has overlooked the fact
that it is syntactically irrelevant whether the substantive, which is
the subject of the infinitive, be nominal or pronominal. It may
now be added that the Qumran literature contains several examples
of an infinitive with pronominal subject, as in Manual of Discipline
7:16: ואיש ברבים ילך רכיל לשלח הוא מאתם ולוא ישוב עוד Damascus
Scroll 9:1 בחוקי הגוים להמית הוא. (³) Are we to assume that the Qumran

---

(¹) Cf. " The Social Background of Wisdom Literature " in HUCA,
1944, vol. 18, pp. 77-118.
(²) The reference to Est. 4:2 was obviously a mistake in our hand-
written manuscript, preserved in the typescript. I appreciate Dr. Dahood's correction of this error.
(³) The Qumran examples exhibit another stylistic peculiarity, the
use of the Piel and Hiphil infinitive with passive force: לשלח הוא " that
he may be sent away, from them, " להמית הוא " that he may be killed. "

community on the shore of the Dead Sea is also to be given a North
Syrian provenance along with *Leviticus, Deuteronomy* and *Esther*?

Finally, we can only reiterate our conviction that the phrase
'*erek rūaḥ* " patience " in 7:8 is thoroughly and adequately explained
by the existence of the authentic Hebrew idiom *qōṣer rūaḥ* in *Exodus*
6:9 meaning " impatience. " That one phrase occurs in an early
Biblical text and the other in a late, is purely a matter of chance,
which is to be expected since only part of ancient Hebrew literature
has reached us in the Bible.

Koheleth uses '*ādām* in 7:28 as meaning " man, male " in contradistinction to '*iššāh* " woman. " The Phoenician inscription of
Azitawaddu (8th century B.C., Col. 2, 11.4-5) offers a welcome parallel, but this is no evidence of a borrowing between a royal Phoenician
king and a Jewish writer some six centuries later.   As we have pointed
out in our commentary, (¹) we have here a widespread semantic process
which can be expressed in Hebrew by imitating the language of a
Rabbinic principle of Biblical hermeneutics: כלל ופרט אין בכלל אלא מה
שאן בפרט, " When both a general and a specific term occur in a given
context, the general term will include only what is *not* comprehended
by the specific term. " (²)   We may note *Gen.* 3:1: והנחש היה ערום
מכל חית השדה where חית השדה refers to all creatures *except* the serpent.
In *Gen.* 3:14-15 we may note the contrast of אשה and אדם, where the
latter term refers only to the male member of the human race. Rabbinic usage offers several additional illustrations of the principle.   In
Jewish law, all Jews fall into three categories: priests, Levites and
Israelites. Manifestly, the term " Israelite " normally includes all
Jews; but when it is used in juxtaposition to *Kohen* and *Levi*, it means

---

That the pronouns are to be construed as the subject and not as the object
of the infinitive, is clear from the fact that they are in the nominative
and not in the accusative case (אותו).

We have found this same usage in rabbinic Hebrew, in the passage
(*Mishnah Abot* 4:22) cited in the text below: הילודים למות והמתים להחיות
Here the final verb להחיות is in the *Hiphil* and literally means " to make
alive. " The parallel with the first clause makes it clear, however, that
the nouns are both the subjects of their respective verbs, not the objects.
Hence Danby correctly renders והמתים להחיות " and the dead are destined to be made alive " a construction identical with the Qumranite usage!

(¹) Cf. *KMW*, p. 274.

(²) The principle was first noted by A. B. EHRLICH, *Randglossen
zur hebräischen Bibel* (Leipzig, 1908) vol. 1, on Gen. 3:1. The formulation is our own.

" any Israelite, except a Cohen or a Levite. " Similarly, the Biblical term גּוֹי " nation, people, " when used in contradistinction to Israel, means " any people not a member of Israel, hence non-Jew. " The Latin use of " Gentile " illustrates the same principle. Accordingly, when Koheleth uses *'ādām* in juxtaposition to אִשָּׁה, the term means " mankind; exclusive of woman " hence, " the male sex. " The process is, of course, unconscious, but it is adequately illustrated within Hebrew and certainly does not pre-suppose any borrowing.

On *Micah* 6:14 יֶשְׁחֲךָ there is no need to assume with QRD [1] a confusion of *Kaph* and *Nun*, and an emendation of יֶשְׁחַ into שְׁחִין. The etymology of the noun is to be sought in the Arabic cognate وَسَخ meaning " dung, uncleanness " from وَسِخ "befoul. " [2] The passages is to be translated:

" You will eat, but not be satisfied, though your excrement
                              [will be within you.
You will absorb the seed, [3] but not give birth;
And what you will eject, I shall hand over to the sword. "

On the theme cf. *Hos.* 9:11-13. The prophet is pronouncing doom on the rapacity and oppression rampant in the land (cf. 6:12,15).

These critical observations needed to be made in order to evaluate the contention of a North Syrian provenance for Koheleth. They are not intended to obscure the real merit of Father Dahood's paper, his effort to utilize the style of the Qumran Scrolls as a standard of comparison with the Biblical book. QRD alleges that Gordis " prefers to look upon the language of *Ecclesiastes* as normal third-century Hebrew which is explicable in terms of Biblical, proto-Mishnaic and Aramaic influence... The language of *Qoheleth* represents just another step in the normal evolution from classical to mishnaic Hebrew... " Albright is cited as emphasizing that " the Qumran finds have proved that normal literary Hebrew in the last two centuries B.C.

---

[1] He makes two other alternative proposals for changing the text (*ibid.* p. 311, n. 2).

[2] This convincing interpretation was proposed by the late David Yellin. It is cited anonymously by A. S. HARTOM, *Commentary on Twelve Prophets* (Tel Aviv, 1953), p. 102.

[3] וַתִּפֶּן is an aberrant orthography for וַתֵּשֶׁג " you will reach, attain " (cf. *Isa.* 35:10; *Pr.* 2:19; *Job.* 41:18 and the idiom הִשִּׂיגָה יָד *Lev.* 5:11; 14:21 and *passim*; *Numb.* 6:21 etc.).

(including *Ben Sira*) classicized in conscious opposition to the dominant Aramaic..." ([1]) Finally, QRD invokes the dissertation of T. W. Leahy, ([2]) who made a syntactic study of the *Manual of Discipline*, for his own conclusion that " the Hebrew of this scroll (i.e., *Manual of Discipline*) is remarkably similar to the classic Hebrew of the Bible. " Thus a contrast is erected between the alleged " normal third-century Hebrew " attributed to *Qoheleth* on the one hand, and the " normal literary Hebrew of the last two centuries B.C.E. which consciously classicized or archaized. " This contrast QRD uses to buttress his conclusion that *Qoheleth* stand outside the normal stream of indigenous Hebrew literary development.

Now both elements of the suggested contrast need to be analyzed far more precisely, if they are to serve as a fruitful basis for a comprehension of the style of *Qoheleth* and of its place in Hebrew literature. Two principles are fundamental:

A) *The concept of " normal literary Hebrew " has little or no meaning, except within the context of specific literary genres.*

In general, one is reminded of the comment of George Bernard Shaw who tells that he once asked a dentist " What percentage of the population has normal teeth? " He received the answer, "Less than twenty percent. " In the nineteenth century, the little-known Victorian English poet, Thomas Lovell Beddoes (1803-49) wrote in Elizabethan and Jacobean style. His contemporary, the famous novelist W. M. Thackeray wrote most of his novels such as *Vanity Fair* and *The Newcomes*, in the nineteenth-century style characteristic of his age, but in *Henry Esmond* he attempted, and with substantial success, to write a novel in the style of the eighteenth century as a *tour de force*.

B) *The archaizing or " classicizing " process must be understood in terms of the personality of the writer and his motivations.*

Archaizing for art's sake is, of course, not to be expected in ancient times, where literature was always more than a means of per-

([1]) It should be added that after this paper was read at Annual Meeting of the Society of Biblical Literature in New York on Dec. 30, 1959, Professor Albright publicly stated that he accepted the approach and conclusions of our presentation.

([2]) *A Study of the Language of the Essene Manual of Discipline*, a dissertation on deposit at Johns Hopkins Library in Baltimore, Md. (1958). I deeply appreciate the courtesy extended to me in making this excellent study available for my use.

sonal self-expression, but this makes it all the more necessary to analyze an author's motivations.

With regard to the first principal, the complexity of the concept of " normal literary style " may be illustrated by the following examples from Rabbinic literature, which exhibit a variety of patterns, legal, aphorismic, liturgical and poetical.

A) *Legal* – Mishnah, Berakot 1:1:

מאימת קורין את שמע בערבית משעה
שהכהנים נכנסים לאכול בתרומתן עד
סוף האשמורה הראשונה.

" From what time in the evening may the *Shema* be recited? From the time when the priests enter (The Temple) to eat of their heaveoffering until the end of the first watch. "

Here the late traits of Mishnic Hebrew in morphology, vocabulary, and syntax are obvious (מאימתי, קורין, משעה ש..., בתרומתן), though it is noteworthy that the Biblical את is retained, as is the *im* ending on נכנסים.

B) *Aphorismic - Mishnah Abot* 2:12:

יהי ממון חברך חביב עליך כשלך
והתקן עצמך ללמוד תורה שאינה
ירושה לך וכל מעשיך יהיו לשם שמים

" Let the property of thy fellow be dear to thee as thine own; and fit thyself for the study of the Law, for (the knowledge of) it is not thine by inheritance; and let all thy deeds be done for the sake of Heaven. "

Here again, the Mishnic traits are self-evident.

C) *Aphorismic, archaizing-Mishnah* – Abot 4:22:

הילודים למות והמתים להחיות....
ודע שהכל לפי החשבון
ואל יבטיחך יצרך שהשאול בית מנוס לך

" They that have been born (are destined) to die, and they that are dead (are destined) to be made alive, and they that live (after death are destined) to be judged, that men may know and make known and understand that he is God, he is the Maker, he is the Creator he is the Discerner, he is the Judge, he is the Witness, he is the Complainant, and it is he that shall judge, blessed is he, in whose presence is neither guile nor forgetfulness nor respect of persons nor taking of bribes; for all is his. And know that everything is according to the reckoning. And let not thy (evil) nature promise thee that the grave will be thy refuge. "

Here the Mishnic style of the aphorism as a whole has been supplemented by such archaic vocabulary as שאול and בית מנוס, induced by the emotional force of the theme, which lifts the utterance from prose to poetry.

D) *Liturgical – Amidah*:

אתה גבור לעולם אדני
מחיה מתים אתה רב להושיע

" Thou, O Lord, art mighty for ever, thou quickenest the dead, thou are mighty to save. "

The *Amidah* or *Tefillah*, the oldest component of the Jewish liturgy, was basically complete by the 2nd century C.E. (¹) It utilized Biblical language virtually throughout, but without attempting to archaize its syntax or rhetoric. Thus the Vav consecutive is lacking and the relative particle שׁ is used, but the Mishnic plural suffixes are not in evidence. A detailed study of the style of the *Stammgebete*, which is needed, would demonstrate that contemporaneously with the rabbinic Hebrew of the Mishnah, the Prayer Book evolved a special style, drawing both upon Biblical and Mishnic Hebrew but easily identifiable as neither one nor the other.

E) *Poetic*.

In elegies, the practice was common, though not universal, throughout the Talmudic period to archaize, in vocabulary, figures of speech and prosody. Thus at the death of the sixth century Babylonian Amora, Rabina, an elegy was intoned:

(¹) For Rabbinic traditions as to its origins, cf. *Mishnah, Berakhot* 4:3; *B. Ber.* 33a. *B. Megillah* 33a; and see I. ELBOGEN, *Der jüdische Gottesdienst in seiner geschichtlichen Entstehung* (Leipzig 1913); pp. 27-41, for a historical study of the various stages of its composition.

אם בארזים נפלה שלהבת
מה יעשו אזובי הקיר
לויתן בחכה הועלה
מה יעשו דני רקק
בנחל שוטף נפלה חכה
מה יעשו מי גבים

If the flame has fallen upon the cedars,
What shall the hyssop in the wall do?
Leviathan has been trapped in the net,
What shall the fish in the shallow pool do?
Into the swift-flowing river, the net has been dropped,
What shall the stagnant waters do? (*B. Moed Katan* 25b).

At the death of R. Zera, who was born in Babylonian and educated in Palestine, the elegiast chanted:

ארץ שנער הרה וילדה
ארץ הצבי גידלה שעשועיה
אוי נא לה אמרה רקת
כי אבדה כלי חמדתה

The land of Shinar conceived and gave birth
The land of glory raised her delightful child,
Woe unto her, says *Raqqat*
For her beloved vessel is lost! (*ibid*)

At the opposite pole of human experience are the wedding songs, in praise of the bride, referred to in the Talmud:

לא כחל ולא שרק ולא פירכום — ויעלת חן

" No stibium, nor paint nor dye —
Yet a graceful gazelle. " (*B. Kethubbot* 17a)

Here the same general literary, socio-economic and cultural milieu produces no less than four or five distinct types of style, differing because of the personality of the author, his motivation and the particular literary genre involved. The conclusion is clear — *in any given epoch there is no single pattern of normal style*.

We may now revert to the 3rd and 2nd century B.C. in order to evaluate the extant literary documents. In general, an author of average talent and moderate originality will follow the available models in his work. Hence these principles:

A) In *poetic passages*, he will tend to imitate the poetic passages in the Bible and hence " classicize. " This is true of *Ben Sira* as a whole, of the concluding hymn in the *Manual of Discipline* (Column 10) and of the Qumranite *Thanksgiving Hymns*.

Thus the imperfect with cohortative ending occurs 7 times in *Manual of Discipline*, all in the concluding hymn (10^{9-24}) and nowhere else in the text.

B) In *legal and ritual codes*, like the *Manual of Discipline*, the author will " classicize " in another mode — by imitating the style of the Biblical law-codes, in order to give his work the aura of binding authority.

It is noteworthy that the use of the perfect with *Vav consecutive*, which occurs 53 times in the entire *Manual*, is found no less than 25 times in the single passage 6:25-7:25, which sets forth offences and penalties and imitates the style of Biblical " Book of the Covenant " (*Ex.* Chap. 20-23.) The same holds true of the use of *'im* in the protasis of conditional sentences (15 or 17 out of 21 examples), which resemble the structure of the casuistic formulations to be found in the oldest Pentateuchal codes (*Ex.* Chap. 21-22) and *Deut.*, Chaps 20f.)

At the same time, the most characteristic trait of Biblical narrative style, the imperfect with *Vav* consecutive is " strikingly rare in the *Manual of Discipline*, occurring only 3 times. " The reason is obvious — the *Manual* is not narrative in character.

Moreover, the Hebrew of the *Manual* cannot be described, as does QRD, as " remarkably similar to the classical Hebrew of the Bible. " The *Manual of Discipline* gives abundant evidence of its contemporaneous character with Qoheleth in a variety of Aramaisms [1] and proto-Mishnic forms [2] assembled by Leahy. Particularly characteristic of Mishnic Hebrew is the use of the progressive tense, the participle with היה, e.g. מברכים היו [3].

Quite otherwise is the situation with regard to Qoheleth, who is as original in style as he is in content. Incidentally, we cannot understand how QRD can attribute to us the view that Qoheleth represents " just another step in the normal evolution from classical to mishnic

---

[1] On Aramaisms in vocabulary and word order, cf. *op. cit.* p. 82 and Chap. II, n. 37.

[2] Cf. such forms as התאחר, מבקר, התיסר, עָרֵב, נפטר (*op. cit.*, pp. 58ff.).

[3] LOAHY, *op. cit.*, p. 54.

Hebrew. " Time and again we refer to the " unique " style of *Qoheleth* (1) and our researches have highlighted distinctive stylistic features previously unrecognized or insufficiently appreciated. Thus Qoheleth is distinguished by his use of the conventional religious vocabulary of his environment, which he utilizes for his own personal vision and interpretation of life. (2)   We demonstrated the use of quotations from older literature as a widespread rhetorical usage in Biblical and extra-Biblical Literature. (3)   Yet nowhere does this use of quotations develop so many new nuances of thought and contribute so abundantly to the richness and color of the stylistic pattern as in *Qoheleth*. (4)   Even the traditional Biblical texts familiar to him, Qoheleth utilizes in his own special manner, (5)   a procedure which he adopts also with such Greek concepts as that of " the four elements" or " the golden mean. " (6)   In all these instances, Qoheleth does not merely cite his sources, but recreates them after his likeness.   It is therefore quite erroneous to conceive of Qoheleth's style as being *merely* that of his period.

In any age Qoheleth would be an outstanding figure and his style would naturally mirror this characteristic difference.   Moreover, his task was further complicated by the fact that he was a pioneer in the use of the Hebrew for quasi-philosophic purposes, a use to which the language had not been previously applied. (7)   A thousand years later, medieval translators like the Tibbonides, who rendered Saadiah, Maimonides, Judah Helevi and other Jewish philosophers into Hebrew, still found that the language had not yet fully developed the flexibility, precision and vocabulary necessary for the treatment of philosophic themes.

As a linguistic pioneer in this use of the language, Qoheleth found no models in Hebrew literature to imitate, no earlier texts that would lead him to classicize or archaize his style.   He wrote as he thought. Living in Jerusalem at a time when Aramaic was the dominant language of Western Asia and was exerting an ever more pronounced

(1) Cf. *KMW*, pp 87, 88, 94; *JBL* vol. 74, 1955, p. 113.

(2) Cf. *op. cit. supra*, pp. 75-95.

(3) Cf. « Quotations as a Literary Usage in Biblical, Rabbinic and Oriental Literature, " in *HUCA*, 1949, vol. 22, pp. 157-219.

(4) Cf. *KMW*, pp. 95-104.

(5) *Op. cit. supra*, pp. 43-46.

(6) *Op. cit. supra*, pp. 56 f.

(7) *Op. cit. supra*, pp. 88 f.

influence on Hebrew, he naturally employed a plethora of Aramaic words, forms and constructions, as has been noted by scholars since Franz Delitzsch, and even earlier. (¹) In this respect, he was anticipating the linguistic development to be found in Mishnic Hebrew.

His *vocabulary* contains forms and words which occur sporadically in earlier Hebrew, but which became more common and familiar in the Mishnah. (²) It is noteworthy that 'anī occurs to the complete exclusion of 'anōkhī, another respect in which his usage is proto-Mishnic. At the same time, the relative אֲשֶׁר, universal in earlier Biblical Hebrew (except for a few passages with a north-Israel background as e.g. Jud. 5,7) occurs 89 times in Qoheleth along with the particle שׁ, which is used 68 times, and which ultimately replaced the former entirely in Mishnic Hebrew. In *morphology*, we may note such abstract noun-ending as ōn and ūth. (³) With regard to *phonetics*, it is noteworthy that several *tertiae Alef* forms coalesce with *tertiae Yodh*, a usage universal in the Mishnah — but this is not always conclusive for the author, since it often inheres in the vocalization (חוֹטֵא 2:26; 8:12; 9:18; וּמוֹצֵא 7:26). Yet we may compare the *tertiae Yod* orthography of feminine שֶׁיָּצָא (10:5).

That Qoheleth stands intermediate between classical Biblical and later Mishnic, is also clear from his *syntax*. He has already adopted the Mishnic usage of the participle as a present tense (1:4-8; 2:14; 3:20f; 4:5, 6:12; 8:12, 14, 16; 9:5; 10:3) with the pronouns as subject

---

(¹) Cf. הֶבֶל construct (1:2); כבר (1:10 and *passim*); מדינה (2:8; 5:7); שבח (4:2); עֹין (1:13 and *passim*); תקן (1:15; 7:13); שִׁיר (7:5 see Com. ad loc.); תקיף (6:10); על דברת (3:18, 7:14); פֶּשֶׁר (8:1); שלטון (8:4, 8); עֲבְדֵיהֶם (9:1); קרב (9:18); גֹּוֹמץ (10:8); סכן (10:9); בן חורים (10:17); מֹרע (10:20); בטל (12:3).

(²) For כל־עמת (5:15), cf. לעמת (Lev. 3:9) and מלעמת (I Ki 7:20); for נכסים (5:18; 6:2), cf. *Josh.* 22:8; on חשבון (7:25, 27; 9:10), cf. the same noun as an ancient place-name (*Numb.* 21:26 ff., a.e.); for משלחת (8:8), cf. *Ps.* 78:49; for דרבנות (12:11), cf. *I Sam*, 13:21; for אי ("woe") (4:10; 10:16), cf. the folk etymology of Ichabod in *I Sam* 4:21, and cf. *B. Taan* 7:12, אי חכם and elsewhere. For the conjunction שׁ (instead of אשר) in 2:22; 3:18, cf. *Jud.* 5:7; 7:12; 8:26, *Ps.* 144:15; 146:5; *Job* 19:29(?); *Can.* 1:3; restored by Albright also in *Num.* 24:3, 15. On the root כשר (2:21; 4:4; 5:10, etc.), cf. *Est.* 8:5. כשר, חשבון, נכסים and שׁ are exceedingly common in Rabbinic Hebrew.

(³) Nouns in ōn: יתרון, חשבון, שלטון, כשרון; nouns in ūth: רעות (1:14); שכלות (1:17) סכלות (2:3), הוללות (10:13), שפלות (10:18).

(1:5, 7; 7:26).   At the same time he has not totally abandoned what
is perhaps the single, most characteristic feature of the classical Hebrew, the *Vav consecutive*, which occurs three times in his book (4:17;
4:1, 7).

Even more illuminating is a study of the *semantics* of his vocabulary.   In early classical Hebrew, the noun *ḥēfeṣ* means " desire,
delight " (e.g. *I Sam* 15:25; *II Sam*. 23:5, *Isa*. 54:12; *Mal*. 1:10).
In Mishnic Hebrew, the noun has developed the meaning of " object,
thing " and is used very frequently of inanimate objets, as in *Baba-
Mezia* 6:6:

לא יאמר בכמה חפץ זה והוא אינו רוצה ליקח

" A man should not say ' What is the price of this object? ' when
he has no intention of buying. "   In *Qoheleth*, the noun still possesses
at times its earlier biblical meaning " desire " (5:3; 12:1).   Yet in
other passages, its active volitional force has survived in attenuated
degree, so that it means " phenomenon, pursuit, activity, affair "
(3:1, 17; 5:6.)   Incidentally, this later meaning of *ḥēfeṣ* " activity,
affair ", occurs elsewhere in late Biblical Hebrew as in *Isaiah*, 58:
3; 13, (along with the older meaning 53:10; 54:12) and probably also
in *Prov*. 31:13.   The semantic development of the root from the
meaning " desire " to that of " object of desire, hence thing," has
its exact Semitic parallels in the Aramaic (צבו " thing, " from the
verb צבי " desire ") and Arabic (شَیْء " thing " from the verb " to
desire " شَاءَ).

Another illustration of the intermediate position *Qoheleth* occupies
between classical Biblical and Mishnic Hebrew is afforded by the
phrases: רְעוּת רוּחַ (2:11, 17, 26; 4:6; 6:0) and רַעְיוֹן רוּחַ (1:17; 2:22;
4:16), highly characteristic of our author.   The nouns are derived from
the root רעה, so that we have an Aramaism, parallel to the Hebrew
רצה.   That this Aramaism is very early is clear from *Hosea* 12:2
אֶפְרַיִם רֹעֶה רוּחַ וְרֹדֵף קָדִים   "Ephraim chases the wind and pursues
the east wind. "   On the close affinity of the two meanings " desire "
and " pursue " we may also compare the Rabbinic utterance אוהב
שלום ורודף שלום *Abot* 1,12.   In the Aramaic of *Daniel* (2:29, 30;
4:16; 5:6, 10) the noun רַעְיוֹן no longer means " desire, " but simply
" thought, " and it is this meaning alone which has survived in Mishnic and post-Mishnic Hebrew to the present day.   Thus once again
Qoheleth stands between the classical Biblical and Mishnic stages.

Similarly, his Hebraized form בֶּן־חוֹרִים (10:17) is older than the more
strongly Aramaized form בן חורין to be found in the Mishnah.

We may summarize the conclusions of this investigation. When
the unique features of Qoheleth's style are taken into account, as they
must, there remains a substantial residue of morphological, syntactic
and semantic evidence which places him within the framework of
authentic Hebrew literature, later than that of the classical Biblical
period, and earlier than the full development of Mishnic Hebrew.
There is no reason why the isolated Qumran community, living its
own intense religious life and writing its manuals of observance and
its liturgical hymns after Biblical patterns, should employ the same
style as the skeptical, searching Sage of Jerusalem who was pioneering
in speculative thought. That nevertheless both Qoheleth and Qumran contain similar elements in syntax and semantics, which reveal
Aramaic influence and became dominate in later Hebrew, testifies to
the common age in which they lived and to the organic religio-cultural
heritage which they shared, however different their interpretation.

All the evidence demonstrates that *Qoheleth* was written by a
Hebrew sage who lived in Jerusalem approximately at the beginning
of the 3rd century B.C. Drawing upon the resources of his Hebrew
religious tradition, as well as some insights of the prevalent Greek
culture of his time, he succeeded in formulating a view of God, man
and the world, which has remained uniquely his own even to our day.

CONTRIBUTIONS TO
THE BIBLICAL LEXICON

THE ROOT דגל IN THE SONG OF SONGS

Among the many difficulties in the text of the Song of Songs, the root דגל, which occurs twice in the form נִדְגָּלוֹת (6 4, 10), once as דָּגוּל (5 10), and once as דִּגְלוֹ (2 4), has been an outstanding crux.[1] The first two instances in the phrase אֲיֻמָּה כַּנִּדְגָּלוֹת have proved particularly troublesome. The traditional rendering, "terrible as an army with banners" or "striking awe as a bannered host" (Jastrow), has been rightly regarded by most modern interpreters as irrelevant and inappropriate as a tribute to the beauty of the beloved. Generally, they have deleted the phrase in 6 4 as an insertion from 6 10.[2] As for the latter passage, it has been emended כְּנֵרְגַּל ("awesome as Nergal, the red star of Mars").[3]

Several weighty considerations militate against this procedure. There is no evidence in the versions either for the deletion in 6 4 or for the emendation in 6 10. Second, the נֵרְגַּל would be a *hapax legomenon* in Hebrew. Third, we must also assume the meaningless addition of the feminine plural suffix *ōth*. Finally, the new text is far from satisfactory from the standpoint of content. While comparing one's beloved to the dawn, the sun, and the moon, is quite understandable, to speak of her as resembling the red star of Mars is rather strange — except, perhaps, in a Communist society!

In 1953, we proposed a solution to this crux which, unfortunately, escaped the notice of some scholars.[4] We called attention to the Akkadian root *dagâlu*, meaning "look upon, gaze, behold," which obviously explains דָּגוּל in 5 10 ("seen, i. e., distinguished among ten thousand").[5]

We pointed out that the niphal participle נִדְגָּלוֹת would mean "things seen, looked upon, i. e., great sights." In 6 4, the reference is to the capital cities of Tirzah and Jerusalem, which a rustic would find awesome and impressive. In 6 10, the word refers to the heavenly bodies, the moon (לְבָנָה) and the sun (חַמָּה). Hence, the feminine plural is precisely correct in both passages. The demonstrative sense, "these great sights," inheres in the definite article, as in הַיּוֹם ("this day today"), כָּעֵת ("at this time"), אַתָּה הָאִישׁ ("You are this man," II Sam 12 7).

This interpretation derives further support from Akkadian usage. The root *dagâlu* carries the special nuance, "look with astonishment," as in *i-dag-ga-lu* ("they looked

---

[1] Its use in the Song of Songs is obviously distinct from דֶּגֶל ("banner"), used in the disposition of the tribes in the desert (Num 1 52, 2 2, 10 14, 18) and the verbal נִדְגֹּל in Ps 20 6, which is probably a denominative ("we shall unfurl a banner"). The etymology is, however, identical, דֶּגֶל, "banner, being something visible, seen." See below.

[2] So Kittel, *BH⁴*, *ad loc.*

[3] So A. Jeremias, *Das alte Testament in Lichte des alten Orients⁴*, p. 670; M. Haller, *Die Fünf Megilloth* (Tuebingen, 1940), p. 38.

[4] In our study, "The Song of Songs" in *The Mordecai M. Kaplan Jubilee Volumes*, pp. 281–381, republished as a separate volume, *The Song of Songs, A Study, Modern Translation and Commentary*, pp. 7, 90 f., 92.

[5] Already noted in W. Muss-Arnolt, *A Concise Dictionary of the Assyrian Language*, I, p. 24; cf. W. von Soden, *Akkadisches Handwörterbuch*, I, p. 14b, "sichtbar."

astounded")[6], or "look with admiration" as in *bīta šâtim ana tabrâti ušepišma ana da-ga-lum kiššat niše* ("I had that temple built as a structure to be looked at with admiration by all people").[7] This is precisely what our passages require. Hence, נִדְגָּלוֹת in both biblical passages means "astonishing, admirable sights," and the phrase is to be rendered, "these great sights."

Scarcely less difficult has been the passage in 2 4b, וְדִגְלוֹ עָלַי אַהֲבָה. The traditional rendering, "his banner above me is love," is highly resonant, but unfortunately it is virtually meaningless. Some have sought to relate it to a flag placed over taverns, like the signs with which we are familiar today, and render, "He has brought me to the banquet hall, and its banner above me is love." There is no evidence for any such practice. Haller renders, "His shield over me is love," but this is an *ad hoc* meaning for דִּגְלוֹ. Some commentators have revocalized הֱבִיאַנִי and וְדִגְלוֹ as imperatives, הֲבִיאַנִי and וְדִגְלוֹ respectively and then rendered, "Bring me to the banquet hall and serve me with love."

Even after the two changes are introduced, several diffiulties remain: 1) the meaning "serve" for דגל is without parallel in biblical Hebrew; 2) we should expect the preposition לִי not עָלַי; 3) the meaning of the clause "serve me with love" is unclear.

Actually, the primary meaning of the Assyrian root is all we require in this passage, as in *du-gul-an-ni* ("look upon me").[8] The Hebrew noun דֶּגֶל therefore means a) "an object looked upon, hence banner," as in Num 1, 2, 10, and b) "a look, glance," as in our passage, lit. "His look upon me was in love, i. e., loving." The use of a noun as an adverbial accusative or adjectivally is a well-known characteristic of biblical Hebrew; cf. Ps 120 7 אֲנִי שָׁלוֹם (lit. "I am peace, i. e., peaceful"), Hos 14 5 אֹהֲבֵם נְדָבָה (lit. "I shall love them as a free gift, i. e., freely").

The passages in the Song of Songs with the root דגל are therefore to be rendered:

2 4　He has brought me to the banquet hall,
　　　And his glance upon me is loving.

5 10　My beloved is fair and ruddy,
　　　Pre-eminent above ten thousand.

6 4　Thou art beautiful, O my love, as Tirzah,
　　　Comely as Jerusalem,
　　　Awe-inspiring as these great sights.

6 10　Who is she gazing forth like the morning star,
　　　Fair as the moon,
　　　Bright as the sun,
　　　Awe-inspiring like these great sights?

Jewish Theological Seminary and Temple University

---

[6] As in the Nimrod Epic, ed., P. Haupt, p. 456, *apud* Muss-Arnolt.

[7] In *Vorderasiatische Bibliothek*, 4, 118, ii, 53, cited in *The Assyrian Dictionary of the Oriental Institute of the University of Chicago*, iii, pp. 21–24.

[8] Cf. W. von Soden, *op. cit., s. v.*

A NOTE ON טוֹב.

In reading the excellent article on the root טוב in Brown-Driver-Briggs Lexicon, we find that it bears a large variety of meanings, such as 'pleasant, fair, sweet, pleasing, fertile, fat, valuable, happy, prosperous, &c.'

Its Aramaic cognate טובא, however, has one exceedingly common meaning lacking in the Hebrew lexicon, namely, 'good in quantity', i.e. 'very much'. This meaning, which occurs on almost every page of the Talmud, is illustrated in Ber. 30 b מרירת לבא טובא 'very bitter at heart'—Sanh. 41 b טובא אמריתו בה 'you have said much about it.'

Non-Semitic languages likewise illustrate the specific shade of 'much' as derived from 'good'. The French 'bien' means 'well' but also 'much, very'. The German 'gut' in such phrases as 'so gut Schuld als er', 'as much to blame as he', 'gut krank', 'very ill', are also cases in point, showing how 'good' developes the meaning of 'much, greatly'.

By predicating this meaning for the substantive טוֹב and for the adverb הֵיטֵב and by giving the Hiph'il הֵיטִיב the force of 'become many, increase', several Biblical passages become clear and unforced. The full apparatus will be found in the standard commentaries. We shall here content ourselves with a brief comment and a translation of each verse where this meaning of טוֹב is appropriate.

Jer. xv 11 לְטוֹב (Qere שֵׁרִיתִךְ) שׁרותך לא אם.

Most modern scholars rightly accept the Kethibh as a derivative from שרר 'be strong', rather than the Qere which is a hybrid verb-and-noun form, based on שְׁאֵרִית with the elision of the Aleph. שָׁרַר is however intransitive in Aramaic. It is therefore assumed that in Hebrew, שֵׁרוֹתִךְ would be transitive and mean 'I strengthen thee', or, preferably, it is emended to הֲשֵׁרוֹתִיךְ. Yet the rendering, 'I have strengthened thee for good' is meaningless. On our assumption, לְטוֹב would be similar to לָרֹב (see below), and would mean 'in abundance, greatly'. The verse is then to be rendered :—

'The Lord said, Verily, I will strengthen you greatly. Verily, I will

---

[1] *Urform und Fortbildungen des Manichäischen Systems* von H. H. Schäder (from the Bibliothek Warburg, vol. iv): see also the same writer's critique of the Coptic finds in *Gnomon* for July, 1933.

cause the enemy to make supplication unto you in the hour of evil and the time of affliction.'

Micah i 12 ‏כִּי חָלָה לְטוֹב יֹשֶׁבֶת מָרוֹת‎.

The opening phrase has occasioned great difficulty, it has been rendered 'the inhabitant of Maroth waiteth for good', which derives the verb ‏חָלָה‎ from ‏יחל = חיל‎ 'trust, wait' (Targum, Rashi, Authorized Version, Ehrlich in his Hebrew Commentary, Jewish Version). Another view construes ‏חָלָה‎ as the masculine perfect Qal of ‏חָלָה‎ 'to be ill' in spite of the fact that ‏יֹשֶׁבֶת‎ is feminine (Vulgate, Peshitta). Perhaps, however, these versions are tacitly reading ‏חֹלָה‎ instead of ‏חָלָה‎, as does Ehrlich, who reads ‏חֹלָה לָמוּת‎ 'sick unto death'. Ibn Ezra and Ḳimḥi derive the verb from ‏חיל‎ 'tremble', but find great difficulty with ‏לְטוֹב‎. Obviously, the Massoretic text permits only the last interpretation. ‏לְטוֹב‎ is no longer difficult, if we give it the meaning advanced in this paper, 'much, greatly'. ‏לְטוֹב‎ is very similar to ‏לָרֹב‎ which means 'in abundance, greatly', as in Gen. xxx 30, xlviii 16, &c. [See Brown-Driver-Briggs, s.v. ‏רב‎.] The verse is then to be rendered :—'For the inhabitant of Maroth trembles greatly'.

Hosea x 1 ‏כְּרֹב לְפִרְיוֹ הִרְבָּה לַמִּזְבְּחוֹת כְּטוֹב לְאַרְצוֹ הֵיטִיבוּ מַצֵּבוֹת‎.

The parallelism of the verse attests our rendering of ‏טוֹב‎ as meaning 'much'. It is so interpreted by Vulgate, Rashi, and Ibn Ezra, and may be translated :

As his fruit increased,
He increased his altars,
The more fertile was his land,
The more abundant were his pillars.

Jonah iv 4, 9 ‏הַהֵיטֵב חָרָה לָךְ‎.

The ordinary rendering—'Dost thou well to be angry?' is inept and awkward. LXX, Targum, Revised Version Margin, and the Jewish Version render it correctly—'And the Lord said, Art thou very angry?' to which Jonah answers in v 9.'I am very angry, even unto death'.

A NOTE ON *YAD*

$\mathbf{S}$EVERAL years ago, it came to my notice that in some Biblical passages, $b^e yad$ cannot be interpreted in its usual meanings ("in the hand, possession, power of," or "by the agency of"), but apparently represents an abnormal spelling for $b^e ad$ (= "for," etc.). Recently, I learnt that a similar observation had already been published by Prof. N. H. Torczyner,[1] who explained the phenomenon along lines proposed independently by Dr. W. F. Albright.

The following passages in Job are adduced by Torczyner: 8 4, which means: "If your sons have sinned, He has sent them off *for* their transgression" (בְּיַד־פִּשְׁעָם); 15 23: "He knows that the day of darkness is prepared *for* him" (נָכוֹן בְּיָדוֹ); 27 11: "I shall teach you *on behalf of* God (בְּיַד־אֵל) and what is in mind of the Almighty, I shall not conceal."[2]

Similarly in Ez 37 19 the words אֲשֶׁר בְּיַד אֶפְרַיִם are very difficult and are deleted by many interpreters, in spite of the evidence of LXX and Vulgate. The problem disappears if $b^e yad$ is the equivalent of $b^e ad$, used, like the Latin *pro* and the Greek $\pi\rho o$, to mean, not only "on behalf of," but also "instead of, for."[3] The passage is then in harmony with the context:

---

[1] ספר היובל לפרופיסור שמואל קרויס in ביד בדי בכתבי הקדש ובכנענית (Professor Samuel Krauss Jubilee Volume) Jerusalem, 5697, pp. 1 ff.

[2] On $b^e ad$ = "on behalf of," cf. BDB, *s. v.*, 2; and such passages as Job 2 4, 6 22. Our passage may be rendered slightly differently: "I shall teach you in God's stead (*pro Deo*)." Cf. Ez 37 19.

[3] This is the required meaning for $b^e ad$ in Is 32 14 "the hill and watchtower will serve as caves (הָיָה בְּעַד מְעָרוֹת) forever," and $b^e ad$ is not a dittography of *me'aroth* (against Graetz, BDB).

341

315

"Behold, I am taking the stick of Joseph, which *stands for* Ephraim and the tribes of Israel his companions, and I shall place upon it the stick of Judah, and I shall make them into one stick and they shall be one in my hand." The Targum, interpreting likewise, renders: הא אנא מקרב ית שבטא דיוסף די הוא שבטא דאפרים ושבטי ישראל אחידהון.

In explaining the phenomenon, Torczyner called attention to the Canaanite gloss *ba-di-u* for *ba-ya-di-hu* in the Tell-el-Amarna Letter No. 245, line 35. The Ugaritic texts now disclose additional evidence for this spelling of *b*ᵉ*yad* as *bd*, pronounced *bad* in early Canaanite and Hebrew, *bod* in Phoenician.[4] Dr. Albright suggests that *b*ᵉ*yad* may sometimes have been pronounced in Hebrew as *bad* (as in Ugaritic), and thus it became confused with *b*ᵉ*ʻad* — originally pronounced *baʻd*, as in Arabic.[5]

This sporadic equivalence of ביד and בעד seems certain — whether due to phonetic or graphic confusion. It will clarify the following passages, hitherto unnoticed.[6]

The last stich of Is 64 66 (וַתְּמוּגֵנוּ בְּיַד־עֲוֹנֵנוּ) is generally rendered: "And hast consumed us by means of our iniquities"[7] or "Thou hast handed us over into the hand of our sins,"[8] which presupposes the emendation וַתְּמַגְּנֵנוּ. But the analogy of Job 8 4, as well as the context, support the Masoretic text, which may be rendered:

> There is none who calls upon Thy name,
> None stirs to take hold of Thee,
> For Thou hast hidden Thy face from us,
> And hast destroyed us for our sins.

The usual rendering of the second clause of I Sam 21 14 (וַיִּתְהֹלֵל בְּיָדָם) is: "he feigned himself mad in their hands,"

---

[4] Cf. F. Böhl, *Die Sprache der Amarnabriefe* (Leipzig, 1909) p. 83; H. L. Ginsberg, in JPOS, 1936, p. 149, C. Gordon, *Ugaritic Grammar* (Rome 1940), p. 20; Albright, *Archaeology and the Religion of Israel* (Baltimore, 1942), pp. 135 f.

[5] In a private communication dated January 24, 1943.

[6] Torczyner also suggests the same interpretation for Job 12 6c and Is 10 5 (doubtfully), but I cannot follow him.

[7] So Ibn Janaḥ, Kimḥi, followed by the Revised Version (text) and the Jewish Version. The verb should be read וַתְּמוֹגְנֵנוּ, with 7 mss. (Kittel).

[8] So LXX, Peshitta, Targum.

meaning either "when they sought to restrain him" or "when he was in their power."[9] This second interpretation is improbable in view of the position of *b⁰yadam* in the middle of the description of David's actions. The parallelism with בְּעֵינֵיהֶם likewise supports the suggestion that *b⁰yadam* means *ba'adam*, "for their benefit." The meaning is, accordingly, "He changed his behavior in their sight and pretended to be mad for their sake."

Conversely, *b⁰'ad* is apparently used for *b⁰yad* in Joel 2 8b (וּבְעַד הַשֶּׁלַח יִפֹּלוּ לֹא יִבְצָעוּ) which is generally interpreted, "the locusts throw themselves among the weapons and they are not injured."[10] But if *b⁰'ad* is a misspelling of *b⁰yad*, the passage is clearer: "Though they (i. e. many of them) fall by the sword, they do not stop (their advance)."

Moreover, *yad* has been misunderstood in several other passages where it is used metaphorically. So in Job 20 10: בָּנָיו יְרַצּוּ דַלִּים וְיָדָיו תָּשֵׁבְנָה אוֹנוֹ. Zophar has described the end of the sinner in 20 5-9, and declared in 10a that his sons will appease the poor whom their late father had despoiled. At this point *yadav* in 10b can hardly refer to the dead sinner's hands.[11] It has therefore been proposed to read וִידֵיהֶם for וְיָדָיו and make the suffix refer to "sons" in stich *a*, or read וִילָדָיו, in which case תָּשֵׁבְנָה must be emended to יָשִׁיבוּ, an even less likely remedy.[12] A simpler expedient is at hand. The Talmud uses "knee," in the meaning "limb, extension," as in the legal maxim: יורש כרעיה דאבוה (B. *Erub*, 70a), "an heir is the knee (i. e. limb, extension) of his father." From it there has developed the common saying ברא כרעיה דאבוה (a son is the limb of his father). If like "knee," *yad* (=hand) is used metaphorically to mean "limb, off-shoot," hence "offspring," the passage in Job would then exhibit perfect parallelism:

> "His children shall appease the poor,
> And his offspring shall return his wealth."

[9] The former is the view of Thenius and Driver; the latter of Kimḥi.

[10] English Versions, BDB, Bewer in ICC *ad loc.*

[11] So Driver-Gray, who are aware of the difficulties, the Jewish Version, and most commentators.

[12] So Budde in Kittel, *Biblia Hebraica.*

This metaphorical use of *yad* apparently occurs in two other passages. In II Sam 18 18, we are told that Absalom erected a pillar during his life-time, "because he said, 'I have no son to keep my name in remembrance,' — and he called the pillar after his own name, and it is called *Yad Absalom* to this day." The phrase is generally rendered "the monument of Absalom." But Absalom's statement that he is erecting the pillar as a substitute for the immortality conferred by children would indicate that the phrase *Yad Absalom* carries at least the secondary sense, "the offspring of Absalom."

Finally, the same sense gives particular power to the passage in Is 56 5: וְנָתַתִּי לָהֶם בְּבֵיתִי וּבְחוֹמֹתַי יָד וָשֵׁם טוֹב מִבָּנִים וּבָנוֹת שֵׁם עוֹלָם אֶתֶּן לוֹ אֲשֶׁר לֹא יִכָּרֵת. The prophet comforts the God-fearing eunuchs, who, in their despair, have declared "I am but a dried-up tree" (56 3), by assuring them: "I will give them in my house and my ramparts an offspring and a name better than [physical] sons and daughters, an eternal name will I give them that will never be cut off."

Rendering *yad* in these two passages as "memorial," as is generally done, is an adequate translation, but it does not reveal the nuance of meaning inherent in the Hebrew word — which a western language cannot easily express.

THE scholarly world continues to await with eagerness the full publication of the texts, with facsimiles, of the various manuscripts in the possession of the Syrian Orthodox church and of the Hebrew University, which have been hailed as "the greatest manuscript discovery of modern times." In the meantime, we must be grateful for the partial publication of material from the Habbakkuk Scroll with translation and notes by Dr. N. H. Brownlee[1] and above all for Professor E. L. Sukenik's sumptuously printed volume,[2] which contains selections from the "Wars of the Sons of Light and the Sons of Darkness," the "Songs of Thanksgiving," and the "Isaiah Scroll."

I

Even this partial publication makes it possible to offer a few exegetical and textual observations.

In Tablet XIII of the "Songs of Thanksgiving" we read (p. 32):

בנפול קו על משפט
וגורל אף על נעזבים
ובהתך המה על נעלבים
וקץ הרון לכול בליעל

Sukenik interprets naᶜalāmīm (or neᶜelāmīm) in line 3 as "weak, lacking in protection" and cites as a parallel Nah. 3:11:

Gam att tiškᵉrīy tᵉhīy naᶜalāmāh, gam att tᵉbhakkᵉšiy māᶜōz meᵓoyēbh.

[1] Cf. *BASOR*, No. 112 (1948), pp. 8 ff.

[2] *Megillot Genuzot* (Jerusalem, 1948).

Aside from the grave difficulties of the Nahum passage, which the commentators are constrained to emend,[3] the parallelism of naᶜᵃalāmīm with bᵉlīya ᶜal in our text indicates that the word refers to evildoers, not to the victims of injustice.

The true biblical parallel to this passage, which is incidentally confirmed by it, is Ps. 26:4:

Lōᵓ yāšabhtīy ᶜim mᵉthēy šāv vᵉᵓim naᶜalāmīm lōᵓ ᵓābhōᵓ.

Here the word is generally interpreted as meaning "those who conceal themselves, i.e., their thoughts, hence dissemblers."[4] However, we should then have expected an active form like maᶜalīmīm. Moreover, the explanation offered is strained and far-fetched.

Another etymology for na ᶜalāmīm, suggested in part by the usage in Psalms and in the newly discovered texts, may be proposed, which, incidentally, recovers a lost Hebrew word.

The MT of I Sam. 12:3 reads:

וּמִיַּד מִי לָקַחְתִּי כֹפֶר וְאַעְלִים עֵינַי בּוֹ

From whose hand have I received any bribe (or, ransom) to blind mine eyes therewith [AV, Jewish Version].

This rendering "therewith" attempts to evade the difficulty that ᶜālam, "hide," is governed universally by min and not by

[3] Thus Brown, Driver, Briggs, *Lexicon*, *s.v.* pronounces the text "very doubtful"; Driver reads neᶜᵉláphāh. J. M. P. Smith, *ICC on Nahum* (New York, 1911), p. 345, interprets the Massoretic reading, on the analogy of ᶜataph and ᶜalaph, as "be powerless."

[4] So BDB, following the Vss. and the commentators, both medieval and modern.

beth (Lev. 4:13; Num. 5:13; II Kings 4:27; cf. ᵓaᶜlīm ᶜeynay mikkem, Isa. 1:15) The LXX in Samuel has ἐξέλασμα καὶ ὑπόδημα; ἀποκρίθητε κατ᾽ ἐμοῦ, which represents a Hebrew text כֹּפֶר וְנַעֲלִים עֲנוּ בִי. The Greek of Ben Sira 46:19, which refers to the prophet Samuel and is obviously based upon our passage, reads χρήματα καὶ ἕως ὑποδημάτων ἀπὸ πάσης σαρκὸς οὐκ εἴληφα. This has been invoked as evidence for the reading *naᶜalayīm* instead of *veᵓaᶜlīm* in Samuel.[5] This reading is additionally supported by Amos 2:6; 8:6, where *naᶜalayīm* is parallel to *keseph* in the sense of "a bribe in judgment." Recently, the effort to defend the reading "pair of shoes" has been made on archeological grounds.[6]

Nonetheless, Driver's objections to this reading in Samuel are still valid: "*kōpher* and *naᶜalayīm* do not agree very well together . . . and it may be questioned whether a pair of shoes would be a bribe likely to be offered a judge."[7]

The key to the solution lies in the Hebrew Genizah text of Ben Sira, which

[5] So Thenius, Wellhausen, Kittel, *BH*.

[6] Cf. A. E. Speiser, "Of Shoes and Shekels" in *BASOR*, No. 77 (1940), pp. 15 ff. He cites two Nuzi tablets (*Harvard Semitic Series*, V, 76, and V, 17) where a shoe is used as a legal symbol. In the first, in return for a dowry, a daughter gives her father a present of "one pair of shoes, one garment, one sheep, one sow with ten pigs." In the second, a man receives a girl as an outright gift from her father (*makannu*), in return for which the father gets only "a cloak and a pair of shoes." Speiser, following Koschaker, regards the shoes as token-payments to validate special transactions. That this usage is related to the incident in Ruth 4:7 seems probable (though cf. E. R. Lacheman in *JBL*, LVI, pp. 53 ff. for another view). But, especially since a simpler interpretation is available, it is not applicable to the passages in Samuel and Amos, which Speiser is forced to explain as a reference to "the oppression of the poor by means which may be legal, but do not conform to the spirit of the law" (*ibid.*, p. 88). The usage in Amos "for the sake of" *baᶜabhūr naᶜalayim* (for which read *naᶜalam*) militates against such an interpretation, as it clearly indicates that *nᶜlm*, like its parallel *ksp*, is the object of the corrupt practice, not the means.

[7] S. R. Driver, *Notes on the Hebrew Text of the Book of Samuel* (Oxford, 1890), p. 69.

reads כֹּפֶר וְנַעֲלָם בִּמֵי לְקַחְתִּי. Unfortunately, scholars have emended it to read *kōpher vᵉna ᶜalayīm*, "ransom and shoes," to conform with the Greek,[8] ignoring the independent testimony of the Syriac *šuḥādā wᵉkurbhānā*, "bribe and offering." This latter rendering clearly presupposes a noun, probably נַעֲלָם (or נַעֲלֶם) synonymous with *kōpher*. That this uncommon noun might be misunderstood by the Greek translator and taken to be the common dual form for "shoes" is much more likely than that the Syriac failed to recognize the ordinary word for shoes, *naᶜalayīm*.

In sum, the Hebrew of Ben Sira has here preserved a Hebrew noun *naᶜalām*, meaning "bribe, lit. concealing substance" from ᶜ*alam* "hide," for which we may compare *kōpher* (Amos. 5:12; Ps. 49:8; Prov. 6:35) from Hebrew *kāphar*, Arabic *kafara*, "cover," and *kesūth ᶜeynayīm*, "a covering of the eyes, hence, compensation" (Gen. 20:16).[9] This word originally occurred in Amos. 2:6; 8:6, where it is an excellent parallel to *keseph*, and in I Sam. 12:3 which read:

וּמִיַּד־מִי לָקַחְתִּי כֹּפֶר וְנַעֲלָם עֲנוּ בִי

From whose hand have I taken ransom-money or a bribe; testify against me.

Nouns with prefixed nun are uncommon, and this doubtless helped to induce the error. However the *naktāl* form has its analogies in *naphtūlīm*, "wrestlings" (Gen. 30:8), and particularly in such Mishnic forms as *naḥtōm* (from *ḥātam*), "baker of bread in molds"; *naḥšōl* (from *ḥāšal*), "crushing wind," corresponding to the Syriac *maḥšōlā* and *niṣōk* (from *yāṣak*),

[8] So I. Lévi, Smend, *ad loc.*

[9] Similarly, Ben Sira, which alone preserves the correct form of the noun, is our only literary source for the term אֲשִׁיחַ "reservoir" (50:3) which occurs elsewhere only in the Mesha Inscription (1.9) as אֲשִׁיחַ.

"uninterrupted flow of liquid" (M. Toh. 8:9).[10]

Lack of familiarity with this uncommon noun led the vocalizers to assume that the final syllable was the *defectiva* (and older) spelling of the diphthong *ai*. Cf. *l-l-h* and *ṣ-h-r-m*. on Mesha Inscription (l. 15), for Hebrew *lāylāh* and *ṣohᵒrayīm; dōthān* (Gen. 37:17) by the side of *dōthayīm*, and *kartān* (Josh. 21:32) by the side of *kiryāthayīm*; such Moabite examples as *k-r-y-t-n* (l. 10), *b-t d-b-l-tn* (l. 30), and *ḥ-w-r-n-n* (l. 31), corresponding to Hebrew *kiryāthayīm* (Jer. 48:1), *bēth dibhlāthayīm* (*ibid.*, 48:22), and *ḥōrōnayīm* (*ibid.*, 48:34), as well as such Kethib-Qere variations as II Sam. 3:7 לאביגל Kethib; לאביגיל Qere; II Kings 14:2 יהועדין Kethib; יהועדן Qere; and the common *defectiva* spelling of Jerusalem without a yod in the closing syllable.[11]

The noun *naᶜalam*, "bribe," was evidently used synecdochically for "men of bribes, corruption"; cf. *lᵉkhol belīyaᶜal* in the text for *lekhol ʾanšey bᵉlīyaᶜal* and probably *mišpāṭ* for *ʾansey mišpāṭ*. This is its meaning in Ps. 27:7 and it now reappears in the same meaning in the "Songs of Thanksgiving." Thus stichs *a* and *b*, which refer to the righteous (*mišpāṭ* and *neᶜezābhīm*) are parallel, as are stichs *c* and *d*, relating to the wicked (*naᶜalāmīm* and *bᵉlīyaᶜal*).

II

With regard to the Isaiah texts, it is noteworthy that the scroll sheds light on the genesis and character of the Kethib-Qere readings in the Massoretic text.

As has been demonstrated elsewhere,[12] there are three early groups of Kethib-Qere variations: (*a*) those designed to guard against pronouncing the Tetragrammaton, (*b*) those replacing terms felt to be obscene, and (*c*) guides to the reader against mispronouncing words written *defectiva* in the biblical text. The bulk of Kethib-Qere readings, however, represent variants, which early guardians of the text sought to preserve against extinction by writing them upon the margin. The new Isaiah text bears welcome witness to the *variational character* of both the Kethib and the Qere readings and to *their antiquity*.[13] Thus in the Massoretic text of Isa. 42, two Kethib-Qere variations occur. In verse 20 the Kethib is *rāʾithā*, the Qere *rāʾōth*; in verse 24 the Kethib is *limᵉšōseh*,[14] the Qere *limᵉšisāh*. The Jerusalem manuscript has in its text the Kethib reading in verse 20, spelled ראיתה, and the Qere reading לבושיה0 in verse 24.

III

The style of the "Songs of Thanksgiving" is not easily described. It is true that it does not resemble that of the medieval *paiṭanīm*, nor is it identical with that of the early Jewish prayers.[15] The closest analogy is with some of the biblical Thanksgiving psalms, whether in Psalms,

---

[10] On *naktōl* as parallel to *naktāl* cf. such *miktāl–miktōl* forms as *mistār* and *mistōr* (Isa. 4:6) *mišlāḥ* and *mišlōaḥ*, *maʾakhāl* and *maʾakhōleth*, etc.

[11] For other examples, which constitute a special category in the Kethib-Qere, cf. Gordis, *The Biblical Text in the Making* (Philadelphia, 1937) p. 100 and notes.

[12] *Ibid.*, pp. 29–66.

[13] The view is maintained there, pp. 45 ff., that this collation of manuscripts, which produced the bulk of the Kethib-Qere readings, took place in the first century c.e., probably before the destruction of the Temple in 70 c.e. The fact that the Rabbinic schools of Akiba and Ishmael of the early second century c.e. subject the text to detailed scrutiny and frequently differ considerably in their interpretations, but do not raise the question of the reading of the text, is evidence that in their day the official text was already established. To the other considerations there advanced, we hope to add new evidence in the near future.

[14] On the *Poᶜel* form of the Kethib here, cf. *op. cit.*, pp. 135 and 187, n. 322a.

[15] Cf. H. L. Ginsberg, in *BASOR*, No. 112 (1948), p. 22.

Daniel, Nehemiah, or Chronicles. But there is a significant difference.

Thus in Tablet XII (Sukenik, p. 30), we read:

למזורה יבקע אפעה ושוא

Sukenik correctly notes that the author utilized the passage in Isa. 59:5 *v^ehazzūreh tibbāka ʾeph^ceh* but that he uses *ʾeph^ceh* not in the meaning of "viper" as there, but as equivalent to אפע, which occurs, perhaps as an error for אפס, in the meaning of "nothingness" in Isa. 41:24; hence the phrase *ʾeph^ceh vāšāv*. This rhetorical procedure foreshadows the conceits of the medieval Hebrew poets, who indulged in the combination of various biblical passages to produce new and sometimes startling effects.[16]

Only further investigation will determine the significance of this usage for the history of post-biblical Hebrew poetry and for the date and provenance of these "Songs."[17]

[16] The very passage from Tablet XIII discussed above may exhibit another example of this practice, in the juxtaposition of *mišpāṭ* and *na^calāmîm*. In Eccles. 12:12 both substantives are used, the latter of course in its usual meaning "hidden," *yābhîʾ b^emišpāṭ ^cal kol ne^clām*.

[17] This paper was completed in March 1949 and accepted for publication in April 1949. Previous publication commitments by the Editor delayed its publication.

THE BIBLICAL ROOT *ŠDY–ŠD*: NOTES ON 2 SAM. i. 21; JER. xviii. 14; PS. xci. 6; JOB v. 21

I

THE value of the Ugaritic inscriptions for Biblical studies is to-day widely recognized. At times, however, their significance is indirect rather than direct, their importance residing in what they suggest

---

[1] Cf. Stein, 'Die allegorische Exegesis von Philo', in *Ztschr. f. d. A. T. Wiss.*, 1928–9 (51), pp. 20 ff.

[2] For the priority of the Pentateuch in the LXX cf. Thackeray, *The Septuagint and Jewish Worship*, pp. 11 ff.

rather than in what they contain. Such an instance, we believe, occurs in the section of the Dn'il epic (E 1, lines 34–45) recently published by Dr. H. L. Ginsberg.[1] In this passage, Dn'il, grieved by the death of a loved one, pronounces a curse of drought upon the land, in which there occurs the following line (no. 44):

bl-ṭl bl-rbb bl-šr' thmtm.

'Let there be neither dew nor rain nor upsurging of the Deep.'

Both in thought and phrasing, this line resembles, as Ginsberg has noted, the lament of David over Saul and Jonathan in 2 Sam. i, in which ver. 21 a is particularly difficult:

הָרֵי בַגִּלְבֹּעַ אַל־טַל וְאַל־מָטָר עֲלֵיכֶם וּשְׂדֵי תְרוּמֹת

The Masoretic text is usually rendered:

'Let there be no dew nor rain upon you nor fields of offerings.'[2]

This is taken to mean that David lays a curse on the hills of Gilboa that there be no fields bearing fine fruits, worthy of being set aside for sacred imposts. That this is far-fetched and unsatisfactory is obvious, and emendations have therefore been copious, none of which commend themselves. In fact, they amply justify H. P. Smith's judgement that 'the variety of suggestions shows the difficulty of the reading'.[3]

On the basis of the Ugaritic parallel בל שרע תהמתם, Ginsberg now emends וּשְׂדֵי תְרוּמֹת into ושרע תהומות. He interprets שרע from the Arabic عرس 'hasten', meaning here 'surge upward'.

The change of תרומות into תהומות has much to recommend it, the two words being graphically very close. The suggested reading of ושרע for ושדי is, however, unconvincing, Graphically, the words are too far distant, and the testimony of the Versions is unanimous in reading the consonants in the meaning of 'fields'. Moreover, the interpretation of שרע in the meaning of 'upsurge' or 'inrush'[4] is insufficiently attested.

We believe that the solution to the difficulty can be found without

[1] 'A Ugaritic Parallel to 2 Sam. i. 21' in *J.B.L.* lvii, Part II, June 1938, pp. 209 ff.

[2] So LXX, ἀγροὶ ἀπαρχῶν; Aquila, ἀφαιρευμάτων; Vulgate, *nequi sint agri primitiarum.* So Syriac ܣܡܐܠ ܘܚܕܒܝ܏. This view is adopted by the medieval Jewish commentators; cf. Kimhi, *ad loc.*, who is followed by Authorized Version, as above, and the Jewish Version, which renders תרומות as 'choice fruits'.

[3] *I.C.C.*, on Samuel (New York, 1899), p. 262. The suggestions advanced may be studied there and in Brown–Driver–Briggs Lexicon, s.v. תרומה, p. 929 a.

[4] So T. H. Gaster, who edited the same text in *Studi i Materiali di Storia delle Religioni*, 1937, xv, pp. 28, 49.

recourse to such radical emendation of the Masoretic text. Here a brief preliminary discussion is necessary. Both Syriac and Aramaic possess a root ܐܫܕ, אשד meaning 'to pour'.[1] Almost as frequent is the related tertiae-Yod root ܫܕܐ, שדא also meaning 'to throw, pour (of water, blood)'.[2] Arabic also possesses a cognate root سدو, سدى signifying, among other meanings,[3] 'become moist', as in the nouns سَدً 'moisture, especially dew', سَدَى 'night-dew'.

On the basis of this well-attested Semitic root and its derivatives in Arabic, Syriac, and Aramaic, the passage in Samuel becomes clear. We need merely revocalize the Masoretic שְׂדֵי as שְׂדִי,[4] a noun analogous to בְּכִי, דְּלִי, שְׁבִי, צְלִי, חֲרִי, &c. and adopt the reading תְּהֹמוֹת for תְּרוּמוֹת. The text then read as follows:

הָרֵי בַגִּלְבֹּעַ אַל־טַל וְאַל־מָטָר עֲלֵיכֶם וּשְׂדִי תְהֹמוֹת[5]

It now yields a powerful and unforced meaning:

> O hills of Gilboa,
> Let there be no dew nor rain upon you,
> Nor outpouring of the Depths.

---

[1] Pešiṭṭa on Lam. ii. 4; iv. 1, 13 for Hebrew שפך. Cf. T. B. Shabbat 156 a אשיד דמא and often.

[2] For the Syriac usage, cf. Payne-Smith, *Thesaurus Syriacus*, p. 4064, who quotes 'canales quae aquas ܠܥܩܪ̈ܐ ܡܝܐ ducunt ad radices plantarum'. Cf. Targum Onkelos at Lev. xvii. 4 דמא שדא for דָּם שָׁפַךְ. The Targum interprets Eccles. ii. 8 שָׂדָה וְשִׁדּוֹת as מרזבין דשדין מיא פשורי ומרוזבין דשדין מיא חמימי 'gutters discharging lukewarm and hot waters', thus illustrating the use of the root. Cf. also Targ. to Ps. lxii. 9; lxxix. 3 (for שפך), and T. B. Gittin 69 b.

[3] These roots possess two principal meanings, (1) 'stretch forth', (2) 'go at random, heedlessly'. This is of great interest semantically. Dr. Ginsberg (ibid., note 14) quotes the two distinct Arabic roots *šrʿ* 'stretch' and *srʿ* 'hasten'. In *šdy* both meanings exist in the same root, making it not unlikely that the two Arabic roots *šrʿ* and *srʿ* are related. This strengthens the view that a close relationship must originally have existed between *Sin* and *Šin* roots, and that they are the result of later differentiations rather than that the similarity is purely accidental. Cf., on שכל-סכל, our remarks in 'Studies in Hebrew Roots of Contrasted Meanings', *J.Q.R.*, N.S. xxvii, p. 56; also in *A.J.S.L.* vol. lv, July 1938, p. 272.

[4] Cp. Ezek. i. 24. where כְּקוֹל שַׁדַּי ought perhaps to be כְּקוֹל שְׂדִי [G.R.D.].

[5] We are now perhaps in a position to evaluate properly the reading of Theodotion ὄρη θανάτου. Montfaucon derives it from the Masoretic text, תרומות being misread as הָרֵי מָוֶת. So Margolis, *Notes on a New Translation of Hebrew Scriptures* (Philadelphia, 1921). Schleusner, *Lexicon in LXX* (Glasgow, 1822), p. 594 a, equates ὄρη with שְׂדֵי and reads תְּמוּתָה for תְּרוּמָה, hence θανάτου.

It seems far more likely that ὄρη θανάτου is the rendering of שְׂדוֹת הַמָּוֶת, which is derived from שדי תהמות, by misreading the Yod as a Vav and

II

The recognition of the root שדה, and the noun שָׂדַי, meaning 'out-pouring', may shed some light on a passage which has baffled all interpreters. Jer. xviii. 14 reads :

הֲיַעֲזֹב מִצּוּר שָׂדַי שֶׁלֶג לְבָנוֹן   אִם־יִנָּתְשׁוּ מַיִם זָרִים קָרִים נוֹזְלִים

The Ancient Versions testify to the Masoretic text at all doubtful points, even when they err in the reading,[1] but their interpretations are valueless from the exegetical standpoint. The prevailing view of the passage is somewhat as follows :

'Doth the snow of Lebanon fail from the rock of the field, or are the strange, cold flowing waters plucked up ? '[2]

The difficulties of the passage are obvious. The word-order in stich. *a* is exceedingly harsh (verb, modifiers, subject). As Driver well says, 'rock of the field' is a strange expression, even if it refers to Lebanon and נתש 'plucked up' is not a suitable word for water. Moreover, it should be noted that עזב always governs the accusative and never is followed by מִן *loci*.[3]

An alternative view of stich. *a* takes שֶׁלֶג לְבָנוֹן as the object of הֲיַעֲזֹב and supplies an indefinite subject for the verb (הָעוֹזֵב), ren-dering :

'Would any man desert the snow of Lebanon, coming from the rock of the field ? '[4]

This interpretation has the advantage of reducing the harshness of the word-order, but it does not solve the other difficulties.

In the light of the interpretation for the root *šdy* set forth above, we should like to make the following suggestions :

שָׂדַי should be revocalized as שְׂדִי 'outpouring, torrent '.

מִצּוּר cannot be governed by הֲיַעֲזֹב. It is to be connected with שְׂדִי 'the torrent from the rocks '.

joining the Tav to the first word. Incidentally, this would attest the spelling תְּהֹמוֹת, and not תְּהֹמֹת or תְּהֹמֹת, as given by Ginsberg, ibid., p. 213.

[1] Thus שָׂדַי is taken by LXX, Pešiṭta, and Symmachus in the sense of 'breast' (שָׁדַיִם); זָרִים is mistakenly read as זֵדִים by LXX; and קָרִים misread as קָדִים, likewise by LXX.

[2] So Jewish Version, and, essentially, S. R. Driver, *Book of the Prophet Jeremiah* (London, 1909), p. 108, who follows Cocceius in changing ינתשו into יִנָּשְׁתוּ 'be dried up' (cf. Isa. xix. 5; xli. 17; Jer. li. 30). ^

[3] Cf. Isa. xxxi. 7; 2 Kings vii. 7; Jer. xii. 7, xxv. 38; Ezek. viii. 12, ix. 9—and frequently.

[4] So AV, following Kimhi. Rashi (first interpretation) and Kara explain it similarly.

יִנְתָּשׁוּ, as Kimhi already recognized, is equivalent to יִנָּטְשׁוּ. Barth [1] has pointed out that the softer *Ta* frequently appears in Arabic instead of the emphatic *Ta* of other Semitic languages, when a liquid is near by. He compares قتل and קטל, تلتل and טִלְטֵל (Isa. xxii. 17 and Mishnic Hebrew). Nor is this interchange limited to liquids, as شَتم = שָׁטַם demonstrates. Prof. G. R. Driver kindly calls my attention to the identical phenomenon within Biblical Hebrew, as in טעה and תעה, חטף and חתף (Job ix. 12). נתש would then be an aberrant orthography for נטש. This suggestion is considerably strengthened, when it is recalled that the parallelism of עזב ||נטש is frequent in Biblical Hebrew.[2]

With הַיַעֲזֹב, an indefinite subject, הָעוֹזֵב, should be understood.[3]

זָרִים in its normal sense of 'strange' is out of place here. It is, however, attested by all the Versions. Vulgate and Targum, however, derive it from the root זרם, interpreting it as זֶרֶם 'stream' or tacitly emending it thus. Similarly in Isa. i. 7 וּשְׁמָמָה כְּמַהְפֵּכַת זָרִים is interpreted by Saadiah as equivalent to 'desolation like the overthrow of a torrent'.[4] זָרִים in our passage may be an alternative form to זֶרֶם, like קָדִים and קֶדֶם, or it may be preferable to correct זָרִים to זֶרֶם.[5]

Moreover, it is not Israel that is being contrasted with the faithful stream, flowing down from the snows of Lebanon, as Prof. S. R. Driver and other interpreters assert. It seems to us, rather, that the metaphor relates to Jahveh. It is the God of Israel who is being compared to the life-giving waters of the mountain-torrent, which no sensible person would forsake. Yet Israel flies in the face of nature and common sense, in order to betray its Maker. This same idea Jeremiah has forcibly expressed in ii. 12, 13:

> Be astonished, O ye heavens, at this,
> And be horribly afraid, be ye exceeding amazed,
> Saith the Lord.
> For My people have committed two evils:
> They have forsaken Me, the fountain of living waters,
> And hewed them out cisterns, broken cisterns,
> That can hold no water.

---

[1] *Etymologische Studien* (Leipzig, 1893), pp. 35 ff.

[2] Cf. 1 Kings viii. 57; Jer. xii. 7; Ps. xxvii. 9, xciv. 14.

[3] Cf. Gen. xi. 9, xvi. 14, xlviii. 1, 2; Exod. xv. 23 and Ges.–Kautzsch (25th ed.), sec. 144, 3.

[4] Cf. also Dunash, *Teshuvot Dunash 'al Rab Saadiah*, p. 8, as well as Ibn Ezra and Kimhi, *ad loc.*

[5] Would מַיִם זָרִים, as an appositional phrase, be equivalent to זֶרֶם מַיִם (Isa. xxviii. 2; Hab. iii. 10)?

We therefore suggest that our passage be read and interpreted as follows :

שֶׁלֶג לְבָנוֹן   הֲיַעֲזֹב מִצּוּר שָׂדַי[1]

קָרִים נוֹזְלִים   אִם־יִנָּתְשׁוּ מַיִם זָרִים

לַשָּׁוְא יְקַטֵּרוּ   כִּי שְׁכֵחֻנִי עַמִּי

שְׁבִילֵי (ק׳) עוֹלָם   וַיַּכְשִׁלוּ בְּדַרְכֵיהֶם[2]

'Does one leave the torrent from the rocks,
    The snow of Lebanon,
Are the waters of the stream abandoned
    Cold and flowing,
That my people has forgotten me,
    Burning incense to vanity,
And they stumble in their ways,
    The tracks of old?'

Incidentally this view restores the appropriate Kinah-rhythm (3 : 2) for the passage, and for the entire section (xviii. 12–17).

III

The permutations of the root under discussion are not exhausted by *'šd* and *šdy*. In Syriac we also find a well-authenticated root ܫܕܐ meaning (*a*) 'pour', (*b*) 'rush with force'.[3] As a matter of fact, this root occurs in Biblical Hebrew, though it has been confused with *šdd*.

In Ps. xci. 6 מִדֶּבֶר בָּאֹפֶל יַהֲלֹךְ מִקֶּטֶב יָשׁוּד צָהֳרָיִם, יָשׁוּד has been taken as a metaplastic *mediae-Vav* form of the root שדד 'devastate',[4] and the clause has been accordingly rendered: 'Nor of the destruction that wasteth at noonday'.

יָשׁוּד is, however, parallel to יַהֲלֹךְ and requires a more concrete

---

[1] Or שְׂדֵי צוּרִים, to preserve the parallelism of the construction [G.R.D.].

[2] In ver. 15, וַיַּכְשִׁלוּם has no subject, unless taken reflexively (so Kara, *ad loc.*), but this is a dubious procedure. It is therefore best to follow LXX and Pešiṭṭa and read וַיִּכָּשְׁלוּ בְּדַרְכֵיהֶם, the Mem being an erroneous ditto-graphy for the Bet of בדרכיהם. For examples of errors resulting from the similarity of ב and מ, cf. 2 Sam. v. 13 (by the side of 2 Chron. xiv. 3); 2 Kings xiv. 13 (as against 2 Chron. xxv. 23); Ezek. xxvii. 18 (see ver. 16); Isa. xxxviii. 9 (cf. Ps. xvi. 1). Cf. also the Kethib in Joshua iii. 16 באדם and the Qere מאדם, and other examples in Gordis, *Biblical Text in the Making, a Study of the Kethib-Qere* (Philadelphia, 1937), p. 143 f.

Because both words in the stich. (ויכשלו בדרכיהם) are long, they receive three beats in the rhythm. Cf. Ps. ii. 3 ננתקה את מוסרותימו ונשליכה ממנו עבותימו, where stich. *a* likewise receives three beats for the same reason.

[3] See Payne-Smith, *Thesaurus Syriacus*, pp. 4088–9 and references there.

[4] So *B.D.B.*; Ges.-K., sec. 67, n. 3.

sense than 'waste'. Reifman has therefore emended it to יָשׁוֹט, but
the change is unnecessary, if the root שׁוּד be recognized in the meaning 'rush with force'. In fact, Pešiṭta translates the passage by its
cognate: ܘܡܢ ܚܫܐ ܕܒܐܝܡܡܐ.[1]
The verse is rendered:

> (Thou shalt not fear)
> The plague that stalks at night,
> Nor the pestilence that rushes at noon.

IV

The recognition of this root שׁוּד helps to clarify the beautiful but
enigmatic passage in Job v. 19–23, in which Eliphaz pictures the
eventual escape of the righteous from calamity:

ובשבע לא יגע בך רע	בשש צרות יצילך
ובמלחמה מידי חרב	ברעב פדך ממות
ולא תירא משוד כי יבוא	בשוט לשן תחבא
ומחית הארץ אל תירא	לשד ולכפן תשחק
וחית השדה השלמה לך	כי עם אבני השדה בריתך

Commentators have found several problems in these verses:[2]

1. The plagues listed total not seven but nine, if ver. 23 is included
(רעב, מלחמה, שוט לשן, שוד, שד, כפן, חית הארץ, אבני השדה and
חית השדה).

2. If, on the other hand, ver. 23 is not regarded as part of the
enumeration, as some authorities assume, the remaining distresses
are not seven but six or five. For some of the plagues seem duplica-
tions:
שׁוֹד (ver. 21) and שֹׁד (ver. 22); רעב (ver. 20) and כפן (ver. 22);
חית הארץ (ver. 22), and חית השדה (ver. 23).

3. In ver. 21 שׁוֹט לָשׁן is usually interpreted literally as 'the
scourge of the tongue, i.e. slander'.[3] In this sense, however, it
scarcely parallels the other perils, all of which are scourges caused
by nature and not by man, and affecting not one individual but an
entire country-side, at the very least.

4. Another difficulty, not hitherto noticed, affords a clue to the

[1] Cf. also Targum שדיא נשיב 'a tempest blowing'. [Cp. Brockelmann,
Lex. Syr.[2] 762 under ܚܒ.]

[2] For an illuminating discussion of the passage as a whole see Driver–Gray,
I.C.C. on Job, vol. i, pp. 56 ff.; vol. ii, pp. 32 f.

[3] So Ibn Ezra, doubtfully, followed by most moderns. This may have
been the view of our phrase held by Ben Sira, who speaks of μάστιξ γλώσσης
'the scourge of the tongue' (xxvi. 6). In that passage, however, he discusses
various types of slander, where the phrase is appropriate. It occurs, too, in
the extant Hebrew of Ben Sira li. 2 b: פציתני מדבת עם משוט דבת לשן
ומשפת שטי שקר. Cf. Smend, Israel Lévi, and Oesterley-Box (in Charles,
Apocrypha and Pseudepigrapha of the O.T., Oxford 1913), ad loc.

solution of the problem. It is noteworthy that, on the basis of the present exegesis, the long list of distresses .does not mention the scourges of fire and storm. The omission of such outstanding calamities [1] is especially inexplicable in the face of the Prologue, where the 'fire from heaven' (i. 16) and the 'great wind' (ver. 19) play so ominous a role.[2]

To meet these difficulties, various expedients have been suggested, particularly the excision of ver. 22, and other emendations of the text.[3] It seems, however, that the problems raised by the passage may be solved without violence to the received text.

We have noted the apparent absence of 'fire' and 'water' among the 'distresses' mentioned. We believe that they are to be sought in ver. 21. For, as has already been noticed, בְּשׁוֹט לָשׁוֹן is inappropriate in the sense of 'slander'. It is, however, eminently in place as an elliptical expression for בְּשׁוֹט לְשׁוֹן אֵשׁ 'In the scourge of the tongue of fire'.[4] We may compare Isa. v. 24 כֶּאֱכֹל קַשׁ לְשׁוֹן אֵשׁ and ibid. xxx. 27 וּלְשׁוֹנוֹ כְּאֵשׁ אֹכָלֶת. Perhaps, too, בְּשׁוֹט is to be corrected into מִשּׁוֹט (from the scourge),[5] or, preferably, revocalized as בְּשׁוּט [6] (infinitive construct of שׁוּט 'rove, wander ').

As for שׁוֹד in stich. b of ver. 21, we propose that it be taken as a noun derived from the root שׁוּד 'rush with power, pour'. שׁוֹד would therefore mean 'an outpouring of rain or of wind', i.e. a torrent or a tempest.[7]

Including ver. 23, seven distresses are given: (1) famine, (2) war, (3) fire, (4) flood, (5) dearth,[8] (6) the beasts of the field, (7) the stones

---

[1] We may compare the text of the Jewish High Holy Day Prayer: בראש השנה יכתבו וביום צום כפור יחתמון··· מי באש ומי במים מי בחרב ומי בחיה מי ברעב ומי בצמא מי ברעש ומי במגפה (N. M. Adler, *The Service of Synagogue*, Day of Atonement, p. 150).

[2] Even if one does not assume that the author of the Dialogue had a prose *Volksbuch* before him, which he reworked, it is obvious that the storm bulked large in Hebrew consciousness. This the early conception of Jahveh as God of the storm abundantly attests. Cf. Judges v. 4 f.; 2 Sam. xxii. 8 ff.; Nahum i. 4 ff.; Ps. xxix *passim*, lxviii, 8 f.; Job xxxviii. 1, &c.

[3] Beer, Budde, and Duhm eliminate the verse. Cf. also Torczyner (*Das Buch Hiob*, Vienna, 1920) for a brilliant but unconvincing emendation of the verse. For other proposed changes see Driver–Gray, loc. cit.

[4] So Ehrlich, who compares Joshua xv. 2 where הַלָּשׁוֹן represents לְשׁוֹן הַיָּם (cf. ver. 5). Torczyner rejects Ehrlich's interpretation on inadequate grounds.

[5] So LXX, Pešiṭṭa, Vulgate, Driver–Gray.

[6] So Saadiah, Budde, Ehrlich, Torczyner.

[7] שׁוֹד is, incidentally, written plene in ver. 21, and defective in ver. 22 (cf. Kittel, *Biblia Hebraica*, 3rd ed., *ad loc.*).

[8] לְשֹׁד וּלְכָפָן in ver. 22 are to be understood as a hendiadys = לְשֹׁד כָּפָן 'the calamity of dearth' since שֹׁד 'destruction' is too general to belong to this catalogue of specific plagues. As an example of hendiadys, cf. Gen. iii. 16 עִצְּבוֹנֵךְ וְהֵרֹנֵךְ = the pain of thy conception '.

of the field.[1] Verse 21 is then to be rendered as follows:

> When the tongue of fire stalks about, thou shalt be hidden,
> Nor shalt thou fear the coming of the torrent.[2]

V

Perhaps this meaning of שׁוֹד = 'surging of wind or rain, tempest' occurs also in Isa. xiii. 6 : הֵילִילוּ כִּי קָרוֹב יוֹם יהוה כְּשֹׁד מִשַּׁדַּי יָבוֹא.
The usual rendering is:

> Howl ye, for the day of the Lord is at hand,
> As destruction from the Almighty shall it come.[3]

It yields however little meaning to announce that the Day of Jahveh comes like a destruction from God. On our view, it should be rendered:

> Howl, for the day of the Lord is at hand,
> Like a storm from the Almighty[1] will it come.

The same interpretation would, naturally, apply to Joel i. 15, virtually a duplication of the Isaianic passage.

---

[1] Or, 'the gnomes of the field', if Rashi's old suggestion, as revised by Köhler and Beer, to read בְּנֵי or אַדְנֵי for אָבְנֵי, is accepted.

[2] The character of this calamity is vividly described by Professor J. A. Montgomery in his learned and altogether delightful volume *Arabia and the Bible* (Philadelphia, 1934), p. 85, 'Other "bad lands" are the scarred and bare mountains which run parallel to the west coast of Arabia, giving the name Hijáz to the west of that watershed from its nature as a "barrier". The rainstorms break against this long ridge and produce almost in a moment raging torrents—the Arabic *sail*, spate—which sweep away all obstacles without warning and with loss of life of man and cattle, leaving the countryside barer than ever with the destruction of vegetation and the removal of the surface soil. This phenomenon illustrates the many references in the Bible, as in Psalms and Job, to "waters" as symbol of overpouring troubles, dangers, enemies, e.g. Job xxvii. 20; Ps. cxxiv. 4, 5. . . . The Arabic poetry has constant references to this phenomenon, its terrors and dangers. And modern travellers give anecdotes of its instantaneous and destructive character.'
It is highly suggestive that he adds: 'We may indeed have a technical word for this inundating spate in Isa. xxviii. 15, translated in our Versions "overflowing scourge", in which the noun (shot) means a torrent, comparing the Arabic noun سوط (Surah lxxxix. 12) and the Ethiopic verb *sôṭa*'. If it were not for the difficulty of לשׁוֹן, בשׁוֹט in our passages could be rendered as Professor Montgomery interprets Isa. xxviii. 15, and מְשׁוֹד as 'tempest' (rushing of wind). Our verse would then be translated:
'When the torrent . . . rushes in, thou shalt be hidden
Nor shalt thou fear the coming of the tempest.'

[3] So AV, Jewish Version, &c.

EXEGETICAL NOTES

A NOTE ON GEN. 24:21

וְהָאִישׁ מִשְׁתָּאֵה לָהּ מַחֲרִישׁ לָדַעַת וגו'

This verse contains two difficulties. For the first, the hapax legomenon מִשְׁתָּאֵה, several interpretations have been proposed. We may dismiss a very ancient one which derives it from שָׁתָה, and translates "drinks" or "gives to drink."[4]

Most authorities prefer the rendering "gazes," "watches," assuming that שָׁאָה is a parallel form to שָׁעָה.[5] There is, however, no evidence for this view.

A third rendering of מִשְׁתָּאֵה is "wonders," "is astonished."[6] This meaning is arrived at by noting that שָׁמֵם, which, like שָׁאָה, means "destroy," "devastate," develops the force of "be astonished" in the Hithpael, a very frequent use in later Hebrew.[7] As a matter of fact, the English words "astonish" and "astound" illustrate a similar transfer of meaning. In this manner the etymological difficulty of מִשְׁתָּאֵה is removed.

[1] Evidently Forrer also originally considered Kunulua and Kullania as two independent cities, but his localization of Kunulua "in einem grossen Tell 1, 5 km. im O vom Ḥârim, 30 km. im O vom Antakja" (*Provinzeinteilung*, pp. 56 f.) and comparison of Kullania with Balnea (*ibid.*, p. 58) are nothing but guesses.

[2] After Tomkins in *PSBA*, V (1882–83), 61, and similarly Dussaud, *op. cit.*, p. 469.

[3] Professor Olmstead informs me that he withdraws his location of Calneh in Chatal Hüyük, made on the basis of Forrer's identification, on the map in his *History of Palestine and Syria*. I take this occasion to thank him for the kind support and many suggestions he has given me for the present article.

[4] So Peshitta, which gives another rendering as well (משקא ומתבקא). Targum Onkelos, as quoted by Rashi, *ad loc.*, by Ibn Ezra in his שָׂפָה בְרוּרָה, p. 11, and by an unknown commentator, now known as סֵפֶר יָא"ר, *ad loc.*, reads שָׁתָר. The Samaritan reads מִשְׁתָּה, but its meaning is not altogether clear.

[5] So already LXX, Vulgate, Peshitta, Onkelos, and most moderns. See Brown-Driver-Briggs, Skinner, and Spurrell.

[6] So Rashi, Samuel ben Meir, and Ibn Ezra, who are followed by Delitzsch.

[7] See Genesis Rabbah, chap. 4 (end), שֶׁהַבְּרִיּוֹת מִשְׁתּוֹמְמִין, "For people wonder." Cf. also Dan. 4:16.

335

It has not been noted, however, that מַחֲרִישׁ לָדַעַת remains difficult, no matter which interpretation of מִשְׁתָּאֵה we accept. The most common rendering, "The man was watching her in silence, to know, etc.," sounds much smoother in translation than in the original Hebrew. One feels that לָדַעַת is too far removed from מִשְׁתָּאֵה to be governed by it, and that the Masoretic accents, which separate מִשְׁתָּאֵה לָהּ from מַחֲרִישׁ, have sensed the rhythm of the verse correctly. The other rendering, "The man was astonished at her, holding his peace, to know, etc.," is no better.

We therefore propose to interpret מַחֲרִישׁ in the sense of חָרַשׁ "plan," "devise." Though this verb is generally used in an evil connotation, it may be used in a favorable sense, as in Prov. 14:22, חֹרְשֵׁי טוֹב. The Hiphil in the sense of "plan" occurs in I Sam. 23:9, כִּי עָלָיו שָׁאוּל מַחֲרִישׁ הָרָעָה.

The slave is planning to learn whether his quest is successful. The next few verses tell us what his plan is. He gives Rebecca the jewels and asks her regarding her family. The verse now reads smoothly: "And the man was marveling [or gazing] at her, planning to learn[1] whether the Lord had made his journey prosperous or not."

---

[1] יָדַע in the sense of "learn to know," "discover," is very common (see BDB, p. 393b).

CRITICAL NOTES ON THE BLESSING OF MOSES
(Deut. xxxiii)

Deut. xxxiii 21

וַיַּרְא רֵאשִׁית לוֹ כִּי־שָׁם חֶלְקַת מְחֹקֵק סָפוּן

וַיֵּתֵא רָאשֵׁי עָם צִדְקַת ה' עָשָׂה וּמִשְׁפָּטָיו עִם יִשְׂרָאֵל

This verse has proved so difficult to interpret, that Driver [1] remarks 'it can hardly be made to yield tolerable sense'. Three main renderings have been suggested for stichoi b and c. They are as follows :—

1. For *there* was hidden the portion of the Lawgiver (Moses),
  And the heads of the people came. [2]

But סָפוּן really means 'panelled' and not 'hidden', and therefore the Brown-Driver-Briggs Lexicon suggests an emendation to צָפוּן. Moreover, Moses's grave on Mount Nebo was not in the portion of Gad but in that of Reuben, [3] and one fails to see how the existence of a burial plot upon it made the land desirable for settlement.

2. Most authorities therefore interpret מְחֹקֵק in a general sense, as 'commander, military chief' and compare its use in Gen. xlix 10, Judges ix 14. [4] They render :—

  For *there* a portion (worthy) of a ruler was reserved,
  And the heads of the people came.

3. Some scholars who render stichos c—'he came with the heads of the people', emend וַיֵּתֵא into וְאֵת [5] or וַיֵּתֵא אֶת [6] because of the harshness of the accusative after √אתה. This emendation is based on LXX and Vulg.,[7] who were, however, quite in the dark themselves as to the meaning

---

[1] *I.C.C.* on Deuteronomy p. 411.   [2] So Vulgate, Peshīṭṭā, Rashi.
[3] Cf. Num. xxxii 38 ; Josh. xiii 20.
[4] So Ibn Ezra, Ehrlich, Driver, Jewish Publication Society's Version.
[5] Oort, Emendationes, *ad loc.*   [6] Dillmann, Oettli, others.
[7] ἅμα, *cum.*

of the verse. Yet סָפֻן remains intrinsically difficult.[1] Apart from its cryptic sense, it destroys the metrical structure of the verse, since every other stichos has three beats and stichos b has four.

However, a simple expedient is at hand, which restores the rhythm and abolishes the difficulties of ספון and ויתא. Our suggestion is to read וַיִּתְאַסְּפֻן instead of ספון and ויתא. The error can be accounted for in the following manner. In a manuscript, the letters ספון were written above the line somewhat higher than the rest of the text, perhaps because they were omitted by error. The next copyist placed them before ויתא, taking each half as a separate word.

The corrected text has a striking parallel in verse 5 — בְּהִתְאַסֵּף רָאשֵׁי עָם. The meaning is clear:—Gad had proved himself worthy of the fertile Transjordan country, because of his prowess on the field of battle, where he had been in the van, fighting for the conquest of the land, and thus fulfilling the will of God. The rhythm too is excellent :—

כי־שֵׁם חלקת מחקק   וירא ראשית לו

ויתאספון ראשי עם

ומשפטיו עם ישראל   צדקת ה עשה

And he chose him a first part,
For *there* was a noble portion,
And the heads of the people gathered
He executed the righteousness of the Lord,
And his ordinances with Israel.

Deut. xxxiii 27

וּמִתַּחַת זְרֹעֹת עוֹלָם   מְעֹנָה אֱלֹהֵי קֶדֶם
וַיֹּאמֶר הַשְׁמֵד   וַיְגָרֶשׁ מִפָּנֶיךָ אוֹיֵב

Though the Massoretic Text is attested by all the versions, it is not devoid of difficulty. The first half of the verse is interpreted by Ehrlich [2]:—

The dwelling place of the eternal God, but beneath are the everlasting arms.

He takes מעונה as a virtual construct state with אלהי, and compares מוֹרָשָׁה קְהִלַּת יַעֲקֹב in verse 4. In his later work [3], Ehrlich prefers to emend מעונה into מִמַּעַל, feeling that מִתַּחַת in stichos b requires an explicit contrast in stichos a—and he translates :—

Above is the eternal God, but beneath are the everlasting arms.

---

[1] Ehrlich emends it into סְפוֹר.

[2] In his Hebrew commentary Mikra Kipheshuṭo *ad loc.*

[3] Randglossen *ad loc.*

Driver[1] renders :—

The eternal God is a dwelling place, and beneath are the ever-lasting arms.

But even this leaves something to be desired in point of smoothness.

Our suggestion is to derive מתחת from the root מתח 'to stretch, extend' and vocalize מְתָחַת on the analogy of מִשְׁחָה. This root occurs in the strikingly beautiful description of creation in Isa. xl; there, in verse 22, the Lord is described as :

> He that stretches out the heavens as a curtain,
> And spreads them out (וַיִּמְתָּחֵם) as a tent to dwell in.

In medieval Hebrew poetry, God is therefore described as דָּר מְתוּחִים, 'the Dweller of the outstretched (sc. heavens)'. Similarly, our author describes the heavens as 'the out-spreading of the everlasting arms'. Our verse is to be interpreted in apposition to שְׁחָקִים in verse 26. We now obtain a passage of rare power, descriptive of the warlike might of Israel's Defender :—

> There is none like the God of Jeshurun,[2]
> Who rides the skies to your help,
> And in His pride, the heavens . . .
> The dwelling place[3] of God of old,
> And the spreading of the everlasting arms . . .
> He drives the enemy before you,
> And decrees, 'Destruction'.

AN ADDITIONAL NOTE ON DEUT. 33 27

Several treatments of Deut. 33 27 have recently appeared in the columns of this JOURNAL.[1] We are adding briefly to the discussion only in order to correct a basic error in fact. The reader will recall that T. H. Gaster proposed a new interpretation of the "Blessing of Moses." As an alternative to his view, which involves the question of the structure of the poem as a whole, and requires an emendation which creates a *hapax legomenon*, we have urged the retention of the MT. When the first word is revocalized as וּמִתַּחַת "out-stretching" from the root *mātaḥ*, the passage yields a thoroughly satisfactory meaning:

> There is none like the God of Jeshurun,
> Who rides the skies to your help,
> And in His pride, the heavens,
> The dwelling-place of the God of old,
> And the out-stretching of the Everlasting Arms . . .
> He drives the enemy before you,
> And decrees, 'Destruction.'

This approach R. Marcus criticizes in these words: "The reading מְתַחַת is proposed by Gordis in the belief that in Hebrew the meanings 'to spread out' and 'to stretch out' are expressed by the same verb, מתח, and that this

---

[1] T. H. Gaster, LXVI (1947) 53–62; R. Gordis, LXVII (1948) 69–72; R. Marcus, LXVIII (1949) 29–34. My original treatment appeared in the Oxford *Journal of Theological Studies*, 34(1933), 390 ff.

verb can govern as its object a noun like זרעת 'arms,' whether in the literal or figurative sense of 'arms.' This implicit assumption I seriously doubt."

Now, astonishing as this may appear, this was never my assumption, whether implicit or otherwise. Without having had any recourse to Jastrow's *Dictionary* or to Ben Jehudah's *Thesaurus*, to which Marcus refers, it never occurred to me that *mātaḥ*, like *pāras*, might govern *zᵉrōʿōt* "arms" as its *object*. In the phrase מתחת זרעת עולם, which is in apposition with *šᵉḥāḳīm* in 26, זרעת עולם is a *subjective genitive, and not an objective genitive*, exactly as in the parallel stich, "the Dwelling-Place of the God of old," אלהי קדם is a subjective genitive!

That a competent scholar like Marcus could make this error makes it clear that it was not enough merely to propose the revocalization and cite in corroboration Isa. 40 22 and the medieval usage מתוחים "the outstretched (sc. heavens)." Obviously the phrase means, not that God stretched out His arms, but that the Everlasting Arms stretched out the heavens as a tent, a frequent figure in biblical poetry.

The vivid description of the heavens as the tent-dwelling of God, which His Everlasting Arms have stretched out, is so appropriate to the context that we still see no need to adopt Gaster's far-reaching reconstruction, or even the less drastic emendation of Marcus to read *yᵉrīʿōt* for *zᵉrōʿōt*.

To be sure, emendation is an art and scholars will naturally differ in their reaction to a given proposal. We submit that M. T. is here superior to all the suggested alternatives.

A NOTE ON JOSHUA 22:34

וַיִּקְרְאוּ בְּנֵי רְאוּבֵן וּבְנֵי גָד לַמִּזְבֵּחַ כִּי עֵד הוּא בֵּינוֹתֵינוּ

כִּי יְהוָה הָאֱלֹהִים

The syntax of this verse has always proved difficult. The Hebrew, as it stands, exhibits two peculiarities: First, we expect the name of the altar after לַמִּזְבֵּחַ; second, the final clause כִּי י' הָאֱלֹהִים seems fragmentary and incomplete.

Various solutions have been proposed for the first difficulty. The most popular is the insertion of עֵד after לַמִּזְבֵּחַ, accounting for its absence either as a textual error or as an ellipsis (מִקְרָא קָצָר). The verse is then translated: "They called the altar Ed, for it is a witness between us that the Lord is God" (so Targum as quoted by Kimhi, Rashi, the Authorized Version, and many moderns).

The version of the Jewish Publication Society frankly recognizes the lacuna in its rendering: "They called the altar ———, for it is a witness, etc."

The second difficulty is evaded by translating "For it is a witness between us that the Lord *is* God." But students of Hebrew will admit that the Hebrew for the phrase "the Lord is God" is יְהוָה הוּא הָאֱלֹהִים (cf. Deut. 4:35, 39; 7:9). Moreover, this rendering does not suit the context. The tribes of Reuben and Gad are setting up the altar, not to testify to the divinity of Jahveh, but rather to emphasize their rights to take part in his worship, together with the other Israelites. This is clearly affirmed in verse 24: "And if we have not rather done this out of anxiety about a matter, saying: In time to come your children might speak to our children saying: What have ye to do with the Lord, the God of Israel?"

If we now turn to the words כִּי עֵד הוּא בֵּינוֹתֵינוּ, we observe the emphatic position of בֵּינוֹתֵינוּ. We have here a case of "anticipation," a rhetorical device common in the classical languages and noticed by Ehrlich in Hebrew as well. Thus in Gen. 1:4, וַיַּרְא אֱלֹהִים אֶת הָאוֹר כִּי טוֹב, the word הָאוֹר, though formally the object of וַיַּרְא, is in reality the subject of the subordinate clause כִּי טוֹב. The verse is therefore the equivalent of וַיַּרְא אֱלֹהִים כִּי הָאוֹר טוֹב and is to be interpreted on that basis. The removal of הָאוֹר from the subordinate to the main clause is "anticipation."

Our verse likewise contains an instance of this change. בֵּינוֹתֵינוּ, though not the subject of the clause, is undoubtedly the most important word in it,

342

and strictly belongs to the subordinate clause. It is equal to כִּי עֵד הִיא כִּי
בֵּינוֹתֵינוּ יְ׳ הָאֱלֹהִים, "For it is a witness that between us is the Lord God."
The Lord God is not limited to the western tribes; Reuben and Gad have a
portion in him as well.

As to the first difficulty, it would seem that the entire clause from עֵד כִּי
to הָאֱלֹהִים is the name of the altar. The long names of the Assyrian and
Babylonian kings as well as such names as Maher-Shalal-Hash-Baz and
Beer-Lahai-Roi make such an assumption not unlikely for a Semitic people.

The verse ought therefore to be translated: "The sons of Reuben and the
sons of Gad called the altar: A-witness-that-the-Lord-God-is-between-us."
כִּי here as elsewhere introduces *oratio recta*, and need not appear in the translation.

A NOTE ON 1 SAM 13 21

ONCE again Professor Julius A. Bewer has made all OT students his debtors by his lucid and interesting notes on three biblical passages.[1] Particularly valuable is his contribution to the exegesis of the difficult verse, 1 Sam 13 21. His interpretation of *peṣirah* = "price" is as convincing as it is simple, and he is certainly correct in referring back LXX τρεῖς σίκλοι εἰς τὸν ὀδόντα to a consonantal text ושלש שקל לשן (cf. Driver ad. loc.). Finally, his suggestion as to the original Hebrew text is highly ingenious: וּשְׁלֹשׁ שֶׁקֶל לָשׁוֹן הַקַּרְדֻּמִּים וּלְהַצִּיב הַדָּרְבָן "and a third of a shekel for sharpening the axes and for setting the goads."

There are, however, a number of problems raised by this suggestion, which may be briefly listed as follows:

(a) The original text must be assumed to have suffered a good deal of corruption before our present MT emerged: The insertion of the Lamed in ולשלש, the loss of the Šin and the Lamed of שקל, with only the Koph remaining and coalescing with the next word to form קלשון, and the insertion of the Vav-Lamed in ולהקרדמים. (b) The Hebrew partitive use of fractions invariably requires that the principal noun be determined, generally by the article and less frequently by a construct or a suffix.[2] Hence "a third of a shekel" can only be שְׁלֹשׁ הַשֶּׁקֶל. (c) The elimination of the *hapax legomenon kilšon* from the Hebrew lexicon raises some

---

[1] In *JBL*, LXI (1942), 45–9.

[2] For the article, cf. *maḥaṣit haššekel* (Ex 30 13); *ḥaṣi ha'amah* (Ex 26 16); *šelišit hahin* (Num 15 6); *rebhi'it hayyom* (Neh 9 3); for the construct, *vaḥaṣi matteh menaššeh* (Num 34 14); *rebha' šekel keseph* (1 Sam 9 8); for the suffix *ḥaṣi zekanam* (2 Sam 10 4).

doubts. The word itself occurs in the Targum to Ecc 12 11 for *masmerot* (=nails), but this solitary example may, as Driver noted, be borrowed from our passage. The root, however, is quite frequent in Talmudic Aramaic in the meaning "to plane off, smooth, thin down."[3] It would surely be a surprising co-incidence that a scribal error should create a noun of this meaning in a passage dealing with the sharpening of implements! While its precise meaning eludes us, its use in the Targum would imply some simple nail, fork, or handpick, and this is borne out by its proximity to *dorbhanot* "ox-goads."

Perhaps another suggestion may be proposed. Clermont-Ganneau's conjecture that *payim*, the weight found by Barton and by Macalister, means "two-thirds" has been generally accepted, but its etymology is obscure.[4] It is necessary to re-consider the Hebrew use of fractions. The phrase *pi šenayim* occurs three times (Dt 21 17; 2 Kgs 2 9; Zech 13 8). In the first two passages, it is generally rendered "a double portion." Zech 13 8, however, which speaks of the destruction of *pi šenayim* and the remaining of a third is conclusive that the former phrase means "two parts (out of three)." Incidentally, this alone suits the context in Kgs, where Elisha prays not for a double portion of his master Elijah's spirit, but more modestly, and appropri-ately, for two-thirds. The same meaning applies to the phrase in Dt, as Ehrlich noticed. The early law of primogeniture gave the first-born two-thirds of the estate.[5]

This use of cardinal numbers to express fractions where the numerator is one less than the denominator, as e. g. $\frac{2}{3}$, $\frac{3}{4}$, is well attested in Rabbinic Hebrew. Thus in Baba Mezia 1:1 *šelošah ḥalakim* lit. "three portions" means "three out of four,

---

[3] Thus Tar. Ps. Jon. to Num. 7 13 דנילדא קלישא "a charger of thin plate;" T. B. Erub. 3a דאמרינן קלוש "we say 'plane it down' ", B. Ned. 68a. מיקלש קליש "does he plane it down?"

[4] Cf. G. A. Barton, *Archaeology and the Bible*, 1937, 202.

[5] This interpretation is discussed in the Siphre ad loc., but is rejected on Talmudic grounds, in favor of the view that the phrase means "double that of the other brothers." This reduction in the share of the first-born would be in line with the general development of Rabbinic law in the direction of equality for under-privileged groups. Cf. L. Finkelstein, *The Pharisees*, 1938, I, 284 f., 342 f.

i. e. three-fourths." In B. Shab. 34 b, *šene ḥelke mil*, lit. "two
portions of a mile" is specifically explained as "two out of three,
two-thirds." It may be noted that *beka'* in biblical Hebrew
(Gen 24 22; Ex 38 26) has undergone the same semantic development. Literally, it means "fraction, part (cf. *frangere, baka'* =
break) and then "one part (out of two)," hence "one half a
šekel."

It may now be suggested that *payim* is the dual of *pi* = "portion, proportion," as in the phrase *pi šenayim, lephi* (Lev 25 16)
kephi (Lev 25 52 et al.).[6] "*Payim*" would then mean "two parts
(out of three)," exactly like *pi šenayim*, hence "two-thirds of
a shekel."

Similarly, one-third of a shekel would be expressed simply
by *šeliš* without *šekel* after it, exactly like *beka'* = "half a shekel"
and our use of "quarter," and the less usual "half," without
"dollar."

The only change required in the MT is to transfer the Lamed
from *velišloš* to *kilšon*. The error may well have been occasioned
by the succession of preceding words with Lamed. On this view
the original text and its translation are as follows: והיתה הפצירה
פַּיִם לַמַּחֲרֵשׁוֹת וְלָאֵתִים וּשְׁלָשׁ לַקִּלְשׁוֹן וְלַהֳקַרְדֻּמִּים וּלְהַצִּיב הַדָּרְבָן.
"And the price was a payim (i. e. two-thirds of a shekel) for the
mattock and the coulters and a third (of a shekel) for the picks,[7]
and for the axes and for setting the goads."[8]

---

[6] Cf. BDB, *Lexicon*, 805b.

[7] The use of the singular is parallelled by the use of the singular for *dorbhan*
and is probably collective in meaning. It is noteworthy that *kilšon* and
dorbhan are not mentioned in v. 20 (against Driver). Apparently v. 20 lists
the larger and more important implements lacking in Israel, while v. 21 gives
a full price tariff, including the less important iron tools as well.

[8] The writer is grateful to Professor Julius A. Bewer, who was kind enough
to read the paper in an earlier draft and make several valuable comments
which have been taken into account in the above text.

THE TEXT AND MEANING OF HOSEA XIV 3

In his suggestive paper, "Echoes of Canaanite Literature in the Psalms" (*VT*, vol. 4, Apr. 1954) Father Roger T. O'CALLAGHAN, whose untimely death is a great loss to Biblical scholarship, discusses Hos. xiv 3c, among other Biblical passages. The difficulties of the traditional interpretations of MT are patent, whether we render "we will pay the calves of our lips" [2]) or "we will pay, as with bullocks, with our lips" [3]) or "we will render, (as) for bullocks, the offerings of our lips." [4]) He therefore interprets Hos. xiv 3c וּנְשַׁלְּמָה פָרִים שְׂפָתֵינוּ as *pārē-m šᵉphātēnū*, treating the *mem* of Masoretic *pārīm* as the enclitic, which has become familiar from Ugaritic, and rendering the stich as "we shall pay the bullocks of our pens." Incidentally, in explaining *šᵉphātēnū* as "pens, enclosures" he was anticipated by TUR-SINAI [5]) and, even earlier, by DUHM.

However, this interpretation does not commend itself, either from the standpoint of content or of language. In pleading for Israel's ideal repentance, the prophet is hardly likely to urge sacrifices, in view of his stress upon love and inward devotion as the highest forms of worship and his sarcastic reference to animal offerings, as in v 6: "With their flocks and cattle do they go to seek the Lord and they do not find Him." Syntactically, too, the accusative after *šillem* generally represents the debt or obligation being discharged [6],) not the object of payment [7]). Most frequently by far the verb governs *neder* "vow" in the accusative. [8])

---

[2]) So CALVIN, G. A. SMITH, AV.

[3]) So EWALD, CHEYNE.

[4]) So *American Standard Revised Version, Jewish Publication Society Version.*

[5]) Cf. E. BEN JEHUDA, *Thesaurus Totius Linguae Hebraicae*, vol. X, pp. 5129a.

[6]) Cf. e.g. Ex. xxi 36 (*šōr*); Ex. xx 12 (*tᵉrēphāh*); Ex. xxii 5 (*bᵉʿērāh*); 2 Kings iv 7 (*nišyēkh*); 1 Sam. xii 6 (*kibhšāh*); Joel ii 25 (*haššānīm*); Prov. xix 17 (*gemūl*), etc.

[7]) The only instances are in the legal phraseology of the Covenant Code (Ex. xxi 37; xxii 3 ff.).

[8]) Cf. *inter alia* Deut. xxiii 22; 2 Sam. xv 7; Is. xix 21; Nah. i 15; Ps. xxii 26; l 14; lxi 9, lxv 2; lxvi 13; cxvi 14, 18; Prov. vii 14; Job xxii 26; Ecc. v 3.

The exigencies of the passage were recognized by LXX: καὶ ἀντα-
ποδώσομεν καρπὸν χειλέων ἡμῶν and by Pešitta: ܦܐܪ̈ܐ
ܘܢܦܪܥ. A long catena of scholars accordingly emend MT to read
פְּרִי שְׂפָתֵינוּ.[1]

This emendation is, however, unnecessary, if we recognize that
the *mem* is enclitic, and revocalize Masoretic *pārīm* as *pᵉrī-m* rendering
the stich "we shall pay the fruit of our lips, i.e., we shall fulfill our
spoken vows to God." On "the fruit of the lips," as a figure for
"speech" cf. נִיב שְׂפָתָיִם (Is. lvii 19; cf. also Prov. x 31) and פְּרִי פִי
אִישׁ (Prov. xii 14; xiii 2; xviii 20).

The difficulty of the clause כָּל ־ תִּשָּׂא עָוֹן is obviated if we emend
כָּל to בַּל and render the particle, on the basis of the Ugaritic usage,
as an asseverative, "Indeed, forgive our iniquity." [2] We have indicated elsewhere [3] that Biblical *lō'* is likewise used asseveratively,
"indeed," a meaning which probably arose from its use in rhetorical
questions, like the Latin *nonne*. This interrogative-asseverative use
of *lō'* is frequent in Rabbinic literature, where the identical passage
occurs in parallel sources with and without *lō'*. The usage is also to
be met with, we believe, in Hos. x 9; xi 5, as well as in the crux
Isa. vii 27. [4]

The enigmatic וְקַח ־ טוֹב has been variously interpreted as "take
it well that we pay" or "accept what is good, i.e., that we pay", or
"let thyself be gracious" or "take good things." [5] On the basis of
the first two stichs we suggest that the clause is to be rendered
"accept our speech."

The Biblical and Rabbinic root *dbb* "speak" (Cant. vii 10) from
which *dibbāh* "report, evil report" (Gen. xxxvii 2; Num. xiv 37) is
derived (cf. Akkadian *dabâbu* "speak, charge"), apparently has a
cognate *ṭôb*, *ṭbb*. Thus *dibbāh* is rendered as טִיבָא by Onkelos and as

---

[1] So DUHM, OORT, WELLHAUSEN, NOWACK, HARPER, SELLIN, T. H. ROBINSON,
and the Lexicons of BDB, and KOEHLER-BAUMGARTNER.

[2] Cf. O'CALLAGHAN's remarks, *op. cit.* p. 166, where the asseverative use of
bl is suggested for Ps. xvi 2.

[3] Cf. „Studies in the Relationship of Biblical and Rabbinic Hebrew" in the
Louis Ginzberg Jubilee Volumes (New York 1945), English volume, pp. 181-3.

[4] Note that the parallel clause in Hos. xi 5 is in the declarative. See the above
paper for details.

[5] Cf. HARPER, *ICC* on *Hosea* p. 411. ROBINSON emends וְקַח to נִקְחָה „Lass uns
empfangen Gutes", which helps but little.

ܠܟܒܣ̈ܐ by *Pešitta* in Gen. xxxvii 2 and by טאבא by the Targum on Prov. x 18.

In Neh. vi 19 טוֹבֹתָיו is parallel to דְּבָרַי: "His utterances they were wont to repeat to me and my words they would bring to him." This, LXX (B, A and א) recognized, rendering both nouns identically by λόγους "words."

The same meaning for the root *ṭob* would seem to occur in the difficult phrase of Ps. xxxix 3b הֶחֱשֵׁיתִי מִטּוֹב, where many commentators emend to מִכְּאֵב, which is impossible, or delete the word entirely. The phrase is to be rendered literally: "I am silent from speaking" i.e., "I refrain from speaking," and thus it constitutes an excellent parallel to the first stich נֶאֱלַמְתִּי דוּמִיָּה, which is also to be translated "I am quiet in speech." [1]) The same meaning for *ṭōb* may also occur in Job xxxiv 3 and in Hos. iii 5.

Our passage now receives a clear and appropriate meaning, without any radical emendation. The prophet pleads with Israel to voice its repentance before God:

"Take words with yourselves and return to the Lord,
Say to Him,
'Thou wilt indeed forgive our iniquity and accept our speech,
And we shall render (unto Thee) the fruit of our lips.' "

New York

---

[1]) On this meaning of *ṭbb* cf. M. SEIDEL in *Debir* (Berlin 5683 = 1923) page 33. On *dmm* in the meaning of "speak" cf. Ps. xxii 3 (note the parallelism); xxxiv 15; lxii 2?; lxiv 2 and perhaps the famous phrase in 1 Ki. xix 12.

'THE BRANCH TO THE NOSE'

A NOTE ON EZEKIEL VIII 17

ONE of the most interesting and baffling verses in the Bible is Ezekiel viii 17. In this passage the prophet describes twenty-five men standing in the inner court of the Temple, worshipping the sun. Not only are these abominations being committed in the Temple, but violence is widespread 'and they put the branch (*hazzemorah*) to their nose'.

Aside from its intrinsic importance, this *crux interpretum* has recently attracted attention because of the brilliant and learned controversy carried on by Prof. Charles C. Torrey and Prof. Shalom Spiegel regarding the proposed Persian date for Ezekiel.[1] Prof. Torrey sees in the *zemorah* the *baresma*, or bundle of twigs, used by the worshipper in the Persian sun-worship,[2] and therefore finds that the verse 'affords one of the clearest and most conclusive bits of evidence that the book of Ezekiel is a pseudepigraph·'.[3] Prof. Spiegel objected to this view,[4] but his objections proved inconclusive, largely because he failed to support them by an adequate exegesis for the verse.

Nevertheless we believe that Prof. Torrey's proposed identification is untenable and shall suggest a new interpretation for the passage.

Our objection to Prof. Torrey's theory is not based on the desire to avoid a Persian date for Ezekiel. Even if the passage be taken as an allusion to a rite in the sun-cult, it could still be maintained, with J. H. Moulton,[5] that 'the earliest evidence of the activity (of the Magi) as a sacred tribe is in Ezekiel (viii 17), where they are found at Jerusalem, in or before 591 B.C., worshipping the sun, and holding to their face a branch, which is the predecessor of the late *barsom*'. More than once Biblical passages have been shewn to be earlier than was first believed possible through the discovery of additional material. Moreover syncretism and borrowing are widespread in religion, and it is *a priori* likely that the Persian sun-worship took over many elements from older forms of the same cult.

It is therefore not because of the date, but because of two other major considerations that we oppose the identification of the *zemorah* and the *baresma* :

A. The position of the clause makes it impossible to interpret it as

---

[1] Prof. Torrey's views were expressed in his book *Pseudo-Ezekiel* 1931 (= PE). Prof. Spiegel's criticism 'Ezekiel or Pseudo-Ezekiel' appeared in the *Harvard Theological Review* 1931 pp. 245–321 (= EPE). Prof. Torrey's reply, 'Certainly Pseudo-Ezekiel' was published in the *J.B.L.* 1934 pp. 291–320 (= CPE).

[2] PE p. 84.   [3] CPE p. 302.

[4] EPE p. 301 ; EPE pp. 302 ff.   [5] *Early Zoroastrianism* p. x.

a reference to a specific rite in any cult. V. 16 is the end of a long passage (ch. viii 6–16) that describes the abominations in the Temple, while vv. 17, 18 constitute the peroration:

v. 16. And He brought me into the inner court of the Lord's house, and behold, at the door of the temple of the Lord, between the porch and the altar, were about five and twenty men, with their backs toward the temple of the Lord, and their faces toward the east; and they worshipped the sun toward the east.

v. 17. Then He said unto me: 'Hast thou seen this, O son of man? Is it a light thing to the house of Judah that they commit the abominations which they commit here, in that they fill the land with violence, and provoke Me still more, and, *lo, they put the branch to their nose*?

v. 18. Therefore will I also deal in fury; Mine eye shall not spare, neither will I have pity; and though they cry in Mine ears with a loud voice, yet will I not hear them.'

Had the phrase in italics referred to any specific rite, its place was above, in v. 16, where other details of the sun-worship are described. In its actual position, however, it must bear a general meaning or the context is utterly destroyed.

B. There is a widespread Rabbinic tradition that the Massoretic text of our passage was changed to avoid a cacophonous or blasphemous expression, and that the original reading was *'appi* 'My nose' (referring to God) instead of *'appam* 'their nose'.[1] The Tannaitic sources describe these changes as *kinnah hak-kathub*, 'Scripture has used euphemistic language', and actually quote the text in the restored form.[2] These changes are usually known as *tikkune sopherim*, 'emendations of the Scribes'.[3]

To gauge the trustworthiness of this tradition of a changed text, it should be recalled that the fixed purpose of Massoretic activity was the preservation of the received text without change of any sort. Thus the greatest Jewish authorities in medieval times could not believe that the received text might have been changed, and attempted to explain the ancient Tannaitic traditions to mean that the verses were so *interpreted* but not *corrected*.[4] The opposition to change being the dominant tendency, the clear-cut statement that our passage among others has

[1] *Midrash Tanḥuma, Beshallaḥ*, sec. 16; the Massorah at beginning of Numbers and on Ps. 106. These sources quote all the eighteen passages where such a change is predicated. Our passage is also included in the briefer lists given in the *Mechilta* on Exod. xv 7, and *Sifre* on Num. x 35. The Masoretic commentator Norzi on Zech. ii 12 quotes all the instances and discusses them at length.

[2] Cf. especially *Tanḥuma loc. cit.*

[3] A name given to them by Simon ben Pazzi in *Genesis Rabbah* sec. 49, par. 7.

[4] See Norzi on Zech. ii 12 and the Rabbinic commentaries on *Genesis Rabbah* sec. 49, par. 7.

351

undergone change should be accepted as valid.[1] At the very least the suggested reading should be treated with the respect accorded variants derived from the ancient versions, which are often based upon inferior copies and equally inadequate knowledge.

We thus have two criteria for interpreting our passage : (a) the reference to the context, (b) the well-attested variant *'appi* instead of *'appam*. On the basis of the context we believe it justifiable to rule out all interpretations that refer the phrase to some specific rite, such as the Persian sun-cult,[2] phallic worship,[3] the burning of incense,[4] or any apotropaic or healing rite.[5]

Scholars have noted that what is undoubtedly required is some general meaning after the words 'they continue to provoke me'. Several such explanations have been proposed but they are not likely to commend themselves.

Thus the medieval commentator Menaḥem ben Simon of Posquières suggested 'they despise me' but advanced no proof for this meaning.[6] The rendering of LXX μυκτηρίζοντες, 'they turn up their nose', and that of Peshitta, *mafqu'in banḥirayhon*, 'they blow with their noses' undoubtedly suggested by the word *'appam*, imply the sense of contempt, but can scarcely be squared with the Hebrew text.

Haupt[7] arrived at the same sense by claiming that the Syriac *zamara* meaning 'bluish gray', which is used of eyes of that colour,[8] could

---

[1] This assumption is strengthened by the following considerations : (1) In practically all the passages, the proposed reading is by no means homiletical in character, but possesses much to recommend it textually. (2) The changes are slight, such as an altered suffix, as in our passage and in Num. xi 16, Jer. ii 11, Zech. ii 12, Mal. ii 13, Ps. cvi 20, or some other minor changes, as in 1 Sam. iii 13, and elsewhere. This is the natural procedure where the desire is to suggest an idea without expressing it. (3) The same process seems to occur in post-Biblical literature. Cf. *Aboth* ii 4 ' Do His will as if it were thy will, that He may do thy will as if it were His will. Nullify thy will before His will, that He may nullify the will of others before thy will.' Here, as some of the commentators have noted (Bertinoro, Lipschütz), ' the will of others' is a euphemism for ' His will', which is called for by the parallelism.   [2] Maintained by Torrey and others.

[3] Proposed by Graetz in *M.G.W.J.* 1876 pp. 507–508, who based his view on the alleged use of *zemorah* in Talmudic literature as a euphemism for the *membrum virile*. See Kohut *Aruch completum*, Levy *Talmudic Dictionary* s.v. A careful study of these passages shews, however, that the Rabbis did not know the meaning of *zemorah* in Ezekiel, and were interpreting it homiletically. Cf. Ben Yehudah *Thesaurus* vol. iii p. 1350.

[4] So Menaḥem ben Saruk, Rashī, Ibn Janāḥ, Kimḥī.

[5] Cf. Harper *Ass. and Bab. Letters* vol. viii no. 771 ll. 5–7.

[6] Quoted by Marmorstein, *O.L.Z.* 1910 p. 435.

[7] In *A.J.S.L.* 1909 p. 2 ; *Z.D.M.G.* 1911 p. 563.

[8] So also in Talmudic Aramaic ; cf. *Gen. Rab.* sec. 85 : והוין עינוהי זמורא ' His eyes were bluish-gray.'

mean 'nasal mucus'. Hence the phrase is : 'they send the mucus through their nose, i.e. they snort defiance at me.' Gunkel,[1] on the other hand, arrived at the same meaning by emending וְמוֹרָה into זִרְמָה 'stream' which occurs in Ez. xxiii 20, and by reading מֵעַל for אֶל. The passage then means : 'They blow the mucus out of their noses.' Marmorstein[2] equated *zemorah* with the Assyrian *zumru* = 'skin', and, adopting the reading *'appi*, translated : 'They stretch their skin before me'—as a sign of contempt.

That all these renderings are far-fetched and unattractive is evident. We believe that a simpler interpretation is available, based on the original reading *'appi*. 'They send the branch into my nose' is a vivid way of saying, 'they harass and irritate me'. Having a twig or thorn thrust into one's face is an obviously unpleasant sensation. To heighten the vividness of the picture, one speaks of 'a thorn in the eye' or 'a branch in the nose', rather than 'a thorn in one's face'. We may compare the English phrase, 'he placed it under his nose', where the meaning is 'he placed it before him'. The figure is, indeed, so vivid that when referred to God it becomes crudely anthropomorphic. The idiom is therefore changed, and *'appi* 'my nose' becomes *'appam* 'their nose'. The same process is at work in the *tikkun* in Zech. ii 12, where the original 'the pupil of My eye' was changed to 'the pupil of their eye'.

The idiom is of course a *hapax legomenon*, but the figure of thorns as irritants occurs elsewhere in Hebrew :

Num. xxxiii 55. 'Then shall those that ye let remain of them, be as thorns in your eyes, and as pricks in your sides, and they shall harass you in the land wherein ye dwell.'

Joshua xxiii 13. 'But they shall be a snare and a trap unto you, and a scourge in your sides, and pricks in your eyes, until ye perish from off this good land which the Lord your God hath given you.'

Ezekiel xxviii 24. 'And there shall be no more a pricking brier unto the house of Israel, nor a piercing thorn of any that are round about them, that did have them in disdain ; and they shall know that I am the Lord God.'

Proverbs xxvi 9. 'As a thorn that cometh into the hand of a drunkard, so is a parable in the mouth of fools', may well mean that a proverb in the mouth of a fool is as irritating as a thorn in the hand of a drunkard, who in his irresponsible condition uses it to harass his neighbour.

It also occurs in later Hebrew :

Exodus Rabbah i 14 שהיו ישראל דומין בעיניהם כקוצים 'Israel were like thorns in their eyes'.

---

[1] In *Schöpfung und Chaos* (1895) p. 14.   [2] See note 6 on p. 286.

Abodah Zarah 46a ; j. Shabbath ix, 11d an idol is referred to by the derogatory epithet עֵין קוֹץ : 'Thorn in-the-eye'.

It remains to note that וַיָּשֻׁבוּ means either, 'they continue to provoke me',[1] or 'they provoke me still more'.[2]   The entire chapter (vv. 6–16) is a description of the various ritual abominations committed in the Temple.   But Ezekiel would not be a prophet if he failed to see their concomitant in the moral iniquity of the people, which arouses the Divine displeasure even more profoundly.   The passage is now forceful and clear:

'Is it a light thing for the house of Judah to commit the abominations which they commit here, that they fill the land with violence and continue to provoke Me,[3] and irritate Me utterly?[4]   Therefore, I, too, will act in fury, Mine eye shall not spare, nor will I have pity, and though they cry in Mine ears with a loud voice, I will not hear them.'

---

[1] As in Gen. xxx 31, Lam. iii 3, Ecc. i 7, and elsewhere.   See Brown-Driver-Briggs, s.v. שׁוּב sec. 8.

[2] So Jewish version and others.

[3] Or ' provoke me still more '.

[4] Lit. ' put the twig to my nose '.

JOB XL 29 — AN ADDITIONAL NOTE

The elucidation of this verse in the Lord's description of Leviathan
(Job xl 25—xli 26) הַתְשַׂחֶק בּוֹ כַּצִּפּוֹר וְתִקְשְׁרֶנּוּ לְנַעֲרוֹתֶיךָ has been substantially advanced by the recent discussion of the passage by Profes-
sor D. WINTON THOMAS [1]). He points out correctly that the usual
renderings of *lᵉnaʿᵃrōthekhā* as a) "thy maidens, maid-servants" [2])
and b) "thy daughters, children"[3]), are both unsatisfactory in the
specific context.

Professor THOMAS accordingly makes the excellent suggestion that
the noun in MT is not the common *naʿarāh*, but is to be interpreted
in terms of the Arabic نَفَر, fem. نَفَرة, "a species of sparrow, young
sparrow", and that the Hebrew cognate is to be vocalized נֹעַר, נֹעֲרָה.[4])
It thus would serve as an excellent parallel to *ṣippōr*. However, he
finds difficulties in the preposition of לְנַעֲרוֹתֶיךָ as well as in the 2nd
person plural suffix. He accordingly deletes the suffix יך as a dittography from יכרו in v. 30 and then changes the *Lamedh* to a *Kaph*.

---

[1]) *VT*, XIV, Jan. 1964, pp. 114 ff.
[2]) So Vulgate, Targum.
[3]) So BICKELL, KISSANE, PETERS, DRIVER—GRAY, DHORME, *inter alia*.
[4]) The evidence for this vocalization is not overly convincing. The examples
in J. BARTH, *Nominalbildung i.d. semitischer Sprachen*, p. 167, are all of adjectives,
not of substantives, as is the single Hebrew instance *šōʿᵃrim* (Jer. xxix 17) that
BARTH adduces. The vocalization of the Hebrew would also depend on whether
we have a cognate or a direct borrowing from the Arabic. However, the uncertainty as to the vocalization of the noun does not affect the validity of the assumption of its existence. Cf. e.g. our suggestion that in Isa. xlix 14 *mērahēm* is to be
read as a noun meaning "woman, mother", parallel to *iššah* like *raham* in Jud. v
30, and is probably, but not definitely, to be vocalized *mirham*. Cf. our paper
"Studies in Relationship of Biblical and Rabbinic Hebrew" in *Louis Ginzberg
Jubilee Volume*, (New York, 1945), English Section, p. 186.

This assumption of two distinct errors in MT weakens the attractiveness of Professor THOMAS' excellent interpretation. Fortunately we believe that an analysis of the syntax makes both emendations unnecessary.

We suggest that the plural of the noun be recognized as distributive. This usage occurs in prose, as e.g. Judg. xii 7 וַיִּקָּבֵר בְּעָרֵי גִלְעָד "he was buried *in one of the cities* of Gilead[1]), but is more common in poetry. Thus we may cite Isaiah l 4d:

יָעִיר בַּבֹּקֶר בַּבֹּקֶר יָעִיר לִי אֹזֶן לִשְׁמֹעַ כַּלִּמּוּדִים

It is clear from the context that the prophet is not comparing himself to disciples *in the plural*. The passage is to be rendered literally:

"Morning by morning he wakens (me)
He wakens my ear,
So that I may hear, as one of the disciples".

Another instance occurs in Job iii 16:

אוֹ כְנֵפֶל טָמוּן לֹא אֶהְיֶה כְּעֹלְלִים לֹא רָאוּ אוֹר

The parallelism of the plural *ke'ōlelīm* with the singular noun *nephel* makes it clear that the former is to be taken distributively. Obviously Job wishes he could have met the fate of one still-born child, not of many. The passage is therefore to be rendered:

"If only I were an aborted birth,
As one of the infants that have never seen the light"[2])

Other examples of the distributive use of the plural in poetic passages occur in Gen. xxi 7 (*bānīm*); Zec. ix 9 (*ben 'athōnōth*); Song ii 9 (*haḥalōnōth, haḥarākīm*).

The *Lamedh* of *lena'arōtekhā* also requires no emendation. There is ample evidence for the use of *Lamedh* to express "a transition into a new state or condition, or into a new character or office"[3]). It thus

---

[1]) Thus GES-KAUTZSCH, *Hebräische Grammatik*, 25 ed. (Leipzig, 1889) § 124,1, note 2 (p. 387) adduces Gen. viii 4 (*ḥarēi*) ; Ex. xxi 22 (*yeladheha*) and 1 Sam. xvii 43 (*bemakkelōth*).

[2]) Our rendering is based on revocalizing the negative *lō* as the optative particle *lu*. See our forthcoming *Commentary on Job*. The retention of the Masoretic vocalization does not affect our point here.

[3]) Cf. BROWN-DRIVER-BRIGGS, *Oxford Lexicon*, s.v. *Lamedh*, sec. 4 (p. 512a).

has the meaning of "for, as". It occurs with many verbs such as *māšaḥ* "anoint so as to be" (2 Sam. ix 16; xv 1, etc.); *ṣiwwāh*, *(Piel)* "appoint as", (2 Sam. xiii 14; xxv 30); *dibber* (2 Ki. xiv 21) "he spoke of me to be king"; *biqqeš* (2 Sam iii 17), *mākhar* (Ex. xxi 7), "when a man sells his daughter to be a slave", as well as in a variety of idioms [1]. Moreover, this is the only use of *Lamedh* with our verb *kāšar* to be found in the Biblical text. Cf. the classical passage Deut. vi 8, וּקְשַׁרְתָּם לְאוֹת עַל־יָדֶךָ lit. "You shall bind them to be a sign upon your hand" (so also Deut. xi 18).

The fact that bird-trainers generally ply their craft with flocks of birds rather than with a single member of the species also supports the view that the plural in MT is in place [2]. The verse accordingly gives an excellent sense without recourse to emendation:

"Can you play with him as with a bird,
Or can you tie him up as one of your sparrows?"

---

[1] Cf. *loc. cit.* for many more illustrations.

[2] Cf the plural in Isa. lx 8; Baruch iii 17; James iii 7, and the frequent use in Mishnic Hebrew of *maphrihei yōnim*, "flyers of doves" for racing and gambling purposes (Mishnah Rosh Hashanah i 8; Sanhedrin iii 3; Shevuot vii 4; Eduyot ii 7).

A NOTE ON LAMENTATIONS ii 13

מָה־אֲעִידֵךְ (Qere) מָה אֲדַמֶּה־לָּךְ הַבַּת יְרוּשָׁלַ͏ִם
מָה־אַשְׁוֶה־לָּךְ וַאֲנַחֲמֵךְ בְּתוּלַת בַּת־צִיּוֹן וגו׳

THE interpretation of this verse has never been smooth, because of
the difficulty occasioned by the word אֲעִידֵךְ. The Hiphil of עוד is quite
common in Hebrew in the meanings : (a) testify, (b) cause to testify,
and (c) warn. These meanings have been utilized in the interpretation
of the verse.

1. The most popular rendering of the verse is :

> 'What shall I take to witness for you ?
> What shall I liken to you ? &c.'[1]

But this interpretation requires a long and cumbersome explanation :
' Whom shall I call as witnesses who have suffered the same fate as
you ? ' Besides, it is syntactically questionable. הֵעִיד is always construed with the ב *personae* to mean ' testify against '.[2] There is no
warrant to make אֲעִידֵךְ with its direct object mean ' testify for '—a usage
that does not occur elsewhere.

2. Another interpretation would derive אֲעִידֵךְ from the adverb עוֹד
and give it the meaning ' Make like something else (עוֹד), cause to
resemble, compare '.[3] The verb would therefore be parallel to the
following verbs, אֲדַמֶּה and אַשְׁוֶה, and the translation would read as
follows :

> ' What shall I make similar to you,
> What shall I liken to you,
> What shall I equal to you,
> That I may comfort you ?

But this rendering seems to offend against the obviously parallel
structure of the verse, by making the first three verbs synonymous, and
the last one distinct from the others.

3. A simpler expedient is, however, at hand. The verb in question
may be interpreted to mean ' restore, fortify, strengthen ',[4] exactly like

---

[1] So LXX, Rashi (?), Ibn Ezra (see the supercommentaries). Authorized and
Revised (marg.) Versions, and the Translation of the Jewish Publication Society
of America.

[2] As in Deut. iv 26, 2 Kings xvii 15 and elsewhere.

[3] So Ehrlich on Jer. xlix 19 and Dr Seidel in the Hebrew Journal *Leshonenu*
vol. 3 no. 1 p. 10. The Vulgate and Luther translate similarly.

[4] This seems to be the rendering of the Targum, אַסְעִיד בָּךְ. Usually, however,
סְעַד is construed with יָת, a suffix, or ל (see Onkelos and the Jerusalem Targum
to Gen. xxvii 37, Jerusalem Targum to Ex. xvii 12, and Targum to 2 Chron.

the Polel and Hithpolel forms of the same root, יְעוֹדֵד and וַתְּעוֹדָד (Pss. cxlvi 9, xx 9). That Hiphil and Polel forms often have the same meaning is obvious from a comparison of מְשִׁיבַת נָפֶשׁ (Ps. xix 8) and נַפְשִׁי יְשׁוֹבֵב (Ps. xxiii 3). Moreover the Hiphil of עוד occurs in this meaning in Ecclus. xx 4, 11 חכמות למדה בניה ותעיד לכל מבינים בה.[1] In Arabic, too, the fourth conjugation, which corresponds to the Hebrew Hiphil, of غاب means 'restored'.[2]

If this meaning be adopted for אֲעִירֵךְ, the verse will be found to exhibit the frequently used chiastic arrangement, where a (אֲעִירֵךְ) is parallel to d (אֲנַחֲמֵךְ), and b (אֲדַמֶּה) to c (אַשְׁוֶה). A translation would read somewhat as follows:

(a) How shall I fortify you,
(b) What shall I liken unto you,
    O daughter of Jerusalem!
(c) What shall I compare unto you,
(d) And comfort you,
    O virgin daughter of Zion![3]

The closing verse in Lamentations is crucial for the meaning and spirit of the entire poem.[1] In spite of the simplicity of its style and the familiarity of its vocabulary, it has long been a crux. After the plea in vs. 21, "Turn us to yourself and we will return, renew our days as of old," vs. 22 *ki ʾim māʾ ōs mᵉʾastānû qāṣaptā ʿālênû ʿad mᵉʾōd*, seems hardly appropriate, particularly as the conclusion of the prayer.

(1) The extent of the difficulties posed by the verse may perhaps be gauged by the desperate expedient adopted, e.g., in the (1917) JPSV, of virtually inserting a negative into the text, thus diametrically reversing its meaning: "Thou canst not have utterly rejected us, and be exceeding wroth against us."

A variety of other interpretations have been proposed, all of which suffer from grave drawbacks:

(2) To treat the verse as an interrogative: "Or have you rejected us, are you exceedingly angry with us?"[2] There is, however, no evidence for rendering *ki ʾim* as "or," whether interrogatively or otherwise, and this interpretation has found few modern defenders.

(3) To delete *ʾim* on the grounds that it is not expressed by the LXX or the Peš and is missing in six medieval Hebrew MSS. The verse is then rendered: "For you have indeed rejected us, etc." It is probable that the ancient versions, endeavoring to make sense of a difficult phrase, rendered it *ad sensum*. As Hillers notes, the MT is to be preferred as the *lectio difficilior*. Moreover, the idea remains inappropriate at the end of a penitential prayer for forgiveness and restoration.

(4) A better approach is to treat the verse as a conditional sentence: "If you should reject us, you would be too angry against us,"[3] or "If thou hast utterly rejected us, then great has been thy anger against us."[4] Actually, there is no true conditional sentence here, stich *b* being completely parallel to stich *a*, and adding nothing new to the thought.[5] In addition, the difficulty mentioned above inheres in this view as well — it offers a very unsatisfactory conclusion to a penitential poem.

[1] As recognized by D. R. Hillers, *Lamentations* (AB 7A; Garden City: Doubleday, 1973) 100.

[2] So RSV: "Why dost thou forget us for ever, why dost thou so long forsake us?"

[3] So Ehrlich, *Randglossen zür hebräischen Bibel* (Leipzig: Hinrichs, 1914), 7. 854; T. Meek, *IB* (Nashville: Abingdon, 1956), 6. 38.

[4] So NEB.

[5] The verbs in both stichs are virtually synonymous, and the infinitive absolute construction in stich *a* parallels *ʿad mᵉʾōd* in stich *b*.

(5) To understand the *ki ʾim* as "unless," on the basis of such passages as Gen 32:27, *lōʾ ʾᵃšallēhᵃkā ki ʾim bēraktāni*, "I shall not let you go unless you bless me," and to render this passage, "Turn us to yourself . . . unless you have despised us," i.e., completely rejected us.[6] But as Albrektson points out, in all such instances *ki ʾim* is used only after a clause containing or implying a negative. The syntactic difficulty aside, the problem of meaning remains: a plea for divine favor is logically and psychologically incompatible with the idea of a possible total rejection by God. A despairing Job may contemplate the possibility of complete alienation from God; a psalmist, however harried and embittered by misfortune, has not surrendered the hope of succor and restoration.

(6) Having rejected all other interpretations, Hillers finds "one remaining possibility — to render the verse adversatively, "But instead you have utterly rejected us, you have been very angry with us."[7] He seeks to buttress this view by three lines of argument:

(a) This interpretation is supported by Jewish liturgical practice, which ordains that in the synagogue reading of the closing sections of Isaiah, Malachi, Ecclesiastes, and Lamentations the last verse of the text is not to be the conclusion, by having the penultimate sentence repeated, so as not to end with "a somber verse."[8]

But even if the synagogue usage be allowed as evidence, it offers no proof for this interpretation. In each of these instances, the reason for not concluding with the final verse is not "the somber verse," but the negative character of the *closing phrase*. In Isa 66:24, the prophet describes the utter destruction and degradation of the wicked. Malachi 3:24 foretells the restoration of unity between parents and children. Eccl 12:12 declares that God will judge all men's actions. None of these ideas are felt to be negative either in biblical or post-biblical thought. They all deal with manifestations of God's power and justice. What the ancient reader found unpalatable and, therefore, sought to avoid ending with was an unpleasant phrase, "a stench to all flesh," "I shall smite the land in total destruction," "upon every deed, good or evil." Similarly in this passage, the closing phrase, "you have been very angry with us," is the reason for the synagogue practice. Hence nothing can be inferred with regard to the specific meaning assigned to the verse as a whole or to the conjunction and to stich *a* in particular.

(b) In further justification of this rendering, Hillers declares that "other laments similarly end on a low key, e.g., Jer 14:9; Ps 88, 89." However, the description of the passage as being "in a low key," would seem to be an understatement. If it is, as Hillers avers, a statement of present realities, it is strongly negative.

Nor can these other passages cited be adduced in favor of this view. Jer 14:9, far from ending on a low key, has a highly appropriate conclusion, paralleling vs. 21 in this chapter. It is a passionate plea for God's help: "Your name is called upon us, do not forsake us!"

In Psalm 89, the plea is expressed in vs. 51a, while vs. 52 is a subordinate clause, giving the grounds for the urgency of the appeal:

[6] So W. Rudolph, "Der Text der Klagelieder," *ZAW* 51 (1933) 120.
[7] AB, following the Vulgate, Luther, AV and P. Volz (*TLZ* 22 [1940] 82-83).
[8] AB, 101.

> Remember, O Lord, how thy servant is scorned
> How I bear in my bosom the insults of the people
> with which thine enemies taunt, O Lord,
> with which they mock the footsteps of thy anointed.[9]

Of the three passages adduced, Psalm 88 does, indeed, end upon a negative note. It seems clear, however, that the surviving text is incomplete and that we have only part of a description of the poet's estrangement and isolation from his fellows. The theme is very similar to that of Job 19:13-19. The conclusion to Psalm 88 can scarcely be described as a satisfactory close to the poem on any count.[10]

(c) Hillers explains that the verse "merely restates the present fact: Israel does stand under God's severe judgment." However, the alleged matter-of-fact statement contradicts the cry of vs. 20: "Why have you forsaken us so long?" and is totally incompatible with the plea of vs. 22, "Turn us back to you, etc."[11]

In sum, this interpretation, like those cited above, offers what must be described as an inappropriate conclusion to the poem.

I would venture to propose another approach. As we have noted above, Psalm 89 ends with a plea extending over two verses, the petition being expressed by a main clause containing the petition (vs. 51), while the supporting grounds or circumstances are presented in a following subordinate clause (vs. 52). The passage in Lamentations exhibits the same syntactic structure, the plea being expressed by the main clause (vs. 21), and the circumstances surrounding the petition being contained in a subordinate clause (vs. 22).

The problem here has been the precise meaning of the conjunction. I believe that in this passage *kî ʾim* is to be rendered "even if, although." This dual conjunction is used widely and rather loosely in biblical Hebrew in a variety of meanings listed in the lexicons. However, in several instances, the conjunction is best rendered "even if, although."[12] That this meaning has not been clearly recognized is due to the difficult passages in which it occurs:

Jer 51:14: *kî ʾim millēʾtîk ʾādām kayyęlęq wᵉʿānû ʿālayik hêdād*, "though I have filled you with men like the locust (i.e., increased your population), yet they (i.e., your assailants) lift up their shout against you."[13]

---

[9] So RSV.

[10] It is, of course, possible to assume that this poem is also incomplete, but this approach is a procedure to be adopted only when no other is available, and Hillers properly does not include this view among the possible options. In addition, virtually all scholars are agreed that the existence of 22 verses in the chapter, identical with the number of letters in the alphabet, is not accidental; it represents a variant of the acrostic pattern characteristic of chs. 1-4.

[11] As Rudolph correctly points out.

[12] Cf. BDB, *s.v.*, 474-75; KB, 431.

[13] See BDB, 475a, who cite Ewald, Keil, Cheyne; so also W. Rudolph, *Jeremia* (HAT; Tübingen: Mohr, 1947), 266. Other commentators render the clause, "I will surely fill them with assailants" (Hitzig, RSV), but this requires construing *millēʾtîk* as a perfect

Isa 10:22: *kî ʾim yihyēh ʿammᵉkā yiśrāʾēl kᵉḥōl hayyām šᵉʾār yāšûb bô*, "even if your people, O Israel, will be like the sand of the sea, only a remnant will return."[14]

Amos 5:22: *kî ʾim taʿᵃlû li ʿōlôt ûminḥōtêkem lōʾ ʾerṣeh*, "even if you offer up to me your holocausts and gift offerings, I will not accept them."[15]

This meaning is highly appropriate in Lam 3:32 as well: *kî ʾim hôgāh wᵉriḥam kᵉrōb ḥᵃsādāw*, "though he has afflicted, he will have pity according to his great mercies."

The meaning "although, even though" which we have postulated for the double conjunction may be the result of a transposition, *kî ʾim = ʾim kî*. We may cite as an analogy the use of *kî gam* which has the meaning "although" in Eccl 4:14; 8:12, 16. This usage, characteristic of Qoheleth, is equivalent to *gam kî*, "even if, although" (Isa 1:15; Hos 8:10; 9:16; Ps 23:4), and likewise introduces a subordinate clause.[16]

A syntactic change in the use of the conjunction "although" appears to have developed in the post-exilic period. In the pre-exilic usage, the subordinate clause introduced by the conjunction *precedes* the main clause (*kî ʾim*, Amos 5:22; Isa 10:22; Jer 51:14; *gam kî*, Hos 8:10; 9:16; so also Ps 23:4; Prov 22:6). Though post-exilic writers continue this sequence (Lam 3:8, 32), they nevertheless feel free to vary it by having the main clause *precede* the subordinate clause (*kî ʾim* in this passage; *kî gam* in Eccl 4:14; 8:12, 16). Obviously, from the standpoint of logic, either sequence of clauses is entirely proper.[17]

It remains to add that the verbs in this passage are to be understood as pluperfects.[18] We now have a vigorous, clear, and appropriate conclusion to the penitential prayer in the last three verses of Lamentations:

of certitude, which appears awkward in this context. Hence NEB follows the view we have adopted, rendering freely, "Once I filled you with men, countless as locusts, yet a song of triumph shall be chanted over you."

[14] The rendering *kî* as "for" disguises, but does not obviate, the difficulty involved in treating vs. 22 as the reason for vs. 21. Actually, the second verse offers no reason for the first; it expresses the same idea as the first, but with greater emphasis.

[15] Here, too, *kî* does not introduce the reasons for vs. 21.

[16] For a discussion of these passages in Ecclesiastes, see R. Gordis, *Koheleth — The Man and His World* (3rd ed.; New York: Schocken, 1968), 244, 297-98. There is virtually complete agreement on the meaning of *kî gam* in 4:14; on 8:12, see BDB, 169, s.v. § 6. We believe this meaning for the double conjunction most appropriate in all three passages.

[17] It may be added that in medieval Hebrew, *wᵉʾim* is frequently used in the sense, "although, even if." Thus in *Bᵉraḥ Dōdî*, the *Gᵉʾûlāh piyyûṭ* recited on the Second Day (as well as the other days) of Passover, the usage occurs no less than nine times in the meaning "though," e.g., *bᵉraḥ dôdî ʾel mākōn lᵉšibtāk wᵉʾim ʿābarnû ʾet bᵉritāk, ʾānā zᵉkōr*, "Fly, my beloved, to your established dwelling and though we have transgressed your convenant, remember, pray, etc." (*Sabbath & Festival Prayer Book* [New York: Rabbinical Assembly and United Synagogue, 1946], 182-83).

[18] Cf. S. R. Driver, *Hebrew Tenses* (Oxford: Clarendon, 1892), 22: "The perfect is used where we should employ by preference the pluperfect, i.e., in cases where it is desired to bring two actions in the past into a special relation with each other, and to indicate that the action described by the pluperfect was completed before the other took place. The function of the pluperfect is thus to throw two events into their proper perspective as regards each other; but the tense is to some extent a superfluous one — it is an elegance for which Hebrew possesses no distinct form, and which even in Greek, as is well known, both classical and Hellenistic is constantly replaced by the simple aorist."

Why do you neglect us eternally,
  forsake us for so long?
Turn us to yourself, O Lord, and we shall return;
  renew our days as of old,
even though you had despised us greatly
  and were very angry with us.

ECCLESIASTES 1 17 — ITS TEXT AND INTERPRETATION

I

THE testament of disillusion which is the book of Koheleth opens with the majestic description of the unending monotony of nature, wherein no progress or improvement is possible. After this introduction, Koheleth adopts the guise of Solomon, and describes his unsuccessful effort to attain happiness through wisdom and through pleasure. His reason for impersonating Solomon is set forth in 2 12, "for what avail is the man who comes after the King?" What better evidence of the vanity of wisdom and the emptiness of pleasure than the testimony of the great king, who possessed both gifts and found them wanting.

Koheleth accordingly describes his experiences (1 16 — 2 11) in two parts. The second section (2 1–11) is clearly concerned with his attempt to find happiness in beautiful surroundings, fine food, and the enjoyment of the senses. The first section (1 16–18) seems to deal with the pursuit of wisdom (vv. 16, 18), but this is by no means as self-evident, largely because of the difficulties of text and interpretation offered by v. 17:

וָאֶתְּנָה אֶת לִבִּי לָדַעַת חָכְמָה וְדַעַת הוֹלֵלוֹת וְשִׂכְלוּת יָדַעְתִּי שֶׁגַּם זֶה הוּא רַעְיוֹן רוּחַ.

The Masoretic text, as interpreted by the vowels[1] and the accents,[2] construes ודעת as an infinitive like לדעת, and places the caesura after חכמה.

---

[1] ודעת has a sheva under the Vav. *Vide infra.*
[2] A disjunctive accent (*zakeph katan*) is placed at חכמה, and a conjunctive accent (*mercha*) at ודעת,

323

365

This division of the text, however, is not borne out by the versions, which in spite of their divergences, are unanimous in construing ודעת as a noun, and making חכמה ודעת הוללות ושכלות the object of לדעת. They read as follows:

LXX: τοῦ γνῶναι σοφίαν καὶ γνῶσιν παραβολὰς καὶ ἐπιστήμην.
(To know wisdom and knowledge, proverbs and understanding)

Peshitta: ܠܡܕܥ ܚܟܡܬܐ ܘܝܕܥܬܐ ܘܡܬܠܐ ܘܣܘܟܠܐ
(same)

Vulgate: cognoscere prudentiam atque doctrinam, erroresque et stultitiam.

Targum: חוכמתא וחולחלתא דמלכותא ומנדעא וסוכלתנו
(wisdom and disorder of the kingdom, knowledge and understanding).

Of the four versions, only the Vulgate interprets ושכלות correctly as an alternative spelling for סכלות "folly."[3] LXX, P, and T take it to mean "understanding" from שָׂכַל, perhaps because of their desire to avoid imputing foolishness to Solomon. Nevertheless, their erroneous rendering substantiates the Masoretic text.

The most striking aberration of LXX and Peshitta, however, is their common rendering of הוללות as "proverbs." In all the other passages where the word, so typical of Koheleth, occurs, both the Greek and the Syriac translators know that it means "madness, folly," and render it with fair exactitude. Thus LXX interprets it as περιφοράν "error" (2 2, 12), παραφοράν "derangement, distraction" (7 25) and περιφέρεια (περιφέρει) "wandering about, error" (7 7, 9 3, 10 13). Similarly, the Peshitta renders it by ܡܫܒܒܠܘܬܐ "foolishness" (2 12, 7 25),[4] ܛܥܝܘ "wandering, error" (9 3) and ܟܘܦܣܬܐ ',shame", (9 13).[5]

---

[3] Cf. וסכלות in 2 3, 12, 13, 7 25, 10 1, 13 and the spelling מַשְׂמְרוֹת in 12 11 for the usual מסמרות. That שכלות =folly is the view of Knobel, Delitzsch, McNeile, Levy, Plumptre, etc.

[4] The rendering of תַּהְפֻּכוֹת in Pr 2 12.

[5] In 7 7 יְהוֹלָל is rendered by מובד, because of the parallel in the verse וִיאַבֵּד. In 2 2 מְהוֹלָל is given by Peshitta as ܡܕܗ ܗܘ. This Syriac rendering is usually

That both versions depart from their usual rendering and translate הוללות as "proverbs" implies a very close relationship at this point between LXX and Peshitta.[6] The Syriac can only be described as a translation of the Greek, which happens elsewhere in Koheleth as well.[7] It remains therefore to account for the Greek rendering of הוללות by παραβολὰs "proverbs."

Graetz solves the problem by assuming that the original Hebrew word was מְשָׁלוֹת, which the LXX translated correctly as "proverbs," and that שְׂכְלוּת is to be taken as "understanding." He fails to explain how משלות became corrupted to הוללות, nor does he adduce evidence in Biblical Hebrew for ôth as the plural ending of מָשָׁל. For these reasons, most scholars have rejected Graetz's emendation and recognized הוללות as original. They have preferred to assume that the LXX, followed by Peshitta, is giving a free rendering of the Hebrew, with an eye to avoiding an offensive reference to Solomon as "knowing madness."

Undoubtedly tendencious interpretations are not beyond the LXX, but it is not likely that a word correctly translated six times elsewhere in the book would be completely rejected and an altogether different word substituted.

We prefer another explanation for the Greek translation. We should like to suggest that an inner Greek error lies at the basis

---

translated "what do they avail?" with ܗܠܝܢ being construed as a participle from ܗܢܐ "be useful, serve." It is assumed that the Hebrew text underlying the Peshitta was מָה יוֹעִיל. This is graphically too distant from the Masoretic text. We should like to suggest another possibility. ܗܠܝܢ may be taken as the plural pronoun "they," and the Peshitta would mean "what are they?" i. e., "of what good are they?" This goes back perfectly to our Hebrew text מהלל vocalized as מְהַלְּלוּ, a contraction for מָה הַלְּלוּ "what are they." הללו is the common Mishnic form of the plural pronoun, and this type of contraction with מה is illustrated by Ex 4 2 (Kethib) מְזֶּה, Ez 8 6 (Kethib) מְהֵם, and the usual Mishnic form מְהוּ.

[6] Kaminetsky, "Die Pesita in Koheleth," *ZATW*, XXIV (1904), 181–239, does not recognize the full degree of connection between LXX and Peshitta. See especially pages 209, 236, 237 of the essay.

[7] Cf. Ecc 2 25 כי מי יאכל ומי יחוש. LXX read πίεται = יִשְׁתָּה for יאכל, and Peshitta adopts this rendering ܢܫܬܐ. So, too שָׂדָה וְשִׁדּוֹת 2 8 is rendered by LXX as "wine-cup bearers" which is also the rendering of Peshitta.

of LXX. παραβολὰς "proverbs" is a mistake for the word παραφορὰς "errors." The two words are graphically very close; in the uncial script especially, Beta and Phi, Rho and Lambda resemble each other: ΠΑΡΑΒΟΛΑΣ, ΠΑΡΑΦΟΡΑΣ. Once the error entered the text, several factors conspired to keep it in its place. The use of three different words to express the Hebrew הוללות, made additional variation easy. Moreover, "proverbs" suited the traditional character of Solomon far better than "wandering error." Lastly, the desire to avoid an offensive reference to Solomon may have helped to preserve the change in the text. This reading the Peshitta translated when it attempted to cope with our difficult passage.

The same tendency to place Solomon in as favorable a light as possible is particularly characteristic of Targum throughout the book, and appears in our passage as well. שכלות is translated "understanding," and *knowledge* is the rendering for ודעת.[8]

Corresponding to הוללות is the phrase חולחלתא דמלכותא "disorder of the kingdom," which is the Rabbinic paraphrase of the Hebrew. This is proved by the comment in Midrash Leviticus Rabbah, ch. 20 on Ps 75 5 אמרתי להוללים אל תהלו—אלו שלבן מלא חלחוליות רעות. So too, Midrash Koheleth Rabbah 2 12 interprets: הוללות—זו הוללה של מלכות "that means, the disorder in the kingdom" — a Hebrew rendering of the Targum in our passage.[9]

Thus all the four ancient versions are seen to go back to our present Masoretic text, even to the extent of the unusual orthography of ושכלות with a Sin.

Two alternative constructions of the passage are possible. The first, supported by the Masoretic vocalization and the accents, is to be rendered as follows:–

> "And I applied my heart to know wisdom,
> and to know madness and folly."

[8] For some reason, מנדעא has been taken out of its original place, and placed third instead of second in the series.

[9] Undoubtedly the resemblance of sound between Heth and He contributed to this interpretation, especially since Heth and He were not well differentiated in the popular pronunciation. Euringer, *Der Massoretische Text des Koheleth*, 38, recognizes that the Targum follow the Masoretic text, but does not account for its translation.

This interpretation is adopted among others by Rashi, Ibn Ezra, Ludwig Levy, Wright, Plumptre, Authorized Version, and Jewish Version. The second rendering, supported by the unanimous testimony of the ancient versions, reads thus:—

"And I applied my heart,
To know wisdom and knowledge, madness and folly."

This construction is favored by Ginsburg, McNeile, and Barton.

Against the latter construction, it has been urged that יָדַע דַּעַת is unhebraic. Yet this cognate accusation is a frequent Hebrew usage, and occurs in such passages as חוֹשֵׂךְ אֲמָרָיו יוֹדֵעַ דָּעַת (Pr 17 27) and תִּתְבּוֹנְנוּ בָהּ בִּינָה Jer 23 20. Moreover, the verse gains in smoothness and balance by the adoption of the second interpretation with two nouns in each stich, and we therefore accept it as the preferable construction.

II

With the text established, the difficulties of the interpretation still remain. What does Koheleth mean by saying that he set his heart to "know wisdom and knowledge, madness and folly?"

Many commentators[10] explain that Koheleth seeks to know the nature of folly as well as of wisdom, but nowhere are we told what is meant by madness and folly. By its etymology and usage, הוללות means "revelry, mad rejoicing, wickedness,"[11] but the description of his experiments with pleasure do not begin until Chapter Two. Moreover, in the following verse, which justifies the conclusion of v. 17, only wisdom and knowledge are spoken of —

"For in much wisdom is much vexation, and he that increaseth understanding increaseth sorrow."

C. D. Ginsburg therefore feels that only חכמה ודעת belongs to our verse, and he omits הוללות ושכלות as an error due to an imitation of 2 12. Jastrow on the contrary removes חכמה ודעת as

---

[10] So Ludwig Levy, Plumptre, Barton.

[11] Cf. Arabic جل and Akkadian alâlu —"shout, rejoice." Cf. Ps 75 5: אמרתי להוללים אל תהלו.

the insertion of a pious editor, retaining only הוללות ושכלות as
original. McNeile omits all of v. 17a ואתנה . . . . ודעת as a duplication of v. 16, and thus creates a text which reads as follows
(vv. 16, 17b) : ולבי ראה הרבה חכמה ודעת הוללות ושכלות ידעתי שגם זה
הוא רעיון רוח. Ehrlich goes further and omits the entire verse as
based on 2 12, which Zapletal and Haupt do on metrical grounds.

In order to approach the problem properly, it is essential to
keep the following elements clearly in mind:

1.—The text is vouched for by the unanimous testimony of
the versions.

2.—Verse 18, which seems to justify our passage, speaks only
of wisdom and knowledge, as does verse 16.

3.—The entire passage 1 16–18 should concern itself with
wisdom, as the succeeding section on 2 1–11 deals with the experiment with pleasure.[12]

We believe it is possible to solve the problem by recalling a
common usage in Semitic syntax. Verbs of perception (*verba
sentiendi*) may take two direct objects, both of which will be in
the accusative. This is especially common in Arabic,[13] as e. g.

علمت زيدا جاهلا   I know Zaid is a fool.

وجدته شيخا حليما   I found that he was a mild old man.

The same usage occurs in Hebrew,[14] where the second object
may be one of several types:

a) It may be an *adjective*:

מְצָאתִיהוּ טוֹב   I found him (to be) good.

Ecc 7 26   וּמוֹצֵא אֲנִי מַר מִמָּוֶת אֶת הָאִשָּׁה

And I find woman more bitter than death (=And I find
that woman is more bitter than death).

[12] Rashi clearly recognizes the division of the two sections in his comment
on 2 1: הואיל וכן הוא אחדל מן החכמה ואעסוק במשתה תמיד "Since this is so (i. e. wisdom
is vexation) I shall desist from wisdom, and occupy myself with feasting at
all times."

[13] See Caspari-Mueller, *Arabische Grammatik*, 4th ed., 1876, sec. 389.

[14] See Ewald, *Lehrbuch der hebräischen Sprache*, 7th ed., 1863, sec. 284b;
Ges.-Kautzsch, *Hebräische Grammatik*, 25th ed., sec. 117, 1, 6, The discussion
in Ewald is far superior to that of Gesenius-Kautzsch.

b. It may be a *participle*:

II Sam 6 16 וַתֵּרֶא אֶת דָּוִד מְפַזֵּז

She saw David dancing (= that David was dancing).

Ecc 7 21 אֲשֶׁר לֹא תִשְׁמַע אֶת עַבְדְּךָ מְקַלְלֶךָ

That you may not hear your servant cursing you (= not hear that your servant is cursing you).

c) It may be a *clause*:[15]

Gen 1 3 וַיַּרְא אֱלֹהִים אֶת הָאוֹר כִּי טוֹב

And God saw the light that it was good (= and God saw that the light was good).

I Kings 5 17 אַתָּה יָדַעְתָּ אֶת דָּוִד אָבִי כִּי לֹא יָכֹל לִבְנוֹת בַּיִת

You know my father David, that he could not build a house (= you know that my father David could not build, etc.).

d) It may be a *noun*:

Ecc 7 25 יָדַעְתִּי רֶשַׁע כָּסָל

I know that wickedness is folly.

It is worthy of note that practically each type of this construction can be illustrated from Ecclesiastes, in spite of the brief compass of the book. The double accusative after verbs of perception is thus undoubtedly characteristic of Koheleth's style.

We therefore suggest that our passage be understood in the same manner. לדעת is a verb of perception, and has two objects, each of which happens to be compound. The first object is חכמה ודעת, the second הוללות ושכלות—and the clause is to be rendered: "to know wisdom and knowledge as madness and folly."

In the clause ואתנה את לבי לדעת, the infinitive construct represents the result of the action of the main verb.[16] The words

---

[15] Where one of the accusatives is a clause, it is customary to speak of the first object as "anticipated," i. e. drawn out of its subordinate clause, into the main clause. The verses quoted are equivalent to וירא אלהים כי האור טוב and אתה ידעת כי דוד אבי לא יכל לבנות בית respectively. On "anticipation," see the writer's note in *AJSL*, 1931, 287–8.

[16] ידע in the sense to "learn to know," "discover" is very common. See *BDB*, 393b. Cf. also our paper in *AJSL*, LI (1935), 191–2. It may be added

are to be translated, "I applied my understanding so that I knew (or learnt),"[17] or, more idiomatically, "I applied my mind and learnt."

It now becomes possible to interpret the entire passage (vv. 16–18) without recourse to excision or emendation. It summarizes Koheleth's experience with wisdom and his conclusion as to its value as a road to happiness:—

I said to myself, I have gotten great wisdom, over all who were before me over Jerusalem, and my heart has seen much wisdom and knowledge. And I applied my mind and learnt that wisdom and knowledge is madness and folly; I perceived that this too is vanity and a striving after wind. For in much wisdom is much vexation and he who increases knowledge increases sorrow.

---

that our suggested rendering for 1 17 is much less "harsh" than the construction in 7 25 adduced above.

[17] That subordinate clauses of purpose and result are closely related is clear both from the nature of the mental processes involved and from the use of *ut* in Latin, *dass* in German, and *so that* in English in both varieties. The same function is performed by Lamed and the infinitive in Hebrew. According to Ges.-K., 114, 2, 4: "Very frequently the infinitive with Lamed serves in a very loose connection to express cause, condition, or other close relationship." Cf. Gen 3 22; Dt 8 6, 10 15; 1 K 2 3; Ps 104 14, 111 6 etc. On the use of Lamed of reference, see *BDB*, p. 517a, b. So too לְמַעַן "for the purpose of" develops virtually the meaning "with the result that", in such passages as Dt 29 18; Isa 30 1, 44 9; Ho 8 4; Amos 2 7; Mi 6 16. This development *may* be due to irony, as *BDB*, (p. 775b) suggests. Brown-Driver-Briggs Lexicon also compares the Arabic use of ل in Qoran 28 7 ليكون لهم عدوا "that he might become their enemy," where it represents the end result of the main verb.

Since the writing of this paper, the author was privileged to read an abstract of a paper read by Professor T. J. Meek before the Society of Biblical Literature and Exegesis (December 1936), on "The Consecutive Use of *le* and *lemaʿan*." Professor Meek proves that *le* and *lemaʿan* are used to introduce result clauses, by a comparison of Ju 2 12 (וַיַּכְעִיסוּ) on the one hand, and Dt 4 25 (לְהַכְעִיסוֹ) and II Ki 22 17 (לְמַעַן הַכְעִיסֵנִי) on the other. He cites the parallel use of ἵνα in the New Testament, in such passages as Mat 2 15. He interprets II Ki 2 27b (לְמַלֵּא) not as a purpose clause ("in order to fulfill"), but as a consecutive acluse ("so that there was fulfilled") — exactly as we interpret לָדַעַת "so that I knew."

A. INDEX OF PASSAGES

An H before a page number refers to the Hebrew Section.

I. BIBLE

Genesis

1:3	371
1:4	342, 243
1:14	270
1:27	81
2:9	78,81
2:19	76,81
2:21	H20
2:23	H38
3:1	297
3:5	81
3:6	20, 79
3:14-15	297
3:16	127,330
3:17	H41
3:22	78, 372
4:1	79, 82
4:4	87
4:15	214, 217
4:43	243
6:1	243
6:2	81, 87
8:4	356
8:13	243
8:17	34
8:18	243
9:21	36, 70
10:19	128
11:1	257
11:9	327
11:14	87
14:2	36
14:5	H8
14:13	H15
25:17	285
16:5	173
16:13	155
16:14	327
18:5	64, 71
18:26	211
18:32	71
19:5-6	80
19:9	145
19:11	204
19:22-23	80
20:1	36
20:16	320

21:7	356
22:24	241
23:11	98
23:13	98
24:14	H21
24:21	335
24:22	346
24:33	33
24:55	64, 71
25:23	36
25:25	H37
25:26	110
25:30	42
27:29	H46
27:36	110, 164
27:37	358
27:44-45	71-72
28:11	88
28:18	88
29:15	164
29:25	152
29:31	219
30:8	320
30:30	314
30:38	267
32:27	111, 361
33:4	6
37:2	348, 349
37:7	198
37:17	321
37:19	H15
37:20	257
38:16	211
38:23	219
38:26	92
39:20	33
41:14	122, 134
41:43	287
43:31	186
44:4	134
44:16	359
45:1	188
45:11	175
48:1-2	296, 327
48:16	314
49:5	H34
49:10	337
49:13	62
49:22	177
49:24	269

50:13	250
50:21	175
50:26	33

Exodus

1:11	169
1:17	219
1:22	219
2:4	191
2:9	198
3:2	H38
3:19	H13
4:2	367
6:4	41, 71
6:6	96
6:9	287, 297
12:3	206
12:15	H22
12:21	126
12:27	206
12:49	285
13:15	176
14:2	220, 222
15:1	265
15:13	96
16:20	H40
16:35	71
17:2	257
17:13	16
18:9	434
18:20	271
20:20	347
21:7	99, 357
21:8-11	99
21:22	356
21:36	347
22:5	347
22:15-16	219
22:19	246
22:24	71, 72
22:25-26	104
22:30	246
23:4	220
23:5	205
23:9	246
23:20	353
25:5	H47
25:23	327
26:16	344

VII. MIDRASH

B. INDEX OF ROOTS

C. INDEX OF WORDS, PHRASES AND PARTICLES

388

מחקרים
בספרות המקרא

מחקרים
בספרות המקרא

מאת

ראובן גורדיס

הוצאת כתב

ניו יורק

תשל"ו

תוכן

נבואת יונה בן אמתי מגת מגת החפר

(מקורות בלתי־מוכרים לתולדות הנבואה)

הרוצה לעמוד על השקפת עולמם של סופרי המקרא בכלל ושל כותבי ספרי ההיסטוריה
התנ״כית בפרט יעיין בס׳ מלכים. המחבר מקדיש בסך הכל י״ג פסוקים לירבעם בן יואש,
שמלך בישראל מ״א שנה, ולבן־דורו עזריה (עוזיה) בן אמציה, שישב על כסא מלכות
יהודה נ״ב שנה (מלכ׳ ב׳ י״ד, 23—ט״ו, 7) [1]. ידוע היה לו לסופר ס׳ מלכים ששני המלכים
הללו הצליחו להרחיב את גבולות ארצותיהם להיקף ימי מלכות דוד ושלמה. סופר ,,דברי
הימים״ אמנם מוסר לנו ידיעות נוספות על עזריה ומרחיב עליו את הדיבור (דבה״י ב׳ כ״ו,
1—23), אולם מאידך גיסא עובר הוא בשתיקה גמורה על בן דורו בצפון, ירבעם בן יואש [2].
ברור שאבן הפינה של השקפת סופרי המקרא היא האמונה שהצלחתה והשלוה הלאומית
מושתתות על אמונה בה׳ והליכה בדרכיו וכי הכשלון הלאומי נגרם בעטיה של בגידה בה׳
והזנחת מצוותיו [3]. כל מאמציהם של ההיסטוריוני המקרא נועדו אפוא להבליט גישה
דתית־מוסרית זאת, בלא שהתענינו במאורעות פוליטיים, כלכליים וצבאיים אלא במידה
שאלה סייעו למגמה זו.

הבא אפוא לכתוב את דברי ימי התקופה המקראית ברוח אוביקטיבית ובמבט מקיף
וכולל — עד כמה שאפשר לממש אידיאל זה — חייב להתחשב בנטיה יסודית זו שבמקורות
ולתקן את ,,המשפט הקדום״ הזה בתארו את חיי עם ישראל וקורותיו, ולא רק מן הבחינה
החמרית והחיצונית שבהם אלא אף בתופעות הרוחניות והפנימיות, כגון הערכת הנבואה
בישראל [4].

---

1. שנות מלכותו של ירבעם הן 785—745, ושל עזריה 783—742, לפי אולברייט. מרגלית־מרכס
    קובעים את שנות עזריה ל־780—740, הסטיה מן השנים המנויות במקרא יסודה בבעיות התאמת
    הכרונולוגיה המקראית למיסמכים המזרח־תיכוניים האחרים, ולא פה המקום להאריך.

2. הערכה נכונה על הישגיהם של ירבעם ועזריה ימצא הקורא בכל ספרי ההיסטוריה המקראית
    החדשים, כגון A History of Israel, John Bright עמ׳ 238—255.

3. המקור לגישה זו להיסטוריה המקראית הוא ס׳ דברים (ראה ביחוד פרקים י״א, ול״ב) אך אינו
    מצומצם רק בו. השקפה זו עוברת כחוט השני בכל ספרי ההיסטוריה והנבואה, ובשינוי המסגרת,
    בספרות החכמה.

4. אין לפרט כאן אף מקצת מן המקצת על השקפת הנביאים. תמצית גישתנו לנבואה בישראל
    יש למצוא במאמרנו "The Bible as a Cultural Monument" במאסף The Jews
    (בעריכת ל. פינקלשטיין), עמ׳ 783—822. לא כאן המקום לדון בגישתו של פרופ׳ י. קויפמן ז״ל,
    המוצא הבדל יסודי בתורת הגמול של הנביאים מצד אחד וסופרי ,,נביאים ראשונים״, תהלים
    וספרות החכמה מצד שני. דעותיו היסודיות בספרו הקלסי ,,תולדות האמונה הישראלית״ ראויות
    לתגובה מקיפה וכוללת. אציין רק שמכמה נימוקים, אני מסתייג משיטתו בנושא זה ובתחומים
    אחרים. לעצם ענינינו כאן אין בעיה זו חשובה.

1

דברי הנביאים הקלאסיים שהגיעו אלינו בספרי „נביאים אחרונים", ותולדותיהם
המסופרות במקצת בספרי „נביאים ראשונים", משקפים נקודת־ראות של קבוצה קטנה,
יוצאת דופן, בימי בית ראשון. בכללם היו נביאים אלה קטני השפעה ומעוטי מספר כלפי
רוב הנביאים המקובלים בדורותיהם, שהיוו שכבה חשובה במנהיגות הרשמית במדינה. מכל
סוגי הנביאים השונים שפעלו בישראל נשארו רק רישומים מעטים ומקוטעים במקורותינו,
מאחר שסופרי המקרא הביטו עליהם בשלילה גמורה, מתוך האספקלריה של הנביאים
העליונים, שמפיהם אנו חיים עד היום. הידיעות שהגיעונו על הדרגות הנמוכות של הנביאים
מרוכזות כמעט לגמרי בתקופה הקדומה, לפני הופעתם של עמוס והושע במאה השמינית
לפסה״נ.

הסוגים האלה כוללים את „ ה ר ו א י ם", שאליהם פנו בני העם הפשוט עם צרותיהם
ובעיוניותיהם הפרטיות, תפקיד שלא נטש גם שמואל הנביא (שמו' א', ט')[5]. בודאי המשיכו
„רואים" מטיפוס זה לפעול ולהשתכר גם בתקופה מאוחרת, אלא שנקודת התעניינותם של
סופרי המקרא עברה מהם לנביאים הקלסיים, ולכן לא נזכרו הרואים במאות האחרונות
של הבית הראשון. סוג שני של נביאים, שמקורם בראשית ימי האומה, היו נ ב י א י ם ־
מ נ ה י ג י ם, כגון משה, דבורה, ושמואל, שפעלו בתקופה הטרום־ממלכתית כמדריכי העם
ומעוריריו בשעות משבר לאומי. עם קום המלוכה, ירד סוג זה מבמת ההיסטוריה ואת מקומו
תפס במידת מה טיפוס חדש, שפעל בחוג מצומצם יותר. כוונתנו ל נ ב י א י ה ח צ ר, שנספחו
לחוג פקידי המלך, שהיו דרים בכפיפתו וסרים למשמעתו. ברור שנביאים אלה, שהתפרנסו
משולחן המלך, היו ברובם המכריע נכנעים בדעותיהם לאדוניהם ומשמיעים לאזניהם מה
שרצו לשמוע. אופייני מאד הדבר ששמותיהם של נביאי החצר האלה לא נשמרו במקרא —
רק נתן הנביא ידוע לנו, הודות לעוזו המוסרי הנדיר, בתוכחתו לדוד על חטאו עם בת־
שבע ורצח אוריה החתי (שמו' א', י״ב), ואחרי כן הודות לתפקידו הפעיל בהמלכת שלמה
(מלכ' א'—א').

עוד טיפוס אחד, שהתפתחה במישרין מן הנביאים־המנהיגים הקדומים, היו ה נ ב י א י ם
ה ע צ מ א י י ם, בעלי השפעה אישית כבירה, שפעלו בחיי האומה ביחוד בימי משבר
ומהפכה. לסוג זה שייך אחיה השילוני (מלכ' א', י״א, 39—29; י״ד 18—1), שהמליך את
ירבעם בן נבט, מעשה המקביל למשיחת שאול ודוד על־ידי שמואל.

הנעלה ביותר בסוג זה היה אליהו התשבי. מדבריו לא נותר לנו מאומה, אך במעשיו
הכבירים התוה את הדרך שבה הלכו נביאי „הדיבור" הנשגבים. אליהו העלה על נס את
שני עקרונות הנבואה — האמונה הקנאית באלהי ישראל, האחד והמיוחד, ללא שיתוף
ופשרה, אמונה שהתבטאה בהתנגשותו עם נביאי הבעל על הר הכרמל (מלכ' ב', י״ח), והדרישה
המוחלטת לצדק החברתי, ללא ויתורים ויוצאים מן הכלל, שמצאה לה ביטוי בהתקפתו
את אחאב על מעשה נבות היזרעאלי (מלכ' א', כ״א).

תלמידו המובהק, אלישע, שביקש רק שני שלישים[6] מרוח רבו הגדול (מלכ' ב', ב', 9),

---

5. השם „רואה" מוסב רק על שמואל (שמו' א', ט', 9; דבה״י א', ט', 22, כ״ו 28, כ״ט 29)
ועל חנני בימי אסא (דבה״י ב', ט״ז, 7, 10), ואולי גם על צדוק הכהן (שמו' ב', ט״ו, 27), ובלשון
רבים בא לסמן את סוג הנביאים בכלל, בתכבולת ל„חוזים", בישע' ל', 10.

6. כך פירוש הביטוי „פי שנים", כלומר שני חלקים (משלשה), גם בדברים כ״א, 17, וזכריה
י״ג, 8 ויכיח. הצעתו של קלרמון־גאנו שיש לפרש את המשקל „פים", שנחשף בחפירות
מאקאליסטר ואחרים, כ„שתי שלישיות השקל" מסתברת בהחלט. ברם, נראה כי כממשיכים לנקד

לא הגיע לרמתו המוסרית. אף־על־פי־כן המשיך את מסורת הפעולה והמנהיגות הלאומית
של שמואל ואחיה בשעתם. מחזור מעשי הניסים של אלישע (מלכ׳ ב׳, ב׳—ט׳) מכיל קווים
רבים המזכירים את תפקיד ״הרואים״ הקודמים.

מן המובנות שעמדתו העצמאית של אליהו, שהתנגדה ליסודות המשטר המקובל,
לא נשאה חן בעיני השלטונות, ביחוד כשהמדינה התבצרה והסדר החברתי־כלכלי עבר
מדרגת הנגודים־למחצה לתרבות עירונית־טכנית מפותחת ומורכבת. עם עליית כח המלך
והמנגנון הפוליטי־צבאי שמסביבו הצליחה הממשלה במידה רבה להשתיק את קול הנבואה
העצמאית, ששללה את רוב הערכים המקובלים. את עמוס מתקוע גרשו מבית אל וניסו
להשתיקו לגמרי[7]. את ירמיהו כלאו בבית הסוהר ואת בן דורו וחברו לדעה, אוריהו בן
שמעיהו, שלא היו לו תומכים בין שרי החצר, רצחו נפש[8]. ואם זכה ירמיהו במידת־מה
להשפעה על המלך, היה זה פרי העובדה שדעותיו עלו בד בבד עם דעות המפלגה הפרו־בבלית
בחצר המלכות, אף שהנימוקים לכך היו שונים בתכלית. רק הנביא ישעיה בן אמוץ נבדל
לטובה מחבריו הנביאים, אולי מפני יחוסו המשפחתי, ויותר מזאת, מחמת שהמלך חזקיהו
היה קרוב לרוחו. ראוי לציין שהשפעתו מצאה הד בחצר אך ורק מפני שאמונתו בנצחיות
ירושלים, עיר מושב ה׳, היתה זהה עם עמדת מגיני העיר נגד סנחריב. מאידך גיסא,
כשהתנגד הנביא לשיטת הכניעה המופרזת בפני אשור שנקט אחז, לא עלה בידו לכפות
את דעתו על המלך ושרי המדינה (ישע׳ ז׳). אפילו את חזקיהו לא יכול ישעיהו לשכנע,
כשהלה רצה לבוא בברית עם מרודך בלאדן בן בלאדן מלך בבל, לשם מרידה באשור
(מלכ׳ ב׳—כ׳, 12 ואילך: ישע׳ ל״ט).

ברור שהשפעת הנביאים ירדה הלוך וירוד במשך מאה וחמשים השנים האחרונות של
בית ראשון. לכן נאלצו הנביאים להעלות את דבריהם על ספר בעזרת תלמידים הנאמנים
לתורתם, כגון ״הלמודים״ הנזכרים בישע׳ (ח׳, 16) והסופר ברוך בן נריה, מקורבו של
ירמיהו.

את השם בחיריק ״פִּים״, וכך נשאר חסר הסבר מתקבל על הדעת. במאמר שהופיע ב־JBL
(1942), כרך 61, עמ׳ 211–209, הצעתי לנקד את המלה כשם שניי — פים, ופירושו ״שני חלקים
(משלשה), דהיינו שתי שלישיות השקל״, והדבר מתפרש יפה בלוח המחירים שקבעו הפלשתים
לשם השחזת כלי הברזל של בני ישראל, הנתון בכתוב בשמ״א א׳, י״ג 21. המפרשים שינו
פסוק זה וסרסוהו, ויש שראוהו כמשובש כל־עיקר. (השוה קיטל, Biblia Hebraica, שם).
במאמרי הנ״ל הראיתי כי אין צורך בתיקונים מופלגים וכי יש להעתיק את ה,,למד״ מן המלה
,,ולשלש״ למלה הבאה, ותו לא. אז יהא הפסוק מחוור: ,,והיתה הפצירה (= מחיר ההשחזה)
פַיִם (= שתי שלישיות השקל) למחרשות ולאתים וּשְלָש (שליש שקל, חצי פים) לקלשון
ולהקרדומים ולהציב הדרבן״.

7. מקובלת ההנחה בין רוב החוקרים שאחרי גירושו ממקדש בית אל ע״י אמציה הכהן (עמוס ז׳),
נשתתק עמוס ולא ניבא יותר. השערה זו נראית מוטעית וחסרת־יסוד. בעטיה לא הובן מבנה
ס׳ עמוס ומהלך דעותיו, והמפרשים באו לידי השמטות וסירוסים ללא צורך וטעם. ראה מאמרנו
"The Composition and Structure of Amos", שהופיע ברבעון Harvard Theological Review, 1940 כרך 33, עמ׳ 251–239, המציע פתרון לבעיות אלה על ידי גישה חדשה,
שזכתה להתקבל על ידי חוקרים אחדים בזמן האחרון. המאמר מופיע גם בספרי החדש הנזכר
בהערה 14.

8. ירמ׳ כ״ו, 20–24, וכן רצח זכריה בן יהוידע הכהן, כאשר ,,לבשה אותו רוח אלהים״ והתנבא
דבהי״ב, כ״ד, 20). בברית החדשה נתערבב זכריה, זה עם זכריהו בן יברכיהו (ישע׳ ח׳, 2;
ראה מתי כ״ג, 35.

רק לאחר חורבן הבית, גלות ושיבת ציון, נתאמתו דברי הנביאים, ולו גם בצורה מסוימת, הן לשבט והן לחסד, ודברי האיום והנחמה שלהם כאחת הוכרו על-ידי העם בכללו כמוצא פי ה'. מאז היכו דברי הנביאים שרשים עמוקים בלב העם. אבל בעצם זמן פעולתם, היו הנביאים חסרי אונים ומעוטי השפעה.

הנביאים שאכן זכו לכבוד ולפרנסה בחייהם הם אלה הידועים לנו בשם הגנאי "נביאי השקר"[9]. שמותיהם של חוזים אלה, והם היוו את הרוב בימיהם, לא הגיעו עדינו, מחמת השקפתם המיוחדת של סודרי המקרא הנזכרת לעיל. רק במקרים בודדים כותבי העתים את שמו של "נביא השקר", בבואו בהתנגשות ישירה עם "נביא אמת", כגון צדקיהו בן כנענה בימי מיכיהו בן ימלה (מלכ' א', כ"ב) וחנניה בן עזור בדורו של ירמיהו (ירמ' כ"ח).

נביאי שקר אלה, שהיו מכובדים ומוכרים הן על-ידי רבי המלך והן על-ידי ההמון, שיקפו את העמדה המקובלת של החברה. יש להניח שכתומכי המשטר הקיים, לא כאבו ביותר את אי-הצדק החברתי ומעשי האלימות ודיכוי העניים. כמו כן לא קראו תגר על מיזוג עבודת ה' בפולחן האלילות והשחתת המידות הכרוכה בסינקרטיזם זה. ייתכן שאף בתחומים אלה של אי-הצדק החברתי, העבודה הזרה, וההתנוונות המוסרית באו לידי מלחמה גלויה עם נביאי האמת, שדנו את עמדתם ברותחין. אך המקורות המעטים שהגיעונו מראים בעליל שנקודת הכובד בהתנגשות שני טיפוסי הנביאים היתה הפוליטיקה החיצונית. "נביאי השקר", הן באפרים והן ביהודה, תמכו בשיטת ההשתלבות המדינית במהלכי המדיניות שבמזרח התיכון, אם בכריתת ברית וכניעה לאומית כלפי האימפריות השולטות של אשור ובבל, אם בנסיונות של פריקת עולן תוך מרידה משותפת, כגון בימי פקח ורצין במאה השמינית, ואם בהתקשרות עם מצרים, כבסוף המאה השישית לפסה"נ.

"נביאי האמת", על אף ההבדלים האישיים שביניהם, התנגדו בכללם בחריפות לכל שיטה של קשרי ברית בין עמם ושכניהם. אולי הכירו בעיגם הבוחנת והבלתי-משוחדת, כי תכסיסי ברית ומלחמה עלולים להביא את המדינה לכליון גמור. ברור שחששו מפני חדירתן של השפעות זרות לאמונת ישראל ולתרבותו, מתוך יצירת יחסים קרובים עם העמים אשר סביבותם. בתודעת הנביאים היו תכסיסי ברית אלה בגידה בה' וחוסר אמון בכחו המושיע, ודוגמאות אחדות יספיקו:

וירא אפרים את חליו   ויהודה את מזורו
וילך אפרים אל אשור   וישלח אל מלך ירב
והוא לא יוכל לרפוא לכם   ולא יגהה מכם מזור

(הושע ה' 13)

כי כה אמר ה' אלהים קדוש ישראל

בשובה ונחת תושעון   בהשקט ובבטחה תהיה גבורתכם

ולא אביתם

(ישע' ל', 15)

על ציר זה נסבה ההתנגשות בין "נביאי האמת" ויריביהם, שהביטו עליהם בשאט נפש. בתקופה הקדומה עדיין לא הרהיבו נביאי האמת עוז בנפשם לשלול את כנותם של

---

9. הביטוי המדויק הזה אמנם אינו מצוי במקרא. הקרוב לו נמצא בירמ' כ"ג, 26 "הנביאים נבאי השקר", וכן ה, 31, וגם "נביא מורה שקר" בישע' ט, 14. אך הכינוי "שקר" מוסב תכופות על הנביאים המקובלים בדברי הקובלנה של מתנגדיהם, ד"מ ירמ' י"ד, 14, כ"ג, 25, כ"ט, 21, ועוד הרבה, זכריה י"ג, 3.

נביאים אלה, והסבירו את פעולתם המסולפת ועמדתם המסוכנת כפרי רוח שקר שמוצאו
מה'. כך מצהיר מיכיהו בן ימלה על צדקיהו בן כנענה: "ויאמר ה' מי יפתה את אחאב ויעל
ויפל ברמת גלעד ויאמר זה בכה וזה בכה. ויצא הרוח ויעמד לפני ה' ויאמר אני אפתנו
ויאמר ה' אליו במה. ויאמר אצא והייתי רוח שקר בפי כל נביאיו ויאמר תפתה וגם תוכל,
צא ועשה כן. ועתה הנה נתן ה' רוח שקר בפי כל נביאיך אלה וה' דבר עליך רעה" (מלכ'
א', כ"ב, 20—23).

ברם, כעבור דורות אחדים, ובייחוד כאשר השפעתם של "נביאי האמת" הצטמצמה יותר
ויותר, הרחיקו ללכת במשאותיהם וחרצו משפט קשה יותר על "נביאי השקר". מיכה
המורשתי מתקיפם כשקרנים ובדאים הלהוטים אחרי הבצע ותו לא: "כה אמר ה' על
הנביאים המתעים את עמי הנושכים בשניהם וקראו שלום ואשר לא יתן על פיהם וקדשו
עליו מלחמה" (ג', 5). כן מכחיש ירמיהו את סמכותו של חנניה בן עזור: "לא שלחך ה'"
(ירמ' כ"ח, 15).

כה נתרחב הפער בין נביאי האמת המעטים ובין "נביאי השקר", והם הרוב המכריע.
אף-על-פי-כן היה הקו המבדיל ביניהם דק מאוד; הן בסגנון ("כה אמר ה' "), הן בשימוש
הדרמטי במעשים סמליים לא נבדלו צדקיהו בן כנענה וחנניה בן עזור ממתנגדיהם הנבואיים.

חשוב להוסיף שהדמיון לא הצטמצם בצורות הנבואה בלבד. גם בתוכן חזיונותיהם לא
חצץ קיר ברזל בין שני סוגי הנביאים. בתוך ספרי הנבואה המקראיים אנו מוצאים נבואות
זעם על שכניהם-אויביהם של בני ישראל, בישעיה (ט"ו—כ"ג), ירמיהו (מ"ו—נ"א) ויחזקאל
(כ"ה—ל"ב, ל"ה, ל"ח, ל"ט). אמנם השתיכותם של פרקים אלה לספריהם שנויה במחלוקת
וכדי להבהיר את העניין נדרש עיון מיוחד לכל נבואה ונבואה. אפס, תהיינה המסקנות
אשר תהיינה, אין ספק שנביאי האמת ניבאו גם הם על גורל האומות השכנות שעיצבו את
חיי עם ישראל, או השפיעו עליהם במידה חשובה. לא ייתכן שהמאמינים באלהי הצדק
המושל בכל העולם יעלימו עין ממעשי האלימות והרצח של העמים עובדי האלילים שסבבו
את עם ישראל וסיכנו את קיומו. כשהצהיר אייספלדט על הנביא עמוס "Bei ihm ist Gott
alles, Israel nichts", "אצלו (אצל עמוס) ה' הוא הכל וישראל לא כלום", הביע את גישתו
של תיאולוג נוצרי, בייחוד בימי הנאצים. אך בשום אופן לא את השקפתו של נביא בישראל,
שכל הרפתקאותיו וסבלו נבעו מתוך אהבה עמוקה לעמו. ואף מנקודה דתית "טהורה", לא
פקפקו הנביאים, על אף חסרונותיהם המוסריים של בני עמם, כי ישראל נבחר ונועד להיות
הכלי היחיד והמיוחד להעברת קול ה' בעולם ולהשמעת רצונו לבני אדם.

אמנם קיים היה הבדל יסודי בין שני סוגי הנביאים גם בדבר הנבואות "על הגויים".
אצל נביאי האמת המשפט הקשה היה המשפט שחרצו על העמים תוצאה ישירה מאמונתם בשלטון
אלהי הצדק, ולכן העבירו גם את עמם, ובייחוד את עמם, תחת שבט הביקורת הנבואית.
תוכחתו העזה של עמוס על העמים מהווה חלק בלתי-נפרד מחזונו הקשה על יהודה ואפרים
(עמוס א'—ב'). נביאי השקר, מאידך גיסא, ציפו רק לכשלון הגויים ולנצחון עמם. כל עוד
נמשך טקס הפולחן הרשמי כנהוג במקדש, מילא ישראל את חובותיו כלפי מעלה. עם זאת
לא נבדלו חלקי נבואתו של עמוס, למשל, הדנים בארם, פלשתים צור, אדום, עמון, ומואב
(א' 3—ב' 3), הן בצורה והן בתוכן, מנבואות הנביאים המקובלים, שהיו רווחות בלי ספק בזמנו.

*\
*

מתוך אוסף נבואותיו של עמוס, הכלולות בתשעה פרקים, אפשר לנו היום לקבל מושג
מקיף פחות או יותר מהשקפת עולמו בכללותה. לא כן הדבר בנוגע לנביאים אחרים, שנשאר

לנו רק מעט מזער מדבריהם. חזונו של עובדיה על אדום ושל נחום האלקושי על נינוה,
המנבאים חורבן וכליה על אויבי עמם, אינם נבדלים במשהו מדברי הנביאים הפטריוטיים
שבימיהם. ייתכן שבזמן מן הזמנים היה בעזבונם הספרותי של עובדיה ונחום חומר יותר
רב ממה שהגיע עדינו, ושדוקא חומר זה ביסס את זכותם להימנות בין נביאי האמת
הדגולים. ברם, החומר המצוי בידינו דומה לדברי הנביאים הידועים לנו כ„נביאי השקר".

בין הנביאים הפטריוטיים האלה נמנה הנביא יונה בן אמתי מגת החפר, שפעל בימי
ירבעם בן יואש. מה שלא הוכר עד עתה הוא שבתעודה הקצרה על המלך המוכשר הזה
(מלכ' ב' י"ד 23—24) שקועים שני קטעי נבואה, שהם עצם פרי רוחו של הנביא, כלשונם
וככתבם. ואלה דברי הכתוב:

„הוא (ירבעם בן יואש) השיב את גבול ישראל מלבוא חמת [10] עד ים הערבה כדבר ה'
אלהי ישראל, אשר דבר ביד עבדו יונה הנביא אמתי הנביא מגת החפר.

כי — רָאֹה ה' אֶת עֳנִי יִשְׂרָאֵל   מֹרֶה[11] מְאֹד,

וְאֶפֶס עָצֹור וְאֶפֶס עָזֹוב   וְאֵין עֹזֵר לְיִשְׂרָאֵל"

ברור שהפסוק השני כתוב במשקל שירי, ולכן חילקנו את הצלעות [12] וציינו את הנגינה.
הקצב המתקבל מן הפסוק בשתי הצלעות הראשונות הוא 4 || 2, ובשתי הצלעות האחרונות
4 || 3, והוא מאופיין בדלת ארוכה ובסוגר קצר. הראשון שהכיר קצב זה בשירה המקראית
היה קרל בודה, שמצאו לפני תשעים שנה בשירי אבל, והגדיר את משקלו כ-3 || 2. משתי
בחינות נתרחב מושג „קצב הקינה" לגבי מה ששיער בודה בשעתו [13]:

א. המשקל הזה אינו מיועד רק לנושאי אבל וקינה. הוא נמצא גם בדברי תפילה
(כגון תה' כ"ז), גם בשירי אהבה (שה"ש ה' 10 ואילך).

ב. אין משקל זה מצטמצם בקצב 3 || 2 בלבד. עיקרו — הדלת ארוכה מן הסוגר.
מכאן שיש כמה וכמה צורות של קצב הקינה, כגון 4 || 3 או 4 || 2, ואף קצבים יותר מורכבים,
כגון 4 || 4 || 3 או 3 || 3 || 2 או 4 || 4 || 3 || 3. ספר „איכה", במיוחד, מכיל כל צורות רבות
ושונות של „קצב הקינה", שתכליתן למעט את סכנת השעמום הכרוך בשימוש בקצב אחד
בשיר ארוך.

<hr>

10. היום מקובל ש„לבוא" אינו שם עצם, „פתח, בדרך", אלא שם מקום במזרח הירדן הידוע
באכדית בשם לאבו. השוה M. Noth ברבעון DPG כרך 58, עמ' 246—242, Palaestina-
Jahrbuch, כרך 33, ע' 36—51, H. Lewy בשנתון HUCA, כרך 18, ע' 445 ואילך. על
המקביל המצרי ראבו, השוה BASOR, חוברת 102, עמ' 9.

11. השבעים, פשיטא, וולגטה מתרגמים את המלה מלשון מ ר. קיטל ב-BH מציע
לקרוא הַמַּר. כל המצוי אצל השירה המקראית יכיר שהשימוש בה"א הידיעה מיוחד.
נראה יותר לקיים את המסורת ולפרש „מרה" כפעל ל"י המקביל לפעל ע"ע; השוה „רנו — רנה
(איוב ל"ט, 23); שגג — שגה, שסה — שסס" ועוד הרבה. השורש ל"י מופיע גם בברא' כו,
ל"ה „מורת רוח".

12. לשם הבהירות נצייון, כי אנו משתמשים במונח „צלע" לסמן פרזה שירית, כגון „האזינו השמים
ואדברה", ובמונח „חרוז" לסמן פסוק שלם המכיל שתי צלעות (או שלש, ולפרקים ארבע).
13. ראה ZATW כרך 2 שנת 1882 עמ' 1—52 K. Budde, Das hebräische Klagelied,
וכן מאמרו ב-Hastings, Dictionary of the Bible, המאמר „Poetry", כרך 4, עמ' 3—13,
ומני אז, בכל סקירה על השירה המקראית כגון G.B. Gray, Forms of Hebrew Poetry
(1915); O. Eissfeldt, The Old Testament, An Introduction (1965), עמ' 51—64.
מ.צ. סגל, מבוא למקרא, וראה הערה 14 להלן.

עוד סימן מובהק של השירה המקראית, שלא עמדו עליו עד עכשיו, נמצא בקטע
נבואי קצר זה. במקום אחר ייחדנו את הדיבור על תופעה זו [14]: משורר או נביא יש שהוא
רוצה לסיים מזמור או נאום ביתר עוז, כדי להשאיר רושם יותר כביר בלב הקורא או השומע
את דבריו, בחינת השימוש במוסיקה ב־fortissimo או crescendo. כדי להשיג מטרה
זו השתמש המשורר המקראי באמצעי אחד, האארכת הקצב בסוף השיר או בסוף
חלק מסוים. הדבר נעשה באחת מארבע דרכים אלה, ולעתים בשתים מהן יחדיו:

א. הגדלת מספר הצלעות בפסוק האחרון, כגון שלוש במקום שתים
וכו' [15].

ב. הגדלת מספר ההברות בחרוז האחרון, על־ידי מלים ארוכות
יותר או ריבוי מלים קצרות [16].

ג. האארכת הקצב בצלע האחרונה בלבד [17], דרך הגורמת לפרקים לכך
שהסוגר יהיה ארוך מן הדלת. תופעה זו נדירה בדרך כלל, ומצויה בעיקר אך ורק כאן.

ד. האארכת הקצב בחרוז האחרון [18], למשל, בהיות השיר בנוי בקצב הקינה
היסודי (3 || 2), יסתיים בקצב יותר ארוך בפסוק האחרון. כך נגמר מזמור מ״ב—מ״ג בקצב
4 || 4. 3. מזמור כ״ז, הכתוב בקצב הקינה, מסתיים בחלקו הראשון (פסוק 6) בקצב 4 || 3 [19].

בקטע נבואי קצר זה של יונה בן אמתי מתגלם רק הכלל האחרון — האארכת הקצב
בחרוז האחרון. בה בשעה שהצלעות א' וב' הן בקצב 4 || 2, מארכות הצלעות ג' וד' לקצב
4 || 3. ראוי לציין שכדי להאריך את צלע ג' חל שינוי בביטוי המקובל ״עצור ועזוב״, הנמצא
בארבעה מקומות אחרים במקרא (דב' ל״ב, 36: מלכים א' י״ד 10; כ״א, 21; מלכ' ב', ט' 8),
מתוך הכנסת המלה ״ואפס״, המפרידה בין הדבקים [20].

הצורה השירית המובהקת שבה מנוסח פסוק 26 מעידה כמאה עדים שיש לפנינו קטע
נבואי. ברם, גם הפסוק הקודם, הכתוב בפרוזה, אינו דיווח היסטורי אלא קטע מחזיר נבואי.
הכתוב מודיע לנו: ״הוא השיב את גבול ישראל מלבוא חמת עד ים הערבה כדבר ה' אלהי
ישראל אשר דבר ביד עבדו יונה בן אמתי הנביא מגת החפר״. אף־על־פי שירבעם היה מלך

14. ראה מאמרנו ״על מבנה השירה העברית הקדומה״, בספר השנה ליהודי אמריקה, שנת תש״ה,
    עמ' 159—136, ושם פרטים על כמה וכמה מן הדוגמאות המובאות להלן. מאמר זה מופיע
    בתרגום אנגלי ובהרחבה בספרי החדש Poets, Prophets and Sages — Essays in
    Biblical Interpretation (Indiana University Press) (1971).

15. השוה תהלים מזמורים י״ג, י״ד, ט״ז, י״ח, ל״ז, מ״ז, נ״ג, ע״ג, צ', צ״ד, ק״ג, ק״ד, קי״א,
    קי״ט, קכ״ה, קכ״ו, קמ״ח; איוב ר', י״ט, כ״ו, בדברי איוב ופרק י״א בדברי צופר.

16. השוה תהלים מזמורים י״ז, כ״ו, מ״א, ע״א, פ״א, צ״א, קט״ז; איוב פרק ה', בדברי אליפז,
    י״ז, כ״א, בדברי איוב, י״ח, בדברי בלדד, מ״א, במענה ה'.

17. השוה מזמורים ח', כ', ס״ב, ס״ו, פ״ד, וכן מזמורים י״ג, מ״ז, מ״ט, ס״ג, ס״ו, פ״ו, קכ״ג, וכן
    מזמורים ד', ג', נ״ב, וקמ״ה.

18. השוה מזמורים צ״ח, ק״ו, י״ט (פסוק 11), כ״ד, ל״ד, נ״א (פסוק 19), פ״ב, פ״ט, צ', קמ״ט, ק״ן;
    מיכה ר', 6.

19. כמו כן, כשהשיר בנוי צלעות משולשות, יארך החרוז האחרון לקצב מחומש (מזמור צ״ח, ק״ן)
    ובייחוד לקצב מרובע (מזמורים י״ט, פסוק 11; כ״ד, ל״ד, נ״א, פס' 19, פ״ב, פ״ט, צ', קמ״ט,
    ק״ן, וכן מיכה ר' 6—8).

20. ביטוי זה, שאינו מחוור די צרכו, הוא דוגמא של merismus, ופירושו הוא, כנראה: ״כל החי —
    הן העצור (בבית הכלא), והן החפשי״, וראה Oxford Lexicon, BDB עמ' 737.

גבור ומצליח, ספק גדול הוא אם נכללו חמת ודמשק של סוריה בתוך גבולות ממלכתו [21].
וכיון שבן־דורו, עוזיהו, היה גם הוא מושל בכיפה, קשה להניח שמלך מדינת אפרים יפרוש
את מצודתו עד גבול ים המלח בדרום [22]. נראה יותר לפרש פיסקה זו „מלבוא חמת עד ים
הערבה" כביטוי מקובל, המובא מתוך דבריו ממש של יונה בן אמתי. כנביא פטריוטי ניבא
יונה לנצחון מלכות ישראל ולהרחבת הגבולים, והשתמש בביטוי שגור זה להביע את
הרעיון של „תחום הארץ — מן הגבול הצפוני האידיאלי עד הגבול הדרומי האידיאלי", מעין
הביטוי „מדן ועד באר־שבע" שהלם יותר את המציאות (שופ' כ', ו'; שמו' א' ג', 20; שמו' ב',
ג', 10, י"ז, 11, כ"ד, 2, 15; מלכ' א', ה', 5).

גישה זו להבנת הפיסקה שלפנינו ניתן לבסס על־ידי ראיה ממימרה חשובה ומעניינת
מספר עמוס, בן דורו של יונה בן אמתי. בכל מהותו היה עמוס מתנגד עקבי לשיטות
„נביאי השקר", שניבאו גדולות למלכות ישראל בשעה שהוא עצמו חזה לעתידה רק כליון
והרס. די להזכיר את התנגשותו עם הכהן אמציה בבית אל (פרק ז') ואת דבריו החריפים
נגד האומרים „לא תגיש ותקדים בעדינו הרעה" (ט', 10), וביחוד את תוכחתו הקשה על
מלכות אפרים בחזון הפתיחה אשר לו (ב', 6—16). גם הנצחונות שנחל ירבעם בן יואש
לא הפיגו את היאוש העמוק שבלב עמוס על הגורל המר הנשקף למדינה עקב חטאותיה
הפוליטיות והחברתיות. כבר העיר גרץ שיש שיש נופל על לשון שנון בדברי הנביא:

הַשְּׂמֵחִים לְלֹא דָבָר　　הָאוֹמְרִים הֲלֹא בְחָזְקֵנוּ
לָקַחְנוּ לָנוּ קַרְנָיִם　　(עמוס ו', 13).

במימרה זו לועג הנביא לשמחים על כיבושי ירבעם בעבר הירדן, בלוקחו את הישובים
לֹא דָבָר (יהו' י"ג, 26 [23]; שמו' ב', י"ז, 27) ועשתרות קרנים (ברא' י"ד, 5) או קרנים [24].
עמוס מצהיר שמתפארים הם על הישגי־הבל ומתגנדרים בכח מדומה שאין בו ממש.
מה שלא הוכר עד עכשו הוא שיש אירוניה חריפה גם בפסוק הסמוך (עמוס ו', 14) — „כי
הנני מקים עליכם בית ישראל נאם ה' אלהי הצבאות גוי ולחצו אתכם מלבוא חמת
עד נחל הערבה" [25]. בדברים אלה חוזר עמוס על משפטו של יונה בן אמתי

21. ברור שפס' 25: „ואשר השיב את דמשק ואת חמת ליהודה בישראל" הוא מסורס. ההצעה לגרוס
„הוא השיב את חמת ה' מישראל" אין לה שחר, והתיקון „ואת חמתי לישראל" הוא פשוט מדי
ואינו משכנע.
22. „ים הערבה", כידוע, זהה עם „ים המלח" (דברים ד', 49; יה' ג', 16; י"ב, 3).
23. במקום „עד־גבול לדבר" יש לגרוס „עד גבול לא דבר".
24. אף שאין שם זה נזכר במקרא, התקיים לפחות עד אמצע ימי בית שני. השוה Καρναιν
(מכבים א', ה' 43—44); Καρνιον (מכבים ב', י"ד, 12).
25. במקום „ים הערבה" שבדברי יונה המובאים בס' מלכים בא כאן הביטוי „נחל הערבה". בכלל
לא היו סופרי המקרא מדייקים ביותר בהבאת ציטטות או בחזרה על פסוקים ידועים. יש להשוות
בספר איוב את דברי מענה ה' (ל"ח 2—3) המובאים בשינויים קלים בתשובת איוב (מ"ד 3—4),
את הפסוק החוזר „בשיר החכמה" (איוב כ"ח, 12—20), וכן את דברי אליהוא, המביא את דברי
איוב כמה פעמים בשינויים קלים ומגיב עליהם. ראה בנידון זה את ספרנו The Book of God
and Man — A Study of Job (1965), פרק 13, וביחוד עמ' 186 ואילך והההערות שם.
ייתכן ש,נחל הערבה" הוא חלקו הדרומי של הירדן הנשפך אל ים־המלח, אף שנראה
יותר לזהותו את „ים הערבה" עם „נחל הערבה". כן מקביל „ים" אל „נהר" (ישע' י"ט, 5)
ומשמש במובן „נהר" (נחום ג', 8, ישע' כ"ז, 1, יחז' ל"ב, 2), וכן מקביל „נחל" אל „ים"
(ויק' י"א, 9, 10) ובא במובן „נהר" (קה' א', 7; מיכה ו', 7).

והופך את הקערה על פיה — לא שלטון מורחב ומוצלח צפוי למלכות ישראל אלא לחץ
וכליה בכל גבול הארץ.

כל הנסיונות לזהות את „נחל הערבה" עם „נחל מצרים" או עם „נחל הערבים" (ישע׳
ט״ו, 6) הבלתי־ידוע, או עם נחל הגבול שבין מואב ואדום (ואדי אל־חאסי), או לשנות את
הגירסה, כדי להתאים את דברי הנביא עם המציאות ההיסטורית, מיותרים לגמרי.[26] לא
דיווח היסטורי לפנינו, הן בס׳ מלכים והן בס׳ עמוס, אלא שני חזיונות נבואיים המתנגדים
זה לזה מן הקצה אל הקצה.

מדיוננו זה מתברר שהצלחנו לחשוף שני קטעי חזון של הנביא יונה בן אמתי שנשתקעו
בס׳ מלכים, שרידים מעטים מדבריו של אחד מן הנביאים המקובלים הלאומניים. בעיני
מתנגדיהם הנאצלים, הנביאים בה״א הידיעה, נחשבו אלה ל„נביאי שקר", אך בעיניהם
הם, ובעיני העם ברובו המכריע, היו יונה וסיעתו נביאים פטריוטיים, מסורים לעמם ודורשים
שלומו וטובתו.

מתוך דבריו האבתנטיים האלה (ipsissima verba) של יונה בן אמתי אפשר אפשר לנו
לשפוט כמה היטיב לעשות הסופר האלמוני של ס׳ יונה ש„בתרי עשר", בבחרו בנביא
הפטריוטי לשמש גיבור העלילה בסיפורו, בו השתמש הסופר כדי להדגיש את ממשלתו
הבלתי־מוגבלת של אלהי ישראל, המשתרעת על הים ועל היבשה. חמלת ה׳, העצומה
ללא־גבול, פרושה לא רק על בני עמו אלא על כל בני האדם, ובכללם אנשי נינוה, בירת
אשור, אויבת ישראל ומחריבת מלכותו; ורב מזה, רחמי אלהים חובקים את כל היקום,
אנשים, נשים וטף, עולם הצומח והחי. את הרקע לכל השגב והעומק הזה יש למצוא בפעולת
הנביא יונה בן אמתי, ששרידים מעטים מדבריו נשתקעו בס׳ מלכים וכך הגיעו אלינו.

---

26. ראה לכאן את פירושו של W.R. Harper, בסדרה Int. Crit. Com., על עמוס, עמ׳ 157, וכן
T.H. Robinson בפירושו על עמוס, עמ׳ 97, בסדרה Handkom. zum A.T.

לשון המקרא לאור לשון חכמים

ההתקדמות העצומה בהבנת כתבי־הקודש שבימינו, ראשיתה בפריחת
הבלשנות העברית בתחילת ימי הביניים. אמנם נתרחבו אפקי המדע המקראי
עד בלי־קץ, על ידי תגליות הארכיאולוגיה החדישה ופיענוח ספרויות העמים
השמים במאה האחרונה, שהפיצו אור בהיר על תוכן המקרא וצורתו. אבל
בעצם הונחו היסודות של הבלשנות השמית ההשוואתית במאה העשירית
לספירתם, על ידי ר׳ יהודה אבן קוריש (המאה השמינית והתשיעית) ורבנו
סעדיה גאון (882—942). במחברתו "ריסאלה" סלל ר׳ יהודה דרך חדשה
למדע, בהביאו את רכוש המלים שבארמית ובערבית כדי לבאר כמה סתומות
בלכסיקוגרפיה המקראית[1]. בן דורו הצעיר והגדול ממנו שימש חלוץ גם
הוא בחקירת הלשון. בקונטרס "תפסיר אל סבעין לפטה"[2], פנה לאוצרות
לשון חז״ל כדי לבאר שבעים מלים בודדות בכה״ק (hapaxlegomena).

שני חוקרים אלה יצרו, איפוא, את השיטה ההשוואתית, וגילו כל אחד
פן מיוחד בה. את הראשון אפשר לכנות אבי "השיטה ההשוואתית האפקית
(horizontal)", המטפלת בבירור ההקבלות בין הלשון העברית ושאר

---

1 מעט מזער ידוע על חוקר חלוץ זה. ראה הרשימה הקצרה באנציקלופדיה
האמריקאית־אנגלית, כרך ז׳, עמ׳ 345.
2 על המהדורות השונות של קונטרס זה, שאגב, נקרא בטעות "פתרון תשעים
מלים בודדות", ראה בספרו של צבי מאלטר Life and Works of Saadia Gaon,
(Philadelphia 1921) עמ׳ 307 ואילך. [והשווה מאמרו של נ. אלוני על קונטרס
זה להלן].

הלשונות השמיות, שהשתמשו בהן העמים בארצות „הסהרון הפורה". השני
הוא אבי „השיטה ההשוואתית האנכית (vertical)"‎, המבקשת סמוכים לא
במקום אלא בזמן. ומוצאת הקבלות ללשון המקרא בדרגות המאוחרות של
הלשון העברית.

שתי צורותיה של השיטה ההשוואתית נולדו, איפוא, בבת־אחת, אבל
שונה היה גורלן, ביחוד במאה השנים האחרונות. השוואת לשון המקרא לשאר
הלשונות והדיאלקטים השמיים טופחה בכשרון ובמסירות על ידי המון
חוקרים. מאידך, השוואת הלשון המקראית אל הלשון העברית בדרגותיה
המאוחרות הוזנחה כמעט לגמרי. רוב מניינם ורוב בניינם של חוקרי התנ״ך
בימינו אינם מבני ברית ואינם מצויים אצל הספרות התלמודית (והבינאית
לא כל שכן). יתר על כן, ביודעים או בלא יודעים הם מעבירים ממקצוע
התיאולוגיה לענף הפילולוגיה את יחס הביטול ל„ספרות הרבנית" ורואים
ביהדות המאוחרת התנוונות־הרוח, ובספרותה פרי עבודה מלאכותית של
חכמים וסופרים צרי־עין, המנותקים מן המציאות ומן החוויה הדתית החיה.

כל מאמציהם של חוקרים יהודים, החל מר״א גיגר ושד״ל ועד ימינו,
עדיין לא הצליחו לתקן את המעוות הזה. בספר יסודי שיצא לאחרונה ושנועד
להדרכת מלומדים צעירים [3], מקדיש המחבר פרק מיוחד ל„שיטות בקורת
הטכסט". הוא מצהיר שם, בצדק, על הצורך לעיין בשימוש של כל מלה
וביטוי בתנ״ך ובלשונות השמיות האחרות — אבל עובר בשתיקה גמורה
על אוצרות הלשון העברית המאוחרת. חזיון נפוץ הוא למצוא בספרות המדעית
בימינו סמוכים לעברית המקראית מאוגריתית או מערבית, אף ששתי
התעודות הספרותיות המושוות נכתבו בריחוק זמן ומקום זו מזו, ומהשקפה
מיתודולוגית נכונה עדיין יש לגלות את צינורות ההשפעה בין שני העמים
הנפרדים האלה. גישה זו לא באנו לבטל, אבל אסור לנו להאפיל על ההשוואה
הזמנית, שהרי כל דרגה ודרגה בספרות ישראל נוצרה על ידי עם אחד,
וכוח אחד חי בה, כח הלובש צורה ופושט צורה אבל אינו ניתק משלשלת
יחוסו [4].

---

3 עי׳ ‏E Würthwein, *The Text of the Old Testament*, בתרגומו
של ‏P.R. Ackroyd, אוכספורד 1957, עמ׳ 78.
4 על כל הבעיה המיתודולוגית הזאת הערתי במאמרי „Studies in the

ביחוד יש להבליט אמת זו לאור העובדה, שכל תגלית חדשה עשויה
להעלות לפנינו ניבים ושימושי לשון שנחשבו עד עכשיו למאוחרים, אך
ורק מפני שלא נמצאו במקורות עתיקים, והנה באה המציאות ולימדה אותנו
"לא ראינו אינה ראיה"[5]. יש בהכרה זו כדי לבטל כמה מטענות המכחישים
את מוצאן העתיק של מגילות ים המלח, רק מפני שניבים כגון "פשר"
"ערך" ו"יחד" לא היו ידועים לנו עד עכשיו אלא מתקופת ימי הביניים.
כתבי כת המדבר מהווים חוליה אחת, די חשובה, בשלשלת־הארוכה של
ספרות ישראל לכל תקופותיה וגווניה. ואין פלא, איפוא, שהיא זורעת אור
על שאר דרגות הספרות העברית מצד אחד, ומצד שני מקבלת הארה על
ידן[6].

אזהרה אחת בשימוש "השיטה ההשוואתית הזמנית" אולי תהיה מובנת
מאליה. החוקר חייב להיות בטוח, שהמקביל המאוחר אינו חיקוי או מובאה
ישירה מן הפיסקה המקראית אלא מהווה תופעה עצמאית בלשון.

יש לקוות שעם החזרת התורה לאכסניה שלה במדינת ישראל והרחבת
חוג החוקרים היהודים מחוץ לארץ, תתחדש השיטה הזאת ככלי חשוב במדע
המקרא, ושתרומותיהם של בעל היובל, נ. ה. טור־סיני, ומלומדים אחרים
בארץ (כגון משה זיידל, חנוך ילון, י. פ. גומפרץ) במקצוע זה, יעוררו את
תשומת לבם של חוקרי התנ"ך בעולם כראוי. במאמר זה באנו להוסיף
דוגמאות מאלפות בפן זה של מדע המקרא ולהביא נדבך לבנין האחיד של
הרוח היוצר באומה בכל הדורות.

*

"Relationship of Biblical and Rabbinic Hebrew בספר היובל לכבוד
פרופ' לוי גינזבורג, הכרך האנגלי, עמ' 199—173. הצעתי שם מספר לא מעט של
השוואות בין המקרא וספרות חז"ל, כחמשה עשר שרשים, שיש להוסיף ללכסיגרפיה
המקראית. את המאמר הנוכחי יש לראות כהמשך למחקר ההוא.

5 השווה המלה "המאוחרת" "נכסים". המופיעה על פי מקרה גם ביה' כ"ב
ח. מלה עברית החסרה לגמרי מספרות התנ"ך היא "אשיח" (בן־סירא נ' ג), שנודעה
לנו בכתובת מישע (שו' 9) בצורה המקבילה "אשוח". השורש "קבל", המצוי רק
באיוב ב' ואסתר ט' כז, ובספרות חז"ל למכביר, נתגלה על ידי אולברייט במשל
כנעני במכתבי תל אל־עמרנה, במאה הי"ד לפסה"נ (ראה BASOR, מס 89
[1943], עמ' 29 ואילך).

6 דוגמה של שיחזור מלה מקראית בעזרת מגילת ים המלח יש למצוא במאמרי
"Na'alam and Other Observations on the Ain Feshka שהופיע
Scrolls" JNES ברבעון, כרך 9 (1950), עמ' 49 ואילך.

אם לא — ולא

מלת החיבור המשנית „אלא", שכידוע אינה נמצאת בתנ״ך, התפתחה
מן הצירוף „אם לא". ביטוי זה נמצא בתורה, בבר׳ כ״ד לח שיש לבאר רק
במובן של „אלא" המשנית ("but-except")   „לא־תקח אשה לבני מבנות
הכנעני... אם לא אל בית אבי תלך".

בשני מקראות אחרים אנו מוצאים צורה קרובה, „ולא", שיש לפרשה
באותו המובן, ואין להכריע אם יש לגרוס „אלא" ממש — או, מה שמתקבל
יותר, שזאת היא צורה מקבילה למלת החיבור „אם לא". בשמ׳ ג׳ יט : „ואני
ידעתי כי לא־יתן אתכם מלך מצרים להלוך ולא ביד חזקה. ושלחתי את
ידי וגו׳". ברור שהפסוק רוצה לומר, שמלך מצרים לא ירשה לבני ישראל
לעזוב אלא בכפיית ידו החזקה של ה׳, ולכן ישלח את ידו ויכה במצרים.

פסוק קשה יותר, שלא הובן כראוי, הוא שמ״א כ׳ טו־טז, בדברי הברית
והשבועה, שאומר יונתן לרעהו דוד : „ולא תכרית את חסדך מעם ביתי עד
עולם, ולא בהכרית ה׳ את איבי דוד מעל פני האדמה. ויכרת יהונתן עם
בית דוד וביקש ה׳ מיד איבי דוד". החלק השני של פס׳ טו רבו בו תיקונים
קיצוניים [7] ופירושים דחוקים [8], שאינם מניחים את הדעת.

בראשונה יש להכיר שבביטוי „איבי דוד" בפס׳ טו, כמו בפסוק הסמוך,
טז, יש לפנינו לשון נקייה, שימוש שבא פעם שלישית בשמ״א כ״ה כב :
„כה יעשה אלהים לאיבי דוד וכה יוסיף". הכנסת המלה „שונאים" בקללה
מצוייה לרוב בספרות חז״ל, כגון ברכות ז׳ ע״א („שאלמלי כעסתי לא נשתייר

───────

7 ראה בפירושיהם של דרייבר, סמית וסגל. על כן מקבל דרייבר את גירסת
השבעים לנכונה והוא גורס על פיה : „וְלֹא בְּהַכְרֵת ה׳ אֶת אֹיְבֵי דָוִד אִישׁ מֵעַל פְּנֵי
הָאֲדָמָה יִכָּרֵת שֵׁם יְהוֹנָתָן מֵעִם בֵּית דָוִד". ברור שאין זו הגירסה המקורית: א) הריווח
בין „וְלֹא" עד „יִכָּרֵת" אינו מסתבר; ב) יהונתן לא הזדהה מעולם עם בית דוד, עד כדי כך
שישביע את רעהו שלא יכרת שמו של יונתן מביתו של דוד התרגום היוני ניסה להרחיב
את הכתוב הסתום לפניו ועל ידי כך לצאת מן המבוכה. לוציאן והחלגטה ניסו לתקן
מעוּת זה וגרס „יִכָּרֵת שֵׁם יְהוֹנָתָן עִם בֵּית שָׁאוּל", אבל גם בה לא נעזרנו הרבה.
8 כך מפרש סגל, ספרי שמואל, עמ׳ קסד : „אפילו כשיתחזק דויד על כסאו
וימית כל אויביו המתנגדים למלכותו, והם בית שאול ואוהביו... גם אז לא יכרית
את בית יונתן". שני קשיים בדבר : א) לפי פירוש זה תלויה המלה „ולא" באויר;
ב) הביטוי „איבי דוד" בפס׳ טו מקבל פירוש הפוך משימושו בפס׳ טז, שהרי שם
מקבל סגל, בצדק, את פרושם של רש״י ורד״ק, שמפרשים את הביטוי כלשון נקיה.

משונאיהם של ישראל כלום"); סוכה כ"ט ע"א („לבנה לוקה סימן רע
לשונאיהם של ישראל") וכן הרבה. ויפה הגדיר כאן רש"י את התהליך
הפסיכולוגי, „כאדם שמקלל עצמו ותולה קללתו באחרים" [9].

ההערה השניה בקשר עם הפסוק דידן היא ביאור „ולא", שפירושו גם
פה במובן „אם לא, אלא". שיעור הכתוב כך הוא: „אתה דוד לא תכרית את
חסדך מעם ביתי, אלא אם יכרית ה' אותך מעל האדמה". ר"ל, כל עוד תישאר
בחיים, עליך לשמור ברית זו.

ראוי להוסיף, שבפסוק הבא שבפיסקה „ובקש ה' מידי איבי דוד"
כמושא לפעל „ויכרת", כי פראזה זו היא שם הברית הכרותה ביניהם, ודוגמה
מקבילה אנו מוצאים ביה' כ"ב לד: „ויקראו בני־ראובן ובני גד למזבח כי
עד הוא בינותינו כי ה' האלהים". שם מהווה הפיסקה האחרונה את שם
המזבח [10]. כאן כרת יונתן עם בית דוד ברית בשם „ובקש ה' מיד דוד", זאת
אומרת, „ה' ינקם נקמת יונתן מדוד אם יעבור על שבועתו".

בונן

בשירת „האזינו" מופיע הפועל „בין" בבנין „פועל" בפעם היחידה
במקרא: „יסבבנהו יבוננהו יצרנהו כאישון עינו" (דב' ל"ב י). הביאור
המקובל, „יתן לו בינה" (אונקלוס, רש"י, ראב"ע ורוב המפרשים), אינו הולם
פשוטו של מקרא, שהרי בא הפועל באמצע תיאור שמירת ה' את עמו, המורחב
עוד יותר בפסוק הבא: „כנשר יעיר קנו על גוזליו ירחף, יפרש כנפיו יקחהו
ישאהו על אברתו". על כן ניסו החדשים לתת לפועל זה את המובן של
שמירה וטיפול, כגון "he cared for him" [11]. אבל יש לשים לב לסמיכת
הפועל אל „יסבבנהו" וגם אל השימוש החד־פעמי של השורש בבנין „פועל",
בה בשעה שההתפעל, „התבונן", מצוי לרוב. יש מקום להסתפק אם יש
בכלל קשר בין המלה שלנו והשורש השכיח „הבין". להפך, התמונה החיה
של הנשר השומר על גוזליו בפסוק הסמוך מחזקת את ההשערה, שגם צלעות

---

9   פירושו לשמ' ב' י.

10   ראה מאמרנו ברבעון AJSL, 1931, "A Note on Josh. 22:34".

11   ר' S.R. Driver (ICC, 1916), בפירושו לס' דברים עמ' 356 ואילך.
וכן הלכסיקון האוכספורדי "He attentively considereth him". עמ' 107. ומלון
קוהלר־בומגרטן, עמ' 120, טור 2. "he takes care of him".

אלו של הפסוק מהוות חלק של תיאור השאול מחיי הנשר ובניו הממריאים
בשחקים. לעתים מתעופפת האם מסביב (יסבבנהו) לקבוצת הגוזלים, ולעתים
היא טסה ביניהם (יבוננהו) כדי להגן ולפקח עליהם. הצורה החד-פעמית של
הפועל כאן מיוסדת, איפוא, על מלת-היחס „בין" ואין לה קשר ישיר לפועל
„הבין"[12].

הקבלה מאלפת לשימוש לשוני זה מצויה בספרות הפיוט. „בשיר היחוד
ליום השני", שורות מד—מה, אנו קוראים: „אין צד וצלע יצליעוך, ורחב
וארך לא ימציעוך / אין פאה לסביבותיך, ואין תוך מבדיל בינותיך"[13].
הפיטן בא לומר, שאין להשיג את מידותיו של הקב"ה. ההקבלה בין
„סביבותיך" ו„בינותיך" כשלעצמה מעניינת מאד, אבל יותר חשוב לעניננו
הוא השימוש בפועל „יצליעוך" מל׳ „צלע", ופירושו „יגבילוך במקום",
ובייחוד בפועל „ימציעוך" מל׳ „אמצע" ופירושו „יקיפוך במקום"[14]. המשורר
הבינאי משתמש בפעלים אלה במובן מופשט, כדי להסביר את אין-סופיותו
של האלהים, בה בשעה שהתורה משתמשת בהם במובן ממשי, לתיאור אהבתו
הבלתי-מוגבלת של אלהי ישראל לעמו, אבל כלי שימושם אחד הוא.

פירוש הכתוב הוא, איפוא: „ה׳ שומר על עֹמו כנשר על גוזליו, יסובב
אותם ויעבור ביניתם ואינו מעלים עין מהם לרגע".

ב ע ל

המלה המצויה „בעל" מסמנת „מי ששולט או משתמש בחפץ ידוע",
ומזה מסתעפות כל ההוראות הרגילות, „בעל אשה", „בעל ברית" (בר׳ י"ד
יג), „בעל החלומות" (בר׳ ל׳ ז יט), „בעל שער" (מל"א א׳ ח) ועוד. אמנם
משמעות זו אינה מתאימה לפיסקה בס׳ משלי ג׳ כח—כט: „אל תמנע-טוב
מבעליו בהיות לאל ידיך לעשות. אל תאמר לרעיך לך ושוב ומחר אתן ויש
אתך". כאן דורש העניין לא את ההוראה „השולט בדבר", אלא להיפך, „הרוצה

---

12 מובן מאליו, שהפועל „הבין" גם הוא מוצאו ממלת היחס „בין". „להבין"
פירושו „הכיר את ההבדלים בין דבר אחד לשני". השווה מאמר חז"ל: „אם אין
דעה הבדלה מנין" (ירו׳ ברכות ה׳ ב). הסתעפות ההוראה היסודית לשני כוונים:
א) „ידיעה וחכמה"; ב) „הליכה בתוך קבוצה", היא תופעה מצויה לרוב בלשון.
13 ראה א.מ. הברמן, שירי היחוד והכבוד (ירושלים תש"ח), עמ׳ כא—כב.
14 ראה אברהם ברלינר, כתבים נבחריב, כרך א׳ (ירושלים תש"ה), עמ׳ 164.

בדבר ואין לו" 15. התרגומים הארמי והסורי עוברים על המלה בשתיקה. יש
המציעים תיקונים, כגון "מרֵעך" 16, "מאבֵיון", "מִשְׁאַלֵיו" ועוד. גרינסטון מקיים
את נוסח המסורה בדרוש יפה: "הטוב השייך לך אינו שלך, אלא שייך לנצרך
לו, שהנהו הבעל האמיתי" 17, אבל ספק אם הפשט סובל פירוש זה.

ברור שהענין דורש ביאור מיוחד למלה "בעל". לא כמשמעותה הרגילה,
"השולט ומשתמש בחפץ ידוע", וגם לא "מי שראוי לדבר מנקודה מוסרית",
אלא "מי שרוצה ומצפה לדבר". שימוש כזה אינו ידוע לי מספרות חז"ל,
אבל יש מקביל בלשון האידית המדוברת וממנה נכנסה לספרות החסידים.
זהו בדיוק ביאור המלה "בעלן" — "מי שחפץ בדבר, שיש לו תשוקה לזה".
כגון "הייתי בעלן להתעסק תמיד להעמיד העננים כדי שאקדש הלבנה" (זכרון
טוב, סיפורי מעשיות של הצדיק מנעסכאיז) 18 וידועה המלה לכל המצוי אצל
הלשון האידית.

הסימנטיקה אינה מובנת לנו היום 19, אבל העובדה די ברורה. מספרות
החכמה המקראית ועד ספרי החסידים — מפכים מעינות הלשון העברית
בחשאי ומקור אחד למימיהם. שיעור הכתוב: "אל תמנע טוב מן המשתוקק
לו".

<h2 style="text-align:center">לא</h2>

כבר העירונו במקום אחר 20, שמלת השלילה "לא" משמשת לפרקים
למונה אישור וחיזוק. ההתפתחות הסימנטית היא דרך השאלה "לא־הלוא",

---

15 ראה בפירושו של C. H. Toy לס משלי (ICC ,1902), עמ' 79. וכן
W.O.E. Oesterley, בפירושו לס' משלי (לונדון 1929), עמ' 26.

16 על פי השבעים, ἐνθέῇ גורס אורט "אביון" וגרץ רואה בזה סמוכים
להצעתו "שאליו".

17 ראה Proverbs with Commentary, J.W. Greenstone (פילדלפיה
1950), עמ' 34.

18 קטעים אלה מובאים במלון בן יהודה, כרך א', עמ' 578 בהערה, ושם
הוא מוסיף: "י"א כי זו המלה השגורה בפי ההמון ושל האשכנזים היא לא בעלן
אלא בלען". דעה זו מופרכת מטעם פוניטי. רגילים היהודים הליטאים לבטא את
המלה "בילן", והיו"ד הזאת סימן מובהק היא לעי"ן שואית, השווה הביטוי העממי
של כעסן=כיסן, מעלה=מילה, דעתי=דיתי וכן עוד רבים.

19 אולי "השואף להיות בעל".

20 השווה המאמר הנזכר בהערה 4, שם, עמ' 181 והלאה. על השימוש של
מלת השלילה "בל" בתור מלת האישור השווה T.H. Gaster, JRAS, 1944,

ומן השימוש בשאלה יוצא השימוש המאשר את דברי הכותב. דוגמאות לרוב
נמצאות בספרות חז״ל. השווה מדרש תנחומא (הוצאת בובר, כרך ג׳, עמ׳
12) : „אמר הקב״ה אלו הייתי מבקש קרבן לא הייתי אומר למיכאל שהוא
אצלי להקריב קרבן ... אמר לו הקב״ה רשע אם הייתי מבקש קרבן הייתי
אומר למיכאל ולגבריאל והיו מקריבים לי״.

ברור שהניבים „לא הייתי אומר״ ו„הייתי אומר״ מקבילים זה לזה
במלואם. על־פי שימוש זה הצעתי במאמר הנ״ל פירושים לפיסקאות אחדות
סתומות במקרא, כגון יש׳ ז׳ כג—כה, הוש י׳ ט, י״א ה. ויש להוסיף עליהן
איוב כ״ג יז : „כי לא נצמתי מפני חושך ומפני כסה אפל״.

נראה לנו, שיש בהכרת שימוש זה כדי להאיר פיסקה קשה בתעודות
לכיש, שהתלבטו בה החוקרים. בחרס 3, מתנצל הושעיהו לפני אדוניו,
יאוש, בקשר עם מכתב שנשלח אליו על ידי השר העליון ורוצה להוכיח
שלא במזיד עבר על רצון שר הראש. שורות 5—13 מכילות קושי יסודי,
ביחוד בשורות 8—9 :

לספר — אשר
שלחתה. אל עבדך אמש. כי. לב
[ע]בד[ך] דוה. מאז. שלחך. אל. עבד
ך וכיאמר. אדני. לא. ידעתה.
קרא ספר היהוה. אם. נסה. א
יש לקרא לי ספר לנצח. וגם
כל ספר אשר יבא. אלי אם
קראתי אתה [אף] ראת מנהו
כל מאומ[ה]

מה ביאור המימרא „וכי אמר אדני לא ידעתה קרא ספר״ ? פרופ׳
טור־סיני [21] פירש „לֹא יָדַעְתִּי קְרֹא סֵפֶר״, ומוסיף שלא כל אדם ידע לכתוב
ולקרוא בזמן ההוא״. שני קשיים בדבר, שעמד עליהם המהדיר הנכבד

עמ׳ 45 הע׳ 29 ; JAOS כרך 70 (1950), עמ׳ 11. לשימוש מקביל בערבית השווה
ZDMG, H. Bauer כרך 74 (1920), עמ׳ 9—208.
21 השווה H. Torczyner, The Lachish Letters (1938) עמוד 51, 65.
ובספרו העברי תעודות לכיש (ירושלים ת״ש), עמ׳ 69, מנקד המהדיר „לֹא יָדַעְתָּ
קְרֹא סֵפֶר״, מפני הקשיים הכרוכים בפירוש הראשון.

156

עצמו: א) הפיסקה בחרס 4, שורה 3 („כן עשה עבדך כתבתי על הדלת, ככל
אשר שלח אדני"), שבאורה הטבעי ביותר הוא שהושעיהו אמנם ידע לכתוב
ודבר זה אף מסתבר בדרך כלל. ב) הכתוב „ידעת" בתור גוף ראשון הוא
קצת מסופק.

אולברייט [22] מנקד את הפיסקה דידן: „לֹא יָדַעְתָּה? קְרָא סֹפֵר!" פירוש
זה אינו מתקבל על הלב. מסופק הוא מאד אם הניב „קרא ספר" המופיע
כאן פעמים אחדות מוסב על סופר, ביחוד אחרי השימוש הודאי של „לספר
אשר שלחת" (שורה 7), וחשוב מזה — אם השר העליון מצווה עליו לקרוא
לסופר, איזו התנצלות היא זו מצד הושעיהו להישבע, ששום איש לא ניסה
לקרוא לו סופר ושהיה דוחה בידים כל סופר שהיה מנסה לבוא אליו? בתרגום
אולברייט:

"and as for any scribe who might have come to me, truly I did
not call him, nor would I give anything at all to him!"

פתרון הפיסקה הסתומה יש למצוא, לפי דעתנו, בהכרת שימוש האישור
של „לא", ויש לנקד את המלים „וְכִי אָמַר אֲדֹנִ לֹא יָדַעְתָּה קְרָא סֵפֶר!".
יאוש מתמרמר על הושעיהו ואומר לו — „הלא אתה ודאי יודע לקרוא".
על זה מתנצל האחרון ונשבע שאיש לא ניסה לקרוא לו מכתב מיאוש.

ומה היה חטאו? זה יש לבאר באחד משני אופנים: א) הפקיד הנמוך לא מילא
פקודות השר העליון, שהיו כלולות במכתב שהלה שלח לו ושהוא טוען כי
לא הגיע אליו. לפי פירוש זה יש לבאר שורות 10-11, „וכל ספר אשר יבא
לי" — כל מכתב שהיה צריך להגיע אלי. ב) הפקיד הנמוך קרא מכתבים
סודיים מיאוש שהיו עוברים דרך ידו ושלא היה צריך לקרוא, ויאוש מאשים
אותו ישירות או בעקיפין בעבירה זו, „הלא אתה יודע לקרוא (וקראת!)".
על זה הוא אומר, ששום מכתב כזה לא קרא, לא כולו ולא מקצתו. כך מבאר
פרופ' טור-סיני את חטאו של הושעיהו והתנצלותו [23], אלא שלא ביסס אותו
בפירוש הכתוב במדה מספקת. יוצא שיש לבאר „לא ידעת" כגוף שני „ודאי
שאתה יודע"!

---

22 השווה תרגומו אצל J.B. Pritchard, ANET עמ' 321—322. וראה
המסקנות שמסיק מפיסקה זו E. Nielsen בספרו Oral Tradition (לונדון
1954), עמ' 55, בדבר המסורת שבעל-פה בתקופת התנ"ך. מסקנותיו בשלילת
מקורות כתובים כמעט לגמרי, מרחיקות לכת יותר מדי.
23 ראה תעודות לכיש, עמ' 63 והלאה.

מ ש כ י ם

פעמיים בספרו משתמש הנביא הושע בתמונה של „ענן בקר, טל משכים
הלך" (ו' ד, י"ג ג), כדי לסמן תופעה חולפת ובלתי־מתמדת. את הצלע
השניה בשתי הפיסקאות מבארים המפרשים „טל הממהר להתנדף" ובאמת
אין יסוד לומר שהפועל „השכים" יהיה מוסב על טל, ולו גם בהשאלה,
ושביאורו הוא „מהר".

מה שיש לפנינו, וההקבלה תוכיח, הוא מונח נרדף ל„בקר". „משכים" —
„זמן הקימה, הבוקר". ביטוי זה נמצא לא רק במשנה (ביכורים ג, ב :
„ולמשכים הממונה אומר"), אלא גם בספרות המאוחרת, כמו שהעיר בצדק
פרופ' ש. ליברמן[24], בסדר עולם (הוצאת מרכס, עמ' 31) ובמגלת כת דמשק
(הוצאת שכטר, עמ' 10). כך הצלחנו להחזיר שלש חוליות בשלשלת דברי
ימיה של מלה עברית, שכמעט נשכח זכרה, במקרא, במשנה ובספרות שמחוץ
לשתיהן.

ס ת ר

בשמ"א כ"ה כ מסופר, שאביגייל היתה „רוכבת על החמור וירדת בסתר
ההר", כשדוד ואנשיו נפגשו בה. מקובל הפירוש, שברדתה היתה מכוסה
בהרים[25], אף שאינו מחוור כלל מה היה נסתר בשיפוע ההר ומהו הדבר
המסתיר, כיון ש„דוד ואנשיו ירדים לקראתה", באותו הגיא[26].

ביאור הביטוי הזה יש למצוא בשני ניבים מקבילים : „צד ההר" (שמ"ב
י"ג לד, כ"ג כו) ו„צלע ההר" (שם ט"ז יג). הניב „סתר ההר" הנהו צורה
מוחלפת ל„סתר הר" — „צד ההר". הטי"ת המקורית בשורש, שיש במקביל
הארמי „סטר", נתחלפה כאן לתי"ו, תופעה נפוצה שבאה ע"פ רוב בקירוב
לאותיות למ"ד, או רי"ש (liquidae)[27]. די להביא קטל كَتَل קיטור
قِطَار   טרף طَرِيف   טרח طَرَح   טלטל تَلَّ• בעברית

---

24 בספרו Greek in Jewish Palestine (ניו־יורק 1942), עמ' 135.
25 ראה מלונותיהם של Kohler-Baumgarten : "Under cover of the
mountain". Brown-Driver-Briggs : "covered by the mountain.
26 ראה לבטיו של מ. צ. סגל, ספרי שמואל, עמ' קצח, המבאר : „שביל היורד
בצדי ההר ונסתר מעין רואים".
27 ראה J. Barth Etymologische Studien (לייפציג 1893), עמ' 35
והלאה, המאסף חומר רב בפרט זה.

מאוחרת נכנסה המלה „סטר" במובן „צד", „עמוד של כתב או לוח", וכן
הפועל „סטר" — לפנות הצידה.[28] בארמית־יהודית משמשת המלה הארמית
„סטרא" לא רק במובן ממשי אלא מושאל.[29] בלשון הקבלה „סטרא אחרא"
הוא כינוי לשטן, הצד שכנגד לקב״ה. הוראה מושאלת זו של „סתר־סטר",
לסמן „צד בסכסוך" מאפשרת לנו להבין פיסקה קשה בס' איוב, שרבו בה
הפירושים והסירוסים, כפי שיש לראות בספרות המדעית.

באיוב י״ג ו—י״א בא קטע שלם, בו מרבה איוב במרי נפשו לשאול שאלות
מחבריו, המנסים להגן על כבוד האלהים בתכסיסים בלתי־מוצדקים. הוא
מאשים אותם בדברי שקר ורמאות ובהטיית הדין לטובת יריבו הכל־יכול
של איוב. איוב הנלחם באל־הכח בשם אל־הצדק, שאמונתו בו עדיין נטועה
בלבו, בטוח שעיוות האמת לשם שמים אינו חשוב בעיני ה' ככבוד, אלא
כלעג וגידוף ושעתידים מליצים־ליצנים אלה ליתן את הדין על מעשיהם
המכוערים. כל זה מביע איוב בשטף רוגזה ובגיבוב שאלות ריטוריות
שמדהימות את נפש הקורא:

ולו תדברו רמיה	הלאל תדברו עולה
אם לאל תריבון?	הפניו תשאון,
אם־כהתל באנוש תהתלו בו?	הטוב כי־יחקר אתכם,
אם־בסתר פנים תשאון.	הוכח יוכיח אתכם
ופחדו יפל עליכם."	הלא שאתו תבעת אתכם

בשורה ארוכה זו של שאלות מרות, נראה פס' י כיוצא דופן, ומוקשה
בתוכנו ובצורתו: א) איזה סתר יש במעשיהם ובדבריהם של הרעים המדברים
קבל־עם את דבריהם המופרכים? ב) מדוע אין סימן שאלה בצלע א' של
הפסוק? פרופ' טור־סיני, בחריפותו ומקוריותו, מנקד „בַּסֵתֶר פָּנִים תִּשָׂאוּן־
ומבאר „אם תשאו סתר־פנים, ז״א מסוה על פניכם", אבל קשה לראות מה

---

28 השווה מלון בן־יהודה, כרך ח', עמ' 4014, המביא שלל מובאות. וכדאי
לציין כאן: „אלו בנות... שהיו פורעות ראשיהן ופורטות סטריהן ויושבות בשוק
ובדרכים" (גנזי שכטר, א', הוצאת גינזברג, עמ' 198). וכן מבאר רש״י „מצלעותיו"
(בר' ב' כא): „מסטריו, כמו לצלע המשכן". ולשימוש הפועל השווה מגילה ט״ז
ע״א: „בא מלאך וסטר ידה כלפי המן". וראה חילוף הגירסה בין „מסתר" ו„מסתיר"
בירו' ברכות ב' א (בן־יהודה, מלון, שם, הערה 1).
29 השווה שבועות מ״ב ע״א: „הנהו סיטראי ניניהו", שפירושו „המעות האלה
מצד אחר הם, לפרוע חוב אחר ניתנו".

ענין מסוה פנים לרעים שטוענים מה שטוענים בלי בושה או כיסוי כלשהו.

נראה לנו לבאר צלע א' של פס' י כשאלה, בלי ה"א השאלה, או להוסיף ה"א שנפלה בהפלוגרפיה, "ההוכח". הפועל "יכח" בהפעיל משמש גם להצהרה (declarative) — "הודיע שפלוני צודק או נכון". השווה "הצדיק, הרשיע", ולא רק לגרם פעולה (causative) 30. שימוש זה של הפועל אפייני לסגנון ספר איוב. דוגמה מאלפת לכך מצויה בפרקנו, פס' טו: "הן יקטלני לא איחל (כ'), אך דרכי אל פניו אוכיח". שיעורו: "אני אוכיח, אגלה את יושר מעשי, צדקת דרכי אל פניו, ויעבר עלי מה". וכן איוב י"ט ה: "אם אמנם עלי תגדילו ותוכיחו עלי חרפתי". בדעתנו להוכיח במקום אחר, שהניב "הגדיל על" המצוי במקרא מקביל לבטוי הערבי جدل בבנין ‏II, שביאורו "ריב, התקוטט" (השווה جدك — מריבה, جدلى קנתרן). שיעור הכתוב הוא, איפוא: "אם אמנם ברצונכם לריב אתי ולהצדיק את חרפתי עלי, כלומר, לומר שכלימתי היא נכונה ומוצדקת".

וכן באיוב כ"ב ד: המיראתך יוכיחך", יש להבין: "האם מפני שה' ירא מפניך, אתה מצפה שיצדיק אותך?". קרובה המשמעות לכתוב בבר' כ"ד יד: "אתה הכחת לעבדך, ליצחק", ששיעורו: "בתולה זו מצאת כנכונה וראויה לעבדך ליצחק".

בשובנו לפיסקה שלנו, יש להבין "הוכח יוכיח אתכם" כשאלה ריטורית המושכת תשובה שלילית אתה, כשאר הפסוקים בפיסקה: "האם יאמר ה' עליכם שאתם נכוחים וצדיקים, האם יצדיק אתכם, אם תשאו פנים לסתר, לצד אחד, במשפט הזה שביני לבין קוני?". אין צורך, איפוא, לשנות את "פנים" ל"פניו", כפי שעשו כמה מן התרגומים והמפרשים. הביטוי "נשא פנים" ידוע למדי (דב' י' יז, משלי י"ח ה, איוב ל"ב כא ועוד).

על־פי גישה זו יוצאת לנו קריאה מחרידה מעמקי לב הסובל, שעל אף מרי־נפשו נשאר נאמן למצפונו. מגיב הוא בשורה ארוכה של שאלות ריטוריות כלפי רעיו המסלפים את האמת. בטוח הוא איוב, שה' לא יקבל ברצון שקריהם המוסמכים לטובת עמדתם הדתית, שכבר עבר עליה כלח. "האם לא יפחדו מפני שאתו?". מאידך מחזיק איוב באמונתו, שגאולתו והצדקתו סופן לבוא. "גם הוא לי לישועה, כי לא לפניו חנף יבוא" (י"ג טז).

---

30 לשימוש הידוע השוה תה' ה' ב, ק"ה יד, משלי ט' ח; וכן וי' י"ט, יז, יש' י"א יד ועוד, בהוראת "העד איש לתקן מעשיו".

בורח הוא „ממנו, אליו״, כי „גם עתה בשמים עדי״ (ט״ז יד) „ואני ידעתי
גאלי חי״ (י״ט כה).

ערב

דיני הפסח הנשנים במקומות שונים בתורה, אינם עולים בד בבד בכל
המקורות. בשמ' י״ב, בתיאור פסח מצרים, תופס קרבן הפסח מקום בראש.
בסיכום הקצר בדב' ט״ז מודגשת ביחוד אכילת המצות, וקרבן הפסח הוא
פחות חשוב. בקשר עם הקרבן כתוב שם, פס' ד : „ולא ילין מן הבשר
אשר תזבח בערב ביום הראשון לבקר״. מה פירוש „יום הראשון״ ?
רש״י מזהה את הביטוי עם י״ד ניסן כדי להתאימן עם החוק היסודי
ומנמק את זיהויו על־ידי המקרא שמ' י״ב טו : „אך ביום הראשון תשביתו
שאר מבתיכם״. אבל הראיה עצמה טעונה חיזוק, שהרי סוף הפסוק מלמדנו
„כי כל אכל חמץ ונכרתה הנפש ההוא מישראל מיום הראשון ועד יום
השביעי״, וברור, איפוא, שיום הראשון הוא ט״ו ניסן, כיון שיום השביעי
על כרחך חלק החג הוא. אם כן, איך אפשר להבין את הביטוי „בערב ביום
הראשון״ בדברים ? מפס' ג, „שבעת ימים תאכל עליו מצות״, ומפס' ח,
„ששת ימים תאכל מצות וביום השביעי עצרת לה' אלהיך״, ברור שביאור
„יום הראשון״ הוא לשבעת ימי החג, ולא היום הקודם למנין. מתי
קרב, איפוא, חג הפסח ? הבא המקרא בדברים כאן לסתור דברי שמ' י״ב,
ולהודיע על הקרבת הקרבן ביום ט״ו לניסן ? אתמהה.

התשובה נראית לנו פשוטה. ידוע השימוש הנפוץ של „ערב״ בלשון
חז״ל לסמן היום הקודם לשבת או לחג, ואין צורך להביא סמוכים לו. אם
נגרוס בדב' ט״ז ד „וְלֹא יָלִין מִן הַבָּשָׂר אֲשֶׁר תִּזְבַּח בָּעֶרֶב יוֹם הָרִאשׁוֹן
לַבֹּקֶר״ [31], נבין את הבטוי כשימושו המשני. הרי המקרא יוצא לפי פשוטו,
שאסור להלין לבוקר את בשר הזבח הקרב בערב יום הראשון של החג, ז״א
הקרב בי״ד בניסן.

---

31 להכפלת הבי״ת אין צורך להביא ראיות רבות, וראה „כי ככתוב״ (דה״ב
כ״ה ד) המקביל אל „ככתוב״ (מל״ב י״ד ו) ; ההרותיה (מל״ב ט״ו טו) וראה
F. Delitzsch, Schreib- und Lesefehler in A.T. (ברלין־לייפציג 1920), עמ'
81 והלאה.

ק י ם

מלה זו נמצאת פעם אחת בכה״ק, בתאור חורבן הרשעים על ידי אליפז
באיוב כ״ב כ: „אם־לא נכחד קימנו ויתרם אכלה אש". רבו ההצעות
והתיקונים: קמינו (דוהם) יקמם (מרץ, בודה) קנמו (=הקן, הזרע שלהם,
טור־סיני), קַנְיָנֵם (פרלס). רוב המפרשים הכירו, בצדק, שיש כאן צורך במלה
ל„עושר" המקבילה אל „יתרם" (השווה יתרה, יש׳ ט״ו ז = יר׳ מ״ח לו).

יש לתקן את הכינוי לגוף שלישי רבים „קימם", תיקון קל המתבאר
על דמיון „נו" ומי״ם (השווה „תשמרם ותצרנו" תה׳ י״ב ח). חז״ל מבארים
את הביטוי בדב׳ י״א ו, „ואת כל היקום אשר ברגליהם, א״ר אליעזר זה
ממונו של אדם שמעמידו על רגליו" (סנהדרין ק״י א׳) וקשר הרעיונות של
„עמידה" ו„הון" מצוי בכמה ניבים כגון wealth, substance.

השם „קים" או „קימה" באיוב אינו טעון שום שינוי, אם נבין אותו
במשמעות „הון".

ר ב

איוב כ״ו ג: „מה יעצת ללא־חכמה, ותשיה לרב הודעת". הביאור המקובל
לצלע השניה הוא: „ואיזו עצה מרובה הודעת"? אבל פירוש זה אינו יוצא
ידי ההקבלה, ולכן רבו ההצעות לתיקונים, כגון „לבער" (גרץ) או „לרד"
(בר, טורטשינר). [33]

לנו נראה לזהות במלה „רב" או „רבה" (בחסרון ה״א, שנפלה מפני
הה״א של המלה הבאה) את המונח המשני „רובה", שפירושו „נער, בחור",
כגון „אין לי רובה שנשא ריבה, מנין רובה שנשא אלמנה" וגו׳ (ירו׳ סוטה
ח׳ ו) „והרובים שומרים שם" (משנה תמיד א׳ א) ועוד הרבה. [34]

הסימנטיקה של „צעיר, בחור" מסתעפת לשני כיוונים: א) „משרת,
עוזר"; 2) „חסר־נסיון וחכמת החיים, שוטה". כך היא הסמנטיקה של „נער"
במשמעותה א) „משרת" (במד׳ כ״ב כב, שו׳ ז׳ י, יא ועוד); 2) „שוטה", השווה

32 השווה, למשל, התרגום היהודי־האמריקאי:
"and plentifully declared sound knowledge".
33 בפירושו לס׳ איוב, שנת תש״א, מפרש פרופ׳ טור־סיני את המלה במובן
„נדהם" ומביא את הכתוב באיוב ד׳ ג ואת השרש הערבי رعب „קפא, הבהל,
הדהם" (ראה עמ׳ 50).
34 ראה מלון בן־יהודה, כרך י״ג, עמ׳ 6367.

משלי א׳ ד: ״לתת לפתאים ערמה, לנער דעת ומזמה״. גם ״פתי״ יסודה
בשורש המופיע בערבית   = נער, צעיר, ובעברית במובן ״שוטה״.
״רובה״ ביאורו היסודי הוא ״צעיר, ההולך וגדל״ וכאן מתפתח המושג
של ״חסר נסיון בחיים, שוטה״. שיעור צלע ב׳ הוא: ״איזו עצה טובה הענקת
לרובה, לצעיר חסר־נסיון ובינה בחיים״? יש, איפוא, הקבלה מצויינת לשתי
צלעות הפסוק.

ר צ ה

השורש המקראי ״רצה״ במובנו היסודי, ״קבל בחסד ובחפץ לב״, הוא
כל כך שכיח שלא הכירו הבלשנים שלא בכל פיסקה מתאים ביאור זה. כך
מנסה הלכסיקון האוכספורדי [35] להסביר את השימוש בוי׳ כ״ו לד, ״אז תרצה
הארץ את שבתותיה... והרצת״ ; שם פס׳ מ״ג ותירץ ; בדה״ב ל״ו כא, ״עד רצתה
הארץ״ — כתולדה מן השורש הרגיל ״satisfy by paying make acceptable״
והקשר דחוק ומסופק למדי.

בלכסיקון החדש של קוהלר־בומגרטן [36] נעשה צעד קדימה, בהבחנתם
בין ״רצה״ היסודי ושורש ״רצה״ שהם מתרגמים enumerate (מנה), ובצדק
הם מזההים שורש מקראי זה עם השורש המשני, כגון ״אסור להרצות מעות
נגד הנר״ (שבת כ״ב ע״א, השווה עירובין י״ח ע״ב, סנה׳ ס״ח, א׳). בתוכחה
ב״ויקרא״ באה התורה להזהיר, שאם בני ישראל לא ימנו את שבתות השנה
כפי׳ מצות ה׳ ייענשו מדה כנגד מדה, והארץ בשוממותה תספור את השנים
שהיתה צריכה להיות בלתי־זרועה. וכדאי לציין שבביאור זה בא הפועל גם
בקל וגם בהפעיל.

בזה עוד לא נגמרה הסתעפות הוראותיו של השורש. בכל הלשונות,
קרובים הרעיונות של ״מנין״ וסיפור דברים״, השוה בעברית, סָפַר וסַפֵּר:
גרמנית zählen, erzählen; אנגלית tell (כגון teller — פקיד הבנק,
והגיד), צרפתית raconter, compter ;recount, count ועוד הרבה. בזה
יש לפתור את הויכוח הארוך על ביאורו היסודי של השורש ״ספר״. כך שולל
רולי כל קשר בין הפועל העברי־כנעני ״ספר״־מנה ובין השם ספר [37].

35 ראה Brown-Driver-Briggs, Lexicon, עמ׳ 953.
36 ראה Kohler-Baumgarten, Lexicon in V.T., עמ׳ 906, טור 2.
37 ראה H.H. ,"The Semitic Sources of Cipher and its Cognates"
Rowley בקובץ Werden und Wesen des A.T. (1936) עמ׳ 175—190.

המלונות מזהים את השם ספר עם ל׳ אכדית „סיפירו" „מכתב, בשורה"
וגוזרים את הפועל ספר מן השם ספר.[38] אמנם מסתבר שהוראה כפולה יש
לשורש ספר, „מנה", „והגיד". ומזה מסתעף מובן השם ספר, בעיקרו „מכתב
בשורת דברים", ולבסוף „הגדה ארוכה, ספר" במובננו אנו היום.

בכל אופן, הקשר הגלוי בין „מנין" ו„סיפור" יש לראות בשורש „רצה".
השווה „הרצאת דברים" בלשון חז״ל. מה שלא הוכר עדיין הוא שמשמעות
זו של רצה-דבר, הגיד, יש בידה להאיר כמה מקראות סתומים, בס׳ תהלים.

תה׳ ס״ב ה : „ירצו כזב בפיו יברכו, ובקרבם יקללו, סלה". לא בא
המשורר לומר שרצונם בשקר, אלא הם מדברים כזב, בפה מהללים ובלב
מקללים את זולתם.

תה׳ נ׳ יח : „אם ראית גנב ותרץ עמו ועם מנאפים חלקך". כאן מורה
מלת-היחסד „עם", שהביאור הרגיל של „רצה" לא יתאים, שכן אין „רצה"
באה אלא עם „ב" או עם מושא ישיר (השווה תה׳ פ״ה ב, קמ״ט ד, יש׳ מ״ב
י, איוב ל״ג כו). גם ההקבלה מלמדת, שהמשורר מתאר כאן התרועעות עם
חטאים — הרשע משוחח עם גנבים ומתחבר עם מנאפים.

תה׳ מ״ט יד : „זה דרכם כסל למו ואחריהם בפיהם ירצו, סלה". פסוק
קשה זה במזמור עמוק ומעורפל לא על נקלה הוא מתפרש, ורבו השינויים
והסירוסים בו, מימיהם של עקילס והיורונימוס, שגרסו „ירוצו", ולא עזר
תיקונם הרבה. קיטל סימן את הביטוי „בפיהם ירצו" כמעוות שאין לתקן,
ומשנה „ואחריהם" ל„אורחותם". המנסים לפרש את הכתוב אינם מצליחים
ביותר.[39] התרגום היהודי-האמריקאי : those who come after approve''
their sayings'' כלומר, „אלה הבאים אחריהם מקבלים ברצון את דבריהם".

נראה שיש להיעזר גם פה בפירוש „רצה-דבר". במלה „דרכם" יש
לראות את „המים" כהוספה (enclitic), הידועה לנו מאוגריתית ואכדית
והוכרה תכופות במקרא בשנים האחרונות.[40] שיעור הפיסקה יהיה, איפוא,
כך : המשורר מתאר את סופו המר של האדם הבא לקבר שלא בטובתו ומשאיר

38 כך Brown-Driver-Briggs, Gesenius-Buhl, Kohler-Baumgarten.

39 ראה תוספתא נידה ר׳ 6, עבודה זרה ל״ו ע״ב, חגיגה י״ד ב׳ ועוד.

40 ראה H.D. Hommel, "Enclitic Mem in Early Northwest
Semitic Especially Hebrew" JBL כרך 76 (195), עמ׳ 10—15. אף שהרבה
מן הדוגמאות המובאות אצלו מסופקות ומתבארות באופן אחר, אין להכחיש במציאות
מי״ם זה, שחברי פרופ׳ ח. א. גינזברג היה הראשון לגלותה באוגריתית ובעברית.

כל רכושו ועמלו לאחרים, ואין מפלט לא לחכם ולא לעשיר מיד המות
האכזרי. „זה דרך הכסל של בני האדם אשר יספרו עליו בפיהם בני דורם
אחריהם". ואולי יש לגרוס „ואחריתם", ואז ביאורו: „ואחריתם אשר יספרו
עליה בני הדור".

כדאי לציין, שרש"י, בחושו הלשוני המופלא, הכיר בביאור המוצע כאן
לפועל „רצה" והסביר את הפסוק על פי דרכו [41].

ש ל ף

בתה' קכ"ט ו מקלל המשורר את הרשעים: „יהיו כחציר גגות, שקדמת
שלף יבש". השורש המקראי „שלף" משמש ברובו המכריע בקשר עם חרב
(שו' ג כב והרבה) ובמקצתו להסרת הנעל מעל הרגל (רות ד' ז—ח). שימוש
בקשר עם צומח אין לו סמוכים בתנ"ך ולכן הוצעו תיקונים רבים, כגון
„שלם" (הוכפלד-נובק), „חלף" (ולהאוזן, דוהם), „שחלף" (וון אורנטברג),
„קדים תשדף" (קוהלר-בומגרטן). שינויים אלה אינם משביעים רצון ובאמת
מיותרים לגמרי.

בלשון חז"ל משמש הפועל „שלף" לקטיפת פירות, כגון „אדם משליף
שדהו" (מדרש בר' רבה, כ), „זול שלוף" (עירובין י"א ע"ב), „מדלין שלופי"
(מועד קטן ד' ע"ב) [42]. המשורר אומר, איפוא, שהרשעים יהיו כחציר הגדל
על הגג לפני השמש, שלפני הגיע זמן הקטיפה כבר מתיבש [43]. השווה איוב
ח' יב, „עודנו באבו לא יקטף ולפני כל־חציר יבש".

כ י נ ו י   ה ג ו ף   ה ח ו ז ר

ביח' כ"ט ג אנו קוראים: „לי יארי ואני עשיתני". ורוב המפרשים
החדשים נגררים אחרי התרגומים וגורסים „עשיתיו" (פשיטא), או „עשיתים"
(שבעים), ובזה הם מבארים כרש"י ורד"ק. קוק דוחה בהחלט את האפשרות,
שהכינוי יהיה חוזר (reflexive) מפני שהשימוש הזה חסר במקרא [44]. ואמנם

---

41 ראה פירושו לשבת ל"א ע"ב, ד"ה זה דרכם: „...בפיהם ירצו ויספרו
תמיד ואעפ"כ אינן חוזרין", ובבהירות יתירה בפירושו לפסוק בתהלים: „והבאים
אחריהם ידברו בהם ויספרו מה איֵרע לראשונים".

42 ראה רש"י שם: „כשהירקות רצופין נוטל מהם מבינתם".

43 ואולי יש לגרוס „ששלף" או „שלף" אחרי מלת היחס „קדמת".

44 ראה G.A. Cooke, בפירושו לס' יחזקאל (ICC, 1936), עמ' 330:

יש לו סמוכים בלשון המאוחרת, שהיתה לגמרי מחוץ למסגרתו. השווה „בדקה
היום ומצאתה טהורה" (רש"י שבת ט"ו ע"א, ד"ה מפקידה לפקידה), „שבדקה
עצמה שחרית ומצאתה טהורה וחזרה ובדקה ערבית ומצאתה טמאה" (רש"י
נדה ב' ע"א, ד"ה ומפקידה לפקידה). „מצאתה" מכילה כינוי הגוף החוזר
על עצמו וזהה עם „מצאה עצמה".

ועוד זאת. הדוגמה השניה, המובאה לעיל, יש בידה ללמד על השימוש
ביח' כ"ט ט ששם כתוב „לי יארי ואני עשיתי", בלי כינוי הגוף. גם בפיסקה
השניה, ברש"י, בא הניב „בדקה עצמה" בפעם הראשונה ורק „בדקה", בלי
המושא, בפעם השניה, ממש כמו ביח' פס' ג ו"ט, כיון שהכינוי מובן
בפעם השניה.

את פסוקנו יש לבאר „אני עשיתי את עצמי", תיאור גאותו של פרעה,
המזדהה עם תנין הנילוס ומתיימר להיות אלוה.

שימוש זה של כינוי חוזר מאפשר לנו לעמוד על פירוש חרוז קשה
בס' ירמיה (ל"א א): „מצא חן במדבר עם שרידי חרב, הלוך להרגיעו
ישראל". חרוז זה נתפרש על־ידי רש"י ורד"ק והנגררים אחריהם (דרייבר,
AV   „האל הלך לפניהם במדבר להמציא להם מנוחה" (רד"ק). אך הפירוש
דחוק, כיון א) שאין הנושא המוצע (ה') כלל בנמצא בשתי הצלעות; ב) השם
„ישראל" נמצא יוצא דופן אחרי הכינוי בפועל; ג) וההקבלה אינה עולה יפה
עם חרוז א' לפי גישה זו. על כן נטו החדשים (כגון SRV) לבאר „כאשר
הולך ישראל לבקש לו מנוחה", וכיון שמתקשים עוד בפועל ובכינוי יש
מגיהים את הכתוב ל„מרגוע" או „למרגועו" (קיטל, BH).

כל הבעיה נפתרת על־ידי הבנה בתחביר החרוז. המקור „הלוך" הוא
„מקור רצוף" (infinitive consecutive) הנוטל את זמן הפועל הקודם לו
בפסוק (מצא),[45] אלא שיש לפרש את הפעלים לא כמוסבים על יציאת
מצרים, כדעת רד"ק, אלא כבר כעבר נבואי המראה על הגאולה העתידה לבוא.

"The sufix, if used in a reflexive sense *made myself* is most anomalours,
hardly less so if taken as a dative made it for myself".

45 השווה דברי רד"ק וראה ברא' מא, מג, (ונתון) ירמ' יד, ה (ועזוב) י"ט, יג
(והסך) קה' ח' ט (ונתון) ועוד הרבה. השווה גזניוס—קוטש, דקדוק, מהדורה 28, פרק
113, קטע a.

הפועל "רגע" בהפעיל הבא גם כעומד וכיוצא [46] בא כאן כפועל יוצא, כמו שמוכח מן הכנוי. השם "ישראל" הוא הנושא למקור "הלוך", שימוש הידוע גם מכה"ק ומצורית [47]. כל הסגולות הדקדוקיות שבחרוזנו נמצאות בקה' ד' ב: "ושבח אני את המתים" [48] (מקור רצוף, נושא, מושא), אלא שבפיסקתנו המושא הוא לא שם אלא כנוי חוזר.

דברי הנביא מקבלים פירוש טבעי ופשוט: "העם הנשאר מחרב האויב ימצא לו חן; ישראל ילך להרגיע את עצמו, להשיג מנוחה לו".

מי"ם המצב

כיון שהלשון העברית לשון אחת היא, יש ללמוד לא רק ביאורי מלים וניבים מתקופה אחת לחברתה, אלא גם לרדת לעומק התחביר (סינטכסיס) בשיטה ההשוואתית. בלשון המשנה משמשת אות היחס מי"ם לסמן את מצב הפועל. השווה: "כל המקיים את התורה מעוני סופו לקיימה מעושר" (אבות ד' ט), "דבר צניעות ראה בו עומדות מעומד נופלות מיושב" (שבת קי"ג ע"ב) [49].

ראוי לציין, שהמלים "עומד" ו"יושב" משמשות כאן כתארי-הפועל ולכן אינן משתנות לנקבה, אף שמוסבות על רות.

שימוש זה של "מי"ם המצב" לא הוכר די צרכו בלשון המקרא. השווה הושע ט' יא—יב: "אפרים כעוף יתעופף כבודם מלדה מבטן ומהריון. כי אם יגדלו את בניהם ושכלתים מאדם". הנביא מאיים על עמו שכל כבודו יתנדף, בהיות בניהם במצב הלידה או במשך זמן היותם בבטן, או בשעת ההריון, בחינת זו אף זו קתני. ואם יימלטו מכליה — ישכל ה' אותם בהיותם כבר במצב של אדם, זאת אומרת בני קיימא.

בתה' כ"ב יא בא שימוש זה: "עליך השלכתי מרחם, מבטן אמי אלי אתה". שיעור הכתוב: מזמן היותי ברחם, בבטן אמי הייתי מוטל רק עליך.

---

46 השווה דברים, כ"ח, סה; ישע' ל"ד יד (עומד); ירמ' נ' לד "למען הרגיע את הארץ" (יוצא).

47 השווה ויקר' ו' ז "הקרב אתה בני אהרן. דבר י' ב "שמוט כל משה ידו"; ובכתובת עזיתוד (Journal of Near Eastern Studies) vol. 8, 1949, (pp. 112 ff.

48 ראה דיוננו על פסוק זה בספרנו Koheleth, teh Man and World (New York. 1951), עמ' 229.

49 "רות היתה מלקטת השבלים שעומדים ממצב עמדה ואלה שנשרו מן הקוצרים לוקטת מיושב ואינה שחה ליטלן משום צניעות", (רש"י, שם, ד"ה נופלות).

167

רשימת הפסוקים במקרא המפורשים

שמ' ג, יט.

יה' כב, לד.

ויק' כו, לד.

דב' טז, ד ; לב, י.

איוב יג, ר־יא ; יג, טו ; יט, ה ;
כב, ד ; כב, כ ; כג, יז ; כו, ג.

דבר״ה ב' לו, כ.

יח' כט, ג.

יר' לא, א.

הו' ו, ד ; ט, יא־יב ; י, ט ; יא, ה ;
יג, ג.

תה' כב, יא ; מט, י ; נ, יח ; סב, ה ;
קכט, ו.

יש' ז, כג־כה

משלי ג, כח־כט.

שמו' א' כ, טו־טז ; כה, כ.

לסגולות המליצה בכתבי הקודש

שנים רבות חלפו מאז ישבנו בכיתה, לפני מורנו ד"ר משה זיידל והוא
פירש לנו את דברי הנביאים והמשוררים שבכתבי הקודש, ואף נטע בלבנו
אהבת נצח לתנ"ך. רושם הימים האלה לא יימחה עולמית. גם צעירים
שכמותנו, יכלו להכיר בו מידות תרומיות — בתור אדם, מורה, חוקר ומחדש.
בו נתאחדו ידיעה קפדנית ורחבה בדקדוק הלשון והכרת יפי הצורה הנעלה
של התנ"ך מצד אחד, עם ירידה לעומק המחשבה והרגש של סופרי המקרא
מצד שני. ועל־הכל רחפה יראת הרוממות בפני קדושת ספר הספרים
והרועה הנאמן ממנו ניתנו כולם.
במאמר זה, באנו להביע מקצת מן המקצת של תודתנו למורה נעלה
ונערץ, בברכת שנים רבות של עבודה פוריה ושמחת החיים.

* *

*

הראשונים, שהכירו את סגולות הלשון והמליצה בספרות, היו המדקדקים
והריטוריקנים היונים, בבואם לפרש את ספרי הומירוס. הם הם שהמציאו
את המונחים לתופעות שונות במליצה שבספרות הקלסית, והם השפיעו על
הבלשנים הערבים בימי הבינים. המפרשים והמדקדקים העברים של אותה
תקופה סללו להם דרך מיוחדת בשדה זה, והכירו את סגולות המליצה בספרות
המקרא. ובמשך מאתים השנים האחרונות, מימיהם של הרדר ולות, כשלמדו
להכיר את השיא הספרותי של כתבי הקודש, התבוננו חוקרים שונים, אל

253

תורת השירה המקראית, וספרות מדעית, בעלת היקף רב, נוצרה במקצוע זה[1];
ולה תרם גם חתן היובל — ד"ר משה זיידל — בכמה ממאמריו וכתביו[2].
תרומה חשובה, הן מפאת היקפה והן מצד ניצול חומר מן הספרות הערבית,
הוא ספרו של ר"ד ילין[3]. גם כותב הטורים האלה, ניסה להעיר על כמה
תופעות בשדה זה, שטרם הוכרו די צרכן[4].

מן הראוי לציין, כי אף בשעה שהעובדות היו ברורות, לרוב לא ניסו
החוקרים לעמוד על התהליך הפסיכולוגי, המונח ביסוד שימושי המליצה
השונים. במאמר זה, באנו להעיר על כמה צורות של הריטוריקה המקראית,
שעל־ידן יש להבין כמה סתומות בכתבי־הקודש שעל מקצתן עמדו מכבר,
ואילו מקצתן — לא הוכרו עדיין; ונוסף על כך — להבהיר את הנתיב הפסיכו־
לוגי, שגרם ליצירת סוגי מליצה אלה.

---

1 לא באנו לפרוט כאן את הספרות הדנה בשאלה המסובכת של תורת השיר והקצב
התנ״כי, החל מר' עזריה מן האדומים בספרו "מאור עיניים", פרק ס' י, ג. הרדר
(Herder) "המקורות הראשונים של האנושיות" (1778), רוברט לות (Lowth), "השירה
הקדושה של העברים" (1741), ג'. ב. גריי (1939) G. B. Gray: The Forms of Hebrew
Poetry. דעותיו של אדורד סיורס (Sievers) על קצב שקול בכה״ק, הובעו בשורה של
ספרים Metrische Studien; אבל, בדרך כלל, לא נתקבלו. סיכום קצר של המקצוע הזה,
בהוספת חידושים בפרטים אחדים יש למצוא במאמר כותב הטורים האלה "על מבנה השירה
העברית הקדומה" בספר השנה ליהודי אמריקה שנת תש״ה, עמ' 136—159.

הערות חשובות בתורת המליצה מפוזרות בפירושיהם של רש״י, ראב״ע ורד״ק,
וב"ספר הרקמה" של ר' יונה אבן־ג'נאח. וכן בס' השרשים של רד״ק. עבודה מקיפה
במקצוע זה היא E. König: Stilistik, Rhetorik, Poetik (Leipzig 1908).
2 השחה "דביר" כרך א' (ברלין 1923), וספרו "חקרי לשון" (ירושלים תרצ״ב)
[ורבים משאר כתביו, המנויים בקובץ זה בעמ' 3—8].
3 "כתבים נבחרים", כרך ב', "לתורת המליצה בתנ״ך והשירה העברית בספרד"
(ירושלים תרצ״ט).
4 יורשה לו להזכיר כאן אחדים, שמפאת לשונם הלועזית — אינם מצויים בנקל לפני
הקורא העברי:
"Some Effects of Primitive Thought on Language" in AJSL, vol. 55,
1938, pp. 270—284.
"A Rhetorical Use of Interrogative Sentences in Biblical Hebrew",
AJSL, 1933, vol. 49, pp. 212—217.
"The Heptad as an Element of Biblical and Rabbinic Style", JBL.
vol. 26. 1943, pp. 17—26.
"Quotations as a Literary Usage in Biblical, Rabbinic and Oriental
Literature", HUCA, vol. 22, 1949, pp. 157—219.

254

תלחין

בין סגולות המליצה המקראית, יש שימוש שעוד לא הכירו בו כראוי: המדקדקים הערבים כינו אותו „תלחין‟ לַצְּחִין [5]. אולם יש להבדיל בין „תלחין‟, ובין „לשון נופל על לשון‟ הידוע מכבר, שימוש הקרוב אמנם אליו, אבל אינו זהה אתו. ב„לשון נופל על לשון‟ בוחר לו הסופר במלה אחת במשמעות אחת; ובחירתו במלה זו דוקא — ולא באחרת — נגרמת על-ידי קירבתה בצלצול למלה אחרת באותה פיסקה, דרך-משל ישעי' ה', ז: „וַיְקַו לְמִשְׁפָּט וְהִנֵּה מִשְׂפָּח‟ וגו'; או במיכה א', יד: „בָּתֵּי אַכְזִיב לְאַכְזָב‟ כאן נגרמת ההנאה האסתטית לקורא — על-ידי הכרת הצלצול הדומה בין שתי המלים [6].

אולם בשמוש ה„תלחין‟, בוחר לו הסופר במלה אחת בעלת שתי משמעויות, ובחירתו במלה זו דוקא — ולא בנרדפת לה — נגרמת על-ידי רצון הסופר להעלות את שתי המשמעויות בבת אחת על סף-תודעתו של הקורא; האחת תשמש כהוראה עיקרית, ואילו השניה — כמושג-לואי, המוסיף נופך מיוחד למחשבה ולהרגשה.

דוגמה מאלפת ל„תלחין‟ יש למצוא באיכה ב', יג: „כִּי גָדוֹל כַּיָּם שִׁבְרֵךְ מִי יִרְפָּא לָךְ‟ — כאן בחר המקונן דוקא במלה „שֶׁבֶר‟ ולא בשם נרדף כגון: „הרס, כליון, חורבן, מכה, נגע‟; מפני שהמלה „שבר‟ מעלה את הרעיון של „מִשְׁבָּר, גל‟ — המתאים כה יפה לתמונת הים: „כִּי-גָדוֹל כַּיָּם שִׁבְרֵךְ.‟ [7].

ההנאה האסתטית המורגשת מ„תלחין‟ — היא הרבה יותר עדינה מזו הנגרמת בעקב „לשון נופל על לשון‟, שהרי אינה תלויה בצלצול חיצוני גרידא, אלא בתוכן הפנימי; והדוגמאות הבאות יוכיחו. ומן העניין להוסיף, כי אותו עונג נובע מתוך ההכרה הפתאומית של שני מובנים, המבצבצים ועולים לפני הקורא ברגע אחד: הראשון כיסודי, והשני כמלווה.

---

5 למלה ערבית זו יש הרבה הוראות וביניהן: „אופן דיבור, דיאלקט, שגיאה בבטוי המביאה לידי שנוי במובן או מבנה המלים‟. המשמעות הטכנית תתבאר בגוף מאמרנו.

6 מחקר מקיף על „לשון נופל על לשון‟ יש למצוא בספרו של I. M. Casanowicz Paronomasia in the O—T. (Boston 1894), וחומר רב נמצא בספרו של ילין הנזכר בהערה 3.

7 בדרך כלל אי אפשר לתרגם שעשועי לשון כאלה מלשון ללשון. אולם דוקא בדוגמה זו יש יוצא מן הכלל, כיון שבאנגלית ישנו שם נרדף לגל ''wave'' שהנהו ''braeker'' ואת הפיסקה יש לתרגם איפוא ''Thy break is great as the sea.''

255

הפסיכולוגיה בימינו לימדה אותנו להכיר, שפתאומיות ההכרה — היא
היא מיסודות ההנאה שבהומור; כי ההלצה מגלה — כהארת־ברק — את הקשר
(בין של דמיון ובין של סתירה) בין שתי תופעות שונות, שלכאורה אין ביניהן
ולא כלום; ובזה עוקצה, חריפותה וחינה של ההלצה. גם מליצת „לשון נופל
על לשון" ניזונה מפתאומיות ההכרה של קשר המאחד שתי מלים, הדומות
בצלצולן. ב„תלחין" פתאומיות זו חשובה פחות, אף שהיא תופסת עדיין מקום
ניכר כגורם להנאה האסתטית. כאן העיקר הרחבת אופק המחשבה והעמקת
ההרגשה, הבאות בעקבות מליצה זו. לכן קרובה מליצת „לשון נופל על לשון"
אל ההלצה; ואילו התלחין — רחוק ממנה.

לא יפלא אפוא, שהמשורר הגאוני מחבר „ספר איוב" השולט בכל
מכמני הלשון העברית, הצטיין בשימוש בשמנה זה. דוגמה מצויינת של תלחין יש
באיוב ז׳, ו:

יָמַי קַלּוּ מִנִּי־אָרֶג   וַיִּכְלוּ בְּאֶפֶס תִּקְוָה.

למלה „תקוה" יש כאן מובנה היסודי — „סכוי לעתיד". אבל גם משמעותה
השניה, הנדירה, מבצבצת ועולה: „חוט", השווה (יהושע ב׳, כ״א, כג) תִּקְנַת
חוּט הַשָּׁנִי (מלשון קו)[8]. מושג משנה זה מתאים כאן באופן מצויין למשל
של המשורר, המדמה את החיים לחוט העובר ונטווה בכלי ארג עד שנגמר,
ובזה נחתך גורלו של האדם. רעיון זה ידוע מספרות יון ורומי, המתארת את
שלש אלות הגורל (Parcae, Moirae) וביחוד קלותו (Clotho), היושבת
ואורגת בכישור עד שעת חיתוך החוט, כשחייו של האדם כלים. רעיון זה,
הידוע לנו מאמונתם הקדומה של היונים[9], היה בודאי נפוץ בכל העולם
העתיק. וכך יוצאת תמונה מחרידה של חיי הקצרים של האדם, הנגזרים
ע״י כח זולתו והנגמרים — באפס תקוה.

דוגמאות נוספות ל„תלחין" בספר איוב ג׳, ו—ז:

הַלַּיְלָה הַהוּא יִקָּחֵהוּ אֹפֶל

---

8 מליצה זו הוכרה על ידי ר׳ דוד ילין בספרו הנ״ל, עמ׳ 103, המביא דעתו של
ש״נ שטיינברג שקדם לו.

9 השחה הסיודוס, Theognis, 219, ו־ E. M. Blakeney, A Smaller Classical
Dictionary (London 1926) p. 346. P. Harvey, Oxford Companion to Classical Literature (Oxford 1937) p. 124.

אַל יֵחַדְּ בִּימֵי שָׁנָה   בְּמִסְפַּר יְרָחִים אַל־יָבֹא

הִנֵּה הַלַּיְלָה הַהוּא יְהִי גַלְמוּד   אַל־תָּבֹא רְנָנָה בוֹ

בפעל יֵחַדְּ התלבטו המפרשים: על פי נקוד המסורה, שרשו הוא „חדה"
(השוה שמות י״ח, ט „וַיִּחַדְ יִתְרוֹ"); אבל על־פי הקבלה, יש לפרשו מלשון
„יָחד" (השוה בראשית מ״ט, ה: „בְּסֹדָם אַל־תָּבֹא נַפְשִׁי, בִּקְהָלָם אַל־תֵּחַד
כְּבֹדִי"). על כן העדיפו רוב המפרשים את השורש „יָחד" לפסוקנו, ודחו את
ניקוד המסורה לגמרי 10. אבל בשיטה זו לא יצאנו עוד ידי חובתנו, שהרי אז
תהיינה מקבילות צלעות ב׳ וג׳ (אל יחד, אל יבא) אבל לא צלעות ד׳ וה׳
(גלמוד, אל תבוא רננה בו). ומאידך גיסא, אם נפרש „יֵחַדְ" מל׳ „שמחה"
יוצאת לנו הקבלה מצויינת בצורת כיאסמוס (א, ב, ב, א) שאינו מכנים בשם
„שתי וערב" 11 (אל יחד // אל תבוא רננה; במספר... אל יבא // יהי גלמוד).
עשירות התוכן השלימה שבבטוי מתגלית, כשמכירים אנו את ה„תלחין" —
„יחד", על שתי משמעויותיו; העיקרית „ישמח" והשנית „יהיה יחד", ושתיהן
מרחפות בעת ובעונה אחת לפני הסופר והקורא.

איוב כ״א, יג:

גורלם המאושר של הרשעים מתואר בפיסקה זו:

יְכַלּוּ (יבלו כתיב) בַטּוֹב יְמֵיהֶם   וּבְרֶגַע שְׁאוֹל יֵחַתּוּ 12

השם „רגע" מכיל בקרבו את הרעיון היסודי של „הרף עין — זמן קצר מאד",
וגם את הרעיון המשני — „במנוחה": כשמגיע קיצם של הרשעים — הם מתים
חיש מהר, ובלי מכאובים ממושכים.

איוב י״ב, ו:

יִשְׁלָיוּ אֹהָלִים לְשֹׁדְדִים   וּבַטֻּחוֹת לְמַרְגִּיזֵי אֵל

לַאֲשֶׁר הֵבִיא אֱלוֹהַּ בְּיָדוֹ.

בפיסקה קשה זו, מודיע לנו המשורר שמשכנות הגזלנים עומדים בשלוה.
המלה „בטחות" יש לפרש מן השורש השמי היסודי — הבא בערבית بَطَحَ

---

10 כך למשל, דוחה לגמרי טור־סיני בפירושו את הקשר עם „חדה".

11 השוה מאמרנו הנזכר, בהערה 1, עמ׳ 152 ואילך; וראה למשל ל„הקבלת שתי
וערב" משלי כ״ג, טו—טז; איוב כ׳ ב—ג.

12 „יֵחַתּוּ", כפי שהוכר על ידי רוב המפרשים החדשים הוא משורש נָחַת = יָרַד
הבא באיוב פעמים אחדות; השוה י״ז, טז; ומשלי י״ז, י.

„נפל, שכב, רבץ", והנמצא במובן זה גם בעברית המקראית[13]. אם כן
יש לפרש „בְּטָחוֹת" במשמעות של „מעונות, משכנות" כמקביל לשם „אהלים"
בצלע א׳.

מכל הנרדפים ל„דירה, מעון" בוחר לו המשורר דוקא במונח הנדיר
„בטחות", מפני שיש בו כאן גם משמעות לואי של „בטחון ומנוחה".

הצלע האחרונה של פסוק קשה זה — סתומה; ורבו עליה סירוסים
ופירושים שאינם מניחים את הדעת. הוצע למשל „לַאֲשֶׁר הֵבִיא בָּאֱלוֹהַּ
יָדוֹ". „לַאֲשֶׁר הֵנִיף בָּאֱלוֹהַּ יָדוֹ". „לֵאמֹר הֲכִי אֱלוֹהַּ בְּיָדִי" ועוד אחרים
המרחיקים-לכת מאלה[14]. רצוננו להעיר, שבלשון האנגלית הקלסית —
בתקופתו של שקספיר — יש בטוי המזדהה, באופן מפליא, עם הצלע שבאיוב,
ופירושו „רָמָה, הוֹנָה, גָּנַב דַּעַת". השווה המחזה „המלך הנרי הרביעי"
חלק ב, מערכה א׳, 2, 34.   "to bear a gentleman in hand,

and then to stand upon security".

שמובננו הוא „לרמות את האדון, ואחרי-כן לדרוש ערבון"[15]. בטוי זה
אינו נדיר בתקופה זו כלל. הוא נמצא גם ב„מקבת", מערכה ד׳, א׳ 79:

"How you were borne in hand"

וכן ב„המלט", מערכה ב׳, 2, 67:   "He was falsely borne in hand".

את מהות הבטוי לא קשה להבין: „לקחת מי שהוא ביד" משמש כתאור
לאחיזת עינים ורמאות; וסימנטיקה זהה יש להניח לבטוי המקראי, שאינו
דורש שום סירוסים ותיקונים, ויהא זה פירוש הפסוק:

„שקטים הם האהלים של השודדים
מעונותם של אלה המכעיסים את אלהים
של אלה המרמים את אלוה".

---

13 ראה S. L. Skoss במאמרו "The Root בקובץ Jewish Studies in Memory of G. A. Kohut (N. Y. 1935) pp. 549—53, המעיר שפירוש „נפל" — הוצע
על ידי הבלשן הקראי, דוד בן אברהם אלפאסי, בקשר לירמיה י״ב, ה (וּבְאֶרֶץ שָׁלוֹם אַתָּה
בוֹטֵחַ); משלי י״ד, טז; תהלים כ״ב, י (מַבְטִיחִי עַל שְׁדֵי אִמִּי). בעקבותיו מפרש שלמה
אבן פרחון את איוב מ׳, כג, ששם לא נראה לפרש כך; ואין כאן המקום להאריך. ויש
להוסיף איוב י״א, יח—יט: „וּבָטַחְתָּ כִּי-יֵשׁ תִּקְוָה, וְחָפַרְתָּ לָבֶטַח תִּשְׁכָּב, וְרָבַצְתָּ וְאֵין
מַחֲרִיד". ההקבלה „בטח, חפר, רבץ" — מורה על שכיבה.
14 אלה הן הצעותיהם של סיגפריד, בער ודוהם; וראה השגותיהם של Driver-
Gray; והשוה טור-סיני, המציע פירוש מיוחד.
15 ראה הערותיו של הפרשן Sidney Lee במהדורתו למקום זה.

258

לסגולות המליצה בכתבי הקודש

הקבלת הצלעות היא מענינת: א. ב, ג; / / ב, ג, ג; כמוֹדגם:

יַשְׁלִיו אֹהָלִים לְשֹׁדְדִים   וּבַטֻּחוֹת לְמַרְגִּיזֵי־אֵל.

לַאֲשֶׁר הֵבִיא אֱלוֹהַ בְּיָדוֹ.

איוב ה׳, כד:

וְיָדַעְתָּ כִּי־שָׁלוֹם אָהֳלֶךָ   וּפָקַדְתָּ נָוְךָ וְלֹא תֶחֱטָא

מן ההקבלה, ברור הוא כי "תחמא" בצלע ב׳ יש לפרש "לא תמצא דבר
חסר בו"; והשווה משלי ח׳, לו ("וְחֹטְאִי חֹמֵס נַפְשׁוֹ"): שופטים כ׳, טז (וְלֹא
יַחֲטִא"[16]. בצלע ב׳ בוחר לו המשורר דוקא בשורש "פקד", שבאורו העיקרי
הוא "בקר"; אבל הוא מעלה על לב הקורא גם את המשמעות השניה "היה
חסר"[17] (השווה שמואל־א׳, כ׳, יח: "וְנִפְקַדְתָּ כִּי יִפָּקֵד מוֹשָׁבֶךָ"; וכן ישעיה
ל״ד, טז). בספר "איוב", אומר המשורר: "תפקד את מעונך, ושום בריה או
חפץ — לא תמצא חסר".

איוב ג׳, כב:

הַשְּׂמֵחִים אֱלֵי־גִיל   יָשִׂישׂוּ כִּי יִמְצְאוּ קָבֶר

רבו המגרסים כאן "אֱלֵי־גַל", כדי להקביל את הצלעות, אבל שינוי זה
מיותר לגמרי. המשורר השתמש בבטוי "שָׂמַח אֶל גִּיל" (הושע ט׳, א); (השווה
גם תהלים מ״ג, ד: "שִׂמְחַת גִּילִי") — מפני שהמלה גיל מזכירה גם את המושג
"גל־קבר", כהוראת לואי.

איוב כ״ב, כה:

וְהָיָה שַׁדַּי בְּצָרֶיךָ   וְכֶסֶף תּוֹעָפוֹת לָךְ.

מכל הנרדפים ל"הון", כגון: "עשר, כח, חיל, שפע" — וכיוצא בהם —
בוחר לו המשורר במלה הנגדירה בָּצֶר (ראה הפסוק הקודם שם), מפני שיש בה

---

16 אולי מורה הכתיב החסר על ניקוד "יחטא" — בקל, ולא בהפעיל.
17 כדאי להעיר שבשימושנו "עיקרי" ו־"משני" — אין אנו באים לחרוץ משפט על
השתלשלות המובנים השונים במקורם "הפרוטושמי", אלא בשימוש החי שבלשון המקרא.
"פקד" ברובו המכריע בתנ״ך הוא "בקר, השגיח, מנה"; ובמיעוטו "מצא חסר". לא
האטימולוגיה ההיסטורית, אלא התודעה של הקורא — היא היא הקובעת ב־"תלחין" לשורש
"פקד" יש סמוכים באכדית, בצורית ובארמית, באבור "בקר, השגיח"; וכן גם בערבית,
לפי דוזי; ויש גם שורש ערבי فقد "אבד, החסיר", והכרעת המוקדם והמאוחר
בסמנטיקה כאן היא די קשה, ואולי מן הנמנעות (ראה גישותיהם הנגודות במלונותיהם של
Brown-Driver-Briggs עמ׳ 823, Kohler-Baumgartner עמ׳ 773).

259

36

ראובן גורדיס

המושג המשני „מבצר, משגב", „ה׳ יהיה מבצרך". ואולי מושג־הלואי הוא
אחר: צָרֶיךָ עם תוספת בית, ופירושו: „ה׳ יקום נגד צריך, אויביך".

השימוש ב„תלחין" אינו מצומצם לספר „איוב"; דוגמא מצויינת בספרי
הנבואה יש בעובדיה פסוק ו:

אֵיךְ נֶחְפְּשׂוּ עֵשָׂו   נִבְעוּ מַצְפֻּנָיו

כבר העירו איתן וילין, שמלבד ההוראה הרגילה של „עשה" יש שורש
שני בעברית, המקביל לערבי غَلَ — שבאורו „כסה"; השווה ישעיה ל"ב, ו;
איוב כ"ג, ט[18]. השם „עֵשָׂו" = „מכוסה שער" בראשית (כ"ה, כה) מתיחס
לשורש זה, ואין לו עם הוראת „עשה" הרגילה ולא כלום.

בהצלחה מרובה משתמש הנביא כאן, בשם אבי עם אדום כ„תלחין",
שהרי באורו הוא „המכוסה"; ולא זו בלבד אלא שעל־פי צלצולו נשמע כשם
עצם ברבים (=המכוסים שלו), ולכן בא הפועל בלשון רבים (נֶחְפְּשׂוּ) ומובן
הכתוב:

איך נתגלו סודותיו של עשו, המכוסה, נחקרו כל נסתרותיו?

הושע ז׳, ט:

אָכְלוּ זָרִים כֹּחוֹ, וְהוּא לֹא יָדָע; גַּם־שֵׂיבָה זָרְקָה בּוֹ, וְהוּא לֹא יָדָע.

ההוראה הרגילה של הפועל „זרק" — השליך, הזה — אינה מתאימה לפסוק.
עיין באורו של הלקסיקון האוקספורדי „שערות שחומות מרובות אצלו"
(‏"are profuse"). לכן הציעו לגרוס „זָרְחָה בו" על פי הכתוב בדברי־הימים־ב
כ"ו, יט (וְהַצָּרַעַת זָרְחָה בְמִצְחוֹ). אבל אין הנידון דומה לעניין. על־כן במקום
התיקון, הציע דרייבר[19] לפרש על פי השם הערבי أَزْعَقَ שהוראתו
blue-white, greyish white. והוא מבאר את הצלע בפסוקנו: „שיבתו
נעשתה שחומה, לבנה". אולם גם בפירוש זה אינו מניח את הדעת, מפני שעל־
פיו אין הפסוק מודיע לנו כלום אלא צבע שיבתו של ישראל, ולא את זה רצה
הנביא להשמיע. עיקר תוכחתו הוא, שהעם אינו מרגיש במצבו המסוכן,
שנתהווה אצלו לפתע פתאום, ואין איש שם על לב.

והנה הפסוק מתבאר על בוריו, כשמכירים אנו בו „תלחין". המשמעות

---

18   ראה ישראל איתן A Contribution to Biblical Lexicography (New-York
1924) ואחריו ר"ד ילין „חקרי־מקרא, איוב" (ירושלים, תרפ"ז עמ׳ 57).

19   ראה G. R. Driver בברבעון Journal of Theological Studies, vol. 33,
p. 38.

260

37

העיקרית היא „הושלכה, קפצה עליו פתאום" ומושג־הלואי, שגרם לבחירת
מלה זו דוקא „נעשתה לבנה. שחומה".

אין לבאר את הפועל „זֹרְקָה" כבנין קל רגיל, שהרי הפועל בבנין זה
הוא יוצא ולא עומד. את הצורה שבמסורה יש לראות כסביל עתיק של הקל,
שרק שרידים ממנו נשארו בלשון המקרא [20], אף שרגיל הוא בלשון הערבית
בבנין הראשון קָטַל‎. השוה: לֻקֳחָה (בראשית ב׳, כג) אֻכַּל (שמות ג׳, ב)
עֻבַּד (דברים כ״א, ג) יֻלַּד (ישעיה ט׳, ה). הקמץ הראשון בפועל שלנו יש
לראותו כקמץ קטן במקום חולם או קיבוץ (זֹרְקָה = זֻרְקָה או זָרְקָה [21]), וכן:
„הִנֵּה בָרֵךְ לָקָחְתִּי (= לֻקַּחְתִּי)" במדבר כ״ג, כ.

ישעיה י׳, טז:

לָכֵן יְשַׁלַּח ה׳ צְבָאוֹת בְּמִשְׁמַנָּיו רָזוֹן.

כאן בוחר הנביא במלה „רזון", מפני שנוסף על הוראתה העיקרית
„כחישות, חולשה" — היא מעלה גם כן את המושג־של „שררה, ממשלה",
שנמצא בשמות רָזוֹן (משלי י״ד, כח), וְרוֹזֵן (שופטים ה׳, ג; חבקוק א׳, 10;
ישעיה מ׳, כג; תהלים ב׳, ב; משלי ח׳, טו, ל״א, ד), ועל־ידי־כך מתבלט
הניגוד: במשמנים, בשרים — יבוא רזון וכחש.

ישעיה א׳, לא:

וְהָיָה הֶחָסֹן לִנְעֹרֶת וּפֹעֲלוֹ לְנִיצוֹץ
וּבָעֲרוּ שְׁנֵיהֶם יַחְדָּו וְאֵין מְכַבֶּה.

שימוש ה„תלחין" מגלה פה את עתיקותה של מלה עברית הידועה לנו
רק מספרות חז״ל. הנביא רוצה לומר, שהתקיף עם כל מעשיו — ישמד כליל,
והוא משתמש במשל הנאה של פשתן הנשרף מהר. הוא בוחר במלה הנדירה
„חָסֹן" (הנמצאת רק בעמוס ב׳, ט, השוה „חַסִין" תהלים פ״ט, ט; „חֹסֶן"
ישעיה ל״ג, ו) ולא ב„גבור" או „חזק", כי המלה „חסון" מזכירה את המונח
הדומה לה „חוסן" — „פשתן לפני שנופץ"; השוה משנה שבת ב׳, א: „במה
מדליקין... לא בחוסן". על עתיקות המלה, מעידה העובדה, שאמוראי בבל

---

20 צורה דקדוקית זו הוכרה על ידי Boettcher בספר הדקדוק שלו Ausführ-
liches Lehrbuch פרקים 904, ו־1022, וראה Gesenius — Kautzsch דקדוק עברי
(מהדורה כ״ה, 1889) פרק 52, סעיף ו׳ הערה 3, שמביא שורה ארוכה של פעלים בבנין זה.
21 השוה „טָרֹף טֹרַף יוֹסֵף" (בראשית ל״ז, לג).

נחלקו בבאורה; ומענין שהביאו את הפסוק דידן, בקשר עם דבריהם בתלמוד בבלי שבת. כ׳ ע״ב: „ולא בחוסן — אמר רב יוסף: נעורת של פשתן; אמר ליה אביי: והכתיב „והיה החסון לנעורת" (מכלל דחוסן לאו נעורת הוא); אלא אמר אביי: כיתנא דדייק ולא נפיץ". ההוראה העיקרית של „חסון" היא „חזק" ומרשג הלואי — „פשתן בלתי מנופץ".

גם משורר תהלים השתמש ב„תלחין", בבחרו בניבים ידועים מפני דו־משמעותם המורגשת:

תהלים קל״ב, יג—יד:

אַנָּה לְמוֹשָׁב לוֹ... פֹּה אֵשֵׁב כִּי אִוִּתִיהָ

השורש הערבי أوى‎ פירושו „הָתָק למקום לשם דירה" [22]; ולכן מרחפות לפני המשורר שתי ההוראות „רצה, התגעגע", וגם „התישב".

תהלים כ״ז, ד:

לַחֲזוֹת בְּנֹעַם ה׳ וּלְבַקֵּר בְּהֵיכָלוֹ

כבר באו לתקן את הגירסה אל „בְּמְעוֹן ה׳". להקבילה אל „היכלו"; אבל שנוי זה מיותר, ובאמת מרושש סירוס זה את המליצה. המשורר רוצה להרגיש את נועם ה׳, את חדותו בקירבת בוראו, והוא בוחר במלה זו דוקא, מפני שמעלה היא לפני הקורא גם את המונח „מעון" (השוה כ״ו, ח).

מאוחר ומוקדם (hysteron proteron)

חז״ל הכירו, כי חויה נפשית מיוחדת במינה באה לידי בטוי בקריאתם הנלהבת של בני ישראל במעמד הר סיני: „נַעֲשֶׂה וְנִשְׁמָע" (שמות כ״ד, ז), שהרי לפי ההגיון, צריכה השמיעה לבוא לפני העשייה. בביטול הסדר ההגיוני והכרונולוגי הרגיל ראו סימן להתמסרותם העילאית של יוצאי מצרים לפקודת ה׳ ודרשו את התלהבותם לשבח, בזה ש„הקדימו ישראל נעשה לנשמע" (שבת פ״ח ע״א). גם בפיסקה מקבילה באסתר ט׳, כז, „קָיְמוּ וְקִבְּלוּ הַיְּהוּדִים", הכירו, ש„קבלה" צריכה להקדים ל„קיום"; ולכן דרשו: „קימו מה שקיבלו כבר" (שבת שם).

שתי מימרות מפורסמות אלה משקפות שימוש מליצי, הידוע בספרות היונית־רומית בשם hysteron proteron (אחרון—ראשון). הסופר מתאמץ

---

22 השוה Brown-Driver-Briggs עמ׳ 15.

262

39

להביע שני רעיונות העומדים בסדר הגיוני או זמני זה אחר זה, אבל
בחשיבותם — עולה האחרון על הראשון ; ולכן מתפרק הרעיון השני מתוך
מסגרת ההגיון והזמן ובא לידי בטוי לפני חבירו הקודם לו. הפרעת הסדר
מתוך הרגשה עמוקה כזו, עשויה להתפתח יותר בשירה מבפרוזה — אבל מצויה
היא בשתיהן.

חשוב לציין, שאין כאן סירוס מקראות על־ידי סופר טועה ומטעה ; אלא
תהליך פסיכולוגי כביר בנפש הסופר, החותר מתחת לסף ההכרה, ובא לידי
גילוי ספרותי[23]. כשמכירים את מציאות השימוש הזה, מתברר הפשט מאליו ;
ונסתפק רק ברשימת פיסקאות אחדות, חוץ משתים אלה שהובאו לעיל. את
שלל התיקונים והסירוסים שהוצעו לפיסקאות השונות, יש לראות אפוא
כמיותרים לגמרי :

שמות ט״ז, כ׳:	נָיָרֻם תּוֹלָעִים וַיִּבְאַשׁ
ישעיה מ״ד, טז:	עַל־חֶצְיוֹ בָּשָׂר יֹאכֵל יִצְלֶה צָלִי וְיִשְׂבָּע
תהלים כ״ו, יא:	וַאֲנִי בְּתֻמִּי אֵלֵךְ פְּדֵנִי וְחָנֵּנִי
תהלים ס׳, ז; ק״ח, ז:	לְמַעַן יֵחָלְצוּן יְדִידֶיךָ הוֹשִׁיעָה יְמִינְךָ וַעֲנֵנִי
איוב י״ד, י:	וְגֶבֶר יָמוּת וַיֶּחֱלָשׁ וַיִּגְוַע אָדָם וְאַיּוֹ[24]
איוב ט״ז, ט:	אַפּוֹ טָרַף וַיִּשְׂטְמֵנִי
איוב כ׳, יט:	כִּי־רִצַּץ עָזַב דַּלִּים[25]

אֶחָד־דֶּרֶךְ־שְׁנַיִם (hendiadys)

במליצת ״מאוחר ומוקדם״, ראינו שעומדים לפני הסופר שני רעיונות
הדורשים ביטוי, ומכיוון שאחד חשוב מחבירו — דוחה הוא את רגלי אחיו,
ומפרכס לצאת לעולם לפניו, בניגוד לסדר ההגיון. כאן מנצח העיקר את
הטפל לו. תהליך פסיכולוגי הפוך יש לראות בתופעה המליצית הידועה

---

23 ר״י אבן־ג׳נח דן בתופעות כאלה ב״ספר הרקמה״ (עמ׳ 212), אבל אינו מבחין
בין דוגמאות של ״מאוחר ומוקדם״ — אשר תהליך פסיכולוגי ביסודם, ובין אלה שטעות
סופרים ומעתיקים גרמה להן.

24 ואין צורך בתיקונים לךְ״וַיַּחַ״ או ״וַיַּחֲלֹף״ (תרגום השבעים) או ״וַיַּחַ״ (רייט, גרץ, בודה,
דרייבר־גריי), ״וַיִּשְׁלָח״ (טור־סיני) או אפילו ״וַיַּחֲלֹשׁ״ ע״פ שורש ערבי خلس
״חטף בסתר״ (איתן) ״וַיֶּחֱלָשׁ״ מקבל באופן מצויין אל ״ויגוע״, במובנו הרגיל, והכוונה:
״האדם נעשה חלש ומת״.

25 דוגמה זו מסופקת, כי על־פי הקבלה היה אפשר לצפות לשם לפני ״דלים״, השחה
צלע ב׳ ״בַּיִת גָּזַל וְלֹא יִבְנֵהוּ״. לכן, יש מציעים עֹזֵב, ומשמחים את המונח ללשון
המשנה: ״מַעֲזִיבָה״ (עהרליך), ויש משנים וקוראים ״זָרוֹעַ דַּלִּים״, וראה טור־סיני, לפסוק.

בשם היוני hendyadys: הסופר רוצה להביע רעיון אחד, אלא שרעיון זה
הוא בעל שני פנים: אחד עיקר ואחד טפל. כאן מנצח הטפל את העיקר,
הרעיון עצמו מתפצל לשני חלקיו; והטפל בא לידי בטוי עצמאי, שוחה
במעלה עם חבירו החשוב ממנו.

בעברית יש אמצעי מיוחד להבעת רעיון אחד בעל שני פנים, עיקר
וטפל. זו הסמיכות, שהשם הנסמך — הוא העיקר; והסומך — הטפל. בתופעה
מליצית, שאנו דנים בה עכשיו — מתבטלת הסמיכות, ובמקומה יבואו שני
שמות קשורים בו״ו החיבור. גם כאן, כשמכירים בשימוש זה, נראים כל
הסירוסים והתיקונים כמיותרים לגמרי; ונסתפק ברשימה קצרה של דוגמאות
ל״רעיון אחד דרך שנים״:

בראשית ג׳, טז:	עִצְבוֹנֵךְ וְהֵרֹנֵךְ (=עצבון הריונך).
דברים ז׳, יב:	וְשָׁמַר הַ׳ אֱלֹהֶיךָ לְךָ אֶת הַבְּרִית וְאֶת־הַחֶסֶד אֲשֶׁר נִשְׁבַּע לַאֲבֹתֶיךָ (=את ברית החסד אשר נשבע)[26].
שמואל־א ט״ו, כג:	כִּי חַטַּאת־קֶסֶם מֶרִי, וְאָוֶן וּתְרָפִים הַפְצַר (=און של תרפים, חטא של תרפים)[27]
ישעיה נ״ג, ח:	מֵעֹצֶר וּמִמִּשְׁפָּט לֻקָּח (=מעצירת המשפט, על ידי מניעת הצדק נשבה עבד ה׳)[28].
ירמיה כ״ט, יא:	אַחֲרִית וְתִקְוָה (=אחרית של תקוה).
ירמיה י״ד, יד:	חֲזוֹן שֶׁקֶר וְקֶסֶם וֶאֱלִיל (קרי) (=קסם של הבל)[29].
איוב ה׳, טו:	וַיֹּשַׁע מֵחֶרֶב מִפִּיהֶם וּמִיַּד חָזָק אֶבְיוֹן (=מחרב פיהם)[30].

---

26 ברור הוא שהפעל ״נשבע״ אין להסב על ״החסד״ — ״ברית החסד״ היא ״ברית
הנובעת מתוך אהבה״.

27 הרלב״ג הרגיש בבאור הזה וחשב את הו״ו של ״וּתְרָפִים״ כמיותרת, וכל
החדשים משמיטים את האות. פירושו של סגל ל״און״ = ״אלילים״ אינו מתקבל על
הדעת, כי ראיתו מישעיה ס״ו, ג מסופקת. ההקבלה מוכיחה ש״און״ פירושו ״חטא״ ושיחסו
ההגיוני אל ״תרפים״ הוא יחס של סמיכות.

28 וכן ״עֹצֵר רַחַם״ (משלי ל׳, טז) = ״מניעת הרחם, עקרות״.

29 השוה זכריה י״א, יז ״רֹעִי הָאֱלִיל״. איוב י״ג, ד ״רֹפְאֵי אֱלִיל״.

30 כעשרים כ״י גורסים ״מֵחֶרֶב פִּיהֶם״ אבל אין זה אלא תהליך ההשואה וההקבלה
(levelling), ואין בכך עדות לגירסה מקורית השונה משלנו. ההצעות ״מֵחֶרֶב״ ⟵ ״הָאִישׁ
השומם״ (עֹחֶלד) ״מַפָּאֵיהֶם״ (טור־סיני) ״מֵחֲרָבִים יָתֵם״ (בודה) ״מִפִּיהֶם יָתֵם״ (בודה)
אינן מחוייבות כלל. צורת ההקבלה כאן, רווחת בספרות אוגרית ובשירה התנ״כית; והיא
מכונה בפי רוב החוקרים Climactic. אנו מעדיפים את המונח ״מַשְׁלֶמֶת״ (-complemen
tary), כיון שהצלע השניה משלמת את הראשונה א ב ב ג // א ב ג ד; למשל תהלים

264

41

איוב י׳, יב :   חַיִּים וָחֶסֶד עָשִׂיתָ עִמָּדִי וּפְקֻדָּתְךָ שָׁמְרָה רוּחִי (=נתת לי
חיים של חסד, לא לפי זכויותי — אלא מתנת חנם,
הנובעת מתוך אהבתך אלי ; ומצותך זו, גזרת המלך,
שמרה את רוחי בחיים) [31].

איוב י׳, יז :   תְּחַדֵּשׁ עֵדֶיךָ נֶגְדִּי וְתֶרֶב כַּעַשְׂךָ עִמָּדִי חֲלִיפוֹת וְצָבָא עִמִּי.
(=חליפות של צבא) [32].

איוב כ״ה, ב :   הַמְשֵׁל וָפַחַד עִמּוֹ (=ממשלה של פחד, המעוררת יראת
הרוממות).

קהלת ח׳, ו-ז :   וְעֵת וּמִשְׁפָּט יֵדַע לֵב חָכָם כִּי לְכָל-חֵפֶץ יֵשׁ עֵת וּמִשְׁפָּט..
(=עת של משפט, השעה הנכונה, המתאימה) [33].

קהלת י״ב, ב :   עַד אֲשֶׁר לֹא-תֶחְשַׁךְ הַשֶּׁמֶשׁ
וְהָאוֹר וְהַיָּרֵחַ וְהַכּוֹכָבִים
וְשָׁבוּ הֶעָבִים אַחַר הַגָּשֶׁם

כאן יש לכאורה קושי במלה „אור״ כיון שהשמש, הירח והכוכבים כולם
נזכרים לחוד. הקצב של שלש נגינות בכל צלע (3:3:3) שולל מחיקת המלה
(קיטל) או התקון (של גלינג) „הַשֶּׁמֶשׁ הַמְּאִירָה״. כאן הכיר תרגום הפשיטטא

צ״ב, א: אֵל נְקָמוֹת ה׳ // אֵל נְקָמוֹת הוֹפִיעַ; תהלים כ״ט, א: הָבוּ לה׳ בְּנֵי אֵלִים // הָבוּ לה׳ כָּבוֹד וָעֹז, ועוד הרבה. ראה מאמרנו הנ״ל בהערה 1, עמ׳ 148 ואילך.

31 רעיונו היסודי של איוב הוא, שעד פרשת היסורים שבאה עליו היה ה׳ מתנהג עמו בחסד ובאהבה. כל עצמו של רעיון זה מתעמם ומתנדף על ידי התיקונים השונים שהוצעו כגון חֵן וָחֶסֶד (בר, דרייבר, גריי-קיטל) „אוֹ חַיִּים וָחֶלֶד שַׁתָּ עִמָּדִי״ (הלשר) הפעל „עָשִׂיתָ״ בא כאן מפני קירבתו ל„חסד״. דוגמה של zeugma (זיווג מלים), השׂחה איוב ד׳, י שַׁאֲגַת אַרְיֵה וְקוֹל שָׁחַל וְשִׁנֵּי כְפִירִים נִתָּעוּ, שהפועל מתאים רק לשם הקרוב אליו, „שני כפירים״ ולא לשאר השמות המוחים את הנושא שלו.

32 על פי תרגום השבעים εγαγες ηπε (תביא עלי) גורסים רוב החדשים פעל בצלע כגון „וַתַּחֲלֹף בְּבָאֶיךָ עִמִּי״ (דרייבר-גריי) או „תַּצְבָּא״ (קיטל). באמת אין שום ראיה לגירסה אחרת מתוך התרגום היוני, שמוסר את ענין הפסוק באופן חפשי, מפני קשיו; והתרגום הארמי שמביא גם הוא פועל „מתחלף מחתאתא מתחיילין גבאי״ יוכיח שבפירוש ולא בחילופי גירסה עסקינן. הקושי אשר דרייבר-גריי מוצא בנוסח ("the combination of relays and a host is strange) בטל, כשמכירים אנו את המליצה של hendiadys; מחזור אחרי מחזור של לוחמים בא עלי״ או „תור של עבדות אחרי תור בא אצלי״. יפה מוסר התרגום האמריקאי-היהודי את הפיסקה לפי הפירוש הראשון "Host succeeding host against me", והלקסיקון האוקספורדי, לפי הפירוש השני: "relays of hard service".

33 ראה על ענין כל הפיסקה הזאת את דברינו בספרנו Koheleth. The Man and His World, p. 279 (New-York, 1951).

265

42

את הצורה המליצית, ופירש (לא שינה) כראוי: „האור של הירח והכוכבים".
שתי הוו"ים „והירח והכוכבים" משמעותם „גם... גם", שמוש השכיח
בערבית ﺍﻭ...ﻭ ונמצא לעתים גם בעברית.[34]

הכרת השימוש ב„הנדיאדון" מאפשרת לנו להבין את הפסוק באור פשוט
ומתקבל על הדעת: „בימי הזקנה, תחשך השמש והאור של הירח והכוכבים,
ואפילו אחרי גשם יעמדו העננים בעינם ואין זוהר ואין נוגה".

דברי הימים־ב ל"ב, א: אַחֲרֵי הַדְּבָרִים וְהָאֱמֶת הָאֵלֶּה (=דברי האמת האלה).

* * *

ייתכן שיש מקום לחלוק על פרטי הפירושים שהוצעו כאן, ובודאי ישנן
דוגמאות נוספות, שלא הובאו כאן; אבל על עצם שימושי מליצה אלו אין —
לפי דעתנו — מקום לערער, ועל ידם הוספנו כלי חשוב — להכרת עושר
המליצה המקראית.

<hr/>

34 ראה הדיון בספרנו הנ"ל, עמ' 331. על שימוש שתי הוו"ים השחה בראשית
ל"ד, כח; במדבר ט', יד; יהושע ט', כג; ישעיה ל"ח, טו; ירמיה י"ג, יד; איוב ל"ד, כט;
נחמיה י"ב, כח ועוד; וראה הלקסיקון האוקספורדי, עמ' 253.

רשימת המקראות שנדונו במאמר

בראשית	ג' טז	משלי	ח' לו
	כ"ה כה		י"ד טז
שמות	ט"ז כ	איוב	ג' ז-ח
	כ"ד ז		ג' כב
במדבר	כ"ג כ		ה' טו
דברים	ז' יב		ה' כד
שמואל-א	ט"ו כג		ז' ו
ישעיה	א' לא		י' יב
	ל"ב-טז		י יז
	מ"ד טז		י"א יח-יט
	נ"ג ח		י"ב ו
ירמיה	י"ב ה		י"ד י
	י"ד יד		ט"ז ט
	כ"ט יא		כ' יט
הושע	ז' ט		כ"א יג
עובדיה	פס' ו		כ"ב כה
תהלים	כ"ב י		כ"ג ט
	כ"ו יא		כ"ה ב
	כ"ז ד	איכה	ב' יג
	ס' ז	קהלת	ח' ר-ז
	ק"ה ז		י"ב ב
	קל"ב יג-יד	אסתר	כ"ד ז
דברי-הימים ב' לא א			

267

44

"אמי ואחותי" ו"אחאב"

במאמרו "עבדך ובנך אני"[1] דן פרופ' שמואל ליונשטאם בנוהג הדיפלומטי במזרח התיכון להשתמש במונחים "אב" ו"אדון" יחד בפניית שרים אל מלכים[2]. הוא מעיר בצדק, שהצימוד "אב – בן" בא לציין פנייה אל גדול בין שום primus inter pares, כגון שני מלכים, השונים בחשיבותם, ובכל זאת עומדים על אותה דרגה פחות־או־יותר. ואילו השימוש "אדון – עבד" משמש לשון פנייה מקטן אל גדול, כגון שר אל מלכו.

בייחוד חשובה הערתו של פרופ' ליונשטאם, שלשונות אלה נתרוקנו מתוכנם המקורי אגב שימוש, עד כדי שהיה אפשר לשלב שניים מהם יחד, כדי לציין עמדתו המדויקת של הכותב, שמצד אחד שוה הוא למקבל מכתבו, ומצד שני נמוך הוא ממנו במקצת כגון "אחי – בני", המופיע במכתבים אוגריתיים[3].

ראוי להוסיף, שׁשימוש זה נתקבל אע"פ שנוצרה על ידו "סתירה הגיונית". לשימוש זה מוצא פרופ' ליונשטאם שימוש מקביל במקצת במלכים ב' טז, ז: "וישלח אחז מלאכים אל תגלת פלסר מלך אשור לאמר עבדך ובנך אני".

והנה יש דוגמה מקבילה בהחלט לשימוש זה, שהיה נפוץ בעולם השמי הקדמון – באיוב יז, יד:

לַשַּׁחַת קָרָאתִי אָבִי אָתָּה אִמִּי וַאֲחֹתִי לָרִמָּה.

כבר רבו המפרשים והמתרגמים, שנתקלו ב"קושי ההגיוני" של הביטוי הכפול בחרוז ב', השמיטו את המלים "אבי אתה" וגרסו:
לשחת קראתי אמי, ואחתי לרמה[4].

---

1. לשוננו לד (תש"ל) עמ' 146.

2. כגון במכתב תל־אל־עמארנה מס' 44, שורה 7–8. "אל אדון מלך מצרים אבי" (תרגומו של א"פ ריריני בלשוננו. לג, תשכ"ט, עמ' 306–308).

3. ראה ליונשטאם שם הערה 2 למקורות.

4. כן בודה, דוהם, בער, ביקל (בספק). דרייבר־גריי משמיט רק את המלה "אתה" מנימוקים הקשורים בקצב, אף שמודה הוא, שהקצב שבמסורת 3:4 מצוי לא־מעט באיוב כגון ה, ג; ט, י; יו, י; יח, ב; יט, כג ועוד (International Critical Commentary on Job, כרך 2, עמ' 114). על קצב זה ראה מאמרנו "על מבנה השירה העברית הקדומה" בספר השנה ליהודי אמריקה תש"ה, עמ' 136–159. מאמר זה מופיע בצורה מורחבת באנגלית בספרי: Poets, Prophets and Sages — Essays in Biblical Interpretation, 1971, Indiana University Press, עמ' 61–94.

45

המקיימים את גרסת המסורה מעלימים עין מן הבעיה⁵, או מפרשים "אמי
או אחותי לרמה"⁶. ולא עמדו על השאלה, מה הוסיף הניב השני על הראשון.

מתוך השימוש שהעיר עליו פרופ' ליונשטאם יש בידנו להוכיח את צדקת
הנוסח המסורתי. ולא זו בלבד, בביטויים האלה מוסיף איוב נופך חשוב להגדרתו.
הוא רואה במות גם את השליט עליו וגם את הקרוב לו. בחינה ראשונה מובעת
על ידי התארים "אבי" ו"אמי", ובחינה שנייה על ידי "אחותי" – שהרי הרימה
קרובה למדיי לגופו של המת.

הרי שיש לנו מקביל שלם בספרות ישראל לשימוש "אב – אח" שבמכתבי
תל־אל־עמארנה ואוגרית. מכל האמור למעלה, מתברר שהשם אַחְאָב אין לבארו
כ"אחי האב", כלומר הדוד מצד האב⁷, אלא כשם תיאופורי. כן מנדיר אותו
פרום' בנימין מזר, שמפרש את השם "האח (היינו האל) הוא אב"⁸.

ואמנם הצימודים "אב – אח" ו"אם – אחות" נותנים יסוד לפרש את ש נ י
חלקי השם אחאב כ כינויים לאל. האל הוא גם אח, הקרוב למאמינים בו, וגם
א ב, המושל ושומר עליהם. שמות תיאופוריים כפולים כאלה יש גם להכיר
בשמות כגון אַבְרָם ואַבְשָלום. בכל השמות המכילים את היסוד "אח" אין לראות
אפוא שמות יחוסיים־משפחתיים־אנושיים, אלא שמות תיאופוריים: חִירָם וַאֲחִירָם
(במד' כו, לה) מקבילים אל אַבְרָם ואֲבִירָם; אֲחִיטוּב (שמ"א יד, ג) מקביל אל
אֲבִיטוּב (דהי"א ח, יא); אֲחִימֶלֶךְ (שמ"א כא, ד) אל אֲבִימֶלֶךְ; אֲחִינָדָב אל
אֲבִינָדָב; אֲחִינֹעַם אל אֲבִינֹעַם; חִיאֵל (מל"א טז, לד; השוה תרגום השבעים Αχειλ)
אל אֲבִיאֵל (שמ"א ט, א) ועוד. וכולם כינויים לאל, המוגדר על ידי שני המושגים
"אב" ו"אח".

---

5. כגון מ' פּוֹפ ב– Job — Anchor Bible, המתרגם את הפסוק כצורתו "My mother
and sister", ומצטט משלי ז, ד, שאינו מקביל לפסוקנו כלל.
6. השוה Standard Revised Version: 'My mother' or 'My sister', and to the worm,
וכן New English Bible שהוסיע מקרוב.
7. כן דעת גלדקה ונות.
8. ראה אנציקלופדיה מקראית, כרך א' עמ' 195, ע' אַחְאָב.

הערות למקרא

ישעיה מד. יא

וְהָרָשִׁים הֵמָּה מֵאָדָם   הֵן כָּל חֲבֵרָיו יֵבֹשׁוּ

יִפְחֲדוּ יֵבֹשׁוּ יָחַד.   יִתְקַבְּצוּ כֻלָּם יַעֲמֹדוּ

קשה לחבר את חרוז ב' אל שאר הפסוק, וידוע שכל התרגומים העתיקים מסכיבים כאן אל המסורה; מֵאָדָם. [1] רש"י מבאר את המשמעות הכללית של המלים האלה: "אותם יוצרים ונוסכים מבני אדם הם ק"ו ליצירתם שהיא הבל" — ופירוש זה נתקבל על ידי רוב המפרשים. [2] אבל הקושי שבו נראה לעין, ראשית פוגם באור זה בהקבלת הפסוק, שנית אין מקום כאן, כשהנביא מציר את סופם המחפיר של יוצרי האלילים, להאור אפסותם וחולשתם,

על כן יש להציע שנוי קטן — מֵאָדָם במקום מֵאָדָם — בינוני פָּעַל של השרש אָדָם. צורה זאת מצויה בשמות כ"ה, ה, ועוד, נחום ב' ד'. במקומות אלה משמשת מלה זו מובן של "מֵאָדָם ע"י צבע או ע"י דם". בפסוק זה יש לה משמעות "מתאדם מתוך בושה". על פי רוב כידוע, מביעים רעיון הבושה ע"י חָוַר בל' התנ"ך וְהֶלְבִּין בלשון המשנה. בכל זאת נמצא שורש אָדָם בהוראה זו במדרש [3] ובעברית החדשה.

ויש לפרש את "יתקבצו" בחרוז ג' לא במובן הרגיל של "התאסף" אלא כצורה קרובה לשרש קָוַץ. המצוי בשפה המאוחרת. גם לשורש הערבי קָבַץ המקביל בדיוק אל קבץ העברי יש ההוראה "התכוץ, התכנס, 4]

באותו החרוז יש לבאר "עמד" בבאור המסתתף (derivatire) מן הבאור העיקרי: "עמד מְדַבֵּר, שתק". השוה במדבר ט, ח, איוב לב, טז.

אין לתמוה על שהנשוא (מאדם) הוא כמספר יחיד, בה בשעה שהנושא (הָרָשִׁים) הוא ברבים. שמוש זה אנו מוצאים לפרקים תכופים, כגון בראשית כז, כט, במדבר כד, ט ארָרֶיךָ אָרוּר וּמְבָרְכֶיךָ בָרוּךְ, ישעיה ג, יב, עַמִּי נֹגְשָׂיו מְעוֹלֵל [5].

מן האמור למעלה יוצא פשט הפסוק כך

וחרשיו יתאדמו מבושה   כל חברי האלילים יכלמו

יפחדו ויבשו יחד.   כלם יתכוצו ויאלמו

1) כן הע' הולגטה, הפשיטא, והתרגום.

2) אין ספק, שזוהי, תמצית פירוש התרגומים. אחרי באור זה נגררו ר"י קרא, רד"ק, ר"ש ברטן (אור בהיר), תרגומי תנ"ך האנגלים, משיין, סקינר, דוהם (הטשנה את נקודות וחרשים). עהרליך, הנומה מן הפירוש המקובל, דחוק מאד.

3) כגון שהאדים את פני דוד — במדבר רבה, פרק ד', החצי השני של הפרק.

4) ראב"ע פרגיש, שהבאור הרגיל של "יתקבצו" אין לו טעם פה, ולכן הוא מפרש: יתקבצו כלם ויכלמו"'.

5) השוה עוד ישעיה ב, יח, זכריה יא, ה; קהלת י, א, דברי"ה א' ג' ד', וה א' המקיף של ר' יוסף מיוחס בַּלְשׁוֹנֵנוּ' תשרי, תרפ"ט צד 145 והלאה.

47

חבקוק ב, ה

גֶּבֶר יָהִיר וְלֹא יִנְוֶה   וְאַף כִּי הַיַּיִן בֹּגֵד

וְהוּא כַמָּוֶת וְלֹא יִשְׂבַּע   אֲשֶׁר הִרְחִיב כִּשְׁאוֹל נַפְשׁוֹ

על פסוק קשה זה, רבו הפירושים והתיקונים. נראה שהתרגום הע' גרם: "והנא
והבוגד גבר יהיר לא יועיל" — או קרוב לזה, וכן האיטלא. הוּלְגָטָה והתרגום הארמי
מבארים: כשם, שהיין בוגד בשותהו כן יבגד האיש היהיר" — והטכסט המסורתי אינו
סובל פירוש יפה מזה, וְלַהֲוֹזַן גורם ירוה במקום ינוה, וא. קרוכמל — יָנוּחַ.

למרות הקושי הרב, יש להבין את הרעיון הכללי של הפסוק. הנביא מתאר את
הגאוה ושאיפת השררה הבלתי מוגבלת של בבל. לכן מציעים אנו לקרוא את "הדלת"
של בֹּגֵד כ"תָיו" בחילוף דלית ותיו בַּנַת. כי באה במובן כף הדמיון. [6] יִנְוֶה הוא פעל
נגזר מן השם נָוֶה ובאור "יִשְׁכֹּן, שקט". [7]

הגת העברית העתיקה הכילה שתי שקתות. "בעליונה, הקרויה גת (במובן צר) או
פֻּגְרָה, היו דורכים את הענבים. והתחתונה, היקב, היתה מקבלת את העסיס". [8] יואל
ד, יג, נותן לנו מושג ברור של מכונה עתיקה זו: כִּי מָלְאָה גַת, הֵשִׁיקוּ הַיְקָבִים".

בפסוק זה נותן חבקוק שני דמיונות נפלאים. לשאיפת השלטון הנפרזה של
הכשדים. הוא מדמה אותה אל הקבר שאינו אומר די, ואל היין החמר ועובר על גדות
הגת. ככה מונה הַמְמַשֵׁל ארבעת הדברים שלא ישבעו: שאול ועצר רחם, ארץ לא
שבעה מים, ואש לא אמרה הון (משלי ל, טו).

באור הפסוק יוצא כך:

הוא עם בכל היהיר שלא ישקט   כמו חיין בגת
ואינו שבע רצון כמות   המרחיב תאותו כקבר

---

[6] עוֹלַד חושב שכף הדמיון נגזרה מן מלת החבור כי — ganz — So wird das Mörtchen כי
(צד 271 מהדורה, שביעית (Jehigehäude, kurz wie präposition gesprochen כְּ).
לאידך גיסא, חושב עהרליך שהמלה כי התפתחה מכף הדמיון. (Raudglersen, כרך א', צד 16).
בכל אופן יש למלה כי הוראת "כְּ" במקומות אחרים בתנ"ך — ישעיה מד, ג; נד, מ; סב, ה, ולעתים
תכופות בלשון המאוחרת כגון בי סיד סוטה לה, ב ועוד. בארמית התלמודית מצוי שמוש זה של "כי"
למאות. ראה המלונים התלמודיים, ביחוד קהוט "ערוך השלם" ערך "כי".

[7] כן ברון — דריבר, — בריגס, — hexien of the O. T. — דף 627 b.

[8] כן סטים — Dictionary of Bible — ערך Winepress. השוה גם כן בֶּנצִינגֶר:
Hebräesche Archäologie מהדורה ראשונה צד 217.